ISSUES IN MEDIA

4TH EDITION

Sara Miller McCune founded SAGE Publishing in 1965 to support the dissemination of usable knowledge and educate a global community. SAGE publishes more than 1000 journals and over 800 new books each year, spanning a wide range of subject areas. Our growing selection of library products includes archives, data, case studies and video. SAGE remains majority owned by our founder and after her lifetime will become owned by a charitable trust that secures the company's continued independence.

Los Angeles | London | New Delhi | Singapore | Washington DC | Melbourne

ISSUES IN MEDIA

SELECTIONS FROM *CQ RESEARCHER*

4TH EDITION

Los Angeles | London | New Delhi
Singapore | Washington DC | Melbourne

FOR INFORMATION:

SAGE Publications, Inc.
2455 Teller Road
Thousand Oaks, California 91320
E-mail: order@sagepub.com

SAGE Publications Ltd.
1 Oliver's Yard
55 City Road
London EC1Y 1SP
United Kingdom

SAGE Publications India Pvt. Ltd.
B 1/I 1 Mohan Cooperative Industrial Area
Mathura Road, New Delhi 110 044
India

SAGE Publications Asia-Pacific Pte. Ltd.
3 Church Street
#10–04 Samsung Hub
Singapore 049483

Printed in the United States of America

Library of Congress Control Number: 2018953434

ISBN: 978-1-5443-5053-0

This book is printed on acid-free paper.

Acquisitions Editor: Terri Accomazzo
Editorial Assistant: Sarah Wilson
Production Editor: Astha Jaiswal
Typesetter: C&M Digitals (P) Ltd.
Cover Designer: Anupama Krishnan
Marketing Manager: Allison Henry

MIX
Paper from
responsible sources
FSC® C005010

18 19 20 21 22 10 9 8 7 6 5 4 3 2 1

Contents

Annotated Table of Contents

instituted in 2015 when Democrats controlled the Federal Communications Commission (FCC), were repealed in December 2017 after Republicans regained control of the agency. The FCC is led by former telecommunications lawyer Ajit Pai, a free-market champion of deregulation who has criticized the net neutrality rules as burdensome and unnecessary. More than 20 states are suing to preserve net neutrality, arguing that federal regulations are needed to keep the large ISPs from becoming too powerful. But defenders of the FCC vote say net neutrality harms the ability of the ISPs to improve their networks and ultimately hurts consumers and businesses. The European Union, meanwhile, has passed laws protecting net neutrality and labeled equal access to the internet a basic right.

3. DIVERSITY IN HOLLYWOOD

Charges of gender and racial bias and sexual stereotyping continue to plague the film and broadcast entertainment industries despite decades of complaints from women, minorities and civil rights advocates. White males still dominate virtually all aspects of the business, from writers, directors and producers to actors starring in leading roles. But the movie industry may have reached a tipping point this year following a controversy over the Academy Awards nominations for best actor and actress: For the second consecutive year, all the nominees were white. Television, meanwhile, is becoming somewhat more inclusive than movies, as are emerging internet-based shows. Still, the Equal Employment Opportunity Commission is investigating claims of bias against female directors, and many minorities remain unpersuaded by recent Hollywood diversity initiatives. Skeptics say significant industry change is unlikely, especially in the high-cost, high-risk movie business, where box-office favorites rather than untested newcomers typically determine which films receive financing.

4. TECHNOLOGY ADDICTION

Some addiction specialists contend that the overuse of video games, social media or other online technology can affect the brain in the same way drug or alcohol dependency does. But other experts question whether an obsessive use of technology meets the clinical definition of addiction. They argue that overuse of technology typically stems from an underlying condition, such as anxiety, depression or attention deficit disorder. Some industry insiders say technology companies such as Facebook design their products to be addictive, which company executives deny. Child advocates and some politicians want the government to do more to address the potential harm of technology overuse, and countries such as South Korea and China have established government-sponsored treatment centers for teens and young adults considered tech-addicted. The American Psychiatric Association has not linked technology overuse with standard medical definitions of addiction but says internet gaming needs further study. The National Institutes of Health, meanwhile, is funding a study on whether online gaming is addictive.

5. TRUST IN MEDIA

Journalism is facing a credibility crisis. Declining faith in government and other institutions and a decades-long assault by conservatives have hurt mainstream news outlets. And President Trump has called journalists "the enemy of the American people." Recent incidents involving public figures, including a Montana congressional candidate's alleged assault on a reporter, have underscored the hostility that journalists face. Some traditional media also have suffered from self-inflicted wounds by blurring the lines between news and commentary and ignoring the interests of rural readers to focus on well-off urbanites. Ad revenue and subscriptions at newspapers have plummeted, in part due to the rise of the internet and changing consumer habits. Meanwhile, social media have fostered "echo chambers" in which people seek out news that affirms their beliefs. Journalists and those studying the news business say mainstream outlets must be more transparent about how they do their jobs and more skillful at explaining events to survive.

6. SOCIAL MEDIA EXPLOSION

From Facebook to the photo-sharing site Pinterest to virtual adventure games, software that helps people meet, converse, work and compete with others is drawing billions online. The use of social media comes with a price, however. Every photo upload or click of a "like" button deposits users' personal data online, much of which is sold to help businesses target advertising. To some, such data mining endangers long-cherished privacy rights, but social media supporters say it is a small price to pay for the benefits of online socializing. Meanwhile, critics of social media express concern that many members of the digital generation may fail to develop vital communication skills because they prefer virtual contact over face-to-face conversations. But proponents say most people use social media not to avoid others but to stay in touch with them.

7. INTERNET AND SOCIAL MEDIA

The internet continues to pummel newspapers, which are losing advertisers to online media and failing to earn enough from their own digital operations to cover operating costs. Internet sites have proliferated, but a handful — led by Google — have corralled the vast majority of visitors and income. Privacy advocates are increasingly concerned about online companies collecting vast amounts of personal information about users. The federal government is attempting to figure out how to thwart cyber attacks by criminals, terrorists and unfriendly nations. The proposed Cyber Intelligence Sharing and Protection Act (CISPA) would allow businesses and government to share cyberthreat information without violating antitrust and privacy laws, but President Obama has threatened to veto the measure, saying it would violate consumer privacy. Meanwhile, debate rages over how to protect intellectual property in the digital age.

8. SOCIAL MEDIA AND POLITICS

Social media, including Facebook, Twitter and YouTube, have become major battlegrounds in this year's elections. Candidates are using the platforms to identify and organize supporters and raise funds. They bypass traditional news media to send their messages unfiltered to the public. They target niche audiences with growing precision, contact hard-to-reach voters, extend their influence as online supporters forward their messages and carry out many campaign tasks at much lower cost than before. The increasing ability of campaign strategists to collect and analyze information about individual voters has raised privacy concerns, and many worry that the social

networks' insular nature contributes to political polarization. But social media's low cost, ease of use and wide reach also raise hopes that they can level the campaign-spending playing field.

9. INTERNET REGULATION

Lawmakers are struggling with tough questions about how to regulate digital media and the internet. With digitized versions of feature films and recorded music playable on personal computers and cell phones, the film, television and music industries have repeatedly complained that global "pirates" use cheap, widely available computer technology and the internet to steal their intellectual property and profits. A bill to require internet service providers (ISPs) to shut down websites suspected of posting or distributing copyrighted material stalled in Congress. Meanwhile, ISPs are fighting government attempts to bar them from discriminating against certain websites. Advocates say such "net neutrality" rules are needed to prevent situations in which, for example, a cable TV-owned ISP that also sells video content might slow the flow of video that customers buy from other companies. But ISPs argue that it wouldn't be in their financial interest to conduct business that way.

10. INTERNET AND MEDIA

As public reliance on the internet grows, courts and government officials are facing new challenges on how best to regulate access to digital information. In Washington, the Federal Communications Commission has proposed rules that could create a dual system that would allow big companies, such as online retailers, to have faster internet connectivity than most consumers and internet entrepreneurs would enjoy. Civil rights and consumer advocates say such a system would squeeze out small websites and steer profit to big corporations. Meanwhile, critics of a proposed merger between cable giants Comcast and Time Warner Cable argue that the deal would reduce programming choices and raise consumer cable rates. And in June the Supreme Court ruled that Aereo Inc., a small company that grabbed broadcast transmissions from the airwaves and stored them in the cloud for access by consumers using a simple antenna, was violating broadcasters' copyright protections.

11. BIG DATA AND PRIVACY

Big data — the collection and analysis of enormous amounts of information by supercomputers — is leading to huge advances in such fields as astrophysics, medicine, social science, business and crime fighting. And big data is growing exponentially: According to IBM, 90 percent of the world's data has been generated within just the past two years. But the use of big data — including tweets, Facebook images and email addresses — is controversial because of its potential to erode individual privacy, especially by governments conducting surveillance operations and companies marketing products. Some civil liberties advocates want to control the use of big data, and others think companies should pay to use people's online information. But some proponents of big data say the benefits outweigh the risks and that privacy is an outdated concept.

12. MEDIA VIOLENCE

Recent accounts of mass school shootings and other violence have intensified the debate about whether pervasive violence in movies, television and video games negatively influences young people's behavior. Over the past century, the question has led the entertainment media to voluntarily create viewing guidelines and launch public awareness campaigns to help parents and other consumers make appropriate choices. But lawmakers' attempts to restrict or ban content have been unsuccessful because courts repeatedly have upheld the industry's right to free speech. In the wake of a 2011 Supreme Court ruling that said a direct causal link between media violence — particularly video games — and real violence has not been proved, the Obama administration has called for more research into the question. Media and video game executives say the cause of mass shootings is multifaceted and cannot be blamed on the entertainment industry, but many researchers and lawmakers say the industry should shoulder some responsibility.

13. DIGITAL JOURNALISM: IS NEWS QUALITY BETTER OR WORSE ONLINE?

More and more people in the United States and around the world are getting their news online instead of in print or via radio or television — the so-called legacy media. Digital news sites allow news to be continually updated, with few if any of the space or other constraints that apply to print publications or radio and television newscasts. With lower upfront costs, journalism entrepreneurs can start businesses more readily than in the past: Witness the new digital-only news sites just started by high-profile journalists who left prestigious traditional newspaper companies. Yet some observers complain about the increased partisanship seen in digital publications and the increased risk of error with less careful editing than in traditional news media. And the business plans for the new digital sites are works in progress, with uncertain long-term prospects. Meanwhile, traditional news organizations are reinventing themselves to remain relevant and profitable in the digital age.

14. MEDIA BIAS

An unprecedented number of Americans view the news media as biased and untrustworthy, with both conservatives and liberals complaining that coverage of political races and important public policy issues is often skewed. Polls show that 80 percent of Americans believe news stories are often influenced by the powerful, and nearly as many say the media tend to favor one side of issues over another. The proliferation of commentary by partisan cable broadcasters, talk-radio hosts and bloggers has blurred the lines between news and opinion in many people's minds, fueling concern that slanted reporting is replacing media objectivity. At the same time, newspapers and broadcasters — and even some partisan groups — have launched aggressive fact-checking efforts aimed at verifying statements by newsmakers and exposing exaggerations or outright lies. Experts question the future of U.S. democracy if American voters cannot agree on what constitutes truth.

15. FREE SPEECH AT RISK

Governments around the globe have been weakening free-speech protections because of concerns about security or offending religious believers. After a phone-hacking scandal erupted in the British press and Muslims worldwide violently protested images in the Western media of the Prophet Muhammad, European nations enacted new restrictions on hate speech, and Britain is considering limiting press freedom. Autocratic regimes increasingly are jailing journalists and political dissidents or simply buying media companies to use them for propaganda and to negate criticism. Muslim countries are adopting and rigidly enforcing blasphemy laws, some of which carry the death penalty. Meanwhile, some governments are blocking or monitoring social media and cybertraffic, increasing the risk of arrest for those who freely express their thoughts online and dashing hopes that new technologies would allow unlimited distribution of information and opinion.

Preface

Who hat is the future of television? Do social media and big data threaten privacy rights? Do children have too much access to violent media content? Is reporting on global conflict worth the risk? These questions — and many more — are at the heart of today's media landscape. How can instructors best engage students on these crucial issues? We feel that students need objective, yet provocative, examinations of these issues to understand how they affect citizens today and will for years to come. This collection aims to promote in-depth discussion, facilitate further research, and help readers formulate their own positions on crucial issues. Get your students talking inside and outside the classroom about *Issues in Media*.

This fourth edition of *Issues in Media* includes fifteen up-to-date reports by *CQ Researcher*, an award-winning weekly policy brief that brings complicated issues down to earth. Each report chronicles and analyzes the background, current situation and future outlook of a policy issue or societal topic. This collection covers a range of issues found in most mass communication and media literacy courses.

CQ RESEARCHER

CQ Researcher was founded in 1923 as *Editorial Research Reports* and was sold primarily to newspapers as a research tool. The magazine was renamed and redesigned in 1991 as *CQ Researcher*. Today, students are its primary audience. While still used by hundreds of journalists and newspapers, many of which reprint portions of the reports, *Researcher*'s main subscribers are now high school, college and public libraries. In 2002, *Researcher* won the American Bar Association's coveted Silver Gavel Award for magazine excellence for a series of nine reports on civil liberties and other legal issues.

Researcher writers — all highly experienced journalists — sometimes compare the experience of writing a *Researcher* report to drafting a college term paper. Indeed, there are many similarities. Each report is as long as many term papers — about 11,000 words — and is written by one person without any significant outside help. One of the key differences is that the writers interview leading experts, scholars and government officials for each issue.

Like students, the writers begin the creative process by choosing a topic. Working with *Researcher*'s editors, the writer identifies a controversial subject that has important public policy implications. After a topic is selected, the writer embarks on one to two weeks of intense research. Newspaper and magazine articles are clipped or downloaded, books are ordered and information is gathered from a wide variety of sources, including interest groups, universities and the government. Once the writers are well informed, they develop a detailed outline and begin the interview process. Each report requires a minimum of ten to fifteen interviews with academics, officials, lobbyists and people working in the field. Only after all interviews are completed does the writing begin.

CHAPTER FORMAT

Each issue of *CQ Researcher,* and therefore each selection in this book, is structured in the same way. A selection begins with an introductory overview, which is briefly explored in greater detail in the rest of the report.

The second section chronicles the most important and current debates in the field. It is structured around a number of key issues questions, such as "Can traditional television thrive in the Internet Age?" and "Do social networking sites threaten privacy rights?" This section is the core of each selection. The questions raised are often highly controversial and usually the object of much argument among scholars and practitioners. Hence, the answers provided are never conclusive, but rather detail the range of opinion within the field.

Following those issue questions is the "Background" section, which provides a history of the issue being examined. This retrospective includes important legislative and executive actions and court decisions to inform readers on how current policy evolved.

Next, the "Current Situation" section examines important contemporary policy issues, legislation under consideration and action being taken. Each selection ends with an "Outlook" section that gives a sense of what new regulations, court rulings and possible policy initiatives might be put into place in the next five to ten years.

Each report contains features that augment the main text: sidebars that examine issues related to the topic, a pro/con debate by two outside experts, a chronology of key dates and events and an annotated bibliography that details the major sources used by the writer.

This volume also includes two "Short Reports" (Chapter 7: Internet and Social Media and Chapter 10: Internet and Media) that provide brief coverage of timely media issues paired with a timeline of significant dates and events.

ACKNOWLEDGMENTS

We wish to thank many people for helping to make this collection a reality. Thomas J. Billitteri, managing editor of *CQ Researcher,* gave us his enthusiastic support and cooperation as we developed this edition. He and his talented editors have amassed a first-class collection of *Researcher* articles, and we are fortunate to have access to this rich cache. We also thankfully acknowledge the advice and feedback from current readers and are gratified by their satisfaction with the book.

Some readers may be learning about *CQ Researcher* for the first time. We expect that many readers will want regular access to this excellent weekly research tool. For subscription information or a no-obligation free trial of *Researcher,* please contact CQ Press at www.cqpress.com or toll-free at 1-866-4CQ-PRESS (1-866-427-7737).

Contributor Bios

Ellen Kennerly has worked as a journalist for more than three decades, mostly with the *Atlanta Journal-Constitution* where she held editing and managerial positions in print and digital. Since then, she worked as professional in residence for the Office of Student Media at Louisiana State University and as an editorial department director for WebMD. She is now a communications consultant in Atlanta.

Jane Fullerton Lemons is a freelance writer in Northern Virginia with more than 25 years of journalism experience. A former Washington bureau chief for the *Arkansas Democrat-Gazette* and *Farm Journal* magazine, she has covered the White House, Congress, food policy and health care. She is currently seeking a master's degree in creative nonfiction from Goucher College in Towson, Md.

Christina Hoag is a freelance journalist in Los Angeles. She previously worked for *The Miami Herald* and The Associated Press and was a correspondent in Latin America. She is the co-author of *Peace in the Hood: Working with Gang Members to End the Violence.*

Susan Ladika is a freelance writer in Tampa, Fla., whose work has appeared in *HR Magazine*, Workforce, Bankrate.com, CreditCards .com, *Science, The Wall Street Journal-Europe* and *International Educator.* She previously worked as a writer and editor for newspapers in the Southeast, including *The Tampa Tribune*, and also reported from Europe for The Associated Press.

Chuck McCutcheon is a former assistant managing editor of *CQ Researcher.* He has been a reporter and editor for *Congressional*

Quarterly and Newhouse News Service and is co-author of the 2012 and 2014 editions of *The Almanac of American Politics* and *Dog Whistles, Walk-Backs and Washington Handshakes: Decoding the Jargon, Slang and Bluster of American Political Speech.* He also has written books on climate change and nuclear waste.

Staff writer **Marcia Clemmitt** is a veteran social-policy reporter who previously served as editor in chief of *Medicine & Health* and staff writer for *The Scientist.* She has also been a high school math and physics teacher. She holds a liberal arts and sciences degree from St. John's College, Annapolis, and a master's degree in English from Georgetown University. Her recent reports include "Computer Hacking" and "Internet Regulation."

Tom Price, a Washington-based freelance journalist and *CQ Researcher* contributing writer, has written about the Internet's impact on public affairs since the mid-1990s. Last year the Foundation for Public Affairs published his report, "Beyond Control: How Social Media and Mobile Communication Are Changing Public Affairs." Before he began freelancing, Price was a correspondent in the Cox Newspapers Washington Bureau and chief politics writer for the *Dayton Daily News* and *The* (Dayton) *Journal Herald.* He is author or coauthor of five books, including *Changing the Face of Hunger* and, most recently, *Washington, DC, Free & Dirt Cheap* with his wife Susan Crites Price.

Carol Kaufmann is a freelance writer living in the Washington, D.C., area.

Christina L. Lyons, a freelance journalist based in the Washington, D.C., area, writes primarily about U.S. government and politics. She is a contributing author for CQ Press reference books, including *CQ's Guide to Congress* and *Congress and the Nation*, and is a contributing editor for Bloomberg BNA's *International Trade Daily.* A former editor for Congressional Quarterly, she also was coauthor of CQ's *Politics in America 2010.*

Lyons began her career as a newspaper reporter in Maryland and then covered environment and health care policy on Capitol Hill. She has a master's degree in political science from American University.

Kenneth Jost has written more than 160 reports for *CQ Researcher* since 1991 on topics ranging from legal affairs and social policy to national security and international relations. He is the author of *The Supreme Court Yearbook* and *Supreme Court from A to Z* (both CQ Press). He is an honors graduate of Harvard College and Georgetown Law School, where he teaches media law as an adjunct professor. He also writes the blog Jost on Justice (http://jostonjustice.blogspot.com). His previous reports include "Blog Explosion" and "Future of Newspapers" (both 2006).

Robert Kiener is an award-winning writer based in Vermont whose work has appeared in *The London Sunday Times, The Christian Science Monitor, The Washington Post, Reader's Digest*, Time Life Books and other publications. For more than two decades he worked as an editor and correspondent in Guam, Hong Kong, Canada and England. He holds an M.A. in Asian studies from Hong Kong University and an M.Phil. in international relations from England's Cambridge University.

Alan Greenblatt covers foreign affairs for National Public Radio. He was previously a staff writer at *Governing* magazine and *CQ Weekly*, where he won the National Press Club's Sandy Hume Award for political journalism. He graduated from San Francisco State University in 1986 and received a master's degree in English literature from the University of Virginia in 1988. For the *CQ Researcher*, he wrote "Confronting Warming," "Future of the GOP" and "Immigration Debate." His most recent *CQ Global Researcher* reports were "Rewriting History" and "International Adoption."

1

Privacy and the Internet

Ellen Kennerly

Tara Nicolson of Lawrenceville, N.J., discovered last year that hackers had stolen her personal information and tried to open more than a dozen credit card accounts, just months after a massive data breach at the Equifax credit bureau. Although threats to privacy are escalating, Congress has yet to act, partly because of concern that too much regulation might hurt online commerce and stifle innovation.

From *CQ Researcher,*
February 9, 2018

Just before Christmas last year, Tara Nicolson received a call from a credit card company, which said it had received an application for a card in her name.

After long hours on the phone, she discovered that someone was using her personal information to try to set up accounts with 17 different companies. "I didn't know where to turn," says Nicolson, of Lawrenceville, N.J. "It just felt very overwhelming."

The fraudulent credit card applications in Nicolson's name occurred only months after a massive data breach at the Equifax credit-reporting firm. While she suspects the Equifax breach, in which the records of 145 million Americans were stolen, is to blame for her experience, it is impossible to know for sure whether that breach was where the thieves got her data. "We're just so vulnerable," Nicolson says.

Nicolson's trials are part of a growing struggle over online privacy and data security. More and more companies are collecting consumer data and sharing it with third parties. As the volume of online personal information has grown, so have massive data breaches — 2017 saw a record number in the United States. Although the hacking threat is escalating, Congress has yet to act, partly because of divisions over how much regulation to impose on the internet without hurting online commerce and stifling innovation.[1]

The Identity Theft Resource Center, a victims' advocacy group in San Diego, tracked 1,579 breaches last year, up 44.7 percent over the previous year's record total of 1,091.[2] And, according to the

Electronic Privacy Information Center (EPIC), an independent research group focused on privacy issues, 73 percent of all U.S. businesses have now been breached.[3]

Five of the most significant breaches in recent years involved a variety of U.S. companies:

- The Equifax breach lasted from mid-May until July and resulted in hackers stealing the names, Social Security numbers, birth dates and addresses of almost half the U.S. population. The company did not reveal the breach until September.[4]
- Yahoo disclosed last year that all of its 3 billion accounts, including its email, Yahoo Fantasy Sports, the Tumblr blogging and social-networking site and the Flickr photo-sharing site, were breached in 2013; hackers made off with email addresses and passwords.[5]
- At Uber, a 2016 hack that affected 57 million accounts worldwide was concealed for about a year, and the ride-sharing company paid the hackers a ransom of $100,000 to delete the driver's license numbers and email addresses they had stolen.[6]
- A 2013 breach of credit- and debit-card records of 110 million Target customers prompted the retailer's CEO to resign.[7]
- A 2014 cyberattack at eBay exposed the names, addresses, birthdays and passwords of all 145 million of its users.[8]

Hackers have a variety of tools at their disposal, according to experts. "Phishing" and "keylogging" are two of the most popular. With phishing, someone poses as a trusted company or person — either online or on the phone — to lure the user into giving up personal information. Keylogging involves the use of software to record what the targeted consumer types on a keyboard, including passwords.[9]

Although the massive breaches and the unwillingness of some companies to report them quickly have triggered worry among businesses, regulators and lawmakers, the federal government has taken little action and, in fact, has loosened Obama-era privacy restrictions.

The Federal Communications Commission (FCC) in October 2016 approved rules to limit how internet service providers (ISPs) could use and sell customer data in what many called an important step toward giving consumers the right to control their own information. The

rules would have given consumers the right to bar providers from sharing location data, browsing history or data about app usage.

But in March Congress passed, and in April President Trump signed, a bill that killed those rules. Tech firms such as Google and Facebook had joined the ISPs in pressing for the rules to be overturned, arguing that they were too restrictive.[10]

In December, the FCC overturned net neutrality, instituted in 2015 to bar ISPs from throttling or otherwise prioritizing access to the internet and defining ISPs as utilities, and thus under FCC purview. Republicans argued that the Federal Trade Commission (FTC), and not the FCC, was the appropriate regulator of ISPs and the December FCC ruling restored the FTC to that role.[11]

A bill introduced in January by Democratic Sens. Elizabeth Warren of Massachusetts and Mark Warner of Virginia would create an office of cybersecurity within the FTC to give it direct authority over credit agencies. The Data Breach Prevention and Compensation Act would impose mandatory penalties for breaches and require compensation to consumers.[12]

Other proposed bills include mandating penalties for companies that fail to report a breach in a timely manner and requiring opt-in consent by consumers before broadband cable companies and ISPs could share personal data. But lawmakers from both parties agree that passage of such regulations is unlikely this year, given the president's and the GOP majority's opposition to additional business regulations.

While Congress has yet to act, the 28-member European Union (EU) has adopted far-reaching privacy regulations that go into effect in May that will apply to any U.S. corporations doing business with EU citizens. The General Data Protection Regulation will require simple, easy-to-understand consent language for consumers, who will need to "opt in" before companies can use their data.[13]

Experts say the sheer volume of data and the speed of its growth increase the urgency for action in the United States. IBM estimates 90 percent of all data in 2017 had been created in the past two years. That is 2.5 quintillion bytes of data every day.[14]

In the absence of government action, some U.S. companies are seeking solutions. Google's parent company,

Alphabet, is launching a cybersecurity-focused business to help companies protect themselves against hackers. The new firm, Chronicle, is "dedicated to helping companies find and stop cyberattacks before they cause harm," said CEO Stephen Gillett. Talent shortages and tight budgets prevent businesses from maintaining top-notch data security, he said.[15]

But consumers also are freely giving up their personal data in exchange for the convenience of using the Web. "People are really selling their information cheaply," says consumer credit adviser Liz Weston, a columnist at NerdWallet, a personal finance website. "I'm not sure all of them understand that when you're getting something for 'free' that you're giving something up."

Cybersecurity expert Bruce Schneier agrees. "Data is collected, compiled, analyzed and used to try to sell us stuff," he said. "Personalized advertising is how these companies make money and is why so much of the internet is free to users. We're the product, not the customer."[16]

The development of algorithms to analyze personal information that is then used to determine mortgage approvals, college admissions and other life-changing decisions raises concerns as well. The Future of Privacy Forum, a Washington think tank that studies data privacy, said potential harms include discrimination in employment, benefits, housing and education.[17]

In the United States, banks and financial institutions are free to share consumer data with their affiliates. While they must tell consumers they are sharing their information, the consumer has no right to stop them from sharing with their affiliates. But if the institutions wish to share the data with third parties, consumers have a right to opt out. Few have chosen to do so, but many say the policies are difficult to understand and sometimes misleading.[18]

Yahoo, Equifax Hacks Among Biggest Breaches

The largest data breach thus far this century involved all 3 billion accounts held by Yahoo, affecting hundreds of millions of users of Yahoo email, Yahoo Fantasy Sports, the Tumblr blogging and social-networking site and the Flickr photo-sharing site. While the Yahoo hackers stole email addresses and passwords, last year's breach of the Equifax credit-reporting agency involved the theft of far more consequential data: private financial information and Social Security numbers of 145.5 million Americans.

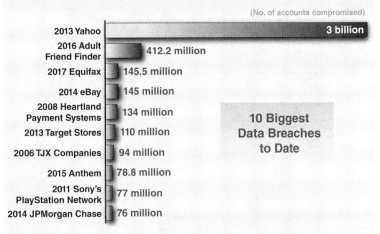

(No. of accounts compromised)

2013 Yahoo	3 billion
2016 Adult Friend Finder	412.2 million
2017 Equifax	145.5 million
2014 eBay	145 million
2008 Heartland Payment Systems	134 million
2013 Target Stores	110 million
2006 TJX Companies	94 million
2015 Anthem	78.8 million
2011 Sony's PlayStation Network	77 million
2014 JPMorgan Chase	76 million

10 Biggest Data Breaches to Date

Sources: Taylor Armerding, "The 17 biggest data breaches of the 21st century," CSO Online, International Data Group, Jan. 26, 2018, https://tinyurl.com/yajr5eem; Robert Hackett, "Equifax Underestimated by 2.5 Million the Potential Number of Breach Victims," *Fortune*, Oct. 2, 2017, https://tinyurl.com/yd6lgv8o

The Supreme Court will provide guidance on digital privacy issues this year. In *Carpenter v. United States*, the court will decide whether cellphone data held by a third party, the carrier, is protected by Fourth Amendment privacy rights against warrantless searches by government agencies.

Meanwhile, most experts agree the United States needs a new identification system to replace the Social Security card number. Some argue its use should be prohibited in the private sector to lessen the chances of identity theft. Technological advances — ranging from encryption to biometrics and facial recognition — could also be part of a more secure system.

The increasingly popular Internet of Things, which connects such things as refrigerators and toys to the internet and sometimes enables them to communicate

Web-Linked Devices to Rise Nearly Fivefold

The number of interconnected devices — known as the Internet of Things (IoT) — is projected to nearly quintuple worldwide between 2015 and 2025. The IoT connects TVs, fitness bands, appliances and other items to the Web and sometimes to each other.

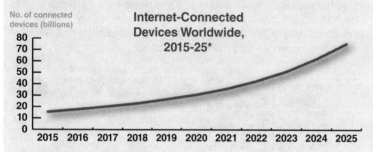

No. of connected devices (billions)

Internet-Connected Devices Worldwide, 2015-25*

* Figures for 2017 to 2025 are projections.

Source: "Internet of Things (IoT) connected devices installed base worldwide from 2015 to 2025 (in billions)," Statista, November 2016, https://tinyurl.com/j3t9t2w

with each other, will likely top 11 billion devices in 2018. But it continues to raise privacy questions because some devices may also be recording users' words and behaviors.[19]

"These products raise significant consumer privacy concerns," says Marc Rotenberg, president of the Electronic Privacy Information Center. For instance, he says, the Google Home Mini virtual assistant "was manufactured in the 'always on' position," which means it was recording conversations without being prompted. The device, which according to Google has sold at a rate of one per second since its release on Oct. 19, 2017, has been updated to address the glitch, but Rotenberg has called for an investigation of such devices that are "always-on."[20]

Industry experts agree data security is the biggest challenge in cloud computing, where information is stored on a remote, instead of a local, server. "The responsibility for protecting . . . information from hackers and internal data breaches then falls into the hands of the hosting company rather than the individual user," said the Privacy Rights Clearinghouse, a consumer advocacy group. "Privacy and security can only be as good as its weakest link."[21]

Technology known as de-identification holds promise because it would allow companies to remove key identifiers

linking individual records to consumer data, says John Verdi, vice president of policy for the Future of Privacy Forum think tank. "De-ID is increasingly important . . . as technologies evolve," he says.

As privacy experts, consumer advocates, lawmakers and others debate how to protect online data, here are some of the questions they are asking:

Should consumer consent be required before data can be shared?

The use of consumers' information without their explicit consent is one of the most controversial practices in the data privacy debate.

When the California software company Alteryx left an unsecured database online late last year, it contained millions of records about U.S. households, including addresses, finances, car and home ownership and even data about children. Much of the information reportedly had originated with Experian, one of the big three credit bureaus in the United States, which had collected the data and sold it.[22]

Experian was not required to get consent from those consumers before sharing their data with Alteryx. While Experian stressed that the information did not include any personally identifiable information, the researcher who discovered the unsecure database said the data would be a "gold mine" for unscrupulous marketers or identity thieves.

The United States, unlike the European Union, gives consumers limited privacy protection. Under the new EU regulations, companies will need to keep track of how and when citizens give consent to use their data. The penalty for breaking the rule is steep — up to 4 percent of a company's annual global revenues.[23]

The United States has no similar federal regulation. The new rules created by the FCC in 2016 that were overturned by the current Congress would have forced ISPs to give consumers the opportunity to "opt in" before collecting personal information such as financial information, children's information and location data. The rules also would have forced ISPs to let customers decide whether service providers could share additional information, including browsing and app usage data, with advertisers and third parties.[24]

ISPs, such as Verizon, which lobbied to get the rule repealed, want to expand their digital advertising opportunities, and the browsing history data is key to doing that.

Last fall, Rep. Marsha Blackburn, R-Tenn., introduced the BROWSER Act (Balancing the Rights of Web Surfers Equally and Responsibly) that would prohibit either ISPs or content providers (such as Google or Facebook) from selling data without opt-in consent.

The Internet Association, which represents Facebook, Google, Twitter and other big internet companies, opposes the bill, saying it could "upend the consumer experience online and stifle innovation." It also argues the bill is unnecessary because websites and apps must comply with "strict FTC privacy enforcement [rules]."[25]

But some in business want Congress to take the lead rather than the regulatory agencies. "Regulators under four different presidents have taken four different approaches," said AT&T Chairman and CEO Randall Stephenson on Jan. 24. "Courts have overturned regulatory decisions. Regulators have reversed their predecessors."

"Congressional action is needed to establish an 'Internet Bill of Rights' that applies to all internet companies and guarantees neutrality, transparency, openness, non-discrimination and privacy protection," he said. "It would provide consistent rules of the road for all internet companies across all websites, content, devices and applications."[26]

Others argue that AT&T's proposal is a way to eliminate the regulatory distinctions between ISPs and content providers. They also say a common set of regulations for ISPs and content providers would be akin to regulating farms and grocery stores in the same way.[27]

Technology security expert Schneier said lawmakers must act. "Congress needs to give the Federal Trade Commission the authority to set minimum security standards for data brokers and to give consumers more control over their personal information," he said. "This is essential as long as consumers are these companies' products and not their customers."[28]

Most consumers automatically click "I agree" to terms-of-service agreements online, choosing functionality over privacy and sometimes unknowingly giving up their personal data for use in behavioral targeting.

"I have never met anyone who has read those terms of service," says Priscilla Regan, a professor in the Department of Public and International Affairs at George Mason University and author of *Legislating Privacy: Technology, Social Values, and Public Policy.* "When we go online to do something, we . . . are focused on [the transaction]," she says. "We don't always operate in a way that protects our privacy."

Most consumers are unaware they are exchanging their private data for the use of online services or functionality, Regan says. "We go online and do something and we think we're doing it for free," she says. "But it's not free. We've become the commodity. Our behavior is of interest to the companies so they can target us better."

Behavioral targeting, which tailors online ads to individuals' preferences, has been found to be effective for both marketers and consumers. In a marketing analytics study, 71 percent of respondents preferred ads tailored to their interests and shopping habits, and users were twice as likely to click on unknown brands if the ads were tailored to them.[29]

But when a company loses personal data, regardless of whether it's from a newsletter sign-up or from a credit bureau, who is liable?

The responsibility for privacy does not rest solely on consumers' shoulders, some argue. "Strong consent is beside the point," says Rotenberg of EPIC. If a "company chooses to collect your personal data, they take on the responsibilities" of ensuring that it is secure.

In congressional testimony last November, Schneier argued that protecting consumer data is more important than just protecting the rights of the individual. It is also vital for national security. "In a world where foreign governments use cyber capabilities to attack U.S. assets, requiring data brokers to limit collection of personal data, securely store the data they collect, and delete data about consumers when it is no longer needed is a matter of national security," he said.[30]

And as biometrics such as facial recognition become more commonplace, consent becomes more nebulous. "When there's a billboard that watches who's walking by

Getty Images/Bloomberg/Andrew Harrer

A computer monitor at a House Financial Services Committee hearing on Oct. 25, 2017, tallies the damage from last year's Equifax data breach. Hackers stole the names, Social Security numbers, birth dates and addresses of nearly half the U.S. population, but the company did not reveal the breach until more than three months later.

it and shows ads related as to who you are [by facial recognition] there's no way of doing consent," he says.

"Choice is supposed to be given expression by explicit consent," says Jim Harper, executive vice president of the Competitive Enterprise Institute, a libertarian think tank in Washington. "But try implementing that. . . . It would fail."

Should the Social Security card be replaced as a primary means of identification?

Social Security numbers (SSN) were never intended to be used as a national identifier. When the first card was issued in 1936, the number was designed simply to keep track of the earnings of U.S. workers for benefits and entitlement programs.

Today, it is the most commonly used identifier in the country.

"SSN is a completely archaic identifier," says Tim Edgar, a privacy lawyer and former White House cybersecurity adviser. Edgar is a senior fellow at Brown University who helped put together its Executive Master in Cybersecurity program.

"It's incredibly insecure," he says. "It's perfectly fine as a number, but it provides no security whatsoever."

White House Cybersecurity Coordinator Rob Joyce agrees. "It's a flawed system," he told *The Washington Post* recently. Joyce supports seeking an encryption solution.[31]

The Trump administration is seeking ways to replace the Social Security card system. One possibility is two-factor authentication involving public and private "keys." When people want to access their account, they would use their public key and would then be sent a message that could only be decrypted with the private key.[32]

Some experts see Estonia's national cryptographic identifier system as a promising model. Every citizen receives a smartcard that securely identifies the user for services and transactions — all online. Its public key infrastructure and auditing system undergoes constant upgrades to keep pace with technology. If a breach occurs no private information is exposed because data backups are stored at "data embassies" around the world.[33]

Congress last fall took a small step toward reducing the SSN's exposure to potential fraud by passing the Social Security Number Fraud Prevention Act. It prohibits federal agencies from listing Social Security numbers on any mailed documents except in special circumstances.[34]

Most experts agree the number works perfectly well as an identifier but not as an "authenticator." No secure system would use the same number as both your log-in and password, said Alessandro Acquisti, an information technology professor and privacy expert at Carnegie Mellon University in Pittsburgh. Yet that is how the Social Security number is used.[35]

Some university databases, for instance, rely on the number to identify students. And credit card companies use it as an authenticator.

"Your email address is a form of identification," said Acquisti. "You can share it publicly, so that people can contact you via that address. The password you use to access your email, instead, is a form of authentication: It should stay secret, because you want to be the only one who can access your emails."[36]

Businesses bear some of the blame for the security problems surrounding the SSN, said Steven M. Bellovin, a professor of computer science at Columbia University in New York City, who focuses on security and privacy questions. The problem is not with the number, he said, but with businesses that use it without instituting additional security standards, Bellovin said.[37]

"Make credit providers liable for the full damages, including ongoing inconvenience, suffered by victims of identity theft," he wrote. "SSNs are not the problem; authentication commensurate with the risk to all parties, including especially individuals, is."[38]

Testifying before the Senate Banking Committee late last year, EPIC's Rotenberg said Congress should ban private sector use of the number unless a company has explicit legal authority to use it.[39]

The ability to prove one's identity is the crux of the matter, says technology security expert Schneier. "The real problem is we need to authenticate ourselves again and again, and we don't have a secure way to do it."

Some experts have proposed biometric solutions. But Rotenberg says a national biometric identifier "raises serious privacy and security risks." While passwords can be completely private, known only to the user, biometrics are inherently public.

"I do know what your ear looks like, if I meet you, and I can take a high-resolution photo of it from afar," said Alvaro Bedoya, a professor of law at Georgetown University in Washington, D.C. "I know what your fingerprint looks like if we have a drink and you leave your fingerprints on the . . . glass." That makes biometrics easily hackable and trackable.[40]

The solution may lie in using more than only one number or one imprint for authentication. "This needs to be a little bit painful," says Eva Casey Velasquez, president and CEO of the Identity Theft Resource Center. She says biometrics should be just one piece of a secure authentication system.

"Things like how I hold my phone . . . not just your passcode, but the pressure that is applied. That data can be captured and analyzed. That doesn't feel deeply private to me, but it can serve as an initial authenticator."

Other countries have adopted biometrics as part of their authentication systems. Australia's tax office, for instance, uses voice-based biometrics to authenticate identities. Other countries are using biometrics to secure

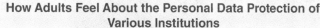

Mixed Confidence in Data Protection

Sixty-six to 70 percent of Americans in 2016 were confident their cellphone, credit card and email providers were protecting their personal data, but fewer than half of those surveyed had the same confidence in the federal government or social media companies.

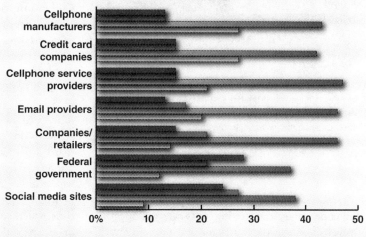

How Adults Feel About the Personal Data Protection of Various Institutions

Note: Refusals and "does not apply" responses not shown.

Source: Kenneth Olmstead and Aaron Smith, "Americans and Cybersecurity," Pew Research Center, Jan. 26, 2017, https://tinyurl.com/zj6f3qx

their data together with other techniques, such as blockchain software. Blockchain is essentially a shared digital ledger that exists across a network of computers with no central authority so no single party can tamper with the records, and there is no single point of failure. Estonia and Dubai are in the process of moving all of their medical records to a blockchain system.[41]

India has an identity biometrics program that has digital information on more than 1 billion people in its database. Its 12-digit Aadhaar number links to a central database housing biometrics, including an iris and fingerprint scan, a photo and demographic information. Citizens will need the number to open a bank account or to get basic services.[42]

Paul Romer, a former chief economist at the World Bank, has called it "the most sophisticated system" he has seen.[43]

A new Visa credit card that can be authenticated through biometrics is displayed at the National Retail Federation's Big Show on Jan. 16, 2018, in New York City. Some experts say biometrics and other technology could make data more secure and better prevent identity theft, but others say the technology presents serious privacy and security concerns.

Harper of the Competitive Enterprise Institute says another option may be creating "self-sovereign" identities in which "I become the warehouse of data about myself."

"That might really change up the game," he says. "Rather than proving my existence by referring to a government card or government number," each person would create identities for different things. "One for online, one for political participation, one for real-world social purposes."

Should police be allowed to use cellphone data gathered without a warrant?

Few dispute that laws, and the court decisions based on them, have failed to keep up with the speed of technological change and unforeseen threats to privacy. Laws written before the Web's inception reflect a time when one's privacy was defined within solid walls, not virtual ones, and a "reasonable expectation of privacy" largely existed only within those tactile structures.

The Supreme Court will hear a case this fall, *Carpenter v. United States*, that legal experts say can clarify the rules on government surveillance and privacy.

Timothy Carpenter was found guilty of involvement in six Michigan robberies after cellphone records placed him near four of the crime scenes. He is currently serving a 116-year prison sentence.[44]

The Fourth Amendment protects the right of citizens to be secure in their "persons, houses, papers and effects against unreasonable searches and seizures" by government agents or entities and requires authorities to show "probable cause" before a search warrant is granted. Despite the amendment's prohibition against warrantless searches, government entities have been obtaining such records without a warrant for years. Verizon Communications said it received more than 20,000 requests from the government for data on cellphone locations during the first half of last year. Only a quarter of those were submitted with a warrant.[45]

Lower courts have upheld the practice largely based on the so-called third-party doctrine, which states that such records can be obtained without a warrant if the individual gave the information voluntarily to a third party. In the *Carpenter* case, the government is arguing that Carpenter gave MetroPCS and Sprint, as the cellphone carriers, his cellphone's location information, which authorities wanted to search.

Rulings from the 1970s reinforced the third-party doctrine, when courts held that individuals had no "legitimate expectation of privacy" from warrantless searches if they gave their data to a third party. But much has changed since then, privacy advocates say, and today third parties hold massive amounts of information from individuals. Supreme Court Justice Sonia Sotomayor signaled her unease with the doctrine in a recent opinion, saying it is "ill-suited to the digital age, in which people reveal a great deal of information about themselves to third parties in the course of carrying out mundane tasks."[46]

The Carpenter case is "the occasion for the Supreme Court to bring the Fourth Amendment into the 21st century," says Erwin Chemerinsky, dean of Berkeley Law. "Getting rid of third-party doctrine is crucial."

Arguing against warrantless searches, the Electronic Privacy Information Center is urging the Supreme Court to extend constitutional protection to cellphone data. It has asked the court to reverse a decision in a 1970s case, *Smith v. Maryland*, which has been the basis for allowing authorities to collect calling data. That case is from an era "when rotary phones sat on desk tops," EPIC said.[47]

EPIC and 36 technical experts and legal scholars filed an amicus brief in the *Carpenter* case recommending that the high court extend Fourth Amendment protection to cellphone data.[48]

"The vast majority of Americans carry cellphones with them in their everyday lives, and the question posed by this case is whether the traditional protections of the Fourth Amendment — including requiring a warrant — will apply to prevent the pervasive location-tracking of any one of us," said American Civil Liberties Union (ACLU) attorney Nathan Freed Wessler, who is representing Carpenter.[49]

But Justice Department attorneys counter that "the government has a compelling interest in obtaining cell-site records to identify suspects, clear the innocent, and obtain information in the preliminary investigation of criminal conduct."[50]

In its brief in the *Carpenter* case, the department pointed to the U.S. Court of Appeals' conclusion that there is a distinction between the content of personal communications, which is private, and the information needed to get those communications from one place to another, which is not. "Historical cell-site records 'fall on the unprotected side of this line,' the appeals court said, 'because they contain routing information' and 'say nothing about the content of any calls.' "[51]

A cellphone user, as a result, has no reasonable expectation of privacy, the Justice Department argued. "Just as a person who dials a number into a phone 'voluntarily convey[s] numerical information to its equipment in the ordinary course of business,' . . . a cellphone user must reveal his general location to a cell tower in order for the cellular service provider to connect a call," attorneys wrote.[52]

The speed of innovation in the digital space has made it "very hard for the Supreme Court, with the Fourth Amendment, to keep up," says Chemerinsky.

"My sense is that the Supreme Court needs to take a lot more of these cases, and needs to lay out some broad principles," says Edgar, the former White House cybersecurity adviser. "If these decisions are decided very narrowly and things just continue . . . then we will be deciding not to decide, and that is in itself a decision."

BACKGROUND
Home as Castle

The roots of privacy in the United States date to the 17th and 18th centuries, when colonists inherited a strong belief from their English forebears that their homes were sacrosanct and could not be illegally searched; nor did they want troops quartered in their houses without their permission.

As democratic norms spread in the colonial period and the newly independent nation drew up a constitution in 1787, the notion of privacy came to encompass the protection of liberty from governmental authority.

In a landmark 1890 *Harvard Law Review* article, 34-year-old lawyer Louis Brandeis of Boston, who would become a Supreme Court justice in 1916, and a co-author argued that the United States needed to formally recognize a right to privacy. Spurring his call was the growing use of photography and the expansion of a muckraking press that was aggressively investigating the excesses of the age.

"Recent inventions and business methods call attention to the next step which must be taken for the protection of the person, and for securing to the individual . . . the right 'to be let alone,' " they wrote. "Numerous mechanical devices threaten to make good the prediction that 'what is whispered in the closet shall be proclaimed from the house-tops.' "[53]

The Constitution's framers had sought to protect Americans in their "beliefs, their thoughts, their emotions and their sensations," Brandeis and Samuel D. Warren wrote.

They proposed that invasions of privacy be classified as a tort — a wrong for which someone can sue in court and obtain economic damages.

In 1928, the growing popularity of two new technologies — the telephone and wiretapping — led Brandeis to argue in a dissenting opinion in *Olmstead v. United States* for a constitutional right to privacy. Brandeis became the first Supreme Court justice to recognize such a right under the Fourth Amendment's prohibition against "unreasonable searches and seizures" by the government and to recognize the threat that technology posed to citizens.[54]

Meanwhile in Europe, to help with its planning, the Dutch government in the 1930s compiled a comprehensive registry of its population that contained the names, addresses and religions of its citizens. But when Nazi Germany invaded the Netherlands in 1940, the Nazis used the registry to track down Jews and Gypsies.[55]

In 1948, the United Nations passed the Universal Declaration of Human Rights, proclaiming that privacy is a fundamental human right. And in 1950, the Council

CHRONOLOGY

1920s-1950s *Privacy rights evolve through court decisions on the Fourth Amendment's prohibitions against unreasonable searches and seizures.*

1928 Supreme Court says warrants are not required in wiretapping cases because no governmental search or seizure is involved.

1948 U.N. passes Universal Declaration of Human Rights, calling privacy a fundamental human right.

1950 European Convention on Human Rights includes the right to "private and family life."

1960s-1970s *Supreme Court rules that the Constitution protects a "zone of privacy" for individuals.*

1965 Supreme Court cites an individual's right to privacy in establishing the right to use contraception *(Griswold v. Connecticut).*

1970 Fair Credit Reporting Act allows individuals to access their credit reports and challenge inaccuracies but immunizes credit agencies from invasion-of-privacy suits.

1972 Federal panel releases the Code of Fair Information Practices, protecting use of consumer data.

1974 Privacy Act outlines how federal agencies should handle individuals' data.

1978 Foreign Intelligence Surveillance Act (FISA) creates a separate court to oversee government surveillance and covert searches.

1980s-1990s *Internet service providers and advertisers develop tools for tracking consumer behavior.*

1986 Electronic Communications Privacy Act extends restrictions on telephone wiretaps to computer data.

1989 Tim Berners-Lee, a British scientist, invents the World Wide Web.

1990 Virtually all U.S. states recognize a right to privacy in civil suits.

1996 Health Insurance Portability and Accountability Act is the first federal statute to directly regulate the privacy of personal health data. . . . European Union requires various entities to protect personal information.

1998 Children's Online Privacy Protection Act regulates the collection of children's personal information online.

1999 Gramm-Leach-Bliley Act allows financial institutions to share customers' information with affiliates.

2000-Present *Data breaches and government surveillance become common.*

2001 After the 9/11 terrorist attacks, the USA Patriot Act allows authorities to investigate and detain suspected terrorists.

2005 *New York Times* reports the George W. Bush administration secretly authorized warrantless surveillance of U.S. citizens by the National Security Agency (NSA).

2008 FISA is expanded to allow warrantless surveillance. . . . Heartland Payment Systems is hacked, exposing information on more than 134 million credit cards.

2011 In one of the worst-ever gaming hacks, 77 million Sony PlayStation network accounts are compromised.

2013 Former NSA contractor Edward Snowden begins leaking classified documents, revealing that the NSA was illegally collecting data. . . . Hackers steal email addresses and passwords from all 3 billion Yahoo accounts.

2015 USA Freedom Act extends parts of the Patriot Act and ends bulk collection of phone data.

2017 Hackers steal personal information of 145 million Americans from Equifax, but the credit agency waits weeks to report it. . . . Uber admits to paying $100,000 ransom after hackers stole 57 million records, including driver's license numbers.

May 2018 European Union's General Data Protection Regulation takes effect.

of Europe, a human rights organization, adopted the European Convention on Human Rights, including the right to "private and family life." The European Court of Human Rights — which adjudicates allegations of human rights violations — has interpreted that right to include the protection of personal data. The convention requires the council's 47 member states to ensure their national laws adhere to its principles.[56]

In the United States, privacy rights did not begin to gain momentum until the 1960s. In 1965 and '73, the Supreme Court cited an individual's right to privacy in landmark decisions establishing the right to use contraception (*Griswold v. Connecticut*) and to have an abortion (*Roe v. Wade*). In 2003 in *Lawrence v. Texas*, the court recognized the right to privacy in homosexual relations.[57]

The U.S. Constitution does not explicitly mention privacy, but Justice William O. Douglas, writing for the majority in *Griswold*, called privacy a "penumbral right," meaning it was implicit in the Bill of Rights. For example, he wrote, the Fourth Amendment and its prohibition against "unreasonable searches and seizures" created a zone of privacy in the bedroom.

"Would we allow the police to search the sacred precincts of marital bedrooms for telltale signs of the use of contraceptives?" he asked.[58]

In the 1970s Congress also began to address the issue. In 1970, it passed the Fair Credit Reporting Act, which regulated information included in credit reports. It stipulated that after seven years — and 10 years for bankruptcy — information about debt collections, civil lawsuits, tax liens and arrests for criminal offenses must be removed from such reports.[59]

Congress also approved the 1974 Privacy Act prohibiting federal agencies from disclosing personal information about an individual without the person's consent, except for purposes such as law enforcement, census statistics and congressional investigations.[60]

And in 1978, Congress passed the Foreign Intelligence Surveillance Act (FISA), creating a separate court to oversee requests for surveillance and covert searches, with looser rules for obtaining permission to conduct such surveillance.

Internet Age

The internet — a network that allows computers to communicate with each other — can be traced to the 1960s when the RAND Corp., a think tank in California focused on military issues, devised a communications network that could survive a nuclear war. With funding from the Defense Department's Advanced Research Projects Agency (DARPA), the fledgling network grew from seven university computers in 1969 to several thousand by the early 1970s.[61]

As computers became smaller, cheaper and more powerful, the internet exploded in popularity after Tim Berners-Lee, a British scientist at CERN, a scientific research center in Switzerland, invented the World Wide Web in 1989 — allowing the interconnection of documents and photos with hypertext links. The software was offered for free along with a browser and code library, ensuring the software's rapid, widespread adoption.[62]

The internet's dramatic growth presented a new set of challenges for Congress. The Electronics Communication Privacy Act (ECPA), passed in 1986, set standards for how the government could access digital information. It required that authorities get a warrant before digital communications could be intercepted or read, but only on public servers and only for 180 days, after which only a subpoena was necessary.[63]

But technology has outpaced the ECPA, which was written before the existence of search engines, Facebook, smartphones and other technologies. "The outdated Electronic Communications Privacy Act," the ACLU said, "allows the government to intercept and access a treasure trove of information about who you are, where you go, and what you do, which is being collected by cellphone providers, search engines, social networking sites, and other websites every day."[64]

Spurred by the 9/11 terrorist attacks, Congress in late 2001 passed the Patriot Act, expanding authorities' ability to conduct warrantless searches and access information about Americans' online and offline communications. The act was updated with the 2015 Freedom Act, which extended the Patriot Act through 2019 but eliminated the bulk collection of Americans' phone records.

The Patriot Act includes a "roving" wiretap provision that allows the FBI to eavesdrop on suspects who use and dump cellphones. The government's ability to collect business records in investigations continues but is limited in scope.

Internet of Things Raises a Web of Worries

Experts say connected devices are easy to hack.

Nathan Ruser, a 20-year-old Australian studying security and the Middle East, noticed something strange in late January when he zoomed in on an interactive online map showing two years of activity by runners and walkers wearing Web-connected fitness devices.

A desert area in Syria that normally would have been dark on the map "sort of lit up like a Christmas tree," Ruser said, leading him to wonder, "Does it show U.S. soldiers?"

Indeed, the Global Heatmap — posted by a GPS tracking company showing fitness device users' activity between 2015 and 2017 — revealed the movements of U.S. soldiers in the Middle East, Afghanistan and elsewhere who were wearing fitness trackers. After news of the security oversight broke, the U.S. military vowed to revise its guidelines on the use of all wireless devices by service members.[1]

Such revelations have raised concerns about the security, and privacy, of devices that are part of the Internet of Things (IoT). The digital innovation connects consumer devices, including lights, refrigerators, DVRs and even toys, to the internet and through it to each other. Based on the rapidly growing popularity of such devices — 127 new ones join the IoT network every second, according to one study — experts predict there will be more than 50 billion IoT devices worldwide by 2020.[2]

However, many of those devices leave their users wide open to hacking, surreptitious monitoring and other privacy intrusions. A study by privacy advocates found, for example, that nearly one-third of the apps on the top wearable fitness devices lack privacy policies covering how user data will be handled.[3]

Some toys also pose concerns. U.S. privacy advocates filed a complaint in 2016 with the Federal Trade Commission (FTC) about a microphone-equipped doll named My Friend Cayla. The advocates said the toy, which is able to "talk" to children by establishing wireless internet connections with a third-party voice-recognition software company, is easily hackable and violates child-protection regulations and laws.

"A stranger or potential predator within a 50-foot range can easily establish a Bluetooth connection with the doll, eavesdrop on the child and even converse with the child through the doll," warned Josh Golin, executive director of the Campaign for a Commercial-Free Childhood, a coalition of educators, health care professionals, parents and others. The group asked Amazon and Walmart to stop selling the doll; both companies have complied, although the doll is still marketed in the United States.[4]

Germany, where wireless devices with hidden cameras or recorders are illegal, has banned the dolls and directed parents to destroy them. A German university student, Stefan Hessel, had raised legal concerns after he found that an eavesdropper could listen in to the doll's conversations with the child "through several walls."[5]

Genesis Toys, the doll's manufacturer, said on its website it "is committed to protecting you and your family's personal information." And Vivid, a U.K.-based toy distributor that sold the dolls in Germany, said it was determined to comply "with all applicable rules and regulations" and was "working with our German partners to resolve this issue."[6]

Advocates of IoT devices say virtual assistants such as Amazon's Alexa and Apple's Siri offer not only convenience but also enormous benefits. "The voice control for Alexa is convenient for me, but if you're blind, Alexa is a game-changer," says John Verdi, vice president of policy for the

Net Neutrality

The internet's growth in size and sophistication spawned a new debate: How much control should internet service providers have over how consumers experience the internet and how their data is handled? An ISP is basically the pipe that delivers the internet to a business or a home, as well as a person's phone or computer.

The Telecommunications Act of 1996 was the first major overhaul of telecommunications law in almost 62 years, according to the FCC website. The goal was to allow any communications business to compete in any market, including telephone services, cable and broadcast.[65]

But a few years later, Democrats warned of potentially monopolistic behavior among ISPs, which led to

Future of Privacy Forum, a think tank that advocates for data privacy.

Meanwhile, so-called smart TVs, or televisions connected to the internet, have come under scrutiny for collecting data on consumers. Vizio, the second-largest manufacturer of smart TVs, was fined $2.2 million by the FTC for collecting and selling data without the knowledge or consent of its TV users. Some of the company's TVs recorded what viewers watched "on a second-by-second basis," said the complaint. Under the settlement, Vizio neither confirmed nor denied wrongdoing, but company general counsel Jerry Huang pledged Vizio will "get people's consent before collecting and sharing television-viewing information."[7]

Most consumers do not realize that their internet-connected devices can be hijacked for use in a major digital attack, such as a 2016 incident that knocked Twitter, Reddit, Netflix and many other sites off the Web. The attackers used millions of unsecured internet-connected webcams, routers and DVRs to create a chain reaction.[8]

Technology security expert Bruce Schneier says the dangers posed by the IoT are so great that a federal agency should be created to deal with them.

While a data breach may be serious, "the IoT can kill people," he says. He cites a situation in which hackers take control of self-driving cars, which use wireless internet connections to guide them. "Crashing all the cars in Pittsburgh is a perfectly reasonable attack scenario," Schneier says.

— *Ellen Kennerly*

Getty Images/Fitbit/Dave Kotinsky

Fitness bands, such as the Fitbit Alta HR, above, and other devices that are part of the Internet of Things can leave their users open to hacking and surreptitious monitoring.

[3] "Best Practices for Consumer Wearables & Wellness Apps and Devices," Future of Privacy Forum, August 2016, https://tinyurl.com/yav3xl8u.

[4] Aimee Picchi, "Amazon, Walmart urged to stop selling 'spying' doll," CBS News, Dec. 20, 2016, https://tinyurl.com/ybmetwml.

[5] *Ibid.*; "German parents told to destroy Cayla doll over hacking fears," BBC, Feb. 17, 2017, https://tinyurl.com/j3hrwrq.

[6] Alanna Petroff, "Germany tells parents to destroy microphone in 'illegal' doll," CNNtech, Feb. 17, 2017, https://tinyurl.com/hf8jlmh; "Privacy Policy," Genesis Toys, Feb. 23, 2015, https://tinyurl.com/ybtry5zs.

[7] Sapna Maheshwari, "Is Your Vizio Television Spying on You? What to Know," *The New York Times*, Feb. 7, 2017, https://tinyurl.com/yahyoleg; "Vizio agrees to pay $2.2 million to settle FTC's television-spying case," *The Washington Post*, Feb. 6, 2017, https://tinyurl.com/yaqa7kjr.

[8] Jeff John Roberts, "Who to Blame for the Attack on the Internet," *Fortune*, Oct. 23, 2016, https://tinyurl.com/hq3p6yd.

[1] Liz Sly, "U.S. soldiers are revealing sensitive and dangerous information by jogging," *The Washington Post*, Jan. 29, 2018, https://tinyurl.com/yb8buo6t.

[2] Louis Columbus, "2017 Roundup Of Internet Of Things Forecast," *Forbes*, Dec. 10, 2017, https://tinyurl.com/ybe5zu7z; Mark Patel, Jason Shangkuan and Christopher Thomas, "What's new with the Internet of Things?" McKinsey & Company, May 2017, https://tinyurl.com/y8fk4sft.

the idea of "net neutrality," where providers would be required to treat all internet traffic equally and not charge for faster speeds. "Net neutrality is an important concept on which the internet has been built upon," said Google CEO Sundar Pichai, at the World Economic Summit on Jan. 24. Moving away from it "can actually favor big companies," he said.[66]

Republicans argued that no regulation was needed, and that internet businesses should evolve freely as the market saw fit. "President Clinton got it right in 1996 when he established a free market-based approach to this new thing called the Internet, and the Internet economy we have is a result of his light-touch regulatory vision," said FCC Chairman Ajit Pai, who was nominated by

For One Family, Identity Theft Hits Home

"This will never be over for us."

The trouble began at the end of 2015. Amy Wang, an occupational therapist in Miami, and her husband started receiving credit card approvals and rejections from stores like electronics retailer hhgregg, Walmart and Bloomingdale's. "Every day it was a different card," she says. Her husband would get on the phone each night and try to tell the companies they had not applied for any cards.

Then the bills began arriving. Macy's and Bloomingdale's said they owed a total of $20,000 for goods the Wangs never bought on cards they did not possess. The couple filed a police report.

"Anything that anyone told us to do, we did," says Wang.

Then they received a change-of-address confirmation form in the mail in early January 2016. "I just thought it was a mistake," she says. Wang called the U.S. Postal Service's 800 number listed on the form and explained they had not moved.

She assumed their mail would start arriving again, but it did not. When Wang talked to their letter carrier about it, he told her their mail was still being forwarded and advised her to go to the post office near her house.

There, she was told it would take seven to 10 days to restore her mail service. About two weeks later, when the couple were still not receiving mail, she started calling the Postal Service's district office. "A trickle" of mail finally started to appear around the end of February, nearly two months after they had received the notice.

It was frustrating, she says, because nothing seemed to work. "We felt like we were in some weird sci-fi movie," says Wang. The Postal Service did not respond to *CQ Researcher* requests for comment.

The timing of the identity theft was not accidental, says Wang. The thieves got "all of our tax information, our kids' Social Security numbers" on documents mailed to them by the IRS in January.

Like Wang and her family, more than 16.7 million Americans had their identities stolen in 2017, costing them $16.8 billion, up from $15.3 billion stolen from 13.1 million victims in 2015, according to Javelin Strategy & Research, a Pleasanton, Calif.-based financial research group. In 2006, in comparison, the number of victims was 10.6 million.[1]

Michigan has the highest per capita rate of reported identity theft fraud, followed by Florida and Delaware.[2]

"It is inevitable that each and every one of us is going to have [our identity] compromised in our lives," says Adam Levin, founder and chairman of CyberScout, a business focusing on identity theft services.

Levin advises consumers to follow what he calls the three M's:

- Minimize the risk of exposure: Reduce the number of credit cards you carry, secure your wireless devices and limit your sharing of personal details on social media.
- Monitor your money: Check you bank accounts daily, get a free credit report annually, sign up with credit monitoring services for free transactional alerts.
- Manage the damage: Alert the authorities, and freeze your credit if appropriate.[3]

"Know as quickly as possible that you have a problem, and then have a plan," he says.

President Trump. "We saw companies like Facebook and Amazon and Google become global powerhouses precisely because we had light-touch rules that apply to this Internet."[67]

During the Obama administration, and after years of heated debate, the FCC — which then had a Democratic majority — approved the 2015 Open Internet Order prohibiting ISPs from attempting to block, throttle or prioritize website speeds. It defined the Web as a utility — something everyone needs, similar to running water or electricity. "Like the air that we breathe [the internet] belongs to the people," says Rep. Hank Johnson, D-Ga. "Therefore, the people's interest must be protected."

Opponents said the FCC gained too much power under the Open Internet Order, including authority over privacy policies, which previously had belonged to the

In 2015, credit card companies introduced cards with microchips, making the cards harder to counterfeit. Credit card companies also use text messages and email alerts to notify cardholders when they suspect thieves are using a credit card number in what is known as a "card-not-present" transaction.[4]

The Postal Service has said it takes several steps to determine whether an address change is legitimate. When a request is made online, a $1 fee must be paid with a credit or debit card. The name and address on the card have to match the name and one of the addresses on the change form. When a change-of-address form is submitted in person, the Postal Service requires "verification," but on its website it does not define the term.[5]

The use of microchips in credit cards led many criminals to switch to identity theft and to open new charge accounts in other people's names, according to the Identity Theft Resource Center, a victim's advocacy group. As a result, fraud in which the thief is actually holding a card is declining while fraud involving a card that is not in the thief's physical possession is rising.[6]

To prevent identity theft, consumers must be armed with better information, says Wang. "Somebody has to be five steps ahead of these guys," she says. "Otherwise we're going to be eight steps behind."

Wang says she and her husband had been notified of a data breach and heard of the possibility of another before their troubles began.

But they have no idea whether either had anything to do with the identity theft. The whole experience, they say, was bewildering and frightening. "You don't understand it until it happens to you," Wang says.

She says the hardest part is that it is not behind them. "They have our information. They have our kids' information."

"To me, they're just waiting," says Wang. "They're like sleeper cells. This will never be over for us."

— *Ellen Kennerly*

Amy Wang of Miami and her family experienced a nightmarish breach of their privacy after someone stole their personal data. More than 16.7 million Americans had their identities stolen in 2016, costing them $16.8 billion.

[1] Al Pascual, Kyle Marchini and Sarah Miller, "2017 Identity Fraud: Securing the Connected Life," Javelin Strategy & Research, Feb. 1, 2017, https://tinyurl.com/y7salnbj; Peter Rudegeair and AnnaMaria Andriotis, "Identity Fraud Hits Record Number of People," *The Wall Street Journal*, Feb. 7, 2018, https://tinyurl.com/y8f2h2hq.

[2] "Consumer Sentinel Network Handbook Data Book for January-December 2016," Federal Trade Commission, March 2017, https://tinyurl.com/juk8uvd.

[3] Adam Levin, "Privacy is Dead, 3 Ways to Protect Yourself," Cyberscout. com, Aug. 28, 2015, https://tinyurl.com/ycnh8fvt.

[4] "Are You a Victim of 'Card-Not-Present' Fraud?" Identity Theft Resource Center, https://tinyurl.com/y7mvaaf8; Jodi Helmer, "New industry tools fight credit card fraud," CreditCards.com, Sept. 19, 2014, https://tinyurl.com/y85ruebo.

[5] Karin Price Mueller, "Bamboozled: Have a mailbox? See the scary 'identity takeover' that could happen to you," NJ.com, Feb. 27, 2017, https://tinyurl.com/yazanaxg; Paul Muschick, "Postal Service change of address system exploited by identity thief," *Morning Call*, Nov. 10, 2017, https://tinyurl.com/yalkxkpn.

[6] "Are You a Victim of 'Card-Not-Present' Fraud?" *op. cit.*

Federal Trade Commission. "The FTC has been our nation's privacy enforcer, and we think [we should] leave that authority with them," says Rep. Blackburn.

Because the Open Internet Order designated the internet a utility, the FTC could no longer regulate the ISPs, because it lacked authority to regulate "common carriers" — companies providing utility services — as the internet was now defined. However, in late 2017, the Republican-dominated FCC rescinded the Obama-era net neutrality rules and returned regulatory power over privacy issues to the FTC.[68]

A recent appeals court ruling found that if an ISP provides a common-carrier service such as mobile phone service — which many of them do — the FTC is not allowed to enforce its regulations against them. The case is on appeal.[69]

The ISPs have pledged to follow the FTC's recommendations on opt-in consent for sensitive information.

The states might have the final word on all this. After the repeal of the FCC's more stringent privacy regulations, legislatures in at least 22 states and the District of Columbia have proposed bills tightening consumer privacy rules. Nevada and Minnesota already require ISPs to get opt-in permission before sharing personal information. And Minnesota requires permission before disclosing data about browsing habits.

The marketplace may also offer some solutions to consumers seeking privacy. "We anticipate the return of 'pay-for-privacy,' " in which consumers can pay more for internet services that keep their browsing information private, according to Fatemah Kahtibloo, a principal analyst at the market research firm Forrester. She predicted the development of "tiered pricing models that would effectively make privacy a privilege for those who could afford to pay more for these services every month."[70]

Surveillance Policy

The debate surrounding privacy rights ramped up after former NSA contractor Edward Snowden leaked classified information about the NSA's global surveillance programs, including previously unknown programs involving Americans. But the only bill that Congress has passed as a result of those revelations was legislation in 2015 to stop the bulk collection of phone records of millions of citizens.

The USA Freedom Act was praised by Snowden and others as the most significant surveillance reform bill since 1978.

But Senate Majority Leader Mitch McConnell, R-Ky., called the act "a resounding victory for those who currently plotted against our homeland. . . . It does not enhance the privacy protections of American citizens, and it surely undermines American security by taking one more tool from our war fighters, in my view, at exactly the wrong time."[71]

Two years later, privacy advocates had hoped to stop the reauthorization of Section 702 of the FISA Amendments Act, due to expire at the end of 2017. Congress had added the section in 2008 to allow warrantless surveillance of suspects and to legalize a post-9/11 secret surveillance program. It included gathering communications between those suspects and Americans, as well as communication among Americans if foreign suspects were mentioned.

Snowden had criticized the surveillance program. "People should be able to pick up the phone and call their family . . . buy a book online . . . without wondering how these events are going to look to an agent of the government," he said in a 2014 TED talk. "More communications are being intercepted in America about Americans than there are in Russia about Russians."[72]

Some members of Congress agreed with him. "We are collecting vast amounts of data," said Rep. Zoe Lofgren, D-Calif., in January on the House floor. "Under [Section] 702 you can search that for Americans for crimes that have nothing to do with terrorism," she said.[73]

Those in favor of the program argued that the United States should do all it could to fight terrorism. Section 702 is a "critical national security tool used by our intelligence community," said Rep. Chris Stewart, R-Utah.[74]

CURRENT SITUATION
Data Hacks

Massive data breaches and invasive surveillance technology are accelerating the discussion about the need for better privacy protections. Among other things, security experts and privacy advocates are proposing consumer education, tighter regulation and stronger oversight.

Numerous lawsuits against Equifax accusing the company of negligence are pending after last year's enormous data breach. More than four months passed between the time Equifax failed to install a security patch and the time the issue was resolved.

Among the lawsuits is a national class action suit, filed in Atlanta, that names plaintiffs from every state and the District of Columbia. In addition, 240 individual class-action suits have been filed and numerous investigations are in process, including one by the FTC. Equifax and its attorneys have declined to comment on the litigation.[75]

According to the national class action lawsuit, thieves may already be using the stolen data. It alleges violations of federal and state laws and includes dozens of complaints indicating that criminals are using the information to make fraudulent credit card charges and apply for loans and mortgages.[76]

But some criminals bide their time. "Thieves know you may set up fraud alerts so they can wait for a period of time until using the data," according to Velasquez of the Identity Theft Resource Center. "We hear anecdotally through our call center that victims of the Anthem breach from 2015 are just now contacting us because their information is beginning to be used."

Anthem, the biggest U.S. health insurance company, agreed to pay $115 million last summer to settle a lawsuit over the hacking of about 79 million people's records in the largest data breach settlement to date.[77]

Action in Congress

In the wake of massive data breaches, Congress is considering several measures.

Under the Data Security and Breach Notification Act, introduced by three Democratic senators in December, business executives have 30 days to report data breaches or face up to five years in prison. The bill also would require the FTC to establish best practices for businesses to improve the protection of customer data.[78]

Rep. Johnson of Georgia is backing the Cyber Privacy Fortification Act, which would establish criminal penalties for those who intentionally conceal security breaches. "We must have measures in place that provide accountability to the public when corporations and their executives do the wrong thing and it hurts people," he says.

Other bills focus on consumer education and the creation of best-practices for businesses and individuals. The FTC would be required to develop cybersecurity resources for consumer education about the Internet of Things under a bill introduced by Sens. Roger Wicker, R-Miss., and Maggie Hassan, D-N.H.[79]

And under a bill co-sponsored by Sen. Orrin Hatch, R-Utah, and Rep. Anna Eshoo, D-Calif., a "cyber hygiene best practices" list would be developed to help consumers navigate data privacy issues.[80]

While it was widely thought the growing number of data breaches would spur quick passage of legislation, none has yet passed. One reason, says Johnson, is that Congress "has no appetite for the exercise of regulatory power."

Regan of George Mason University also sees the Trump administration as a potential roadblock. "With the current administration [in power], I think we're highly unlikely to see any legislation passed," she says.

During his first year in office, President Trump has been moving aggressively to reduce government regulations, but White House press secretary Sarah Huckabee Sanders said shortly after the Equifax breach that the administration will look at the situation "extensively" to decide whether more rules are needed to protect data.[81]

Overseas Rules

Meanwhile, under the EU's stringent data privacy laws going into effect in May, businesses must get explicit consent from consumers before using or sharing their data. In addition, if consumers wish to withdraw their consent at any time, the procedure must be clearly explained and easily accomplished.[82]

The new regulations codify "privacy by design," in which systems storing data must include privacy protections from inception — not as an afterthought.

The regulations will apply to any business processing the data of someone living in the EU, regardless of where the company itself is located.

Other key changes include:

- An organization out of compliance will face fines of up to 4 percent of annual gross revenues or 20 million pounds, whichever is greater.
- Businesses must use clear and easily understandable language on forms requesting data. The forms also must include the purposes for which the data will be used.
- Organizations must reveal a breach within 72 hours of its discovery.

In a significant shift, EU citizens will have the right to find out whether any of their personal data is being collected, and if so, what and where. In addition, they will be entitled to an electronic copy of the data free of charge.

Citizens will have the right to erase their personal data.[83]

"Right now, Europe is the regulatory superpower," says technology security expert Schneier.

Microsoft, Facebook and other U.S. companies are preparing for the new regulations because of the compliance costs and the steep fines they could face if they suffer data breaches involving EU citizens. For example, Equifax could have been fined 4 percent of its annual

Can consumers' online data be protected?

YES

Priscilla Regan
Professor of Policy and Government, George Mason University; Author, Legislating Privacy: Technology, Social Values, and Public Policy

Written for *CQ Researcher,* February 2018

Protecting consumer data is not only possible but essential. Despite repeated claims that "privacy is dead," people value their individual privacy and living in a society that protects privacy. They also want their online data protected and are outraged by data breaches such as those at Equifax (2017), Uber (2016) and Yahoo (2013).

However, the current policy for protecting privacy, based on a 1970s idea of "fairness" and captured under the mantra of "notice and consent," does not provide the necessary protection. Privacy-consent policies are long, unclear and legalistic — and unrealistically burden the individual who is focused on a transaction or activity. Hence the paradox that people care about privacy but act in ways that compromise it. And state laws provide redress only after a data breach occurs, leave consumers vulnerable to future harms and provide no real consequences for the companies.

As consumers' online and offline lives continue to blend into seamless data streams, protecting consumer data will be critical to innovations such as those promised by the Internet of Things and "big data." Contrary to popular, but largely untested, beliefs that regulation of cyber activities will stifle online innovation, effective privacy and security regulation is now necessary to foster innovation.

Consumers are becoming more wary and skeptical as media coverage of privacy issues increases. In 2017, a *Guardian* reporter asked Tinder, a dating app, what information it had about her only to learn it had amassed, in her words, "her deepest, darkest secrets." This is one of numerous examples ranging from concerns about reported misuse of personal data by many popular online companies to unauthorized surveillance and questionable security by nanny cameras, Alexa and driverless cars.

Effective privacy and security policies that consumers trust will require government regulation to hold companies accountable and render significant consequences for bad actors. Self-regulation by companies has not proven effective, and calls for more rigorous self-regulation are unlikely to improve the situation because real protections are expensive and not necessarily in the company's interest.

Instead, we need requirements for designing privacy and security into online systems; clear standards for appropriate uses of information; outside audits to ensure that personal data are being maintained with security and integrity; and a way for individuals to learn what types of their information are being held and delete irrelevant or outdated details.

NO

Bruce Schneier
Security Technologist; Author, Data and Goliath: The Hidden Battles to Collect Your Data and Control Your World

Written for *CQ Researcher,* February 2018

Everything online is hackable. This is true for Equifax's data and the federal Office of Personal Management's data, which was hacked in 2015. If information is on a computer connected to the internet, it is vulnerable.

But just because everything is hackable doesn't mean everything will be hacked. The difference between the two is complex, and filled with defensive technologies, security best practices, consumer awareness, the motivation and skill of the hacker and the desirability of the data. The risks will be different if an attacker is a criminal who just wants credit-card details — and doesn't care where he gets them from — or the Chinese military looking for specific data from a specific place.

The proper question isn't whether it's possible to protect consumer data, but whether a particular site protects our data well enough for the benefits provided by that site. And here, again, there are complications.

In most cases, it's impossible for consumers to make informed decisions about whether their data are protected. We have no idea what sorts of security measures Google uses to protect our highly intimate Web search data or our personal emails. We have no idea what sorts of security measures Facebook uses to protect our posts and conversations.

We have a feeling that these big companies do better than smaller ones. But we're also surprised when a lone individual publishes personal data hacked from the infidelity site Ashley Madison.com, or when the North Korean government does the same with personal information in Sony's network.

Think about all the companies collecting personal data about you — the websites you visit, your smartphone and its apps, your internet-connected car — and how little you know about their security practices. Even worse, credit bureaus and data brokers like Equifax collect your personal information without your knowledge or consent.

So while it might be possible for companies to do a better job protecting our data, you as a consumer are in no position to demand such protection.

Government policy is the missing ingredient. We need standards and a method for enforcement. We need liabilities and the ability to sue companies that poorly secure our data. The biggest reason companies don't protect our data online is that it's cheaper not to. Government policy is how we change that.

profits, or $124 million, if the EU regulations had been in place in 2017 when its breach occurred.[84]

China, meanwhile, is expanding its use of facial recognition to build a national surveillance and data-sharing platform. In a test of the far-reaching "Sharp Eyes" program, authorities are alerted if targeted people move more than 330 yards outside of designated areas.

"A system like this is obviously well-suited to controlling people," Harper of the Competitive Enterprise Institute told Bloomberg Businessweek. " 'Papers, please' was the symbol of living under tyranny in the past. Now, government officials don't need to ask."[85]

"Surveillance technologies are giving the government a sense that it can finally achieve the level of control over people's lives that it aspires to," said German academic Adrian Zenz.

China's goal is to effectively track its people's locations, activities and associations in order to gauge their trustworthiness and ultimately assign them a "social credit" score, he said. The score could then be used to determine what schools their children attend and whether they could borrow money.[86]

In the United States, meanwhile, concerns are growing about automated decision-making (based on algorithms) for credit applications and other uses. Consumer reporting companies collect data and provide reports to other companies about consumers. These reports then help companies decide whether to provide people with credit, employment, rental housing, insurance and other things.[87]

"Lots of online companies are employing algorithms for a whole range of business practices," says Verdi of the Future of Privacy Forum.

The group said algorithms can discriminate against applicants based on race, gender or health. It urged companies to design algorithms that "ensure proxies are not used for protected classes [under the law] & [that] data does not amplify historical bias."[88]

Law enforcement also is using algorithms for such things as deciding where to patrol or who should be offered bail, Verdi says. In New York, Chicago and other cities, for example, police are using algorithms in computerized maps to predict crime trends and deploy resources. Defenders of the practice say the technology has helped reduce the city's crime rate to historic lows.[89]

The question, Verdi says, is whether "these algorithms are lawful or just discriminatory."

Washington state Attorney General Bob Ferguson announces a multimillion-dollar lawsuit against Uber on Nov. 28, 2017. He says the ride-sharing company broke state law when it failed to notify more than 10,000 drivers in the state that their personal information was accessed as part of a major hack in 2016 that affected 57 million Uber accounts worldwide. Uber concealed the hack for a year. The company acknowledges the problems and says it paid the hackers a $100,000 ransom to delete the data.

Personal data that may be shared is becoming even more personal than name and address. Newly popular DNA kits are raising privacy red flags over the danger of companies sharing a person's genetic information with third parties, such as health insurance companies.

Sen. Chuck Schumer, D-N.Y., has asked the FTC to investigate companies such as 23andMe, a personal genomics and biotechnology company, as well as genealogy websites such as Ancestry.com and MyHeritage. 23andMe and Ancestry.com both said they do not sell DNA data without consent. MyHeritage said it has never sold such data to a third party.[90]

OUTLOOK
Growing Threats

Privacy advocates and many lawmakers from both political parties agree that danger lies ahead if the United States does not take steps soon to safeguard consumer privacy.

"Data breaches and identity thefts are increasing," says Rotenberg of the Electronic Privacy Information Center, and "obviously it's out of control."

"It's hard to build political pressure for the changes," says Chemerinsky, dean of Berkeley Law. "In order for Congress to respond, it will likely take political pressure."

"We can't just rely on the courts," he says. "Some of the most important things that protect privacy come from legislation."

The danger reaches beyond U.S. borders, says Rotenberg. "Increasingly, we see today that the data is being targeted by foreign adversaries," he says. "This actually ups the stakes."

The growing threat will make digital security even more important in the years ahead. "There will be a horrific shortage of qualified cybersecurity professionals" in the coming years, says Adam Levin, founder and chairman CyberScout, which focuses on preventing and dealing with identity theft. He believes the nation will need "a cybersecurity [agency] equivalent to the Consumer Financial Protection Bureau."

"There has to be a much saner policy on disclosure of discovered vulnerabilities," he says. "I am worried [that by] 2022, we may have entered the movie 'Minority Report,'" about a world where people are arrested based on computer projections, before they actually commit crimes.

Despite the growing concerns over privacy, Rotenberg says he is "cautiously optimistic" that solutions can be found. "I don't think you can afford to give up on the future," he says.

Companies such as Alphabet's Chronicle are emerging to offer businesses better protections against data breaches. And universities are beginning to offer specialties such as Brown University's Executive Master in Cybersecurity program to address a growing need for professionals.

The most oft-cited problem — using Social Security numbers to identify individuals and authenticate their data — has gained national urgency. Of all of the separate identifiers being discussed to replace the Social Security card system — biometrics such as facial recognition or retina scans, encryption, blockchain or two-factor authentication — the solution may be an amalgam of most or all of these options. Combining standard identifiers such as name, address and birth date along with dynamic factors such as biometrics could pull a range of identities into one central — and much more secure — consumer "identity."[91]

"There are always going to be risks, and really bad things will happen, but we will muddle through," says Harper of the Competitive Enterprise Institute. It may take a while, he adds.

In five years, he says, society will be in "about the same place." But in "15 to 50 years, we will be much better off." Why? "Because the solution to all of these privacy problems is generational."

"Society will just get good at figuring this out," says Harper.

Others are not so optimistic. If society fails to solve its burgeoning privacy issues, "we are going to face some kind of 'Cybergeddon,'" says Levin. "Self-regulation simply isn't working."

NOTES

1. "2017 Data Breaches," Privacy Rights Clearinghouse, https://tinyurl.com/y9pw3pvq.
2. "2017 Annual Data Breach Year End Review," Identity Theft Resource Center, Jan. 25, 2017, https://tinyurl.com/yb3epaf9.
3. "Data Breaches on the Rise," Electronic Privacy Information Center, Jan. 25, 2017, https://tinyurl.com/ybl5bn97.
4. Kenneth Harney, "Data breach at Equifax prompts a national class-action suit," *The Washington Post*, Nov. 22, 2017, https://tinyurl.com/ybg4h4q9.
5. Selena Larson, "Every single Yahoo account was hacked: 3 billion in all," CNNtech, Oct. 4, 2017, https://tinyurl.com/ydevl9e9.
6. Eric Newcomer, "Uber Paid Hackers to Delete Stolen Data on 57 Million," Bloomberg, Nov. 21, 2017, https://tinyurl.com/y8zpdrcw.
7. Michael Kassner, "Anatomy of the Target Data Breach," ZDNet, Feb. 2, 2015, https://tinyurl.com/lp7y8rt.
8. Taylor Amerding, "The 17 biggest data breaches of the 21st Century," CSO, Jan. 26, 2018, https://tinyurl.com/yajr5eem.
9. Selena Larson, "Google says hackers steal almost 250,000 web logins each week," CNNtech, Nov. 9, 2017, https://tinyurl.com/yaaluvje.
10. Kimberly Kindy, "How Congress dismantled Internet privacy rules," *The Washington Post*, May 30, 2017, https://tinyurl.com/yc36et8f.
11. Brian Fung, "The FCC just voted to repeal its net neutrality rules, in a sweeping act of deregulation,"

The Washington Post, Dec. 14, 2017, https://tinyurl.com/y7h2u3k8.

12. "Warren, Warner Unveil Legislation to Hold Credit Reporting Agencies Like Equifax Accountable for Data Breaches," press release, Office of Sen. Elizabeth Warren, Jan. 10, 2018, https://tinyurl.com/y8dr8shz.

13. "GDPR Portal: Site Overview," European Union, https://tinyurl.com/ybhn3f5d.

14. "Domo Releases Annual 'Data Never Sleeps' Infographic," GlobeNewswire, Nasdaq, July 25, 2017, https://tinyurl.com/ybz5hqvb; "10 Key Marketing Trends for 2017," IBM, https://tinyurl.com/y9xrkesl.

15. Selena Larson, "Alphabet launches cybersecurity firm Chronicle," CNNtech, Jan. 24, 2018, https://tinyurl.com/yar3e8ts.

16. Liz Mineo, "On internet privacy, by very afraid," *The Harvard Gazette*, Aug. 24, 2017, https://tinyurl.com/ydblamx2.

17. Lauren Smith, "Unfairness by Algorithm: Distilling the Harms of Automated Decision-Making," Freedom of Privacy Forum, Dec. 11, 2017, https://tinyurl.com/yd3mepk6.

18. Daniel J. Solove, "A Brief History of Information Privacy Law," George Washington University Law School, Feb. 9, 2017, https://tinyurl.com/ya2fe7ta.

19. Bernard Marr, "The Internet Of Things (IOT) Will Be Massive In 2018: Here Are The Four Predictions From IBM," *Forbes*, Jan. 4, 2018, https://tinyurl.com/ybwnbxnj.

20. Ray Downs, "Google Home Mini caught 'spying' on owner," UPI, Oct. 13, 2017, https://tinyurl.com/yav3uzl6; Frederic Lardinois, "Google says it sold a Google Home device every second since October 19," Tech Crunch, Jan. 5, 2018, https://tinyurl.com/yccumv4o.

21. "The Privacy Implications of Cloud Computing," Privacy Rights Clearinghouse, Sept. 27, 2017, https://tinyurl.com/ybjk7rq9.

22. Robert Hackett, "Data Breach Exposes 123 Million Households," *Fortune*, Dec. 22, 2017, https://tinyurl.com/y7v7acxk.

23. "GDPR Portal: Site Overview," *op. cit.*

24. Jeff Dunn, "Trump just killed Obama's internet-privacy rules — here's what that means for you," *Business Insider*, April 4, 2017, https://tinyurl.com/lshv6au.

25. "Statement On The BROWSER Act," Internet Association, May 23, 2017, https://tinyurl.com/y74bqjos.

26. "Consumers Need an Internet Bill of Rights," AT&T, Jan. 24, 2018, https://tinyurl.com/ybg9ev8u.

27. Devin Coldewey, "AT&T's 'Internet Bill of Rights' idea is just a power play against Google and Facebook," TechCrunch, Jan. 24, 2018, https://tinyurl.com/yd5wzelg.

28. Bruce Schneier, "Testimony before the House Subcommittee on Digital Commerce and Consumer Protection," Nov. 1, 2017, https://tinyurl.com/ybax987q.

29. Krystal Overmyer, "The Psychology of Behavioral Targeting Goes Deeper Than You'd Think," *Skyword*, June 28, 2016, https://tinyurl.com/yccny5ao.

30. Schneier, *op. cit.*

31. Paige Hymson, "White House Cybersecurity Coordinator Rob Joyce calls Social Security identification system 'flawed,' " *The Washington Post*, Oct. 4, 2017, https://tinyurl.com/y9uapmbc.

32. Nafeesa Syeed and Elizabeth Dexheimer, "The White House and Equifax Agree: Social Security Numbers Should Go," Bloomberg, Oct. 3, 2017, https://tinyurl.com/yba8pyf9.

33. Kalev Leetaru, "Replacing US Social Security Numbers With Estonia's Cryptographic Model?" *Forbes*, Oct. 15, 2017, https://tinyurl.com/y8o5nhjn.

34. "H.R.624 — Social Security Number Fraud Prevention Act," CongressGov, Sept. 15, 2017, https://tinyurl.com/ydxfj2w6.

35. Farai Chideya, "The Way We Use Social Security Numbers Is Absurd," *FiveThirtyEight*, Oct. 15, 2015, https://tinyurl.com/yddn2tbs.

36. *Ibid.*

37. Steven Bellovin, "Replacing Social Security Numbers Is Harder Than You Think," *Motherboard*, Oct. 5, 2017, https://tinyurl.com/y7dy43ro.

38. *Ibid.*

39. Marc Rotenberg, Testimony before Senate Banking Committee, Electronic Privacy Information Center, Oct. 17, 2017, https://tinyurl.com/y7qjaar4.

40. April Glaser, "Biometrics are coming, along with serious security concerns," *Wired*, March 9, 2016, https://tinyurl.com/y9cwyqdq.

41. Suzanne Wooley, "Want to Ditch Social Security Numbers? Try Blockchain," Bloomberg, Oct. 9, 2017. https://tinyurl.com/ybbkbpfz.

42. *Ibid.*

43. *Ibid.*

44. Robert Snell, "Detroiter's case sparks Supreme Court privacy battle," *Detroit News*, Nov. 28, 2017, https://tinyurl.com/y99jb6bm.

45. Jess Bravin and Ryan Knutson, "Supreme Court to Weigh Warrantless Cellphone Data Searches," *The Wall Street Journal*, Nov 28, 2017, https://tinyurl.com/y9gjs573.

46. John Villasenor, "What You Need to Know about the Third Party Doctrine," *The Atlantic*, Dec. 30, 2013, https://tinyurl.com/ydg9gfms.

47. EPIC amicus brief to the U.S. Supreme Court, Aug. 14, 2017, https://tinyurl.com/y8de6kk6.

48. "International Working Group on Data Protection in Telecommunications," Electronic Privacy Information Center, Nov. 27-28, 2017, https://tinyurl.com/ybkk7nt9.

49. Steven Nelson, "Major Cellphone Privacy Case Accepted by Supreme Court," *U.S. News & World Report*, June 5, 2017, https://tinyurl.com/y75d5zq5.

50. Bravin and Knutson, *op. cit.*

51. Brief to the U.S. Supreme Court, *Timothy Ivory Carpenter v. United States of America*, p. 7, https://tinyurl.com/y7d7msll.

52. *Ibid.*, pp. 11, 15.

53. Samuel D. Warren and Louis D. Brandeis, "The Right to Privacy," *Harvard Law Review*, Dec. 15, 1890, p. 195, https://tinyurl.com/qavzf2b.

54. Leah Burrows, "Brandeis: To Be Let Alone," *Brandeis Now*, July 24, 2013, https://tinyurl.com/pyhcqgg.

55. Viktor Mayer-Schönberger, *Delete: The Virtue of Forgetting in the Internet Age* (2009), p. 141.

56. European Convention on Human Rights, https://tinyurl.com/qywhyns.

57. Mayer-Schönberger, *op. cit.*

58. *Griswold v. Connecticut* (1965) Opinion, Justia, https://tinyurl.com/orrrxc4.

59. "A Summary of your Rights under the Fair Credit Reporting Act," Federal Trade Commission, https://tinyurl.com/narqyf8.

60. Privacy Act of 1974, Department of Justice, https://tinyurl.com/nox2xpf.

61. For background, see Marcia Clemmitt, "Controlling the Internet," *CQ Researcher*, May 12, 2006, pp. 409-32.

62. For background, see Marcia Clemmitt, "Internet Regulation," *CQ Researcher*, April 13, 2012, pp. 325-48, and Sarah Glazer, "Privacy and the Internet," *CQ Researcher*, Dec. 4, 2015, pp. 1009-32.

63. "Internet Privacy Laws We Need to Be Aware of in 2017," *National Law Review*, Oct. 12, 2017, https://tinyurl.com/ydg2uou4.

64. "Modernizing Electronic Communications Privacy Act (ECPA)," American Civil Liberties Union, https://tinyurl.com/y9m8vhbl.

65. The Telecommunications Act of 1996, https://tinyurl.com/ydy8j4n3.

66. "Google CEO: Net neutrality a principle we all need to fight for," CNN Money, Jan. 24, 2018, https://tinyurl.com/y97hsr7o.

67. Laurel Wamsley, "FCC's Pai: Heavy-handed Net Neutrality Rules are Stifling the Internet," NPR, Nov. 22, 2017, https://tinyurl.com/ybgvt9w7.

68. Cecilia Kang, "F.C.C. Repeals Net Neutrality Rules," *The New York Times*, Dec. 14, 2017, https://tinyurl.com/y9wngf7y.

69. Gigi Sohn, "The FCC's plan to kill net neutrality will also kill internet privacy," *The Verge*, April 11, 2017, https://tinyurl.com/yayr9dde.

70. Dunn, *op. cit.*

71. Sabrina Siddiqui, "Congress passes NSA surveillance reform in vindication for Snowden," *The Guardian*, June 3, 2015, https://tinyurl.com/yd4mbr64.

72. "Edward Snowden," TED talk, March 18, 2014, https://tinyurl.com/o2wpjca.

73. Floor testimony, House of Representatives, Congressional Record, Jan. 11, 2018, https://tinyurl.com/yc6elm66.

74. *Ibid.*

75. Harney, *op. cit.*

76. *Ibid.*

77. Brendan Pierson, "Anthem to pay record $115 million to settle U.S. lawsuits over data breach," Reuters, June 23, 2017, https://tinyurl.com/ycptxz9q.

78. Selena Larson, "Senators introduce data breach disclosure bill," CNNtech, Dec. 1, 2017, https://tinyurl.com/y7zdj7nw.

79. "S. 2234 — IoT Consumer Tips Act of 2017," CongressGov, https://tinyurl.com/ycbcoofl.

80. "S. 1475: Cyber Hygiene Act," GovTrack, https://tinyurl.com/ybeu4oqa.

81. Elizabeth Dexheimer and Jesse Hamilton, "Equifax's Seismic Breach Tests Trump's Pledge to Dismantle Rules," Bloomberg, Sept. 12, 2017, https://tinyurl.com/y77hu3e9.

82. "GDPR Portal: Site Overview," *op. cit.*

83. *Ibid.*

84. Henry Kenyon, "European Privacy Becomes a U.S. Problem," *CQ*, Jan. 29, 2018, https://tinyurl.com/yc6l7fz8.

85. "China Uses Facial Recognition to Fence in Villagers in Far West," Bloomberg Businessweek, Jan. 17, 2018, https://tinyurl.com/yd777jx2.

86. Simon Denyer, "China's watchful eye," *The Washington Post*, Jan. 7, 2018, https://tinyurl.com/y7bodsme.

87. "List of consumer reporting companies," Consumer Financial Protection Bureau, 2016, https://tinyurl.com/l2wjq8j.

88. Lauren Smith, "Unfairness by Algorithm: Distilling the Harms of Automated Decision-Making," Future of Privacy Forum, Dec. 11, 2017, https://tinyurl.com/yd3mepk6.

89. For background, see Barbara Mantel, "High-Tech Policing," *CQ Researcher*, April 21, 2017, pp. 337-60; Timothy Mclaughlin, "As shootings soar, Chicago police use technology to predict crime," Reuters, Aug. 5, 2017, https://tinyurl.com/yd4bsawl.

90. Daniella Silva, "Senator calls for more scrutiny of home DNA test industry," NBC News, Nov. 26, 2017, https://tinyurl.com/y747kanx.

91. Ryan Francis, "Has fraud met its match?" CSO, Feb. 24, 2017, https://tinyurl.com/y7ug9ufc.

BIBLIOGRAPHY
Selected Sources
Books

Edgar, Timothy H., *Beyond Snowden: Privacy, Mass Surveillance, and the Struggle to Reform the NSA*, **Brookings Institution, 2017.**
Although surveillance programs pose a profound threat to privacy, it need not be sacrificed for intelligence agencies to do their jobs, writes a former intelligence official in the George W. Bush and Barack Obama administrations.

Levin, Adam, *Swiped: How to Protect Yourself in a World Full of Scammers, Phishers, and Identity Thieves*, **PublicAffairs, 2016.**
A longtime consumer advocate says that to protect against identity theft, consumers must focus on minimizing risk, monitoring their identity and managing the damage.

Schneier, Bruce, *Data and Goliath: The Hidden Battles to Collect Your Data and Control Your World*, **W.W. Norton, 2016.**
A cybersecurity expert outlines how to reform government programs and create business models that protect privacy.

Articles

Hymson, Paige, "White House Cybersecurity Coordinator Rob Joyce calls Social Security identification system 'flawed,' " *The Washington Post*, **Oct. 4, 2017, https://tinyurl.com/ycxnwadd.**

Government agencies have been asked to explore a more secure cryptographic identifier to replace the Social Security number.

Kastrenakes, Jacob, "Most smart TVs are tracking you, Vizio just got caught," *The Verge*, Feb. 7, 2017, https://tinyurl.com/ydckvapo.
The author provides tips on how consumers can control whether smart TVs and other streaming devices capture their data.

Rosic, Ameer, "What Is Blockchain Technology? A Step-by-Step Guide For Beginners," *Blockgeeks*, undated, https://tinyurl.com/mkmf62o.
An easy-to-understand guide describes blockchain technology, which allows digital information to be shared but not copied.

Rotenberg, Marc, "Equifax, the Credit Reporting Industry, and What Congress Should Do Next," *Harvard Business Review*, Sept. 20, 2017, https://tinyurl.com/y9spbfvg.
Congress needs to address fundamental flaws in the use of the Social Security number system and in the credit industry, says the president of the Electronic Privacy Information Center, which studies privacy issues.

Savage, Charlie, Eileen Sullivan and Nicholas Fanidos, "House Extends Surveillance Law, Rejecting New Privacy Safeguards," *The New York Times*, Jan. 11, 2018, https://tinyurl.com/yckjajl2.
The House voted to continue the National Security Agency's warrantless surveillance program for another six years, despite bipartisan calls for more privacy protections.

Schneier, Bruce, "Click Here to Kill Everyone," *New York Magazine*, Jan. 27, 2017, https://tinyurl.com/jztq8yz.
A cybersecurity expert argues that the Internet of Things, which connects household and other devices to the internet, is equivalent to a world-size robot that needs to be controlled.

Sorkin, Amy Davidson, "In Carpenter case, Justice Sotomayor tries to picture the smartphone future," *The New Yorker*, Nov. 30, 2017, https://tinyurl.com/ydf4fbpk.
The author explains the nuances of *Carpenter v. United States*, which some consider the most significant privacy case in decades, and Supreme Court Justice Sonia Sotomayor's role in the case.

Reports and Studies

"Data Breaches Database," Privacy Rights Clearinghouse, 2005-Present, https://tinyurl.com/yc8x3xe2.
A database maintained by a privacy rights advocacy group identifies data breaches by type and year.

Rotenberg, Marc, "Testimony and Statement for the Record, Hearing on Consumer Data Security and Credit Bureaus," Committee on Banking, Housing and Urban Affairs, U.S. Senate, Oct. 17, 2017, https://tinyurl.com/y7qjaar4.
The president of the Electronic Privacy Information Center outlines steps Congress could take to minimize the risk of another major data breach in the wake of the massive Equifax hack.

Schneier, Bruce, "Testimony Before the House Subcommittee on Digital Commerce and Consumer Protection," U.S. House of Representatives, Nov. 1, 2017, https://tinyurl.com/ybax987q.
A noted cybersecurity expert argues that effective regulation of data brokers is vital to protect citizens and national security.

Smith, Lauren, "Unfairness by Algorithm, Distilling the Harms of Automated Decision-Making," Future of Privacy Forum, Dec. 11, 2017, https://tinyurl.com/yd3mepk6.
Automated decision-making can cause economic and social harm and restrict liberty, argues a report by a think tank focused on data privacy issues.

For More Information

Cato Institute, 1000 Massachusetts Ave., N.W., Washington, DC 20001; 202-842-0200; www.cato.org. Libertarian think tank that studies privacy issues, especially data privacy.

Competitive Enterprise Institute, 1310 L St., N.W., 7th floor, Washington, DC 20005; 202-331-1010; cei.org/. Libertarian think tank whose executive vice president and senior fellow Jim Harper was a founding member of the Department of Homeland Security's Data Privacy and Integrity Advisory Committee. Harper has written amicus briefs in Fourth Amendment cases.

Electronic Freedom Foundation, 815 Eddy St., San Francisco, CA 94109; 415-436-9333; www.eff.org. Advocacy group focused on digital civil liberties; opposes illegal surveillance and advocates for the protection of data privacy.

Electronic Privacy Information Center, 1718 Connecticut Ave., N.W., Suite 200, Washington, DC 20009; 202-483-1140; www.epic.org. Research group that focuses on privacy issues involving digital data, surveillance and civil liberties.

Future of Privacy Forum, 1400 I St., N.W., Suite 450, Washington, DC 20005; 202-768-8950; fpf.org. Think tank seeking solutions for privacy issues concerning data use.

Identity Theft Resource Center, 3625 Ruffin Road, #204, San Diego, CA 92123; 888-400-5530; idtheftcenter.org. Advocacy group that supports identity theft victims and works to educate the public about how to protect against identity theft, data breaches, scams and frauds.

2

The Fight Over Net Neutrality

Jane Fullerton Lemons

Ajit Pai, appointed by President Trump as Federal Communications Commission chairman, says the FCC's repeal of net neutrality regulations, enacted in 2015 when Democrats controlled the agency, represents a shift from "pre-emptive regulation" to "targeted enforcement." Democratic FCC Commissioner Mignon Clyburn said, however, that by rescinding net neutrality, "we have basically handed the keys to the internet to large internet service providers."

From *CQ Researcher,*
March 16, 2018

Comedian John Oliver is not exactly known for his calm demeanor as he discusses the leading issues of the day on his expletive-filled HBO show "Last Week Tonight." But one topic really gets him worked up: the future of the internet.

In two widely viewed episodes in 2017 and 2014, Oliver explored a fundamental question: Should government regulate the internet to ensure all digital traffic is treated equally, known as net neutrality, or should telecom companies be in control?

Like other defenders of net neutrality, Oliver worries that Comcast, Verizon, AT&T and other companies that provide online access are becoming so big and powerful that they will soon be determining who sees what on their computers, at what price and at what speeds. His conclusion: Internet providers "should not be able to engage in any [expletive] that limits or manipulates the choices you make online."

Oliver's shows each went viral, drawing more than 21 million total views online and fueling so many public comments to the FCC that its website crashed — twice.[1]

With almost 90 percent of Americans online — and the telecom industry generating $750 billion in annual revenues — both sides of the net neutrality debate agree on the importance of an open internet to consumers and the U.S. economy. The dispute centers on how much regulation is needed.[2]

Consumer advocates and content providers argue that because the internet plays a central role in American life, the government must ensure that it remains open and accessible to everyone equally. That means that internet service providers (ISPs) should not have

Many States Seek to Reverse Repeal

A coalition of attorneys general in 22 states and the District of Columbia has sued to block the Federal Communications Commission's repeal of net neutrality, saying it would hurt consumers and businesses. Proponents of repeal say it will encourage investment in the internet.

States Suing to Block Net Neutrality Repeal

Source: New York State Attorney General Eric T. Schneiderman, "Petition for Review," Feb. 22, 2018, https://tinyurl.com/ya4nu7yc

"light-touch regulatory framework." It also removed broadband providers from the utility-type classification, meaning the government will no longer subject broadband service to the stringent rules that utilities face.[4]

The loss of net neutrality is "awful for consumers and it's awful for citizens. I tend to see this from a small 'd' democratic perspective," says Michael Copps, a former Democratic member of the FCC, who argues the internet has become just as important as the telephone was for previous generations and should be regulated as such. "Surrendering to anybody the gatekeeper control is not only bad for consumers, it's antithetical to democracy."

But the ISPs say they are committed to net neutrality and will ensure equal access to all. Anything less, they say, would hurt their bottom lines.

"Our companies have committed to consensus net neutrality principles very publicly — no blocking, no throttling, no unreasonable discrimination, and transparency of how they operate their networks," says Brian Dietz, senior vice president of NCTA — The Internet & Television Association, the trade association representing the cable and broadband industry.

The real threat to a vibrant internet, ISPs say, is heavy-handed government regulation that stifles innovation and investment in new technologies. Rescinding the net neutrality rules restores "a regulatory regime that emphasizes private investment and innovation over lumbering government intervention," said Joan Marsh, AT&T executive vice president of regulatory and state external affairs.[5]

The FCC's new rules were published in the *Federal Register* on Feb. 22. Although they are months away from being fully implemented, foes of the new rules have filed a host of lawsuits. The coming legal battles will pit ISPs against groups that want an unfettered internet, including state and local elected officials, consumer groups and content providers, including tech industry giants such as Amazon, Facebook and Google.[6]

wide latitude over what people can see online or the speed with which they can access it. Without net neutrality, they say, ISPs could block content or charge companies like Netflix and Twitter more for using internet "fast lanes" to reach consumers.

The stakes were dramatically highlighted in December 2017 when the Federal Communications Commission (FCC), with a new Republican majority, scrapped net neutrality regulations that the same commission, with a Democratic majority, had adopted in 2015. The earlier rules had barred ISPs from blocking or slowing consumer access to the internet and from charging content providers a fee to reach their customers. The 2015 rules also had placed broadband providers — Comcast, Verizon, AT&T and others that provide high-speed internet service — into the same legal category as telephone companies, requiring them to provide equal access and internet speeds to all websites and applications.[3]

The FCC's 2017 action replaced those rules with what commission Chairman Ajit Pai characterized as a

So far, a coalition of attorneys general from 22 states and the District of Columbia has sued to reinstate the net neutrality rules. They joined other companies that have filed similar suits, including Mozilla, developer of the Firefox Web browser and the video-sharing website Vimeo, as well as open-internet advocacy groups such as Free Press, Public Knowledge and the Open Technology Institute.[7]

In addition, more than half the states have introduced legislation to enact their own net neutrality regulations, with Washington state in early March becoming the first to pass a law protecting net neutrality.[8]

Pai, a former Verizon general counsel who was appointed FCC chairman by President Trump, has become a lightning rod for the issue because he voted against the 2015 rules and led the fight for their repeal when he became chairman last year.

The new policy, Pai said, represents a shift from "preemptive regulation" to "targeted enforcement based on actual market failure or anti-competitive conduct." He stressed that this is "not a completely hands-off approach. Nobody gets a free pass."[9]

The two Democratic FCC members disagree. Commissioner Mignon Clyburn said that by rescinding the rules, "we have basically handed the keys to the internet to large internet service providers. . . . They have the ability to do all the things that we fear the most."[10]

After the FCC repealed net neutrality, The Associated Press (AP) asked seven major ISPs about their plans, and several promised not to block or throttle lawful content.

But when the AP asked the ISPs whether they might charge websites for faster access to consumers, known as "paid prioritization," none of the seven companies — Verizon, AT&T, Comcast, Charter, Cox, Sprint and T-Mobile — would rule out that possibility. Most said they had "no plans" for paid prioritization, while a few declined to answer the question.[11]

Open-internet advocates dismiss the ISPs' promises to abide by net neutrality principles by pointing to examples when they violated it. One instance involved Comcast, the nation's largest ISP, which blocked or slowed file-sharing applications in 2005. "The problem is very real," says Timothy Karr, senior director of strategy and communications at Free Press, which has compiled examples of ISPs violating net neutrality principles.[12]

The FCC's reversal on net neutrality shifts much of its historical internet oversight role to the Federal Trade Commission (FTC). The two agencies issued an agreement in December pledging cooperation in the enforcement of net neutrality principles.[13]

The FCC's action will allow the FTC to play a larger enforcement role, says Margaret McCarthy, executive director of Mobile Future, the trade association representing the mobile telecom industry. "The FCC and the FTC are working together to be the cops on the beat, which we think is really critical."

But net neutrality advocates say the FTC is not up to the task. FTC Commissioner Terrell McSweeny, a Democrat, agrees. While her agency is good at many things, she said, don't count on it to protect the internet. The FTC, McSweeny said, does not have telecommunications expertise.[14]

Consumer advocates say the loss of net neutrality could particularly hurt areas with limited access to broadband service or with fewer ISP choices.

Currently, the top six ISPs control more than 71 percent of the U.S. internet market. But because the market is regionalized, the ISPs do not usually compete directly with each other. Thus, unlike in other countries, most Americans — especially in rural areas — have only one choice when it comes to internet service. The United Kingdom, by contrast, has more than 50 ISPs.[15]

The FCC's decision to repeal net neutrality "will have an outsized impact on rural and poor communities because these are the communities that don't have choices for how they access the internet," says Heather West, senior policy manager for Mozilla.

In fact, many Americans have no access to internet service. The most recent FCC data found that 39 percent of the rural population — or 23.4 million people — lacked access to what the agency regards as basic fixed broadband service. That compares to 4 percent of the urban population.[16]

Public opinion polls show overwhelming bipartisan support for retaining net neutrality regulations. Various polls have found from 52 percent to 83 percent of those responding favored retaining the 2015 FCC rules.[17]

The partisan divide on the issue exists only in Washington, West says. "We've seen an amazing groundswell of grassroots activism and engagement on this," she says. "It's been really clear, survey after survey, that

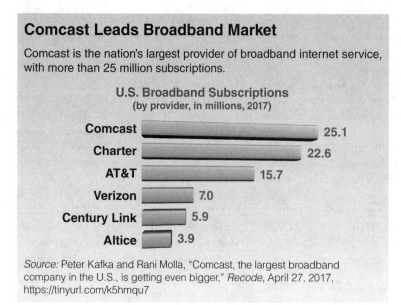

Comcast Leads Broadband Market

Comcast is the nation's largest provider of broadband internet service, with more than 25 million subscriptions.

U.S. Broadband Subscriptions
(by provider, in millions, 2017)

Comcast	25.1
Charter	22.6
AT&T	15.7
Verizon	7.0
Century Link	5.9
Altice	3.9

Source: Peter Kafka and Rani Molla, "Comcast, the largest broadband company in the U.S., is getting even bigger," *Recode*, April 27, 2017, https://tinyurl.com/k5hmqu7

outside of Washington there's incredible support for enforceable net neutrality protections."

As consumer advocates, internet companies, regulators and others debate net neutrality, here are some of the questions they are asking:

Is ending net neutrality good for consumers and businesses?

Advocates of net neutrality contend the FCC's about-face on the 2015 rules will harm internet users.

"Potentially, these changes could affect everyone," says West of Mozilla. "Taking these rules back means the ISPs are in a position to determine what I have access to, whether that's fast access or access at all."

Democratic FCC Commissioner Jessica Rosenworcel, who voted to retain the 2015 regulations, said overturning them "hands broadband providers the power to decide what voices to amplify, which sites we can visit, what connections we can make and what communities we create."[18]

But Mobile Future's McCarthy says repealing the 2015 rules "really isn't the end of net neutrality. There's widespread agreement across all the players in the internet ecosystem that protecting openness online is really critical — for consumers, for small businesses and entrepreneurs — and that it's been a critical ingredient for the internet becoming the great American success story that it is."

Despite the ISPs' repeated assurances they will follow net neutrality principles, consumer advocates fear ISPs could charge content providers and tech companies a fee for access to internet "fast lanes." Or they could give priority to preferred content, such as television shows produced by their subsidiaries. Or they could offer bundled packages to consumers providing access to specific sites, much like the channel packages offered by cable television companies.[19]

Asked recently about net neutrality, Sprint CEO Marcelo Claure said he does not see anything wrong with charging internet content providers — such as Netflix, Facebook or Google — for faster service, much like consumers can choose internet service at different speeds. The difference is that the ISP controls the content provider's access to their customers.[20]

"I don't think there's anything wrong for you to eventually charge a higher price for a faster access to your network," he said at a mobile industry trade show in Barcelona, Spain. He compared the concept to a toll road: "In the United States in many roads you drive, you have a faster road and you pay more. There's nothing wrong with that."[21]

Such a prospect worries net neutrality advocates. Besides hurting consumers who cannot afford higher monthly rates, fast-lane pricing could give larger businesses an advantage over smaller businesses or startup companies that might not be able to afford it. They cite Google and Facebook, noting that if those companies had had to pay for access to broadband networks when they were starting out, they might not have developed into the giant tech companies they are.

Reed Hastings, Netflix chief executive officer, argued forcefully for net neutrality rules in 2015. While he still supports the concept, his company has since grown large enough that it can negotiate with ISPs. But he said smaller players could be hurt by the FCC policy change, noting that "where net neutrality is really important is the Netflix of 10 years ago."[22]

Indeed, Netflix already has entered into "peering" agreements with Comcast, Verizon and AT&T that let the movie provider connect directly to their networks to reach its customers more quickly — which some observers say amounts to the kind of fast lanes that ISPs could impose on content providers.[23]

Similar worries led a coalition of small businesses to send a letter to FCC Chairman Pai last year, calling for the FCC to retain the 2015 net neutrality rules.

"The open internet has made it possible for us to rely on a free market where each of us has the chance to bring our best business ideas to the world without interference or seeking permission from any gatekeeper first," they wrote on behalf of more than 500 small businesses. "This is possible because the principle of net neutrality ensures that everyone has unimpeded access to the internet."[24]

Small businesses could be hampered if ISPs impose fees to access their customers, charge their customers for access to their websites, provide competitors with faster internet speeds or slow down their online traffic.

For consumers, the results could be similar if ISPs charge them for faster access to specific sites or services that they own or favor. An ISP, for instance, could favor one movie service over another, letting Netflix load faster than Hulu or Amazon.

"Right now all your content comes at the same speed," says Benjamin Hermalin, an economics professor and a vice provost at the University of California, Berkeley. With no net neutrality rules, "your content could come at different speeds."

Does net neutrality impede investment and innovation?

FCC Chairman Pai frequently says the net neutrality rules adopted in 2015 created regulatory uncertainty, causing ISPs to delay the investments necessary to improve their networks and pursue innovations in the telecom industry. Such an outcome harmed the internet and, ultimately, consumers, he said.

Removing those rules, the argument goes, will reduce uncertainty and encourage spending on things like expanding broadband infrastructure and access.

The 2015 regulations that classified ISPs as a "common carrier" — a transportation or communication network subject to a more stringent level of federal oversight. Under Title II of the 1934 Communications

Students at Monroe Intermediate School in rural Lower Peachtree, Ala., work in the computer lab, which lacks a high-speed internet connection. Repealing net neutrality "will have an outsized impact on rural and poor communities," says Heather West, senior policy manager for Mozilla. According to the FCC, 39 percent of the nation's rural population lacks high-speed service.

Getty Images/The Washington Post/Michael S. Williamson

Act, common carriers "are like the proverbial sledgehammer being wielded against the flea," Pai said, and do not match the internet marketplace. "Let the marketplace evolve organically," he said, "and if you see any harm to consumers, then take targeted action to address that problem."[25]

According to the U.S. Telecom trade association, the telecom industry's investment dropped by $2.4 billion from 2014 to 2016, partly because of the net neutrality regulations. Comcast, for instance, said it delayed introducing a streaming TV service because of the more stringent regulatory environment.[26]

"For decades, the internet flourished under a bipartisan regulatory approach that allowed it to operate, grow and succeed free of unnecessary government controls," said Kathy Grillo, a Verizon senior vice president, adding that net neutrality rules were outdated and unnecessary. "It undermined investment and innovation, and posed a significant threat to the internet's continued ability to grow and evolve to meet consumers' needs."[27]

A group of economic researchers concluded that reducing regulatory barriers could make it more profitable for broadband providers to reach underserved areas, especially in rural and lower-income communities. Their analysis of FCC data found that although broadband adoption increased from 68 percent of the population in

Key Net Neutrality Terms

Broadband — High-speed data transmission, typically through a single cable or optical fiber, that can handle large amounts of data simultaneously. Wireless broadband is known as Wi-Fi.

Common carrier — A public utility, transportation or telecommunication company that provides the public with essential services, such as electricity; placing internet providers in this category means they face the same regulatory scrutiny as utilities.

DSL — A digital subscriber line provides high-speed internet access by using unused higher frequencies in telephone lines.

5G — Fifth-generation wireless technology, projected to be much faster than the current 4G standard. It could launch in 2018.

ISPs — Internet service providers are companies that build the "pipes," or lines, that bring the internet to homes and businesses.

Net neutrality — The principle that ISPs should treat all internet traffic equally in terms of speed, access and cost.

Paid prioritization — The practice of ISPs charging higher fees to companies that want consumers to be able to reach their websites more quickly.

Title II — Communications Act provision that can be used to classify internet service providers as common carriers, subjecting them to tougher utility-style regulations.

2012 to 73 percent in 2017, "high-speed access tends to be skewed toward denser, urban centers where the economics are more favorable to a network operator, resulting in large areas with limited broadband access." As a result, the analysis found, more than 10.6 million households have no access to high-speed landline internet or have access to only one high-speed provider.[28]

Smaller ISPs have come down on both sides of the issue. An ISP in Arkansas said it delayed a planned expansion to make sure it was complying with the 2015 rules. But a group of more than 40 small providers told the FCC they "encountered no new additional barriers to investment or deployment," and said the rules were needed to ensure a level playing field as they try to compete with the large ISPs.[29]

Net neutrality advocates deny that the 2015 regulations hampered broadband investment. Based on an analysis of company filings with the Securities and Exchange Commission (SEC), the Free Press said the telecommunications industry increased its capital investments following adoption of the 2015 rules.[30]

"We found that not a single publicly traded U.S. ISP ever told its investors (or the SEC) that Title II negatively impacted its own investments specifically," according to the Free Press report. The group found total capital investment by publicly traded ISPs was more than 5 percent higher during the two-year period following the FCC's vote than it was in the two years before the vote.[31]

In January, three leading telecommunications companies filed their quarterly earnings reports. Comcast and AT&T reported earnings and revenue that topped analysts' expectations. Verizon's earnings missed expectations, but its revenue exceeded estimates. All three companies are in the midst of transforming their business model from one based on phone service into one combining data and internet services.[32]

The media industry is watching Comcast's earnings report particularly closely because the company has business interests on both sides of the net neutrality debate. It produces content through NBC and Universal Pictures, and as the nation's largest ISP it owns the "pipes" to deliver that content to consumers. Verizon has a digital content and advertising arm that includes Yahoo and AOL. AT&T hopes to finalize its acquisition of Time Warner this year, although the Justice Department has challenged the merger.

During a public call discussing its earnings report, AT&T Chairman Randall Stephenson praised the FCC's "rationalized" regulation, but said the industry needs long-term predictability of the rules of the internet in the form of legislation.

"We obviously believe this is a step in the right direction," he said, "but this regulatory pendulum is going to keep swinging back and forth unless Congress steps forward and writes new laws to govern all internet companies and to protect the consumer. We believe that we need clarity."[33]

Net neutrality advocates say the FCC's decision to rescind the rules will hurt internet content providers;

money sent to ISPs for faster access to online consumers will leave content providers with less money to invest in new products, they say.

The loss of net neutrality could especially hurt small businesses and startups, because ISPs could charge them more for faster delivery of content, says Nicholas Economides, an economics professor at New York University.

"When innovative companies have higher costs, they will have a much harder time becoming established and growing and contributing to U.S. growth," Economides says. In the long term, "that will have the effect of slowing down U.S. growth in the tech sector and U.S. growth in general."

Does repealing net neutrality encourage internet censorship?

Proponents of net neutrality regulations worry that without them, ISPs will be able to censor internet content.

"The internet is the public square of the 21st century," said New York state Attorney General Eric Schneiderman, who has sued the FCC, contending the agency's decision to revoke net neutrality violates federal law. "But without net neutrality, it will become a private square — with massive corporations deciding what people and ideas get in."[34]

By removing the sanctions against blocking or slowing online content, the new rules do not prohibit ISPs from discriminating among different kinds of content, net neutrality advocates say. With no requirement to treat all online content equally, ISPs could favor their own content over a competitor's. Comcast, for instance, could prioritize shows on NBC, which it owns, while slowing those from rival networks.

"There's nothing in the books now going forward to keep that from happening," says Copps, the former FCC commissioner. "Censorship is a strong word, but that's what it is."

But broadband companies insist they will not do it. "We do not block websites, nor censor online content,

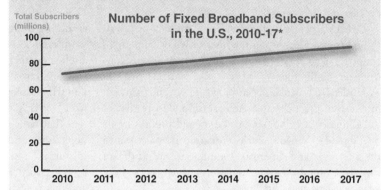

Broadband Links on the Rise

The number of subscribers to internet broadband services delivered via phone lines, fiber optic cable and other fixed equipment rose nearly 30 percent between 2010 and 2017, to 94 million.

Number of Fixed Broadband Subscribers in the U.S., 2010-17*

* Fixed wired broadband includes technologies with download speeds of 256 kilobits per second or greater delivered via telephone line-based DSL, cable modem, fiber-to-home lines and other fixed equipment such as power lines and leased lines.

Source: "Number of quarterly fixed broadband subscribers in the United States from 2010 to 2017 (in millions)," *Statista*, November 2017, https://tinyurl.com/y7y9c8uk

nor throttle or degrade traffic based on the content, nor unfairly discriminate in our treatment of internet traffic," said Bob Quinn, AT&T senior executive vice president of external and legislative affairs.[35]

Like other free-market advocates, Andrew Magloughlin, a regulatory policy intern at FreedomWorks, a conservative advocacy group, thinks censorship concerns are a false narrative. If a company were to engage in anticompetitive censorship of website content, it would be subject to antitrust regulations enforced by the FTC — and would face further penalties from the public backlash that would follow.

"Fears of a content-restrictive internet are fantasy," he said. "This is a problem that simply doesn't exist. Content-based censorship provokes backlash from customers who appreciate such content. Comcast would face a consumer exodus if it blocked the New England Patriots website just because it prefers the Miami Dolphins."[36]

Hermalin, the Berkeley professor, acknowledges that censorship is possible, but says ISPs will be wary of a public reaction. He predicts that a kind of economic censorship is more likely.

"The bigger fear is they will block content for economic reasons," he says, adding that "one of the dangers is that that they will favor their own content at the expense of other content."

Other observers express concern about censorship of thoughts and ideas along the lines of what happens in countries like China, where the government retains control over the internet.

"Indeed, a broadband carrier like AT&T, if it wanted, might even practice internet censorship akin to that of the Chinese state, blocking its critics and promoting its own agenda. Allowing such censorship is anathema to the internet's (and America's) founding spirit," said Tim Wu, the Columbia Law School professor who coined the term network neutrality.[37]

The internet's development in the United States has been a democratizing force, particularly for underrepresented groups, said Willmary Escoto, a Google policy fellow at Public Knowledge, a public interest group that advocates for an open internet. The internet has enabled marginalized communities to illuminate social injustices that were once in the shadows.[38]

The internet, for example, played a key role in helping the tea party become a potent conservative political movement and in transforming the Black Lives Matter from a hashtag into a liberal movement against racism and police shootings of unarmed black men.[39]

"Live streaming is transforming the growth of citizen journalism, providing a distressing view of shootings like these, and empowering citizens to share their story without the fear of censorship," Escoto said.

Carmen Scurato, director of policy and legal affairs for the National Hispanic Media Coalition, said dismantling net neutrality opens the door for corporations to limit free expression, organizing efforts, educational opportunities and entrepreneurship. "An open internet is the primary destination for our communities to share our stories in our own words — without being blocked by powerful gatekeepers motivated by profit," she said.[40]

The power those gatekeepers wield became apparent last year after several companies ended their affiliation with the American neo-Nazi website The Daily Stormer in the aftermath of a violent white nationalist rally in Charlottesville, Va.

Cloudflare, a security company that protects websites from being taken down by hackers or extortionists, ended its relationship with The Daily Stormer, which meant the website could not continue to stay online.[41]

Cloudfare's action was tantamount to kicking The Daily Stormer off the internet — a form of censorship, according to observers of the net neutrality debate who wondered how and whether such actions could be applied to other viewpoints across the political spectrum.

Cloudfare itself was uncomfortable with its actions, said Chief Executive Officer Matthew Prince. The power to censor is "terrifying," he said, calling for a review system that would allow such decisions to be made with objectivity and consistency. "The internet is a really important resource for everyone," Prince said, "but there's a very limited set of companies that control it, and there's such little accountability to us that it really is quite a dangerous thing."[42]

The key to avoiding internet censorship is to keep the people who control the networks from controlling the content, says Robert McChesney, a communications professor at the University of Illinois, Urbana-Champaign.

"This is about the control of information, all information — journalism, entertainment, the works," he says. Without net neutrality regulations, that control will rest in the hands of a few companies.

"The core principle of democracy is, you don't want monopolists to have control over anything remotely close to your means of information," he says. "That is a recipe for disaster."

BACKGROUND
Expanding Regulations

The principle of common carriage, which underlies the debate over net neutrality, has played a central role in regulating transportation and communications worldwide for centuries. Under common carriage laws, ship owners, innkeepers, stable keepers and others engaged in "public callings" must serve any and all customers who reasonably seek their services.[43]

Common carriers in the United States have included railroad, shipping, utility and telecommunications companies. In 1887, Congress responded to a public outcry over the growing power and wealth of the railroads by passing the Interstate Commerce Act, which required that shipping rates be "reasonable and just." The rail-roads were accused of forming trusts to set prices and of discriminating against smaller businesses by charging higher prices per mile for short hauls than for long ones.

The new law also established the Interstate Commerce Commission (ICC), the first federal agency established to regulate a private industry.[44]

In 1910, Congress expanded the ICC's jurisdiction to cover the telecommunications industry, including a new technology, the telephone, and an older one, the tele-graph. It defined both as common carriers.

The pioneering days of radio in the 1920s paralleled the early days of the internet, with little regulation of the new medium. As the number of licensed broadcast sta-tions grew from five in 1921 to 500 in 1924, Congress created the Federal Radio Commission in 1927 to regu-late the public airwaves.[45]

Less than a decade later, Congress passed the Communications Act of 1934, which consolidated all radio, television and telephone regulations under the new Federal Communications Commission, which replaced the Federal Radio Commission. The FCC was charged with overseeing interstate and foreign commu-nications. Telecommunications companies were regu-lated as common carriers under Title II of the act, thus requiring phone companies and others to provide access to their networks at reasonable rates.[46]

In the 1940s, the FCC addressed the growing power and commercialization of radio by asserting that radio stations were to serve the public interest. The agency published the "Public Service Responsibility of Broadcast Licensees" — commonly known as the Blue Book — to outline how broadcasters should fulfill that obligation.[47]

In 1949, as radio and television broadcasting contin-ued to grow, the FCC instituted the Fairness Doctrine, requiring stations licensed by the FCC to provide time for controversial subjects and to air opposing views on those issues.[48]

Computer Revolution

During the 1960s and '70s, technology developed in two key ways that laid the groundwork for today's inter-net. First, computers advanced from specialized scien-tific uses to tools the public could use. Second, a "network of networks" began evolving into what would become the internet.[49]

As FCC chairman, Tom Wheeler successfully pushed the FCC to adopt net neutrality rules in 2015. The rules, he said, would ensure "the rights of internet users to go where they want, when they want, and the rights of innovators to introduce new products without asking anyone's permission."

Computer advances in the 1960s forced the FCC to face its earliest decisions about how to regulate the bur-geoning technology. The agency debated whether such communications systems fell under the same common-carrier legal framework as telephone communications.

After undertaking "Computer Inquiries" in the 1970s and '80s, the FCC concluded the new technologies were an "enhanced service," meaning they would be regulated less stringently under Title I of the 1934 Communications Act, rather than as a common carrier "basic service" such as the telephone.[50]

The Defense Department, meanwhile, was develop-ing the precursor to the internet, the ARPANET (Advanced Research Projects Agency Network). Created in 1969, it consisted of seven research-university com-puters that exchanged packets of information over tele-phone wires. But the phone companies showed no interest in the new technology.[51]

After the government completed its research in 1971, AT&T turned down an offer to take over operation of the ARPANET — an offer that would have amounted to monopoly ownership of what became the internet. Like

CHRONOLOGY

1880s-1920s *Federal regulatory powers grow.*

1885 Inventor Alexander Graham Bell establishes American Telephone & Telegraph Co., which achieves a virtual monopoly on U.S. telephone service that lasts until 1982.

1887 Public outcry over railroads' high prices prompts Congress to pass the Interstate Commerce Act to regulate rail operators as "common carriers" — companies providing an essential public service.

1927 Congress creates Federal Radio Commission to regulate the public airwaves.

1930s-1940s *Debate over access to airwaves foreshadows net neutrality controversy.*

1934 Communications Act of 1934 establishes Federal Communications Commission (FCC) to oversee interstate and radio communication. The law classifies telephone companies as common carriers.

1949 FCC's Fairness Doctrine requires radio and TV stations to provide airtime for controversial subjects and opposing views.

1960s-1990s *Rise of the internet leads to net neutrality debate.*

1960s Defense Department's Advanced Research Projects Agency Network (ARPANET) paves the way for development of the internet.

1980s Studying the growing convergence of telecommunications and computers, FCC concludes the new technologies are an "enhanced service," meaning they would be regulated less stringently under Title I of the Telecommunications Act.

1995 The U.S. government turns the internet over to the private sector.

1996 Congress overhauls the 1934 Communications Act, drawing a regulatory distinction between phone and cable companies. . . . Fewer than 20 percent of Americans have cellphones or internet service at home.

2000s-Present *Net neutrality is passed, then rescinded.*

2002 FCC takes first steps toward deregulating broadband services by deciding not to force cable companies to share their infrastructure with competitors.

2003 Tim Wu, a University of Virginia law professor, coins the term "network neutrality."

2005 FCC issues net neutrality as a policy, but not a rule.

2008 FCC rebukes Comcast for blocking or slowing access to popular file-sharing software — the only time the agency found a U.S. broadband provider in violation of net neutrality principles. Comcast appeals.

2010 Federal appeals court rules in Comcast's favor, saying the FCC's action exceeded its authority. The FCC subsequently adopts the first net neutrality regulations, prompting a lawsuit from Verizon.

2014 Federal appeals court sides with Verizon, saying the FCC legally can regulate broadband but that it relinquished its authority by not classifying broadband the same as telephone service.

2015 Democratic-controlled FCC enacts "Open Internet Order," subjecting internet service providers (ISPs) to a more stringent regulatory framework by putting them in the same public-utility classification as telephone service.

2016 Federal appeals court allows the FCC regulations to take effect.

2017 Now Republican-controlled, FCC rescinds the 2015 net neutrality rules. . . . FCC and FTC agree to jointly police the internet.

2018 In the wake of net neutrality repeal, Washington state passes a law protecting net neutrality. . . . State attorneys general from 22 states and the District of Columbia file court challenge to FCC's actions.

many at the time, AT&T officials did not see its commercial value.[52]

But explosive growth was just around the corner. In 1991, British computer scientist Tim Berners-Lee and colleagues at CERN, the European Organisation for Nuclear Research, in Geneva, created the World Wide Web, allowing documents and photos to be sent via hypertext links. After the first website went online in 1991 at CERN, the number of internet-connected computers jumped from 2,000 in 1985 to more than 2 million in 1993, and the number of internet users exploded — to 14 million worldwide.[53]

In the early 1990s, the federal government began turning over operation of its computerized networks to the private sector. By 1995, the internet was fully privatized.[54]

In the mid-1990s, Congress undertook the first significant overhaul of telecommunications policy since 1934. The Telecommunications Act of 1996 drew a regulatory distinction between traditional phone companies and cable companies. Phone companies continued to be regulated as "telecommunications services" and subject to the utility-style Title II regulations of the original law. But cable companies were classified as "information services" and therefore subject to less stringent oversight. The act also attempted to reduce regulatory barriers to entry and competition in the telecommunications industry.[55]

Dawn of Broadband

In 1999, Democratic FCC Chairman William Kennard advocated "vigilant restraint" when regulating the internet.

"The internet is really blossoming, but some policymakers and politicians want to control it and regulate access to it," Kennard said. "We should not try to intervene in this marketplace. We need to monitor the rollout but recognize we don't have all the answers because we don't know where we're going."[56]

Those comments came at time when people primarily got their internet over their phone lines. Cable television operators were just beginning to offer internet services. Two factors were at play: Cable could offer faster internet connections, so the companies offering internet access over phone lines wanted access to the cable lines, too. And cable services were regulated less stringently than phone lines.

This situation began the debate about whether broadband service was as essential as phone or electric services and, therefore, should be subject to the same level of regulation. Supporters of net neutrality regulations argued that internet service, regardless of whether provided by phone or cable companies, met the threshold to be classified as a common carrier: It provides an important service, is transmitted over a common network infrastructure and has few suppliers.

But the telecom industry and free-market advocates denied that the internet is a monopoly and said it doesn't fit the mold for regulation as a public utility.

Over the next two decades, the FCC struggled with how to classify emerging broadband services and how to regulate the internet. The companies providing access battled each other in court in an attempt to gain competitive advantage. And several of those companies merged.

In 2002, the FCC under Republican Chairman Michael Powell took the first steps toward keeping broadband services deregulated when it decided cable companies would not be forced to share their lines with competitors. That was a departure from the treatment of telephone operators, which had to allow competitors to use their networks.

The FCC classified cable internet access as an interstate information service under Title I of the 1934 Communications Act, rather than a telecommunications service under the act's Title II. That meant cable broadband services would not be subject to utility-style regulation as a "common carrier" under Title II.[57]

In June 2003, Wu, who was then an associate professor at the University of Virginia, first used the phrase "network neutrality" in a prescient paper for an academic journal. "Communications regulators over the next decade will spend increasing time on conflicts between the private interests of broadband providers and the public's interest in a competitive innovation environment centered on the Internet," he wrote.[58]

Powell, meanwhile, challenged the broadband industry to preserve four "internet freedoms." In a February 2004 speech, he said internet customers should expect the freedom to access any legal content, to use applications, to attach personal devices to their home connections and to obtain meaningful information about their service plans.[59]

FCC Chair Uses Humor to Parry Critics

Ajit Pai stirred passions in fight to repeal net neutrality rules.

To his many critics, Federal Communications Commission (FCC) Chairman Ajit Pai is Darth Vader reincarnated.

They have branded Pai, who pushed the agency to rescind Obama-era rules protecting net neutrality, the destroyer of a free and open internet, and a scoundrel who "murdered Democracy in cold blood."[1]

But Pai's supporters say he has taken highly effective actions as chairman, such as removing regulations that stifle industry growth and innovation.

Pai, 45, a former lawyer at telecommunications conglomerate Verizon Communications, laughs off his critics. The day before the contentious vote in December rescinding the rules, he recorded a tongue-in-cheek video, promoted on YouTube, listing "7 things you can still do on the Internet" after the demise of net neutrality. "You can still ruin memes," he tells viewers in the final segment, gyrating to music while wielding a lightsaber. And a week before the vote, he joked during a speech that "we only have seven more days to use the internet."[2]

Pai and Michael O'Rielly were the only Republicans on the FCC when the agency voted 3-2 along party lines in 2015 to adopt the net neutrality rules. Pai, a strong believer in deregulation and free markets, said at the time that the rules gave the FCC "the power to micromanage virtually every aspect of how the internet works. It's an overreach that will let a Washington bureaucracy, and not the American people, decide the future of the online world."[3]

Pai was born in Buffalo, N.Y., after his parents immigrated to the United States from India in 1971, and he was raised in Kansas. He graduated from Harvard University in 1994 and got his law degree from the University of Chicago, where he was editor of the law review.

From 1998 to 2001, Pai was a telecommunications lawyer in the Justice Department's Antitrust Division. He then worked as associate general counsel at Verizon, one of the internet service providers (ISPs) that has fought net neutrality, from 2001 to 2003. Pai was a lawyer at the FCC from 2007 to 2011.[4]

With a Republican seat on the FCC open, President Barack Obama appointed Pai to the agency in 2011 at the request of Senate Republican Leader Mitch McConnell of Kentucky, and the Senate confirmed him in 2012. President Trump made Pai chairman in January 2017 to replace Democratic Commissioner Tom Wheeler, who resigned after Trump took office, in keeping with agency custom. Trump renominated Pai in March 2017 to a full term as chairman, and the Senate voted 52-41 in October to confirm him.[5]

Since becoming an FCC commissioner, Pai has criticized what he sees as the agency's heavy-handed approach to regulation. "We need to fire up the weed whacker and remove those rules that are holding back investment, innovation and job creation," he said in December 2016.[6]

The intense national debate over net neutrality has obscured many of Pai's other actions as FCC chairman. "I would wager he's been the most productive of any FCC chair," Roslyn Layton, a visiting scholar at the American Enterprise Institute, a conservative think tank in Washington, said of Pai. "He's removed unnecessary regulations, promoted innovation and improved public safety."[7]

Pai has worked to bring the latest broadband technology to unserved areas, increased transparency at the FCC, taken steps to help minority businesses enter the broadcasting industry and toughened enforcement of laws targeting robo-callers, according to the FCC.[8]

The following year saw several developments. In March 2005 the FCC found that Madison River Communications, a phone company providing dial-up internet service in the Southeast and Midwest, had had been blocking subscribers from using Vonage, an internet phone service that competed with its traditional calling options — the kind of action advocates contend could happen without net neutrality regulations. The company negotiated an agreement with the FCC in which it agreed to end the practice.[60]

In June 2005, the U.S. Supreme Court overturned a lower-court ruling that would have forced cable companies to share their infrastructure with competitors delivering internet service via phone lines. The Supreme Court's

But some of his other actions have prompted angry reactions from consumer advocacy groups, which say Pai is allowing too much consolidation in the broadcast industry.

"Every single thing they're doing is for incumbent telephone cable and media companies," said Gigi Sohn, a distinguished fellow at the Georgetown University Institute for Technology Law & Policy and a former counselor to Wheeler at the FCC. "Pai wants to make the big bigger and the rich richer."[9]

Pai's critics note that the same day the FCC held its net neutrality vote it voted to move ahead with a proposal to modify or eliminate rules barring broadcast companies from owning TV stations that reach more than 39 percent of all TV households in the country.[10]

The FCC's inspector general is investigating whether that and other rules changes pushed by Pai were designed to clear the way for right-leaning Sinclair Broadcast Group — known for adding conservative content to its local programming — to buy 42 TV stations from Tribune Media. An FCC spokesman called the accusation "absurd."[11]

Under Pai, the FCC also did away with a rule, first instituted in 1975, that had prevented entities from owning a radio or TV station and a newspaper in the same market. And it brought back the "UHF discount," which allows broadcasters to understate the reach of their stations for purposes of complying with the 39 percent rule.[12]

— *Val Ellicott*

Federal Communications Commission Chairman Ajit Pai appears in a Twitter sketch he created to poke fun at critics of the commission's repeal of net neutrality rules.

[1] Hamza Shaban, "FCC chairman Ajit Pai says his children are being harassed over net neutrality," *The Washington Post*, Nov. 27, 2017, https://tinyurl.com/y852jqqy; Dwight Adams, "FCC's Ajit Pai ruined Christmas, Twitter says. And now he deserves a new job," *IndyStar*, Dec. 21, 2017, https://tinyurl.com/ycuep5cl.

[2] Hamza Shaban, "Watch FCC's Ajit Pai dress up as Santa and wield a lightsaber to mock net neutrality rules," *The Washington Post*, Dec. 15, 2017, https://tinyurl.com/y9cjr4wg; David Z. Morris, "FCC Head Ajit Pai Jokes About Being Verizon's 'Puppet' Ahead of Net Neutrality Rollback," *Fortune*, Dec. 9, 2017, https://tinyurl.com/y7erxgrs.

[3] "Dissenting Statement of Commissioner Ajit Pai," Ajit Pai, undated, https://tinyurl.com/ke8d2pd.

[4] "Ajit Pai, FCC Chairman," Federal Communications Commission, undated, https://tinyurl.com/n75qoqw.

[5] Ted Johnson, "Senate Votes to Confirm Ajit Pai for New FCC Term Despite Democrats' Objections," *Variety*, Oct. 2, 2017, https://tinyurl.com/y7pltcdc.

[6] Jim Puzzanghera, "Trump names new FCC chairman: Ajit Pai, who wants to take a 'weed whacker' to net neutrality," *Los Angeles Times*, Jan. 23, 2017, https://tinyurl.com/j2tk3xe.

[7] Melissa Quinn, "FCC Chairman Ajit Pai wins praise for progress, criticism over deregulation," *Washington Examiner*, Oct. 30, 2017, https://tinyurl.com/ycmf78ym.

[8] "Chairman Pai Leads A Year of Action and Accomplishment," Federal Communications Commission, undated, https://tinyurl.com/y7oadbh5.

[9] Seth Fiegerman, "Trump's FCC moves quickly to upend internet, media rules," CNN, Nov. 22, 2017, https://tinyurl.com/yaect63d.

[10] Margaret Harding McGill, "FCC votes to repeal net neutrality rules," *Politico*, Dec. 14, 2017, https://tinyurl.com/yclxgtcd.

[11] Margaret Harding McGill and John Hendel, "How Trump's FCC aided Sinclair's expansion," *Politico*, Aug. 6, 2017, https://tinyurl.com/y92nwa83; Todd Shields, "FCC Chairman's Ties to Sinclair Are Subject of Probe, Source Says," Bloomberg, Feb. 15, 2018, https://tinyurl.com/y8pwp6j4.

[12] Fiegerman, *op. cit.*

decision was based on whether the FCC had the authority to determine how to classify an internet provider — not on how cable operators should be classified.[61]

As a result, in September 2005 the FCC reclassified internet access via phone lines as a Title I interstate information service under the Telecommunications Act. That put DSL — a technology that provides high-speed internet access over telephone lines — in the same category as cable broadband services, which were no longer considered a Title II common carrier.[62]

That same month, Republican FCC Chairman Kevin Martin expanded on Powell's "internet freedoms" speech with a policy statement outlining principles to ensure broadband networks were operated in a "neutral manner."

European Union Backs Net Neutrality

"Access to the internet is a basic right."

In the debate over net neutrality, the European Union (EU) has come down firmly on the side of consumer choice.

"Internet providers must treat all traffic equally. I do not want a digital motorway for the lucky few, while others use a digital dirt track," EU technology chief Andrus Ansip said in February. "Access to the internet is a basic right. It has to stay open for everybody."[1]

Current EU policy prohibits internet service providers (ISPs) in all 28 member states from blocking or slowing any content, services or applications — a far different stance from that of the Republican-controlled Federal Communications Commission (FCC). The agency voted in December to scrap net neutrality rules implemented in 2015 during the Obama administration because it said those rules would harm innovation.[2]

"I think Europe and the U.S. can agree on the need to preserve the freedom of the internet economy," Ansip said. "Where we may differ is how to do it."[3]

A key difference between the United States and Europe is the number of companies offering internet access to homes or on mobile phones. In Britain, more than 50 companies offer access. France has four major broadband operators and nine low-cost options. That compares with just six major internet service providers in the U.S. market.[4]

Canada currently has a "robust" net neutrality policy, said Michael Geist, founder of the Canadian Internet Policy and Public Interest Clinic, a legal clinic at the University of Ottawa focused on technology policy. But Canada's proximity to the United States means it could be affected by the U.S. policy change, particularly if ISPs implement plans that give priority to some websites over others.

"The most profound impact will be on businesses attempting to break into the large American market," Geist

said. "If a two-tier internet is put in place, it could allow internet service providers to pick and choose which sites and applications get preferential treatment, which could seriously hamper innovation and the growth of new businesses."[5]

As the FCC has wrestled with how to regulate the internet, other countries have been watching, says Nicholas Economides, an economics professor at New York University.

When the FCC, then under Democratic control, enacted its net neutrality rules in 2015, countries such as Brazil, Chile and India did so as well, says Timothy Karr, senior director of strategy and communications for the Free Press, an advocacy group in Washington pressing for an open internet. "Now that the United States is stripping away those protections, I think there's reason to be concerned that these other countries and regional bodies will follow suit."

That was on the minds of Europeans, too. When the FCC was considering reversing the net neutrality rules last year, more than 200 European civil society organizations and companies signed a letter to FCC Chairman Ajit Pai warning him the move "could negatively impact the world's shared internet ecosystem." Access to the entire internet is vital for people and businesses outside the United States, they said.

"The open internet makes it possible for all of us to bring our best business ideas to the world without interference or seeking permission from any gatekeeper first," the business leaders wrote. "This is possible because the principle of net neutrality ensures that everyone, no matter where they are located, has unimpeded access to internet opportunities."[6]

France's top internet regulator, Sébastien Soriano, argued net neutrality is a worldwide responsibility for

The statement represented the agency's first attempt to establish a formal net neutrality policy, but it stopped short of implementing the guidelines as rules.[63]

Two months later, AT&T CEO Edward E. Whitacre Jr. suggested that he wanted to charge internet companies such as Yahoo for delivering their content to

customers through AT&T's "broadband pipe" — thereby voicing what net neutrality advocates feared would happen without regulations to prevent it.

"Now, what they would like to do is use my pipes free, but I ain't going to let them do that because we have spent this capital, and we have to have a return on it," he democracies. Soriano also is chairman of the regulatory body that oversees EU net neutrality policy.

"Having net neutrality rules in one country creates benefits for all others — because innovators and people from all over the world will enjoy an open access to the end users of this country," he said. "The worldwide openness of the internet has been a great factor in its success, and it is now a global responsibility to preserve it."[7]

At a February global technology trade show in Barcelona, Spain, Pai defended the FCC's actions, saying America's internet economy "became the envy of the world thanks to a market-based approach that began in the mid-1990s," but that the 2015 net neutrality regulations had hampered ISPs' ability to make investments.

"The United States is simply making a shift from pre-emptive regulation, which foolishly presumes that every last wireless company is an anticompetitive monopolist, to targeted enforcement based on actual market failure or anti-competitive conduct," he said.[8]

But other experts say the FCC vote hurts the United States' reputation as a global internet leader and sets a negative example for countries still developing their internet policy.

"This will be another instance of the U.S. ceding leadership in a global area," said Nick Frisch, a resident fellow at Yale Law School's Information Society Project. "It is going to set a bad example for other countries, coming from the country that invented the internet."[9]

— *Jane Fullerton Lemons*

At a trade show in Barcelona, Spain, in February, European Union technology chief Andrus Ansip criticized the U.S. stance on net neutrality. "Internet providers must treat all traffic equally," he said.

[1] Catherine Stupp, "Tensions over net neutrality shake up Mobile World Congress," EURACTIV, Feb. 27, 2018, https://tinyurl.com/y974moz3; Edward C. Baig, "FCC Chair Ajit Pai defends net neutrality repeal to doubters at Mobile World Congress," *USA Today*, Feb. 26, 2018, https://tinyurl.com/yb7yjqup.

[2] "All you need to know about Net Neutrality rules in the EU," Body of European Regulators for Electronic Communications, https://tinyurl.com/y7skdvrp.

[3] Roger Cheng, "FCC chairman defends net neutrality's end as he opens 5G door," CNET, Feb. 26, 2018, https://tinyurl.com/y9l6rscg.

[4] Liz Alderman and Amie Tsang, "Net Neutrality's Holes in Europe May Offer Peek at Future in U.S.," *The New York Times*, Dec. 10, 2017, https://tinyurl.com/ybmjso78.

[5] Mack Lamoureux, "How America Rolling Back Net Neutrality Will Affect the Rest of the World," *Vice*, Nov. 28, 2017, https://tinyurl.com/y8722hel.

[6] Maryant Fernández Pérez, "Letter to the FCC: The world is for net neutrality," European Digital Rights, Sept. 26, 2017, https://tinyurl.com/ycdvcd5y.

[7] Sébastien Soriano, "Europe Has a Message for Americans on Net Neutrality," *Slate*, Dec. 12, 2017, https://tinyurl.com/ycbgmrfw.

[8] Ajit Pai, "Remarks Of FCC Chairman Ajit Pai At The Mobile World Congress," Federal Communications Commission, Feb. 26, 2018, https://tinyurl.com/yd4kwtqr.

[9] Sherisse Pham, "What does the end of U.S. net neutrality mean for the world?" CNN, Dec. 15, 2017, https://tinyurl.com/ybcu687t.

said. "The internet can't be free in that sense, because we and the cable companies have made an investment, and for a Google or Yahoo or Vonage or anybody to expect to use these pipes [for] free is nuts!"[64]

In August 2008, the FCC rebuked Comcast for blocking or throttling access for some customers using the popular BitTorrent software to download online files, including music and videos. The FCC said the action was unlawful, marking the first and only time the FCC officially found a U.S. broadband provider in violation of net neutrality principles. But Comcast appealed the decision, and a federal court ruled in

April 2010 that the action was outside the FCC's authority.[65]

Net Neutrality

The FCC headed by Democratic Chairman Julius Genachowski adopted its first formal regulations on net neutrality in 2010. The Open Internet Order prohibited cable and DSL providers from blocking or throttling internet services, but it imposed fewer restrictions on the new wireless technology.

Verizon challenged the order, and a federal court in January 2014 sided with Verizon, saying the FCC had relinquished its authority by not classifying broadband as a Title II carrier. The court, however, did say the FCC should be able to regulate broadband and told it to come up with better rules that would be enforceable.[66]

The Verizon decision marked the second time courts handed the FCC a setback in its efforts to implement net neutrality policy. But the issue got a push from comedian Oliver, who in June 2014 first discussed net neutrality on his HBO show. The episode went viral, drawing more than 14 million views online. It helped fuel so many public comments that the FCC's website crashed as a filing deadline approached for the proposed net neutrality regulations.[67]

The issue got a second push from President Barack Obama, who in November 2014 urged the FCC to "implement the strongest possible rules to protect net neutrality" by reclassifying broadband providers as Title II common carriers.[68]

In February 2015, the FCC adopted formal net neutrality regulations after Democratic Chairman Wheeler announced support for regulating all broadband under the Title II regulations that govern phone companies. "These enforceable, bright-line rules will ban paid prioritization, and the blocking and throttling of lawful content and services," he wrote. This will ensure, he continued, "the rights of internet users to go where they want, when they want, and the rights of innovators to introduce new products without asking anyone's permission."[69]

Later that month, the FCC approved a new Open Internet Order, on a 3-2 party-line vote, applying the Title II standards to both wired and wireless internet providers, thereby subjecting those ISPs to the more stringent regulatory framework.[70]

Cable, telecom and wireless internet providers and others challenged the legality of the regulations, but a federal court in June 2016 allowed the new rules to take effect.[71]

After taking office in January 2017, President Trump named Pai as FCC chairman. Pai quickly announced plans to reverse the agency's 2015 net neutrality rules, which he had voted against as a commission member. In May, comedian Oliver again used his HBO show to defend net neutrality.[72]

The FCC voted Dec. 14, 2017, again on a 3-2 party-line vote, to rescind the 2015 net neutrality regulations.

CURRENT SITUATION

Flurry of Lawsuits

The battle over net neutrality is heading to the courts.

As soon as the *Federal Register* published the rules implementing FCC's December 2017 repeal of net neutrality on Feb. 22, consumer groups, internet companies and attorneys general from 22 states and the District of Columbia began suing the agency.

Repealing net neutrality would have "dire consequences for consumers and businesses" because it would "allow internet service providers to put corporate profits over consumers by controlling what we see, do, and say online," New York Attorney General Schneiderman said. He led the coalition of attorneys general in supporting the suit filed earlier by Mozilla and Vimeo.[73]

Public interest groups Free Press, Public Knowledge and the Open Technology Institute also have filed lawsuits seeking to protect net neutrality.[74]

"This rule defies the will of a bipartisan majority of Americans and fails to preserve a free and open internet," said Michael Beckerman, president of the Internet Association, a trade group representing tech companies.[75]

States Act

On March 5, Democratic Gov. Jay Inslee of Washington signed a net neutrality bill, setting up a potential clash with the FCC. It bans ISPs from blocking or slowing content, and from speeding up apps and services in exchange for money from developers and website owners.[76]

The measure was among 61 bills introduced in 27 states aimed at retaining net neutrality in their states. Although most of those efforts have been initiated by Democrats, a number of Republicans are supporting net neutrality. The bill signed by Inslee, for instance, was sponsored by Republican state Rep. Norma Smith, who represents a rural district with constituents concerned about retaining open internet access for their homes and businesses.

"This is not a partisan issue here," Smith said. "Everyone is concerned about equal access to the internet and being able to participate in the 21st-century economy."[77]

Taking another approach, a Republican governor and four Democratic governors — from Vermont, Montana, Hawaii, New Jersey and New York — have signed executive orders forbidding their states from doing business with ISPs that violate net neutrality principles.[78]

"This is a simple step states can take to preserve and protect net neutrality," said Democratic Gov. Steve Bullock of Montana. "We can't wait for folks in Washington, D.C., to come to their senses and reinstate these rules."[79]

State officials will continue to take action on the issue, said Danielle Dean, a policy director for the National Conference of State Legislatures. "Net neutrality is going to be a big issue for states in 2018. We expect more and more bills to be filed," she said "The issue will be contentious, and there will be heated conversations about what role states should take."[80]

Municipalities have joined the fray, too. In December, 68 mayors and county leaders signed a letter opposing the FCC's rollback of the 2015 net neutrality rules. In particular, they took issue with the part of the FCC order that seeks to prevent states and localities from enacting their own net neutrality rules, saying they were "deeply disturbed by the Commission's efforts to preempt our ability to protect consumers and businesses in our communities."[81]

These state and local efforts will likely lead to a separate legal battle over whether states and municipalities have the authority to circumvent the FCC's order. The wireless communication industry trade group CTIA argues that broadband internet service is an "interstate offering" that makes it the purview of the FCC and not individual states.[82]

Bret Swanson, a visiting fellow at the American Enterprise Institute, a conservative Washington think tank, said internet access and applications are "inherently nonlocal services" that fall under federal jurisdiction. "If ever there were an economic activity that met the definition of interstate commerce," he said, "it is the internet."[83]

Republican FCC Commissioner Michael O'Rielly agreed, saying broadband is "an interstate information service" that should be subject to "a uniform, national framework." This position, he said, is consistent with the U.S. Constitution.[84]

"A hodgepodge of state rules could severely curtail not only the next generation of wireless systems that we have been working so hard to promote," he said, "but also the technologies that may rely on these networks in the future."

Senate Debate

In addition to the lawsuits, the FCC's December action is sparking debate in Congress, most notably leading to a long-shot Democratic-backed effort to reverse the new rules. The action could have ripple effects on other legislative issues aimed at extending the reach of broadband networks, particularly in underserved rural areas, or reauthorizing the FCC for the first time since 1990.[85]

In the Senate, Democrats have enough support to force a vote on a resolution reversing the FCC repeal of net neutrality. They would use a legislative tool called the Congressional Review Act, which gives Congress the power to reverse a federal agency's ruling within 60 legislative days of its publication in the *Federal Register* — in this case, Feb. 22.

Sen. Ed Markey, D-Mass., who sponsored the resolution calling for repeal of the rule, said he has "a tsunami" of support. "The internet doesn't belong to big internet service providers and special interests who want to turn it into a toll road where consumers will pay more while the biggest corporations get to ride in the fast lane," he said.[86]

All 49 senators who caucus with the Democrats plus one Republican, Susan Collins of Maine, back the measure. Democrats need one more Republican to support the bill for it to pass. But even if it does, the measure is unlikely to pass in the House. The bill's supporters aim to force Republicans to take a public stand on the issue during an election year.[87]

Senate Minority Leader Chuck Schumer, D-N.Y., began the countdown to that vote with a Feb. 27 opinion piece in *Wired* magazine, urging another Republican senator to vote for the measure and avoid the FCC's "dystopian vision for the future of the internet."[88]

Is regulation necessary to ensure unfettered online access?

YES
Heather West
Senior Policy Manager, Mozilla

Written for *CQ Researcher*, March 2018

In 2015, the Democratic-controlled Federal Communications Commission (FCC) issued an order ensuring meaningful, enforceable protections for a free and open Web. But in 2017 the new Republican FCC chairman, Ajit Pai, decided to remove those protections. This is an existential threat to the internet. His order ending net neutrality will benefit internet service providers (ISPs) at the expense of users, innovators and small businesses.

We believe the FCC order also erodes free speech, competition, innovation and user choice. This order should, and will, result in efforts in Congress and challenges in the courts to protect a neutral and open internet.

Net neutrality is two interconnected problems: rules, and the authority to enforce them. Most experts agree on what rules are needed for an open internet. Ensuring authority to enforce these rules has been the topic of the latest net neutrality debate, with some stakeholders objecting to the FCC's use of its Title II authority under the Telecommunications Act. Under Title II, the agency can treat ISPs as "common carriers" that must give other companies unfettered access to the internet.

The rules should apply to all types of network connections — fixed, mobile, wired and wireless. ISPs should not be able to block or throttle lawful traffic, nor should they be allowed to charge more for preferential treatment, such as providing faster access to content.

People must be able to run applications and to access the content of their choice via their internet provider. Such protections should apply regardless of the sender, receiver, content, website, platform, application, feature, device or equipment.

Title II regulatory authority, with appropriate forbearance, is still the best way to protect net neutrality. It also ensures other important goals, such as universal service, assistive services, infrastructural protections and privacy of browsing history.

The FCC should adopt and enforce net neutrality rules, including receiving and processing complaints, assigning liability to ISPs for violations and recovering those penalties.

It should also adopt universal service rules in the context of broadband services.

Finally, the FCC should take later action, including rulemaking and adjudication, to evaluate future practices that might undermine neutrality, and if necessary to prohibit them.

We will continue to work in Congress, the courts and with our allies and internet users against the FCC's decision to destroy net neutrality.

NO
Margaret McCarthy
Executive Director, Mobile Future

Written for *CQ Researcher*, March 2018

Open internet access is essential for full participation in American life. Consumers should be able to use their broadband connection to see the legal content of their choosing, and innovators should continue to have low barriers to entry in the broadband economy.

The United States has consistently employed regulatory restraint when it comes to federal oversight of internet service providers (ISPs), and this restraint has helped make our communications and technology sector the envy of the world. Dating back to the Clinton administration, policymakers focused on the power of competition and markets to spur investment in faster, higher-capacity networks. The result was a huge boon for the American economy. "Edge" companies like Google, once small startups, grew into household names without the need for regulations circumscribing ISPs' behavior.

That changed in 2015, when the Federal Communications Commission (FCC) classified broadband internet access as a common-carrier service under Title II of the Communications Act. We have moved light years from the dial-up dark ages of 1996, the year of the last meaningful update to the law. The legal gymnastics required to construct the 2015 Title II order show how ill-suited it is to treat ISPs like a utility.

Further, the vitriol of the net neutrality debate obscures the impact of the 2015 decision. The application of Title II turned the internet ethos of "permissionless innovation" on its head. There are real examples of services that carriers declined to bring to market, to the detriment of consumers who could have reaped new benefits and efficiencies.

The FCC's decision to remove the specter of Title II in December 2017 restored our historically successful regulatory approach. This is critical, as the wireless industry is poised to invest billions of dollars to deploy 5G technology, enabling connectivity that will power the Internet of Things and rival today's wired broadband speeds.

We can recognize the centrality of internet access to prosperity in the digital age and protect its hallmark openness without demanding the use of an outdated legal tool.

Instead of shoehorning today's dynamic broadband and mobile technologies into a regulatory regime written for monopoly telephone service, we should work toward a comprehensive law for the entire internet ecosystem. Congress can build on the consensus around an open internet to protect consumers and incentivize continued investment in a broadband economy that works for everyone.

Later that day, dubbed a "day of action" by net neutrality advocates, Democrats introduced bills in both chambers. In the Senate, Markey predicted that grassroots support for reinstating net neutrality rules would grow and nudge senators to vote for passage.

"When we take this vote on the Senate floor," Markey said, "every one of my colleagues will have to answer this question: 'Whose side are you on?' "[89]

A Republican who could be the tie-breaking vote on the Congressional Review Act introduced his own bill to codify some elements of net neutrality. The measure from Sen. John Kennedy, R-La., who has not announced his position on the resolution, would prevent ISPs from "slowing down and controlling Web content." It does not, however, block paid prioritization.[90]

On the House side, Rep. Mike Doyle, D-Pa., introduced a companion bill to the Democratic effort. (Rep. Marsha Blackburn, R-Tenn., introduced a companion bill to Kennedy's measure last year.)[91]

In December, Blackburn and more than 100 fellow House Republicans sent a letter to the FCC in support of the repeal. "This proposal is a major step forward in the effort to clear the way for the substantial investment necessary to advance our internet architecture for the next generation and close the digital divide," they said.[92]

Internet service providers characterized the Democratic effort to overturn the FCC decision as a step backward in the policy-making process.

The process "only delays us from really providing consumers some basic protections on the internet," said AT&T's Quinn. He and other telecom industry representatives called for bipartisan legislation to solve the "vexing issue" of net neutrality.[93]

In January, AT&T took out full-page newspaper ads calling for a national net neutrality law that would govern not just ISPs like itself but also tech companies and content providers such as Google and Facebook. ISPs are concerned about the potential for a patchwork of state laws. They support efforts to ban blocking or slowing internet content, but would stop short of prohibiting paid prioritization. That issue is a key difference between the Republican and Democratic bills currently pending. Congress has tried before to come up with such a law but failed to reach an agreement.[94]

"We should work together on comprehensive legislation that will preserve the open internet ecosphere and finally end this arduous debate," said Robert M. McDowell, chief public policy adviser at Mobile Future and a former Republican FCC commissioner.[95]

The intensified congressional activity comes as members gear up for this fall's midterm elections. Given the widespread public interest net neutrality has generated, the seemingly arcane topic appears likely to become a key campaign issue.

"Net neutrality will be a major issue in the 2018 campaigns," Sen. Schumer said.[96]

OUTLOOK
Continuing Battle

Given how rapidly technology has changed over the past 50 years, experts say it is difficult to predict what the future holds for net neutrality. But they expect the battle in the courts and legislatures over internet regulation to continue for years.

Meanwhile, the new FCC policy of light-touch regulation will begin this spring after the Office of Management and Budget completes a review of the repeal.

"My bet is that the broadband companies will manage to be good for about 15 minutes," says Harold Feld, senior vice president of the public interest group Public Knowledge. "Then the problem of having a system that is built on 'you can do what you want until you run into trouble' means the only way you find your limits is when you run into trouble."

Some observers say it is time to update the 1996 Telecommunications Act. After all, as futurist and technology researcher Richard Adler wrote, "Two decades is a long time in the world of technology, and telecom is vastly different today than it was then." In the 1990s, fewer than 20 percent of Americans had cellphones or residential internet service, and internet service was provided through dial-up connections.[97]

While some in Congress and the industry would like to revamp the law, says Carr of Free Press, it would be a complicated process involving countless lawyers and lobbyists. "It's become a bit of a hot potato," he says, "not only because of the issue of net neutrality, but there are a whole host of contentious issues."

Technological change could further complicate things.

In the world of telecommunications, Verizon and AT&T plan to begin offering fifth-generation, or 5G, wireless services this year that will bring customers faster speeds and the ability to connect to more devices at once.

In addition, a number of new technologies are on the horizon, such as voice activation, augmented reality, artificial intelligence and automated cars. And the Internet of Things, in which "smart" household objects can send and receive data via the internet, will continue to expand.[98]

From using smart transportation to reduce traffic fatalities to creating prosthetic limbs with 3D printing, McCarthy, of Mobile Future, says the future of technology is intertwined with the internet — and therefore with the rules that govern it.

"How we use that connectivity," she says, "is going to be so much more than just looking at the screen of your smartphone. That all requires dollars and wires and all kind of technology deployment, and the regulatory environment can have a huge impact on that."

NOTES

1. "Net Neutrality II: Last Week Tonight with John Oliver," HBO, May 7, 2017, https://tinyurl.com/md2a9v8. He also devoted an earlier show to the topic; see "Net Neutrality: Last Week Tonight with John Oliver," HBO, June 1, 2014, https://tinyurl.com/pxemfjj.

2. Monica Anderson, Andrew Perrin and Jingjing Jiang, "11% of Americans don't use the internet. Who are they?" Pew Research Center, March 5, 2018, https://tinyurl.com/yce4gme5; "Research and Markets: US Telecom Industry Revenues Total $750 Billion Reveals New Market Research Report from Signals and Systems Telecom," *Business Wire*, Jan. 4, 2012, https://tinyurl.com/ycd2o3yw.

3. Rebecca R. Ruiz, "F.C.C. Sets Net Neutrality Rules," *The New York Times*, March 12, 2015, https://tinyurl.com/y8znxd9w.

4. "Restoring Internet Freedom," Federal Communications Commission, https://tinyurl.com/ybueyl3n.

5. "AT&T Statement on FCC's Restoring Internet Freedom Draft Order," AT&T, Nov. 21, 2017, https://tinyurl.com/ycp2nvnj.

6. "Restoring Internet Freedom," *Federal Register*, Feb. 22, 2018, https://tinyurl.com/y8veagfp.

7. Cecilia Kang, "Big Tech to Join Legal Fight Against Net Neutrality Repeal," *The New York Times*, Jan. 5, 2018, https://tinyurl.com/y72q7tu2.

8. Chris Boyette and Madison Park, "Washington becomes first state to pass law protecting net neutrality," CNN, March 6, 2018, https://tinyurl.com/y8c5y4eb.

9. "Remarks Of FCC Chairman Ajit Pai At The Mobile World Congress," Federal Communications Commission, Feb. 26, 2018, https://tinyurl.com/yd4kwtqr.

10. Terrence O'Brien, "FCC Commissioner Clyburn talks about net neutrality at CES," *Engadget*, Jan. 11, 2018, https://tinyurl.com/y9pmwpj3.

11. Tali Arbel, "After net neutrality, brace for Internet 'fast lanes,' " The Associated Press, *USA Today*, Dec. 20, 2017, https://tinyurl.com/ybvjcn4j.

12. Timothy Karr, "Net Neutrality Violations: A Brief History," Free Press, April 25, 2017, https://tinyurl.com/y8hu2dts.

13. Harper Neidig, "FCC, FTC announce partnership to police internet after net neutrality repeal," *The Hill*, Dec. 11, 2017, https://tinyurl.com/ya3gborc.

14. Terrell McSweeny, "The FCC plans to kill the open internet; don't count on the FTC to save it," *Quartz*, Dec. 5, 2017, https://tinyurl.com/ybd3e2vd.

15. "Market shares of internet service providers in the United States in the fourth quarter of 2013," *Statista*, https://tinyurl.com/y7366zpm.

16. Blair Levin and Carol Mattey, "In infrastructure plan, a big opening for rural broadband," Brookings Institution, Feb. 13, 2017, https://tinyurl.com/y9mcu58y.

17. "Overwhelming Bipartisan Majority Opposes Repealing Net Neutrality," Program for Public Consultation at the University of Maryland, Dec. 12, 2017, https://tinyurl.com/yafav2nc; James K. Willcox, "Survey: Consumers Favor Strong Net Neutrality Rules," *Consumer Reports*, Sept. 27, 2017, https://tinyurl.com/y8q3w3kb; and Edward Graham, "Majority of Voters Support Net Neutrality Rules as FCC Tees Up Repeal Vote," *Morning Consult*, Nov. 29, 2017, https://tinyurl.com/y9rxlmnh.

18. Jessica Rosenworcel, "Rosenworcel Statement on FCC Plan to Roll Back Internet Rights," Federal Communications Commission, Nov. 21, 2017, https://tinyurl.com/yaps2bqh.

19. Jacob Kastrenakes, "ISPs won't promise to treat all traffic equally after net neutrality," *The Verge*, Dec. 15, 2017, https://tinyurl.com/y9z29p35.

20. Daniel Golightly, "Sprint Keynote May Stir Net Neutrality Controversy — MWC 2018," *Android Headlines*, Feb. 27, 2018, https://tinyurl.com/y9fnhgfo.

21. Mike Dano, "Sprint CEO on net neutrality: There's nothing wrong with charging for faster service," *Fierce Wireless*, Feb. 27, 2018, https://tinyurl.com/y8ocmnn7.

22. Dieter Bohn, "Netflix CEO says net neutrality is 'not our primary battle,' " *The Verge*, May 31, 2017, https://tinyurl.com/yclawpz9.

23. Timothy B. Lee, "The FCC's net neutrality debate is irrelevant — the internet already has fast lanes," *Vox*, May 16, 2014, https://tinyurl.com/yc3wpd3v.

24. "Letter to FCC Chairman Ajit Pai," American Sustainable Business Council, https://tinyurl.com/y7qhdlf4.

25. David Greene, "FCC Chief Makes Case For Tackling Net Neutrality Violations 'After The Fact,' " NPR, May 5, 2017, https://tinyurl.com/yc2eg236.

26. Patrick Brogan, "Broadband Investment Dropped in 2016," USTelecom, Oct. 31, 2017, https://tinyurl.com/y82utjgf; David L. Cohen, "Reconfirming Comcast's Commitment To An Open Internet And Net Neutrality," *Comcast Voices*, Dec. 13, 2017, https://tinyurl.com/y9t5rhhf.

27. Marguerite Reardon, "FCC chief moves to eliminate net neutrality regulations," CNET, Nov. 21, 2017, https://tinyurl.com/y7jh8dpe.

28. Jon Brodkin, "50 million US homes have only one 25Mbps Internet provider or none at all," *Ars Technica*, June 30, 2017, https://tinyurl.com/yassokb6; Hal Singer, Ed Naef and Alex King, "Assessing the Impact of Removing Regulatory Barriers on Next Generation Wireless and Wireline Broadband Infrastructure Investment," Economists Incorporated, June 2017, pp. 9-10, https://tinyurl.com/yb4cnzh2.

29. Klint Finley, "The FCC Says Net Neutrality Cripples Investment. That's Not True," *Wired*, Dec. 8, 2017, https://tinyurl.com/y7m3zwps.

30. Jon Brodkin, "Title II hasn't hurt network investment, according to the ISPs themselves," *Ars Technica*, May 16, 2017, https://tinyurl.com/lzjl3hs.

31. S. Derek Turner, "It's Working: How the Internet Access and Online Video Markets Are Thriving in the Title II Era," Public Knowledge, May 2017, https://tinyurl.com/ycfsq8ux.

32. Anita Balakrishnan, "Comcast beats earnings expectations, adding 350,000 high-speed internet customers," CNBC, Jan. 24, 2018, https://tinyurl.com/y95ce9qs; Christine Wang, "AT&T earnings: 78 cents per share, vs expected EPS of 65 cents," CNBC, Jan. 31, 2018, https://tinyurl.com/yb3or7fw; and Anita Balakrishnan, "Verizon earnings: 86 cents a share, vs. 88 cents EPS expected," CNBC, Jan. 23, 2018, https://tinyurl.com/yb7bnqbe.

33. "AT&T's CEO Randall Stephenson on Q4 2017 Results — Earnings Call Transcript," Seeking Alpha, Jan. 31, 2018, https://tinyurl.com/y7z48yzv.

34. Kristin Houser, "Exclusive: N.Y. Attorney General on Why He Refuses to Let Net Neutrality Die," *Futurism*, Dec. 16, 2017, https://tinyurl.com/y9eupmjw.

35. Bob Quinn, "AT&T Statement on FCC Vote to Restore Internet Freedom," AT&T, Dec. 14, 2017, https://tinyurl.com/y7prx6yl.

36. Andrew Magloughlin, "Net Neutrality Has Nothing to Do With Censorship," Freedom Works, June 5, 2017, https://tinyurl.com/yalbdplz.

37. Tim Wu, "Tim Wu: Why the Courts Will Have to Save Net Neutrality," *The New York Times*, Nov. 22, 2017, https://tinyurl.com/y757pou5.

38. Willmary Escoto, "Net Neutrality: The Social Justice Issue of Our Time," Public Knowledge, July 19, 2017, https://tinyurl.com/y74eexyf.

38. Deana A. Rohlinger, "How Social Movements Are Using The Internet To Change Politics," Scholars Strategy Network, January 2012, https://tinyurl.com/y8dltqf7.

40. Escoto, *op. cit.*

41. Kate Klonick, "The Terrifying Power of Internet Censors," *The New York Times*, Sept 13, 2017, https://tinyurl.com/yc9vn9k7.

42. Jon Russell, "Cloudflare CEO calls for a system to regulate hateful internet content," *TechCrunch*, Aug. 17, 2017, https://tinyurl.com/yb6gtsmv.

43. Eli M. Noam, "Beyond Liberalization II: The Impending Doom of Common Carriage," *Telecommunications Policy*, August 1994, https://tinyurl.com/y8e64pka.

44. "The Interstate Commerce Act Is Passed," U.S. Senate, https://tinyurl.com/y859jkz8.

45. Stephen Smith, "Radio: The Internet of the 1930s," American RadioWorks, Nov. 10, 2014, https://tinyurl.com/zql79mk; Clive Thompson, "The Debate Over Net Neutrality Has Its Roots in the Fight Over Radio Freedom," *Smithsonian*, October 2014, https://tinyurl.com/ybnrh8r6.

46. "Communications Act of 1934," Roosevelt Institute, https://tinyurl.com/y98g4by6; Communications Act of 1934, https://tinyurl.com/y8d536nd.

47. Theresa Riley, "The FCC, the Public Interest and the Blue Book," Moyers and Company, Dec. 19, 2012, https://tinyurl.com/y8stzjzv.

48. Dylan Matthews, "Everything you need to know about the Fairness Doctrine in one post," *The Washington Post*, Aug. 23, 2011, https://tinyurl.com/ycx7lgt2.

49. Tim Wu, "How the FCC's Net Neutrality Plan Breaks With 50 Years of History," *Wired*, Dec. 6, 2017, https://tinyurl.com/y7wzucx4.

50. Tom Struble, "The FCC's Computer Inquiries: The Origin Story Behind Net Neutrality," *Morning Consult*, May 23, 2017, https://tinyurl.com/y8hx-lc4p; "Computer Inquiries: Internet over Telecom," CyberTelecom, updated March 1, 2017, https://tinyurl.com/8m26ef6.

51. "ARPANet 1970s: Experimental to Operational," CyberTelecom, updated Sept. 21, 2017, https://tinyurl.com/yap7rtun.

52. Janus Kopfstein, "AT&T Could Have Bought the Internet in 1971," *Motherboard*, Jan. 17, 2012, https://tinyurl.com/ybsowowx.

53. Julia Murphy and Max Roser, "Internet," Our World In Data, https://tinyurl.com/y7v2hd6b; "A Brief History of NSF and the Internet," National Science Foundation, Aug. 13, 2003, https://tinyurl.com/jv48rs6.

54. Peter H. Lewis, "U.S. Begins Privatizing Internet's Operations," *The New York Times*, Oct. 24, 1994, https://tinyurl.com/yaqp822e.

55. Hanlong Fu, David J. Atkin and Yi Mou, "The Impact of the Telecommunications Act of 1996 in the Broadband Age," *Advances in Communications and Media Research*, 2012, https://tinyurl.com/y8uxy6bv.

56. Deborah Solomon, "FCC Chief Says Keep Hands Off the Internet or Risk Stifling Advances," *San Francisco Chronicle*, July 20, 1999, https://tinyurl.com/ybr4gfom.

57. "FCC Classifies Cable Modem Service As 'Information Service,'" news release, Federal Communications Commission, March 14, 2002, https://tinyurl.com/ybpq9zp5.

58. Tim Wu, "Network Neutrality, Broadband Discrimination," *Journal of Telecommunications and High Technology Law*, June 5, 2003, https://tinyurl.com/k6p52bq.

59. Michael K. Powell, "Preserving Internet Freedom: Guiding Principles For The Industry," remarks at Silicon Flatirons Symposium, as prepared for delivery, Feb. 8, 2004, https://tinyurl.com/ydaptkrr.

60. Jonathan Krim, "Phone Company Settles in Blocking of Internet Calls," *The Washington Post*, March 4, 2005, https://tinyurl.com/y9pu6szj.

61. *National Cable & Telecommunications Association v. Brand X Internet Services*, Oyez, https://tinyurl.com/ybq3xheg.

62. "FCC Eliminates Mandated Sharing Requirement on Incumbents' Wireline Broadband Internet Access Services," news release, Federal Communications Commission, Aug. 5, 2005, https://tinyurl.com/ybd5rldt.

63. "FCC Policy Statement," Federal Communications Commission, Sept. 23, 2005, https://tinyurl.com/mbpbg82.

64. "Online Extra: At SBC, It's All About 'Scale and Scope,'" *Businessweek*, Nov. 7, 2005, https://tinyurl.com/ycjvyq5p.

65. Cecelia Kang, "Court rules for Comcast over FCC in 'net neutrality' case," *The Washington Post*, April 7, 2010, https://tinyurl.com/ylhzukc.

66. Marguerite Reardon, "Appeals court strikes down FCC's Net neutrality rules," CNET, Jan. 14, 2014, https://tinyurl.com/ybjpe738.

67. Soraya Nadia McDonald, "John Oliver's net neutrality rant may have caused FCC site crash," *The Washington Post*, June 4, 2014, https://tinyurl.com/ybaxjbt7.

68. Edward Wyatt, "Obama Asks F.C.C. to Adopt Tough Net Neutrality Rules," *The New York Times*, Nov. 10, 2014, https://tinyurl.com/y9w6ydkm.

69. Tom Wheeler, "FCC Chairman Tom Wheeler: This Is How We Will Ensure Net Neutrality," *Wired*, Feb. 4, 2015, https://tinyurl.com/y9mgsz3n.

70. FCC Report and Order, Federal Communications Commission, March 12, 2015, https://tinyurl.com/nh8d4yk.

71. Kang, *op. cit.*

72. Elahe Izadi, "John Oliver revives his signature fight — net neutrality — in an ingenious way," *The Washington Post*, May 8, 2017, https://tinyurl.com/ycwlmpat.

73. "A.G. Schneiderman Leads Coalition Of 23 AGs In Suit To Block Illegal Rollback Of Net Neutrality," news release, Office of New York Attorney General, Feb. 22, 2018, https://tinyurl.com/yblnw7af.

74. Klint Finley, "Tech Giants to Join Legal Battle Over Net Neutrality," *Wired*, Jan. 5, 2018, https://tinyurl.com/ydxrv8og.

75. "Statement Announcing Intention To Intervene In Judicial Action To Preserve Net Neutrality Protections," Internet Association, Jan. 5, 2018, https://tinyurl.com/ya4gzoa5.

76. Brian Fung, "Washington state's net neutrality law is the beginning of a big headache for Internet providers," *The Washington Post*, March 6, 2018, https://tinyurl.com/yd3zmsy2.

77. Cecilia Kang, "States Push Back After Net Neutrality Repeal," *The New York Times*, Jan. 11, 2018, https://tinyurl.com/y9v9t8kt.

78. Klint Finley, "States and Cities Keep the Battle for Net Neutrality Alive," *Wired*, Jan. 23, 2018, https://tinyurl.com/y9p7k4d9.

79. "Governor Bullock Protects Net Neutrality In Montana," news release, Montana Governor's Office, Jan. 22, 2018, https://tinyurl.com/ycszajxx.

80. Jenni Bergal, "Net Neutrality Fight Shifts to the States," *Stateline*, Jan. 24, 2018, https://tinyurl.com/y95lyghz.

81. Martin J. Walsh, "Net Neutrality Letter From Mayor Walsh, Other Local Leaders," news release, Boston Mayor's Office, Dec. 7, 2017, https://tinyurl.com/ybpcmyd3.

82. Harper Neidig, "With rules repealed, what's next for net neutrality?" *The Hill*, Feb. 23, 2018, https://tinyurl.com/yaqavzl3; Jon Brodkin, "FCC will also order states to scrap plans for their own net neutrality laws," *Ars Technica*, Nov. 21, 2017, https://tinyurl.com/ycadj827.

83. Bret Swanson, "If any economic activity meets the definition of interstate commerce, it's the internet," American Enterprise Institute, Oct. 13, 2017, https://tinyurl.com/y9jn84f9.

84. Michael O'Rielly, "Statement Of Commissioner Michael O'Rielly," Federal Communications Commission, Jan. 4, 2018, https://tinyurl.com/y9ch9cn5.

85. Harper Niedig, "Congress pushes broadband access ahead of Trump infrastructure proposal," *The Hill*, Jan. 25, 2018, https://tinyurl.com/y7e5fdlc; Mariam Baksh, "Net Neutrality Advocates Fear Implications of FCC Reauthorization," *Morning Consult*, Aug. 17, 2017, https://tinyurl.com/ya6msynt.

86. "Senator Markey: Clock Starts Ticking Today in Push to Fully Restore FCC's Net Neutrality Protections," news release, Office of Sen. Ed Markey, Feb. 22, 2018, https://tinyurl.com/y8qc2wng.

87. Cecilia Kang, "Senate Democrats Push for a Net Neutrality Vote. Do They Have a Chance?" *The*

New York Times, Jan. 16, 2018, https://tinyurl.com/ycvkcbvz.

88. Charles E. Schumer, "Senate Democrats Have a Plan to Save Net Neutrality," *Wired*, Feb. 27, 2018, https://tinyurl.com/ycgqr7vw.

89. Ali Breland, "Dems introduce legislation to stop FCC net neutrality repeal," *The Hill*, Feb. 27, 2018, https://tinyurl.com/yb8p898z.

90. Harper Neidig, "GOP senator offers his own net neutrality bill," *The Hill*, March 7, 2018, https://tinyurl.com/yarlnw33.

91. Tracie Mauriello, "Rep. Mike Doyle introduces legislation to preserve net neutrality," *Pittsburgh Post-Gazette*, Feb. 27, 2018, https://tinyurl.com/y92tdrep; Brian Fung, "Days after the FCC repealed its net neutrality rules, the GOP has a bill to replace them," *The Washington Post*, Dec. 19, 2017, https://tinyurl.com/y6wcrlg5.

92. Harper Neidig, "GOP lawmakers urge FCC to repeal net neutrality rules ahead of vote," *The Hill*, Dec. 13, 2017, https://tinyurl.com/y782acgw.

93. "Broadband for America Statement On Effort To Overturn FCC Order," Broadband for America, Feb. 27, 2018, https://tinyurl.com/y8bccqhy; Bob Quinn, "Let's Take Action and Enact a Federal Consumer Bill of Rights," AT&T, Feb. 27, 2018, https://tinyurl.com/ybn2sxf8.

94. Brian Fung, "AT&T wants Congress to draft a net neutrality law. Here's why that's a big deal," *The Washington Post*, Jan. 24, 2018, https://tinyurl.com/y9mc7bwq.

95. Robert M. McDowell, "Statement: CRA is not the Best Way to Bring Broadband Access to Every American," *Mobile Future*, Feb. 27, 2018, https://tinyurl.com/y9mttujd.

96. Marguerite Reardon, "Democrats force Senate vote on net neutrality repeal," CNET, Jan. 9, 2018, https://tinyurl.com/y7sx2rng.

97. Richard Adler, "Will the Telecommunications Act get a much-needed update as it turns 21?" *Recode*, Feb. 8, 2018, https://tinyurl.com/y9o6mdtg.

98. Daniel Burrus, "The Internet of Things Is Far Bigger Than Anyone Realizes," *Wired*, https://tinyurl.com/y8d7kxlq.

BIBLIOGRAPHY

Selected Sources

Books

Blum, Andrew, *Tubes: A Journey to the Center of the Internet*, Ecco, 2013.
A journalist describes Americans' digital lives.

Crawford, Susan, *Captive Audience: The Telecom Industry and Monopoly Power in the New Gilded Age*, Yale University Press, 2014.
A Harvard law professor analyzes how government policies have led to consolidation in the telecom industry and says the United States has lost its competitive advantage in the internet revolution.

Hazlett, Thomas W., *The Fallacy of Net Neutrality*, Encounter Books, 2011.
An economist argues net neutrality regulations inhibit innovation and says the marketplace should be allowed to develop spontaneously.

MacKinnon, Rebecca, *Consent of the Networked: The Worldwide Struggle for Internet Freedom*, Basic Books, 2012.
An internet policy specialist says corporations are misusing their digital power and calls for regulations to support the rights of internet users around the world.

Tufekci, Zeynep, *Twitter and Tear Gas: The Power and Fragility of Networked Protest*, Yale University Press, 2017.
A sociologist examines how the internet has transformed 21st-century protest and social movements by allowing them to connect globally.

Articles

Downes, Larry, "The Tangled Web of Net Neutrality and Regulation," *Harvard Business Review*, March 31, 2017, https://tinyurl.com/ycv7rf9z.
An internet-industry analyst explains the regulatory issues surrounding net neutrality.

Economides, Nicholas, "A Case for Net Neutrality," *IEEE Spectrum*, Dec. 13, 2017, https://tinyurl.com/y7aqfdc4.
A New York University professor of economics argues that repealing net neutrality rules will harm the U.S. economy and technology sector.

Goode, Lauren, "Netflix CEO says he isn't worried that Trump administration will gut net neutrality," *The Verge*, March 16, 2017, https://tinyurl.com/y9hedbnw.
The head of Netflix says internet openness is well established and will survive no matter what the Federal Communications Commission (FCC) does regarding net neutrality.

McMillan, Robert, "What Everyone Gets Wrong in the Debate Over Net Neutrality," *Wired*, June 23, 2014, https://tinyurl.com/yaymr38g.
A journalist argues that internet service providers (ISPs) have long had favorites and that the net neutrality debate is misleading.

Schrodt, Paul, "What the End of Net Neutrality Means for You," *Money*, Dec. 15, 2017, https://tinyurl.com/ycejhh8w.
The FCC's 2017 vote ending net neutrality could lead to higher costs for consumers.

Stone, Brad, "Father of the Web Confronts His Creation in the Era of Fake News," Bloomberg, Nov. 13, 2017, https://tinyurl.com/ybclz64f.
Web inventor Tim Berners-Lee lobbied to keep net neutrality regulations, warning the United States' tech leadership could be lost if regulators do not preserve the separation between content creators and telecommunications companies.

Wu, Tim, "How the FCC's Net Neutrality Plan Breaks With 50 Years of History," *Wired*, Dec. 6, 2017, https://tinyurl.com/y7wzucx4.

The Columbia University law school professor who coined the term "network neutrality" reviews the history of internet regulation.

Reports and Studies

"Decoding the Net Neutrality Debate," Knight Foundation, Dec. 10, 2014, https://tinyurl.com/ycw933sw.
A democracy-advocacy group looks at how various parties sought to influence opinion on net neutrality, concluding public support for internet regulation is overwhelming.

Gilroy, Angele A., "The Net Neutrality Debate: Access to Broadband Networks," Congressional Research Service, Dec. 20, 2017, https://tinyurl.com/ydyc2xgb.
A telecommunications policy specialist details the history of internet regulation and congressional actions surrounding it.

Mayo, John W., *et al.*, "An Economic Perspective of Title II Regulation of the Internet," *Economic Policy Vignettes*, July 2017, https://tinyurl.com/ycgqy4df.
A report produced for Georgetown University makes the economic case against net neutrality regulations, warning that regulating the internet as a public utility violates standard economic principles.

Wu, Tim, "Network Neutrality, Broadband Discrimination," *Journal of Telecommunications and High Technology Law*, June 5, 2003, https://tinyurl.com/k6p52bq.
In this research paper from the internet's early days, a legal scholar first uses the term "network neutrality," comparing different approaches that could be taken to regulate the internet as he makes the initial case for ensuring the principles of net neutrality.

For More Information

Federal Communications Commission, 445 12th St., S.W., Washington, DC 20554; 888-225-5322; www.fcc .gov. Federal agency that regulates interstate and international communications by radio, television, wire, satellite and cable.

Free Press, 1025 Connecticut Ave., N.W., Washington, DC 20036; 202-265-1490; www.freepress.net. Independent organization advocating for open internet access.

Internet Association, 1333 H. St., N.W., Washington, DC 20037; 202-869-8680; internetassociation.org. Trade association representing the internet industry.

Mobile Future, 607 14th St., N.W., Washington, DC 20005; 202-772-0453; mobilefuture.org. Trade association representing the wireless communications industry.

NCTA — The Internet & Television Association, 25 Massachusetts Ave., N.W., Washington, DC 20001; 202-222-2300; www.ncta.com. Trade association representing the cable and broadband industry.

Open Technology Institute, 740 15th St., N.W., Washington, DC 20005; 202-986-2700; www.newamerica .org/oti. Technology arm of the New America think tank.

Public Knowledge, 1818 N St., N.W., Washington, DC 20036; 202-861-0020; www.publicknowledge.org. Public interest group that advocates for an open internet.

U.S. Telecom Association, 601 New Jersey Ave., N.W., Washington, DC 20001; 202-326-7300; www.ustelecom .org. Trade association representing the wired and wireless telecommunications industries.

3

Diversity in Hollywood

Christina Hoag

Comedian Chris Rock, host of the 2016 Academy Awards, pointedly acknowledged the controversy over Hollywood's lack of racial and ethnic diversity in his opening bit at the ceremony: "I'm here at the Academy Awards, otherwise known as the White People's Choice Awards." For the second year in a row, only white performers were nominated for top actor and actress Oscars.

From *CQ Researcher,*
August 5, 2016

When African-American comic Chris Rock took the stage to host the 2016 Academy Awards, he wasted no time in confronting the issue of the day.

"I'm here at the Academy Awards, otherwise known as the White People's Choice Awards," Rock quipped. His blunt monologue reflected public outrage that the academy's 7,000-plus predominantly older, white and male members had nominated an all-white slate of actors and actresses for Hollywood's most prestigious prizes — for the second year in a row.[1]

Yet Rock himself didn't escape charges of bias and stereotyping. In a spoof that fell flat for many viewers, he introduced a group of Asian children as the accountants who tally the award votes, and Latino activists were piqued that he addressed the exclusion of blacks but not of other minorities.

"Who OK'd that script?" asks Alex Nogales, president of the National Hispanic Media Coalition. "Diversity is more than one group." Still, Rock underscored the point made by the #OscarsSoWhite hashtag that had erupted on social media in January as soon as the academy announced its 2016 nominees. "How is it possible for the second consecutive year all 20 contenders under the acting category are white?" director Spike Lee wrote on Instagram.[2]

Black Hollywood A-listers, including Lee and actor Will Smith, whose performance as a Nigerian doctor in *Concussion* had been widely considered Oscar-worthy, announced they would boycott the globally televised awards ceremony.[3] Activists holding signs saying "Shame on You" and "Hollywood Must Do Better" picketed the event.[4]

Minorities Trail Whites in Leading Roles

The percentage of minorities playing leading roles in films and broadcast shows edged up in recent years, but blacks, Hispanics and other minorities continue to fall far short of whites. Minorities filled about 13 percent of lead-actor film roles in 2014, up from 10.5 percent in 2011. In scripted broadcast programs, minorities filled about 8 percent of lead roles in the 2013-14 season, up from 5 percent in 2011-12. Minorities make up about 38 percent of the U.S. population.

Lead Actor Roles by Race in Theatrical Films, Broadcast Scripted Programming, 2011-2014

(Percentage)

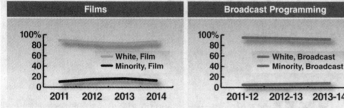

Source: "2016 Hollywood Diversity Report: Busine$$ as Usual?" Ralph J. Bunche Center for African American Studies at UCLA, Feb. 25, 2016, http://tinyurl.com/hhrdltn

Even President Obama weighed in, saying, "As a whole, the industry should do what every other industry should do, which is to look for talent and provide opportunity to everybody."[5]

The outcry highlighted long-festering charges of bias against racial and ethnic minorities and women in the film and television industries — both in front of and behind the camera — despite decades of complaints, studies and diversity programs.

"This is a long-term problem that has proven somewhat intractable," says Darnell Hunt, professor of sociology and director of the Ralph J. Bunche Center for African American Studies at the University of California, Los Angeles (UCLA).

The issue of diversity in the film and television industries, which employ 302,000 people directly and 1.9 million indirectly, increasingly is being scrutinized as the United States becomes more heterogeneous.[6] In 2014, minorities represented 38 percent of the population; by 2060 they are projected to account for 56 percent.[7] But whites and men dominate nearly every facet of the industry, from the corporate suite to cinematography, although studies show

TV has become somewhat more diverse than movies.

A 2015 study by the Bunche Center found minorities, predominantly African-Americans, had 13 percent of lead film roles in 2014.[8] In television shows, white men filled about 70 percent of scripted roles.[9] And research by the Center for the Study of Women in Television and Film at San Diego State University said that women, who make up 51 percent of the population, occupied 19 percent of major behind-the-scenes movie jobs, such as director, writer and producer.[10] The trend is more pronounced among industry powerbrokers. The UCLA study reported that talent agents — who make the deals placing actors, writers, directors, producers and others in productions — are 91 percent white and 68 percent male.[11]

"The film industry still functions as a straight, white, boys' club," stated another study by the University of Southern California's Institute for Diversity and Empowerment at Annenberg (IDEA) that had similar findings.[12]

Studio executives admit more could be done to include women and minorities. Stacey Snider, co-chair at 20th Century Fox, said she could mentor more women and "enable young female writers and directors to have access" to studios.[13] Harvey Weinstein, co-chair of the Weinstein film studio, said, "The truth is that the industry needs to, and must, do better. And we will, too," he said.[14]

Activists say mass entertainment has a particular responsibility to mirror the population at-large because it wields considerable influence over popular culture and public perceptions, especially by those who may not personally know people different from themselves. Movies and TV "reflect our values but they also shape them," says Megan Townsend, entertainment media strategist for GLAAD, an LGBT rights organization known by its acronym. Adds Nogales, "The way we are perceived is the way we'll get treated."

Several factors explain why racial, ethnic and gender imbalance remains an issue in film and television, experts say. The industries' allure of glamor, wealth and fame leads to a talent supply that far outstrips demand. Thus, breaking into and advancing in the industry are highly contingent on personal relationships, which has led to the development of a clubby circle of insiders.

"It's not a merit system. Most people are disadvantaged by that," says John W. Cones, a California entertainment attorney who has written 16 books on access issues in Hollywood.

Because white males broker most deals at studios, networks and talent agencies, they tend to choose from their own circles to fill major positions, such as directors, writers and producers, Hunt and Cones say. In turn, they add, producers and directors fill production jobs with people who also tend to look like them.

"It's based on relationship and comfort zones, which is not to say that plain, old-fashioned racism isn't alive and well, too," Hunt says. "But it's very insular."

A similar dynamic appears to play out with regard to gender. In movies directed by men in 2015, women made up only 10 percent of writers, 19 percent of editors and 10 percent of cinematographers, according to the San Diego State University study. But in movies directed by women, more than half the writers were women, as were 32 percent of the editors and 12 percent of the cinematographers, the study found.[15]

Such trends are amplified in the movie business because box-office returns are unpredictable and films can cost hundreds of millions of dollars to make, researchers say. As a result, executives tend to hire people with proven success. "They go back to the same white men who have a track record," Hunt says. Because women and minorities don't get the experience they need to land the prestige studio jobs, he and others say, they end up working on smaller, independent productions.

Meanwhile, many professionals have been reluctant to complain about the system out of fear of being labeled troublemakers in a highly competitive industry, in which employment goes from project to project, researchers say.

Signs of change are afoot, however. The Oscars controversy has stirred a new push for inclusivity from Hollywood insiders. The Academy of Motion Picture Arts and Sciences, which runs the Oscars, revamped its voting rules and this year added its most diverse group of

Critics blasted the selection of Hispanic actress Zoe Saldana, right, to portray beloved African-American singer Nina Simone, left, as a return to "blackface" in the movies. Saldana wore a prosthetic nose and her skin was darkened with makeup (not shown) in a trailer for the film released this year.

new members ever, with the goal of nominating more women and minorities for awards. And prominent producers J. J. Abrams and Ryan Murphy announced initiatives to hire more people from underrepresented groups as cast and crew.

Outside of Hollywood, a new generation of internet media, such as Amazon and Hulu, is providing new platforms for underrepresented groups and original story lines. They include Netflix's "Master of None," a TV comedy created by and starring an American Muslim of Indian descent, Aziz Ansari, and *Beasts of No Nation,* a searing drama about African child soldiers. Mainstream TV also is adding new shows, such as ABC's "Fresh Off the Boat," an Asian immigrant comedy, with largely ethnic casts and stories.

Actresses increasingly are speaking out against discrimination based on age, the dearth of female roles and the on-screen sexualization of women, which activists say reflect male points of view. One study shows that female characters were more likely than males to be attractive or shown nude or sexily or scantily attired.[16] Pay gender inequity also surfaced as an issue in December 2014 after hackers publicized emails from Sony Pictures that revealed Jennifer Lawrence was paid less than her male co-stars in *American Hustle* (2013).[17] Lawrence said she was shocked and angry at the disparity. And the U.S. Equal Employment Opportunity Commission is investigating

Off-Camera Jobs for Women Remain Stagnant

The share of behind-the-scenes jobs filled by women on the 250 top-grossing American films between 1998 and 2015 remained below 20 percent. In 2015, women comprised 19 percent of all directors, writers, producers, executive producers, editors and cinematographers, only 2 percentage points more than in 1998.

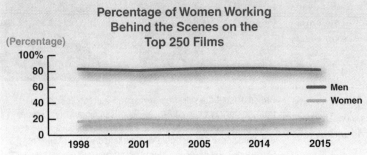

Percentage of Women Working Behind the Scenes on the Top 250 Films

Source: "The Celluloid Ceiling: Behind-the-Scenes Employment of Women on the Top 100, 250, and 500 Films of 2015," Center for the Study of Women in Television and Film, 2016, http://tinyurl.com/h5gmn7p

allegations of bias against female directors after the American Civil Liberties Union (ACLU) of Southern California filed a complaint against the industry.[18]

"As a result of this rapidly growing and increasingly vociferous public conversation, the explicit denial or implicit disregard of the embarrassing statistics by high-profile individuals is no longer possible," said Martha M. Lauzen, executive director of San Diego State University's Center for the Study of Women in Television and Film.[19]

As Hollywood insiders and outsiders discuss diversity in the entertainment industry, here are some of the questions being debated:

Does Hollywood discriminate against female and minority actors?

When the trailer of an upcoming movie about African-American singer Nina Simone was released this year, critics blasted it as a return to "blackface" — using makeup on white actors so they can play black characters. Hispanic actress Zoe Saldana, who had been chosen to portray Simone, was wearing a prosthetic nose and her skin had been darkened with makeup.

"There are many superb actresses of color who could more adequately represent my mother," Simone's daughter Lisa Simone Kelly said.[20]

Using white actors to portray minorities is an established practice in Hollywood. In *Exodus: Gods and Kings* (2014), English actor Christian Bale played the Middle Eastern Jewish character Moses, and white actors portrayed Egyptian characters.[21] Emma Stone portrayed a Hawaiian-Asian woman in *Aloha* (2015).[22] Joseph Fiennes plays the late pop singer Michael Jackson in *Elizabeth, Michael & Marlon* (2016).[23]

And television is not exempt. Fox's "Tyrant" stars Adam Rayner, a white actor, as the show's sympathetic Middle Eastern hero.[24]

Hollywood insiders say the problem is the bottom line: To get a movie financed, backers need a "bankable" star who can increase the film's box-office return — and most big stars are white. Director Ridley Scott responded to *Exodus* critics: "I can't mount a film of this budget, . . . and say that my lead actor is Mohammad So-and-So from such-and-such. I'm just not going to get it financed. So the question doesn't even come up."[25]

Research has shown, however, that diverse casts can boost returns. A Bunche Center study of 2014 movies found that global box-office returns for films with a 40- to 50-percent minority cast were twice that of movies with a 10 percent or less minority cast. TV shows showed similar patterns.[26]

Critics charge that it is unfair to exclude minority actors from racial and ethnic roles, especially since there are far fewer such parts and minority actors can give more nuanced performances drawn from their own experience. "How else can it be authentic?" asks Nogales of the National Hispanic Media Coalition. And playing those roles could help minority actors become bankable stars, critics say.

But Indian-American actor Ansari said in casting his Netflix series "Master of None," that it was hard to find minority actors because there are fewer of them than white actors, which leads to casting white actors in "brownface." "But I still wonder if we are trying hard enough," he said.[27]

Members of other underrepresented groups say when roles for them do arise, they often involve only limited story lines. People with disabilities, for example, are primarily played by ablebodied actors and story lines often are based on overcoming adversity or recovering from the disability, says Johnson Cheu, assistant professor at Michigan State University who studies culture, disability and media.

Rarely are people with disabilities portrayed as fully realized characters outside of their disability, Cheu says. "Disability makes for good tension and conflict, as long as [the disability] is not long-term and permanent in Hollywood. That's not progress, and it's not reality," he says.

Activists with other underrepresented groups also say their community members often are stereotyped: Transgender people are almost always women; Asian men rarely get to play romantic swashbucklers; Hispanics tend to be brown-skinned and occupy low-paying jobs. "Judges are the only role black women get to play" on television, says Rashad Robinson, executive director of ColorOfChange.org, a civil rights organization. "It makes us feel like a box was checked."

Women also face age discrimination, with fewer parts for women as they age. Maggie Gyllenhaal said that at age 37 she was deemed too old to play the love interest of a 55-year-old man.[28] The 27-year-old Stone said she's had to play opposite romantic male leads her father's age.[29]

Studies bear out their statements. Female characters in their 30s represent 28 percent of female roles, while female characters in their 40s make up only 20 percent of roles, according to research by the Center for the Study of Women in Television and Film at San Diego State University. The opposite is true for men, the study found: The percentage of older male characters increases slightly as men age: Men in their 30s represent 27 percent of male roles, while those in their 40s make up 30 percent of roles.[30]

"Portraying female characters in their 20s and 30s tends to keep the emphasis on their physical traits," said study author Lauzen.

Women actors also are speaking up about gender-based pay disparities, after WikiLeaks published the Sony emails, hacked in 2014 by the North Korean government in retaliation for the lampooning of leader Kim Jong Un in the movie *The Interview.* Lawrence learned not only that she was paid less than her male co-stars in *American Hustle* but also that she and co-star Amy Adams received 7 percent of profits while their three male co-stars each earned 9 percent.[31]

Other actresses have spoken out as well: While Jack Nicholson received profit-sharing pay for *Something's Gotta Give* (2003), his co-star Diane Keaton did not, and triple Oscar winner Meryl Streep said she routinely is paid less than her male co-stars. Shortly after the Sony hacking revelations, Patricia Arquette underscored the issue during her acceptance speech for Best Supporting Actress at the 2015 Oscars: "It's our time to have wage equality once and for all."[32]

Lawrence, the highest-paid movie actress in 2015, earned $52 million, far less than top-paid actor, Robert Downey Jr, who made $80 million.[33]

Pay disparities also exist in television, although they are less pronounced. The two highest-paid female TV actresses — Sofia Vergara ("Modern Family") and Kaley Cuoco ("The Big Bang Theory") — each earned $28.5 million in 2015, nearly as much as the industry's highest paid actor, "Big Bang" star Jim Parsons ($29 million). But the cut-off to make *Forbes'* list of highest-paid TV actresses was $5 million — $4.5 million less than the cutoff for male actors.[34]

Is television more diverse than film?

Many experts say diversity is making visible progress in television. Fox's "Empire," a melodrama about the music industry, features a nearly all-black cast. ABC's sitcom "Fresh Off the Boat" is based on the memoir of a Taiwanese immigrant chef. The CW network has "Jane the Virgin," a comedy about a Latina who accidentally becomes pregnant.

"Television is much further along than film," says Nogales of the National Hispanic Media Coalition.

TV production companies score better on diversity overall than movie companies. Two dozen film companies were rated as not inclusive, while nine out of 10 TV companies were found to be largely or fully inclusive, according to a study by the University of Southern California's Institute for Diversity and Empowerment at Annenberg, which studies media inclusivity. The study listed the Walt Disney Co. networks (ABC, Disney, Disney Jr. and Freeform) and CW as the most diverse because they hired more women and minorities in key positions.[35]

Getty Images/FOX

Many experts say the nearly all-black cast of Fox's "Empire," a drama about the music industry, shows that diversity is making visible progress in television. Above, Taraji P. Henson and Terrence Howard in the show's "Et Tu, Brute?" episode.

TV always has been ahead of movies in diversity, observers say, primarily because networks, which must fill a lot of programming slots, constantly are seeking fresh stories. "There's just so much more being produced in TV than in film," says Tery Lopez, director of diversity at the Writers Guild of America West, the industry group representing screenwriters.

Television also is more nimble. Production costs tend to be lower than for movies, giving networks more latitude to try new concepts, experts say. A new show that does not attract good ratings can be yanked quickly, allowing networks to cut their losses. And television shows, which typically are produced in a matter of months as opposed to years for feature films, can incorporate fast-changing societal attitudes and current events, says GLAAD's Townsend.

Reliance on overseas sales also differs between the industries. Both studios and networks license their content abroad, but foreign sales are a vital consideration in movie financing decisions. Foreign revenue from American movies last year ($40 billion) represented 73 percent of box-office receipts — up 10 percent from 2010. By contrast, domestic movie ticket sales increased by only $4 million during the same period.[36]

As a result, studios produce more star-studded, action-driven, blockbuster movies that appeal to international audiences. Those films also appeal to the biggest U.S. movie-going demographic — 12- to 39-year-olds, who make up more than half of frequent American

moviegoers.[37] Controversial themes, such as LGBT issues, thus tend to be avoided.

"There's some concern as to how films play around the world," Townsend says. "That affects the stories they are choosing to tell, or not tell."

Television, on the other hand, does not typically develop shows with foreign audiences in mind, and some U.S. ethnic shows do not translate well overseas. "Empire," for example, flopped in the United Kingdom, Germany, Australia and Canada.

"These shows are a reflection of our society, but not a reflection of all societies," said Marion Edwards, president of international TV at Fox. However, shows with mainstream themes featuring diverse casts or leads, such as ABC's "Grey's Anatomy" and "How to Get Away with Murder," have done well overseas.[38]

But ethnic content on TV could be affected as foreign sales become increasingly important to help defray rising television production costs — about $3 million for an hourlong drama in 2013.[39] "We are telling our units that they need to be aware that . . . creating too much diversity in the leads in their show means . . . problems having their shows translating to the international market," Edwards said.[40]

Behind the camera, however, television remains dominated by whites and males. During the upcoming 2016-17 season, showrunners — those who oversee everything on a show from hiring to creative direction — at the five biggest broadcast networks are 90 percent white and 80 percent male, according to a study by the trade journal *Variety*.[41]

Industry insiders say that while most networks have programs to develop talent from diverse backgrounds, they have mostly led to tokenism rather than wide change. NBC's Diverse Staff Writing Initiative, for instance, pays a series to employ a minority staff writer, but typically only one hire is made.[42] Writer Amy Aniobi said she has seen staff lists with employees labeled "diversity writer." "Everyone knows who the diversity writer is. You're the one who's the only one," she said.[43]

That lack of minority inclusion also trickles down to production jobs. "You rarely see diversity in the crew," says Jaquita Ta'le, an African-American actress in Los Angeles.

But minorities are popular with the population at-large, says UCLA's Hunt, noting the success of African-American showrunner Shonda Rhimes, whose hit series, such as

"Scandal" and "Grey's Anatomy," use minority actors, writers and crew members.

"If more networks took that lead, they'd be more in sync with their audience," Hunt says.

Will streaming outlets lead to greater diversity?

Katie Elmore Mota was tired of seeing Latinos absent from TV so she created her own show. "East Los High," a hit soap opera depicting Hispanic teens in a fictional Los Angeles high school was recently renewed for a fourth season by the Hulu internet streaming service. Executive producer Mota says the show's 60 percent non-Latino audience underscores to the mainstream industry that TV characters don't have to all be "rich, white teenagers."[44]

To overcome barriers to hiring, women and minorities are finding internet viewing platforms — such as Amazon, Netflix, Hulu, Snapchat, Yahoo and YouTube — more welcoming than the mainstream industry. These new digital media seek different kinds of shows to lure viewers from traditional broadcast and cable channels.

In addition, many internet outlets operate under business models — such as subscriptions and limited advertising — that differ from network or cable models, so online outlets can appeal to niche audiences marginalized in the mainstream media. "Media is changing and that is . . . improving visibility for artists of color," says actress Ta'le, who has appeared in ABC's "Castle," among other shows, and voiced animated productions. "It's become the best way to get your stories told."

Some shows, such as Amazon Studios' "Transparent," created by Jill Soloway and featuring a transgender dad and his family, have turned into Emmy-winning hits. Others have helped their creators break into the mainstream industry. HBO snapped up the rights to Issa Rae's YouTube series "The Misadventures of Awkward Black Girl," which features a shy, middle-class black woman modeled on Rae, after its first webisode scored 2 million views.[45]

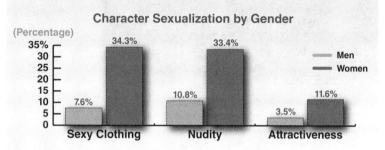

Females More Sexualized in Media Than Males

Female characters were far more likely than males to be portrayed in a sexualized manner in films, TV shows and digital series, according to a 10-year study of 10 major entertainment-media companies. The study defines sexualization as displays of sexy clothing, nudity or references to a person's physical attractiveness.

Character Sexualization by Gender

(Percentage)

Sexy Clothing: Men 7.6%, Women 34.3%
Nudity: Men 10.8%, Women 33.4%
Attractiveness: Men 3.5%, Women 11.6%

Source: "Inclusion or Invisibility? Comprehensive Annenberg Report on Diversity in Entertainment," Media, Diversity, & Social Change Initiative, Annenberg School for Communication and Journalism, University of Southern California, Feb. 22, 2016, http://tinyurl.com/jxjyj2p

The internet also has evolved into a go-to place for Hollywood agents seeking fresh talent, giving exposure and critical experience to underrepresented groups, says the Writers Guild's Lopez. "The Web does give opportunities to people who put up their work," she says.

A USC study ranked Amazon and Hulu as strongly inclusive, with Amazon hiring the most female directors.[46]

Underrepresented groups also are benefiting from a boom in TV production. From 2009 to 2015, the number of scripted shows doubled — from just over 200 to 409 — leading to a shortage of experienced producers and writers and thus creating opportunities for less experienced entrants, insiders say.[47]

That's especially true in new media. Writer Gloria Calderon Kellett is making her debut as a showrunner with the Netflix remake of the 1970s sitcom "One Day at a Time," featuring a Latino family. "The fact that there is so much work is huge," she said. "People who don't normally get a chance, who are very talented, get seen."[48]

Internet companies also are producing movies. At the Cannes Film Festival in May, Amazon Studios unveiled its first slate of five feature films designed to be viewed online, including one directed by Park Chan-wook of South Korea.[49] While Netflix's first motion picture,

Getty Images/Hulu/Todd Williamson

The hit Hulu soap opera "East Los High" depicts Hispanic teens in a fictional Los Angeles high school. Creator Katie Elmore Mota said the show's 60 percent non-Latino audience proves that TV characters don't have to all be "rich, white teenagers." Above, the cast gathers to celebrate the Season 4 premiere on July 6, 2016.

Beasts of No Nation, was not a box-office hit it scored more than 3 million views via online streaming in the months after its initial release.

The internet movie trend creates "opportunities for movies to get made that audiences are going to love but are increasingly difficult to get made," said Netflix Chief Content Officer Ted Sarandos. These are "films of a certain budget, of a certain nature and certain topics."[50]

Amazon Studios' acquisition methods underscore how the internet gives underrepresented groups a chance, insiders say. While few Hollywood talent agents and producers accept unsolicited screenplays, perpetuating the insider nature of the business, Amazon Studios invites writers to submit scripts online and bases its final choices on customer feedback.[51]

Nevertheless, internet shows can be susceptible to the same tropes and criticism as traditional productions. The Netflix comedy "Unbreakable Kimmy Schmidt" has been both praised and criticized for a subplot revolving around a Lakota Indian woman disguising her heritage and then rediscovering it. Some have taken issue with a blond, white actress (Jane Krakowski) playing the role but have noted that Native Americans have been cast as her parents. Likewise, some Indians say a few of the jokes have been cringe-worthy but also reflect the truth. Others are simply glad an internet TV show features Native Americans.[52]

"There were a few moments where I cringed because it seemed like we were supposed to laugh at Native American stereotypes, which really aren't that funny," said Cutcha Risling Baldy, assistant professor of American Indian studies at San Diego State University.[53] Executive producer Robert Carlock defended the plot, saying that because some of the show's writers have Native American heritage, "we felt like we had a little room . . . to go that direction."[54]

Still, the internet is welcome news to women and minorities locked out of the traditional Hollywood system, activists say. "We have no choice but to create our own destiny," says Nogales of the National Hispanic Media Coalition.

BACKGROUND

Stereotypes and Exclusion

D. W. Griffith's *The Birth of a Nation* (1915) is famed as the first feature-length motion picture. But its use of white actors in blackface and portrayals of heroic Ku Klux Klansmen and oversexed black slaves ushered in another trend, film scholars say: Hollywood's use of racial and ethnic stereotypes.

"More than any other film, *The Birth of a Nation* gave birth to the shocking and degrading stereotypes that were to plague African-American movie images throughout the twentieth century," wrote Donald Bogle, author of *Bright Boulevards, Bold Dreams: The Story of Black Hollywood.*[55]

From Hollywood's earliest years, racial and ethnic groups — who were also battling deeply entrenched racism in society — have protested their depiction on screen and exclusion from decision-making roles. Mexican-Americans were portrayed as villains in films such as *Tony the Greaser* (1911). By 1922 the Mexican government threatened to ban Hollywood movies in Mexico, leading Hollywood producers to agree not to present Mexicans in an objectionable manner, and after that light-skinned Hispanics were cast as "Latin lovers."[56] Asian-Americans were typically laundry workers or seductresses. Fed up with Hollywood's limited roles for Asians, Anna May Wong, the biggest Asian star of the period, moved to Europe for several years in 1928.[57]

But before the studio system became entrenched — with production companies holding actors, directors, writers and others under exclusive contract and enforcing rigorous rules — the industry's initial years were years of opportunity. Women, for instance, wrote, directed, produced and edited movies and founded their own studios. "Women had a major role in the early days of the American film industry because no rigid role distinctions had yet been set. . . . Whoever could achieve a desired effect or result, male or female, got the job."[58]

Japanese actor Sessue Hayakawa, a heartthrob of silent cinema, had his own production company in 1918, writing, directing, producing and acting in 23 films.[59] African-Americans formed companies to produce "race films," with "all colored casts" in roles such as bankers and businessmen, to be shown in segregated theaters.[60] More than 30 companies produced some 500 race films by the time the genre faded around 1940.[61]

The most successful African-Americans in that era were the child actors of *Our Gang* (1922-44), which featured white and black youngsters as equals — unusual for the period.[62]

Studio Era

As silent films gave way to talkies in the 1920s and movies' popularity and profitability increased, the studio system emerged, and over the next two decades, independent filmmakers were edged out and minorities relegated to sideline roles.

Women were pushed out of behind-the-scenes jobs except writing, but then that also dropped off. In 1928, women wrote 52 of 238 screenplays. By 1940, they penned just 64 of 608 scripts.[63] Instead, women were deemed to be more suited to on-screen roles. Actresses, who fell into two main camps — sex goddesses and career women — proved to be more popular than male stars.

"The film industry during the first part of the 20th century was responsible for reinforcing patriarchal norms; with men occupying most of the positions as directors and producers, female actresses were often cast in roles and publicized in ways that led them to become the objects of the male gaze," according to a history of women in film.[64]

Faced with a backlash against "loose morals" in movies, the studios in 1930 adopted the Motion Picture Production Code, a list of 36 prohibitions designed to hold producers to high moral standards.[65] The code,

Getty Images/John Kobal Foundation

In the early days of movies, white actors typically filled minority roles, including lead characters. In 1928, fed up with limited parts for Asians, Anna May Wong, perhaps the biggest Asian star of the period, moved to Europe for several years. She later was offered, and turned down in disgust, the role of a "dragon lady" in MGM's *The Good Earth*. The 1937 film notoriously cast Caucasian actors Paul Muni and Luise Rainer in "yellowface" makeup as the leads.

which banned such things as lustful kissing, crime, nudity, suggestive dancing and interracial relationships, was voluntary and carried no penalties for violation. But theaters would not show films that did not adhere to it. The code would be abandoned in 1968 after becoming increasingly obsolete.[66]

Even when the code wasn't an issue, white actors filled minority roles, including lead characters. One of the most notorious instances was MGM's *The Good Earth* (1937). Caucasian actors Paul Muni and Luise Rainer played the married sympathetic Chinese male and female leads, in "yellowface" makeup, while Anna May Wong was offered the role as a "dragon lady," which she refused in disgust.[67]

In addition, most heroic roles went to whites, even when the heroes were minorities. Douglas Fairbanks and Tyrone Power at different times played Zorro, the Mexican masked avenger of Spanish colonial injustice.[68] Likewise, the popular Chinese-American detective Charlie Chan was played by white actors in more than 40 movies in 1930s and '40s.[69] African-Americans were cast mostly as servants, but they won some recognition. Hattie McDaniel became the first African-American to win an Oscar, albeit for her stereotyped role as Mammy in the 1939 classic *Gone with the Wind*.

CHRONOLOGY

1910s-1930s *Stereotyped characters and "blackface" are common in films.*

1915 D. W. Griffith's *Birth of a Nation,* the first feature-length film, sparks protests over its use of white actors in blackface.

1927 The first sound film, *The Jazz Singer,* stars Al Jolson in blackface.

1939 *Gone With the Wind* actress Hattie McDaniel becomes the first African-American to win an Oscar.

1950s *Racially tinged political movies stir controversy.*

1951 Situation comedy "I Love Lucy," featuring an Anglo woman (Lucille Ball) married to a Cuban bandleader (Desi Arnaz), becomes television's most-watched show.

1952 Boxing drama *The Ring* depicts discrimination against Mexican-Americans with Latino actors in lead roles.

1954 Congress denounces *Salt of the Earth,* a film depicting striking Mexican-American mine workers, as subversive because of its creators' alleged involvement in communist politics.

1960s-1970s *Minorities and women make strides in film and TV roles.*

1961 In a widely criticized example of "yellowface," Mickey Rooney plays a stereotyped Japanese character in *Breakfast at Tiffany's.*

1962 African-Americans picket the Oscars to protest discrimination. . . . Congressional hearings are held on Hollywood bias against blacks.

1967 Sidney Poitier becomes the first black movie star with *In the Heat of the Night.*

1968 NBC's "Julia" stars Diahann Carroll, an African-American, in a non-stereotypical TV role (nurse).

1975 ABC debuts "Hot L Baltimore," featuring TV's first gay couple.

1979 Female members of the Directors Guild of America criticize the lack of opportunities for women.

1980s-1990s *Minority groups gain mainstream audiences; women enter studio executive ranks.*

1983 Directors Guild sues Warner Bros. and Columbia Pictures, alleging hiring discrimination against women and minorities.

1985 Directors Guild lawsuit is dismissed after a judge says it does not meet requirements for class-action lawsuits.

1990 Native Americans praise *Dances with Wolves* for what they call its fair depiction of tribes.

1991 Network TV's first kiss by a gay couple airs on "L.A. Law."

1994 ABC's "All-American Girl" is the first situation comedy featuring an Asian-American family.

2000-Present *Complaints rise over diversity, ageism, gender pay inequities and sexualization of women.*

2000 A group of 165 film and TV writers sue 51 studios, TV networks and talent agencies for age discrimination.

2001 Disney/ABC launches program aimed at fostering minority and female directors.

2005 *Brokeback Mountain,* one of the first movies featuring a gay love story aimed at a mainstream audience, is a critical and box office hit.

2010 Writers' age discrimination lawsuit is settled for $70 million.

2014 Networks and studios launch programs to foster careers of underrepresented directors and writers. . . . Hacked Sony Pictures emails fuel outrage over gender pay gap.

2016 Oscar nominations excluding nonwhite actors spur Academy of Motion Picture Arts and Sciences to overhaul voting rules (January) and diversify its membership (June).

Roles for African-Americans changed after 1942, when the NAACP, a civil rights organization, won pledges from studios to end stereotyped casting and hire more blacks for production jobs. The result was a raft of films featuring popular black entertainers, such as Louis Armstrong, Duke Ellington and Lena Horne, and other African-Americans who were hired as musicians and dancers.

Latin culture also boomed during this period, and depictions of Latinos changed considerably, with actors such as Cesar Romero and Ricardo Montalban portraying upper-class, educated characters in a variety of roles.

From 1947 through the 1950s, the House Un-American Activities Committee targeted political diversity in Hollywood, holding high-profile hearings aimed at rooting out communism in popular culture. Ten people, mostly writers, eventually went to prison for contempt of Congress for refusing to answer questions at the hearings, while dozens of others saw their careers ruined after being "blacklisted," or blocked from working in Hollywood.[70]

In the 1950s white filmmakers began making minority-sensitive movies. *Salt of the Earth* (1954) and *Giant* (1956) broke new ground by addressing discrimination against Hispanics, while *Viva Zapata!* (1952) depicted the life of Emiliano Zapata, with Marlon Brando playing the Mexican revolutionary. Dorothy Dandridge became the first black pinup star after her Oscar nomination for best actress for *Carmen Jones* (1954), which featured an all-black cast.[71]

By the late 1950s, the studio system had collapsed, in part due to a 1948 Supreme Court ruling in an antitrust case that forced the five major studios to sell their theater chains. The ruling allowed room for independent filmmakers and smaller studios to distribute their movies. Stars became more savvy about contracts and increasingly opted to work as free agents.

The industry also began to face significant competition from television and foreign films.

Television's Advent

Women and minorities did not fare well in early-1950s television. Women filled traditional housewife roles in shows such as "The Donna Reed Show" (1958-66), and females working off-camera were rare. Caricature-style stereotypes of blacks returned with two short-lived shows,

"The Beulah Show" (1950-53) and "The Amos 'n' Andy Show" (1951-53), which spurred NAACP protests.[72]

There were exceptions. One of the decade's biggest hits, "I Love Lucy" (1951-57) featured an ethnically mixed couple: Cuban Desi Arnaz and his zany white wife, Lucille Ball. CBS executives were initially skeptical that the mixed couple would be well received, but the show became one of television's most enduring.

"The Lone Ranger" (1949-57) TV series represented a breakthrough for Native Americans, who had largely lost major roles to white actors and had been stereotyped as whooping savages since cinema's early days. Tonto was played by Jay Silverheels, making him the first Native American star.[73]

With the civil rights movement growing powerful in the next decade, Hollywood developed more complex roles for minorities. In 1965, NBC cast Bill Cosby as a secret agent in "I Spy" (1965-68) in one of the first lead roles for an African-American. By the decade's end more than two dozen TV shows featured black actors in lead or prominent supporting roles.[74] One was "Star Trek" (1966-69), which featured a black woman (Nichelle Nichols) and an Asian man (George Takei) in what was considered revolutionary casting at the time.

Women began making inroads in other aspects of the industry, such as comedy and variety shows. After being told that women writers were not wanted on "The Smothers Brothers" comedy show (1967-70), Gail Parent was hired by another comedy program, "The Carol Burnett Show" (1967-78), the only female on CBS' staff of 100 variety show writers.[75]

The era's social tumult over civil rights and women's rights inspired moviemakers to tackle controversial themes, leading to more story lines involving minorities and women in major roles. Sidney Poitier, the first black actor to gain star status, starred in the groundbreaking 1967 interracial-relationship story *Guess Who's Coming to Dinner?* The first feature film written and directed by an African-American (Gordon Parks) was released by a major studio: *The Learning Tree* (1969).

Homosexuality, which had been featured in few films due to bans by the Motion Picture Production Code, emerged in *Inside Daisy Clover* (1965), an early-mainstream movie with a gay character who is not killed or does not commit suicide, although his sexuality is not overtly displayed.[76]

Muslims Struggle to Counter Terrorist Stereotypes

"They've been the most vilified group in the history of Hollywood."

President Obama has a message for the television and movie industry: Write more scripts depicting Muslims as regular people, not as terrorists and fanatics.

"Most Americans don't necessarily know — or at least don't know that they know — a Muslim personally," he told the Islamic Society of Baltimore in February in a speech aimed at countering negative stereotypes of Muslims and assuring them that they "fit in here" in American society.

"Many only hear about Muslims and Islam from the news after an act of terrorism, or in distorted media portrayals in TV or film, all of which gives this hugely distorted impression," Obama said. "Our television shows should have some Muslim characters that are unrelated to national security. It's not that hard to do."[1]

Muslims and Arabs have been portrayed on screen as villains and evildoers for decades. In 1,200 depictions of Arabs and Muslims in Hollywood from the early 1900s to Sept. 11, 2001, 97 percent of the portrayals were negative, said Jack Shaheen, a visiting scholar of Near East studies at New York University who has been tracking the portrayals of Arabs in popular culture since the 1970s.[2] "They've been the most vilified group in the history of Hollywood," said Shaheen.[3]

Since the 2001 terrorist attacks in New York and Washington and subsequent U.S. involvement in wars in Iraq and Afghanistan, negative stereotypes have mushroomed, particularly on hit TV shows such as Showtime's "Homeland" and Fox's "24." Such dramas have depicted both Arabs and American Muslims as terrorists threatening U.S. security.

"Hollywood and television have created an even more dangerous precedent by vilifying American Arabs and American Muslims in particular," Shaheen said. "They've blended the old stereotypes from 'over there' with new stereotypes from 'over here.'"[4]

Some say shows and movies simply reflect the current global reality of Middle East unrest and extremist bombings. "Stereotyping is common in Hollywood but tends to be factually based," wrote Melbourne University history fellow Daniel Mandel in *Middle East Quarterly.* "Because terrorism against Americans is carried out by Muslims and Arabs, there is a basic truth to the movies."[5] But others, including *Middle East Monitor* columnist Noura Mansour, say that reflection has devolved into a catch-all stereotype based on misperceptions, as well as ignorance about the Islamic religion and culture.[6] For instance, Hollywood often uses the words "Arab" and "Muslim" interchangeably, when in fact Muslims hail from 57 countries, only 22 of which are predominantly Arab.[7]

"There's a lot of misinformation about Islam and the Koran," says Suhad Obeidi, director of the Hollywood bureau of the Muslim Public Affairs Council in Los Angeles.

The Hollywood tropes help contribute to a negative view of Muslims, say Mansour, Obeidi and others. In a 2014 study by the Pew Center, Americans ranked Islam as the least favorable religion, while 58 percent associated Muslims with fanaticism and just 22 percent said they were respectful of women.[8]

The stereotypes also play into anti-Muslim sentiments expressed by some politicians, including Republican

The Hollywood Production Code, weakened by a 1952 Supreme Court ruling that movies were protected under the First Amendment right to free speech, became obsolete as societal attitudes liberalized and studios became reluctant to clamp down on filmmakers. When the code was officially abandoned in 1968, the Motion Picture Association of America replaced it with a ratings system that determines the age-appropriateness of movies based on the amount of sex, adult language or violence.[77]

As social attitudes became increasingly liberal in the 1970s, more opportunities opened for underrepresented groups — in both film and television.

presidential candidate Donald Trump, who has proposed registering Muslim Americans and banning foreign Muslims from entering the country.[9] Hollywood "has been presenting and reinforcing stereotypical images, which line up with belligerent and orientalist American policies towards Arabs and Muslims," wrote Mansour in the *Middle East Monitor.*[10]

Some progress has occurred, however. In ABC's "Quantico," Lebanese actress Yasmine Al Massri, who plays an FBI trainee who wears a hijab, said she took the role partly to dispel the image of a repressed, submissive Muslim woman.[11] Other shows, including Fox's "Bones," ABC's "Lost" and NBC's "Community," have featured positive Arab-American characters. And while progress in recent films has been scant, the 2009 film *Star Trek* featured a Pakistani character played by Pakistani-American Faran Tahir.[12]

Activists are working to improve Hollywood portrayals. The Muslim Public Affairs Council has been working with producers of Fox's "Tyrant," which was widely criticized for negatively stereotyped characters, to improve how it depicts Arabs. The council also has established programs to get more Muslims into the entertainment industry, which Obeidi says is the key to solving the problem.

"We want to shift it from other people telling stories about us to us telling our own stories," she says. "It's vital for us to be in the industry. TV and movies change hearts and minds."

— Christina Hoag

Getty Images/ABC/Johnathan Wenk

Lebanese actress Yasmine Al Massri, who plays a hijab-wearing FBI trainee in ABC's "Quantico," said she took the role partly to dispel the image of repressed, submissive Muslim women.

[1] Barack Obama, "Remarks by the President at Islamic Society of Baltimore," Office of the Press Secretary, White House, Feb. 3, 2016, http://tinyurl.com/jfocpth.

[2] Steve Rose, "Death to the Infidels! Why It's Time to Fix Hollywood's Problem with Muslims," *The Guardian,* March 8, 2016, http://tinyurl .com/j2sw86k.

[3] *Ibid.*

[4] *Ibid.*

[5] Daniel Mandel, "Muslims on the Silver Screen," *Middle East Quarterly,* Spring 2001, www.meforum.org/26/muslims-on-the-silver-screen.

[6] Noura Mansour, "Hollywood's Anti-Arab and Anti-Muslim Propaganda," *Middle East Monitor,* Jan. 29, 2015, http://tinyurl.com/ zl28xek.

[7] Helena Vanhala, *The Depiction of Arabs in Hollywood Blockbuster Films: 1980-2001* (2011), p. 119, http://tinyurl.com/zpm3cy2.

[8] Michael Lipka, "Muslims and Islam: Key findings in the U.S. and around the world," Pew Research Center, Dec. 7, 2015, http://tinyurl .com/gsmjpzj.

[9] Trip Gabriel, "Donald Trump says He'd 'Absolutely' Require Muslims to Register," *The New York Times,* Nov. 20, 2015, http://tinyurl.com/ jglm42v.

[10] Mansour, *op. cit.*

[11] Mohamed Hassan, "Yasmine Al Massri on Fighting Arab-American Stereotypes as Twins on 'Quantico,' " NBC News, March 4, 2016, http://tinyurl.com/zrm2pun.

[12] Josie Huang, " 'Tyrant': Are there any positive portrayals of Arab-Americans?" KPCC-FM, June 25, 2014, http://tinyurl.com/jha7b9a.

Chief Dan George became the first Native American to be nominated for an Oscar for his supporting role in the 1970 film *Little Big Man,* which won praise for its sensitive portrayal of American Indians.

The feminist movement also resulted in breakthrough feminist films such as *An Unmarried Woman* (1978) and *The Stepford Wives* (1975). Meanwhile, a cadre of women emerged as set and costume designers and editors, and a few as directors. Actresses such as Jane Fonda and Anne Bancroft formed their own production companies, and women attained ranking studio positions.[78] In 1976, Lina Wertmuller became the

Activists' Plea: Stop Killing Off Minorities

"Minority characters are expendable because they're not main characters."

When Lexa, a lesbian character, was killed off during a March episode of CW's hit post-apocalyptic drama "The 100," thousands of fans took to social media to protest her demise.

Tweets under the hashtags #LGBTFansDeserveBetter and #BuryTropesNotUs became trending topics nationally, with some fans writing on Twitter and Tumblr that they couldn't sleep and threatened self-harm over the loss of Lexa.[1]

A similar social media backlash occurred when Abbie Mills, an African-American female character, met an untimely death in Fox's supernatural drama "Sleepy Hollow" in April.[2] AMC's hit zombie drama "The Walking Dead" also faced criticism when three main black characters were killed in its fifth season in 2015.[3]

Along with underrepresentation of minorities on screen and a gender pay gap, treatment of minority characters is another facet of Hollywood's diversity problem, activists say. "Minority characters are expendable because they're not main characters," says Chandler Meyer, spokesperson for LGBT Fans Deserve Better, a group advocating for more protagonists from underrepresented groups. "It's part of the diversity problem behind the scenes. Most writers are straight white males."

Activists say while writers are incorporating more minority characters into story lines in an effort to be diverse, they are resorting to tropes and stereotypes when inventing plot lines for those characters, creating a more subtle pattern of discrimination.

"It's a way of being progressive without being too out there," Meyer says. "For example, bisexual women always end up with the man. Heroes are always straight and white" on television. According to LGBT group Autostraddle, 10 lesbian or bisexual characters were killed off in March alone, in shows including CW's "Jane the Virgin," AMC's "The Walking Dead" and Syfy's "The Magicians," with 20 in the first three months of 2016.[4] For LGBT people, the untimely demises hit a raw nerve, because for decades gay people have been portrayed as conflicted and rarely as happy, productive or heroic, activists say.

"When you have so few LGBT characters on TV, you're sending a message to people who identify with them that they never get a happy ending," say Megan Townsend, entertainment media strategist for GLAAD, an advocacy group that monitors how LBGT people are represented in the media.

Producers respond that plots can be a difficult balance between fans' wishes and the dramatic aims of the show.

In "The Walking Dead," two of the three black male characters who were killed — Tyreese, Bob and Noah — were white in the graphic novels on which the show is based, said producer Scott Gimple. "It's tough because I also want to be sensitive to how people feel. Two of those

first woman to be nominated for a Best Director Oscar for *Seven Beauties*.[79]

Influenced by the black power movement, African-American filmmakers, who had had little access behind the camera since the race films of the 1920s, started a genre of "blaxploitation" movies, which portrayed African-Americans as violent avengers of white injustice in movies such as *Shaft* (1971), *Super Fly* (1972) and *Foxy Brown* (1974).

In 1973, CBS appointed television's first woman executive, vice president Ethel Winant.[80] More female-centric programming came into vogue, such as the wildly popular "The Mary Tyler Moore Show" (1970-77) — the first show featuring a single career woman — and "Mary Hartman, Mary Hartman" (1976-77).

Minorities and social issues became more visible, particularly in comedies. Sitcoms depicting African-American life became a hallmark of the era, such as "The Jeffersons" (1975-85), featuring a middle-class black family, and "What's Happening!!" (1976-79), portraying life in Los Angeles housing projects. "Chico and the Man" (1974-78), with Hispanic actor Freddie Prinze in the lead role, was a Latino sitcom in a similar style and was the first show set in a Mexican-American neighborhood, East Los Angeles.

characters were destined to die, and they could've been cast in any direction, and I just cast the best people — or at least the people I just felt were best and I loved what they did with the role. It's weird to imagine not using them. But I did know those characters were dying, and I did cast those people," he said.[5]

The furor over Lexa's death has made "The 100" producers more sensitive to how characters are written, said Executive Producer Jason Rothenberg, noting that Lexa was killed off after she consummated her relationship with a female lover to heighten the sense of tragedy. The death was prompted because the actress who played Lexa, Alycia Debnam-Carey, was leaving the show for a role in AMC's "Fear the Walking Dead."[6]

"The end result became something else entirely — the perpetuation of the disturbing 'bury your gays' trope," Rothenberg wrote in an apology to fans. "Our aggressive promotion of the episode, and of this relationship, only fueled a feeling of betrayal. . . . I am very sorry for not recognizing this as fully as I should have. Knowing everything I know now, Lexa's death would have played out differently."[7]

While activists say they recognize that characters will die, especially in shows that pivot on violence, they hope producers can be more sensitive to the reasons for writing in deaths while also hiring more writers from underrepresented groups who can bring greater nuance to plot lines. "We're asking producers to consider the plot reasons for killing off characters, but it's also part of the larger problem of diversity," Townsend says.

— *Christina Hoag*

The TV death of Lexa, a lesbian character played by Alycia Debnam-Carey on CW's post-apocalyptic hit drama "The 100," sparked an outcry by thousands of fans.

[1] Bethonie Butler, "TV keeps killing off lesbian characters. The fans of one show have revolted," *The Washington Post*, April 4, 2016, http://tinyurl.com/jhq8oj2.

[2] Bethonie Butler, "After a shocking death on 'Sleepy Hollow,' fans are questioning how the show treats characters of color," *The Washington Post*, April 12, 2016, http://tinyurl.com/z3vn9s3.

[3] Dalton Ross, "Walking Dead showrunner on the prominence of black character deaths last season," *Entertainment Weekly*, Sept. 22, 2015, http://tinyurl.com/h4e9wta.

[4] Butler, "TV keeps killing off lesbian characters," *op. cit.*

[5] Ross, *op. cit.*

[6] Maureen Ryan, " 'The 100' Showrunner Apologizes for Controversial Character Death," *Variety*, March 24, 2016, http://tinyurl.com/zgapxrj.

[7] *Ibid.*

Groundbreaking television producer Norman Lear tackled tough social issues, such as bigotry and feminism, in his hit sitcoms, "All in the Family" (1971-79) and "Maude"(1972-78).

Minority Filmmakers

In 1980, Sherry Lansing became president of 20th Century Fox, the first female to lead a major studio.[81] Her appointment heralded an age when women and minorities asserted themselves as executives, producers, directors and writers and created public awareness of hiring disparities.

Still, women were rarely found behind the camera. When Parent landed a job writing for "The Golden Girls" (1985-92), a series about a group of older women living in Miami, she was the only woman. "They allowed one of you, period," she said. "Even on shows about women."[82]

In 1983, the Directors Guild of America, the labor organization that represents film and TV directors, filed an anti-discrimination suit against Warner Bros. and Columbia Pictures on behalf of women and minority members. Although the suit was dismissed in 1985 on grounds that the guild had no a standing to sue, it drew

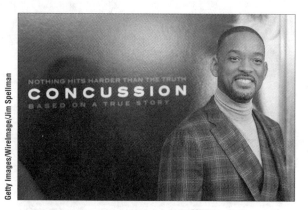

Actor Will Smith was among the Hollywood A-listers who boycotted the Academy Awards ceremony this year to protest entertainment industry diversity policies, including the nominations for best actor and actress that included no blacks for the second straight year. Smith's performance as a Nigerian doctor in *Concussion* had been widely considered Oscar-worthy.

attention to an uneven playing field and for a short time spurred the hiring of more female directors.[83]

By the late 1980s, a wave of independent black and Latino filmmakers, such as Spike Lee and Luis Valdez, emerged, winning acclaim with movies such as *She's Gotta Have It* (1986) and *La Bamba* (1987), which reflected their communities' experience but had crossover audience appeal. That coincided with a growing A-list of black actors, such as Denzel Washington and Eddie Murphy. In 1990, *Dances with Wolves* turned the tables on Native American stereotypes, depicting whites as the villains and the Lakota Indians as a benevolent people.

The television landscape changed dramatically in the 1990s, with the steady expansion of cable and satellite channels and new broadcast networks emerging. This created more programs that catered to smaller audiences.

In movies, independent filmmakers such as Quentin Tarantino became an increasingly key part of the industry.

Still, women and minorities saw only incremental progress. In 1999, the National Council of La Raza called on Hispanics to boycott TV to pressure the networks to hire more Latinos.[84] The Hispanic advocacy organization said that in two decades the percentage of Latinos playing primetime TV characters had risen only marginally — from 1 percent to 1.6 percent.[85]

In the 21st century, several barriers have been broken, but progress remains stalled, and new bias allegations

have emerged. In 2002, older writers filed a class-action suit alleging age discrimination against 51 major TV networks, studios and talent agencies. It was settled in 2010 for $70 million.[86]

Movies with gay themes received a huge boost in 2005 when *Brokeback Mountain's* male cowboy love story scored a box-office hit and three Oscars. In 2010, Kathryn Bigelow became the first woman to win a Best Director Oscar for *The Hurt Locker.*

In recent years, Mexican directors Guillermo del Toro, Alfonso Cuarón and Alejandro González Iñárritu have earned Oscar nomination and awards for mainstream movies.[87] And independently-financed African-American-themed films, including *12 Years a Slave* (2013), have been box-office hits.

In 2015, an all-white slate of acting nominees for the Academy Awards sparked a huge public outcry, and the hashtag #OscarsSoWhite lit up social media, focusing attention on Hollywood's lack of diversity. A year later, the hashtag was revived amid another wave of outrage when the nominee slate again consisted of all white actors.

CURRENT SITUATION
Gathering Momentum

Officials from the U.S. Equal Employment Opportunity Commission (EEOC) are questioning an expanded list of people in the gender discrimination investigation. The list now includes studio executives, agents, producers, actors and male directors.[88] The investigation began in 2015 after the ACLU of Southern California filed a complaint alleging that the Hollywood entertainment industry is biased against female directors.

Women accounted for 6.4 percent of motion picture directing in 2013-14, and they tend to direct less lucrative films, according to the Directors Guild of America, the industry group representing film and TV directors.[89] In television, women directed 16 percent of episodes in 2014-15, the guild said.[90] The EEOC investigation could spur a lawsuit against employers, mediation to increase the ranks of female directors or result in no action at all.

The inquiry is a sign that the push for more diversity in Hollywood is gathering momentum. The Academy of Motion Picture Arts and Sciences' new voting eligibility rules for Oscar nominations, announced after the

Is Hollywood taking steps to become more diverse?

YES Rashad Robinson
Executive Director, Color of Change

NO John W. Cones
Author, Hollywood Wars:
How Insiders Gained and Maintain Illegitimate
Control Over the Film Industry

Written for *CQ Researcher*, August 2016

Written for *CQ Researcher*, August 2016

Last year more than 51,000 Color Of Change members called for an overhaul of the Academy of Motion Picture Arts and Sciences membership process and the release of accurate diversity numbers. Since then, we have continued to work with artists and the industry to ensure that we can move toward a collective vision that promotes a standard for Hollywood that is truly representative of the diversity and intricacies of moviegoers.

We applaud the academy board for acting expediently to fix a problem that was 100-plus years in the making. But this important step cannot be the end. This isn't about "seeking validation" but about rejecting a discriminatory system that sends a message to far too many that they are unwelcome. At a time when our news media continue to make clear how little the lives of black Americans matter, and our rights continue to be rolled back on several fronts, it is especially important that we are at the center of our own narratives and that our stories receive the wide release and support they deserve.

Award recognition matters. With it comes increased financial and creative opportunities for artists and those they employ. It also provides power to confront negative depictions of our communities that shape how we're perceived.

Research continues to show that negative perceptions of black and brown men and women or the erasure of people of color from movies and television programs translate into greater chances of us being shot by the police and receiving diminished attention from doctors and less consideration when applying for jobs, loans and educational opportunities.

Let's not forget that this is about a completely flawed system — from the lack of diversity among critics who determine which movies get Oscar buzz to discrimination in casting and white-washing of historical figures to underfunding of projects helmed by people of color. Studios, guilds and agencies have a lot of work to do. The onus can't strictly be on Academy president Cheryl Boone Isaacs to create change.

Hollywood is a reflection of power structures in our country. We must take more steps to ensure real change that creates a better reality for our people both in and out of the industry.

We want actions that provide a consistent pipeline of people of color in internships, middle management and at the executive level across the industry.

Some say Hollywood is changing, but I submit the words of anthropologist Hortense Powdermaker, in her groundbreaking 1950 book, *Hollywood, the Dream Factory*: "Rarely in the history of mankind has any group with power given it up voluntarily."

Hollywood's lack-of-diversity problem finally became obvious at the two most recent Academy Awards presentations, when no African-American was nominated for an acting award. Besides some rather shallow nods toward reform, Hollywood pretty much continues to ignore the issue.

Even worse, the discrimination at the academy is just the tip of the iceberg. Hollywood's lack of diversity includes women, Latinos, Asian-Americans, Native Americans, Irish-Americans, Italian-Americans, Christians, Muslims, Mormons and many other "Hollywood outsiders." Furthermore, this massive discrimination occurs not only in the acting arena but in all professions involved in developing, producing and distributing movies.

For more than 100 years, millions of hard-working and talented people who sought employment opportunities in the film industry have been arbitrarily denied those opportunities in favor of someone else who was better connected to a narrowly defined Hollywood insider group.

And that's not all. The U.S. Supreme Court found in the 1952 *Burstyn v. Wilson* case that the motion picture is a "significant medium for the communication of ideas." That's important to a democracy that supposedly values the free marketplace of ideas. As my studies show, Hollywood movies contain patterns of bias with regard to which ideas are portrayed positively or negatively. That's because movies tend to mirror the values, interests, cultural perspectives and prejudices of their makers.

Thus, when the Supreme Court held in *Burstyn v. Wilson* that movies are protected by the First Amendment right of free speech and eliminated government censorship of movies, official censorship was simply replaced by private censorship, applied by a small group of Hollywood insiders who have used this powerful communications medium to promote their own private propaganda interests.

Many have been outraged recently by the revelation that a U.S. presidential candidate may be a racist. But it is just as outrageous for the entire government and our nation to continue to accept the massive and ongoing discrimination perpetrated by Hollywood insiders through nearly five generations.

Oscars-so-white controversy erupted in January, are aimed at enabling younger, more diverse active members to cast votes, decreasing the dominance of older, retired members who skew white.

In June, the academy unveiled a record 683 new members — 46 percent of them female and 41 percent people of color. With the new members, women now make up 27 percent of the academy's members, and people of color, 11 percent.[91]

Some said the changes were symbolic and doubted they will change nominations or hiring practices overall. "You can keep adding members — pack it like the Supreme Court — but I don't think that answers the question" of how to increase diversity, said Mike Medavoy, a producer whose movies include *The 33* (2015) and *Shutter Island* (2010).[92]

But others saw the academy's moves as important. "One good step in a long, complicated journey for people of color + women artists," tweeted Ava DuVernay, whose lack of a directing nomination for the civil rights drama *Selma* (2014) sparked an outcry in 2015. "Shame is a helluva motivator."[93]

The 2016 Oscars controversy also sparked greater awareness of Hollywood's gender and racial imbalance and spurred efforts to combat it. In February, Murphy, the producer of TV shows such as "Glee" and "American Horror Story," announced that he would fill half the directing slots on his shows with women, people of color and LGBT people, and would start a mentorship program for students. "I personally can do better," he said.[94]

Abrams, producer of the Star Wars and Star Trek movies and TV series, said his company has asked agents to include women and minorities among their candidates for acting and writing jobs. "The Oscars controversy was a wake-up call," Abrams said.[95]

The Writers Guild's Lopez said the organization has been receiving more calls from agents, managers and executives seeking minority talent. "They're asking, 'Do you have an Asian comedy writer' or 'a Latino drama writer?'" she says. "They're seeing that now is the time to really make this change and stray out of their comfort zones and open up."

But others doubt the momentum will be sustained, noting that previous efforts have resulted in little more than tokenism and an eventual return to business as usual.

"The fact that the many industry programs to encourage a more diverse workforce have not achieved their desired goals speaks volumes about how deeply entrenched gender and racial bias are across an industry driven by fragmented, relationship-driven and word-of-mouth hiring practices," the directors' guild said on its website. "We continue to approach this matter from a number of angles to convince employers to take ownership of the issue. Until that happens, there may never be substantive change."[96]

Resistance to change exists. The academy's new voting rules sparked a firestorm of criticism, largely from older members. "Obviously, it's a thinly veiled ploy to kick out older, white contributors — the backbone of the industry — to make way for younger, 'politically correct' voters," said actor Tab Hunter, 84. "The academy should not cave in to media hype and change the rules without talking to or getting votes from all members first."[97]

Some members of the public also have objected to Hollywood's attempts at diversity. A 2016 remake of the 1984 hit *Ghostbusters,* with an all-female lead cast, netted a wave of criticism from fans who claimed the women would ruin the movie.

African-American actress Leslie Jones, who plays one of the ghostbusters, quit Twitter in July after being subjected to hundreds of racist and sexist tweets, saying she did not believe Twitter should be used to abusively target someone. Twitter responded by barring Milo Yiannopoulos, a prime mover of the campaign against Jones and an editor with the conservative news website Breitbart.com.[98]

Role of Government

Activists say governments can do more to encourage diversity. For instance, Illinois is the only state to give a tax credit (30 percent) to production companies that hire local minorities and women.[99] But critics say the program has a loophole that allows producers to merely show they made "a good-faith effort" to obtain a diversified workforce.

"People think you have to hire people of color. You do not. You can interview 50 minorities and you don't have to hire any of them," said Michele McGhee, a tax credit specialist with the Illinois Department of Commerce and Economic Opportunity, which runs the Illinois Film Office.[100]

Other states are considering similar programs. A pending New York bill would allot $5 million of the

$420 million Empire State Film Production Tax Credit as incentives to TV producers who hire women or minority writers or directors who are New York taxpayers, with a maximum credit of $50,000 per hire. The bill was introduced in 2013 but stalled in a Republican-controlled Senate after passing the Assembly. Backers now hope that with a Republican sponsor and the recent Oscars controversy, the measure has a better chance of passage.[101]

Robinson of ColorOfChange.org says such incentive programs would help boost minority hiring but that guilds representing Hollywood professions also must be pushed to do more. The Screen Actors Guild-American Federation of Television and Radio Artists (SAG-AFTRA), which represents the bulk of the industry's experienced actors, includes anti-discrimination provisions in the contracts producers must sign to use guild-member employees, he notes.

SAG-AFTRA also provides financial incentives for movies with budgets of up to $3.75 million that meet diversity standards. If half of the speaking roles go to actors of color, women, actors with disabilities or those who are over age 60, the union will allow concessions on how much all actors must be paid. That can include reduced overtime rates, no premiums for six-day work weeks and fewer background actors who must be paid union scale.[102] Some form of the SAG-AFTRA program and contracts could be replicated with other guilds, Robinson says.

The Motion Picture Association of America, which represents major studios, should also be pushed to take a stand, says Lauzen of San Diego State. The association could create an independent organization that aims to increase diversity on studio films, particularly in key hiring positions because they can then hire more diverse staffs, she says.

But some experts say that since the industry has not improved diversity despite years of public outcry, more forceful measures may be needed, such as lawsuits, contract provisions and more robust financial incentives.

"Because those in the industry have demonstrated little will to change, it seems likely that pressure from some external source, such as the EEOC, will be necessary to achieve significant and sustained change," says Lauzen.

OUTLOOK
Turning Point

Experts generally agree that Hollywood, particularly the movie industry, will be forced to include more women and minorities in the coming years, but they differ on what will decisively push the industry to move from tokenism to meaningful change.

If movie-going is to remain a relevant mass entertainment option, the film industry will have to echo the general trend of diversification in the U.S. population, some experts predict, especially as competition from online-viewing grows. "Diversity is a smart business decision," says Suhad Obeidi, director of the Hollywood bureau of the Muslim Public Affairs Council. "People want to see people who look like them."

The 2016 #OscarsSoWhite backlash was a watershed moment that is boosting the momentum for change, say some Hollywood observers. The Academy of Motion Picture Arts & Sciences' revised award voting rules and the admission of a new, more diversified class of members were important and symbolic first steps, they note.

"Call me a cautious optimist," says Hunt, of UCLA's Bunche Center for African American Studies. "But business as usual is really not sustainable. We've reached a turning point."

But others say it's going to take more than academy moves to prod studios out of deeply entrenched practices. Cones, the entertainment attorney, says executives are unlikely to change their business models unless compelled by government actions, such as legislation or an EEOC ruling. Over the years, he says, outcries over the lack of diversity have resulted in little progress once the initial media attention faded. "People with power do not give it up voluntarily," he says.

Jonathan Glickman, president of MGM's motion-picture group, said Hollywood is changing but slowly. "It takes time to turn the ship around to the right direction because of the amount of time it takes to produce and market a film," he said.[103]

As for television, observers are optimistic that it will continue to use more diverse characters and stories, but they say it still has a long way to go to move beyond cultural stereotypes and increase opportunities for underrepresented groups behind the camera. "We've got miles and miles to go on that frontier," Hunt says.

The push by leading producers to hire more women and minorities, plus the success of minority producers such as Rhimes, could spur other producers and networks to seek out more diverse crews, staffs and casts, experts say.

In the meantime, internet-based entertainment increasingly will become an outlet for women and minorities and make it easier for studios and networks to find diverse talent with demonstrated success. Independently produced TV shows and movies, including those made solely for online viewing, will help boost the number of diverse stories on screen, some industry observers predict, and provide needed competition for the traditional industry.

"They'll realize they're leaving a lot of money on the table," says Nogales of the Hispanic Media Coalition. "It doesn't stand to reason to not bring us in."

The programming success on newer viewing channels eventually will force the industry to open up to diverse points of view from plots to producers, says Lopez of the Writers Guild. "It'll transfer into [the mainstream business] little by little," he says. Ultimately, consumers, who can vote with their wallets and remote controls, can force progress in both the film and television industries, some experts say.

But, says actress Ta'le, "if audiences remain complicit and watch what they're given, then there's no reason to change."

NOTES

1. Michael Schulman, "Chris Rock's Oscars," *The New Yorker,* Feb. 29, 2016, http://tinyurl.com/zhruuru.

2. Brandon Griggs, "Jada Pinkett Smith, Spike Lee to boycott Oscars ceremony," CNN.com, Jan. 19, 2016, http://tinyurl.com/h6c65hk.

3. Cynthia Littleton, "Will Smith Won't Attend Oscars," *Variety,* Jan. 21, 2016, http://tinyurl.com/hjy64u6.

4. "Al Sharpton Leads Oscars Protest Rally in Hollywood," The Associated Press, Feb. 28, 2016, http://tinyurl.com/hg4mttu.

5. Michael Pearson, "Obama: Oscars diversity call part of broader issue," CNN.com, Jan. 28, 2016, http://tinyurl.com/jd3hk74.

6. "Creating Jobs," Motion Picture Association of America, undated, http://tinyurl.com/heyox9z.

7. Noor Wazwaz, "It's Official: The US Is Becoming a Minority-Majority Nation," *U.S. News & World Report,* July 6, 2015, http://tinyurl.com/p4hhart.

8. Darnell Hunt, Ana-Christina Ramon and Michael Tran, "2016 Hollywood Diversity Report: Busine$$ as Usual," University of California Los Angeles, February 2016, http://tinyurl.com/hhrdltn, p. 10.

9. *Ibid.,* p. 21.

10. Martha M. Lauzen, "The Celluloid Ceiling: Behind-the-Scenes Employment of Women on the Top 100, 250, and 500 Films of 2015," Center for the Study of Women in Television and Film, San Diego State University, 2016, http://tinyurl.com/h5gmn7p.

11. *Ibid.,* p. 40.

12. Stacy L. Smith, Marc Choueiti, Katherine Piper, "Inclusion or Invisibility: Comprehensive Annenberg Report on Diversity in Entertainment," University of Southern California, http://tinyurl.com/jxjyj2p, p. 16.

13. Justin Morrow, "6 Hollywood Executives Discuss the State of the Film Industry," No Film School, Nov. 20, 2015, http://tinyurl.com/hd53hry.

14. Maria Puente and Andrea Mandell, "Hollywood Diversity Report Brings mostly Silence from Studios," *USA Today,* Feb. 23, 2016, http://tinyurl.com/jeweolp.

15. Lauzen, *op. cit.,* p. 5.

16. Smith *et al., op. cit.,* p. 3.

17. Inkoo Kang, "THR Roundtable Actresses on Ageism, the Pay Gap and Playing 'Strong Women' & Gender-Swapped Roles," *IndieWire,* Nov. 24, 2015, http://tinyurl.com/j9zcglk.

18. Martha M. Lauzen, "MPAA Must Lead — or Be Led — in Battle to Improve Diversity," *Variety,* March 17, 2016, http://tinyurl.com/hw37gpf.

19. *Ibid.*

20. Daniel Kreps, "Nina Simone's Daughter Defends Zoe Saldana, Slams Biopic," *Rolling Stone,* March 5, 2016, http://tinyurl.com/zg5zxpr.

21. Megan Gibson, "Ridley Scott Explains Why He Cast White Actors in Exodus: God and Kings," *Time.com,* Nov. 27, 2014, http://tinyurl.com/jf8577m.

22. Nigel M. Smith, "Emma Stone Says Aloha Casting taught her about whitewashing in hollywood," *The Guardian,* July 17, 2015, http://tinyurl.com/hrxzjnb.

23. Stereo Williams, "Joseph Fiennes as Michael Jackson: A Symptom of Hollywood's Deep-Seated Race Problem," *The Daily Beast,* Jan. 27, 2016, http://tinyurl.com/gqtk9qn.

24. Daniel Fienberg, "Why It Matters that FX's Tyrant Didn't Cast a Middle Eastern Actor in its Lead Role," *HitFix,* June 24, 2014, http://tinyurl.com/zmujruy.

25. Gibson, *op. cit.*

26. Hunt *et al., op. cit.* pp. 50-53.

27. Aziz Ansari, "Aziz Anzari on Acting, Race and Hollywood," *The New York Times,* Nov. 10, 2015, http://tinyurl.com/oc6nraj.

28. Ben Childs, "Dakota Johnson hits out at 'brutal' Hollywood over ageism," *The Guardian,* Jan. 5, 2016, http://tinyurl.com/j8pa6on.

29. Nigel Smith, *op. cit.*

30. Martha M. Lauzen, "It's a Man's (Celluloid) World: Portrayals of Female Characters in the Top 100 Films of 2015," 2016, http://tinyurl.com/zlxqvul.

31. Madeline Berg, "Everything You Need To Know About The Hollywood Pay Gap," *Forbes,* Nov. 12, 2015, http://tinyurl.com/j8r2zgp.

32. *Ibid.*

33. Peter Sciretta, "The Highest Paid Actresses and Actors Of 2015," *Slash Film,* Aug. 20, 2015, http://tinyurl.com/gsdbfyv.

34. Maggie McGrath, "World's Highest Paid TV Actresses 2015," *Forbes,* Sept. 8, 2015, http://tinyurl.com/hdn84tl.

35. Stacy L. Smith *et al., op. cit.,* p. 17.

36. Ryan Faughnder, "$40 billion in global box office? Thank China and 'Star Wars,' " *Los Angeles Times,* Dec. 30, 2015, http://tinyurl.com/zpk4p9e.

37. "Theatrical Market Statistics 2014," Motion Picture Association of America, undated, http://tinyurl.com/kr3vmlq, p.12.

38. Scott Roxborough, "America's TV Exports Too Diverse for Overseas?" *The Hollywood Reporter,* March 30, 2016, http://tinyurl.com/jz3yw7d.

39. Amol Sharma, "TV Studios Court Licensing Deals in Bustling Foreign Markets," *The Wall Street Journal,* Nov. 19, 2014, http://tinyurl.com/h3kbzmo.

40. Roxborough, *op. cit.*

41. Maureen Ryan, "Showrunners for New TV Season Remain Mostly White and Male," *Variety,* June 7, 2016, http://tinyurl.com/zmjm7ah.

42. Aisha Harris, "Same Old Script," *Slate.com,* Oct. 18, 2015, http://tinyurl.com/om2aslu.

43. *Ibid.*

44. Maanvi Singh, " 'East Los High' Isn't Just a Soapy Teen Drama — It's Also A Science Experiment," NPR, Jan. 11, 2016, http://tinyurl.com/z6kahak.

45. Jenny Wortham, "The Misadventures of Issa Rae," *The New York Times Magazine,* Aug. 4, 2015, http://tinyurl.com/p4eq4k4.

46. "Frequently Asked Questions," Amazon Studios, undated, http://tinyurl.com/glu8mqo.

47. Josef Adalian and Maria Elena Fernandez, "The Business of Too Much TV," *Vulture.com,* May 2016, http://tinyurl.com/h5supdd.

48. *Ibid.*

49. Matt Donnelly, "How Amazon Studios became the New Star of Cannes," *The Wrap,* May 10, 2016, http://tinyurl.com/zot5a5o.

50. Mike Fleming Jr., "Netflix's Ted Sarandos Says 'Beasts Of No Nation' Has Been Seen By Over 3 Million Viewers So Far: Q&A," *Deadline,* Oct. 26, 2015, http://tinyurl.com/p3jsd98.

51. "Submissions Guidelines," Amazon Studios, undated, http://tinyurl.com/j2tzho6.

52. Claire Fallon, "The Native Plot On 'Kimmy Schmidt' Makes Us Cringe, But Is It All Bad?" *The Huffington Post,* April 29, 2016, http://tinyurl.com/j86kqu6.

53. *Ibid.*

54. Alyssa Rosenberg, "Unbreakable Kimmy Schmidt's Lakota plot and the fight for diversity in TV," *The Washington Post,* March 12, 2015, http://tinyurl.com/gpqxuuk.

55. Donald Bogle, *Bright Boulevards, Bold Dreams: The Story of Black Hollywood* (2005), pp. 11-13.

56. Matthew Bernstein, *Controlling Hollywood: Censorship and Regulation in the Studio Era* (2000), p. 112, http://tinyurl.com/z9qkbn8.

57. Anne Helen Petersen, "The Forgotten Story of Classic Hollywood's First Asian American Star," *Buzzfeed,* Sept. 30, 2014, http://tinyurl.com/gm2jell.

58. Dawn B. Sova, *Women in Hollywood: From Vamp to Studio Head* (1998), p. 2.

59. "Sessue Hayakawa: The Legend," Gold Sea, undated, http://tinyurl.com/hnmvl7q.

60. Jennifer Thompson (curator), "From Blackface to Blaxploitation: Representations of African Americans in Film," Duke University Libraries, undated, http://tinyurl.com/jzszdjw.

61. Hansi Lo Wang, "Restored Race Films Find New Audiences," NPR, March 6, 2016, http://tinyurl.com/jkh749y.

62. Bogle, *op. cit.,* p. 41.

63. Sova, *op. cit.,* p. xii.

64. *Ibid.*

65. Bob Mondello, "Remembering Hollywood's Hays Code 40 Years On," NPR, Aug. 8, 2008, http://tinyurl.com/5rku7d.

66. *Ibid.*

67. Lucy Fischer and Marcia Landy, *Stars: The Film Reader* (2004), p. 189, http://tinyurl.com/ju9m9ag.

68. Markus Heide, "From Zorro to Jennifer Lopez: US-Latino History and Film for the EFL-Classroom," *American Studies Journal,* 2008, http://tinyurl.com/jpxucuv.

69. "Charlie Chan Biography," Internet Movie Database, undated, http://tinyurl.com/hjyz7ky.

70. Dan Georgakas, "The Hollywood Blacklist," *Encyclopedia of the American Left* (1992), http://tinyurl.com/pjvqara.

71. "Dorothy Dandridge," *Encyclopaedia Britannica,* undated, http://tinyurl.com/j264wwk.

72. J. Fred MacDonald, "Blacks and White TV: The Golden Age of Blacks in Television," undated, http://tinyurl.com/hsexjgl.

73. Jay Tavare, "Hollywood Indians," *The Huffington Post,* May 18, 2011, http://tinyurl.com/6y47gt7.

74. MacDonald, *op. cit.*

75. Jennifer Armstrong, "The Secret History of Women in Television," *Bust,* undated, http://tinyurl.com/zns4ksq.

76. Guy Walters, "Lesbian Gay Bisexual and Transgender Movies since 1894," *The Telegraph,* March 20, 2015, http://tinyurl.com/japw6cb.

77. Mondello, *op. cit.* For background on movie ratings system, see Brian Hansen, "Movie Ratings," *CQ Researcher,* March 28, 2003, pp. 273-296.

78. Sova, *op. cit.,* pp. 154-157.

79. "Lina Wertmüller Biography," Internet Movie Database, undated, http://tinyurl.com/zgxvjwv.

80. Pat Saperstein, "Ethel Winant," *Variety,* Dec. 3, 2003, http://tinyurl.com/zk3mkq6.

81. "Sherry Lansing Biography," Internet Movie Database, undated, http://tinyurl.com/zxnhkt8.

82. Armstrong, *op. cit.*

83. David Robb, "Feds Officially Probing Hollywood's Lack of Female Directors," *Deadline,* Oct. 6, 2015, http://tinyurl.com/j3jace6.

84. Michael A. Fletcher, "Latinos Plan Boycott of Network TV," *The Washington Post,* July 28, 1999, http://tinyurl.com/j85lm8x.

85. Dana E. Mastro and Elizabeth BehmMorawitz, "Latino Representation on Primetime Television," *Journalism and Mass Communication Quarterly,* Spring 2005, http://tinyurl.com/h9w4pfd.

86. Nikki Finke, "Huge $70M Settlement in TV Writers Age Discrimination Lawsuit," *Deadline,* Jan. 22, 2010, http://tinyurl.com/hw4c3wf.

87. Lorraine Ali, "Oscars 2015: Brutal honesty marks Inarritu's bond with Cuaron, del Toro," *Los Angeles Times,* Feb. 21, 2015, http://tinyurl.com/hrveaoo.

88. Rebecca Keegan, "Gender Bias in Hollywood? U.S. Digs Deeper to Investigate the Industry's Hiring Practices," *Los Angeles Times,* May 11, 2016, http://tinyurl.com/hznwgvq.

89. "DGA Publishes Inaugural Feature Film Diversity Report," Directors Guild of America, Dec. 9, 2015, http://tinyurl.com/qgsg438.

90. "DGA TV Diversity Report," Directors Guild of America, Aug. 25, 2015, http://tinyurl.com/ohrg2d6.

91. Alex Stedman, "Academy Invites 683 New Members in Push for More Diversity," *Variety*, June 29, 2016, http://tinyurl.com/j9vfxoh.

92. Scott Feinberg, "Academy's New Voting Rules Raise Questions, Concerns and Anger Among Members," *The Hollywood Reporter*, Jan. 23, 2016, http://tinyurl.com/j9wtbsl.

93. *Ibid.*

94. Lacey Rose, "Ryan Murphy Launches Foundation to Tackle Hollywood's Diversity Problem," *The Hollywood Reporter*, Feb. 3, 2016, http://tinyurl.com/heps8cb.

95. Rebecca Ford, "How J. J. Abrams' Bad Robot Is Bringing More Diversity to Hollywood," *The Hollywood Reporter*, March 2, 2016, http://tinyurl.com/gqm3s5f.

96. "DGA Diversity: Frequently Asked Questions," Directors Guild of America, undated, http://tinyurl.com/j56vgy5.

97. Feinberg, *op. cit.*

98. Mike Isaac, "Twitter bars Milo Yiannopoulos in Wake of Leslie Jones' Reports of Abuse," *The New York Times*, July 20, 2016, http://tinyurl.com/jzkdpwk.

99. "Welcome to The Illinois Film Office," Illinois Department of Commerce and Economic Opportunity, http://tinyurl.com/nwpacw4.

100. La Risa Lynch, "Lights, camera but little action for blacks in film industry," *Austin Weekly News*, Sept. 13, 2014, http://tinyurl.com/he7275v.

101. Addie Morfoot, "New York Looks to Remedy Hollywood's Diversity Problem," *Crain's New York*, April 11, 2016, http://tinyurl.com/j3ze6z5.

102. R. B. Jefferson, "The Ultimate Guide to SAG-AFTRA Low-Budget Film Signatory Agreements for Indie Filmmakers-Part 2," *Lawyers Rock*, Oct. 20, 2014, http://tinyurl.com/jxbmv2u.

103. Puente and Mandell, *op. cit.*

BIBLIOGRAPHY
Selected Sources
Books

Cheu, Johnson, *Diversity in Disney Films: Critical Essays on Race, Ethnicity, Gender, Sexuality and Disability,* McFarland, 2013.
An assistant professor of American culture at Michigan State University edits an essay collection about diversity in Disney films, including race, gender, sexuality, masculinity and disability.

Cones, John W., *Patterns of Bias in Hollywood Movies*, Algora Publishing, 2012.
An entertainment lawyer studies why consistent complaints of bias in Hollywood have had little impact on racial and ethnic stereotyping.

Najera, Rick, *Almost White: Forced Confessions of a Latino in Hollywood,* Smiley Books, 2013.
A Latino writer, actor, director, comedian, playwright and producer explains how he broke into the entertainment industry and struggled against typecasting.

Scott, Ellen C., *Cinema Civil Rights: Regulation, Repression, and Race in the Classical Hollywood Era,* Rutgers University Press, 2014.
An expert in African-American cultural history and film explores how black audiences, activists and lobbyists influenced the representation of race in Hollywood before the 1960s.

Shaheen, Jack, *Reel Bad Arabs: How Hollywood Vilifies a People,* Southern Illinois University, 2014.
A Middle East scholar documents a century of offensive stereotypes about Arabs and Muslims in a review of 900 films, showing how the image of the "dirty Arab" has reemerged over the last 30 years.

Articles

Dargis, Manohla, "Lights, Camera, Taking Action," *The New York Times*, Jan. 21, 2015, http://tinyurl.com/nandeyz.
A film critic explores women directors' efforts to land jobs and finance their productions.

Dowd, Maureen, "Women of Hollywood Speak Out," *The New York Times Magazine,* **Nov. 20, 2015, http:// tinyurl.com/p2rtjqp.**
A columnist examines gender bias in the film industry.

Ford, Rebecca, and Borys Kit, "Hollywood's Casting Blitz: It's All About Diversity in the Wake of #OscarsSoWhite," *Hollywood Reporter,* **March 2, 2016, http://tinyurl.com/zqvag8w.**
Writers for an entertainment industry trade journal detail how colorblind casting is gaining momentum.

Kang, Cecilia, Krissah Thompson and Drew Harwell, "Hollywood's race problem: An insular industry struggles to change," *The Washington Post,* **Dec. 23, 2014, http://tinyurl.com/jxgwdap.**
Business reporters examine movie studios' reluctance to finance films featuring African-American stories, which has forced producers to adopt creative means to make such projects.

Scott, Ellen C., "Most Timely: Hooray for Hollywood," *Common Reader,* **Jan. 26, 2016, http:// tinyurl.com/z7runzo.**
An expert in African-American cultural history and film argues that racism in awarding the Academy Awards is not new and details the history of black actors protesting Hollywood bias in the 1960s.

Reports and Studies

Hunt, Darnell, Ana-Christina Ramon and Michael Tran, "2016 Hollywood Diversity Report: Busine$$ as Usual," UCLA Ralph J. Bunche Center for African-American Studies, February 2016, http://tinyurl .com/hhrdltn.
Researchers at an African-American academic research center analyzes films and TV shows for percentages of women and minorities in acting, writing and directing roles and looks at audience ratings and awards in the context of race and gender.

Lauzen, Martha M., "The Celluloid Ceiling: Behind-the-Scenes Employment of Women on the Top 100, 250, and 500 Films of 2015," Center for the Study of Women in Television and Film, San Diego State University, January 2016, http://tinyurl.com/h5gmn7p.
A scholar at a university academic center studying women in television and film tracks the employment of women directors, writers, producers, cinematographers and editors in the top 250 films of 2015.

Smith, Jason, "Between Colorblind and Colorconscious: Contemporary Hollywood Films and Struggles Over Racial Representation," *Journal of Black Studies,* **December 2013, http://tinyurl.com/zt4dpga.**
A George Mason University scholar in sociology examines the advances made by African-Americans in the film industry and the difference between playing colorblind and colorconscious roles.

Smith, Stacy L., Mark Choueiti and Katherine Pieper, "Inclusion or Invisibility? Comprehensive Annenberg Report on Diversity in Entertainment," Media, Diversity, & Social Change Initiative, University of Southern California, February 2016, http://tinyurl .com/jxjyj2p.
Professors at the University of Southern California's Annenberg School for Communication and Journalism look at diversity in film and television and rate entertainment companies for gender and racial balance.

For More Information

Academy of Motion Picture Arts and Sciences, 8949 Wilshire Blvd., Beverly Hills, CA 90211; 310-247-3000; www.oscars.org. Professional association whose members award the annual Oscars.

Center for the Study of Women in Television and Film, San Diego State University, 5500 Campanile Drive, San Diego, CA 92182; 619-594-6301; womenintvfilm.sdsu.edu. Research center that studies gender issues in the film and TV industry.

ColorOfChange.org; www.colorofchange.org. A civil rights group that works to promote racial justice and economic equality for African-Americans.

Directors Guild of America, 7920 Sunset Blvd., Los Angeles, CA 90046; 310-289-2000; www.dga.org. Labor union that represents film and TV directors.

Media, Diversity, & Social Change Initiative, Annenberg School for Communication and Journalism, University of Southern California, 3502 Watt Way, Los Angeles, CA 90089; 213-740-6180; annenberg.usc.edu/pages/DrStacyLSmithMDSCI. Think tank that researches gender, ethnic and racial imbalance in the entertainment industry.

Motion Picture Association of America, 1600 I St., N.W., Washington, DC 20006; 202-293-1966; www.mpaa.org. Trade association that represents major movie studios and TV networks.

Ralph J. Bunche Center for African American Studies, University of California, Los Angeles, 160 Haines Hall, Los Angeles, CA 90095; 310-825-7403; www.bunchecenter.ucla.edu. Academic research center that examines racial and ethnic bias in film and television.

Screen Actors Guild — American Federation of Television and Radio Artists, 5757 Wilshire Blvd., 7th floor, Los Angeles, CA 90036; 323-549-6644; www.sagaftra.org. Labor union that represents actors.

Writers Guild of America, 7000 W. Third St., Los Angeles, CA 90048; 323-951-4000; www.wga.org. Labor union that represents television and movie writers.

4

Technology Addiction

Susan Ladika

Courtesy of Charles Bracke

Charlie Bracke, a gamer from Redmond, Wash., entered a rehab center after he realized his addiction to online video games was out of control and ruining his life. Now, after more than a year in treatment, he has a full-time job and is studying accounting. As part of his treatment, Bracke attends 12-step support groups, meets with a therapist and shares his story about battling technology addiction.

From *CQ Researcher*,
April 20, 2018

After spending much of his childhood playing video games, Charlie Bracke realized that his constant gaming as an adult was out of control: He says he had flunked out of three colleges, lost a girlfriend and washed out as a real estate agent.

Twice, recalls the 29-year-old from Redmond, Wash., he tried to quit gaming. Then, one day as he contemplated suicide, he says, his parents showed up unannounced and found him and his apartment a wreck.

They began calling treatment centers and help lines and found reSTART, a rehab center for internet, gaming and virtual reality addiction based in Fall City, Wash. After more than a year in treatment, Bracke now has a full-time job as a Costco merchandiser and is studying accounting. He attends 12-step support groups, meets with a therapist and shares his story about battling technology addiction with others at reSTART.

Before he went to rehab, Bracke says, "I didn't know how to deal with my feelings of failure. I was intentionally medicating my emotions with gaming."

Some addiction specialists say people like Bracke are addicted to technology, which they say can affect the brain in the same way an over-dependence on alcohol or drugs does. Others say tech overuse is not an addiction in the medical sense but rather is a manifestation of underlying conditions such as anxiety or depression.

The debate is occurring as several former technology industry insiders have accused software companies of intentionally creating addictive products, although defenders of the companies say they should not be blamed for making products that keep users

Half of U.S. Teens Feel Tech Dependent

One in two youths ages 12 to 18 say they feel addicted to their smartphones or other mobile devices, and an even higher percentage of parents believe their children are hooked. More than one-fourth of parents feel that they themselves are addicted.

How Young Adults and Their Parents View Their Tech Use

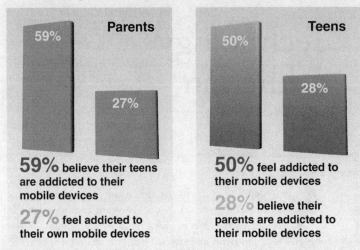

59% believe their teens are addicted to their mobile devices

27% feel addicted to their own mobile devices

50% feel addicted to their mobile devices

28% believe their parents are addicted to their mobile devices

Source: "Dealing With Devices: The Parent-Teen Dynamic," Common Sense Media, May 3, 2016, https://tinyurl.com/ydb86tlb

engaged. Several parent groups and child development experts want the government to address the potential negative effects of technology overuse, especially on young children.

There is "a fairly even split in the scientific community about whether tech addiction is a real thing," said Michael Bishop, a psychologist and director of Summerland Camps, which runs summer camps in North Carolina and California for children with what Bishop calls "screen overuse" habits. Bishop says he prefers the term "habit" over an "addiction," because, "When teens think about their behavior as a habit, they are more empowered to change."[1] Addiction occurs when something becomes all-consuming and has a negative impact on one's life, such as interfering with relationships, sleep patterns, work, hobbies or eating habits.

"Technology, like all other 'rewards,' can over-release dopamine [a neurotransmitter], overexcite and kill neurons, leading to addiction," said Robert Lustig, a University of California, San Francisco, emeritus professor of pediatric endocrinology and author of *The Hacking of the American Mind*, a book about what he says is a corporate scheme to sell pleasure that is creating an international epidemic of addiction, depression and chronic disease. Technology is "not a drug, but it might as well be," Lustig said. "It works the same way. . . . It has the same results."[2]

But Michael Rich, an associate professor of pediatrics at Harvard University, says, "we don't think the word 'addict' is the correct word to use. There's not a measurable physiological change when you're using or withdrawing, unlike alcohol, heroin or tobacco."

The American Psychiatric Association (APA), a professional organization representing psychiatrists, academics and researchers, did not define technology addiction as a diagnosable disorder in its latest edition of the *Diagnostic and Statistical Manual of Mental Disorders* (*DSM-5*), published in 2013. However, the manual, used by health professionals to make diagnoses and by insurance companies to determine medical coverage, did say that internet gaming disorder needs further study.[3]

But Dan Hewitt, a vice president of the Entertainment Software Association, a trade group of gaming software companies, in Washington, says in an email interview that "legitimate science, objective research and common sense all prove video games are not addictive. By misusing the word addiction, which is a medical term, society demeans real compulsive behaviors, like alcoholism and drug abuse, which deserve treatment, compassion, and care."

The World Health Organization (WHO), which held its fourth annual meeting on tech addiction in 2017, wrote that the increased use of technology is associated "with documented cases of excessive use, which often has negative health consequences." In a growing number of countries and jurisdictions, said the WHO, "the problem has reached the magnitude of a significant public health concern."[4]

Several former employees of companies such as Google and Facebook say tech companies intentionally created technology designed to hook users in order to make money by selling their data. "We talk about addiction and we tend to think, 'Oh, this is just happening by accident,'" said Tristan Harris, a former design ethicist at Google who has accused the companies of creating addictive software. "This is happening by design. There's a whole bunch of techniques that are deliberately used to keep the auto play [going] on YouTube to keep you watching the next video."[5]

Some scientists and child advocates worry that children and young adults may be particularly susceptible to tech addiction. Adolescents, says Lustig, are particularly vulnerable to almost every psychiatric disease — schizophrenia, anxiety, addiction, depression — in part because their prefrontal cortex, which controls executive function and decision-making, is the last part of the brain to fully develop. Thus, "teens exposed to addictive substances or behaviors are more likely to become addicted" than adults, Lustig says.

According to an open letter to Apple by a group of concerned investors, the average American child receives his or her first smartphone at age 10, and teens spend more than 4.5 hours per day on their smartphones, not counting time spent texting and talking. Nearly 80 percent of teens said they check their phones at least every hour.[6]

But Stanford University communications professor Byron Reeves said his research has found that some college students turn their phones on and off 300 times in a 24-hour period. "And that's just the average," he said. "There are a lot of people that are turning it on and off 500, 600, 700, 800 times a day. So it's going on, going off for an average of ten seconds." Reeves said he worries that such habits could lead to shortened attention spans.[7]

Regardless of what experts say about whether tech addiction exists, a January poll found that nearly half of parents with children under 18 feared their kids were addicted to their mobile devices. About 20 percent of the parents said they were extremely or very concerned that the devices were affecting their children's mental health, and more than a quarter said they considered themselves addicted to their devices.[8]

The poll was sponsored by Common Sense Media, which advocates for safe technology and media use by children. "We are not anti-tech," said James P. Steyer, founder of the group. "We are into the appropriate and balanced use of technology. We are calling out the industry for their excesses and their intentional effects to manipulate and addict."[9]

Another survey, of 400 parents published in March by *Fast Company* magazine, found that they were more concerned about their children being harmed by tech addiction than about online bullying, data privacy or sexual predators.[10]

A smartphone "takes over a child's daily consciousness," a father of three from Chicago said in response to the survey. Children who are naturally "voracious, inquisitive curiosity seekers slowly, invariably and inevitably become . . . indifferent to discovery in favor of scrolling. Smartphones numb creativity, intellectual critical thought and social growth."[11]

The mother of a 1-year-old from New York City wrote: "I see myself reaching for my phone out of habit anytime I'm the least bit bored or have a moment to spare. I hate this and yet can't seem to stop myself. I figure at least my brain patterns were formed without this influence and am terrified of what growing up with smartphones and tech will do to my daughter."[12]

Rich, director of the Center on Media and Child Health at Boston Children's Hospital, says the center has dealt with a few hundred cases of children and young adults whose families were worried about their internet use. "Every case so far has underlying psychological issues driving behavior," such as attention deficit/hyperactivity disorder or anxiety, he says. The center, which educates families on healthy media use, recently opened the Clinic for Interactive Media and Internet Disorders to treat children with internet use issues.

Boys, according to Rich, who teaches social and behavioral sciences in addition to pediatrics, are more likely to overindulge in gaming; girls to overuse social media. Gamers tend to have attention deficit/hyperactivity disorder, while those who overuse social media tend to have anxiety, he says. The genders are evenly split, though, when it comes to binging on information and viewing pornography, he says. Some politicians and religious leaders have raised concerns about the excessive use of online pornography in recent years, especially violent porn.

Profile of a Tech-Addicted Nation

U.S. smartphone owners check their phones an average of **47** times a day.

More than **80** percent check their phones within an hour of waking or going to bed — more than a third within 5 minutes.

47 percent have tried to limit their phone use, but only **30** percent have succeeded.

Source: Felix Richter, "America's Smartphone Addiction," Statista, March 12, 2018, https://tinyurl.com/ybf8kux3

Some tech insiders and politicians say the government should help to combat the potential for tech addiction. The National Institutes of Health (NIH) is funding its first study on technology addiction — an examination of online gaming.[13]

Several other countries recognize tech addiction as a disorder, and some have declared it a public health crisis. In France, for instance, proposed legislation would require children under 16 to obtain parental approval to open accounts on social media sites such as Facebook, Snapchat or Instagram. And the government plans to ban mobile phone use at primary and junior high schools, starting this fall.[14]

As researchers, technology company executives and parents examine tech addiction, here are some of the questions they are asking:

Can technology use be addictive?

Addiction occurs when the brain recognizes substances or behaviors that create pleasure by releasing dopamine, a chemical that passes information from one neuron to the next — signals that the brain associates with anticipation of a reward. Being repeatedly exposed to the substance or behavior can make a person want more. Eventually, the person builds up tolerance, needing more of the substance or activity to feel the pleasurable effect.[15]

Some experts say the still-developing brains of children and young adults, in particular, can respond to technology similarly to how they would respond to other addictive substances, such as drugs and alcohol. "From a central nervous standpoint, there's no difference," says Lustig, at the University of Southern California. MRIs and PET scans have found changes in the brains of those with internet addictions similar to those with other addictions, he says, adding, "If it looks like a duck and walks like a duck and quacks like a duck, it's a duck."

Larry Rosen, a professor emeritus of psychology at California State University, Dominguez Hills, also believes technology can affect the brain. With addiction, the brain releases, besides dopamine, the mood-affecting neurotransmitter serotonin. With anxiety, the brain releases hormones that react to stress by producing a surge of energy and heightened mental focus. People can feel compelled to do an activity, such as check Facebook, to reduce their anxiety, Rosen says. "We act like Pavlov's dog when we get a notification on our phones," he says. "Technology can impact" anxiety or addiction, or both.

With technology, as with other types of addictions, he said, problems arise if a person requires more of the addictive substance to feel the same level of satisfaction. And being away from the substance or activity can prompt depression, stress or anxiety, typical symptoms of withdrawal.[16]

The Hazelden Betty Ford Foundation, which operates drug and alcohol addiction treatment centers, defines teen technology addiction as "frequent and obsessive technology-related behavior increasingly practiced despite negative consequences to the user of the technology." In addition, the foundation says, teen dependence on technology can lead to consequences ranging from "mild annoyance when away from technology to feelings of isolation, extreme anxiety and depression."[17]

Researchers in South Korea, one of several countries that recognize tech addiction as a disorder, have found that teens obsessed with their smartphones or the internet experience changes in their brain chemistry similar to those found in other types of addiction. Using a type of MRI that measures the brain's chemical composition, researchers examined 19 young men diagnosed as addicted to technology and compared them with 19 young men who were not.

The teens diagnosed with tech addiction had more neurotransmitter activity in the region of the brain tied to rewards, mood regulation and control of inhibition and rated higher for depression, anxiety and impulsivity. The researchers also found that the psychotherapy treatment known as cognitive behavioral therapy could help normalize the chemical imbalance.[18]

Christopher Whitlow, chief of neuroradiology at the Wake Forest School of Medicine in Winston-Salem, N.C., said the area of the brain where the imbalance was found — the anterior cingulate — has been found to play a role in addictive behavior. "In that way, smartphone and internet addiction appears to have some similarities with addiction to other things," he said.[19]

Max Wintermark, chief of neuroradiology at Stanford, said of the South Korean findings: "It's a very small study, so you have to take it with a grain of salt." However, he added, "It's the first study that I read about internet addiction, but there are many studies that link alcohol, drug and other types of addiction to imbalances in various neurotransmitters in the brain."[20]

However, professor of psychology Christopher Ferguson at Stetson University in DeLand, Fla., said, "Sometimes with new technology you see these heightened claims of harm. . . . In my opinion, they're not comparable to, say, methamphetamine addiction or heroin addiction." Technology "is a tool," he adds. "It's really about how you use it. It's not heroin. That's not to say you can't overdo it."[21]

Harvard's Rich agrees that tech overuse is not a classic type of addiction. But, he says, computer applications "are designed to continually grab and re-grab information and give us just enough frustration, followed by satisfaction, to give us the little shots of dopamine we so crave. We need to learn how to develop self-regulation and encourage tech companies to design more human-friendly apps."

Michael Robb, director of research for Common Sense Media, acknowledges that it is impossible to gauge whether tech addiction actually exists. "There is no way to measure it right now," he says. "There's no agreement on a definition. There needs to be less ambiguity." But for some kids, he says, their tech use "is so disruptive it causes significant harm in other parts of their lives" such as sleep, school and social relationships.

Dean Eckles, a communications and technology professor at the Massachusetts Institute of Technology, said that because nearly everyone uses technology and each person uses it in different ways, "it's really hard to do purely observational research into the effects of something like screen time or social media use." Rather than dividing participants into those with smartphones and those without, for example, researchers must compare differences in use, while considering differences in race, income and parental education.[22]

Even expert organizations are not sure technology addiction is real. While the APA has not said internet or social media overuse is an addictive disorder, it has said internet gaming disorder needs to be studied further. The organization cited studies indicating that when some individuals are engrossed in internet games, certain brain pathways are triggered "in the same direct and intense way that a drug addict's brain is affected by a particular substance."[23]

The WHO plans to list "gaming disorder" as a mental health disorder in its next edition of the International Classification of Diseases (ICD), scheduled for release this year. The ICD sets international standards for reporting health conditions and diseases.[24]

Hewitt, of the Entertainment Software Association, said his organization rejects the WHO's conclusion but supports the APA's call for more research into computer and video games. "Video game 'addiction' is a colloquial, loaded term with no real scientific or medical definition or broad support," he said. "And it is important to remember that video game enthusiasm is often misinterpreted as 'addiction.' "[25]

Nancy Petry, a University of Connecticut professor of medicine, is leading the two-year, $416,000 NIH study that may ultimately help determine whether online gaming is a disorder. "Tech addiction is a hot topic," she said, "but we need to clearly define and differentiate what constitutes a mental disorder that is causing major adverse consequences and distinguish it from just a bad habit that people just wish they weren't doing."[26]

Getty Images/LightRocket/Zhang Peng

Teenagers play the popular video game "Arena of Valor" at a shopping mall in China. In 2008 China became the first country to recognize internet addiction disorder. South Korea and China have established government-sponsored treatment centers for teens and young adults considered tech-addicted.

Are companies intentionally making technology addictive?

Some ex-employees of big tech companies have accused their former employers of purposely getting consumers hooked on technology, and profiting in the process.

Former Google employee Harris, whose job was to advise the company on how its technology should "ethically" steer the thoughts and actions of customers using their products, has been one of the most outspoken on the subject. He has likened a smartphone to a slot machine, since people repeatedly check their phones each day to see how many "likes" they have received on Facebook or how many new followers they have on Twitter. "This is one way to hijack people's minds and create a habit," he said. "When someone pulls a lever, sometimes they get a reward, an exciting reward."[27]

Technology companies want consumers constantly to be drawn back to their phones, he said. "They want you to use it particular ways and for long periods of time. Because that's how they make their money."[28]

Tech companies have teams of experts whose goal is to keep users habitually engaged, wrote Adam Alter, an associate professor of marketing and psychology at New York University and author of the 2017 book *Irresistible: The Rise of Addictive Technology and the Business of Keeping Us Hooked.* Software developers use a variety of techniques to addict users, he said, including "compelling goals that are just beyond reach; irresistible and unpredictable positive feedback; a sense of incremental progress and improvement; [and] tasks that become slowly more difficult over time."[29]

Ramsay Brown, the co-founder of Dopamine Labs in Venice, Calif., which produces apps for financial firms and fitness companies, said programmers write computer code intended to trigger a neurological response by selectively doling out rewards to make consumers return for more. Someone may suddenly get 30 likes on an Instagram post, but the program holds "some of them back [in order] to let [them] know later in a big burst," Brown said.[30]

"There's some algorithm somewhere that predicted for this user right now, . . . we can see an improvement in his behavior if you give it to him in this burst instead of that burst," Brown said. "You're part of a controlled set of experiments that are happening in real time across you and millions of other people."[31]

Similarly, Harris said, Snapchat's Snapstreak feature lets users see how many days they have exchanged messages with someone else. Some teens get so stressed over keeping those streaks going, he said, that when they go on vacation they give their password to friends so they can keep their streaks going for them. "You could ask, when these features are being designed, are they designed to most help people live their life?" Harris asked. "Or are they being designed because they're best at hooking people into using this product?"[32]

In fact, say industry insiders, keeping people as engaged as possible is the corporate model for tech companies, particularly social media companies such as Facebook, which provide services for free in exchange for users' personal data, which the companies then sell. Sandy Parakilas, a former Facebook manager who now is an adviser to the Center for Humane Technology, said Facebook has "an incentive to try to attract as many users, get those people to view as much content as possible, collect as much data as possible and then sell that."[33]

Sean Parker, the founding president of Facebook, said the intent behind social media was: "How do we consume as much of your time and conscious attention as possible? And that means that we need to sort of give you a little dopamine hit every once in a while, because someone liked or commented on a photo or a post or whatever. . . . It's a social-validation feedback loop. . . ., exactly the kind of thing that a hacker like myself would come up with, because you're exploiting a vulnerability in human psychology."[34]

But Antigone Davis, head of global safety for Facebook, said, "There's a lot of misinformation and miscommunication about the concept of addiction and how people are engaging online. We really care at Facebook about making sure people are engaging in a positive, safe way."[35]

"We do not build products based on research about creating addictions," Facebook said in a statement. "We are doing research on issues like excessive use of social media to make sure we're giving people the tools they need to better manage the time they spend on Facebook."

Tech writer Steve Kovach wrote that rather than addiction, "the problem most tech users face is their devices and services are annoying and disruptive. It's easy to feel stressed out or overloaded because of them. In other words, the tech industry doesn't need to worry about making its products less addictive. It needs to focus on making them better."[36]

Those who disagree with the claim that software writers intentionally made addictive products say coders merely made products that encourage the user to stay engaged, but that some people become obsessed with the products. That is not the same as clinically addicting people, they say.

Gabe Zichermann, an expert on gamification, says software companies use "various addicting algorithms and approaches" to take advantage of the users' own psychological state in order to "make something obsession-oriented more powerful."

Nir Eyal, the author of *Hooked: How to Build Habit-Forming Products*, told the 2017 Habit Summit conference, "We're not freebasing Facebook and injecting Instagram here." Showing a slide of sweet baked goods, he said. "Just as we shouldn't blame the baker for making such delicious treats, we can't blame tech makers for making their products so good we want to use them."[37]

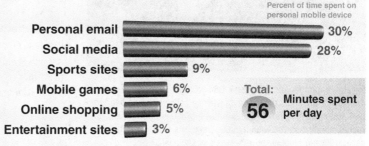

Personal Email, Social Media Sap Productivity

Workers say they spend nearly an hour each workday using their mobile phones for nonwork activities. Thirty percent say they spend the most time on personal email, and 28 percent on social media.

Activities Employees Spend the Most Time On, Using Their Smartphones, While at Work

Percent of time spent on personal mobile device

Activity	Percent
Personal email	30%
Social media	28%
Sports sites	9%
Mobile games	6%
Online shopping	5%
Entertainment sites	3%

Total: **56** Minutes spent per day

Source: "Working Hard or Hardly Working? Employees Waste More than One Day a Week on Non-Work Activities," OfficeTeam, Robert Half, July 19, 2017, https://tinyurl.com/ybwlosfx

"Of course that's what tech companies will do. And frankly: do we want it any other way?" he asked. "The idea is to remember that we are not powerless. We are in control."[38]

Should the government help curb the potential for tech addiction?

Even as tech insiders and some investors are pushing technology companies to address internet addiction, some advocacy groups — and a handful of politicians — are beginning to call for government action.

Sen. Edward Markey, D-Mass., said in February that he planned to introduce a bill calling for a federal study to examine the impact of electronic media on children's health and behavior.[39] He was speaking at a conference organized by Truth About Tech, a campaign to educate consumers about the potential pitfalls of technology, cosponsored by the nonprofit Common Sense Media and the Center for Humane Technology. The center was cofounded by former Google ethicist Harris to advocate for technology that aims to improve the well-being of humanity.

Tweeting about the proposed study, which would be conducted by the National Institute of Child Health and

Getty Images/Alex Brandon

Facebook founder and CEO Mark Zuckerberg apologized for his company's missteps regarding its privacy policies during hearings on Capitol Hill in April. "We didn't take a broad enough view of our responsibility, and that was a big mistake," he said. In addition, several former employees of companies such as Google and Facebook say tech companies intentionally created technology designed to hook users in order to make money by selling their data.

Human Development, Markey said: "Children are immersed in a digital world that can ennoble and enrich or degrade and debase."[40]

Sen. Mark Warner, D-Va., says he believes there is evidence that technology can be addictive, although he's unsure about government regulation. "I'd much rather do this in a collaborative effort with the companies, but with the notion that if they don't acknowledge this, I think public unease is going to dramatically undermine consumer's trust."[41]

Tech companies have come under increased scrutiny following revelations that Russia meddled in the 2016 U.S. presidential election, largely using social media. Facebook, Google and Twitter executives came to Capitol Hill in October and acknowledged their role in the meddling.[42]

Facebook also faced political and consumer backlash this year regarding its privacy policies, after the British data collection company Cambridge Analytica, which was working on President Donald Trump's election campaign, accessed the personal data of more than 50 million Facebook users, including Facebook chairman and CEO Mark Zuckerberg.[43] During hearings on Capitol Hill in April, Zuckerberg apologized for his company's missteps.

"We didn't take a broad enough view of our responsibility, and that was a big mistake. It was my mistake, and I'm sorry," Zuckerberg said. But Rep. Jan Schakowsky, an Illinois Democrat, said, "you have a long history of growth and success, but you also have a long list of apologies. This is proof to me that self-regulation simply does not work."[44]

Common Sense spokeswoman Corbie Kiernan says, "Clearly, tech is not going to regulate themselves, as they've shown with their 'move fast and break things' approach, so it is up to policymakers, advocates and citizens to hold them accountable. Hopefully, they will see the light and work with Common Sense and others like us to move fast and fix things instead."

Jeff Kagan, an independent mobile industry analyst, agreed that "companies are not going to self-regulate" but that the threat of legislation could pressure them to take action.[45]

But Larry Downes, a senior industry and innovation fellow at Georgetown University, doubts Congress will take action. "When something goes wrong, there's a call for legislation," he says. "Ninety-nine times out of 100 it just dies away. What crisis is going to be big enough that it just won't go away?"

Some industry critics have called for social media to be regulated similar to traditional media. But broadcasters and other media are only lightly regulated, Downes points out, largely because of the Constitution's guarantee of free speech. "The First Amendment looms very large over any effort to regulate anything having to do with speech," he says.

"Government is profoundly ineffective in creating fair regulations and enforcing restrictions," says Harvard's Rich. Instead, he says he would like to see the government play a bigger role in educating and empowering consumers to "help build our literacy and mastery of the digital environment."

Common Sense said it plans to conduct research on the magnitude of digital addiction among young people and evaluate its impact, and will work with other groups and tech insiders to develop ethical design standards "to prevent, avoid and discourage digital addiction." In addition, groups said they plan to pursue an aggressive agenda for regulation of tech companies that use manipulative practices on consumers.[46]

Internet and TV providers Comcast and DirecTV are donating $50 million worth of air time for public service announcements focusing on such things as a potential link between depression and heavy social media use. The ads are patterned after anti-smoking campaigns.[47]

Marc Benioff, CEO of the customer relationship management platform Salesforce.com, suggested social media overuse be treated as a public health issue like smoking.

"I think that you do it exactly the same way that you regulated the cigarette industry: 'Here's a product: Cigarettes. They're addictive, they're not good for you,' " Benioff said. "Technology has addictive qualities that we have to address, and product designers are working to make those products more addictive, and we need to rein that back." Meanwhile, he said, the government should provide clarity on whether social media use is harmful for people.[48]

Downes is skeptical about using tobacco-style public service announcements because the health effects of tobacco have been thoroughly studied, while very limited research has been conducted on the impact of technology overuse. "Research takes years," Downes says. "Even when you have all the facts, it still takes years for people to accept the facts."

Sponsoring studies such as the one NIH is funding on gaming addiction, he says, "is a completely appropriate role for the government."

BACKGROUND
Early Qualms

Concerns about the impact of technology are nothing new. When radio emerged on the scene in the 1920s, some feared it would distract kids from reading and hurt their school performance. The magazine *Gramophone* claimed in 1936 that radio was "disturbing the balance of their (kids') excitable minds."[49]

Then when television became popular after World War II, some feared it would hurt reading, conversation, family life and "result in the further vulgarization of the American culture."[50] Even famed American television journalist Edward R. Murrow warned in 1957 that television was becoming the "opiate of the people."[51]

The debate over whether television was addictive continued in ensuing decades. As late as 1990, Richard Ducey, senior vice president of research and planning with the National Association of Broadcasters in

A family watches TV in the 1950s. When radio, and later TV, emerged on the scene, many people worried — much as they worry today about high-technology use — that the new devices would distract children from schoolwork. In 1957, influential TV journalist Edward R. Murrow warned that television was becoming the "opiate of the people."

Washington, told *The New York Times*: "I've never seen anything conclusive that shows television to be psychologically addictive. It's a proposition with no support, except in some metaphorical sense, the same way you might be addicted to dessert."[52]

The first computers were massive, requiring a team of specialists to keep them functioning. One of the earliest and best known was the Electronic Numerical Integrator Analyzer and Computer (ENIAC), built to make ballistics calculations for the U.S. military during World War II. It weighed 30 tons and covered almost 2,000 square feet.

The invention of microprocessors, developed by Intel in 1971, paved the way for smaller and smaller computers. The chip, which was just one-sixteenth of an inch by one-eighth of an inch, had computing power equal to the huge ENIAC. This led to the development of personal computers, an industry that began to gain traction in 1977, with the mass-produced Apple II, Tandy Radio Shack TRS-80 and Commodore Business Machines Personal Electronic Transactor.[53]

By 1990, some laptop computers were on the market, and computer ownership boomed in the next decade. In 1993, less than 25 percent of U.S. households owned a computer. By 2000, more than half of all households had

C H R O N O L O G Y

1920s-1950s *As new technologies are introduced, concerns emerge about overuse and addiction.*

1920 First U.S. commercial radio station, KDKA in Pittsburgh, goes on the air. After radio becomes a common household object, some fear it will distract children and hurt their school performance.

1927 Television is invented.

1928 First U.S. television station, W3XK, begins broadcasting from suburban Washington, D.C.

1944 Two University of Pennsylvania professors build the Electronic Numerical Integrator and Calculator, considered the grandfather of computers.

1957 TV journalist Edward R. Murrow warns that television is becoming the "opiate of the people."

1970s-1980s *Personal computers and mobile phones are invented.*

1971 An Intel engineer creates the first microprocessor.

1973 The first mobile phone call is made — between a Motorola employee and Bell Labs headquarters.

1976 Steve Jobs and Steve Wozniak build the Apple I desktop computer.

1981 First laptop computer, the Epson HX-20, is introduced.

1990s-2000s *Computer ownership soars and social media companies form.*

1993 Fewer than one in four U.S. households owns a computer.

1995 Psychologist Kimberly Young begins first study on internet addiction in the United States.

1997 First social media site, Six Degrees, is founded.

1998 Congress passes Children's Online Privacy Protection Act.

2000 Half of U.S. households have a computer.

2003 MySpace social media site is created.

2004 Mark Zuckerberg launches Thefacebook — the predecessor of Facebook — from his Harvard dorm room.

2006 Twitter is founded.

2008 China becomes the first to recognize internet addiction disorder.

2010-Present *Social media use soars; some consumer groups and tech insiders begin to push back against tech companies.*

2010 Instagram founded.

2011 Snapchat launches.

2013 *Diagnostic and Statistical Manual of Mental Disorders* lists "Internet gaming disorder" as a condition worthy of further study.

2014 World Health Organization (WHO) holds the first international meeting on internet addiction.

2016 More U.S. households have cellphones than landlines.

2017 South Korean researchers find that technology overuse affects the brain in ways similar to other addictions. . . . National Institutes of Health funds first U.S. study on gaming addiction. . . . WHO announces it will include gaming disorder in its next International Classification of Diseases.

2018 Common Sense Media and the Center for Humane Technology start the Truth About Tech campaign. . . . Apple shareholders JANA Partners LLC and the California State Teachers' Retirement System urge the company to develop tools to help parents control children's iPhone use. . . . Sen. Edward J. Markey, D-Mass., says he will propose that Congress fund a study on the impact of electronic media on children's health and behavior.

a computer, and 41.5 percent had internet access.[54] By 2016, 80 percent of U.S. households had a laptop or desktop computer.[55]

But long before then, *The Journal of Organizational Behavior Management* in 1985 ran an article on computer fear and addiction, noting: "The advent of the computer has given rise to several types of reactions, ranging from fear, avoidance and sabotage, on the one hand, to patterns of headlong involvement and overuse comparable to addiction, on the other."[56]

In 1998, Congress approved the Children's Online Privacy Protection Act (COPPA) requiring the Federal Trade Commission to issue regulations related to children's online privacy.[57] The law, which took effect in 2000, was designed to give parents control over what information is collected about their children online. It also required that children be at least 13 years old before opening a social media account.[58]

Video games began gaining in popularity in the late 1970s, with the introduction of Atari; Nintendo advanced the demand for gaming in the 1980s. In 2000, Sega began offering consoles that could connect to the internet, opening the door to the next generation of devices, Microsoft's Xbox Live and Sony's PlayStation. Nintendo's Wii entered the scene in the mid-2000s, allowing people to do things such as bowl, golf or play tennis, virtually. Sales eventually topped 100 million units worldwide.[59]

Games moved to handheld devices with the introduction of the iPhone in 2007 and iPad in 2010. The "Angry Birds" game was introduced in 2009 and skyrocketed in popularity: By 2011 it had been downloaded 50 million times. In 2010, consumers spent $17.5 billion on video game content, a figure that rose to $24.5 billion by 2016. About two-thirds of U.S. households include someone who plays at least three hours of video games per week. By 2017, some of the top-selling video games of all time were "Grand Theft Auto" (80 million copies), "Minecraft" (122 million) and "Tetris" (170 million).[60]

Although the term "smartphone" was not used until 1995, the first internet-connected phone came out in 1992. Called the Simon Personal Communicator, the $899 device was developed by IBM, and had the features of a cellphone and a personal digital assistant. While it had no web browser, it did have email access.[61]

By 2011, 35 percent of adults had smartphones, but only a quarter used them (rather than computers) to access the internet, while 23 percent of teens, most of them age 14 and older, had a smartphone, according to the Pew Research Center.[62] Within five years, according to Pew, 84 percent of households had smartphones — more than had landlines — and a third of households had three or more smartphones.[63]

Pew's last survey of teens, in 2015, found that 88 percent had access to a cell phone or smartphone, and nearly one-quarter said they are online "almost constantly."[64] By 2016, according to the marketing consulting firm Influence Central, the average age for kids to get their first cell phone was 10.3 years.[65]

The first social media site, Six Degrees (based on the notion that there are "six degrees of separation" between all people), was created in 1997. Users could create a profile and "friend" other people.[66] Social media has had a major impact on society since the 2000s. MySpace, created in 2003 and the most visited website in 2006, was valued at $12 billion in 2007. After the rise of Facebook, however, MySpace dwindled in popularity; it now focuses on music and culture.[67]

Mark Zuckerberg launched Thefacebook from his Harvard dorm room in February 2004. The site quickly spread to other universities, and in 2004 Zuckerberg dropped out of Harvard to run the company, which became known as Facebook and was headquartered in a Palo Alto, Calif., office. PayPal co-founders Peter Thiel and Elon Musk invested $500,000 in Facebook, which had its initial public offering in 2012.[68]

Meanwhile, Twitter was founded in 2006, followed by Instagram in 2010 and Snapchat in 2011.[69] As of 2015, more than 70 percent of teens said they used Facebook, while more than half used Instagram. Girls were more likely to use social media sites, while boys were more likely to play online games.[70]

Even though under COPPA children must be at least 13 years old before opening a social media account, 11 percent opened their first account by age 10, and 39 percent got their first account between the ages of 10 and 12, according to a 2016 survey.[71]

Concerns Emerge

In the 1980s and '90s, people were said to have computerphobia if they experienced "resistances, fears, anxieties

A Variety of Programs Treat Tech Overuse

Clients must "learn how to delay gratification."

As treatment centers crop up around the country to address technology overuse, the Clinic for Interactive Media and Internet Disorders in Boston is trying not only to help adolescents regulate their technology use but also to collect data to learn more about the problem and how best to treat it.

"What we want to do actually is to identify these problems much earlier — much farther upstream — before they become disabling," said Michael Rich, the clinic's founder, who is also director of the Center on Media and Child Health at Boston Children's Hospital, which investigates the positive and negative health effects of media on children. Both the center and the clinic are located at Children's Hospital, but the clinic is the only such facility for adolescents located at an academic research center.[1]

The center has treated a few hundred kids, but Rich and his staff cannot handle the volume of requests for help, he says. So they are working to train primary care physicians, pediatricians and therapists on how to treat internet overuse, says Rich, who is also an associate professor of pediatrics and of social and behavioral sciences at Harvard University.

Rich is only one soldier in what he and some other therapists see as a battle against technology overuse.

One of the first adult residential treatment centers in the country began operations outside Seattle in 2009. Hilarie Cash, a psychologist and licensed mental health counselor, moved to the Seattle area in 1993. Shortly after opening her practice she had a 25-year-old patient about to lose both his marriage and his job at Microsoft because he constantly played the online game "Dungeons and Dragons."

"He opened my eyes to this problem," Cash says. "I was very ignorant and naïve."

Over time, Cash dealt with others hooked on tech — some on online video games, some on internet pornography and some who had had affairs with people they met in chat rooms.

"There was no place to send young people who needed a higher level of care" beyond traditional treatment for depression, anxiety or other psychological problems that might drive an over-reliance on technology, she says.

In 2009, Cash and psychotherapist Cosette Rae launched reSTART, an inpatient facility in Fall City, Wash., a rural community east of Seattle. Initially treating only adults, the center expanded to include teens in 2016.

The first phase of treatment begins at a house in the woods, where clients are kept away from any kinds of screens in a process called "detoxing." Clients need to "learn how to delay gratification," Cash says. "Their brains are wired for immediate gratification."

They also have to learn life skills, time management and emotional regulation, and counseling helps them to find the root cause of their problems. Typically, young

and hostilities" about computers, including fears of touching or damaging one, of being replaced by computers and of becoming a slave to them, according to the 1996 book *Women and Computers*.[72] Similar concerns about the internet began to crop up in the 2000s, with headlines such as "Email 'Hurts IQ More than Pot,' " and "How Using Facebook Could Raise Your Risk of Cancer."[73]

Kimberly Young, currently the program director of the master's in strategic leadership program at St. Bonaventure University in New York State, was the first U.S. expert to begin focusing on internet addiction. In 1994, her friend's husband was spending 40 to 50 hours a week in AOL chat rooms. Besides running up hefty bills — chat room use cost $2.95 an hour — the man's life was out of balance and his relationship with his wife was in trouble.[74]

Young began the first study on internet addiction in 1995. In 1998 she wrote the book *Caught in the Net*, identifying internet addiction and its impact on families and society. She also founded the first U.S. inpatient clinic for internet addiction at Pennsylvania's Bradford Regional Medical Center, and the Center for Internet Addiction, using cognitive behavioral therapy to treat patients.[75]

adults who finish rehab move to an apartment with others who attended reSTART. They work part time and take a college class.

At this stage, technology is largely off limits. Clients receive a phone without an internet connection and may only work on computers in a monitored computer lab. Eventually they move to another apartment, where they can work full time and take additional college classes as they learn to reintegrate technology into their lives.

They also are required to attend 12-step meetings — similar to the system used by Alcoholics Anonymous — that are designed to help them recover from their addictive behavior. The reSTART program costs tens of thousands of dollars for the three phases of treatment.

Cash says many clients come from homes in which technology is heavily used, and many started playing video games at age 4 or 5. "Parents are handing kids this digital drug," Cash says.

A 2015 survey by reStart found mixed results for its program. The survey of almost 50 family members of reSTART clients found that 93 percent said their loved one was unable to control digital media use before entering the treatment program. After treatment, up to one-third were unable to control their behavior.[2] In comparison, 40 percent to 60 percent of those who go through drug addiction treatment relapse, according to the federal government.[3]

Other tech-addiction treatment centers have sprung up around the country. Some offer conventional addiction therapy. Others are summer camps that treat youngsters with individual counseling sessions and information on how technology affects physical and mental health.

At Summerland Camps, with locations in North Carolina and California, tweens and teens take part in activities such as rock climbing, zip lining, arts and music, as they learn to communicate and socialize without their cellphones. There are group discussions on tech overuse and coaching sessions to learn new habits, as well as individual sessions with licensed therapists.[4]

Camp co-founder Michael Bishop, a psychologist, said, "Kids are spending less time doing neighborhood games of basketball, hide and seek — the games we used to play as kids. They're just spending more time on cellphones. So as the environment changes, as parents, we have to change as well. And we have to prepare our kids for the environment we're going off to. So ultimately the goal for our camp is to create habits with your child so when they leave you no longer have to be the screen police."[5]

— *Susan Ladika*

[1] Steve Tellier, "7News Investigates Gets Exclusive Look Inside New Child Internet Addiction Center," 7News Boston, Feb. 26, 2018, https://tinyurl.com/y9qtnes2.

[2] "2015 Treatment Outcome Results," reSTART, 2015, https://tinyurl.com/ydhoncax.

[3] "Principles of Drug Addiction Treatment: A Research-Based Guide," National Institute on Drug Abuse, January 2018, https://tinyurl.com/hq62gk6.

[4] "Summer Camp for Gaming Overuse, Technology Overuse, and Co-occurring Issues," Summerland Camps, undated, https://tinyurl.com/yayjqhdd.

[5] Marcus Leshock and Mike Ewing, "Are We Addicted to Our Smartphones? Experts Weigh in," WGN, Feb. 19, 2018, https://tinyurl.com/y6twlhj7.

During an American Psychiatric Association meeting in 1996, Young presented "Internet Addiction: The Emergence of a New Clinical Disorder," in which she discussed the results of her interviews with people viewed as "dependent" and "non-dependent" on the internet.[76]

Only 17 percent of those rated as "dependent" had been online for a year or more, compared to 71 percent of those considered "non-dependent," Young said. That suggests that for some people internet addiction can develop "rather quickly from one's first introduction," she said. Those labeled as dependent spent nearly eight

times as many hours per week on the internet for pleasure as those considered non-dependent, she said.[77]

"Dependents gradually developed a daily Internet habit of up to ten times their initial use as their familiarity with the Internet increased," Young said, adding, "This may be likened to tolerance levels which develop among alcoholics who gradually increase their consumption of alcohol in order to achieve the desired effect."[78]

By the late 2000s and early 2010s, online gaming, which had moved to social media platforms and mobile devices as well as in-home consoles, was raising concerns about overuse.[79] A Pew Research Center study from

From Asia to Europe, Tech Addiction Is Raising Alarms

Online games are called "the new opium to poison the growth of teenagers."

Concerns about tech addiction are a global phenomenon — and so are efforts to deal with it. At least seven countries — Australia, China, India, Italy, Japan, South Korea and Taiwan — consider addiction to technology a disorder.[1]

In South Korea, about 10 percent of teens are considered addicted to the internet, according to surveys. To address the problem, the government has established roughly 200 treatment programs at counseling centers and hospitals. The government helped fuel internet addiction by promoting advances in mobile and other technology, said Shim Yong-chool, a director at the National Center for Youth Internet Addiction Treatment camp in Muju. "Now," he said, "the government is trying to help solve it."[2]

Yoon Yong-won, 18, had to turn in his smartphone when he was sent to the camp, where activities include hiking and stress-reduction classes. "I'm so frustrated. I feel like I'm being held captive," he said during his first day there. But Kim Sung-min, 14, said the camp was better than he thought it would be. "At home, I just used to play games," he said. "But here, we talk to each other."[3]

South Korea also passed the so-called Cinderella law, which prevents video gamers from logging onto the internet after midnight.[4]

In Japan, officials in 2013 began to establish internet "fasting camps," where internet addicts receive counseling and are barred from accessing technology. China, which in 2008 became the first country to recognize internet addiction as a disorder, has more than 300 treatment centers.[5]

Li Yan, who with her husband runs an internet addiction treatment camp in Huai'an, about 250 miles north of Shanghai, said solitude drives the problem. "They feel emptiness in their hearts," she said of technology addicts. "They can't live up to their parents' expectations. So they go to the internet cafe." Li's camp offers classes in ballet, music, stand-up comedy and other cultural skills.[6]

But as China tries to tackle tech addiction, some treatment centers have come under scrutiny.

Trent Bax, an assistant professor of sociology at Ewha Womans University in South Korea who has researched Chinese internet addiction centers, said they advertise "a quick-fix solution." Parents send their children "in response to a very real fear that [their] only child's successful future may never be realized because they refuse to stop gaming and start studying," he said. From the 1970s until 2015, the Chinese government allowed families to have only one child.[7]

Some centers have been accused of beating patients or conducting electroshock therapy on them. Last year, an 18-year-old man died while receiving treatment at an internet addiction "boot camp" in China. Authorities are investigating the incident, which left the man with multiple injuries and, according to his mother, covered with scars.[8]

Yu Xinwen, a vice president of Guangzhou University and delegate to the National Committee of the Chinese People's Political Consultative Conference, a government advisory council, wants China to develop a system to classify online games by appropriate age. "Some online games have become the new opium to poison the growth of teenagers," she said.[9]

Tencent, a Chinese internet service and video game company, plans to issue digital contracts so parents and their children can agree on an appropriate amount of game-playing time. Under the contracts, children could earn more playing time as a reward for doing chores or getting good grades.[10]

Inpatient treatment centers are less common in Europe than in Asia, but concerns about tech addition are no less prevalent. In December, French education officials announced they planned to ban the use of mobile phones during breaks in elementary and middle schools this fall, fulfilling a 2017 campaign pledge of President Emmanuel Macron. Since 2010 French students have been prohibited from using phones in elementary and middle school classrooms.[11]

"These days the children don't play at break time anymore; they are just all in front of their smartphones, and from an educational point of view, that's a problem," Education Minister Jean-Michel Blanquer said. He cited studies warning against screen time for children under age 7.[12]

"Together with school principals, teachers and parents, we need to find ways to protect our children from spending hours on their cellphones," Blanquer said.[13]

But the proposed ban has skeptics. "Can you imagine school supervisors having to check the pockets of about 400 students every morning?" said Valérie Sipahimalani, a spokeswoman for the National Union of Secondary School Teachers. The measure will be impossible to enforce, she said.[14]

Some French parents oppose the proposed ban as excessive and instead advise teaching students how to moderate their phone use. "Cellphones are tools, and it's their excessive use that poses problems," said Gerard Pommier, head of the Federation of Parents in State Schools.[15]

France also has proposed requiring parental permission for children under 16 to open an account on social media sites such as Facebook, Snapchat or Instagram. The three companies require subscribers to be at least 13 years old to open an account.[16]

In Italy, which hosted the First International Congress on Internet Addiction Disorders in 2014, officials rescinded a ban on cellphones in schools in 2016. Education Minister Valeria Fedeli said the phones "are an extraordinary tool to facilitate learning."[17]

— *Susan Ladika*

Shinsei Noguchi, a gamer known as Mayo, plays "Splatoon" at a gaming competition in Chiba, Japan, on Feb. 10, 2018. Japan is among at least seven countries that consider addiction to technology a mental health disorder.

[1] Barbara Booth, "Apple Urged to Take Action on Smartphone Addiction Some Call 'Digital Heroin,' " CNBC, Jan. 8, 2018, https://tinyurl.com/y8ls9bfb.

[2] *Ibid.*; Anna Fifield, "In South Korea, a Rehab Camp for Internet-Addicted Teenagers," *The Washington Post*, Jan. 24, 2018, https://tinyurl.com/yboeo9hw.

[3] Booth, *op. cit.*; Fifield, *ibid.*

[4] Fifield, *ibid.*

[5] Booth, *op. cit.*

[6] Tom Phillips, "'Electronic Heroin': China's Boot Camps Get Tough on Internet Addicts," *The Guardian*, Aug. 28, 2017, https://tinyurl.com/ybs8erk3.

[7] "Teen's Death at Chinese Internet Addiction Camp Sparks Anger," BBC News, Aug. 14, 2017, https://tinyurl.com/ybpyo288; Chris Buckley, "China Ends One-Child Policy, Allowing Families Two

Children," *The New York Times*, Oct. 29, 2015, https://tinyurl.com/jbv8a53.

[8] "Teen's Death at Chinese Internet Addiction Camp Sparks Anger," *op. cit.*

[9] Alyssa Abkowitz, "Tencent to Introduce Video Game Contracts for Parents and Children," *Morningstar*, March 3, 2018, https://tinyurl.com/yb4fa39f.

[10] Brian Crecente, "Massive Game Publisher Rolling Out Digital Contracts to Help Limit Kids' Gameplay," *Rolling Stone*, March 5, 2018, https://tinyurl.com/yanlpk7p.

[11] Jenny Anderson, "France is banning mobile phones in schools," *Quartz*, Dec. 11, 2017, https://tinyurl.com/ychboj79; Paul Pradier, "France to Ban Mobile Phones in Primary, Middle Schools Starting in September 2018," ABC News, Dec. 13, 2017, https://tinyurl.com/yauew9au.

[12] Laurel Wamsley, France Moves to Ban Students from Using Cellphones in School," NPR, Dec. 12, 2017, https://tinyurl.com/yatdtcec.

[13] *Ibid.*

[14] Pradier, *op. cit.*

[15] Alice Tidey, "France Grapples with whether to Ban Cellphones in Schools," NBC News, Jan. 14, 2018, https://tinyurl.com/ybhdsab9.

[16] Harriet Agnew, "France Takes Phones Away From Tech-Addicted Teenagers," *The Financial Times*, Dec. 15, 2017, https://tinyurl.com/y9vlk2oo.

[17] Tidey, *op. cit.*; Christie Barakat, "Internet Addiction Around the World," *Adweek*, June 16, 2014, https://tinyurl.com/ybvddaz3.

Some addiction specialists say the obsessive use of technology, including virtual reality headsets, above, can affect the brain in the same way an overdependence on alcohol or drugs does. Others say tech overuse is not an addiction in the medical sense but rather a manifestation of underlying conditions such as anxiety or depression.

2015 found almost 60 percent of teen-age girls and 84 percent of teen-age boys played video games online.[80]

Another Pew study from that same year found that half of U.S. adults played video games, and 10 percent considered themselves "gamers." But gaming was much higher among younger adults. More than three-quarters of men between the ages of 18 and 29, played video games, and one-third consider themselves "gamers." In comparison, 57 percent of women in that age range played video games, and just 9 percent considered themselves to be gamers.[81]

Similar concerns have been raised about people who obsessively view online pornography. Some social scientists, feminists and anti-porn groups say pornography's evolution from a subscription-based or pay-per-view system to a ubiquitous, largely free online commodity has created a public health crisis, undermining male-female relations and "normalizing" sexual violence against women. They also worry that because porn is now easily accessible to users of any age, children as young as 11 are learning about sex by viewing explicit, often violent, sex scenes.[82]

In recent years, experts have voiced concerns about the age at which children are being exposed to screens. In 2016, the American Academy of Pediatrics recommended that children under the age of 18 months not

have screen time, except for video chats. Tots between 18 and 24 months can be introduced to high-quality programming on digital media, the academy said, and for those between the ages of 2 and 5, screen time should be limited to one hour per day.[83]

Even after the age of 24 months, screen time should not "take the place of face-to-face interaction," says Yolanda S. (Linda) Reid-Chassiakos, an assistant professor of pediatrics at the University of California, Los Angeles and director of the Student Health Center at California State University Northridge. "There's some research that kids learn more effectively in 3D than 2D and retain information longer," she says. "But if you're going to use media, use good media."

Power of Addiction

For decades after research on addictive behavior began in the 1930s, researchers thought addicts lacked willpower or were morally flawed. Many believed that those not strong enough to break their habit should be punished.[84]

Alcoholism was recognized as a disease by the American Medical Association in 1956. The American Psychiatric Association's early versions of the *DSM* required a person to exhibit increased tolerance for alcohol or a drug and withdrawal symptoms before being diagnosed with dependence. The *DSM-IV*, published in 1994, included a loss of control and the failure to abstain even when the substance abuse was causing problems in a user's life.[85]

Researchers now define addiction as a chronic disease that changes the brain structure and function. Researchers also believe activities such as gambling and shopping, considered behavioral addictions, can impact the brain. The brain recognizes all pleasures by releasing the neurotransmitter dopamine in the nucleus accumbens, made up of nerve cells under the cerebral cortex. Substances ranging from nicotine to methamphetamines release extremely powerful surges of dopamine.

But after a while, as tolerance to addictive drugs and behaviors develop, the brain produces less dopamine, and people need more of a substance to get the same "high." The memory of the pleasurable results can lead to intense cravings.

Genetics also come into play: Research has shown that about 40 percent to 60 percent of those who are susceptible to addiction inherited the tendency.[86]

CURRENT SITUATION

Gaming Addiction

While experts have yet to define technology overuse as an addiction, internet gaming disorder could be included in future versions of the American Psychiatric Association's *Diagnostic and Statistical Manual of Mental Disorders*. The APA's decision on whether gaming is a disorder will depend, at least in part, on the results of the NIH study, expected to be completed in 2019.

In discussing internet gaming, the APA has said: "The 'gamers' play compulsively, to the exclusion of other interests, and their persistent and recurrent online activity results in clinically significant impairment or distress." Behaviors that would be considered in making such a diagnosis include: preoccupation with internet games; withdrawal symptoms when not playing; buildup of tolerance so more time is spent playing games; loss of interest in other activities; and putting relationships or opportunities at risk because of gaming.[87]

The World Health Organization's definition of a gaming disorder includes impaired control over gaming, increasing priority for gaming over other activities and continued gaming despite negative consequences.[88]

So far, most of the studies on online gaming have focused on males in Asian countries. "The studies suggest that when these individuals are engrossed in Internet games, certain pathways in their brains are triggered in the same direct and intense way that a drug addict's brain is affected by a particular substance," the APA said in 2013. Gaming prompts a neurological response "that influences feelings of pleasure and reward, and the result, in the extreme, is manifested as addictive behavior."[89]

A 2017 study in *The American Journal of Psychiatry* examined data on almost 19,000 online gamers from the United States, Canada, the United Kingdom and Germany and found just 0.3 percent to 1 percent might qualify for a diagnosis of internet gaming disorder.[90] That "suggests that video game addiction might be a real thing, but it is not the epidemic that some have made it out to be," wrote Stetson University's Ferguson and Patrick Markey, a psychology professor at Villanova University, in a joint commentary on the study.[91]

"It's less clear — did games do this, or is there something about the person that makes it hard for them to regulate these things," Ferguson says. "In most cases, tech addicts had an underlying mental health problem. Tech is a way to self-medicate. Games didn't really do it."

Reducing Tech Overuse

The potential link between technology overuse and children's mental health has been the subject of particular scrutiny.

According to Jean Twenge, a psychology professor at San Diego State University, teens who spend the most time looking at screens are more likely to report symptoms of depression. Eighth-graders who use social media heavily increase their risk of depression by 27 percent. Teens who spent three hours or more on an electronic device are more likely to have a risk factor for suicide, such as making a suicide plan.[92]

Social media "exacerbate the age-old teen concern about being left out," said Twenge, author of *iGen: Why Today's Super-Connected Kids Are Growing Up Less Rebellious, More Tolerant, Less Happy — and Completely Unprepared for Adulthood — and What That Means for the Rest of Us.* "Today's teens may go to fewer parties and spend less time together in person, but when they do congregate, they document their hangouts relentlessly — on Snapchat, Instagram, Facebook. Those not invited to come along are keenly aware of it."[93]

However, research is needed on the link between technology and mental health. "What causes what? Is it that screen time leads to unhappiness or unhappiness leads to screen time?" Twenge asked.[94]

Harvard's Rich says parents should "introduce a smartphone to a child in much the same way they would introduce a power saw to a child — when it's needed and they can use it responsibly."

Concerns about tech overuse have spread outside the tech and research communities. In January, the California State Teachers' Retirement System and the investment firm JANA Partners LLC, both Apple shareholders, wrote to Apple urging it to develop tools to help parents control children's iPhone use. The letter, which Rich helped craft, states that the average American teenager spends 4.5 hours a day on his phone, excluding texting and talking, and half of teens say they feel "addicted" to their phone.

"It would defy common sense to argue that this level of usage, by children whose brains are still developing, is not having at least some impact, or that the maker of such a powerful product has no role to play in helping

Is 'technology addiction' a valid diagnosis?

YES   Robert H. Lustig, M.D., M.S.L.
Emeritus Professor, Division of Pediatric Endocrinology, University of California, San Francisco

Written for *CQ Researcher*, April 2018

An apocryphal story: It's 1955, and the Yankees' Yogi Berra is at the plate. The pitch arrives; Berra takes. The umpire doesn't react. The catcher yells, "Well, is it a ball or a strike?" The ump says, "Ain't nothin' till I call it."

The American Psychiatric Association (APA) has been the umpire of U.S. addiction. In 1993, its *Diagnostic and Statistical Manual* (DSM)-IV listed "substance use disorder" as requiring two criteria for addiction: tolerance (decreased sensitivity to a substance in the "reward center" of the brain); and withdrawal (measurable physiological symptoms and signs of abstinence due to the systemic effects of these drugs). Most if not all recreational drugs, including cocaine, opioids, nicotine, alcohol and caffeine, exhibited both. Under this rubric, behaviors that lacked withdrawal because they did not exert systemic physiologic effects could not be labeled as addictive.

However, as public health difficulties stemming from behavioral addictions grew, the APA expanded the definition of addiction to include "behavioral addictions," characterized by nine criteria: craving or a strong desire to use; recurrent use resulting in a failure to fulfill major role obligations; recurrent use in physically hazardous situations (e.g. driving); use despite social or interpersonal problems caused or exacerbated by use; taking the substance or engaging in the behavior in larger amounts or over a longer period than intended; attempts to quit or cut down; time spent seeking or recovering from use; interference with life activities; and use despite negative consequences.

Under this new rubric, gambling is now labeled an addiction in order to provide clinical services. But despite an extensive literature and similar criteria, the APA relegated "Internet Gaming Disorder" to the DSM appendix as "requiring further study." And because the APA couldn't come up with universally accepted diagnostic criteria, it refused to label social media or pornography as addictions.

Nonetheless, we have empirical brain-scan data for all of these. Perhaps not surprisingly, the World Health Organization (WHO) has added the following behavioral addictions to the next International Classification of Diseases, due out this year: gambling disorder, gaming disorder and other specified or unspecified disorders "due to addictive behaviors."

So, which umpire do you want for your game: one who calls balls and strikes as he sees them, or one who sits on the call and can't make up his mind?

NO   Christopher Ferguson
Professor of Psychology, Stetson University

Written for *CQ Researcher*, April 2018

There is little question that a small percentage of individuals, likely 1 percent or less, overuse technology. But it is less clear that this is due to an addiction in the same sense as over-dependence on alcohol, nicotine or illicit drugs.

Technology use doesn't have the same biochemical processes as substance use, and there are no clear parallels to the tolerance (needing more to get the same high) and withdrawal (physiological symptoms that result from stopping use) typical of substance abuse. Some scholars have tried to find ways to make tolerance and withdrawal fit into conceptualizations of technology misuse, but these don't seem to work well.

One misunderstanding arises from the observation that technology use activates some of the same dopaminergic centers of the brain involved with pleasure as does substance abuse. However, these centers are involved in anything fun, so finding that a fun activity (whether technology use, exercising, eating a candy bar, getting an "A" on a test, etc.) activates these areas, just as cocaine and methamphetamine do, is hardly surprising. These are, in fact, natural processes.

However, illicit substances such as methamphetamine activate these centers to a much greater degree than do normal activities such as technology or exercise. That is what makes these substances dangerous, a detail often left out of these discussions.

Although groups such as the American Psychiatric Association and World Health Organization have proposed technology addiction diagnoses, these have been controversial, with many scholars opposed to such classifications. This is because current evidence suggests these are not unique disorders but rather arise as symptoms of underlying mental health problems, such as depression or attention problems.

Nor is there evidence that technology is uniquely addictive, as other research has focused on everything from exercise to dance addictions. Finally, evidence is clear that on most behavioral indices, youths today are actually pretty healthy. No evidence has emerged to suggest an epidemic of tech-addicted youths.

Every generation of older adults tends to freak out about new technology and exaggerate its potential harms. This is something we understand as "moral panic theory." In the 1950s the fear was centered on comic books; in the 1980s, rock music and the game "Dungeons and Dragons."

Current concerns about technology addiction, given the evidence, are better understood as a new moral panic rather than a legitimate concern supported by data.

parents to ensure it is being used optimally," the letter said. "It is also no secret that social media sites and applications, for which the iPhone and iPad are a primary gateway, are usually designed to be as addictive and time-consuming as possible, as many of their original creators have publicly acknowledged."

The letter called on Apple to offer new tools for parents to limit screen time to age-appropriate levels for their children. "Apple can play a defining role in signaling to the industry that paying special attention to the health and development of the next generation is both good business and the right thing to do," the letter said.[95]

Apple spokesman Ted Miller cited a company statement that said Apple devices give parents "the ability to control and restrict content including apps, movies, websites, songs and books, as well as cellular data, password settings and other features. Effectively, anything a child could download or access online can be easily blocked or restricted by a parent."

The company also recently launched a new Families page, which pulls all of the company's parental controls together in one place. It enables parents to approve or reject app purchases, limit content on their children's devices and restrict their browsing to pre-approved websites.[96]

A group of concerned parents organized a movement last year — called Wait Until 8th — which asks parents to sign a pledge not to give their child a smartphone until he or she is in the eighth grade.[97]

Child development experts, health advocacy groups, educators and others also have written to Facebook CEO Zuckerberg, urging him to shut down the controversial Messenger Kids app, which is designed for children between the ages of 6 and 12. "Younger kids are simply not ready to have social media accounts," according to the letter. "At a time when there is mounting concern about how social media use affects adolescents' well-being, it is particularly irresponsible to encourage children as young as preschoolers to start using a Facebook product."[98]

Facebook's spokesperson Davis responded that the company had worked with child health experts to make the app as safe as possible.

Some companies are taking a different tack. The Brooklyn-based company Light is introducing a sleek new "dumb phone," which allows people only to call, message and get directions. The phones cost $250.[99]

Other companies are rolling out apps designed to help consumers limit or monitor their phone use. Gaming expert Zichermann, for example, developed the app Onward, which lets individuals set limits on phone features that might be addictive, such as those for gaming, pornography and shopping. In a study of about 2,500 pornography users, he says, Onward helped almost 90 percent reduce their use, and nearly 50 percent said it stopped their addiction.

Zichermann calls it a "bottom up" approach, rather than having others impose limits. "It's not possible to build something to give everyone what they need to help them," he says. "We can only really help people that want help."

OUTLOOK
A Growing Problem

Given the dearth of research on tech addiction, and the lack of a clear definition of the problem, experts are hoping for more clarity and consensus in the coming years. The APA and WHO "don't even agree on how to conceptualize this thing," says Stetson's Ferguson.

Randomized, controlled trials are needed to determine the links between technology and its effects. "That's where longitudinal studies come in," said Twenge, of San Diego State University.[100]

Harvard's Rich has helped to establish the Clinic for Interactive Media and Internet Disorders (CIMAID) in Boston, which he hopes will present a clearer path forward in treating kids who he says display "problematic interactive internet usage." Because CIMAID is located at an academic research center (Boston Children's Hospital), Rich says the focus will be on collecting data on treatment outcomes, which he says is lacking at many other treatment centers. Such information can be used to determine the best course of treatment for the disorder.

While treatment facilities are springing up around the country, cost can be an obstacle for treatment because it is not covered by insurance. Health insurers rely on the *DSM* when determining which conditions to cover, University of Southern California pediatrician Lustig says. Historically, the *DSM* is seldom updated, a process that typically takes more than a dozen years, although the APA said it can make incremental updates as new medical breakthroughs occur.[101]

Lustig says he is concerned that it will take years before the APA recognizes internet addiction as an official disorder. "It's a big deal when the *DSM* comes out," he says. "It determines if insurers will pay."

Gaming specialist Zichermann says the government should require health insurers to cover treatment for tech addiction. But he does not think the government can rein in the proliferation of such addictions. With artificial intelligence and algorithms designed to keep people coming back to their smartphones and computers, he says, "even the engineers who craft these things don't understand how it's working."

Rosen, of California State University, says rather than the government, it's up to tech companies to address the concerns. "They're responsible for figuring out ways to not get you sucked in. I don't see a government role in this," he says. "I see this as a very large social responsibility issue" for the companies.

Columbia University Law School professor of communications law Tim Wu said the tech world needs "to designate the deliberate engineering of addiction as an unethical practice. More broadly, we need to get back to rewarding firms that build technologies that augment humanity and help us do what we want, as opposed to taking our time for themselves."[102]

Lustig expects the problem to get worse as today's youngsters grow up. "This is an existential crisis because tech is not going away."

Bracke, the 29-year-old gamer who is in recovery, agrees the problem will get worse. In his volunteer work in 12-step groups and at the reSTART rehab program, most of the gamers are much younger than he is and grew up with the internet.

When he was very young, Bracke remembers, there was no internet in his home. For those growing up now, he says, "they don't have any concept of life without it and what a normal life is."

NOTES

1. Anya Kamenetz, "Screen Addiction Among Teens: Is There Such a Thing?" NPR, Feb. 5, 2018, https://tinyurl.com/y7z95v6b.

2. Jenny Anderson, " 'It's Not a Drug, but It May as Well Be,': Expert Opinions on Whether Kids Are Addicted to Tech," *Quartz*, Feb. 9, 2018, https://tinyurl.com/y9smeswu.

3. Stephanie A. Sarkis, "Internet Gaming Disorder in DSM-5," *Psychology Today*, July 18, 2014, https://tinyurl.com/y9kkus5j.

4. "Public Health Implications of Excessive Use of the Internet and other Communication and Gaming Platforms," World Health Organization, March 2018, https://tinyurl.com/ybl239lx.

5. Center for Humane Technology, undated, http://humanetech.com/.

6. "Open Letter from JANA Partners and CALSTRS to Apple Inc.," JANA Partners LLC, Jan. 6, 2018, https://tinyurl.com/ychlreby.

7. "Overload: How Technology Is Bringing Us Too Much Information," CBS News, April 1, 2018, https://tinyurl.com/y7yg9skz.

8. "Common Sense Media/Survey Monkey YouTube Poll Topline," Common Sense Media, undated, https://tinyurl.com/y8thpppm.

9. Sara Ashley O'Brien, "Silicon Valley Employees Launch Campaign to Combat Tech Addiction," CNN.com, Feb. 6, 2018, https://tinyurl.com/yblxphaf.

10. Kathleen Davis, "Sorry, Silicon Valley Won't Save Your Kids from Tech Addiction," *Fast Company*, March 26, 2018, https://tinyurl.com/y7jjhykg; "Survey: Parents Are More Worried about Tech Addiction than Online Predators," *Fast Company*, March 26, 2018, https://tinyurl.com/ya4kaw4j.

11. *Ibid.*

12. *Ibid.*

13. Barbara Booth, "Internet Addiction is Sweeping America, Affecting Millions," CNBC, Aug. 29, 2017, https://tinyurl.com/y89y5yz5.

14. Harriet Agnew, "France Takes Phones away from Tech-Addicted Teenagers," *Financial Times*, Dec. 15, 2017, https://tinyurl.com/y9vlk2oo.

15. "How Addiction Hijacks the Brain," *Harvard Health Publishing*, July 2011, https://tinyurl.com/yb7fo7e9.

16. Angie Marcos, "Are You Addicted to Your Smartphone?" California State University, April 26, 2017, https://tinyurl.com/ya65ka5b.

17. "Teen Technology Addiction," Hazelden Betty Ford Foundation, undated, https://tinyurl.com/y8degrx9.

18. Dennis Thompson, "Does 'Smartphone Addiction' Show up in Teens' Brains," CBS News, Dec. 4, 2017, https://tinyurl.com/y832smtb; Booth, *op. cit.*; "Smartphone Addiction Creates Imbalance in the Brain, Study Suggests," *Science Daily*, Nov. 30, 2017, https://tinyurl.com/ydhfc2nh.

19. A. Pawlowski, "Kids Who Are Addicted to Smartphones May Have an Imbalance of the Brain," *Today*, Nov. 30, 2017, https://tinyurl.com/y7mbuh2a.

20. Sandee LaMotte, "Smartphone addiction could be changing your brain," CNN, Dec. 1, 2017, https://tinyurl.com/yc2j9fo6.

21. Lesley McClurg, "Is 'Internet Addiction' Real?" NPR, May 18, 2017, https://tinyurl.com/y8qm-jngh.

22. Robbie Gonzalez, "It's Time for a Serious Talk about the Science of Tech 'Addiction,' " *Wired*, Feb. 1, 2018, https://tinyurl.com/y9ernkpy.

23. "Internet Gaming Disorder," American Psychiatric Association, 2013, https://tinyurl.com/ydfl4g9l.

24. "Gaming Disorder," World Health Organization, January 2018, https://tinyurl.com/y9byw2ze.

25. Blake Hester, "Academics Rebuke World Health Organization's Video Game Addiction Classification," *Rolling Stone*, March 1, 2018, https://tinyurl.com/yaop4aag.

26. Booth, *op. cit.*

27. Anderson Cooper, "What is 'Brain Hacking?' Tech Insiders on Why You Should Care," 60 Minutes, June 11, 2017, https://tinyurl.com/y8aubrdx.

28. *Ibid.*

29. Adam Alter, "Tech bigwigs know how addictive their products are. Why don't the rest of us?" *Wired*, March 24, 2017, https://tinyurl.com/lkms2hy.

30. Cooper, *op. cit.*

31. *Ibid.*

32. *Ibid.*

33. Noah Kulwin, "Facebook is a Fundamentally Addictive Product," *New York*, April 10, 2018, https://tinyurl.com/y9lpmxsq.

34. Mike Allen, "Sean Parker Unloads on Facebook: 'God Only Knows What It's Doing to Our Children's Brains," *Axios*, Nov. 9, 2017, https://tinyurl.com/ychmh478.

35. "What is Facebook Doing to Address Tech Addiction," CBS News, Feb. 6, 2018, https://tinyurl.com/y85wb96s.

36. Steve Kovach, "We Don't Need Tech to Become Less Addictive — We Just Need it to be Better," *Business Insider*, Jan. 21, 2018, https://tinyurl.com/ya9op7vp.

37. Paul Lewis, "Our Minds Can Be Hijacked: The Tech Insiders Who Fear a Smartphone Dystopia," *The Guardian*, Oct. 6, 2017, https://tinyurl.com/ycaqv9ad.

38. *Ibid.*

39. Jack Corrigan, "Lawmakers Want to Curb Big Tech's Influence on Kids," Nextgov, Feb. 8, 2018, https://tinyurl.com/yacjg46w; David Morgan, " 'Truth about Tech' Campaign Takes on Tech Addiction," CBS News, Feb. 5, 2018, https://tinyurl.com/y8ggr9up.

40. Ed Markey, Twitter, Feb. 7, 2018, https://tinyurl.com/ydyxjgms.

41. David McCabe, "Top Democrat Sees Evidence that Tech Can Become Addictive," *Axios*, Feb. 7, 2018, https://tinyurl.com/ydgd3pl8.

42. Cecilia Kang, Nicholas Fandos and Mike Isaac, "Tech Executives Are Contrite, about Election Meddling, but Make Few Promises on Capitol Hill," *The New York Times*, Oct. 31, 2017, https://tinyurl.com/ybgly8sq.

43. Tiffany Hsu and Cecilia Kang, "Demands Grow for Facebook to Explain its Privacy Policies," *The New York Times*, March 26, 2018, https://tinyurl.com/y92m7d7r.

44. Jena McGregor, "Facebook CEO Mark Zuckerberg Has Apologized — Again," *The Washington Post*, April 11, 2018, https://tinyurl.com/ybnbqm6w.

45. Todd Spangler, "Hooked on Hardware? Tech Giants Face Tough Questions over Device Addiction," *Variety*, 2018, https://tinyurl.com/y8pmr9pf.

46. "Common Sense Partners with the Center for Humane Technology; Announces 'Truth About Tech' Campaign in Response to Escalating Concerns about Digital Addiction," Common Sense Media, Feb. 5, 2018, https://tinyurl.com/y7eop3yp.

47. Nellie Bowles, "Early Facebook and Google Employees Form Coalition to Fight What They Built," *The New York Times*, Feb. 4, 2018, https://tinyurl.com/yal47zde; "Public Service Campaigns," Common Sense Media, undated, https://tinyurl.com/yapkqpoy.

48. Anita Balakrishnan, "Facebook Should Be Regulated Like a Cigarette Company," Says Salesforce CEO, CNBC.com, Jan. 23, 2018, https://tinyurl.com/y7cxrxur.

49. Vaughan Bell, "Don't Touch that Dial," *Slate*, Feb. 15, 2010, https://tinyurl.com/bbraumc.

50. *Ibid.*

51. Spangler, *op. cit.*

52. Daniel Goleman, "How Viewers Grow Addicted to Television," *The New York Times*, Oct. 16, 1990, https://tinyurl.com/yc7g2l8y.

53. "Invention of the PC," History, undated, https://tinyurl.com/yan3qmd2.

54. *Ibid.* "Home Computers and Internet Use in the United States: August 2000," U.S. Census Bureau, September 2001, https://tinyurl.com/y8o6sza5.

55. Kenneth Olmstead, "A Third of Americans Live in a Household with Three or More Smartphones," Pew Research Center, May 25, 2017, https://tinyurl.com/y94s8re5.

56. Robert S. Davidson and Page B. Walley, "Computer Fear and Addiction," *Journal of Organizational Behavior Management*, 1985, https://tinyurl.com/ycl2qzmu.

57. "Complying with COPPA: Frequently Asked Questions," Federal Trade Commission, March 20, 2015, https://tinyurl.com/y7rmg6sp.

58. "What Age Should My Kids Be Before I Let Them Use Instagram, Facebook and Other Social Media Services," Common Sense Media, undated, https://tinyurl.com/kw32dkw.

59. For background, see Alicia Ault, "Video Games and Learning," *CQ Researcher*, Feb. 12, 2016, pp. 145-168.

60. "2017 Sales, Demographic and Data Usage. Essential Facts about the Computer and Video Game Industry," Entertainment Software Association, April 2017, https://tinyurl.com/ybnm8b7h. Also see "Top Ten Best-Selling Games of All Time," MoGi Group Entertainment, undated, https://tinyurl.com/yb2t42jx.

61. Steven Tweedie, "The World's First Smartphone, Simon, Was Created 15 Years Before the iPhone," *Business Insider*, June 14, 2015, https://tinyurl.com/j6shk89.

62. Aaron Smith, "Smartphone Adoption and Usage," Pew Research Center, July 11, 2011, https://tinyurl.com/kmosrbu; Amanda Lenhart, "Cell phone ownership," Pew Research Center, March 19, 2012, https://tinyurl.com/yb4d9uww.

63. Olmstead, *op. cit.*

64. Amanda Lenhart, "Teens, Social Media & Technology Overview 2015," Pew Research Center, April 9, 2015, https://tinyurl.com/mrf2cxw.

65. "Kids & Tech: The Evolution of Today's Digital Natives," Influence Central, undated, https://tinyurl.com/ybo9c4of.

66. "The History of Social Media: Social Networking Evolution," History Cooperative, undated, accessed April 2, 2018, https://tinyurl.com/hvxfglp.

67. "Then and Now: A History of Social Networking Sites," CBS News, undated, https://tinyurl.com/y8kqbksz.

68. Matt Weinberger, "33 Photos of Facebook's Rise from a Harvard Dorm Room to World Domination," *Business Insider*, Sept. 7, 2017, https://tinyurl.com/jhpt548.

69. Amanda MacArthur, "The Real History of Twitter, in Brief," *Lifewire*, Nov. 7, 2017, https://tinyurl.com/ycnv9ozq; Raisa Bruner, "A Brief History of Instagram's Fateful First Day," *Time*, July 16, 2016, https://tinyurl.com/ycnv9ozq; Mark Molloy, "Who Owns Snapchat and When Was it Created?" *The Telegraph*, July 25, 2017, https://tinyurl.com/ya6ntuo9.

70. Lenhart, "Teens, Social Media & Technology Overview 2015," *op. cit.*

71. "Kids & Tech: The Evolution of Today's Digital Natives," *op. cit.*

72. Adrienne LaFrance, "When People Feared Computers," *The Atlantic*, March 30, 2015, https://tinyurl.com/yb9myese.

73. Bell, *op. cit.*

74. Harvey Schachter, "Click Till You're Sick: The Growing Problem of Internet Addiction," *The Globe and Mail*, March 26, 2017, https://tinyurl.com/ydxbwfaz.

75. "About Us," Net Addiction, undated, https://tinyurl.com/ydel8e6n.

76. Kimberly S. Young, "Internet Addiction: The Emergence of a New Clinical Disorder," paper presented at the American Psychological Association meeting, Aug. 15, 1996, https://tinyurl.com/ycgntrxo.

77. *Ibid.*

78. *Ibid.*

79. "Video Game History," History, undated, https://www.history.com/topics/history-of-video-games.

80. Lenhart, "Teens, Social Media & Technology Overview 2015," *op. cit.*

81. Maeve Duggan, "Gaming and Gamers," Pew Research Center, Dec. 15, 2015, https://tinyurl.com/qdva6xf.

82. For background, see Sarah Glazer, "Pornography," *CQ Researcher*, Oct. 21, 2016, pp. 865-888.

83. "American Academy of Pediatrics Announces New Recommendations for Children's Media Use," American Academy of Pediatrics, Oct. 21, 2016, https://tinyurl.com/jcyoong.

84. "How Addiction Hijacks the Brain," *op. cit.*

85. David J. Mersy, "Recognition of Alcohol and Substance Abuse," *American Family Physician*, April 1, 2003, https://tinyurl.com/y7vvahy2.

86. "How Addiction Hijacks the Brain," *op. cit.*

87. Sarkis, *op. cit.*

88. "Gaming Disorder," World Health Organization, *op. cit.*

89. "Internet Gaming Disorder," *op. cit.*

90. Andrew K. Przybylski, Netta Weinstein and Kou Murayama, "Internet Gaming Disorder: Investigating the Clinical Relevance of a New Phenomenon," *The American Journal of Psychiatry*, March 1, 2017, https://tinyurl.com/y7bylhse.

91. Patrick M. Markey and Christopher J. Ferguson, "Internet Gaming Addiction: Disorder or Moral Panic," *The American Journal of Psychiatry*, March 1, 2017, https://tinyurl.com/yc9mcl7g.

92. Jean M. Twenge, "Have Smartphones Destroyed a Generation?" *The Atlantic*, September 2017, https://tinyurl.com/yacrkvtu.

93. *Ibid.*

94. Gonzalez, *op. cit.*

95. "Open Letter from JANA Partners and CALSTRS to Apple Inc.," *op. cit.*

96. "You Want to Do What's Best for Your Family. So Do We," Apple, undated, https://tinyurl.com/yba4wb8n.

97. "We Empower Parents to Say Yes to Waiting for a Smartphone," Wait Until 8th, https://www.wait-until8th.org/.

98. Natt Garun, "Facebook Should Shut Dow Messenger Kids, Child Advocates Say," *The Verge*, Jan. 30, 2018, https://tinyurl.com/y7xmfm4h.

99. Avery Hartmans, "This Beautifully Designed 'Dumb Phone' Can Only Make Calls and Send Texts — and It Might be the Key to Curing Our Addiction to Apps," *Business Insider*, March 1, 2018, https://tinyurl.com/ybyywz6z.

100. Gonzalez, *op. cit.*

101. "DSM History," American Psychiatric Association, undated, https://tinyurl.com/y9vcv6nj; "DSM-5: Frequently Asked Questions," American Psychiatric Association, undated, https://tinyurl.com/hgcyzov.

102. Tim Wu, "Subtle and insidious, technology is designed to addict us," *The Washington Post*, March 2, 2017, https://tinyurl.com/y9rlyw63.

BIBLIOGRAPHY
Selected Sources
Books

Alter, Adam, *Irresistible: The Rise of Addictive Technology and the Business of Keeping Us Hooked*, Penguin Books, 2017.
A psychology and marketing professor at New York University examines the rise of behavioral addictions.

Gazzaley, Adam, and Larry Rosen, *The Distracted Mind: Ancient Brains in a High-Tech World*, MIT Press, 2016.
Human brains have a limited ability to pay attention, making people vulnerable to technology-related interruptions, according to a professor in the neurology, physiology and psychiatry departments at the University of California, San Francisco (Gazzaley) and a professor emeritus of psychology at California State University, Dominguez Hills (Rosen).

Lustig, Robert, *The Hacking of the American Mind*, Avery, 2017.
A professor of pediatrics at the University of California, San Francisco, examines how technology and other addictive pleasures affect brains and physical and psychological health.

Twenge, Jean M., *iGen: Why Today's Super-Connected Kids are Growing Up Less Rebellious, More Tolerant, Less Happy — and Completely Unprepared for Adulthood — and What that Means for the Rest of Us*, Simon & Schuster, 2017.
A psychology professor at San Diego State University argues that those born in the mid-1990s or later, the first generation to spend their entire adolescence with smartphones, are different from their predecessors.

Articles

"How Addiction Hijacks the Brain," Harvard Health Publishing, July 2011, https://tinyurl.com/yb7fo7e9.
A Harvard Medical School article explains the impact of addiction on the brain.

"Smartphone Addiction Creates Imbalance in the Brain, Study Suggests," *Science Daily*, Nov. 30, 2017, https://tinyurl.com/ydhfc2nh.
South Korean researchers present evidence that technology can affect the brain in ways similar to other addictions.

Anderson, Jenny, " 'It's not a drug, but it may as well be': Expert opinions on whether kids are addicted to tech," *Quartz*, Feb. 9, 2018, https://tinyurl.com/y9smeswu.
Experts discuss tech addiction at a conference sponsored by Common Sense Media and the Center for Humane Technology.

Cooper, Anderson, "What is 'Brain Hacking?' Tech Insiders on Why You Should Care," "60 Minutes," CBS News, June 11, 2017, https://tinyurl.com/y8aubrdx.
Tech company insiders explain how companies get consumers hooked on technology and the impact that has on individuals.

Davis, Kathleen, "Sorry, Silicon Valley Won't Save Your Kids from Tech Addiction," *Fast Company*, March 26, 2018, https://tinyurl.com/y7jjhykg.
Parents describe their concerns about their children's use of technology.

Fifield, Anna, "In South Korea, a Rehab Camp for Internet-Addicted Teenagers," *The Washington Post*, Jan. 24, 2018, https://tinyurl.com/yboeo9hw.
A reporter looks inside a camp in South Korea designed to rehabilitate teens addicted to technology.

Gonzalez, Robbie, "It's Time for a Serious Talk about the Science of Tech 'Addiction,' " *Wired*, Feb. 1, 2018, https://tinyurl.com/y9ernkpy.
Experts discuss tech addiction and the limitations of scientific research on the issue.

Kamenetz, Anya, "Screen Addiction Among Teens: Is There Such a Thing?" NPR, Feb. 5, 2018, https://tinyurl.com/y7z95v6b.
A journalist discusses the views of the American Psychiatric Association, World Health Organization and other researchers on whether to classify tech addiction as a disorder.

Reports and Studies

Argyriou, Evangelia, Christopher B. Davison and Tayla T.C. Lee, "Response Inhibition and Internet Gaming Disorder: A Meta-analysis," *Addictive Behaviors*, August 2017, https://tinyurl.com/yb8rf99k.
Researchers find a link between internet gaming disorder and impaired inhibition among participants.

Olmstead, Kenneth, "A Third of Americans Live in a Household with Three or More Smartphones," Pew Research Center, May 25, 2017, https://tinyurl.com/y94s8re5.
Nearly 85 percent of Americans live in a home with at least one cellphone, and cellphone ownership outpaces landline ownership.

Twenge, Jean M., Thomas E. Joiner and Megan L. Rogers, "Increases in Depressive Symptoms, Suicide-Related Outcomes and Suicide Rates Among U.S. Adolescents after 2010 and Links to Increased New Media Screen Time," *Clinical Psychological Science*, Nov. 14, 2017, https://tinyurl .com/yc5mv4ch.
Adolescents who spend the most time on social media and electronic devices are more likely to report mental health issues.

For More Information

American Academy of Pediatrics, 345 Park Blvd., Itasca, IL 60143; 800-433-9016; www.aap.org. Professional organization representing pediatricians.

American Psychiatric Association, 800 Maine Ave., S.W., Suite 900, Washington, DC 20024; 888-357-7924; www .psychiatry.org. Professional organization representing psychiatrists, academics and researchers; publishes *Diagnostic and Statistical Manual of Mental Disorders.*

Center for Humane Technology, http://humanetech.com. Organization of technology experts concerned about technology's impact on individuals and society.

Center on Media and Child Health, 300 Longwood Ave., Boston, MA 02115; 617-355-5420; http://cmch.tv. Academic research center at Boston Children's Hospital that promotes healthy media use by children.

Common Sense Media, 650 Townsend, Suite 435, San Francisco, CA 94103; 415-863-0600; www.commonsense media.org. Research and advocacy organization focused on media use, digital literacy and other aspects of technology's role in children's and families' lives.

Internet Association, 1333 H. St., N.W., Washington, DC 20005; 202-869-8680; internetassociation.org. Trade group that represents the internet industry on public policy issues.

National Institutes of Health, 9000 Rockville Pike, Bethesda, MD 20892; 301-496-4000; www.nih.gov. U.S. Department of Health and Human Services agency that is backing the first government-funded study related to internet addiction.

5

Trust in Media

Chuck McCutcheon

Fox News proclaims its clout at its New York studios. Attitudes about media outlets, particularly Fox and *The New York Times,* reflect partisan views. According to a recent poll, 73 percent of Republicans found Fox credible – compared to 45 percent of Democrats. *The Times* drew a 76 percent credibility rating from Democrats versus 52 percent from Republicans.

From *CQ Researcher,*
June 9, 2017

The annual White House Correspondents' Dinner is known for its movie stars and not-so-gentle ribbing of the president. But this year's event was different. For the first time in 36 years, the president didn't attend. And one of journalism's legendary figures offset the glamour and jokes with a sober assertion countering criticism of the mainstream media as biased.

"Journalists should not have a dog in the political fight except to find that best obtainable version of the truth," *Washington Post* reporter Bob Woodward, whose work uncovering the Watergate scandal in the 1970s helped spur President Richard M. Nixon's resignation, said in a speech at the April gala.[1]

That same night, 95 miles away, at a rally in Harrisburg, Pa., to mark his 100th day in office, President Trump delivered a different message about journalists. "Their priorities are not my priorities, and not your priorities," Trump told a cheering, partisan crowd. "If the media's job is to be honest and tell the truth, the media deserves a very, very big fat failing grade."[2]

Woodward's and Trump's remarks illustrate the conflicting views that confront traditional news outlets as they try to rebuild public trust in the media that polls show has hit bottom. Those outlets — newspapers, magazines, websites and broadcast networks with professional, nonpartisan staffs — are victims of an overall decline of faith in government and nongovernmental institutions, as well as constant assaults from politicians that have put them in the crosshairs of today's polarized political climate. Trump is the latest leader of the assaults, labeling journalists "the enemy

Views of Media's Performance Show Partisan Divide

Democrats are more likely than Republicans to say the national news media do a very good job of keeping people informed. The percentage of Republicans with that view dropped 6 points over the last year, while the percentage of Democrats who feel that way increased by 5 points.

Percentages of U.S. adults who say national news media do "very well" or "fairly well" at keeping them informed:

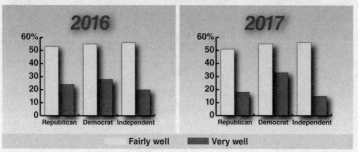

Fairly well ■ Very well

Source: Surveys conducted March 13-27, 2017, and Jan. 12-Feb. 8, 2016, "Americans' Attitudes About the News Media Deeply Divided Along Partisan Lines," Pew Research Center, May 10, 2017, https://tinyurl.com/lwvktsu

aggressively challenge the unfounded claim that Iraq had weapons of mass destruction. In addition, competition for readers has led some outlets to focus on "clickbait" — frivolous and incendiary stories, some untrue — at the expense of substantive topics.

Journalists and those studying the news business say mainstream media outlets must rise to the challenge by performing skillfully in the face of greater outside pressure and shrinking resources. They also must devote more energy to educating readers, listeners and viewers about how they operate.

"Journalism has a trust problem. . . . There's a growing rift between news organizations and the consumers they exist to serve," said Benjamin Mullin, managing editor of Poynter.org, the website for the Poynter Institute, a journalism-training center in St. Petersburg, Fla.[4]

Recent Gallup polls suggest the rift is wide:

of the American people" and dismissing unfavorable coverage of him as "fake news."[*3]

The media also have deeply fragmented as the internet has given rise to a cacophony of voices casting doubt on traditional-media staples — notably the use of anonymous sources and the concepts of neutrality and dispassionate reporting. Facebook and other social media have fostered that cacophony by creating "echo chambers" that affirm people's beliefs and enable them to spread information — accurate and inaccurate — faster than ever.

But trust in the media also has been hurt by self-inflicted wounds, including blurred lines between news and commentary; fabricated stories written by rogue reporters; a focus on well-off urbanites while giving less attention to rural Americans; and the post-9/11 failure to

- Just 32 percent of Americans trust the media, the lowest level recorded since Gallup began asking the question in 1972.[5]
- Forty-one percent of the respondents to another survey asking about the honesty and ethical standards of 22 professions ranked journalists "low" or "very low." Only members of Congress and car salespeople scored lower.[6]
- Sixty-two percent of Americans said the media favor one political party over the other, compared with 50 percent in past years.[7]

News organizations' failure to engender trust could cause society to splinter even further, warns Tom Rosenstiel, executive director of the American Press Institute and a senior fellow at the Brookings Institution, a centrist Washington, D.C., think tank.

"The press needs to rebuild its trust with the public," Rosenstiel says. "We've got to create [news stories] in such a way that people will say, 'I don't like the tone of that,

---

* While Trump defines unfavorable coverage as "fake news," the accepted definition is fabricated stories, posted on obscure websites, intended to disparage politicians and generate ad revenue through clicks after readers share them.

but yeah, I'll accept it, because it's probably true.'"

The two biggest reasons people do not trust news are that they consider it one-sided or inaccurate, according to a 2016 poll by the Press Institute — a nonpartisan media-research organization in Arlington, Va.[8]

Yet the entire notion of "wrong" has become politicized. Trump made so many assertions judged false that the Oxford Dictionaries named "post-truth" its 2016 word of the year.[9] One of his advisers, Kellyanne Conway, caused an uproar in January when she described a questionable assertion about the size of Trump's inauguration crowd as an "alternative fact."[10] Another aide defended giving Trump a false magazine cover warning of a forthcoming ice age instead of global warming at a briefing by contending the information it contained was "fake but accurate."[11]

But more than most issues, Gallup and other polls show, media mistrust reflects the country's entrenched political divide.

A Pew Research Center poll in May found a 47 percentage-point gap between Democrats and Republicans over whether criticism from the media helps keep politicians honest — the largest gap since Pew began asking the question in 1985.[12] And according to a Morning Consult poll in December, 73 percent of Republicans found GOP-leaning Fox News credible — compared to 45 percent of Democrats. *The New York Times* drew a credibility rating of 76 percent from Democrats versus 52 percent from Republicans.[13]

Mistrust of the media is not a strictly partisan issue. African-Americans have accused the media of failing to recognize the Black Lives Matter movement as well as the importance of events fueling its rise.

Media scholars say some outlets have fueled the divide by coarsening discourse and lambasting news organizations whose politics differ from theirs. They also say the growth of watchdog groups, such as Media

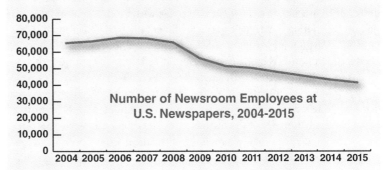

Newspapers Slashing Editorial Staffs

Newspapers in the United States cut more than 24,000 newsroom jobs — a decline of 37 percent — between 2004 and 2015, the most recent year data were available. Layoffs and buyouts among reporters and editors are expected to continue as newspapers struggle with falling circulation and ad revenue.

Number of Newsroom Employees at U.S. Newspapers, 2004-2015

Source: "Newspapers Fact Sheet," Pew Research Center, June 1, 2017, p. 8, https://tinyurl.com/yb8g77ht

Matters and the Media Research Center, has added to the divide. Wealthy partisans finance many of those groups, which track inaccurate reporting, media bias and political gaffes.

Journalists of late have had to endure additional abuse. Four incidents occurred in May:

- A Federal Communications Commission (FCC) guard allegedly pinned a reporter for *CQ Roll Call* against a wall as he sought to ask commissioners a question at FCC headquarters in Washington, then forced him to leave a public meeting. An FCC commissioner apologized for the incident.
- In Montana, Republican congressional candidate Greg Gianforte was charged with misdemeanor assault after he allegedly threw a reporter to the ground who asked him a question. After winning the special election for the state's at-large House seat, Gianforte apologized for his conduct.
- Dan Heyman, a Public News Service reporter in West Virginia, was arrested after trying to question Health and Human Services Secretary Tom Price in a state Capitol hallway. Heyman said he was holding his phone toward Price to record him; police said he was trying to bypass Price's security detail.

• Reporter Nathanial Herz of the *Alaska Dispatch News* said state Sen. David Wilson (R-Wasilla) slapped him across the face after he asked the senator a question. Herz filed a police report, and the case has been turned over to the state's Office of Special Prosecution.[14]

Also in May, several windows were shattered at the offices of Kentucky's *Lexington Herald-Leader*, with investigators attributing the damage to small-caliber bullets, or possibly a BB gun. Newspaper publisher Rufus M. Friday cited a rise in hostile rhetoric toward journalists.[15]

For some media veterans, the media's role in uncovering inaccurate statements by Trump and other politicians while serving as the public's government watchdog is the biggest barometer of the media's future credibility.

"If the media for whatever reason fails to meet this challenge, then democracy as we have known it will slowly die," longtime television network correspondent Marvin Kalb, a professor emeritus at Harvard University's Kennedy School of Government and founding director of its Shorenstein Center on the Press, Politics and Public Policy, said in March.[16]

Those on the political right, however, see the mainstream media — or what they call the "legacy media" — as facing an insurmountable obstacle to rebuilding public trust. Above all, perhaps, they consider the media guilty of hypocrisy for its perceived bias against Republicans while insisting it favors neither party.

"The biggest challenge facing journalists today is a self-inflicted problem: too many activists with bylines posing as neutral observers, and they've been found out," says John Bicknell, executive editor of Watchdog.org, a network of websites covering local and state government funded by the Franklin Center for Government & Public Integrity, a news organization based in Alexandria, Va., with a free-market, limited-government perspective. "Once you've destroyed your own credibility, it's very difficult to get it back — and we see that in many, if not most, legacy newsrooms."[17]

Both conservative and liberal journalism observers say generalizing about "the media" is difficult, in large part because it encompasses an ever-growing array of news and information sources, each with its own mission and leanings.

"Lumping these disparate entities under the same single, bland label is like describing the denizens of the ocean as 'the fish,'" wrote *Washington Post* media reporter Paul Farhi.[18]

Despite such media diversity, the public tends to focus on national — not local — outlets when expressing mistrust. Joy Mayer, a consulting fellow at the University of Missouri's Donald W. Reynolds Journalism Institute, says she noticed this when speaking with readers and viewers around the country for a project she leads on media trust-building.

"I couldn't believe how quickly, in most people's minds, 'the media' jumps to national political coverage," Mayer says. "I tell them, 'The media are people who cover your local school board and high school sports.' "

The notion of "journalist" also is being expanded with the phenomenon of cellphone video capturing news incidents and social media's ability to give members of the general public the power to give direct on-the-scene reports while sharing information among friends.

Social media have created what Rosenstiel calls the "atomization of the news," in which people place more trust in who shared information with them than in the quality of news brands. That phenomenon, he says, helped fuel the "fake news" phenomenon.

As journalists, academics and others debate trust in the news media, here are some of the questions being raised:

Are traditional standards of objective journalism outdated?

One of the bedrock principles of traditional journalism is objectivity, generally defined as not playing favorites despite one's personal views. But the notion of objectivity has come under attack from critics of President Trump, who say his unfitness for the presidency demands the media take up an advocacy role to portray the truth more directly and accurately.

Many veteran journalists say objectivity is essential to developing trust. Media outlets, they say, have an obligation never to identify with any side in a conflict or other issue.

"Journalists in this tradition [of objectivity] have plenty of opinions, but by setting them aside to follow the facts — as a judge in court is supposed to set aside prejudices to follow the law and the evidence — they can often produce results that are more substantial and more credible," former *Times* executive editor Bill Keller said.[19]

In January, Lewis Wallace was fired from his job as a reporter for the syndicated business radio show "Marketplace" after publishing an article on the website *Medium*.[20] Journalists, Wallace wrote, "need to become more shameless, more raw, more honest with ourselves and our audiences" instead of simply reacting passively to what he predicted would be arrests and other attempts to curtail media freedom of speech under Trump.[21]

Among the most vocal critics of objectivity is American journalist Glenn Greenwald, whose articles in London's *Guardian* contained classified information on U.S. government surveillance in 2013 released by former national-security contractor Edward Snowden. "This voice that people at NPR and PBS and CNN are required to assume, where they're supposed to display this kind of non-human neutrality about the world in which they're reporting, is a deceitful, artificial one," said Greenwald, editor of the national-security website *The Intercept*.[22]

Kerry Lauerman, executive editor of the liberal-leaning news and commentary website *Mic*, which targets Millennials, encourages reporters not to hide their views. "We're stronger by having people with different points of view approach things with those points of view," Lauerman said. "It probably does further erode the sort of old-fashioned notion of objectivity. But I think that's better for journalism, too."[23]

Some critics of traditional media point to earlier eras to argue that mainstream journalism never has been truly objective — and should stop pretending it is.

Objectivity "has seldom existed in American history, and has especially been scarce since the 1960s, when activist journalism came out of the closet with its ideological coverage of Vietnam and then Watergate, all perfumed with the spurious claim to journalistic integrity and public service," said Bruce Thornton, a fellow at Stanford University's Hoover Institution.[24]

Other critics fault the language of objectivity. *National Review* columnist Jonah Goldberg pointed to The Associated Press stylebook's barring the use of "illegal immigrants," though "illegal immigration" is still permitted. Instead, The AP and other outlets have recommended terms such as "unauthorized" and "undocumented" for immigrants.

That usage, Goldberg said, is part of left-wing pro-immigration activists' agenda "to blur the distinctions between legal and illegal immigration. . . . As a matter of fact and logic, the difference between an 'unauthorized immigrant' and an 'illegal immigrant' is nonexistent."[25]

Many journalists say absolute objectivity is impossible, given the inherent subjective nature of choosing one fact over another in telling a story.

But they say that something close to it can be achieved by doing rigorous reporting offering deep insights. That includes weeding out extremist voices and specious claims in favor of provable facts.

"Objectivity is all about doing your job well as a journalist," says Ken Paulson, a former editor of *USA Today* who is president of the First Amendment Center, which studies free-expression issues. He also is dean of Middle Tennessee State University's College of Media and Entertainment. "The question is, can you get up every morning and write what you find out — accurately write about what you've discovered?"

Paulson and many journalists say objectivity is rooted in fairness — conveying the arguments of all sides of an issue. But, they add, fairness does not mean "he said, she said" reporting — the oft-criticized practice of unquestioningly giving both sides equal weight.

"Good journalism doesn't require perfect balance," said Michael Kinsley, founding editor of *Slate* magazine. "In fact, perfect balance may be a distortion of reality. But journalism gains credibility when it gives all sides their due."[26]

The American Press Institute's Rosenstiel says one means of bolstering media trust — greater transparency — is enhancing objectivity by borrowing the methods of science and demonstrating to readers and viewers how news outlets arrive at their conclusions.

The Post, in publishing an e-book biography of Trump last year, put online an archive of most of its research materials, including thousands of pages of interview transcripts, court filings, financial reports, immigration records and other material.[27]

"There's this discipline of verifying — making sure you have enough sources and describing as much as can about your sources, like showing your math in a school assignment that proves to the teacher that you did the work yourself," Rosenstiel says. "That's what the idea of an objective method of journalism is about."

Are the national news media out of touch with ordinary Americans?

Critics of mainstream journalism question whether staffers at national outlets are disconnected from people in

Edgar Maddison Welch surrenders to police in Washington, D.C., on Dec. 4, 2016. Armed with an assault rifle, the Salisbury, N.C., man drove to Washington to try to stop what online conspiracy theories falsely said was a child sex ring being run by Democratic presidential candidate Hillary Clinton out of a local pizza restaurant. Media experts and scholars say many voters were swayed during the presidential campaign by the proliferation of so-called fake news spread by alternative news websites and social media.

blue-collar jobs who often live outside of the metropolises of the East or West coasts. But journalists at those outlets dispute the charge.

The debate is an old one. In a 1996 article, "Why Americans Hate the Media," *Atlantic* national correspondent James Fallows said national political journalists fixate on tactical matters at the expense of issues that the public cares about more deeply.

"When ordinary citizens have a chance to pose questions to political leaders, they rarely ask about the game of politics," Fallows wrote. "They want to know how the reality of politics will affect them — through taxes, programs, scholarship funds, wars."[28]

Those tendencies have only worsened over the last two decades with the explosion of the internet and interest in polls and celebrity at the expense of more time-consuming, deeply reported pieces, media observers say. As the news business has shrunk, it has concentrated in New York, Washington and California.

The result, those observers say, helps explain the traditional media's failure to anticipate the outcome of 2016's election, in which Trump defied almost all polls and pundits to win the Electoral College despite losing the popular vote.

"Much of the East Coast-based media establishment is arguably out of touch with the largely rural population that voted for Trump," said Mathew Ingram, a *Fortune* senior writer covering the media.[29]

Dean Baquet, the *Times'* executive editor, said he is proud of his paper's campaign coverage. But he said after the election: "The New York-based and Washington-based media powerhouses . . . don't get the role of religion in people's lives."[30]

Veteran reporter and author David Cay Johnston, former board president of the group Investigative Reporters and Editors, said today's journalists no longer closely share their audience's concerns.

"There's been a tendency in the news to focus very much on, 'What's going on with the internet? What's going on with these exciting new gizmos?' As opposed to, 'What's happening to people who work in factories in Iowa and Michigan and their concerns?'" Johnston said.

Johnston attributed the shift to changing demographics. In 1960, nearly one-third of reporters and editors had never attended a single year of college; in 2015, that figure was down to 8 percent — 38 percentage points below the number of adults 25 and older nationwide.[31]

College-educated journalists "began making newspapers move up the income ladder and the wealth ladder in terms of readership and lost sight of this mass audience they used to have," he said. "And a result, the coverage and what newspapers defined as important tended to be the concerns of the upper-middle class."[32]

Too many of the journalists are liberal, putting them further out of touch, says Watchdog.org's Bicknell. "If mainstream news organizations want to regain credibility with the public, they should begin by hiring young conservative journalists," he says.

The White House Correspondents' Dinner, which has evolved from an intimate gathering in 1921 into a televised gala of hundreds of journalists and politicians — and the celebrities they invite — often is cited as symbolizing the gulf between the national media and public. *The Times* stopped attending the dinner in 2008, saying it sent a misleading signal that the paper was too chummy with politicians.[33]

Criticism of the national media's aloofness from America extends beyond economic class and politics into race.

African-American talk show host Tavis Smiley cited the Trayvon Martin case as evidence that newsrooms have "the same unconscious bias that exists in police departments" because they lack staffers who understand black America. Martin, an unarmed 17-year-old African-American, was shot and killed in 2012 by neighborhood-watch volunteer George Zimmerman in a gated Florida community. Zimmerman, who is white, pleaded self-defense and was acquitted of second-degree murder.[34]

"The reality is that that story would never have made it to the front pages were it not for black media," Smiley said. "Oftentimes the mainstream media — particularly where people of color are concerned — is on the late freight."[35]

However, a number of academics and journalists say major news outlets are responding to such criticisms.

"That is something that needs a correction, and the correction has begun," former *Post* executive editor Leonard Downie, now a professor of journalism at Arizona State University, says of the accusation of being out of touch.

Downie and other media observers cite *The Times'* and other newspapers' detailed stories explaining the impacts of Trump's policies. That includes the White House's proposed budget, which calls for slashing or eliminating federal programs important to small communities and rural areas that backed Trump.

They also note that while the number of minorities at media outlets is still too low, it is on the rise. An American Society of News Editors survey found the minority workforce rose 5.6 percent from 2015 to 2016 among the 433 news organizations that took part in both years' surveys. Overall, minorities made up 17 percent of workers at daily print newspapers and 23 percent of employees at digital-only publications.[36]

Media observers are encouraged by journalists' willingness to "crowd-source" reporting — asking the public directly for help, expanding their networks and building credibility. *Post* reporter David Fahrenthold won a Pulitzer Prize in April for his work investigating Trump's charitable contributions, in part by soliciting information

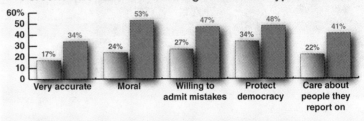

People Most Trust Media They Use

Americans tend to trust the news sources they rely on but distrust "the news media" as an abstract concept. For example, just over half of those surveyed viewed the news sources they consult as moral, but only 24 percent said that about the media in general.

Source: "'My' media versus 'the' media: Trust in news depends on which news media you mean," American Press Institute, May 24, 2017, p. 2, https://tinyurl.com/ya32z2za

from readers about whether they belonged to organizations that had been promised or received contributions.

When looking into whether Trump used $10,000 of charitable money to buy a portrait of himself, Fahrenthold recalled, "I asked my readers and Twitter followers for help, and they amazed me with their ingenuity. They found things that I never would have thought to find on my own."[37]

Times domestic-affairs correspondent Sheryl Gay Stolberg also cites "Anxious in America," a 2016 series to which she contributed, as another example of reporting about everyday Americans. It explored economic and social concerns in rural Appalachia, among African-Americans at a Philadelphia food pantry and evangelical Christians in small-town Iowa as well as other places.[38]

While acknowledging that the national media focuses too much on polls and "horse-race" journalism, Stolberg says of her paper, "I disagree that we don't reflect America."

Does the use of anonymous sources erode trust in journalism?

Critics of the use of anonymous sources call it a significant contributor to the erosion of trust in the media, while the practice's defenders say that — when done

Getty Images/NBC/NBCU/Will Heath

Comedian Melissa McCarthy parodies White House press secretary Sean Spicer on "Saturday Night Live" on May 13, 2017. In recent weeks, assistant press secretary Sarah Huckabee Sanders has been giving press briefings instead of Spicer, who has had a rocky relationship with the press. Spicer faced withering criticism after President Trump pulled out of the Paris climate accord, telling reporters he did not know whether Trump accepted climate change science.

judiciously — it gets closer to the truth than quoting people only by name.

The use of such sources requires the public to place considerable faith in journalists, said Mary Louise Kelly, who covers intelligence agencies for NPR. "If I am using an anonymous source, I have given my word that I will not reveal their identity," Kelly said. "But I am asking you, the listener, to trust me that I have done everything in my power to make sure this person is who they say they are, that they have access to the information and also to weigh what's their motive."[39]

A Morning Consult/*Politico* poll in March found that 44 percent of those surveyed said it is likely reporters make up unnamed sources. As with other polls involving media trust, the poll showed a deep partisan split: 65 percent of Republicans said journalists made up sources, while just 24 percent of Democrats agreed.

The poll also showed that half of those surveyed didn't consider it appropriate for the media to use anonymous sources when reporting on government business. That issue also broke along partisan lines: 66 percent of Republicans considered it inappropriate compared to only 36 percent of Democrats.[40]

Trump has fed public mistrust about the practice. Reporters "have no sources; they just make them up when there are none," he said in February.[41]

The Times tightened its requirements for the use of unnamed sources in 2016 in response to two erroneous articles. One was based on unnamed officials who said inspectors general asked the Justice Department to open a criminal investigation into whether Hillary Clinton had mishandled sensitive information on a private email account she used as secretary of State. *The Times* later clarified that the referral was not criminal and did not name Clinton as a focus.[42]

Nevertheless, when *The Times* this year published a string of exclusive stories about Trump, the paper drew a warning from Liz Spayd, the paper's public editor.* She noted the articles relied heavily — some entirely — on unnamed sources. "The descriptions [of sources' identities] generally tilt far more toward protecting the sources than giving readers confidence in what they said," Spayd wrote.[43]

Conservative political commentator Mollie Hemingway, a senior editor at the *Federalist* magazine, responded to a slew of critical articles about Trump in May with a sarcastic tweet: "I didn't go to journalism school, but should our media really privilege unaccountable, anonymous sources to on-the-record accountable ones?"[44]

However, many in the news business say mainstream media outlets do a largely successful job in drawing a distinction between unnamed sources with a partisan ax to grind and those wanting to provide helpful information without risking their jobs.

Of those in the latter camp, "These are not people who pull us aside because they want to screw Donald Trump," *The Times'* Baquet said. "These are people who are worried about the direction of government."[45]

Reporters who make the most frequent use of anonymous sources have accumulated considerable trust with those sources, which should persuade the public to have confidence in those reporters, said Dana Priest, a Pulitzer Prize-winning national security reporter at *The Post.*

---

* *The Times* announced on May 31 that it was eliminating the public editor position, and Spayd resigned. The paper has recently created the Reader Center, which it described as a way to "build even stronger bonds with our readers."

Those reporters "are pretty good at judging the character of somebody that they actually quote without their name," Priest said. "And that's how we do that business. It would not happen without it, because they're really not supposed to be talking to us."[46]

The use of anonymous sources declined in the half-century between 1958 and 2008, reaching its peak in the 1970s, according to a 2011 study.

The study found journalists increasingly described the backgrounds of anonymous sources in some way rather than simply identifying them as "reliable sources." In 1958, 34 percent of stories with unnamed sources used that type of vague language, but that figure fell below 3 percent in 2008. It also found reporters more frequently explained the reasons why they grant anonymity.[47]

Paulson of the First Amendment Center says procedures to discourage reliance on anonymous sources — including having reporters share the names of sources with senior editors — led to a 70-percent reduction in their usage during his stint as *USA Today's* editor from 2004 to 2009.

Relying on unnamed sources while sustaining trust is "a balancing act," he says. "It has to be offset by the importance of the story. We were not going to use anonymous sources to find out the name of the new Taylor Swift album — only to reveal important information about national security."

BACKGROUND
Early Press Coverage

The First Amendment's guarantee of press freedom makes the news media "the only business in America specifically protected by the Constitution," as President John F. Kennedy once observed.[48] Nonetheless, journalists seldom have been held in high public regard.

Thomas Jefferson famously championed free expression: "Were it left to me to decide whether we should have a government without newspapers or newspapers without a government, I should not hesitate a moment to prefer the latter," the author of the Declaration of Independence and the nation's third president once said. Yet he griped about how those papers covered him.

"Nothing can now be believed which is seen in a newspaper," Jefferson wrote in 1787. "Truth itself

CBS News anchor Walter Cronkite, considered the country's most trusted figure during his long tenure, helped change public perception of the Vietnam War when he declared in a 1968 commentary that it was destined "to end in a stalemate."

becomes suspicious by being put into that polluted vehicle."[49]

For much of the 19th century, journalists stressed sensationalism over accuracy, with papers serving as mouthpieces for political parties. "He lies like a newspaper" became a common criticism.[50]

"Editors ran their own candidates — in fact they ran for office themselves, and often continued in their post at the paper while holding office," historian Garry Wills wrote. "Politicians, knowing this, cultivated their own party's papers, both the owners and the editors, shared staff with them, released news to them early or exclusively to keep them loyal, rewarded them with state or federal appointments when they won."[51]

Ulysses S. Grant, the commanding Union general during the Civil War, later served two scandal-filled presidential terms. During his second inaugural address in 1873, Grant railed against reporters, saying he had been "the subject of abuse and slander scarcely ever equaled in political history."[52]

The New York Press in 1897 coined the term "yellow journalism" to describe the fiercely competitive and sensationalistic New York newspapers owned by titans Joseph Pulitzer and William Randolph Hearst. The term came from the comic strip "The Yellow Kid," about a mischievous boy in a yellow nightshirt.[53]

The splashy reporting of Hearst's and Pulitzer's papers was offset by *The New York Times*. Tennessee publisher

Adolph S. Ochs acquired the paper in 1896 and vowed "to give the news impartially, without fear or favor, regardless of party, sect or interests involved."[54]

The emergence of investigative journalists — muckrakers — in the early 20th century helped boost trust. The best known was Upton Sinclair, whose 1906 novel *The Jungle* exposed labor and sanitary abuses in the meatpacking industry. Thirteen years later, Sinclair's *The Brass Check,* a work of nonfiction, compared the brass token used by patrons of prostitutes to wealthy newspaper owners' buying off journalists' credibility.[55] It sold more than 150,000 copies.[56]

Legendary journalist Walter Lippmann helped found *The New Republic* magazine in 1914 and became one of the world's most widely respected columnists.[57] Lippmann warned in a 1920 book that without a "steady supply of trustworthy and relevant news," then "all that the sharpest critics of democracy have alleged is true."[58]

During the 1920s, radio became common in American households. In 1934, President Franklin D. Roosevelt signed a bill into law stipulating that stations could lose their licenses if their broadcasts were considered too controversial. It required stations to offer equal time for political candidates.[59]

With the advent of television after World War II, the federal government again became involved in regulating journalistic content. Lawmakers became concerned that the three TV networks of the era — NBC, ABC and CBS — could misuse their broadcast licenses to advance a biased agenda. The Federal Communications Commission issued the Fairness Doctrine in 1949 requiring radio and TV stations to devote some of their programming to controversial issues and allow the airing of opposing views.[60]

During the 1930s and '40s, polls showed "at best only modest levels of trust in the news media," according to Georgetown University public policy professor Jonathan M. Ladd.[61]

But around midcentury, competition from television led newspapers to expand coverage and offer more deeply sourced and interpretive reporting. Papers also developed, along with magazines, a commercial model that led many of them to be hugely profitable through classified and display advertising.

It was during this period that a few newspapers, including the *Milwaukee Journal* and *Washington Post,* questioned accusations by Wisconsin GOP Sen. Joseph McCarthy, who led the "Red Scare" investigations of alleged communists in the United States during the 1950s. CBS News reporter Edward R. Murrow, in a 1954 special report, said of the senator: "He didn't create this situation of fear — he merely exploited it, and rather successfully."[62]

By 1956, two-thirds of Americans said in polls that newspapers were fair. Of those charging unfairness, most thought they were too favorable toward President Dwight D. Eisenhower (1953-61) and other Republicans.[63]

Vietnam and Watergate

The Vietnam War hardened partisan attitudes toward the media. Reporters found struggles on the battlefront at odds with the upbeat assessments of military leaders, while TV news broadcast vivid combat images directly into American homes. CBS News anchor Walter Cronkite, considered the country's most trusted figure, changed the public perception of the war when he declared in a 1968 commentary that the war was destined "to end in a stalemate."[64]

Republican Nixon (1969-74) and his first vice president, Spiro T. Agnew, often accused reporters of untrustworthiness. On Vietnam, Nixon said "our worst enemy seems to be the press," while Agnew blasted "the tiny, enclosed fraternity of privileged men elected by no one."[65]

Reed Irvine, a Republican journalist and press critic, in 1969 founded the conservative watchdog group Accuracy in Media to provide what he saw as a check against the media's liberal excesses. It grew within two decades into a 30,000-member organization with a $1.5 million annual budget, drawing praise from GOP lawmakers for its work exposing alleged biases, errors and distortion.[66]

Journalists played the central role in the era's other most significant controversy—the 1972 break-in at Democratic National Committee headquarters in Washington's Watergate office building and subsequent events that culminated in Nixon's resignation in 1974.

Relying on anonymous sources, *Post* reporters Woodward and Carl Bernstein uncovered many of the developments tying Nixon and top aides to the break-in, a cover-up and other misdeeds. A 1976 movie portrayed

CHRONOLOGY

1900s-1950s *Newspapers draw competition from radio, television.*

1919 Celebrated muckraker Upton Sinclair, known for attacking his era's social and economic institutions, publishes *The Brass Check,* a nonfiction book equating the brass tokens that brothel patrons used to buy prostitutes' services with the money that newspaper owners paid journalists to influence their reporting.

1949 Federal Communications Commission (FCC) issues "Fairness Doctrine" requiring radio and TV stations to devote some programming to controversial issues and the airing of opposing views.

1954 CBS News correspondent Edward R. Murrow wins praise for commentary highly critical of Wisconsin Sen. Joseph McCarthy's "Red Scare" investigation of suspected communists in the United States.

1956 Two-thirds of Americans say in polls that newspapers are fair, more than twice the percentage as those who consider them unfair.

1960s-1980s *Partisan attitudes harden toward media.*

1968 CBS News anchor Walter Cronkite helps turn public opinion against the Vietnam War by predicting it will end in a stalemate. . . . Republican Richard M. Nixon is elected president and attacks the media's credibility.

1969 Conservative media critic Reed Irvine starts Accuracy in Media to provide what he calls a check against liberal media excesses.

1972 After a break-in at Democratic National Committee offices at Washington's Watergate complex, *Washington Post* reporters Bob Woodward and Carl Bernstein write numerous articles tying Nixon and his aides to the break-in, a subsequent cover-up and other misdeeds, all leading to Nixon's resignation.

1976 Gallup Poll shows public confidence in the media at an all-time peak of 72 percent.

1980 Republican Ronald Reagan is elected president, serving two terms during which his aides sought to aggressively shape media coverage through staged events and other means. . . . Business tycoon Ted Turner launches CNN, the first TV channel providing 24-hour news coverage.

1981 *Washington Post* reporter Janet Cook wins Pulitzer Prize for "Jimmy's World," an article about an 8-year-old heroin addict that is later exposed as a fabrication.

1987 FCC abolishes "Fairness Doctrine," paving the way for talk radio to become a platform for conservatives and others to regularly attack perceived media bias.

1990s-Present *Internet reshapes public's perception of the media.*

1994 Matt Drudge, an unknown political commentator, starts the news-aggregation website *Drudge Report,* among the first of a number of conservative-leaning media outlets.

1996 Fox News launched; within six years it is the most-watched cable network.

2003 Critics of the Iraq War bash news outlets, saying they didn't aggressively challenge President George W. Bush's assertions that Iraq possessed weapons of mass destruction.

2004 Facebook social network launched; it quickly becomes a massively popular alternative to news outlets by taking their content and tailoring it to users' preferences.

2008 Alaska Gov. Sarah Palin, the GOP vice presidential nominee, lambastes what she calls "the lamestream media."

2016 During the presidential campaign, conservatives accuse mainstream media of under-covering Hillary Clinton's perceived misdeeds and Democrats accuse them of overcovering Donald Trump's rallies in order to boost ratings and online traffic. Some Democrats also accuse Fox News of pro-Trump bias.

2017 President Trump calls the media "the enemy of the American people" amid constant clashes with reporters.

Catching Politicians With Their 'Pants on Fire'

Fact-checking sites perform "very important journalism."

In the media-trust debate, two phrases have become part of the lexicon: "Pants on Fire" and "Pinocchios." The colorful expressions are used, respectively, on the fact-checking websites PolitiFact and Fact Checker, which evaluate the truth of government officials' statements. The sites' popularity has both irked their targets and raised questions about how the administrators of the sites choose which statements to parse.

The two sites are far from alone. U.S. news outlets had 52 separate fact-checking operations in 2016, up by 15 from 2015.[1] The biggest is PolitiFact (www.politifact.com), launched by the *Tampa Bay Times* in 2007, which won a Pulitzer Prize two years later and now has affiliations with news outlets in 18 states, public radio and the Scripps chain of television stations.[*2]

The Washington Post also started its fact-checking site, Fact Checker (https://www.washingtonpost.com/news/fact-checker/), in 2007. Another well-known site, FactCheck .org, was launched in 2003 by the University of Pennsylvania's Annenberg Public Policy Center.[3] On the political right, the website Conservapedia (www.conservapedia.com) — a conservative version of the online dictionary Wikipedia — aims to debunk what it considers overly liberal claims.[4]

At PolitiFact, claims are rated — as shown on an accompanying "Truth-O-Meter" — on a scale from "True" to "Pants on Fire," while Fact Checker assesses the degree of truth of a statement on a scale of zero to four "Pinocchios."

A Fact Checker column on May 18 assigned three Pinocchios to the assertion by House Minority Leader Nancy Pelosi, D-Calif., that 7 million veterans would definitely lose tax credits under the House Republicans' bill to repeal former President Obama's health-care overhaul, the Affordable Care Act. "In reality, it's not so certain," Fact Checker said.[5]

On May 12 PolitiFact gave a "Pants on Fire" rating to President Trump's assertion that allegations that his campaign may have colluded with Russia was a "made-up story" that Democrats used as an excuse for his victory. "Democrats did not create the story, nor do they control the agenda of the House and Senate committees, which are conducting their own investigations," the column declared.[6]

Fact-checking has evolved beyond its origins in the 1990s, when news outlets occasionally assessed claims in campaign advertisements, journalism scholars say. Today, TV networks such as CNN also do on-screen fact-checking during debates.

"It is very important journalism, and it's here to stay," says former *Post* executive editor Leonard Downie, now a professor of journalism at Arizona State University. (As a young deputy metropolitan editor of *The Post*, Downie supervised much of the paper's Watergate coverage by Bob Woodward and Carl Bernstein.)

A Pew Research Center survey last fall found 83 percent of voters consider it the media's responsibility to check the statements of candidates and campaigns. And 77 percent of those who said they planned to vote for Trump saw it as either a major or minor responsibility, compared with 89 percent of Hillary Clinton's supporters.[7]

Politicians have noticed. In a 2015 interview, then-Gov. Rick Perry, R-Texas, — now U.S. Energy secretary — said his state had reduced nitrogen-oxide emissions levels by 63.5 percent. Then he added, "Say 63 percent — that way, we won't get PolitiFacted." (The actual figure was 62.5 percent, the site noted.)[8]

But conservatives have criticized such sites because, they say, no public mechanism exists to show which assertions are fact-checked and which aren't, opening the selection process to bias. "When you're only advocating a political agenda, like PolitiFact, I understand, guys, where you're coming from," Fox News commentator Sean Hannity said in 2015 while disputing a "Pants on Fire" rating for an earlier assertion about Syrian refugees.[9]

In a 2016 study, political scientists Stephen Farnsworth of the University of Mary Washington and Robert Lichter of George Mason University examined hundreds of PolitiFact and Fact Checker evaluations and found that PolitiFact's selections were more critical of Republicans than Democrats "to a statistically significant degree." Fact Checker also was more critical of GOP politicians, they found, but not to as significant a degree.

---

* PolitiFact won the Pulitzer Prize for National Reporting for its coverage of the 2008 election, including its use of "probing reporters and the power of the World Wide Web to examine more than 750 political claims, separating rhetoric from truth to enlighten voters."

Farnsworth and Lichter said the sites should better explain how they choose claims to evaluate. "The lack of transparency from the organizations regarding their selection procedures, and the practical difficulties of content analyzing every controversial statement by every lawmaker, make it difficult to untangle the central question of whether partisan differences in fact-checking reflect the values of the fact-checkers or the behavior of their targets," they said.[10]

PolitiFact creator Bill Adair, now a journalism professor at Duke University who remains a contributing editor at the site, says PolitiFact vigorously tries to avoid bias by examining the most significant or newsworthy statements, regardless of political affiliation.

The Fact Checker's Glenn Kessler responded to complaints about Trump getting more fact-checks in 2016 than Clinton by saying the GOP nominee talked more. "We would have liked to publish a lot more fact-checks of Hillary than we did, but she didn't give many interviews, her speeches were rigidly vetted and didn't vary that much," Kessler said. "Meanwhile, Trump would call in to four to five TV shows and go off the script in rallies."[11]

Tom Rosenstiel, executive director of the American Press Institute, a nonpartisan media-research organization, encourages fact-checking that goes beyond cataloguing assertions. "We've heard fact-checking is more effective if it's viewed as 'Help me understand this issue' rather than just right and wrong," Rosenstiel says. "The idea we have is, let's fact-check a broader issue rather than a specific claim. You would pick issues based on how important they are. Like transportation — what are the key facts? Or water — how clean is the water?"

Several efforts are underway to incorporate new technologies into fact-checking and to present the results in various formats. Studies show that charts and other graphical information can make information stick better in readers' minds, Adair says.

"We need to develop different ways of presenting accurate information," he says.

— *Chuck McCutcheon*

Screenshot/CQ Researcher Staff

The online fact-checking site PolitiFact has made "Pants on Fire" part of the media-trust lexicon. Fact Checker, with its "Pinocchio" rating, is another popular site that evaluates the truth of government officials' statements.

[1] Bill Adair, "Keep on Fact-Checking!" *The New York Times,* Nov. 8, 2016, http://tinyurl.com/l9kwxqj.

[2] Mark Stencel, "The facts about fact-checking across America," ReportersLab.org, Aug. 3, 2016, http://tinyurl.com/ya6fqb4n.

[3] Brooks Jackson, "Is This a Great Job or What?" FactCheck.org, Dec. 5, 2003, http://tinyurl.com/ya4w9btx; Glenn Kessler, "About the Fact Checker," *The Washington Post,* Sept. 11, 2013, http://tinyurl.com/ybsf4v9t; The PolitiFact Staff, PolitiFact.com, http://tinyurl.com/yck9q3pw.

[4] "Conservapedia.com," undated, http://tinyurl.com/2ppol7.

[5] Michele Ye Hee Lee, "Nancy Pelosi's claim that 'seven million veterans will lose their tax credit' under the GOP health bill," *The Washington Post* Fact Checker, May 18, 2017, http://tinyurl.com/ybqrlm2z.

[6] Jon Greenberg, "Donald Trump's Pants on Fire claim Russia story 'made-up' by Democrats," PolitiFact.com, May 12, 2017, http://tinyurl.com/yaktmejd.

[7] Michael Barthel, Jeffrey Gottfried and Kristine Lu, "Trump, Clinton Supporters Differ on How Media Should Cover Controversial Statements," Pew Research Center, Oct. 17, 2016, http://tinyurl.com/ybhyyf3f.

[8] W. Gardner Selby, "Rick Perry gets a laugh out of Texas Truth-O-Meter," PolitiFact Texas, Jan. 15, 2015, http://tinyurl.com/y7stbhgj.

[9] Alex Griswold, "Hannity Blasts 'Left-Wing Website' Politifact For Giving Him 'Pants on Fire' Rating,'" *Mediaite,* Oct. 28, 2015, http://tinyurl.com/oncqu6g.

[10] Stephen J. Farnsworth and S. Robert Lichter, "A Comparative Analysis of the Partisan Targets of Media Fact-checking: Examining President Obama and the 113th Congress," paper presented at the American Political Science Association convention, September 2016, http://tinyurl.com/yabwrdx2.

[11] Alexios Mantzarlis, "Fact-checking under President Trump," Poynter.org, Nov. 10, 2016, http://tinyurl.com/jmbg4sn.

the pair as dogged investigators, and a Gallup poll that year showed public confidence in the media at an all-time peak of 72 percent.[67]

But Republican Ronald Reagan's presidency (1981-89) ushered in greater public skepticism. Some Democrats accused reporters of being reluctant to criticize him out of fear of being cut off from the flow of White House information. They also said reporters were too willing to take part in stage-managed events crafted by Reagan aides with an eye toward enhancing the president's popularity.[68]

In 1987, during Reagan's second term, the FCC abolished the Fairness Doctrine, paving the way for talk radio.[69] Rush Limbaugh, a conservative political commentator and host of a talk show in Sacramento, Calif., made perceived liberal bias one of his signature issues and saw his program become nationally syndicated in 1988 and the nation's most popular radio show.[70]

The Reagan era also saw competitive constraints and government regulation of cable channels relaxed by the Cable Communications Policy Act of 1984. The industry boomed, as all-news "24/7" cable channels such as CNN changed the face of television journalism by reaching a wide audience and offering coverage for longer periods than the TV networks.[71]

Media Scandals

Cable increased pressure on print media, which in the post-Watergate era had boosted in-depth reporting. *The Post*'s Janet Cooke won a Pulitzer Prize in 1981 for "Jimmy's World," a lengthy article about an 8-year-old heroin addict that the paper retracted when she admitted the boy was fictitious.[72]

The Cooke controversy was followed by scandals involving other journalists found to have fabricated or embellished their work:

• *The New Republic*'s Stephen Glass, who wrote articles in the 1990s about young conservatives, Wall Street traders and Silicon Valley technology entrepreneurs that were found to be entirely or partially false.[73]
• *USA Today*'s Jack Kelley, who wrote dispatches from Serbia and other war-torn countries in the 1990s and early 2000s that the newspaper found were substantially inaccurate. Editor Karen Jurgensen resigned in 2004 over her failure to detect the fabrications.[74]

• *The Times*' Jayson Blair, who was found in 2003 to have copied material from other publications as well as devising fake quotations, then lying about it. The paper's two top editors subsequently stepped down.[75]
• NBC News anchor Brian Williams, who was suspended without pay for six months in 2015 — and eventually lost his anchor post — following a segment in which he exaggerated details of his travels in a military helicopter during the Iraq War. The story opened a controversy involving other instances in which Williams exaggerated or invented dangers he faced.[76]
• Sabrina Rubin Erdely, a journalist for *Rolling Stone*, the magazine and its parent company were found guilty of defamation of a former University of Virginia administrator in a 2014 magazine article about sexual assault on campus that included a debunked account of a fraternity gang rape.[77]

Media trust levels, as measured by Gallup, fell to just over 50 percent of Americans polled through the late 1990s and into the early 2000s. Media credibility has consistently been below 50 percent since 2007.[78]

Democratic President Bill Clinton was a polarizing figure, especially after his sexual relationship with White House intern Monica Lewinsky led to his impeachment and subsequent acquittal. "The Drudge Report," a conservative news-aggregation website launched in 1994, led the charge against Clinton and other Democrats.

Other right-wing outlets that followed in its wake, such as Breitbart News, were aggressively skeptical of President Barack Obama. The outlets gave voice to the "alt-right," a loose coalition of white nationalists, white supremacists, anti-Semites and others seeking to preserve what they consider traditional Western civilization.[79]

Such outlets "were preaching this is the only place you can get news — this is the only place you can trust," said Ted Newton, president of a Washington political communications firm and an adviser to Republican Mitt Romney's 2012 presidential campaign. "All other media outlets are lying to you [they said], so you need to come to us. And so in an attempt to capture an audience, they almost made them slaves to those news outlets."[80]

Cable news discovered that many viewers were hungry for partisanship. Fox News launched in 1996 with a motto to be "fair and balanced," combining straight news reporting with pro-Republican commentary.

Though critics labeled Fox a GOP soapbox for bigotry and propaganda, it struck a chord with viewers who believed the rest of media displayed an overly liberal tilt to become the most-watched cable channel in 2002.[81] Rival cable channel MSNBC, created in 1996 as a partnership between NBC and Microsoft, sought starting in 2007 to become Fox's liberal counterweight.[82]

Critics of the Iraq War blasted Fox and the rest of the media for not more aggressively investigating GOP President George W. Bush's justification of the 2003 invasion — that Iraq possessed nuclear, chemical or other so-called weapons of mass destruction. One *Times* reporter, Judith Miller, came under criticism for writing articles giving credence to Iraqi and U.S. officials who made that claim.[83]

Some journalists said deep public support for Bush after the Sept. 11, 2001, terrorist attacks influenced how aggressively they challenged his claims.

In the run-up to the war, "There wasn't any reporting in the rest of the press corps, there was stenography," recalled John Walcott, Washington bureau chief for McClatchy Newspapers, which published some of the most skeptical coverage about the decision to invade. "The administration would make an assertion, people would make an assertion, people would write it down as if it were true, and put it in the newspaper or on television."[84]

Social Media

Facebook, Twitter and other social-media sites further lessened the need for Americans to rely on newspapers, TV or other news outlets. Facebook's algorithms assessed what people clicked on and then fed them similar content, a development that many experts say further lessened trust in mainstream outlets.

Politicians began recognizing the power of social media in appealing directly to a mass audience. Alaska Gov. Sarah Palin, the 2008 GOP vice-presidential nominee, inveighed against "the lamestream media."[85]

At the same time, media watchdog groups formed across the ideological spectrum. On the political right, hedge fund executive Robert Mercer and his daughter

Craigslist founder Craig Newmark, whose website has attracted millions of dollars' worth of ads away from local newspaper classified advertising, has joined several private and nonprofit groups and media organizations in supporting projects aimed at developing faith in the media. "As a news consumer, like most folks, I want news we can trust," Newmark said. "That means standing up for trustworthy news media and learning how to spot clickbait and deceptive news."

Rebecca gave $13.5 million between 2008 and 2014 to the Media Research Center, whose projects include a website (CNSNews.com) that publishes stories it says the mainstream media overlooks.[86] On the left, liberal business magnate George Soros gave at least $1 million to Media Matters for America, which also has obtained funding from or formed partnerships with several groups that Soros funds or has funded.[87]

In the 2016 presidential race, traditional media came under attack from all sides. Hillary Clinton's campaign castigated journalists for lavishing too much uncritical attention on Trump, whose colorful candidacy drew far more coverage than any of his Republican primary rivals.[88] Supporters of Vermont Sen. Bernie Sanders, Clinton's main primary opponent, accused the media of not taking him seriously and undermining his campaign.[89]

Neither Trump nor Sanders, however, made media criticism as central to their races as Trump. Three months before the election, Trump named Steve Bannon, a founding member of the board of Breitbart, as head of his campaign. He later tapped the controversial Bannon as his chief strategist in the White House.

Trump made, and continues to make, near-daily use of Twitter as a weapon to bypass and attack traditional

Falling Newsroom Employment Erodes Trust

Reporters are "stretched thinner. That hurts trust."

Journalists are having a tough time building trust, in part because there are fewer of them and those who remain are stretched thin.

Declining circulation and falling advertising revenue have led to dramatic downsizing at print, broadcast and digital outfits. Newspapers, for instance, shed more than 24,000 reporting and editing jobs — a 37 percent drop — between 2004 and 2015, the latest year for which figures exist.[1] And the remaining reporters must not only gather the news and write stories but also shoot videos and constantly update their stories in real time using Twitter, Facebook and other social media.

"As newsrooms shrink, there's less time to do stories and they're doing shorter, more incomplete stories," says Tom Rosenstiel, executive director of the American Press Institute, a nonpartisan media research group in Arlington, Va. "As a consumer, you say, 'This is paper is thinner,'" he says, while journalists are having to "write a tweet and do a video [so] they're stretched thinner. That hurts trust. You don't have as much time to do everything."

Facing plummeting ad income, Gannett Co., the country's largest newspaper chain and owner of *USA Today* and more than 100 other dailies, reduced its workforce about 2 percent last October.[2] The company also cut staff at its Tennessee and New Jersey papers this year, but has refused to publicize recent cuts, according to the *Columbia Journalism Review.*[3] BH Media Group, a subsidiary of Berkshire Hathaway, the conglomerate headed by Nebraska investor Warren Buffett, announced in April it was cutting 289 jobs at its 31 dailies and nearly 50 weeklies.[4]

And the future economic climate for newspapers could get even worse, said Nicco Mele, former *Los Angeles Times* senior vice president. "If the next three years look like the last three years," he predicted in 2016, "somewhere between a third to a half" of the 50 largest metropolitan papers in the country could go out of business. Mele is now director of the Shorenstein Center on Media, Politics and Public Policy at Harvard University.[5]

Staff cuts have decimated coverage of state legislative news. Between 2005 and 2014, investigative and in-depth reporting on state government declined 30 percent at six major papers, according to a 2016 study by a George Washington University graduate student.[6]

Downsizing local and state government coverage means greater secrecy — and potentially increased corruption — because fewer media outlets are holding state and local institutions accountable, several watchdog groups have warned. "The traditional media, particularly newspapers, have always led the open-government charges if the school board is closing a meeting illegally or the city is denying records or a judge is kicking a reporter out," said Jeffrey Hunt, a media lawyer in Salt Lake City. He sees the media "leaving the field in terms of fighting these battles."[7]

Not all of the economic news is bad — especially for the big media outlets such as *The New York Times*, *The Washington Post* and cable network MSNBC that have devoted substantial resources to the unfolding controversy over Russia's alleged involvement in the U.S. presidential election and ties to President Trump's administration.

In January *The Post* generated more new subscriptions than in any other month, beating what had been a record-setting November.[8] The paper has hired hundreds of reporters and editors since Amazon's Jeff Bezos bought the paper a few years ago, and Jed Hartman, chief revenue officer, predicted that 2017 would be its third year of double-digit revenue growth.[9] And during the first three months of this year *The Times* added 308,000 net digital-only news subscriptions — more than in any quarter in its history.[10] First-quarter revenues increased 5.1 percent over the first quarter of 2016, and circulation revenues jumped 11.2 percent.[11]

Stephen Farnsworth, a professor of political science and international affairs at the University of Mary Washington in Fredericksburg, Va., said the two papers are benefiting from a jump in the number of serious news consumers because of Trump. Those people "are appreciating the media more than they did last year at this time," says Fransworth, who directs Mary Washington's Center for Leadership and Media Studies.[12]

Despite those numbers, *The Times* in late May announced a round of newsroom buyouts aimed primarily at editors. The paper also announced it was abolishing the "public editor," or ombudsman, position held by Liz Spayd. Publisher Arthur Sulzberger said the paper would create a "Reader Center" to interact with the public.[13]

Meanwhile, the left-leaning MSNBC was the second-most-watched cable network during prime time during the week of May 15 — behind TNT, which carried several NBA playoff games. MSNBC's weekday prime-time shows averaged 2.44 million, eclipsing Fox News' 2.40 million for the first time ever.[14] Fox has devoted less coverage to the Russia controversy, and its commentary has been solidly pro-Trump. Some industry analysts wonder if its approach will hurt both its credibility and financial situation.[15]

Numerous advertisers backed away from Fox after commentator Bill O'Reilly was forced out in April amid allegations of sexual harassment and popular Fox commentator Sean Hannity had to apologize for advancing a discredited rumor that a murdered Democratic National Committee staffer was targeted for death by Hillary Clinton and liberal philanthropist George Soros.[16]

No one in the industry, however, has an easy solution for how news organizations can boost revenues while maintaining trust. Some foundations are financing investigative reporting, and some wealthy donors are providing millions of dollars to fight fake news and support in-depth reporting.

Another experiment is emulating the Netherlands' *De Correspondent (The Correspondent)*, which recently announced a U.S. prototype. The online news site is funded by 56,000 members, who each pay about $63 a year for work done by its 21 full-time staff and 75 freelancers. The site aims to do in-depth, unique articles without competing against other media for breaking news, said Jay Rosen, a New York University professor of journalism who is helping with the U.S. version's launch.[17]

At journalism conferences, Rosen wrote, he has heard "a very good question: What if news organizations optimized every part of the operation for trust? Not for speed, traffic, profits, headlines or prizes . . . but for trust. What would that even look like? My answer: It would look a lot like *De Correspondent*."[18]

— *Chuck McCutcheon*

[1] "Newspapers Fact Sheet," Pew Research Center, p. 8, June 1, 2017, https://tiny url.com/yb8g77ht.

[2] Philana A. Patterson, "Gannett to reduce workforce by about 2% to help manage costs," *USA Today*, Oct. 24, 2016, http://tinyurl.com/yaknjj3y.

[3] Steve Cavendish, "Gannett Slashes Staffs at Tennessee Papers," *Nashville Scene*, March 28, 2017, http://tinyurl.com/ydff4nfa; Benjamin Mullin, "Layoffs hit North Jersey Media Group, again," Poynter.org, http://tinyurl.com/h8erxqr. Also see David Uberti, "Gannett newspapers are hiding an important local story," *Columbia Journalism Review*, May 5, 2017, http://tinyurl.com/y97jnu7w.

[4] Paul Fletcher, "Berkshire Hathaway's Media Group Cuts 289 Newspaper Jobs Nationwide," *Forbes*, April 4, 2017, http://tinyurl.com/ybwl52l3.

[5] "Nicco Mele — In Search of a Business Model: The Future of Journalism in an Age of Social Media and Dramatic Declines in Print Revenue," Shorenstein Center on Media, Politics and Policy, Harvard University, Feb. 18, 2016, http://tinyurl.com/ya3qes95.

[6] Lauren A. Dickinson, "The Strength of State Government Reporting: How In-Depth News and Investigative Coverage by Six U.S. Newspapers Fared from 2005 Through 2014," master of arts thesis, George Washington University, May 15, 2016, http://tinyurl.com/yb6ajwsl.

[7] Miranda S. Spivack, "Public contracts shrouded in secrecy," "Reveal" (Center for Investigative Reporting), Nov. 16, 2016, http://tinyurl.com/y9jvtrue.

[8] Ken Doctor, "Trump Bump Grows Into Subscription Surge — and Not Just for the New York Times," *TheStreet.com*, March 3, 2017, http://tinyurl.com/y7hu29ff.

[9] James B. Stewart, "Washington Post, Breaking News, Is Also Breaking New Ground," *The New York Times*, May 19, 2017, http://tinyurl.com/y8cs94x2.

[10] Sydney Ember, "New York Times Co. Reports Rising Digital Profit as Print Advertising Falls," *The New York Times*, May 3, 2017, http://tinyurl.com/m72ezr5.

[11] "The New York Times Company Reports 2017 First-Quarter Results," *Business Wire*, May 3, 2017, http://tinyurl.com/y8mr6d8b.

[12] Natalia Wojcik, "Trump has been 'rocket fuel' for NYT digital subscriptions, CEO says," CNBC.com, May 3, 2017, http://tinyurl.com/kyp6y46.

[13] Tali Arbel, "Among the job cuts at The New York Times, the public editor," *Boston.com* (The Associated Press), May 31, 2017, http://tinyurl.com/y88zmdz8.

[14] James Hibberd, "MSNBC weekly ratings beat Fox News, CNN for first time ever," *Entertainment Weekly.com*, May 22, 2017, http://tinyurl.com/m2sntup.

[15] Stephen Battaglio, "Trump-Russia story is a threat to Fox News' ratings dominance," *Los Angeles Times*, May 23, 2017, http://tinyurl.com/y9l5msgq.

[16] Simon Dumenco, "Is the Sean Hannity Advertiser Revolt Bill O'Reilly All Over Again?" *Advertising Age*, May 25, 2017, http://tinyurl.com/ybpayo4k.

[17] Jay Rosen, "Jay Rosen: This is what a news organization built on reader trust looks like," NiemanLab, March 28, 2017, http://tinyurl.com/ktkmpgb.

[18] *Ibid.*

Rachel Maddow, host of the "Rachel Maddow Show" on MSNBC, is celebrated by liberals – and reviled by conservatives – for her partisan commentary. In today's highly polarized political and media climate, 62 percent of Americans say the media favor one political party over the other, compared with 50 percent in past years.

media.[90] House Majority Leader Kevin McCarthy, R-Calif., a Trump supporter, said the president's deployment of Twitter is "like owning newspapers."[91]

Facebook came under heavy criticism during the campaign for tailoring stories in users' online feeds to what those users had previously read. That included a substantial amount of fake news, which made the network "a sewer of misinformation," according to Joshua Benton, director of Harvard's Nieman Journalism Lab.[92]

As polls showed trust in the media plummeting, news organizations and outside groups ramped up efforts to rebuild it.

One effort was the Reynolds Institute's Trusting News project, launched in January 2016 to look at how news outlets could rebuild trust through social media. The project found successful social-media posts shared several traits: They were about familiar topics that people were inclined to interact with; they gave people something specific to react to; and they used informal language to be relatable.[93]

A participant, the *Standard-Examiner* in Ogden, Utah, developed a video for Facebook and its website in which local African-Americans and law enforcement officials met to discuss Black Lives Matter.[94] The project

"was a new way for us to see the importance of having a conversation with the readers and being transparent," says Ann Elise Taylor, the paper's news editor.

The Coloradoan newspaper in Fort Collins, Colo., used a hit-and-run bicycle accident as a way to explain how — contrary to some readers' beliefs — journalists regret having to cover bad news. The Facebook post generated more than 3,500 link clicks — far more than expected.[95]

The Cincinnati television station WCPO-TV also took part, using Facebook to explain its commitment to covering child poverty while acknowledging the challenges in exploring the topic because it cannot show children's faces or use their voices on camera.[96]

"With the state of media and the way people think about media, it's crazy not to get involved with a project like this to win their trust," says Mike Canan, WCPO .com's editor.

CURRENT SITUATION

Trump and the Media

The early months of Trump's presidency have been marked by aggressive news coverage — led by *The Times* and *Post* — about whether Russia's government worked behind the scenes to help his campaign and influence his new administration.

A Quinnipiac University poll in early May indicates the media covering Trump may have gained some ground in winning the public's confidence. But it also showed skepticism of journalists remains entrenched.

When asked whom people trusted more to tell the truth about important issues, 31 percent picked Trump and 57 percent cited the media, a rise of 5 percentage points from mid-February, when the president denounced the media as "the enemy of the American people" in a tweet.[97]

However, the poll also showed that voters disapproved, 58 percent to 37 percent, of the way the media cover the president.[98]

Such a split in attitudes reflects the harm inflicted from Trump's attacks, says Bill Adair, a former *Tampa Bay Times* reporter and founder of the fact-checking site PolitiFact who is now a professor of journalism at Duke University.

"Clearly there's been a hunger for accurate, objective news lately — that's been encouraging," Adair says. "But

Should journalists try to be objective?

YES Thomas Kent
President and CEO, Radio Free Europe/Radio Liberty; Former Standards Editor, The Associated Press

Written for *CQ Researcher*, June 2017

Not every journalist needs to be objective. But if sources of objective journalism disappear, society will suffer a tragic loss.

Some claim it's impossible for journalists to be objective; no one, they say, can report the news without a shade of personal opinion.

This might be true if a journalist's job were simply to provide one version of reality. That would open the way for journalists to impose their views on others. But the real goal of objectivity isn't so much about controlling the information available as about making sure readers get all the facts and interpretations they need to make up their own minds.

Smart journalists draw these facts and interpretations not only from their own investigations but also from reporting and reasonable opinions on social networks — making a well-done objective news story deeply democratic, reflecting input from many places. Objectivity demands only that journalists keep their personal views out of their stories. Personal opinions should be saved for opinion columns, where people expect writers to advocate for their points of view.

Critics sometimes claim objective journalism is a robotic, mindless craft of simply writing down what everyone says. It is nothing of the sort. So-called fake news and fantasy narratives have no place in an objective news article. Some things happened; others didn't. A newsmaker spoke in one context; to put his or her words in another is a lie. Journalists remain responsible for the truth of what they publish.

Some critics also accuse objective journalists of scrubbing humanity and emotion out of stories in a bid to avoid any opinion. But objectivity doesn't mean rejection of human feeling. The slaying of children by a gunman at a school can be fairly referred to as horrific; there is no need for a paragraph saying "on the other hand." A photographer covering a war or disaster can put aside his camera when he has a chance to save a life.

The world will be far poorer if journalism is allowed to become nothing but a stream of opinion pieces, which by their nature shortchange some points of view in order to advance the author's argument.

Society must have a place where thoughtful readers without the time to do extensive personal research can find fair, accurate accounts of events as well as a variety of responsible opinion to put them into context. Objective journalism fills this need.

NO Bruce Thornton
Research Fellow, Hoover Institution; Professor of Classics and Humanities, Fresno State University

Written for *CQ Researcher*, June 2017

So-called objective journalism is another progressive idea based on scientism, the notion that human behavior and action can be as predictable and reliable as science. In earlier times, media reported obvious facts, but the political interpretation of those facts reflected what James Madison called the "passions and interests" of the competing political factions in a diverse country. The numerous newspapers across the country reflected this diversity, which is why they often had the word "Democrat" or "Republican" in their titles.

After World War II, journalism was professionalized and training happened in "J schools" at liberal universities, which biased much reporting toward liberal and urban sensibilities. The advent of television reduced the number of newspapers that once provided diversity, allowing the liberal interpretation to dominate far beyond the media centers in New York, Washington, Chicago and Los Angeles.

In the 1960s journalism became an activist and advocacy business. Coverage of the Vietnam War and the Watergate scandal interpreted events from a partisan and left-wing perspective that saw U.S. intervention as neocolonial adventurism and President Richard Nixon as a budding tyrant out to destroy the Constitution. As a consequence, South Vietnam was abandoned to the communist North, and Nixon was forced to resign, paving the way for Jimmy Carter's disastrous foreign policy of retreat and appeasement.

The repeal of the Federal Communications Commission's Fairness Doctrine in 1987 was followed by the advent of talk radio, which began to erode the monopoly of the big-three television networks and dominant newspapers like *The New York Times* and *The Washington Post*. Then came cable news with shows like Fox News, and the internet. Now thousands of outlets reflect the diversity of opinion that the First Amendment was written to protect. Where once maybe 50 opinion makers dominated political discourse, now there are hundreds of thousands. Their impact became clear when in 2004 CBS icon Dan Rather was brought down by internet sleuths for reporting "fake news" about George W. Bush's National Guard service.

Today we've returned to a true "marketplace of ideas" in which diverse political perspectives can compete, and ideological biases pretending to be "objective" can be exposed within hours. Once more it is up to the citizens to be informed and use their critical judgment rather than taking on faith the reporting of a handful of media outlets. If they misuse that freedom, that's the price always to be paid when people are free.

Pierre Omidyar, founder of eBay, launched a $100 million global project in April aimed at restoring trust in the media and other institutions. The focus will be on strengthening independent media and investigative journalism, confronting misinformation and hate speech and enabling citizens to better engage with government.

Trump has said some incredibly damaging things about the media."

Both *The New York Times* and *Post* have seen financial gains that media analysts say reflect increased trust.[99]

Barton Swaim, a conservative *Post* columnist, said he expected the mainstream media to aggressively cover Trump's presidency after being demonized during the election. "Even so, the sheer visceral animosity from the media, together with the aggressively insurgent opposition by [Democratic] holdovers from within the government, has shocked me as much as the election itself," Swaim said.[100]

Media scholars and journalists say Trump tacitly understands traditional media's importance. They note that when the initial attempt to overturn Obama's Affordable Care Act could not win enough GOP supporters to be brought up for a House vote in March, the first reporters Trump notified were not from a conservative outlet, but *The Times* and *Post*.[101]

Commentators at Fox News, like other GOP-leaning outlets, have remained supportive of Trump, devoting less airtime to the ongoing investigation's into the Trump campaign's possible collusion with Russia than other outlets. Fox's opinion-givers and other conservatives have echoed the president in arguing that the leaking of classified information to the media is far more serious than speculation of any administration wrongdoing.[102]

William Kristol, a conservative pundit and former Fox commentator, criticized the conservative media, particularly Fox News, for "rationalizing everything" Trump does.[103]

The nonprofit investigative website *ProPublica,* founded in 2008, recently has expanded on its collaborations with other outlets, pairing with *The Times* and The Associated Press in March to rapidly collect White House staffers' financial-disclosure forms.[104] *ProPublica* opened a bureau in Chicago this spring, its first outside Washington and New York.[105]

In the Midwest, Cleveland's *Plain Dealer* and *Cleveland.com* launched the reporting collaboration "Ohio Matters," which has sent reporters to six rural, suburban and urban parts of the crucial swing state to hear concerns. Trump carried Ohio by 8 percentage points in 2016, far above most polls' earlier projections.[106]

To try to show its commitment to watchdog journalism, *The Post* in February put the motto "Democracy Dies in Darkness" below its front-page nameplate. The move led the conservative *Washington Times* to launch its own slogan — "Real News for Real Americans."[107]

Trust-Related Projects

Several private and nonprofit groups have joined media organizations on projects aimed at developing trust.

A global coalition of technology leaders, academic institutions and others announced a $14 million undertaking in April, The News Integrity Initiative, to combat declining trust in media and advance news literacy. Supporters include Craig Newmark, founder of the online classified-ad site Craigslist, which, ironically, has severely crippled newspapers' classified revenues.

"As a news consumer, like most folks, I want news we can trust," Newmark said. "That means standing up for trustworthy news media and learning how to spot clickbait and deceptive news."[108]

The program will be administered by the CUNY Graduate School of Journalism. It will focus in part on helping readers better spot fake news and frivolous "click-bait" disguised as news articles.[109]

The philanthropic investment firm Omidyar Network, the brainchild of eBay founder Pierre Omidyar, in April launched a $100 million project over the next three years aimed at restoring trust in the media and other institutions globally. The funding will focus on strengthening independent media and investigative journalism, tackling misinformation and hate speech, and enabling citizens to better engage with government.[110]

The Reynolds Institute recently wrapped up the second phase of its "Trusting News" project with 30 media outlets around the country. That phase — which will conclude with a report this fall — invited local readers and viewers to describe how news outlets can win their confidence, Mayer says.

In Cincinnati, WCPO.com's invitation for readers to take part drew 463 responses in less than a day — a sign Canan says people care about the issue.

"One of the biggest takeaways is, there's a lot of guilt by association," he says. "As I delved into conversations with people, they said, 'I don't trust the media,' but it was really, 'I don't when comes to politics.' Or they don't trust the national media."

Canan says he has started collaborating with the *Cincinnati Enquirer,* a journalistic competitor, on ways to build trust. Peter Bhatia, the newspaper's editor and vice president for audience development, said he and other editors have been trying to "demystify our process" by explaining how the newsroom operates in talks to tea party as well as progressive groups and when publishing investigative projects or deeply reported work.

Transparency "becomes more of an imperative as we work hard to restore trust lost in the last election cycle, regardless of how fair the charges against us may be," Bhatia said.[111]

The *Standard-Examiner's* Taylor, who also took part in the Reynolds Institute project, agrees on the need for increased transparency. She says a surprising number of readers do not make the distinction between news and commentary, with separate staffs handling each as at most outlets.

"That's knowledge a lot of journalists take for granted," she says. "One thing I'd like to address in being more transparent is explain what is an editorial, what is an opinion piece, how do they differ from a news story and how are all these things connected? That would be a valuable tool people could use as they consume news for the rest of their lives."

Facebook and Google

The twin colossi of the information world are trying to bolster confidence in the media in the face of criticism that they have enabled the spread of fake news and profited from sharing journalism content without paying its producers for it.

Facebook has put out new tools to stem the spread of fake news. If users click on a news story, they now have the option of reporting it as being false. If enough users flag such stories, Facebook will send the article to a factchecking organization such as Snopes. com or PolitiFact — and if those outlets agree, the article will appear on Facebook with a red banner that says "Disputed by third-party fact checkers" and include a link to the explanation.

In addition, Facebook has promised to employ software to help identify fake news stories and has its engineers working on finding websites that impersonate actual news sites.[112]

Founder Mark Zuckerberg published a manifesto in February outlining how the social-media giant can contribute to restoring trust in news and information. One of his aims is to encourage the growth of local news and improve the range of business models on which news organizations rely.[113]

Google's News Lab, launched in 2015, seeks to connect journalists with programs, data and other resources to use in their reporting. It started the First Draft coalition to create standards and best practices for verifying eyewitness media content and combating fake news. The coalition expanded last year to include 80 partners, including Facebook and Twitter, and is working with universities and other organizations around the world.[114]

Critics of Google's and Facebook's efforts, however, say their continued dependence on incorporating news articles in their content compels them to do far more to help the media regain trust.

Steven Waldman, founder of Life-Posts.com, where people share personal stories online, said Facebook and Google should devote 1 percent of their profits for five years to create a $4.4 billion permanent endowment to transform local journalism.

"These companies are among the biggest beneficiaries of the digital disruption that has, among other things, caused the crisis in American journalism," Waldman said. "It's time for the disrupters to solve the problems."[115]

OUTLOOK
Unpleasant Truths

With political polarization deeply rooted in society, journalism scholars and those in the news media predict mistrust of journalists will continue — the question is to what degree.

"The media will never be all that popular; it's in the business of telling unpleasant truths," says Stephen Farnsworth, a professor of political science and international affairs at the University of Mary Washington in Fredericksburg, Va., who directs its Center for Leadership and Media Studies.

The American Press Institute's Rosenstiel says trust levels "are going to continue to slip, because we're in a more polarized world, and I don't see a solution to that on the horizon." Part of the problem, he adds, is the inability of the Democratic and Republican parties to produce leaders who are considered trustworthy to a broad bipartisan audience.

"It's ironic that when he left office, Barack Obama had much higher approval ratings than Trump or any politician has now," he says. "I think there's a sort of nostalgia — we can, in retrospect, appreciate people, but when we're on the field of battle, we retreat to our team."

More conservatives need to have their voices heard in traditional media, said former Wisconsin right-wing talk-radio host Charlie Sykes. If that does not happen, he said, those conservatives will continue putting their faith in outlets that mirror their preconceived views.

"You can do the best reporting in the world, but unless you can find a way to restore that credibility . . . it won't even register," said Sykes, now a contributing *New York Times* columnist.[116]

Benton, of Harvard's Nieman Lab, is particularly interested in seeing whether online outlets such as BuzzFeed and Mic that have marketed themselves to younger, urban readers will start courting conservative readers.

"Do they double down on identity-driven stories embracing the values of diversity and multiculturalism?" he asked. "Or — at a time when many are under their own revenue strains . . . do any of them see a market opportunity in the Trump voter?"[117]

Finding ways to finance quality journalism at larger-scale mainstream outlets will be critical, says Arizona State's Downie, the former *Post* editor.

"I'm pleased to see that audiences are beginning to find ways to pay more for digital subscriptions to the *Times*, support events produced by other news organizations and increase membership in public radio," he says. "Foundations are stepping up and philanthropists are stepping up. But whether that's sufficient five or 10 years from now, I can't say."

The Reynolds Institute's Mayer, who leads the Trusting News project, predicts a split between news organizations catering to polarization and those willing to earn more trust. Of the latter group, she expects an increased effort to listen more closely to readers.

"There's no room in journalism any more for people who don't see customer service and understanding the audience as part of the job," she says. "People in journalism have to have an entrepreneurial mindset and a customer-service mindset with a focus on, 'Here's what we do.'"

Duke University's Adair, the PolitiFact creator, estimates that if trust levels do pick up, it will take 10 or 15 years. The media "will do better at labeling types of articles and being more transparent," he says. "There's likely to be a renewed effort to invest in news literacy so that people, particularly young people, have a better understanding of the news ecosystem."

Until then, said *Post* media columnist Margaret Sullivan, a former *Times* public editor, young people going into journalism must accept being mistrusted.

"You have to understand there's a mission attached to our job and that we need to do it well," Sullivan told a student audience at the University of Wisconsin-Madison, "and put on our big-boy and big-girl pants and not worry that we're under attack — because it's going to continue."[118]

NOTES

1. Jennifer Calfas, "Read the Advice Bob Woodward and Carl Bernstein Gave at the White House Correspondents' Dinner," *Time,* April 30, 2017, http://tinyurl.com/n7qvosk.

2. Mark Landler, "Trump Savages News Media at Rally to Mark His 100th Day," *The New York Times,* April 29, 2016, https://tinyurl.com/ycvcq7u9.

3. See Chuck McCutcheon, "Populism and Political Parties," *CQ Researcher,* Sept. 9, 2016, pp. 721-744.

4. Benjamin Mullin, " 'I want to see us take journalism to people where they are': A Q-&-A with Jeff Jarvis about restoring trust in journalism," Poynter.org, April 3, 2017, https://tinyurl.com/y6uugszv.

5. Art Swift, "Americans' Trust in Mass Media Sinks to New Low," Gallup, Sept. 14, 2016, https://tinyurl.com/hda5s4u.

6. "Honesty/ethics in professions," Gallup, Dec. 7-11, 2016, https://tinyurl.com/lcer8a.

7. Art Swift, "Six in 10 in US See Partisan Bias in News Media," Gallup, April 5, 2017, https://tinyurl.com/metlvk6.

8. "How trust can be broken, and the decline of confidence in the press," American Press Institute, April 17, 2016, https://tinyurl.com/yadwe7or.

9. "Oxford Dictionaries Word of the Year 2016 is . . . Post-Truth," Oxford Dictionaries.com, Dec. 12, 2016, https://tinyurl.com/kdgknmd.

10. "Meet The Press 01/22/17," NBC News, Jan. 22, 2017, https://tinyurl.com/y7fuxnjy.

11. Shane Goldmacher, "How Trump gets his fake news," *Politico,* May 15, 2017, https://tinyurl.com/kwlt3yl.

12. Michael Barthel and Amy Mitchell, "Americans' Attitudes About the News Media Deeply Divided Along Partisan Lines," Pew Research Center, May 10, 2017, https://tinyurl.com/ydgclyxx.

13. Laura Nichols, "Poll: Majority Find Major Media Outlets Credible," Morning Consult, Dec. 7, 2016, https://tinyurl.com/ya59mcra.

14. Paul Farhi, "Reporters say they are being roughed up. Observers point to Trump," *The Washington Post,* May 26, 2017, https://tinyurl.com/ycfzvlbj.

15. "Windows shattered at Herald-Leader building; suspected bullet damage found," *Lexington Herald-Leader* (Ky.), May 29, 2017, https://tinyurl.com/ycp3c2ds.

16. "Marvin Kalb on Current Challenges to the Freedom of the Press," National Press Club Journalism Institute speech, YouTube.com, posted April 1, 2017, http://tinyurl.com/ycxubgdd.

17. Andrew Collins, "Meet Watchdog editor John Bicknell: journalist, author, history buff," Franklin Center for Government & Public Integrity, Nov. 3, 2015, https://tinyurl.com/y9pwrkyd.

18. Paul Farhi, "Dear readers: Please stop calling us 'the media.' There is no such thing," *The Washington Post,* Sept. 23, 2016, https://tinyurl.com/y9v84hfb.

19. Mathew Ingram, "Glenn Greenwald vs. the NYT's Bill Keller on objectivity and the future of journalism,"

Gigaom, Oct. 28, 2013, https://tinyurl.com/yd76vw7v.

20. Margaret Sullivan, "How one reporter's rejection of objectivity got him fired," *The Washington Post,* Feb. 1, 2017, https://tinyurl.com/y7e98afx.

21. Lewis Wallace, "Objectivity is dead, and I'm okay with it," Medium.com, Jan. 27, 2017, https://tinyurl.com/y8k56rtw.

22. Adam Ragusea, "Glenn Greenwald on the 'adversarial force' of a free press," *Current*, March 29, 2016, http://tinyurl.com/y8zokx8h.

23. "Objectivity: What Is It Good For?" WNYC-FM's "On the Media" transcript, Feb. 3, 2017, https://tinyurl.com/ybg5hlbe.

24. Bruce Thornton, "We Citizens Have to Guard the Media 'Guardians,'" *FrontPageMag*, Sept. 2, 2016, https://tinyurl.com/ya368tpe.

25. Jonah Goldberg, "The Press Is Not the Enemy," *National Review,* Feb. 24, 2017, https://tinyurl.com/yaox2yj7.

26. Michael Kinsley, "Is It Possible There Is Nothing Nice to Say?" *The New York Times*, May 13, 2017, https://tinyurl.com/ybrufzqw.

27. "'Trump Revealed': The reporting archive," *The Washington Post,* Aug. 30, 2016, https://tinyurl.com/h9g6rgg.

28. James Fallows, "Why Americans Hate the Media," *The Atlantic,* February 1996, https://tinyurl.com/y8y9h3st.

29. Mathew Ingram, "Here's Why the Media Failed to Predict a Donald Trump Victory," *Fortune,* Nov. 9, 2016, https://tinyurl.com/z8db88p.

30. " 'New York Times' Executive Editor On The New Terrain Of Covering Trump," "Fresh Air," NPR, Dec. 8, 2016, https://tinyurl.com/jdo6pxg.

31. Andrew McGill, "U.S. Media's Real Elitism Problem," *The Atlantic,* Nov. 19, 2016, https://tinyurl.com/y9jd3fu6.

32. Carrie Sheffield, "WATCH: Journalism used to fight for the working man, now it's a bastion of 'trust fund kids,'" *Salon.com,* March 19, 2017, https://tinyurl.com/yd8esfe3.

33. "History of the WHCA," White House Correspondents' Association, https://tinyurl.com/csdr45h; Jim Romenesko, "Why NYT doesn't attend White House Correspondents' Association Dinner," Poynter.org, May 4, 2011, https://tinyurl.com/yawpvrp9.

34. See Peter Katel, "Racial Conflict," *CQ Researcher*, Jan. 8, 2016, pp. 25-48.

35. Nick Tabor, "PBS?'s Tavis Smiley on What's Wrong (and Right) With the Media," *New York*, July 24, 2016, https://tinyurl.com/yabdclp3.

36. Shan Wang, "U.S. newsrooms seem to be getting a little more diverse. But minority journalists are still, well, a minority," NiemanLab.org, Sept. 9, 2016, https://tinyurl.com/zqkx9zg.

37. "The President and the Press: The First Amendment in the First 100 Days," Newseum.org event transcript, April 12, 2017, https://tinyurl.com/y8yn3o4w.

38. "Anxious in America," *The New York Times*, 2016, https://tinyurl.com/y8dx7ucp.

39. "Why The Media Use Anonymous Sources," "Morning Edition," NPR, Dec. 16, 2016, https://tinyurl.com/hs9a4v4.

40. Eli Yokley, "Voters Skeptical of Anonymous Sourcing, but Still Trust Political Reporting," *Morning Consult*, March 8, 2017, https://tinyurl.com/y7m6dryj; "Morning Consult National Tracking Poll #170301," *Morning Consult*, March 2-6, 2017, p. 265, https://tinyurl.com/ycvdgy5h.

41. Tara Golshan, "Full transcript: President Trump's CPAC speech," *Vox.com*, Feb. 24, 2017, https://tinyurl.com/ybescrr8.

42. "Following Multiple Debacles, NY Times Is 'Cracking Down On The Use Of Anonymous Sources,'" Media Matters for America, March 15, 2016, https://tinyurl.com/yamapyfc.

43. Liz Spayd, "The Risk of Unnamed Sources? Unconvinced Readers," *The New York Times*, Feb. 18, 2017, https://tinyurl.com/yb2wmu3r.

44. Mollie Hemingway, tweet, May 15, 2017, https://tinyurl.com/y9z4rmgv.

45. Jill Disis, "New York Times editor: Why journalists need to use anonymous sources," CNN.com, Feb. 26, 2017, https://tinyurl.com/ycuvz6hd.

46. "Why The Media Use Anonymous Sources," *op. cit.*

47. Steve Myers, "Study: Use of anonymous sources peaked in 1970s, dropped by 2008," Poynter.org, Aug. 9, 2011, https://tinyurl.com/y98utmk9. The study was by Matt J. Duffy, a professor of international media law at Zayed University in Abu Dhabi, and Ann E. Williams, a professor of communication at Georgia State University.

48. "John F. Kennedy Speeches/The President and the Press: Address before the American Newspaper Publishers Association, April 27, 1961," John F. Kennedy Presidential Library and Museum, https://tinyurl.com/zuxwmen.

49. Lindsey Bever, "Memo to Donald Trump: Thomas Jefferson invented hating the media," *The Washington Post*, Feb. 18, 2017, https://tinyurl.com/ybh5hqro; Daniel Lattier, "Thomas Jefferson Had Some Issues With Newspapers," *Intellectual Takeout*, Aug. 28, 2015, https://tinyurl.com/y76v92bt.

50. Ryan Holiday, "Abraham Lincoln as Media Manipulator-in-Chief: The 150 Year History of Corrupt Press," *The Observer*, Nov. 5, 2014, https://tinyurl.com/ycq45rf6.

51. Garry Wills, "How Lincoln Played the Press," *New York Review of Books*, Nov. 6, 2014, https://tinyurl.com/yaoc27mz.

52. "Second Inaugural Address of Ulysses S. Grant," Yale University Law School, Lillian Goldman Law Library, https://tinyurl.com/yb9okf5b.

53. "Yellow journalism," *New World Encyclopedia*, https://tinyurl.com/yagthwpu.

54. "Our History," New York Times Company, https://tinyurl.com/y7hxev7j; "Without Fear or Favor," *The New York Times*, Aug. 19, 1996, https://tinyurl.com/ybtored9.

55. Upton Sinclair, *The Brass Check: A Study of American Journalism* (1919), https://tinyurl.com/y7zsf7um.

56. "Upton Sinclair," https://tinyurl.com/yc2574cl.

57. "Walter Lippmann," *Encyclopaedia Brittanica*, https://tinyurl.com/y93ffgw5.

58. Walter Lippmann, *Liberty and the News* (1920), p. 11.

59. Stuart N. Brotman, "Revisiting the broadcast public interest standard in communications law and regulation," Brookings Institution, March 23, 2017, https://tinyurl.com/kpugnbz.

60. Dan Fletcher, "A Brief History of the Fairness Doctrine," *Time,* Feb. 20, 2009, https://tinyurl.com/yawejko8.

61. Jonathan M. Ladd, *Why Americans Hate the Media and How It Matters* (2013), p. 62, http://tinyurl.com/mljy8vp.

62. "Joseph R. McCarthy," History.com, https://tinyurl.com/o724hco; David Mindich, "For journalists covering Trump, a Murrow moment," *Columbia Journalism Review,* July 15, 2016, http://tinyurl.com/ybhfryk4.

63. Ladd, *op. cit.*

64. "Final Words: Cronkite's Vietnam Commentary," NPR, July 18, 2009, https://tinyurl.com/3wncqv3.

65. Chester Pach, "Public Learned Less After Media Was Blamed for Failure in Vietnam," *The New York Times,* April 29, 2015, https://tinyurl.com/ycult2yx; Christopher Cimaglio, " 'A Tiny and Closed Fraternity of Privileged Men': The Nixon-Agnew Antimedia Campaign and the Liberal Roots of the U.S. Conservative 'Liberal Media' Critique," *International Journal of Communication 10* (2016), https://tinyurl.com/y86wosuv.

66. "The Retromingent Vigilantes Revel," Accuracy in Media Report, October 1989, https://tinyurl.com/y8h26snb.

67. Swift, "Americans' Trust in Mass Media Sinks to New Low," *op. cit.*

68. Mark Hertsgaard, *On Bended Knee: The Press and the Reagan Presidency* (1988).

69. Fletcher, *op. cit.*

70. "Rush Limbaugh," Biography.com, https://tinyurl.com/ce2e5qh.

71. Michael I. Meyerson, "The Cable Communications Policy Act of 1984: A Balancing Act on the Coaxial Wires," *Georgia Law Review 19,* Spring 1985, https://tinyurl.com/y8kfytwm.

72. Mike Sager, "The fabulist who changed journalism," *Columbia Journalism Review,* Spring 2016, https://tinyurl.com/y7rmfgnh.

73. Michael Hiltzik, "Stephen Glass is still retracting his fabricated stories — 18 years later," *Los Angeles Times,* Dec. 15, 2015, https://tinyurl.com/yb3ryk6r.

74. Jacques Steinberg, "Editor of USA Today Resigns; Cites Failure Over Fabrications," *The New York Times,* April 21, 2004, https://tinyurl.com/y8gdzx53.

75. Isabella Kwai, "Why he did it: Jayson Blair opens up about his plagiarism and fabrication at the New York Times," ReportersLab.org, April 12, 2016, https://tinyurl.com/y8msdlel.

76. Paul Farhi, "At long last, Brian Williams is back — humbled and demoted to MSNBC," *The Washington Post,* Sept. 21, 2015, http://tinyurl.com/y7gnkb6c.

77. T. Rees Shapiro, "Jury finds reporter, Rolling Stone responsible for defaming U-Va. dean with gang rape story," *The Washington Post*, Nov. 4, 2016, http://tinyurl.com/ybhzols8.

78. Swift, *op. cit.*

79. See Marcia Clemmitt, "'Alt-Right' Movement," *CQ Researcher,* March 17, 2017, pp. 241-264.

80. Oliver Darcy, "Donald Trump broke the conservative media," *Business Insider,* Aug. 26, 2016, https://tinyurl.com/j8qprjf.

81. "Roger Ailes Looks Back on 15 Years of Fox News," The Associated Press, Fox News.com, Oct. 5, 2011, https://tinyurl.com/y9anos9o.

82. Alex Weprin, "A Brief History Of MSNBC.com And NBCNews.com," *AdWeek,* July 16, 2012, https://tinyurl.com/ydz8jpqz.

83. Erik Wemple, "Judith Miller tries, and ultimately fails, to defend her flawed Iraq reporting," *The Washington Post*, April 9, 2015, https://tinyurl.com/y8occ74s.

84. Max Follmer, "The Reporting Team That Got Iraq Right," *The Huffington Post,* May 25, 2011, https://tinyurl.com/yo99zz.

85. Andy Barr, "Palin trashes 'lamestream media,'" *Politico,* Nov. 18, 2009, https://tinyurl.com/yc9g7ok7.

86. Matea Gold, "The Mercers and Stephen Bannon: How a populist power base was funded and built," *The Washington Post,* March 17, 2017, https://tinyurl.com/m8gctl3.

87. Keach Hagey, "Soros gives $1 million to Media Matters," *Politico,* Oct. 20, 2010, https://tinyurl.com/29da5l3.

88. Nicholas Confessore and Karen Yourish, "$2 Billion Worth of Free Media for Donald Trump," *The New York Times,* March 15, 2016, https://tinyurl.com/z9jkzcn.

89. Nicole Fisher, "Sanders' Supporters: Why Some Won't Back Clinton," *Forbes,* Aug. 17, 2016, https://tinyurl.com/y7kt698g.

90. Robert Draper, "Trump vs. Congress: Now What?" *The New York Times Magazine,* March 26, 2017, https://tinyurl.com/mxl7vvv.

91. *Ibid.*

92. Joshua Benton, "The forces that drove this election's media failure are likely to get worse," NiemanLab, Nov. 9, 2017, https://tinyurl.com/nrccvms.

93. "Trusting News," Donald W. Reynolds Journalism Institute, February 2017, https://tinyurl.com/kbsgehl.

94. "VIDEO: Discussing race and policing in Northern Utah," *Standard-Examiner* (Ogden, Utah), July 27, 2016, https://tinyurl.com/ybp dzlqd.

95. "Newsrooms Partners: The Coloradoan," Trusting News website, undated, http://tinyurl.com/ycyyjwxu/.

96. "WCPO — 9 On Your Side," Facebook post, Sept. 23, 2016, https://tinyurl.com/yb926w5u.

97. Michael M. Grynbaum, "Trump Calls the News Media the 'Enemy of the American People,'" *The New York Times,* Feb. 17, 2017, https://tinyurl.com/js4uyw5.

98. "May 10, 2017 — U.S. Voters Send Trump Approval To Near Record Low; Quinnipiac University National Poll Finds; No Winner In Media War, But Voters Trust Media More," Quinnipiac University, May 10, 2017, https://tinyurl.com/kebfbpv.

99. Sydney Ember, "New York Times Co. Reports Rising Digital Profit as Print Advertising Falls," *The New York Times,* May 3, 2017, https://tinyurl.com/m72ezr5.

100. Barton Swaim, We're not learning from the Trump story — because we've peeked at the last page," *The Washington Post*, May 18, 2017, https://tinyurl.com/y9pj3tbv.

101. Jackie Strause, "After 'Fake News' Claims, Trump's First Calls After Health-Care Defeat Were to N.Y. Times, Washington Post," *Hollywood Reporter,* March 24, 2017, http://tinyurl.com/kxenhcp.

102. Maxwell Tani, "Here's how Fox News responded to reports Trump leaked classified information to Russian officials," *Business Insider,* May 16, 2017, https://tinyurl.com/ycbbmkor.

103. Aidan McLaughlin, "Bill Kristol: Most of Fox News Has Become 'Ridiculous,'" *Mediaite,* May 15, 2017, https://tinyurl.com/mb87gr4.

104. Eric Umansky, "How We're Learning To Do Journalism Differently in the Age of Trump," *ProPublica,* May 8, 2017, https://tinyurl.com/mk2lvhe.

105. Jackie Spinner, "Q&A: Louise Kiernan says ProPublica Illinois will 'find areas where we can have impact,'" *Columbia Journalism Review,* March 6, 2017, https://tinyurl.com/ybj3zgbh.

106. "Ohio Matters: Redesigning Political Coverage in Ohio," *Cleveland.com*, http://tinyurl.com/mvecskx; "Ohio: Trump vs. Clinton," *Real ClearPolitics.com,* http://tinyurl.com/y923vh3u

107. Rachel Stoltzfoos, "The Washington Times Adopts A New Slogan For Trump Era," *The Daily Caller,* March 13, 2017, https://tinyurl.com/y8etm5nq.

108. Benjamin Mullin, "Can trust in the news be repaired? Facebook, Craig Newmark, Mozilla and others are spending $14 million to try," Poynter.org, April 3, 2017, http://tinyurl.com/nyfkvh4.

109. *Ibid.*

110. Margaret Sullivan, "Omidyar network gives $100 million to boost journalism and fight hate speech," *The Washington Post,* April 4, 2017, https://tinyurl.com/y9a84mes.

111. Peter Bhatia, "To Restore Trust, Enhance Transparency," *Nieman Reports,* Feb. 15, 2017, https://tinyurl.com/yb8jh224.

112. David Pogue, "What Facebook Is Doing to Combat Fake News," *Scientific American*, Feb. 1, 2017, https://tinyurl.com/h26du9a.

113. Mark Zuckerberg, "Building Global Community," Facebook, Feb. 16, 2017, https://tinyurl.com/myq4nkf.

114. Steve Grove, "The Google News Lab in 2016, and where we're headed," *Medium.com,* Dec. 6, 2016, https://tinyurl.com/y747x5bt.

115. Steven Waldman, "What Facebook Owes to Journalism," *The New York Times*, Feb. 21, 2017, https://tinyurl.com/y9kjtyf2.

116. Cadence Bambenek, "Recap: Trust, Truth and the Future of Journalism," Center for Journalism Ethics, University of Wisconsin-Madison, April 13, 2017, https://tinyurl.com/ycdxnwxf.

117. Benton, *op. cit.*

118. "Truth, Trust & the Future of Journalism: Keynote Conversation with Margaret Sullivan," Center for Journalism Ethics, University of Wisconsin-Madison, YouTube video, posted April 5, 2017, https://tinyurl.com/y8dpw97y.

BIBLIOGRAPHY

Selected Sources

Books

Anderson, C.W., Leonard Downie and Michael Schudson, *The News Media: What Everyone Needs to Know,* **Oxford University Press, 2016.**
A media culture professor at the College of Staten Island (Anderson), a former *Washington Post* executive editor (Downie) and a Columbia University journalism professor (Schudson) explain the economic, technological and societal forces that have helped erode trust in journalism.

Carlson, Matt, *Journalistic Authority: Legitimating News in the Digital Era,* **Columbia University Press, 2017.**
A St. Louis University communications professor examines the cultural, structural and technological factors that prompt readers to accept or reject a journalist's version of events.

Graves, Lucas, *Deciding What's True: The Rise of Political Fact-Checking in American Journalism,* **Columbia University Press, 2016.**

A University of Wisconsin professor of journalism and mass communication chronicles the evolution of fact-checking websites and their importance in assessing assertions by government officials.

Stone, Roger, *The Making of the President 2016: How Donald Trump Orchestrated a Revolution,* **Skyhorse Publishing, 2017.**
A political adviser and friend of Donald Trump details how Trump's strategy of castigating mainstream news outlets helped him win the presidency.

Articles

"The Case Against the Media. By the Media," *New York*, **July 25, 2016, https://tinyurl.com/zm2sn6g.**
The weekly magazine interviews dozens of print, broadcast and online journalists about what they see as their profession's biggest flaws.

Benton, Joshua, "The forces that drove this election's media failure are likely to get worse," NiemanLab, Nov. 9, 2017, https://tinyurl.com/nrccvms.
The director of Harvard University's media-research center says the problems that led the media to be blindsided by Trump's victory must be corrected.

Rosenstiel, Tom, "What the post-Trump debate over journalism gets wrong," Brookings Institution, Dec. 20, 2016, https://tinyurl.com/h6pgke5.
A senior fellow at the centrist think tank and executive director of the American Press Institute says journalists must embrace new methods to earn trust, such as making documents and other reporting research available for readers to see firsthand.

Shafer, Jack, "How Trump Took Over the Media By Fighting It," *Politico Magazine*, **Nov. 5, 2016, https://tinyurl.com/jqnhfwn.**
The political website's media writer says Donald Trump went far beyond any other presidential candidate in condemning reporters.

Thornton, Bruce, "We Citizens Have to Guard the Media 'Guardians,'" *Frontpage Mag*, **Sept. 2, 2016, https://tinyurl.com/n86nge5.**
A fellow at Stanford University's Hoover Institution says negative coverage of Trump's presidential campaign reflects the mainstream media's longtime bias against Republicans.

Toffel, Richard J., "The Country Doesn't Trust Us — But They Do Believe Us," NiemanLab, Dec. 12, 2016, https://tinyurl.com/n2vjyzy.

The president of the investigative website ProPublica highlights the importance of trust in an essay accompanying interviews with several dozen journalists, academics and others predicting future media trends.

Umansky, Eric, "How We're Learning To Do Journalism Differently in the Age of Trump," *ProPublica*, May 8, 2017, https://tinyurl.com/mk2lvhe.

ProPublica, a nonprofit online news organization, says it will cover the Trump administration by digging deeper, collaborating, being transparent and being comfortable with uncertainty.

Reports and Studies

"State of the News Media 2016," Pew Research Center, June 15, 2016, https://tinyurl.com/zh7vqdj.

The nonprofit research group says the economic pressures facing the news media intensified in 2015, with average weekday newspaper circulation seeing its biggest drop since 2010.

"Trusting News," Donald W. Reynolds Journalism Institute, February 2017, https://tinyurl.com/kbsgehl.

A research project of the University of Missouri's journalism think tank says news outlets can employ Facebook and other social media to effectively build trust with audiences.

" 'Who Shared It?': How Americans decide what news to trust on social media," American Press Institute, March 20, 2017, https://tinyurl.com/leh49n7.

A collaboration between the American Press Institute and The Associated Press-NORC Center for Public Affairs Research finds that when Americans read news on social media, how much they trust the content is determined less by who creates the news than by who shares it.

Swift, Art, "Americans' Trust in Mass Media Sinks to New Low," Gallup, Sept. 14, 2016, https://tinyurl.com/hda5s4u.

The polling company finds trust in the media at its lowest level since Gallup began asking the question in 1972.

For More Information

Accuracy in Media, 4350 East West Highway, Suite 555, Bethesda, MD 20814; 202-364-4401; www.aim.org. Conservative media watchdog organization that searches for potential liberal bias in news reporting.

American Press Institute, 401 N. Fairfax Drive, Suite 300, Arlington, VA 22203; 571-366-1200; www.americanpressinstitute.org. A nonprofit group that researches journalism trends.

American Society of News Editors, 209 Reynolds Journalism Institute, Missouri School of Journalism, University of Missouri, Columbia, MO 65211; 573-884-2430; www.asne.org. Promotes ethical journalism, supports First Amendment rights and defends freedom of information and open government.

Fairness & Accuracy in Reporting, 124 W. 30th St., Suite 201, New York, NY 10001; 212-633-6700; www.fair.org. Liberal media watchdog organization that monitors bias and censorship in news reporting.

Media Matters for America, P.O. Box 52155, Washington, DC 20091; 202-756-4100; www.mediamatters.org. Liberal

media watchdog group that looks for potential conservative bias in news reporting.

Media Research Center, 325 S. Patrick St., Alexandria, VA 22314; 703-683-9733; www.mrc.org. Conservative media watchdog group that searches for potential liberal bias in news reporting.

Nieman Journalism Lab, Harvard University, 1 Francis Ave., Cambridge, MA 02138; 617-495-2237; www.niemanlab.org. Analyzes the news media's future in the internet age.

Pew Research Center for the People & the Press, 1615 L St., N.W., Suite 700, Washington, DC 20036; 202-419-4300; www.people-press.org. Nonpartisan media research organization funded by the Pew Charitable Trusts.

Poynter Institute for Media Studies, 801 Third St. South, St. Petersburg, FL 33701; 727-821-9494; www.poynter.org. Journalism education and research organization and owner of the *Tampa Bay Times;* ethics section of its website includes articles, discussions, tips and case studies.

6

Linebacker Manti Te'o of the University of Notre Dame is at the center of an Internet hoax involving his two-year online relationship with a non-existent young woman who Te'o said had died of cancer. The situation constitutes "a terrible statement about where we are today and how social media is a tool in some really bad stuff," said Notre Dame athletic director Jack Swarbrick. Te'o says he did not know it was a hoax.

From *CQ Researcher*,
January 25, 2013

Social Media Explosion

Marcia Clemmitt

Randi Zuckerberg — Facebook's former marketing director and sister of Facebook CEO Mark Zuckerberg — should have known better.

After she posted a family photo for her Facebook friends, the picture popped up in the Twitter feed of someone not on Ms. Zuckerberg's "friend" list.[1] "Not sure where you got this photo," she tweeted angrily. "I posted it only to friends. You reposting it on Twitter is way uncool."

But the error was Zuckerberg's. Even though she had guided Facebook's marketing, she hadn't remembered one of the company's complex rules for figuring out which postings are private. The person who tweeted the picture was a Facebook friend of a different Zuckerberg sister in the photo. Because that sister was named — "tagged," in Facebook parlance — as one of the photo's subjects, the picture was visible to all her Facebook friends as well, despite sister Randi's intention to only share it privately.

It's a typical confusion of the social media era, when mushrooming numbers of photos and other personal information are being placed online with no consensus about whether any of it should remain private or viewable by only a few, and, if so, how to accomplish that.

The Internet has been a haven for socializing since its earliest days, but beginning about a decade ago technology developers have focused like a laser on "social media" — software designed primarily to facilitate social interaction — as the key to drawing the public online. Today, social media include social networks such as Facebook that allow people to reach out to friends of friends; the photo-sharing

Sports, Entertainment Dominate Twitter

The Japanese animated movie "Castle in the Sky" was the subject of more than 25,000 tweets per second during its December 2011 broadcast, the most related to any event between January 2011 and February 2012. The most heavily tweeted events during the period, as measured in tweets per second, were in sports and entertainment.

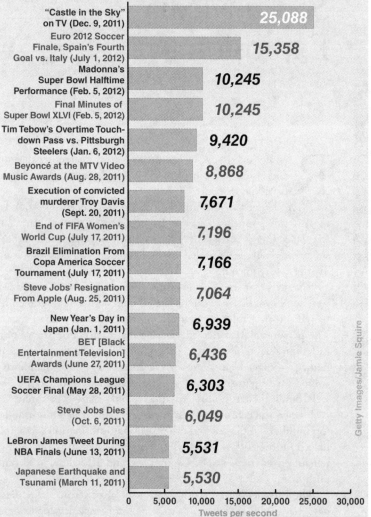

Events With Most Tweets Per Second, January 2011–February 2012

Event	Tweets per second
"Castle in the Sky" on TV (Dec. 9, 2011)	25,088
Euro 2012 Soccer Finale, Spain's Fourth Goal vs. Italy (July 1, 2012)	15,358
Madonna's Super Bowl Halftime Performance (Feb. 5, 2012)	10,245
Final Minutes of Super Bowl XLVI (Feb. 5, 2012)	10,245
Tim Tebow's Overtime Touch-down Pass vs. Pittsburgh Steelers (Jan. 6, 2012)	9,420
Beyoncé at the MTV Video Music Awards (Aug. 28, 2011)	8,868
Execution of convicted murderer Troy Davis (Sept. 20, 2011)	7,671
End of FIFA Women's World Cup (July 17, 2011)	7,196
Brazil Elimination From Copa America Soccer Tournament (July 17, 2011)	7,166
Steve Jobs' Resignation From Apple (Aug. 25, 2011)	7,064
New Year's Day in Japan (Jan. 1, 2011)	6,939
BET [Black Entertainment Television] Awards (June 27, 2011)	6,436
UEFA Champions League Soccer Final (May 28, 2011)	6,303
Steve Jobs Dies (Oct. 6, 2011)	6,049
LeBron James Tweet During NBA Finals (June 13, 2011)	5,531
Japanese Earthquake and Tsunami (March 11, 2011)	5,530

Tweets per second (axis: 0, 5,000, 10,000, 15,000, 20,000, 25,000, 30,000)

Getty Images/Jamie Squire

Source: Brian Anthony Hernandez, "The Top 15 Tweets-Per-Second Records," *Mashable*, February 2012, mashable.com/2012/02/06/tweets-per-second-records-twitter

site Pinterest; the collaboratively written Wikipedia encyclopedia; the "user review" sections at retail websites such as Amazon; "virtual worlds" such as "World of Warcraft" where people from around the world meet, compete, collaborate and play adventure games together, and many more.

Software that helps people meet, converse, work and play with others is king of the online universe, and its popularity keeps growing. As of July 2011, nearly 164 million Americans were using social media, according to the New York City–based media-research company Nielsen, and by July 2012 the number had risen 5 percent, to about 172 million.[2]

While research is in its earliest stages, some analysts believe that because young people, especially, have shifted so much social energy online, social media may end up having profound effects not just on privacy but on both individual human relationships and how people relate to their communities.

Facebook CEO Zuckerberg has famously said that, because of social networks, privacy is no longer a "social norm."

"People have really gotten comfortable not only sharing more information and different kinds, but more openly and with more people," said Zuckerberg. That new social norm is "just something that has evolved over time," he said.[3]

But some analysts argue that privacy protections are crucial. "The No. 1 problem is that the United States doesn't have data-protection" requirements, says Alice Marwick, an assistant professor in communication and media studies at Fordham

University in New York City. "The No. 2 problem," she says, "is that the market impulse goes in the opposite direction" from privacy protection, promising huge financial rewards to social media companies that sell users' information for targeted marketing efforts and the like.

Little is known about how social media may be affecting human relationships. However, some analysts fear that social media are being seen as a replacement for face-to-face conversation. In a survey on favored communication modes, people born between 1990 and 1999 said they prefer texting above all other forms of communication, but in second place — tied with instant messaging and phone calls — is communicating via Facebook. Strikingly, face-to-face conversation is the least favored form of communication for the digital generation. That's a stark reversal of the survey preferences voiced by each generational cohort born between 1946 and 1989. All those groups put face-to-face conversation as their preferred conversational mode, and none even listed a social media technology.[4]

"Many kids say they prefer not to talk face to face," notes Larry Rosen, a professor of psychology at California State University, Dominguez Hills. Instead, he says, they rely on written communication only, mainly via text or social media sites, especially when communicating with adults. That choice might damage young people's communication skills for years to come, Rosen says. When people rely entirely on written messages "where you don't have access to [nonverbal] cues, things are ripe for miscommunication," he says. Furthermore, without enough practice observing how people communicate through tone and gesture, it becomes difficult to accurately read face-to-face conversations that do take place, he says.

Some worry that a preference for social media over face-to-face meetings may make it easier and more tempting to commit identity fraud and hoaxes. For example, although exactly who was involved in the elaborate hoax is not yet clear, it was recently revealed that

Teens Flocking to Facebook

Nine in 10 Americans ages 13 to 17 use Facebook, making it the most popular social networking site. Experts say the multimedia appeal of Facebook and its ease of use are helping to drive its popularity among teenagers.

Most Popular Websites Visited by U.S. Teens Ages 13–17, May 2012

- Facebook: 89.5%
- Twitter: 48.7%
- Google+: 41.5%
- Tumblr: 33%
- 4chan: 23%
- Pinterest: 20%
- MySpace: 18%
- Foursquare or other location-based services: 12.2%

Source: "The Digital Divide," McAfee, June 2012, www.mcafee.com/us/about/news/2012/q2/20120625-01.aspx

star Notre Dame linebacker Manti Te'o engaged in a two-year online relationship with a non-existent young woman who Te'o said died of cancer. He says he did not know it was a hoax. The situation constitutes "a terrible statement about where we are today and how social media is a tool in some really bad stuff," said Notre Dame athletic director Jack Swarbrick.[5]

Others see little reason for worry. Most "digital natives" — the generation that has grown up online — do not appear to be living their personal lives much differently than older generations, says Kaveri Subrahmanyam, a professor of psychology at California State University, Los Angeles. Most use social media mainly "to connect to people already in their lives" and "do the things they'd do anyway" in the physical world, she says. "Socially, I don't think that we need to be too concerned," at least about the average person.

The Internet's potential to ignite a more civically engaged populace by making policy information and political debate easily accessible has excited speculation since the world first went online. Now, the dominance of social media — which spark intense online engagement by many people in social and entertainment matters, for example — has further fueled those hopes.

Research suggests that social media are leading to increased political activity, says Joseph Kahne, a professor of education at Mills College, in Oakland, Calif., and chairman of the MacArthur Foundation's Research Network on Youth and Participatory Politics. In a survey, 41 percent of young people reported engaging in what Kahne terms "participatory politics" — individual efforts to influence public policy outside the sphere of institutions such as political parties.[6] Their methods include tweeting support for a cause or forwarding a news article about an issue. This kind of personal political engagement is "happening more and more" among young people of all races and ethnicities, he says.

An example occurred in January 2012, when the Dallas-based Susan G. Komen Foundation, which supports breast cancer research and treatment, announced it would no longer fund programs offered by Planned Parenthood, Kahne notes. The announcement triggered a storm of furious commentary on Twitter, Facebook and other online sites — some from individuals and some from organizations — and three days later the foundation reversed course.[7]

Participatory politics played a big role in the incident, in which a powerful organization was prodded to change its position, at least partly because of influence from everyday people, says Kahne. The influence "didn't generally run through institutions" such as lobbyists or lawmakers, he says. Instead, "a lot of people posted stuff on Facebook pages. It went viral."

Despite the growing prevalence of such events, social media probably are not causing more people to become interested in politics and policy, as some Internet analysts have long hoped, Kahne says. Most people who engage in the new participatory politics would have been following politics anyway, he says. However, social media have provided new ways for people to turn their interest into deeper involvement and influence, he says.

As Internet users and technology analysts ponder how the burgeoning world of social media may be changing people's lives, here are some of the questions being asked:

Do social media foster greater community engagement?

Through social media such as Twitter and Facebook, friends can urge friends to become involved in causes,

and advocacy groups can reach out to millions. Social-media skeptics, however, wonder how much of this new engagement is useful.

During riots in London in August 2011, triggered by economic unrest and a police shooting, "we have seen extraordinary acts of pro-active social engagement" carried out on social media, wrote Kate Crawford, a principal researcher at the corporate think tank Microsoft Research, in Boston, and an associate professor of media at Australia's University of New South Wales, in Sydney. A Facebook and Twitter campaign under the hashtag #riotcleanup "rallied people to clean up the streets," wrote Crawford. On Twitter and Tumblr — a social network and blog website that makes it easy for users to follow other users' blogs — citizen journalists writing from the field "made substantive contributions to media coverage," she said.[8]

Social media make supporting and organizing causes easier than in the past and are especially effective in getting people already interested in politics to take a more active role, says Daniel Kreiss, an assistant professor of journalism and mass communication at the University of North Carolina, Chapel Hill. For example, thanks to social media, "I can give a small donation much easier — instantaneously" in fact, he says. Debating public issues can now be done from home, for free, via social media channels such as Twitter, Tumblr blogs, and newspaper and blog comment sections. In the past, self-publishing a pamphlet cost at least a bit of cash, and figuring out how to get it to potentially interested people was extremely difficult, Kreiss notes.

President Obama's 2008 and 2012 campaign operations used Facebook effectively to encourage supporters to contact particular Facebook "friends" who analysts determined were promising targets for a vote-Obama pitch, Kreiss says.

"A strong activist community is one that is unified and [has] a sense of camaraderie," wrote Charles Harris, a political science major and 2011 graduate of Western Kentucky University Honors College, in Bowling Green, who organized his local university chapter of a national peace and sustainability group. Facebook is an ideal place to bring activists together because the frequent interaction people experience on social media can increase "comfort levels in interaction during regular meetings" in real life, he said.[9]

Some observers argue, however, that the role of big-name social media such as Twitter has been overblown when it comes to organizing protests.

Western commentators have claimed that Iranians used Twitter to organize protests after a contested June 2009 election. But, in fact, Twitter was used only minimally, according to Golnaz Esfandiari, an Iranian-born blogger and a senior correspondent for the U.S.-funded agency Radio Free Europe, which broadcasts to Eastern Europe, Central Asia and the Middle East. Most of the Twitter feeds Westerners quoted as evidence of Twitter's role were in English, and "no one seemed to wonder why people trying to coordinate protests in Iran would be writing in any language other than Farsi," Esfandiari said. Twitter may actually have had a destructive influence on the protests because it eased the spread of unsubstantiated rumors, she said.[10]

In social media's early days, Internet theorists "had this amazing optimism that as the cost of [becoming engaged and engaging others] falls, then everyone was going to be engaged in public issues," says Kreiss. "But it turns out that there's always a ceiling, in money, in skills, in time." It's now clear that while many who were already interested in public issues are more deeply engaged because of social media, the greatly broadened participation once predicted is highly unlikely to happen, he says.

With ever-increasing amounts of information about individuals available from social networks such as Facebook, political campaigns can target their messages to only the very small slice of the electorate prone to be persuadable, and that could be dangerous to democracy, wrote Kreiss and Philip N. Howard, an associate professor of communication at the University of Washington in Seattle. "Scholars have long feared a 'democratic deficit' " when campaigns communicate only with the handful of voters they believe will respond to specific pitches so that successful candidates, in effect, end up representing only those people, they wrote.[11]

Social media communications and relationships are too short and shallow to spur deep commitment, argues best-selling author Malcolm Gladwell, a journalist who writes about social-science research.

Effective activists for high-stakes causes such as the 1960s civil rights marches almost invariably have a high degree of personal connection to the movement, with many real-life friends — the kind "who talk late into the night with one another" — also involved, he wrote. "The kind of activism associated with social media isn't like this at all," Gladwell argues. Twitter "is a way of following . . . people you may never have met," while Facebook is "for keeping up with the people you would not otherwise be able to stay in touch with." Such acquaintances are useful for passing along new information about causes one might consider supporting, but they aren't personally compelling enough to inspire the hard work of true activism, he argues.[12]

Are social media making personal relationships more difficult?

With many people communicating with friends more online than off these days, debate is growing about whether that trend is healthy for human relationships.

"It's a tough area to study because it's all so new," says California State's Rosen. "There are no answers yet."

Some trends are emerging, however, Rosen and other researchers say.

Teens are showing "a decrease in risk taking" from previous generations when it comes to expressing themselves and interacting with other people, says Katie E. Davis, an assistant professor at the University of Washington Information School in Seattle. "It's hard to know how much of this comes from technology," but many teenagers today hold back on intimacy by forgoing face-to-face conversations whenever possible in favor of writing on a Facebook wall or texting — modes of communication that encourage much briefer and less open-ended dialogue than do more traditional approaches such as face-to-face talk or even email, she says.

"It feels much safer to broach uncomfortable subjects when you don't have to look someone in the eye," says Davis. "It takes a lot of the messiness out of relationships, but it means that you don't make yourself vulnerable," Davis says. That can be a problem because vulnerability is a key to strong relationships, she says.

Many teens also seem constrained when it comes to expressing different aspects of themselves freely, Davis says. Traditionally, "adolescence is a time of experimentation," when people try on many roles and are concerned with self-expression, she points out. But, she adds, in a Facebook-dominated world many say "that how they present themselves online is very public, something that friends" and even parents and college

Social Media Becoming a Worrisome Distraction

"If you take the technology away, you'll lose people in minutes."

The allure of socializing online has created a nation of mobile-device obsessives, many of whom can go barely 10 minutes without checking their smartphones for Twitter or Facebook messages. But the long-term consequences of this behavior are difficult to determine.

Some believe that whatever the psychological and relationship-related changes that may stem from this new form of interaction, social media obsession may already be altering how people think and learn.

Single-minded focus on a person, object or concept seems to be the first casualty, making the age of online socializing also the age of multitasking, says Larry Rosen, a professor of psychology at California State University, Dominguez Hills.

When electronic devices were first becoming ubiquitous, some hoped they would teach a new generation how to multitask better than previous generations did. But research indicates that people who grew up with electronic devices "really can't multitask" either, says Rosen. As a result, the typical technology-obsessed person now gives "continuous partial attention" to just about everything and full attention to almost nothing. "You never do anything in depth," he says.

"You're constantly interrupted, and you're self-interrupting," too, he says. The very nature of the brain seems to decree that, for many activities, people simply can't do two or more tasks at once. In addition, while the brain can switch rapidly from task to task, doing so takes more time to do the tasks. In addition, he says, "You simply don't do as thorough a job," and some tasks simply aren't amenable to being done in a shallow way. The repeated switching of attention also "adds to one's stress."

Some analysts say evidence may already be showing that technology-driven multitasking takes a toll on one's ability to perform the most complex mental tasks. "I'm

admissions officers might scrutinize and judge, she says. Then, because the online and offline social worlds are increasingly intertwined, many teens end up presenting themselves in both arenas as what Davis terms "packaged, polished selves" who conform to whatever image they believe fits best in their social circle, without allowing eccentric pictures or negative emotions or unusual interests to show. "Everything's happy on Facebook" even if it's not, she says.

As the online world migrates to mobile devices through which social media are readily available 24 hours a day, new concerns arise.

A 2011 study found that smartphone users are developing "checking habits" — recurring 30-second glances at social media such as Facebook — as often as every 10 minutes.[13]

"Just the fact that we're constantly pulling our phones out" is evidence "that we're becoming anxious," says Rosen. "An obsession is something that builds up an anxiety so that we have to do something about it to relieve it" — in this case, check for contact from one's social group, he says.

Camp directors interviewed by the University of Washington's Davis see this anxiety growing rampant among "helicopter parents," Davis says. To avoid being out of touch with their away-at-camp children, some parents now equip their youngster with two cell phones so that when the camp director asks for one to be handed over, the child still has a hidden one. "Parents expect to see pictures of their children on a camp's website" daily, something unheard of just a few years ago, Davis says.

"Digital natives" are "always connected, never alone," says Subrahmanyam, at California State University, Los Angeles.

This fact may translate into overblown fears of being alone, according to some analysts. "We have a generation not sure I'm able to write in the same concentrated way" as before the saturation of digital media began, says Kaveri Subrahmanyam, a professor of psychology at California State University, Los Angeles. "And I'm teaching 20-year-olds who seem to have less memory than I do."

The sleep disruptions that accompany social technology may help account for cognitive changes, Subrahmanyam suggests. The "digital native" generation — teens and young 20-somethings who have grown up with these technologies —"sleep with the cell phone and get up in the middle of the night to respond to texts," she says. While the long-term effects of such behavior are unknown, research has shown that "frequent sleep interruptions make it harder for the brain to consolidate the day's learning and memories," she says.

Because technologically aided social connection is not going away, society must figure out how to adapt to these changes, says Rosen. He recommends "tech breaks" — for classrooms and even family dinners — to help people tolerate the anxiety many feel when unable to check their online social worlds.

Banning cell phones from the classroom or dinner table doesn't work, he says. "If you take the technology away, you'll lose people in three to five minutes. They'll start to zone out" because of the anxiety of knowing they can't check their phones, he says. Anxious people aren't able to pay attention, he says.

If, instead, people can check their phones every five minutes, for example, that anxiety is defused, and the intervals between phone-checking time can be increased gradually, he says.

Mental focus matters, and social media may pose a particular threat to it, says Rosen.

His research team conducted detailed observations of 263 middle school, high school and university students while they studied at home for 15 minutes. Not surprisingly, most were surrounded by technology and remained at one task just three to five minutes before losing focus. One finding from the research "stunned" Rosen, though: "If the students checked Facebook just once during the 15-minute study period, they had a lower grade-point average." Thanks to always-available social media, Rosen argues, many young people spend their days constantly simmering in anxiety about whether they've heard from online friends, and "anxiety inhibits learning."[1]

— *Marcia Clemmitt*

---

[1] Larry Rosen, "Driven to Distraction: Our Wired Generation," *Pioneer Press* [St. Paul, Minn.], Nov. 12, 2012, www.twincities.com/opinion/ci_21982260/larry-rosen-driven-distraction-our-wired-generation.

of young adults who, due to no fault of their own, have grown dependent on continuous technological connection," wrote Vivian Diller, a psychologist in New York City. With so little experience dealing with "frustration or loneliness," Diller wonders how a cell phone-dependent generation will deal with such feelings.[14]

The more one's Facebook friends include people from different spheres — such as extended family, school friends and work colleagues — the greater one's social stress, according to researchers at Scotland's University of Edinburgh. "Facebook used to be like a great party for all your friends where you can dance, drink and flirt," said Ben Marder, a fellow at the university's business school. "Now with your mum, dad and boss there, the party becomes an anxious event full of potential social landmines."[15]

But many researchers also note that qualms and difficulties always accompany new technology and that some evidence indicates that much social media use is benign.

In young people's quick embrace of social media, it's clear that they constitute "a primal way to satisfy the eternal need for social connection," says Subrahmanyam.

Social media tools clearly help some people, says Rosen. For example, studies show that for people with mild or major depression, "having many friends on Facebook helps" improve moods, in the same way that talking on the phone does.

In addition, "we've actually found that practicing being empathetic online" — such as by commenting positively on someone's online postings — "can help you learn to be empathetic in the real world," says Rosen. "Now we're looking at whether kids can learn other social skills online," such as taking turns and "expressing what you say in nicer terms," and then translate those skills into offline situations where they're needed.

Social Media Engage Consumers

Social media users are more likely to turn to social networking sites to talk about consumer products (bottom graph) than to engage in discussions about political or social issues (top). Consumers are especially interested in learning about others' experience with products and in researching information on goods and services.

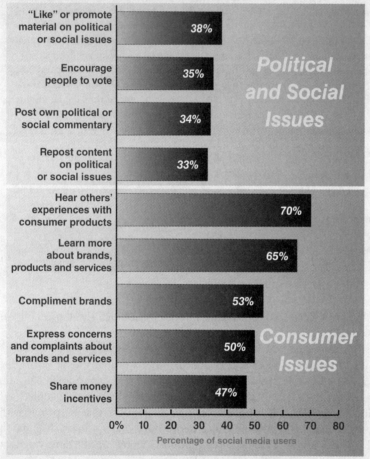

Percent of social media users who . . .

"Like" or promote material on political or social issues — 38%

Encourage people to vote — 35%

Post own political or social commentary — 34%

Repost content on political or social issues — 33%

Political and Social Issues

Hear others' experiences with consumer products — 70%

Learn more about brands, products and services — 65%

Compliment brands — 53%

Express concerns and complaints about brands and services — 50%

Share money incentives — 47%

Consumer Issues

0% 10 20 30 40 50 60 70 80

Percentage of social media users

Sources: "Social Media and Political Engagement: Summary of Findings," Pew Internet & American Life Project, October 2012, pewinternet.org/Reports/2012/Political-engagement/Summary-of-Findings.aspx; "State of the Media: The Social Media Report 2012," Nielsen, 2012, p. 20, blog.nielsen.com/nielsenwire/social/2012

day they log on to websites and whose birthday parties they attend. Statistical analysts aggregate that information into profiles that businesses use to target ads and political campaigns milk for insight into whether voters are persuadable.

To some, this aspect of social media spells the end of the very notion of privacy — the idea that all people have the right and should have the ability to determine for themselves who can see their personal information. But others say allowing such "data mining" for commercial and other purposes is a reasonable price to pay for the services social media provide.

Internet users are likely unaware of how aggressive companies are about using personal information, wrote software developer Dave Winer, who says the current climate "scares" him.

"I have always assumed everything I post to Facebook is public," but companies now use information that we leave behind simply by visiting websites, without ever clicking a "Like" button or posting a comment, Winer wrote. "What clued me in was an article on [the technology blog] *ReadWriteWeb* that says that just reading an article on their site may create an announcement on Facebook" that will go out to all of one's Facebook followers — a group that includes not just one's Facebook "friends" but people, including strangers, who have signed up to get access to public posts. "People joke that privacy is over, but I don't think they imagined that the disclosures would be so proactive."[16]

As the archives of personal data grow, interest increases in examining them for many purposes.

In the past, college admissions officers viewed only information provided by applicants or available from

Are social media eroding privacy?

As people navigate the Internet, social media and data-analysis companies gather information about everything from what magazine articles they read to what times of public sources, such as schools or government agencies. A recent survey of medical school and residency admissions officers, however, found that while only 9 percent said they routinely used material from social networks to make admissions decisions, 53 percent said evidence of unprofessional behavior found on such sites could jeopardize a candidate's spot.[17]

The Obama campaign had access to more than 500 points of data for every member of the public, including data from surveys, commercial and financial transactions, magazine subscriptions and so on, says Kreiss of the University of North Carolina. "None of it is very meaningful" on its own, he says. However, because analysts have data for literally hundreds of millions of people, they can use statistical patterns to construct a profile of the person most likely to be swayed to vote for a candidate, he says.

Kreiss believes campaigns should be required to reveal basic information about how they use personal data. "We don't know if the data is secure or how campaigns target certain people" to receive particular individualized ads, he says.

For example, today campaigns send certain ads to people who access the Internet over a smartphone, different ads to people who use a computer or tablet and very negative ads only to carefully chosen voters. Since the Supreme Court has ruled that it is constitutional to require transparency of political advertisers, "there should be a disclosure on every individually targeted ad that explains: 'Why am I seeing this ad?' " he argues.[18]

Nevertheless, Kreiss doesn't think the data give campaigns a creepy superpower to manipulate voters. "An ad that's specifically targeted to me still won't make me turn into a Republican. Ads work on the margin," convincing only a very narrow subset of people who are ripe for changing their minds, he says.

The difficulty of drawing truly accurate conclusions about people from even the largest amounts of data may

Facebook Use Soars

About half the U.S. population, or 152 million Americans, are expected to log in to Facebook at least once a month this year, up from 84 million in 2009.

Number of Americans Who Use Facebook at Least Once a Month, 2009 and 2013

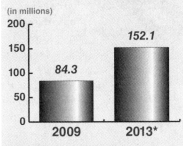

(in millions)

*forecast

Source: "Number of Facebook Users in the United States From 2009 to 2013 (in Millions)," Statista, 2013, www.statista.com/statistics/183089/forecast-of-the-number-of-facebook-users-in-the-us/

be the biggest problem, said Alessandro Acquisiti, an associate professor of information technology and public policy at Carnegie Mellon University's Heinz College.

Companies sell data-mining and profile-assembly services to employers looking for guidance on which job candidates to hire and advertisers seeking to woo customers who might be particularly influential among their peers. Today, some organizations even use facial-recognition software to link people in photos to their Facebook profiles to ferret out more details about them. But analogous experiments carried out by his research team demonstrate that such operations should be regarded with mistrust because it's far too easy to jump to a sure-feeling — but dead wrong — conclusion about someone based on information they reveal online, Acquisiti said. "We tend to make strong extrapolations about weak data," he said.[19]

Other analysts argue that privacy violations are not a problem, even in some of the most massive databases.

Businesses that use social media information to target advertising collect the data and target the ads using numerical customer codes rather than real names, according to companies involved in such work. Contrary to privacy-advocates' fears, therefore, the data collection actually preserves social media users' anonymity and thus their privacy, company representatives say.[20]

An oft-expressed worry is that the "digital-native" generation may forgo traditional concerns about privacy in favor of broadcasting their doings to a social media audience. In fact, however, many young people "are actually being very strategic" and increasingly savvy about social media use, says Fordham University's Marwick.

For example, "we see people using sites like Twitter" — where pseudonyms are allowed —"to post more playfully" than they would on Facebook, knowing that what

AFP/Getty Images/Stan Honda

Competitors in the final round of the LG U.S. National Texting Championship face off in New York's Times Square on Aug. 8, 2012. Austin Wierschke, a 17-year-old from Rhinelander, Wis., left, won for the second year in a row, pocketing $50,000. In 39 seconds he accurately typed a 149-character message with capitalization, punctuation and several symbols.

they post there is "not going to come back to their Facebook identities," Marwick says.

Teens also are shifting to pseudonym-permitted sites to share the kind of private revelations that most people have always restricted to a small circle, according to the blog of mobileYouth, a consulting firm that analyzes marketing for mobile devices.[21]

Recent surveys reveal that more teens now seek out social media sites where they can restrict their postings to friends only. At the same time, many are adding to their social media repertoire Twitter accounts blocked to public viewing. A Twitter account visible to friends only is "the equivalent of having that secret diary you would allow only your closest friends to read. This is where teens post more emotional content — how they feel after a breakup, their latest crush," said the mobileYouth analyst.

One survey found that between 2009 and 2011 teen Twitter users doubled from 8 percent to 16 percent, mainly splitting their online time between Facebook and Twitter, according to the mobileYouth blog.[22]

Some governments are limiting how far companies can go in collecting personal information, although the trend hasn't spread to the United States, says Marwick. The European Union recently required social media sites to turn off their facial-recognition technology. "It's

ridiculous that video store rental is protected and online information" — much of it far more revealing —"is not," she says.

BACKGROUND

Social Life

Over the centuries, people have quickly turned new technologies of all kinds into new and improved ways to meet one of humanity's strongest needs — to socialize. Horse-drawn carriages and automobiles, designed as simple transportation, quickly became dating venues for young lovers. The telephone, intended as a business aid, almost immediately became a favorite means of social chitchat.[23]

In the late 1960s, when the Internet was established, its quick adoption for friendly social interaction surprised its developers. By 1973, e-mail — much of it purely social in nature — made up 75 percent of traffic on ARPANET, the world's first computer network, designed by the Department of Defense to allow researchers to exchange data and access remote computing capability. Early "newsgroups," used by Internet researchers to transmit messages, soon included groups sharing their enthusiasms for subjects such as science fiction and wines.

By the 1990s, technology developers had caught on to the appeal of online socializing and saw it — rather than the lure of interesting content — as key to attracting the public online.

"Community is the Velcro that keeps people [at America Online (AOL)]," said Ted Leonsis, a former top AOL executive. AOL was one of the first tech companies to provide public access to the Internet from home computers.[24]

Among the social features AOL introduced early in its existence were chat rooms that allow users to exchange messages live and "buddy lists" that alert members when their friends are online so they can exchange instant messages.[25]

Social Media

The first social networking site (SNS) similar to those that are popular today — New York-based SixDegrees .com — was launched in 1997.[26] It integrated several

CHRONOLOGY

1990s *As more people go online, companies develop technologies to help them socialize.*

1996 AOL introduces the Buddy List, which alerts users when friends are online.

1997 The early social networking site Sixdegrees.com is among the first to link users to friends of their friends.

2000s *As the popularity of social networking grows, technology to facilitate user-generated content and social interaction spreads to most websites.*

2001 Online social network Meetup is launched to help link people wanting to meet offline. . . . Wikipedia, a collaboratively written and edited encyclopedia, is founded.

2003 MySpace is founded. . . . Vermont Gov. Howard Dean becomes a leading contender for the Democratic presidential nomination with a successful social media-based campaign. . . . Business networking site LinkedIn debuts. . . . Online virtual world "Second Life" debuts.

2004 Thefacebook.com debuts for Harvard undergraduates only. . . . Launch of photo-sharing site Flickr.

2005 Blog-hosting website Xanga adds social networking features. . . . Social news and entertainment site Reddit is founded; content is featured on the site based on member voting. . . . Video-sharing site YouTube is founded.

2006 Facebook opens to anyone age 13 or older. . . . Social network and "microblogging" site Twitter opens.

2007 Facebook introduces Beacon, which updates Facebook members' friends about members' recent purchases, but ends the program after users protest. . . . Social discussion service Disqus is founded; members use the same login details at any website that uses Disqus; member profiles include information about websites a member uses. . . . Microblogging website Tumblr founded to facilitate sharing of videos, graphics, music and links. . . . Good Reads is founded to share book recommendations and reading lists.

2008 Twitter users post 100 million tweets every three months.

2009 Location-based social networking site Foursquare is founded for use on mobile devices; users can search for friends or types of places in their geographical location and leave location-linked commentary for other users.

2010 Privacy advocates dub May 31 "Quit Facebook Day," but fewer than 40,000 people quit. . . . Number of Facebook users passes 500 million. . . . Germany bans employers from checking Facebook pages of potential hires. . . . Library of Congress agrees to archive all Twitter traffic.

2012 Studies find people have become savvier about protecting privacy on social media. . . . Facebook sells stock shares to the public for the first time; the $38 per-share offering price is widely considered too high because it's unclear that selling customer data can raise as much revenue as some expect; the stock quickly loses about half its value. . . . Breast-cancer charity Susan G. Komen Foundation cuts funding to Planned Parenthood but reverses course after criticism explodes on social media. . . . Documentary film "Kony 2012" by advocacy group Invisible Children attracts more than 95 million YouTube views and millions of "shares" on social media websites as Internet users protest atrocities by the African cult leader Joseph Kony; critics note that the film contains inaccuracies. . . . European Union (EU) forces Facebook to turn off facial recognition software for users in EU countries. . . . Senate panel holds hearing on facial-recognition technology. . . . Senate Judiciary Committee approves bill requiring permission for mobile-device applications to share location-based data and another measure requiring the government to obtain warrants before obtaining most e-mail communications.

2013 Library of Congress has archived 170 billion tweets but struggles with how to make them searchable. . . . Six states now prohibit employers or postsecondary schools — or both — from demanding access to individuals' social media information. . . . Facebook introduces new Graph Search feature allowing users to search name-tagged photos and users' online profiles, including "likes."

Online Anonymity Stirs Controversy

Do real-name-only policies stop abusive behavior or shut down difficult debates?

An old joke runs, "On the Internet, nobody knows you're a dog." And until several years into the 21st century, that was largely true, since many — if not most — people who participated in online discussion forums did so under pseudonyms. That changed, however, when Facebook and other social media sites such as Google Plus and YouTube began requiring users to post under their real names.[1]

Supporters of real-name-only policies say they prevent abusive behavior online because they force people to take full responsibility for what they post. Proponents of allowing pseudonyms, however, say their use frees many people to engage in honest online conversation about delicate topics such as politics, sex or health problems without exposing them to offline suspicion or harassment.

"Anonymity on the Internet has to go away," said Randi Zuckerberg, former Facebook marketing director and sister of the company's co-founder and CEO, Mark Zuckerberg. "People behave a lot better when they have their real names down. People hide behind anonymity, and they feel like they can say whatever they want behind closed doors."[2]

Requiring the use of real names in Internet postings would create a more civil online atmosphere, wrote London-based Internet analyst James Cook. "Associate someone's real name to abusive content that they've posted online, and suddenly they aren't so keen on standing by it," said Cook. A requirement for real-name posting "is often accompanied by a rise in quality, and a friendlier community," he said. "Would you scam someone on eBay if they knew your real name? Would you tell someone to go kill themselves via Twitter if everyone who followed that person knew who you were? The odds are that, no, you would not."[3]

But skeptics of the virtue of a real-names-only Web say such arguments ignore salient points. For one thing, posting under a longtime pseudonym, as many veteran Internet posters have done for decades, is different from posting anonymously, says Alice Marwick, an assistant professor in communication and media studies at Fordham University in New York City. Many pseudonymous posters have built up a reputation under their pseudonyms, she says, and preserving that reputation creates many of the same benefits claimed for real-name posting, without opening people to possible harassment because they hold unpopular views.

"The civility argument doesn't tell the whole story," said Eva Galperin, international freedom of expression coordinator at the nonprofit Electronic Frontier Foundation, which advocates for online privacy. For instance, "uncivil discourse [is] alive and well in venues with real-name policies (such as Facebook)," she said.[4]

Furthermore, "offline, people say things appropriate to the group they are in," and the use of online pseudonyms allows people to decide with whom they may openly share which ideas, just as people do in real life, said Bernie Hogan, a research fellow at the Oxford Internet Institute in the United Kingdom. Without that, he said, the freedom to share certain thoughts with only some people vanishes.[5]

Many who prefer pseudonymous postings want to preserve the Internet as a venue for honest discussion of existing software features into a package that closely resembles the later SNS giants, MySpace and Facebook.

Social network sites are unique not because they "allow individuals to meet strangers" with common interests, wrote Nicole Ellison, an associate professor of human-computer interaction at the University of Michigan's School of Information, and Danah Boyd, a senior researcher at Microsoft Research. Online chat rooms and newsgroups always facilitated such interactions, they noted. Instead, social networking sites "enable users to articulate and make visible" to themselves and others their real-world webs of social connections, including friends of friends, thus linking an online social world with a real-life social world, Ellison and Boyd wrote.[27]

Unlike previous online technologies, SNSs alerted people to the "friends of their friends" and allowed users to browse SNSs' membership lists, thus allowing them to reach out socially by the natural-feeling method of contacting people with whom they have mutual acquaintances, wrote Boyd and Ellison.

Others can use the information, too, however, setting up concerns about whether this innovative socializing tool difficult topics as much as they want to make it more civil. Among those who may need the protection of pseudonyms to engage in honest discussion are teachers, those whose relatives don't share their views or circumstances, those who live in intolerant communities, spouses of government workers who must keep their political views to themselves and marginalized people, such as homosexuals, wrote Danah Boyd, a senior researcher at the corporate think tank Microsoft Research. "Not everyone is safer by giving out their real name."[6]

"People also don't seem to understand the history of Facebook's 'real names' culture," noted Boyd. "When early adopters (elite college students) embraced Facebook, it was a trusted community," confined to certain universities. Then "as the site grew larger, people had to grapple with new crowds being present and discomfort emerged. . . . But the norms were set."[7]

Other analysts say the opportunity to take on another character — such as by choosing a so-called avatar to represent oneself on a game site or some other kind of virtual world — can be a valuable learning experience for young people. For safety's sake, many virtual environments created for children and teens bar users from revealing their true names, ages or the cities in which they live, says Deborah Fields, an assistant professor of instructional technology and learning sciences at Utah State University

Former Facebook marketing director Randi Zuckerberg, sister of Facebook co-founder Mark Zuckerberg, says people "behave a lot better" when they use their real names online.

in Logan. The role playing that takes place in virtual environments — under pseudonyms — is valuable, and "research is suggesting that that's especially true for girls" who, in real life, "are often constrained" in their roles. "It's easier to take on a role with people who don't know you because people who know you put you in a box."

— *Marcia Clemmitt*

[1] For background, see Gregory Ferenstein, "Surprisingly Good Evidence that Real Name Policies Fail to Improve Comments," *Techcrunch*, July 29, 2012, http://techcrunch.com/2012/07/29/surprisingly-good-evidence-that-real-name-policies-fail-to-improve-comments, and Ramona Emerson, "Google+ 'Real Names' Policy Gets Revised," *The Huffington Post*, Jan. 24, 2012, www.huffingtonpost.com/2012/01/23/google-plus-real-names-policy_n_1224970.html.

[2] Quoted in Eva Galperin, "Randi Zuckerberg Runs in the Wrong Direction on Pseudonymity Online," Electronic Frontier Foundation, Aug. 2, 2011, www.eff.org/deeplinks/2011/08/randi-zuckerberg-runs-wrong-direction-pseudonymity.

[3] James Cook, "Let's Have an Internet-wide Real-name Policy," *The Kernel*, Jan. 10, 2013, www.kernelmag.com/comment/column/3951/lets-have-an-internet-wide-real-name-policy.

[4] Galperin, *op. cit.*

[5] Bernie Hogan, "Real-Name Sites Are Necessarily Inadequate for Free Speech," Social Media Collective blog, Aug. 8, 2011, http://socialmediacollective.org/2011/08/08/real-name-sites-are-necessarily-inadequate-for-free-speech.

[6] Danah Boyd, "Real Name Policies Are an Abuse of Power," *Social Media Collective blog*, Aug. 4, 2011, www.zephoria.org/thoughts/archives/2011/08/04/real-names.html.

[7] *Ibid.*

exposes SNS members to too much snooping. Among other risks, governments can use the "friends of friends" information to find and watch the social circles of people they suspect of dangerous activity.[28]

Since the first SNSs came on the scene, the online world has included ever more elements of "social media" — loosely defined as technologies that center the online experience on:

- user-created content, both individual and collaborative; (such as the user-written Wikipedia),

- conversation and other interaction among social-media users, such as "liking" fellow users' postings;
- participation in online communities with shared interests, and
- in some cases, publication of individuals' social circles online.

The technologies that enable such activities are known as Web 2.0, a term first used in 2004 to distinguish the new — social — online world from the Web 1.0 paradigm, in which software tools were primarily designed

Social Media's Wide Reach

Pope Benedict XVI sends his first Twitter message during his weekly general audience at the Vatican on Dec. 12, 2012 (top). The pope's tweet, sent from a digital tablet using the handle @pontifex, blessed his hundreds of thousands of new Internet followers. An anti-government demonstrator (bottom) promotes Facebook use during protests at Tahrir Square in Cairo, Egypt, on Feb. 3, 2011. Initial protests against the government were organized using social media.

to facilitate publishing content on the World Wide Web, according to Andreas M. Kaplan and Michael Haenlein, professors of marketing at the Paris campus of ESCP Europe, a business school.[29]

The World Wide Web is the massive Internet-based technology, invented around 1990 by British technology developer Tim Berners-Lee, which allows browsers such as Internet Explorer to use so-called hyperlinks to discover and access the millions of documents and other resources that exist on the Internet's connected computers.

In the Web 1.0 days, the aim behind most online technology was to make it easier and cheaper for individuals and organizations to publish their work online in a way that would be easy for others to discover as they "clicked" website links. As it became clear that socializing is a more compelling human desire than creation, however, Web 2.0 shifted from helping people publish their own blogs to helping them converse, collaborate, compete, meet, socialize and comment on others' online postings, Kaplan and Haenlein wrote. With Web 2.0, online "content and applications are no longer created and published by individuals, but instead are continuously modified by all users in a participatory and collaborative fashion." That occurs, for example, when multiple blog participants create a massive commentary on a single individual post or when YouTube posters create a massive archive of, say, a musician's live and electronic performances.[30]

In Web 2.0, the universe of online "user-generated content" exploded. No longer did a person have to commit to a time-consuming personal blog — which no one might ever see — to be an online content creator. Using social media tools, even time-strapped people and those who aren't interested in writing their thoughts have easy routes to posting content that others are likely to see and respond to. Spurred by the lure of getting responses from others, Internet users have embraced social media.[31]

Social media technologies also include reader-review sections at online retailer Amazon and other commercial sites; increasingly expansive readers'-comment sections on blogs and at newspaper websites; YouTube, where cell phone and other videos are shared by people and businesses; the photo-sharing site Pinterest where people post and categorize favorite images relating to interests such as fashion; and blog websites such as Tumblr, where some bloggers mainly post screen captures and brief animated snippets from favorite TV shows.

In fact, not all social media even require users to create content to participate and collaborate, notes Christopher Peterson, a research assistant at the Massachusetts Institute of Technology Center for Civic Media.

Websites such as Digg and Reddit, for example, engage members in "curating" online content, or filtering the staggering amount of content that appears online daily, elevating the best to a position so others will be likely to see it. Users vote posted content up or down, and, based on an algorithm that weights individual users' ratings, content that's judged most positively rises to prominence, says Peterson. As a result, large numbers of ordinary Internet users daily sift through massive amounts of material and "decide what's good or bad — rather than having editors decide to what our attention should be directed," he says. "We trust the people and the algorithm to surface useful information from a flood of material."

Other social media offer opportunities to interact through role-playing in "virtual worlds."

In multiplayer online role-playing games such as "World of Warcraft," players choose characters — called avatars — to represent themselves and enter a virtual game world to pursue adventures such as fighting monsters or seeking treasure. In the process, they interact with other players' characters, competing, collaborating and forming friendships, rivalries and romances. Players find the social games so compelling that they spend an average 22.7 hours a week in play.[32]

Other virtual social worlds such as "Second Life" don't have game-style rules but allow people to choose animated avatars and "live" in an online video environment as those people. Players socialize and form relationships with other "residents" as they explore the world, create and participate in groups of many kinds as well as create businesses and "sell" one another virtual goods and services such as virtual pets, clothing, jewelry, works of art and parcels of "Second Life" real estate.

Social Everywhere

The use of mobile devices such as smartphones and tablets for accessing the Internet also has helped fuel social media's dominance.

Tweets and Facebook status updates encapsulate a moment's thought or emotion, making them perfect for devices that are always in one's pocket, argues Kaplan, the Paris marketing professor.[33]

As the world has gone mobile, social media have become "an even more integrated part of social life" because mobile-device users are actually connected to social media at all times, even when surrounded by live companions, as in a restaurant with friends or family, says Fordham's Marwick. That gives people's social media

circles increased influence because "you're getting feedback" from them constantly, she observes.

Some social media have been developed to take advantage of the fact that mobile devices reveal their users' exact locations 24 hours a day, wrote Kaplan. At the locally based directory services collectively known as Yelp, users can search for local businesses and post reviews of businesses that are then "tagged" to a location and accessible to other users who visit the spot. Yelp users also gain reputations in the Yelp community as useful or less useful reviewers, based on voting by other users.[34]

Who's in Charge?

Social media facilitate easy communication with friends as well as publication of one's ideas to a potentially wide audience. As of August 2012, nearly 70 percent of U.S. adult Internet users employed social networking sites, for example, including 75 percent of women and 92 percent of people ages 18 to 29.[35] And it's all free.

Free, however, always comes at a price. The bottom line with anything consumers get "free" is this, wrote a commenter pen-named "blue_beetle" on the *MetaFilter* blog: "If you are not paying for it, you're not the customer; you're the product being sold."[36]

When it comes to social media, the presumed value of the customer-as-product lies in the massive amounts of personal information social media users leave online, which businesses hope to use to target ads and marketing. That includes information people post about themselves, information gleaned from analyzing an individual's social media connections and patterns of online activity and information that mobile technology sends out constantly about its users' geographic location and online activities. Debates over how that information is collected, stored and used and who has the right to grant access to it and control its uses have raged throughout the social media age.

"Even more so than television audience members, Facebook users function as workers who look . . . at advertisements but are also, crucially, suppliers of personal information and producers of content — particularly on a platform like Facebook," wrote Tamara Shepherd, a postdoctoral fellow in information-technology management at Toronto's Ryerson University. Unlike with traditional media, the customer information social media produces is so detailed that advertisers not only can determine which products people are likely to buy but can use clues about their economic status to show them different prices for the same goods, Shepherd wrote.[37]

"The privacy concerns surrounding social media are the most important things to pay attention to," says Fordham's Marwick. "We want to connect and share with those we care about, and we want to participate in public life, but we don't want our information to be public," she says.

CURRENT SITUATION
Profits and Control

Social media companies continue looking for ways to turn the public's love of their products into profit, but the process is tough. Meanwhile, struggles continue between marketers hungry for personal data and individuals who want to control how their information is shared.

During the recent holiday shopping season, while store and online sales rose, the number of purchases made after a social media user clicked through to a store from a site such as Facebook or YouTube dropped 26 percent from the previous year. Furthermore, old-fashioned email advertising resulted in $39.40 in sales for each dollar spent in 2012, compared to only $12.90 worth of sales per dollar spent on social media-based promotions.[38]

Social media businesses keep looking for ways to cash in on user-generated content. But users are managing to beat back some initiatives. In December, the photo-sharing site Instagram, owned by Facebook, sparked ire when it announced that it not only claimed full ownership of photos and all other information users leave on the site but would accept cash from companies and other organizations "to display your username, likeness, photos and/or actions you take" in advertising and promotional material "without any compensation to you." For example, Instagram users might find their vacation photos and comments used in advertising for a hotel or resort without getting paid for the content.[39]

After commenters on Instagram and other social media sites reacted angrily, the company quickly changed course, however. "Instagram has no intention of selling your photos, and we never did. We don't own your photos, you do," co-founder and CEO Kevin Systrom backtracked on the company blog.[40]

Still, extending companies' control over user data is a common social media business strategy. In December, Facebook unveiled a revamped system that makes privacy-control tools more easily findable on the site and shows users more details about where and to whom their information is visible — both consumer-friendly moves. However, in the same package, Facebook ended users' rights to mark their profiles off-limits to Facebook's search function.

The ability to hide one's profile from search is being "retired" because only a "single-digit percentage" of Facebook users do so, explained the company's director of product, Sam Lessin. However, because Facebook now has over a billion users, that "single-digit percentage" could mean "tens of millions" of people, remarked Nick Bilton, a technology blogger for *The New York Times*.[41]

This month, Facebook introduced the first version — fledgling and incomplete — of a search tool that ultimately will allow users to search for much more than just names. Using Graph Search, users can dig into Facebook's photo archives as well as the many preferences that people in their social networks have expressed online to find, for example, "photos of friends before 1990" or which Facebook connections are fans of a particular columnist.[42]

In response, some analysts predict a mass rejection of photo tagging and "liking" as people realize that things they casually responded to five years ago are suddenly searchable by anyone in their Facebook network.[43]

Limiting Access

Simmering questions about whether social media facilitate serious invasions of privacy are leading to new legislative proposals.

Last September in Europe, Facebook turned off its facial-recognition software, which links names to photographed faces based on other photos that users have already "tagged" with a name. Facebook said it would delete all facial-recognition data it had stored for European customers. The Irish Data Protection Commissioner, who oversees data-protection issues for the European Union, and privacy officials in some other EU countries demanded the change on the grounds that the software did not comply with privacy laws in some EU countries.[44]

Privacy experts worldwide have voiced concerns about whether the technology might allow rampant government

Will social media's use of facial recognition destroy privacy?

YES Alessandro Acquisti
Associate Professor of Information Technology, Heinz College, Carnegie Mellon University

From testimony before Senate Judiciary Subcommittee on Privacy, Technology and the Law, July 18, 2012

Face recognition could make our lives easier or more secure; conversely, it could limit our freedom, endanger our security and chill free speech by creating a state of constant and ubiquitous surveillance.

Consider, for instance, Facebook. Many of its users choose photos of themselves as their "primary profile" image. Facebook has aggressively pursued a "real identity" policy, under which members are expected to join the network under their real names, under penalty of account cancellation. Using tagging features and login security questions, the social network has successfully nudged users to associate their and their friends' names to uploaded photos. These photos are also publicly available: Primary profile photos must be shared with strangers under Facebook's own Privacy Policy.

Online social networks such as Facebook are accumulating the largest known databases of facial images. Often, those images are tagged or attached to fully identified profiles. Furthermore, many social network users post and tag multiple photos of themselves and their friends, allowing biometric models of their faces, and those of other people as well, to become more accurate. Furthermore, such a vast and centralized biometrics database can be at risk of third-party hacking.

An analysis of recent history in the market for personal data also suggests that firms may engage in more invasive applications of face recognition over time. If recent history is a guide, the current, almost coy applications of face recognition may be "bridgeheads" designed by firms to habituate end-users into progressively more powerful and intrusive services.

Consider the frequency with which, in the past few years, a popular social network such as Facebook has engaged in practices that either unilaterally modified settings associated with user privacy or reflected a "two steps forwards, one step backward" strategy, in which new services were enacted, then taken back due to users' reaction, and then enacted again, after some time had passed.

In the absence of policy interventions, therefore, the patterns we are observing (increasing gathering and usage of individuals' facial biometrics data) are unlikely to abate.

The risk exists that some firms may attempt to nudge individuals into accepting more capturing and usage of facial data — creating a perception of fait accompli which, in turn, will influence individuals' expectations of privacy and anonymity.

NO Robert Sherman
Manager, Privacy & Public Policy, Facebook

From testimony before Senate Judiciary Subcommittee on Privacy, Technology and the Law, July 18, 2012

In the early days of Facebook, we learned how important photo sharing was to our users. One component of our photo management and sharing features is photo tagging — the 21st century's version of handwriting captions on the backs of photographs — and it allows users to instantaneously link photos from birthdays, vacations and other important events with the people who participated.

To help our users more efficiently tag their friends in photos, we built "tag suggestions," which uses facial recognition technology to suggest people they already know and whom they might want to tag.

"Tag suggestions" works by determining what several photos in which a person has been tagged have in common and storing a summary of the data derived from this comparison. When a person uploads a new photo, we compare that photo to the summary information in the templates of the people on Facebook with whom the person communicates frequently. This allows us to make suggestions about whom the user should tag in the photo, which the user can then accept or reject.

"Tag suggestions" has been enthusiastically embraced by millions of people because it is convenient, and the uploader is in control of [his or her] photos.

We launched the feature with several important privacy protections.

"Tag suggestions" only uses data people have voluntarily provided to Facebook — photos and the tags people have applied to them. We do not collect any new information beyond the photos themselves in order for "tag suggestions" to work.

Facebook's technology does not enable people to identify others with whom they have no relationship.

Perhaps most importantly, Facebook enables people to prevent the use of their image for facial recognition altogether. Through an easy-to-use privacy setting, people can choose whether they will use our facial recognition technology to suggest that their friends tag them in photos. When you turn off "tag suggestions," Facebook won't suggest that friends tag you when photos look like you.

Our software cannot be used to compare a photo of an unknown person against our database of user templates. Our technology is designed to search only a limited group of templates — namely, an individual user's friends — and law enforcement agencies accordingly cannot use our technology to reliably identify an unknown person.

AP Photo/Elaine Thompson

Seattle resident Damon Brown is all smiles after Facebook helped give him a new lease on life. Brown, here with his wife and two sons, found a kidney donor after telling of his need on the social media site. His friends and family forwarded the request to everyone they knew, and a woman his wife had known for years offered to make the donation.

surveillance of innocent people as well as potentially invasive or embarrassing commercial-marketing efforts based on the content of photos people consider private.[45]

In November 2012, in a measure that applies mainly to email, the U.S. Senate Judiciary Committee approved a bill requiring the government to get probable-cause warrants to request most stored online communications from companies. And in December the panel approved requiring user consent before an app on a mobile device reports information about its geographic location. Committee leaders are expected to urge further action on the bills this year.[46]

On Jan. 1, laws took effect in Illinois and California barring employers from asking workers and job seekers for their social media account-access information. California also has a new law barring universities and colleges from seeking applicants' or students' social media passwords.

On Dec. 28, Michigan's Republican governor, Rick Snyder, signed legislation barring employers and postsecondary educational institutions from requesting social media access information, effective immediately. In early December, New Jersey Republican Gov. Chris Christie signed legislation barring universities and colleges from seeking applicants' or students' passwords. And in November the New Jersey Senate passed a similar ban on employers, which awaits action by the state Assembly.

Earlier in 2012, Delaware banned postsecondary educational institutions and Maryland barred employers from seeking social media access information.[47]

Federal legislation blocking employers and colleges from seeking social media access information was introduced in the U.S. House last April, but it expired after no committee acted on it during the 112th Congress.[48]

"Our social media accounts offer views into our personal lives and expose information that would be inappropriate to discuss during a job interview due to the inherent risk of creating biases," said Democratic California state Assembly member Nora Campos, author of her state's bill.[49]

But some analysts blame an unfounded "media frenzy" for the legislative interest. In March 2012, The Associated Press reported on some isolated incidents in which employers had either requested or required social media log-in information from workers or job applicants. Yet, wrote bloggers for San Francisco-based Littler Mendelson, a law firm specializing in employment issues, no media article has cited "a single study proving that private employers routinely" do so.[50]

Meanwhile, significant cultural changes — including in how people engage with political issues — are occurring because of the intertwining of media and social networking, says Kahne of Mills College. "We think we see potentially a very important shift — especially for young people" in the way people pass along and learn about the news, he says.

In a survey by his research group, roughly as many young people said they got news through their Facebook and Twitter relationships with friends and family as said they got it from newspapers, he says. This suggests that a fairly large percentage of young people — the 10 to 15 percent who report that they regularly forward news — are "mediating or influencing what their family and friends learn" about the world, Kahne says. "I would argue that's a significant difference" from the past, with the news-forwarders playing a very active role in shaping the political conversation in their networks, he says.

OUTLOOK
Changing Expectations?

Just under a decade into the flowering of social media, early predictions that they would empower people in hitherto unimagined ways and earn billions for social media companies are giving way to more realistic views, analysts say.

Theorists once predicted that, with ever larger numbers of people posting and responding to observations at venues such as Twitter and website comment sections, citizen reporting and analysis might rival if not replace traditional journalism for exposing and opposing official malfeasance, says Kreiss of the University of North Carolina. But that task turns out to be too demanding for unpaid amateurs, no matter how numerous, Kreiss says.

"It's great to imagine that an army of people on Twitter is going to call the government to account," but "professional journalists are paid to sort through databases" and track down elusive sources — actions that social-media users, posting for free in their spare time, simply can't do. "Producing high-quality journalism requires resources to counter power, which itself has huge resources," he says.

Mid-2000s expectations for the earnings potential of social media companies were also overblown, says Fordham's Marwick.

The concept of a "successful" social media website is beginning to change, she says. For one thing, sites where users post under pseudonyms — rather than real names, as Facebook requires — increasingly get millions of hits by providing social centers where people with shared interests, such as parenting, can converse while maintaining privacy, a combination many people find "very freeing," she says. Because these companies don't require people to use their real names or reveal their offline social connections, they'll never collect the masses of individual data that Facebook intends to rely on for ultra-high profits.

Still, Marwick says, "I think a lot of the small companies will be fine because they're not expecting to have billion-dollar IPOs" — initial public offerings of their shares on Wall Street. "It's very sexy and exciting to have these young entrepreneurs" such as Facebook CEO Zuckerberg and Microsoft's Bill Gates, who earned billions in the dot-com boom of the 1990s, "but in reality there's no reason that tech companies should make people millions and millions of dollars. We're moving toward a much more moderate model based on reality," she says.

Having social media as today's predominant communications mode is leading to a significant cultural change — the rise of "participatory culture," which is already baked into the entertainment arena and spilling over into politics, says Kahne of Mills College. Although the change may hardly be noticeable, participatory activities such as public voting to determine the outcome of TV shows, tweeting back and forth with a TV show's writing staff while an episode airs or providing commentary and debate with other fans on a real-time blog during a football game or reality-TV program are now commonplace activities. During the recent presidential campaign both President Obama and GOP candidate Mitt Romney sent special tweets to their followers before debates, bringing people into a closer relationship to the campaigns than in the past, Kahne says.

All this may make the moment ripe for helping young people forge new connections to political life, Kahne says. The teen and 20-something generation can more easily learn the tools of civic engagement than in the past, because institutions such as advocacy groups and government offices use social media, too, he says.

Studies show that young people already are enthusiastically engaged in participatory culture, and now they can become more politically involved just by "doing [what] they are already doing" on social media for other interests, such as music and sports, "drawing on skills they've already developed," Kahne says. "These things are much more friendly" to the digital generations than writing letters to the editor, he says.

NOTES

1. "Oops. Mark Zuckerberg's Sister Has a Private Facebook Photo Go Public," Tech blog, *Forbes*, Dec. 26, 2012, www.forbes.com/sites/kashmirhill/2012/12/26/oops-mark-zuckerbergs-sister-has-a-private-facebook-photo-go-public; and Tom McCarthy, "Mark Zuckerberg's Sister Learns Life Lesson After Facebook Photo Flap," *US News* blog, *The Guardian* [UK], Dec. 27, 2012, www.guardian.co.uk/technology/us-news-blog/2012/dec/27/facebook-founder-sister-zuckerberg-photo.

2. "State of the Media: The Social Media Report 2012," Nielsen, http://blog.nielsen.com/nielsenwire/social/2012.

3. Quoted in Bobbie Johnson, "Privacy No Longer a Social Norm, Says Facebook Founder," *The Guardian*, Jan. 10, 2010, www.guardian.co.uk/technology/2010/jan/11/facebook-privacy.

4. Larry Rosen, "Poke Me: How Social Networks Can Both Help and Harm Our Kids," address, American Psychological Association 119th Annual Convention, Aug. 4-7, 2011, www.fenichel.com/pokeme.shtml.

5. Quoted in Steve Eder, "Te'o Maintains Innocence in Hoax," *The New York Times*, Jan. 19, 2013, www.nytimes.com/2013/01/19/sports/ncaafootball/notre-dame-athletic-director-jack-swarbrick-stands-by-manti-teo.html?hpw.

6. Cathy J. Cohen and Joseph Kahne, "Participatory Politics: New Media and Youth Political Action," MacArthur Research Network on Youth and Participatory Politics, June 2012, http://ypp.dmlcentral.net/sites/all/files/publications/YPP_Survey_Report_FULL.pdf.

7. David Rothschild, "The Twitter Users Who Drove the Furor Over Komen and Planned Parenthood," Yahoo! News/*The Signal*, Feb. 4, 2012, http://news.yahoo.com/blogs/signal/twitter-users-drove-furor-over-komen-planned-parenthood-160326208.html#krwrGyT.

8. Kate Crawford, "Riots, Social Media and the Value of 'First Responders,' " *Social Media Collective Research* blog, Aug. 12, 2011, http://socialmediacollective.org/2011/08/12/riots-social-media-and-the-value-of-%E2%80%98first-responders%E2%80%99.

9. Charles Harris, "Social Media for Social Good: A Guide to New Media for College Activists," Honors College Capstone Experience/Thesis Projects, Paper 320, Western Kentucky University, May 5, 2011, http://digitalcommons.wku.edu/stu_hon_theses/320.

10. Golnaz Esfandiari, "The Twitter Devolution," *Foreign Policy*, June 7, 2010, www.foreignpolicy.com/articles/2010/06/07/the_twitter_revolution_that_wasnt.

11. Daniel Kreiss and Philip N. Howard, "New Challenges to Political Privacy: Lessons from the First U.S. Presidential Race in the Web 2.0 Era," *International Journal of Communication*, 2010, pp. 1032-1050, http://ijoc.org/ojs/index.php/ijoc/article/view/870/473.

12. Malcolm Gladwell, "Small Change," *The New Yorker*, Oct. 4, 2010, pp. 42-49, www.gladwell.com/pdf/twitter.pdf.

13. Antti Oulasvirta, Tye Rattenbury, Lingyi Ma and Eeva Raita, "Habits Make Smartphone Use More Pervasive," *Journal of Personal and Ubiquitous Computing*, June 16, 2011, www.hiit.fi/u/oulasvir/scipubs/Oulasvirta_2011_PUC_HabitsMakeSmartphoneUseMorePervasive.pdf.

14. Vivian Diller, "The Need for Connection in the Age of Anxiety," *The Huffington Post*, Nov. 8, 2012, www.huffingtonpost.com/vivian-diller-phd/technology-anxiety_b_2083475.html?utm_hp_ref=college&ir=College.

15. "More Facebook Friends Means More Stress, Says Report," press release, University of Edinburgh/EurekAlert, Nov. 26, 2012, www.eurekalert.org/pub_releases/2012-11/uoe-mff112612.php.

16. Dave Winer, "Facebook Is Scaring Me," *Scripting* blog, Sept. 24, 2011, http://scripting.com/stories/2011/09/24/facebookIsScaringMe.html.

17. Carl I. Schulman, *et al.*, "Influence of Social Networking Websites on Medical School and Residency Selection Process," *Postgraduate Medicine Journal*, Nov. 8, 2012, www.ncbi.nlm.nih.gov/pubmed/23139411.

18. The case is *Citizens United v. Federal Election Commission*, 588 U.S. 310 (2010), www.supremecourt.gov/opinions/09pdf/08-205.pdf.

19. Quoted in Erica Naone, "When Social Media Mining Gets It Wrong," *MIT Technology Review*, Aug. 9, 2011, www.technologyreview.com/news/424965/when-social-media-mining-gets-it-wrong.

20. Natasha Singer, "Your Online Attention, Bought in an Instant," *The New York Times*, Nov. 17, 2012, www.nytimes.com/2012/11/18/technology/your-online-attention-bought-in-an-instant-by-advertisers.html?_r=0&adxnnl=1&ref=natashasinger&adxnnlx=1355878018-DcmDj3dpu5kPXSMf8kp0GQ.

21. "Facebook vs. Twitter vs. Instagram: What Do Teens Prefer?" *mobileYouth Idea Factory* blog, Nov. 14, 2012, www.mobileyouthideafactory.com/facebook-vs-twitter-vs-instagram-what-do-teen.

22. *Ibid.*

23. For background, see Marcia Clemmitt, "Cybersocializing," *CQ Researcher*, June 28, 2006, pp. 625-648, and "Social Networking," *CQ Researcher*, Sept. 17, 2010, pp. 749-772.

24. Quoted in "Internet Communities," *Business Week Archives*, May 5, 1997, www.businessweek.com/1997/18/b35251.htm.

25. *Ibid.*

26. For background, see Danah M. Boyd and Nicole B. Ellison, "Social Network Sites: Definition, History, and Scholarship," *Journal of Computer-Mediated Communications*, October 2007, article 11, http://jcmc.indiana.edu/vol13/issue1/boyd.ellison.html.

27. *Ibid.*

28. *Ibid.*

29. Andreas M. Kaplan and Michael Haenlein, "Users of the World, Unite! The Challenges and Opportunities of Social Media," *Business Horizons*, 2010, pp. 59-68, www.michaelhaenlein.eu/Publications/Kaplan,%20Andreas%20-%20Users%20of%20the%20world,%20unite.pdf.

30. *Ibid.*

31. For background, see Kenneth Jost and Melissa J. Hipolit, "Blog Explosion," *CQ Researcher*, June 9, 2006 (updated Sept. 14, 2010), pp. 505-528.

32. For background, see Nicholas Yee, "The Psychology of Massively Multi-User Online Role-Playing Games: Motivations, Emotional Investment, Relationships and Problematic Usage," in Ralph Schroeder and Ann-Sofie Axelsson, eds., *Avatars at Work and Play: Collaboration and Interaction in Shared Virtual Environments* (2006), pp. 187-207, http://vhil.stanford.edu/pubs/2006/yee-psychology-mmorpg.pdf. Also see Sarah Glazer, "Video Games," *CQ Researcher*, Nov. 10, 2006, pp. 937-960; updated, Sept. 23, 2011.

33. Andreas M. Kaplan, "If You Love Something, Let It Go Mobile: Mobile Marketing and Mobile Social Media 4 x 4," *Business Horizons*, 2012, pp. 129-139, http://smad341automotive.files.wordpress.com/2012/09/going-mobile.pdf.

34. *Ibid.*

35. "Who Uses Social Networking Sites," Pew Internet: Social Networking, Nov. 13, 2012, http://pewinternet.org/Commentary/2012/March/Pew-Internet-Social-Networking-full-detail.aspx.

36. "User-Driven Discontent," MetaFilter, Aug. 26, 2010, www.metafilter.com/95152/Userdriven-discontent#3256046.

37. Tamara Shepherd, "Desperation and Datalogix: Facebook Six Months After Its IPO," *Culture Digitally* blog, Nov. 12, 2012, http://culturedigitally.org/2012/11/desperation-and-datalogix.

38. Sapna Maheshwari and Matt Townsend, "Email Still Whips Social Media as Marketing Tool," Bloomberg News, *The Columbus Dispatch*, Dec. 24, 2012, www.dispatch.com/content/stories/business/2012/12/24/email-still-whips-social-media-as-marketing-tool.html.

39. Quoted in "User Revolt Causes Instagram to Keep Old Rules About Picture Rights," Agence France-Presse, *Herald Sun* [Melbourne, Australia], Dec. 21, 2012, www.heraldsun.com.au/technology/user-revolt-causes-instagram-to-keep-old-rules-about-picture-rights/story-fn5izo02-1226541837778.

40. Quoted in *ibid.*

41. Nick Bilton, "Facebook Changes Privacy Settings, Again," *Bits* blog, *The New York Times*, Dec. 12, 2012, http://bits.blogs.nytimes.com/2012/12/12/facebook-changes-privacy-settings-again; for background, see Carl Franzen, "Facebook Updates Privacy Controls: Better and Simpler, Or More Invasive?" Idea Lab, *Talking Points Memo*, Dec 12, 2012, http://idealab.talkingpointsmemo.com/2012/12/facebook-changes-privacy-controls-better-and-simpler-or-more-invasiv.

42. Barbara Ortutay, "'Graph Search' Reviewed," The Associated Press/*ABQ Journal* [Albuquerque], Jan. 16, 2013,www.abqjournal.com/main/2013/01/16/abqnewsseeker/updated-facebook-search-tool-a-review.html.

43. *Ibid.*

44. Somini Sengupta and Kevin O'Brien, "Facebook Can ID Faces, but Using Them Grows Tricky,"

The New York Times, Sept. 21, 2012, www.nytimes
.com/2012/09/22/technology/facebook-backs-
down-on-face-recognition-in-europe.html?_r=0;
Loek Essers, "Facebook to Delete All European
Facial Recognition Data," *ComputerWorld*/IDG
News Service, Sept. 21, 2012, www.computer-
world.com/s/article/9231566/Facebook_to_delete_
all_European_facial_recognition_data?taxo
nomyId=70; "Facebook Ireland Ltd: Report of
Re-audit, Data Protection Commissioner," Sept.
21, 2012, http://dataprotection.ie/documents/
press/Facebook_Ireland_Audit_Review_
Report_21_Sept_2012.pdf.

45. *Ibid.* (*New York Times.*)

46. "Senate Judiciary Committee Approves Location
Privacy Bill," Electronic Privacy Information Center,
http://epic.org/2012/12/senate-judiciary-committee
-app.html, and "Senate Committee Updates ECPA,
Modifies Video Privacy Law," Electronic Privacy
Information Center, http://epic.org/2012/11/
senate-committee-updates-ecpa.html.

47. "Employer Access to Social Media Usernames and
Passwords," National Conference of State
Legislatures, www.ncsl.org/issues-research/telecom/
employer-access-to-social-media-passwords.aspx.

48. Sean Gallagher, "Bill Banning Employer Facebook
Snooping Introduced in Congress," *Ars Technica*,
April 28, 2012, http://arstechnica.com/tech-pol
icy/2012/04/bill-banning-employer-facebook-
snooping-introduced-in-congress; and H.R. 5050
(112th), "Social Networking Online Protection
Act," *GovTrack*, www.govtrack.us/congress/
bills/112/hr5050.

49. Quoted in Leslie Katz, "Progress for Calif. Bill to
Stop Employers' Social-media Snooping," *CNET
News*, May 10, 2012, http://news.cnet.com/8301-
1023_3-57432298-93/progress-for-calif-bill-to-
stop-employers-social-media-snooping.

50. Philip Gordon and Lauren Woon, "Re-thinking and
Rejecting Social Media 'Password Protection'
Legislation," *Privacy* blog, July 10, 2012, http://priva
cyblog.littler.com/2012/07/articles/state-privacy-leg
islation/rethinking-and-rejecting-social-media-
password-protection-legislation.

BIBLIOGRAPHY

Selected Sources

Books

Aboujaoude, Elias, *Virtually You: The Dangerous
Powers of E-Personality***, W.W. Norton & Company,
2011.**
A Stanford University psychiatrist recounts his experiences treating people who have created social media
personas that are much more adventurous, risk-taking,
confident, sexy and charismatic than their real-life personalities. Those personas often cause problems in the
relationships — both online and offline — of their
creators.

Castells, Manuel, *Networks of Outrage and Hope:
Social Movements in the Internet Age***, Polity, 2012.**
A professor of communication technology and society at
the University of Southern California, Los Angeles,
explains the role of Internet technology in recent social
movements such as the Occupy Wall Street movement in
the United States and the Arab Spring revolutions in
North Africa and the Middle East.

Keen, Andrew, *Digital Vertigo: How Today's Online
Social Revolution Is Dividing, Diminishing, and
Disorienting Us***, St. Martin's Press, 2012.**
An Internet business executive argues that privacy and
human intimacy are endangered as the networked world
continually increases the amount of information people
inadvertently share about themselves and social media
replace in-person conversation.

Articles

**Angwin, Julia, "The Web's New Gold Mine: Your
Secrets,"** *The Wall Street Journal***, July 30, 2010,
http://online.wsj.com/article/SB1000142405274870
3940904575395073512989404.html.**
This article, the first of a series, reports on the burgeoning tracking technology that social media and other websites are using to collect data on computer users as they
make their way around the Web. On average, each of the
country's 50 most visited websites installed 64 pieces of
tracking software on the computers of each visitor; a few
of the sites, such as the nonprofit Wikipedia, did not
install any, however.

Gillespie, Tarleton, "Is Twitter Us or Them? #Twitterfail and Living Somewhere Between Public Commitment and Private Investment," *Culture Digitally* blog, July 31, 2012, http://culturedigitally .org/2012/07/is_twitter_us_or_them.
A Cornell University assistant professor of communication describes the ethical, political and business issues involved in having private companies such as Twitter and Facebook function as major public communication channels. Are the companies obligated to support free speech or cooperate with government surveillance? How far can they go in serving advertisers' interests before they harm the public interest?

Rosen, Larry, "The Power of Like: We Like Being Liked . . . on Facebook," *Rewired* blog, *Psychology Today*, July 15, 2012, www.psychologytoday.com/ blog/rewired-the-psychology-technology/201207/ the-power.
Is clicking "like" or "share" on a social media site enough to show online friends that we care about them or are such gestures too small to provide meaningful positive feedback?

Singer, Natasha, "Your Online Attention, Bought in an Instant," *The New York Times*, Nov. 17, 2012, p. A1, www.nytimes.com/2012/11/18/technology/ your-online-attention-bought-in-an-instant-by-advertisers.html?pagewanted=all&_r=0.
Marketers increasingly know exactly how people spend their time online and use that information to target them with very specific advertising, including offering different prices to different people. Privacy advocates worry about such scenarios as future marketers targeting shopaholics with low sales resistance with ads tailored to entice them.

Reports and Studies

Boyd, Danah, and Alice Marwick, "Social Privacy in Networked Publics: Teens' Attitudes, Practices, and Strategies," discussion paper for Privacy Law Scholars Conference, June 2, 2011, www.danah .org/papers/2011/SocialPrivacyPLSC-Draft .pdf.
Basing their arguments on interviews with young people, analysts from the corporate think tank Microsoft Research contend that, contrary to myth, young social media users do care about privacy and try to shape their online behavior to protect it in matters of greatest concern to them.

"Participatory Politics: New Media and Youth Political Action," The MacArthur Network on Youth and Participatory Politics, 2012, www.michael haenlein.eu/Publications/Kaplan,%20Andreas% 20-%20Users%20of%20the%20world,%20unite .pdf.
A foundation-funded study by academic researchers finds that more than 40 percent of people ages 15 to 25 engage in political acts such as voicing support for or criticism of interest groups on social media websites or forwarding political news to family and friends. Forty-three percent of white, 41 percent of black, 38 percent of Latino and 36 percent of Asian-American youths say they participate in such activities.

"Photos and Videos as Social Currency Online," Pew Internet and American Life Project, September 2012, http://pewinternet.org/Reports/2012/Online-Pictures.aspx.
Social websites specializing in visual media — such as Instagram, Tumblr and Pinterest — are becoming a much more prominent part of the online experience.

For More Information

Culture Digitally blog, culturedigitally.org. National Science Foundation–funded blog where scholars and researchers discuss information technologies, including social media.

Electronic Frontier Foundation, 454 Shotwell St., San Francisco CA 94110-1914; 415-436-9333; www.eff.org. Nonprofit advocacy, information and legal-support group involved with technology-related privacy and civil rights issues.

Electronic Privacy Information Center, 1718 Connecticut Ave., N.W., Suite 200, Washington, DC 20009; 202-483-1140; www.epic.org. Nonprofit research center that studies privacy and civil liberties issues related to technology.

Facebook blog, blog.facebook.com. Announces and discusses Facebook policy changes.

MacArthur Research Network on Youth and Participatory Politics, ypp.dmlcentral.net. Foundation-funded academic research project that studies cultural participation in the online era and its effects on young people's political engagement.

Mashable, mashable.com. Online magazine that covers social media news.

Pew Internet and American Life Project, 1615 L St., N.W., Suite 700, Washington, DC 20036; 202-419-4500; pewinternet.org. Nonprofit foundation that studies social media use and trends.

Social Media Collective blog, socialmediacollective.org. A blog where researchers at the corporation-funded think tank Microsoft Research New England discuss social media issues.

7

Internet and Social Media

Tom Price

Holding an iPad, U.S. former Federal Trade Commission Chairman Jon Leibowitz announces on Jan. 3, 2013, that the agency had closed an investigation of Google over allegations of uncompetitive conduct. The FTC found that the company had not violated antitrust laws. Google voluntarily agreed to make it easier for advertisers to switch ad campaigns to competitors and ended exclusive search deals with websites.

B owing to the increasing influence, popularity and profitability of the Internet, *The Cleveland Plain Dealer* in April became the latest big newspaper to announce a sharp cutback in personnel and production: The paper, Ohio's largest, plans to curtail home delivery to three days a week and lay off a third of its already-shrunken staff. The paper will continue to publish seven days per week, but will be available only at newsstands on four.

The changes will occur this summer when its parent company, Advance Publications, plans to expand its Internet presence. Advance — which also owns 11 weekly newspapers in the Cleveland area, the Cleveland.com Web site and other media properties around the country — will consolidate content production in a newly formed Northeast Ohio Media Group and create a new website that mimics The Plain Dealer's format. Plain Dealer subscribers will have access to the new site, which will be available to others for a fee.[1]

The decisions illuminate the plight of most U.S. newspapers, which are losing advertisers to online media and struggling to profit from their own Internet activities. Newspaper income from online subscriptions grew last year. But the continuing decline of print advertising dropped overall revenue by 2 percent.[2] The problem is exacerbated by improved targeting that enables large Internet companies to sell local ads to both national firms and local businesses.

Newspapers aren't the only old media affected by the rising popularity of the Internet for news as well as entertainment. Local television viewership continued to drop last year, especially among the young.[3] Television executives also worried about viewers who watch

Maj. Gen. Brett Williams, director of operations at the U.S. Cyber Command, speaks at an Armed Forces Communications and Electronics Association conference in Washington on Feb. 22, 2013. The event focused on cyber preparedness amid growing concerns about attacks by unfriendly nations, terrorists and criminal networks.

shows online, bypassing cable systems that pay for programming. Broadcasters have filed suit against Aereo, a company that captures over-the-air TV signals and sends them to subscribers via the Internet. In April, three major networks — Fox, CBS and Univision, which carries Hispanic programming in Spanish — threatened to become cable channels if the lawsuit fails.[4]

Still, amid all the turmoil traditional media are facing, there is some good news. While Yahoo was the top Internet news site last year, 20 of the next 24 most popular Internet news sources were newspaper or television sites, according to comScore, a company that tracks Internet activity — proof that traditional news organizations remain popular with Web surfers, if not with advertisers.[5]

In the battle for readers and revenue, some old and new media are seeking new income from what they euphemistically term "native advertising" — ads that could be mistaken for regular news material. Native advertising — also more transparently termed "branded" or "sponsored" content — can be prepared by sponsors or a news organization's staff.

The practice raises "huge ethical issues," says Andrew Alexander, former *Washington Post* ombudsman and current visiting professional at the Ohio University journalism school. Native ads that are not labeled as such are "not defensible," he says. Even clear labels don't answer all ethical questions, he says.

"A fundamental tenet of journalism is that quality journalism is truly independent," Alexander explains. Even staff-produced content — when published because an advertiser pays for it — is not totally independent, he argues.

Competition . . . or Not

Meanwhile, the number of Internet sites has grown beyond counting, but a handful dominate the Web. For instance, five companies — Google, Yahoo, Facebook, Microsoft and AOL — earned nearly two-thirds of U.S. digital ad revenue last year. Six companies sold nearly three-quarters of all mobile-device display ads in 2012, and Google accounted for nearly 55 percent of all mobile advertising.[6] The companies are even more dominant within their niches. Facebook now claims a billion members — 100 times that of Google's social media platform Google+.[7] Through YouTube, however, Google overwhelms the online video space with a billion unique visitors each month.[8] And Google controls about three-quarters of the U.S. Internet search market.[9] The company also has moved rapidly into software, installing its Android operating system on 41 percent of all tablets shipped in the third quarter of 2012.[10]

In January 2013, the U.S. Federal Trade Commission (FTC) closed an investigation of Google, saying the company had not violated antitrust laws. However, in a voluntary concession, Google agreed to make it easier for advertisers to switch ad campaigns to competitors and ended exclusive search deals with websites. In Europe, where Google has 95 percent of the search market, the company also has offered concessions in hopes of ending an antitrust inquiry.[11]

Privacy Concerns

Internet users are becoming increasingly worried about expanding online data collection that enables advertisers and others to distribute messages to precisely targeted audiences. The Pew Research Center's Internet & American Life Project reported in November, for instance, that 81 percent of parents expressed concern over the information advertisers can learn about teenagers' online activities.[12]

New technology is raising fears that anyone could use online data to find individuals with specific traits. Facebook is rolling out a tool that enables public

CHRONOLOGY

2012

March Federal Trade Commission urges Internet companies to adopt stronger restrictions on tracking individuals' online activities.

2013

January California and Illinois join four other states banning employers from demanding employees' social media passwords. . . . U.S. Federal Trade Commission closes antitrust investigation of Google, finding no violation of U.S. laws, but European antitrust inquiry continues. . . . Facebook begins rolling out tool that searches for people by such criteria as hometown, hobbies and "likes."

February FTC asks mobile industry to build better privacy safeguards into software and smartphone apps.

March U.S. copyright chief asks Congress to enact comprehensive copyright reform for the digital era.

April *Cleveland Plain Dealer* newspaper announces plans to cut home delivery to three days a week, expand Internet presence. . . . Fox CBS and Univision threaten to become cable channels if they can't stop free transmission of their programming over the Internet. Electronic Frontier Foundation asks Washington state Supreme Court to give text messages the same privacy protections as phone calls.

June Government contractor Edward Snowden leaks news that the National Security Agency has collected phone call data on millions of Americans as part of its anti-terrorism activities.

---

searching of its vast database, for example. Currently, "Graph Search" allows searching by such criteria as hometown, hobbies and "likes." Later the searches might expand to messages and posts.[13] Facebook representatives suggested that journalists could employ the search to find sources — employees of a company going through a contentious strike, for instance.[14] Singles might also be able to locate promising dates, Facebook suggested.[15]

The FTC last year urged Internet companies to adopt stronger restrictions on tracking individuals' online activities.[16] And in February the agency asked the mobile industry to build better privacy safeguards into software and smartphone apps.[17] In April, the Electronic Frontier Foundation asked the Washington state Supreme Court to rule that text messages enjoy the same privacy protections as phone calls.[18] And six states have banned employers from demanding that employees and job applicants reveal social media passwords so the employers can review online activity.[19]

Crime and Sabotage

Privacy advocates also have raised alarms about cybersecurity legislation that passed the U.S. House April 18 but faces Senate opposition and the threat of a presidential veto.

The Cyber Intelligence Sharing and Protection Act (CISPA) is designed to combat what federal intelligence officials term a top national security threat. Criminals, terrorists and unfriendly nations all are attempting to disrupt or steal information from businesses and government agencies, intelligence officials told Congress in March.[20]

CISPA would allow businesses and government agencies to share cyberthreat information without running afoul of antitrust and privacy laws.[21] Privacy advocates argue, however, that would violate the rights of customers who entrust information to companies with the understanding — sometimes in signed contracts — that it would not be shared.[22]

The White House agreed, saying in a veto threat that "citizens have a right to know that corporations will be held accountable — and not granted immunity — for failing to safeguard personal information adequately."

President Obama took his own cybersecurity action Feb. 12, ordering federal agencies to notify businesses of cyberthreats in a manner that protects individuals' civil liberties. He also instructed the National Institute of Standards and Technology to develop best-practice recommendations for protecting against attack.[23]

Copyright for Digital Age

Warning that copyright law is "showing the strain of its age," U.S. Copyright Office chief Maria Pallante has urged Congress to enact comprehensive reform for the digital era.

The latest copyright revision — the Digital Millennium Copyright Act — is 15 years old, she pointed out in March. Much of current copyright law was enacted in 1976, before the Internet existed.[24]

Pallante and other reform advocates note that digital recording and communication have created new opportunities for intellectual-property theft. Digital technology also creates opportunities for dissemination of art and information that can be thwarted by out-of-date laws.

One spur for reform was the January suicide of Aaron Swartz, a cofounder of the Reddit social media platform and an advocate of free access to scholarly publications.

Demonstrating the ease of large-scale online theft, the 26-year-old Swartz hacked into the Massachusetts Institute of Technology's computer system and downloaded 4.8 million documents from JSTOR, a repository for scholarly publications, in 2010 and 2011. Charged with 13 felony counts of violating the Computer Fraud and Abuse Act, which became law in 1986, he faced a maximum 35 years in prison and $1 million in fines. Swartz, who was said to suffer from depression, killed himself after rejecting a plea bargain that would have reduced his jailed time to less than a year.[25]

Swartz clearly committed a felony, according to Orin Kerr, who teaches cyber law at George Washington University.[26] But the proposed punishment was too severe, and the law is "breathtakingly broad," Kerr said.[27] The act outlaws violating a website's terms of service, which most users never read. That means Facebook users could be prosecuted for posting false information about themselves, Kerr explained.

While Swartz's actions were extreme, many advocate free access to the fruits of government-funded research. The National Institutes of Health already requires grantees to provide free access within a year of publication.[28] In February, White House science adviser John Holdren extended that policy to all federal agencies with annual research budgets greater than $100 million.[29]

— *Tom Price is a freelance writer in Washington, D.C.*

NOTES

1. Robert L. Smith, "The Plain Dealer to remain a daily But home delivery will be made only on Sundays and 2 other days," *The* (Cleveland) *Plain Dealer*, April 5, 2013, p. 1.

2. Mark Coddington, "This Week in Review: Network TV threatens to go paid, and newspapers' slow revenue shift, Nieman Journalism Lab, April 12, 2013, www.niemanlab.org/2013/04/network-tv-paid-news papers-revenue-shift/?readnext; and Pew Research Center, Project for Excellence in Journalism, "The State of the News Media 2013," March 18, 2013, http://stateofthemedia.org.

3. "The State of the News Media 2013," Pew research Center, Project for Excellence in Journalism, March 18, 2013, http://stateofthemedia.org.

4. Brian Stelter, "Broadcasters Circle Wagons Against a TV Streaming Upstart," *The New York Times*, April 9, 2013, www.nytimes.com/2013/04/10/business/media/aereo-has-tv-networks-circling-the-wagons.html?pagewanted=al.

5. Pew Research Center, *op. cit.*

6. *Ibid.*

7. Ryan Tate, "Facebook Announces New Search Engine," *Wired*, Jan. 15, 2013, www.wired.com/business/2013/01/facebook-event.

8. *Ibid.*

9. Carol Matlack and Stephanie Bodoni, "Google's EU Antitrust Proposal Will Likely Be Tweaked," *Bloomburg BusinessWeek*, April 15, 2013, www.business week.com/articles/2013-04-15/googles-eu-anti trust-proposal-will-likely-see-tweaks.

10. Pew Research Center, *op. cit.*

11. Matlack and Bodoni, *op. cit.*

12. "Parents, Teens, and Online Privacy," Pew Research Center, Internet & American Life Project, Nov. 20, 2012, www.pewinternet.org/Press-Releases/2012/Parents-Teens-and-Online-Privacy.aspx.

13. Brandon Bailey, "Facebook search may take time to catch on," *San Jose Mercury News*, Jan. 17, 2013, www.insidebayarea.com/breaking-news/ci_2238 9902/facebook-search-may-take-time-catch.

14. Pew Research Center, Project for Excellence in Journalism, *op. cit.*

15. Ryan Tate, "Facebook Announces New Search Engine," *Wired*, Jan. 15, 2013, www.wired.com/business/2013/01/facebook-event.

16. Hayley Tsukayama, "FTC releases final privacy report, says 'Do Not Track' mechanism may be available by end of year," *The Washington Post*, March 26, 2012, http://articles.washingtonpost.com/2012-03-26/business/35446988_1_information-collection-practices-privacy-report-privacy-bill.

17. Edward Wyatt, "F.T.C. Suggests Privacy Guidelines for Mobile Apps," *The New York Times*, Feb. 1, 2013, www.nytimes.com/2013/02/02/technology/ftc-suggests-do-not-track-feature-for-mobile-software-and-apps.html.

18. Electronic Frontier Foundation, "Can Police Read Text Messages Without a Warrant?" April 9, 2013, www.eff.org/press/releases/can-police-read-text-messages-without-warrant.

19. David Kravets, "6 States Bar Employers From Demanding Facebook Passwords," *Wired*, Jan. 2, 2013, www.wired.com/threatlevel/2013/01/password-protected-states.

20. Luis Martinez, "Intel Heads Now Fear Cyber Attack More Than Terror," ABC News, March 13, 2013, http://abcnews.go.com/Blotter/intel-heads-now-fear-cyber-attack-terror/story?id=18719593#.UXW048rHZ-Q.

21. "Pro-business cyber security bill sails through House again, but without clear path ahead," The Associated Press, April 18, 2013, www.washingtonpost.com/business/pro-business-cybersecurity-bill-sails-through-house-again-but-without-clear-path-ahead/2013/04/18/01151846-a84a-11e2-9e1c-bb0fb0c2edd9_story.html.

22. Zach Carter and Sabrina Siddiqui, "CISPA Vote: House Passes Cybersecurity Bill To Let Companies Break Privacy Contracts," *The Huffington Post*, April 18, 2013, www.huffingtonpost.com/2013/04/18/cispa-vote-house-approves_n_3109504.html.

23. Alex Fitzpatrick, "Obama Signs Order Demanding Federal Agencies Share Cyber Threat Info," *Mashable*, Feb. 12, 2013, http://mashable.com/2013/02/12/obama-executive-order-security-cyber-threat.

24. Maria Pallante, "The Register's Call for Updates to U.S. Copyright Law," House Judiciary Subcommittee on Courts, Intellectual Property and the Internet hearing, Congressional Documents and Publications, March 20, 2013.

25. David Uberti, "Inquiry widens into Swartz prosecution," *The Boston Globe*, Feb. 28, 2013, p. 1.

26. *Ibid.*

27. David Uberti, "Activist's suicide echoes in Congress," *The Boston Globe*, Feb. 6, 2013, p. 1.

28. "We Paid for the Research, So Let's See It," *The New York Times*, Feb. 26, 2013, p. 24.

29. Carolyn Y. Johnson, "Free, open access to taxpayer-funded studies in spotlight," *The Boston Globe*, March 4, 2013, P. B4.

8

Social Media and Politics

Tom Price

Mitt Romney

Republican presidential candidate Mitt Romney sleds with one of his grandsons in a family photo posted on Pinterest by his wife, Ann. Mrs. Romney and Michelle Obama, as well as the candidates themselves, have posted recipes, family photographs and other personal information on the site in an effort to humanize the candidates and forge closer links to voters.

From *CQ Researcher*,
October 12, 2012

As Republicans sought to boost Mitt Romney's then-flagging presidential campaign during their August nominating convention in Tampa, this message popped up on the social media website reddit on Aug. 29:

"I am Barack Obama, President of the United States — AMA" (reddit shorthand for "ask me anything").[1]

For the next half hour, Obama fielded questions from reddit participants, generating 5,266 queries and comments. By the morning of Aug. 31, the discussion had logged nearly 5.3 million page views. He wrapped up the unprecedented online session — complete with a photo of him at his computer, shirtsleeves rolled up, tie loosened, to prove he was really answering questions — with a pitch for voting and a link to an online voter-registration form.[2]

In the process, the president asserted his affinity for the rapidly growing world of social media and enrolled more than 10,000 reddit users as potential campaign volunteers, Obama chief digital strategist Joe Rospars said. The president also served notice that he would not allow Romney a solo moment in the sun, even during the GOP convention.

Obama's command of the Internet proved a key to his victory over Arizona Sen. John McCain in 2008. This year, all candidates are striving to emulate Obama's 2008 online success, but there are differences:

- The president's 2012 campaign is doing much more online than it did four years ago.
- The buzz now is about social media such as Facebook, Twitter, YouTube and the many less-prominent platforms such as

Many Voters Ignore Internet Comments

Two-thirds of voters say they are taking little or no account of comments posted on social media and Internet forums before voting for president in November. More consideration is given to conversations with family and friends and opinions voiced by experts on major news outlets.

How much do you consider the following in deciding whom to vote for in the November presidential election?

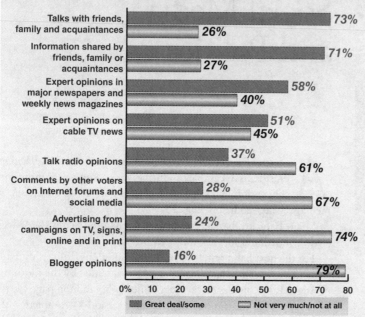

Source: "Heartland Monitor Poll," *National Journal*, June 9, 2012, p. 24, www .allstate.com/Allstate/content/refresh-attachments/Heartland_monitor_XIII_ topline.pdf

reddit, all of which had far less impact — or didn't even exist — in 2008.

- And Romney's camp is determined to keep up.

"The tools people can use to get messages to their friends are much more powerful than they were in 2008," says Joe Trippi, architect of former New Hampshire Gov. Howard Dean's 2004 campaign for the Democratic presidential nomination, which tapped the powers of the Internet more than any candidate had done before.[3] "The sheer size of the networks has exploded. [Prominent Democratic strategist James] Carville used to say: 'It's the economy, stupid.' Now 'It's the networks, stupid.'"

One proof of social media's growing importance, says Vincent Harris, who ran GOP presidential hopeful Newt Gingrich's online activities in some of this year's primaries, is its incorporation as an integral component of many campaigns' operations. No longer is the "new-media guy" sent to a corner to manage the Internet in isolation from the rest of the staff, Harris explains.

Other proof is in the numbers. Twitter users posted 1.8 million tweets on Election Day in 2008, the kind of event that spurs social media activity. Now tweets average 340 million a day — nearly 200 times as much.[4] This year's Republican National Convention generated more tweets the day before it opened than the 2008 convention did during its full run, according to Adam Sharp, head of Twitter's government, news and social innovation operations.

"More tweets are sent every two days today than had had been sent in total from Twitter's creation in 2006 to the 2008 election," he told a panel at the Democratic National Convention in early September. Registered voters who use Facebook today outnumber those who actually voted in the 2008 general election, says Katie Harbath, a Facebook manager who helps Republicans use the platform.

Overall, nearly two-thirds of U.S. adults say they use social media regularly.[5] And "they don't skew as young as you may think," says Michael Reilly, a partner in the Democratic campaign consulting firm Murphy Vogel Askew Reilly in Alexandria, Va.

While younger people are more likely to use social media, the contingent of older adults is growing most rapidly. Eighty-six percent of 18- to 29-year-olds use social media, compared with about a third of those 65 and older. But participation nearly quintupled among those 50 and older between 2008 and 2012. Nearly three times as many 30- to 49-year-olds use social media now as in 2008. Among 18- to 29-year-olds, the increase was just 19 percent, with the same proportion using social media this year as two years ago.[6]

That growing participation increases social media's attractiveness to politicians, who use the platforms to identify and organize supporters, raise funds and spread their messages. Candidates bypass traditional news media to send unfiltered communication to the public. They target recipients of their messages with growing precision. They contact hard-to-reach voters — especially the young — who record television programs and fast-forward through the commercials. They use online communication to organize phone banks, door-to-door canvassing and other offline activities. And they tap into what is believed to be the most effective form of persuasion: friend-to-friend conversation.

Social media's interactive nature allows candidates to engage in what can be — or can appear to be — conversations with individual voters. Those voters can forward the candidates' posts to their friends, extending the candidates' reach and adding the endorsement of the people who pass the messages on.

But the increasing ability of online campaign strategists to collect and analyze detailed personal information about individual voters has raised privacy concerns.

Polled in May about information sources they tap when deciding how to vote, Americans put family, friends and acquaintances at the top. Bloggers ranked at the bottom, just below advertisements and online comments by people voters don't know.[7]

Each social medium offers its own political tools. Trying to label one more valuable than the other is "sort of like asking which is your favorite child," says Phil Noble, a Democratic online political consultant since the 1990s. "Advantage," says George Washington University political scientist Michael Cornfield, "goes to people who can use all of them."

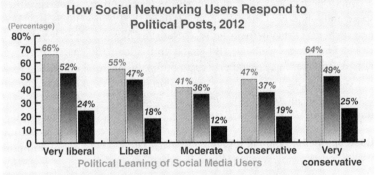

Strongest Views Dominate Political Posts

Social media users who identify themselves as "very liberal" or "very conservative" are more likely than those who identify themselves as less partisan to "like" political posts, write positive comments or "friend" those who share their political views.

How Social Networking Users Respond to Political Posts, 2012

(Percentage)

Very liberal: 66%, 52%, 24%
Liberal: 55%, 47%, 18%
Moderate: 41%, 36%, 12%
Conservative: 47%, 37%, 19%
Very conservative: 64%, 49%, 25%

Political Leaning of Social Media Users

■ Hit "like" button for political post
■ Posted positive comment
■ "Friended" someone with shared views

Source: "Social Networking Sites and Politics," Pew Research Center, March 2012, p. 8, www.pewinternet.org/~/media//Files/Reports/2012/PIP_SNS_and_politics.pdf

But one network clearly dominates. "Facebook is the 800-pound gorilla," with its large number of users and friend-to-friend networks, Harris says. Politicians communicate with journalists through Twitter and use its brief messages for rapid response to political attacks. Television news media often pick up YouTube videos and give them wider distribution.

These interactive media's greatest value comes from how they interact with each other, says Ken Deutsch, who manages the digital practice at the Jones Public Affairs communications firm's Boston office. "If YouTube wasn't shared on Facebook and Twitter and blogs and those other places, it would have no [political] value," Deutsch explains. "If you couldn't link newspaper articles to Twitter, Twitter would have no value."

Social media enable individuals to enter the public political debate in ways previously reserved to politicians and the traditional news outlets. That poses a challenge to candidates, who can't control their messages once social media users start passing them around and commenting on them. But candidates also benefit when supporters rise to the candidates' defense after a social media attack.

Indeed, the millions of citizen postings create an unending barrage of attacks, defenses and counterattacks that demand rapid responses from campaigns. That heightens the likelihood of gaffes, which in turn get amplified in online repostings, adding to the cacophony, and the allure, of social media.

Smart phones and other mobile devices increase the speed and ubiquity of the debate, which individuals can enter whenever they want from wherever they happen to be. The devices' cameras also enable individuals to record candidates' gaffes and post them online instantly.

As campaign 2012 races to its conclusion on Nov. 6, here are some questions being raised about social media's impact on the American political process:

Does online data mining threaten voters' privacy?

Political operatives and political scientists are talking about "Big Data" a lot this year.

The phrase refers to political organizations' ability to collect enormous amounts of information about individual voters — through social media and traditional means — then crunch it and use the results to send finely tuned messages to narrowly targeted audiences. Some critics worry that it's also a highly intrusive invasion of privacy.

By gathering material from social media, other websites and offline sources, campaigns can identify individuals' browsing habits, online purchases, social media discussions, data about friends and friends' interests and other information.[8]

When people signed up for a smart phone app that was to notify them of Romney's vice presidential pick, the campaign gathered their email addresses and other data.[9] Those who joined Obama's campaign by clicking "I'm in" on Facebook gave the campaign their Facebook data plus information on their Facebook friends, according to Trippi, the architect of Howard Dean's Internet-dependent 2004 campaign. "People would want to turn their machines off if they knew everything these campaigns know about them," he says, only partly in jest.

When campaigns target voters now, Democratic online consultant Noble says, "it's not [an anonymous] white male voter in this precinct. It's James Q. Smith on Grand Street."

That so-called "microtargeting" is quite valuable, according to Mike Zaneis, senior vice president of the Interactive Advertising Bureau, a New York–based trade group for companies that sell online advertising. In the commercial sector, he says, targeted ads are 2.5 times as effective as nontargeted ones.

Directly addressing a voter's precise interests through social media allows a campaign to "engage people in detail on issues you might not otherwise have had the time or resources to talk about through traditional media," says Reilly, the Democratic campaign consultant.

"If you want to reach people who are interested in a particular topic, there are groups and sub-groups for everything in social media with their own thought leaders that you can identify and either advertise to or reach out to directly," Deutsch of Jones Public Affairs notes.

The practice carries "great potential for abuses of privacy," according to John Allen Hendricks, chair of the mass communication department at Stephen F. Austin State University in Nacogdoches, Texas, and co-editor of a book about the 2008 Obama campaign. "I don't know that there are prominent enough disclaimers on the politicians' websites to inform the electorate that they are giving up a lot of information that they may not want revealed in the future," he explains. "We do not know what the campaigns will do with that data after the election is over."

Jeffrey Chester, executive director of the Center for Digital Democracy, a consumer-protection and privacy advocacy group in Washington, D.C., argues that the privacy threat is especially serious because it involves voting. "It's not about selling books and music and T-shirts," he says. "It's about the heart of the democratic process. Do we really want giant political parties and well-funded special interest groups like the Super PACs compiling millions of dossiers on voters and becoming a series of private National Security Agencies or FBIs?"

Chester wants the federal government to adopt "new rules that enable the voters to make the decisions about how their data can be collected and used." Voters should have to give permission before organizations could gather information about them online, he says. "Retention limits" should allow data to be used only for a short time and not be archived or sold, he adds.

He also worries that microtargeting will enable politicians to distribute false campaign pitches "under the radar, without being accountable to the public fact-checking process."

Zaneis calls Chester's under-the-radar warning "a bit of a red herring. It's no more of a potential problem in the digital world than it is in the offline world," he says, pointing out that direct-mailers have targeted individuals with postal mail for decades.

Gingrich online director Harris notes that "there's a reason people who subscribe to *Guns* magazine get direct-mail pieces about the Second Amendment."

"If somebody wants to deceive," Zaneis says, "they're going to be able to do that in any medium."

The Interactive Advertising Bureau's code allows consumers to opt out of being tracked and targeted online, he says, although that doesn't apply to political organizations that don't belong to the organization. An opt-in requirement would hinder the operations of the $35-billion online advertising industry, which supports 3 million jobs, he says. Most consumers wouldn't bother to opt in, even though most also don't bother to opt out, he says.

"I'm not sure why the Internet should be the redheaded stepchild of the media," he adds. "You can collect data about people all over the place" offline.

Jim Harper, director of information policy studies at the libertarian Cato Institute, says federal legislation would be too blunt an instrument.

"Legislation is going to produce privacy protection that is too high for many people and too low for many people," he says. "My argument is that privacy is a product of personal responsibility. You don't share what information you don't want others to have. That way you get custom privacy protection, because you've done it yourself."

Douglas Pinkham, president of the Public Affairs Council, an association of public affairs professionals that studies online political activity, observes that many younger Americans are comfortable revealing information on the Internet because they "just don't care about privacy as much as middle-aged and older people do."

Do social media cause political polarization?

"It's constitutional. B----es," Democratic National Committee Executive Director Patrick Gaspard tweeted crudely when the Supreme Court upheld Barack Obama's signature health-care legislation in June.[10]

After Republicans attacked him for the intemperate remark, Gaspard tweeted an apology, explaining that "I

Republican presidential candidate Mitt Romney works online aboard his bus after a campaign stop in Council Bluffs, Iowa, on June 8. In an effort to enhance his social media presence, Romney urged his Facebook friends on Aug. 21: "We're almost to 5 million likes — help us get there! 'Like' and share this with your friends and family to show you stand with Mitt!" By the second week of October, Romney had 8.6 million "likes."

let my excitement [at the Supreme Court's ruling] get the better of me." Then he let his Twitter feed go silent for six weeks.[11]

Gaspard's gaffe is just one example of the polarization and hostility that seem to characterize some online political communication. And the ill feelings are not restricted to political leaders.

A woman in the Houston, Texas, area became so disturbed about the tone of political debate that she declared her Facebook page to be a "Politics-Free zone." "Let's all take a deep breath, step back and remember that we are friends — in spite of our political views," Sandy Mansfield posted.[12]

More than a third of social media users in a Pew Research Center study this year reported receiving a "strong negative reaction" after they posted a political comment.[13]

Explanations for the phenomenon range from the overall polarized political climate to the nature of social media themselves.

The brevity of social media messages tends to "tweak people's impulses rather than cause them to think," said Bill Shireman, president of Future 500, a San Francisco consulting firm that helps businesses work with activist

Social Media Use Declines With Age

More than 70 percent of adults under age 50 say they use social networking sites, with usage highest among those 18 to 29. Only about a third of those 65 and older use social media. Experts say a lower level of technological literacy among seniors is the reason for less social media use, but their participation is increasing rapidly.

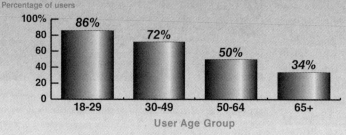

Social Networking Use by Age Group, 2012

Source: "Older Adults and Internet Use," Pew Research Center, June 2012, p. 9, www.pewinternet.org/~/media//Files/Reports/2012/PIP_Older_adults_and_internet_use.pdf

groups. "So prejudice and group-think can appear very quickly with few restraints."[14]

Social media worsen polarization that already exists in American politics, says Deutsch, the online communications manager at Jones Public Affairs. "People follow people they agree with. On Facebook, you're seeing news put up by friends who are reinforcing your own views."

ComScore Inc., which measures online activity, this year released a study that found people tend to visit Internet sites that share their political leanings. Some Republicans visit the liberal TalkingPointsMemo.com, for instance, but Democrats account for 70 percent of the time spent at the site. Conversely, Democrats account for just 9 percent of the time spent at the conservative DailyCaller.com site.[15]

Aaron Smith, who studies politics and the Internet at the Pew Research Center, says most political posts in social media are made by activists with strong views. In one Pew survey, for instance, 66 percent of "very liberal" people said they had "liked" a political post, as did 64 percent of "very conservative" people. Only 41 percent of self-described "moderates" did so. Pew found the same pattern when asking if people had posted political comments.[16]

"They come to this [online] world with a certain set of attitudes and a team mentality, and social networking sites provide a way for them to support their team," Smith says of the activists. "While you can see ways social networking sites can exacerbate [polarization], in a way they're only reflecting that broader political culture."

Social media promote nationalization of politics, just as cable TV news and the Internet in general do, Democratic campaign consultant Reilly says. Nationalization then promotes polarization, as ideological activists from around the country jump into local political debates, he explains.

"No matter where you're running," he says, "the challenge to make it about [often-less-polarized] local issues and local candidates is tremendous," Reilly says.

Former House Speaker Thomas P. "Tip" O'Neill, D-Mass., famously proclaimed that "all politics is local," Reilly noted, but the media now are making it more accurate to say that "all politics is national."

Social media amplify the heated, negative campaigning that often appears in polarized debates, Reilly says. But well-funded independent organizations tend to drive the negativity through the offline advertisements that they purchase, he adds.

Other aspects of social media can combat polarization and negativity.

While Twitter requires micro-comments and Facebook encourages brevity, tweets and Facebook postings can link to longer documents, and long videos can be posted on YouTube, for example.

"On television, you're limited to the sound bite you can get on the news and the 30-second ad," Reilly notes. "On social media, you can be posting as much as you want every day. It's an avenue for getting more information to people that wasn't available before social media came about."

Although people tend to associate with others who have similar beliefs, few people's networks are devoid of diversity.

Asked in a May survey about the political orientation of their social media contacts, 24 percent of those polled said most were the same as their own, 9 percent said most were different, and 60 percent said there was an even mix. The rest didn't know or didn't answer.[17]

"There are plenty of echo chambers, but there also are lots of tunnels among the echo chambers," the Cato Institute's Harper says.

"People are on social media to interact with the drama of their lives," not to form political organizations, Harris says. Their networks tend to be comprised of family and friends. And "not everyone in a family or at a high school or in college agrees on all the same political points." As a result, he says, "the average person on Facebook is friends with people of diverse political views, religions and backgrounds."

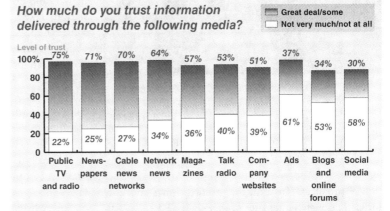

Social Media Lag in Trustworthiness

Americans find traditional news outlets such as public television and newspapers as the most trustworthy sources of news. More than half of those surveyed say social media platforms as well as blog and online forums — which allow anybody to post content — are not very trustworthy.

How much do you trust information delivered through the following media?

Source: "Heartland Monitor Poll," *National Journal,* June 9, 2012, p. 24, www.allstate.com/Allstate/content/refresh-attachments/Heartland_monitor_XIII_topline.pdf

Do social media level the campaign-spending playing field?

Mark McKinnon, chief media adviser for George W. Bush's presidential campaigns, has become an Internet evangelist.

"Americans are leveraging technology to more fully engage in the political process," McKinnon proclaimed earlier this year. "Voters have become more than just passive consumers of these digital messages. . . . 'We the people' can now compete against the near-deafening influence of unlimited campaign contributions."[18]

McKinnon is not alone in his optimism. Low cost and ease of use have led many to view social media as weapons that underfunded candidates and common citizens can use to combat the enormous campaign spending of millionaires and billionaires that was unleashed by the Supreme Court's *Citizens United* decision in 2010.[19] They also view social media as an inexpensive tool for solving problems that defy traditional media.

Social media are "good for niche issues," Democratic online consultant Noble says, noting that television is too expensive for addressing topics of interest to small

groups. Social media offer effective access to young people, who watch less television than their elders, Democratic campaign consultant Reilly says. Because the young are less likely to vote, as well, their cost-per-vote in television advertising can be prohibitive, he adds.

Social media also open an avenue of influence that can't be tapped by traditional, geographically bound media, according to Deutsch of Jones Public Affairs.

Presidential campaigns concentrate their television spending in the handful of states where the race is close. But "most of us are influenced by people who live outside the media market we live in — our friends, our classmates, our colleagues," as well as by advertising and by people who live nearby, Deutsch points out. Social media enable those people to be in touch with each other and allow campaigns to try to influence them no matter where they live, he says.

Social media also have become a leveling tool as television advertising becomes less effective.

Zac Moffatt, digital director of the Romney campaign, has identified "off-the-gridders" — people who avoid television commercials by not watching programs when

President Obama talks with Facebook CEO Mark Zuckerberg during a town hall meeting at the social media company's headquarters in Palo Alto, Calif., on April 20, 2011. A majority of young adults 18 to 29 say Facebook is their top news source, and a fifth name Comedy Central's Jon Stewart and Stephen Colbert, according to a recent survey.

they're broadcast. Instead, they record shows and fast-forward through the ads later, or they get their commercial-free entertainment from such sources as Netflix.

Surveys found that a third of the residents of Ohio and Virginia — key swing states — fall into that category, watching only sporting events at their scheduled broadcast time, Moffatt said in a panel discussion during the Republican Convention. Advertising that runs next to online search results or in social media offers ways to reach these potential voters, Moffatt said. In addition, he noted, recipients of online advertising can share it with friends, thus extending its reach.

Social media will not replace traditional news sources anytime soon, however. One important reason: Other than information they receive from friends and relatives, people — including young people — don't trust what they're told on social media as much as they trust what traditional news outlets tell them.

In a May *National Journal* survey, three-quarters of Americans polled said they have some or a great deal of trust in public television and public radio. Newspapers and cable news followed close behind with 71 and 70 percent. Next came network news (64 percent), magazines (57) and talk radio (53). Social media finished dead last, with just 30 percent.[20]

Television also topped a 2011 Public Affairs Council survey that asked Americans where they get most of their

news. Print newspapers or magazines stood second at 12 percent, well below TV's 70 percent. Just 1 percent picked social media.[21]

In an August survey for the *Los Angeles Times* and the University of Southern California's Annenberg communication school, a majority of young adults ages 18 to 29 said Facebook is their top news source, and a fifth listed Jon Stewart and Stephen Colbert, the Comedy Central cable station's fake news anchor and commentator. But those sources finished below traditional news media in trust.[22]

"An insurgent candidate with little money can use the Web to catch fire," former Gingrich online coordinator Harris says. "But every survey continues to show that television is where people are spending most of their time. So, until those numbers change, television will continue to take the lion's share of the media money."

The candidates with the lion's share of the money will be able to buy the lion's share of television time, which limits social media's ability to level the field, Deutsch says.

"In a world where there was some regulation of size of donations, social media may have leveled it," he says. "But, at this point, with the number of individual donors you have to have to make up for the wealthiest donors who support PACs, I don't think it can be."

Hendricks of Stephen F. Austin State University agrees that "the wealthy's ability to spend unlimited amounts on campaigns may overcome the Internet's people power." But Cornfield of George Washington University suggests that the enormous amount of cash being poured into this year's campaigns may, ironically, limit money's impact in the closing weeks before the election.

"I'm hearing that we're going to see, because of the rise of Super PACs, much less advertising space available, especially in broadcast and cable TV and radio," he says. "All the time's been bought up. That's forcing campaigns to rely more on Web ads. And there are starting to be anticipated shortages on the favorite Web ad spaces."

BACKGROUND
Nascent Revolution

Today's global Internet can trace its birth to the transmission of one word — "log" — from a computer at the University of California, Los Angeles to a computer at

CHRONOLOGY

1990s *The Internet becomes a political instrument.*

1991 Commercial activities are allowed on the Internet. . . . Point-and-click navigation invented. . . . World Wide Web name coined.

1992 Clinton-Gore campaign uses Internet to reach out to prospective voters.

1994 First graphical browser invented. . . . White House website introduced.

1995 Library of Congress creates www.thomas.gov site, named after President Thomas Jefferson, to put legislative information online.

1996 More campaigns go online. . . . Center for Responsive Politics puts campaign finance information on the Web.

1998 Professional wrestler Jesse Ventura demonstrates Internet's value to the underdog by winning Minnesota governorship as a third-party candidate.

1999 Federal Election Commission allows matching federal campaign funds for online credit-card donations. . . . Napster music-sharing network founded. . . . New Jersey Sen. Bill Bradley raises more than $600,000 online in unsuccessful campaign for 2000 Democratic presidential nomination.

2000s *Online campaigning expands, and social media enter politics.*

2000 After upset victory in New Hampshire primary, Republican presidential candidate John McCain raises $2.7 million online in three days.

2001 Accused of violating copyrights, Napster goes offline and is later reborn as a legal online music store.

2002 LinkedIn business networking site and Friendster, a prototypical social networking platform, launched; Friendster later morphs into a gaming website.

2003 Exploiting Internet's fundraising and voter outreach capabilities, former New Hampshire Gov. Howard Dean becomes frontrunner for 2004 Democratic presidential nomination but ultimately loses to Sen. John Kerry.

2004 TheFacebook (later just Facebook) begins business as a networking platform for Harvard undergraduates. . . . Flickr photo-sharing platform created. . . . Dean's 2004 campaign taps power of Internet fund-raising as never before.

2005 YouTube video-sharing platform founded. Facebook expands on college campuses and allows some high school students to participate.

2006 After expanding to more college campuses, Facebook is opened to anyone 13 and older. . . . Twitter established.

2007 CNN and YouTube sponsor Democratic and Republican debates during which viewers submit video questions.

2008 Barack Obama wins presidency after raising $500 million online and conducting most-ever campaign activities online. . . . Twitter records 1.8 million tweets on Election Day.

2009 White House begins posting photos to Flickr. . . . Grassroots conservatives tap social media to find like-minded activists and grow the decentralized Tea Party movement.

2010 Social media contribute to conservative election victories at all levels of government.

2011 In run-up to 2012 election, all major political candidates campaign on social media; GOP presidential candidates debate on Twitter; Obama hosts "Twitter Town Hall" from White House.

2012 Social media play larger campaign role than ever; Twitter averages 340 million tweets a day; U.S. Facebook users outnumber 2008 total voters; Obama leads Romney in most measures of social media activity, but some think Romney's social media supporters may be more engaged; online data-mining raises privacy concerns; researchers study social media activity to evaluate political campaigns' effectiveness. . . . Candidates use social media for on-the-fly tests of campaign tactics' effectiveness. . . . Companies create fake social media followers to inflate apparent size of campaigns' online support.

Twitter: A New Political Weathervane

"We have never had a way to peer into discussions before."

Can social media conversations predict election results? A growing number of organizations are trying to find out.

Twitter launched the Twitter Political Index — or Twindex — on Aug. 1.[1] It's an attempt to measure Twitter users' opinions about the leading presidential candidates by evaluating their tweets.

The index was developed in partnership with two prominent political pollsters — Democrat Mark Mellman and Republican Jon McHenry — and a firm that analyzes social media activity, Topsy.

Topsy uses software to evaluate the sentiments expressed about people or things in tweets by Americans each day. It then compares the results with tweets about Barack Obama and Mitt Romney. Finally, it creates a 0-100 ranking that resembles an SAT percentile. An 80 score means tweets about the candidate were more positive than tweets about 80 percent of all people and things that were tweeted about that day. A score of 20 means the candidate's tweets were more negative than 80 percent of the others.

Computing Obama's Twindex scores for the previous two years, Topsy said they often paralleled his approval ratings in Gallup polls.[2]

Adam Sharp, Twitter's head of government, news and social innovation, said the index offers a peek into "conversations that just an election cycle ago were limited to coffee shops, dinner tables and water coolers."[3]

The most influential conversations are among friends, relatives and colleagues, Mellman said, but "we have never really had a way to peer into those discussions before."

The index can't claim the precision of scientific surveys, both pollsters said. But the way the index has paralleled Obama's Gallup ratings suggests that "what we're seeing in these conversations is not radically divorced from what we're seeing in the country as a whole," Mellman said.[4]

Mining the conversations reveals nuances that aren't captured in yes-or-no or multiple-choice questions in a poll, Sharp said.[5] A campaign could find the Twindex data helpful if the data could show which topics link a candidate to more positive conversations, McHenry said.[6]

Twindex might offer a "leading indicator" of opinion, Sharp said during the Democratic National Convention. In the days following the spike of American good feeling caused by Osama bin Laden's death in May 2011, for instance, Obama's Twindex score dropped more quickly than his approval ratings in polls, "as the Twitter conversation returned to being more focused on economic issues," Sharp said at the index's launch.[7]

Twindex has obvious weaknesses, says Brad Fay, chief operating officer of the Keller Fay Group, a research and consulting firm that specializes in word-of-mouth marketing. For one thing, three-quarters of conversations occur face-to-face and 15 percent by phone, he says. Only about 10 percent occur online, and just a fraction of those on Twitter, he says.

"We know that the Twitter universe skews young whereas the voting universe skews a little older," he says. "Some people participate at a much higher frequency rate than other people. You could tweet once a month or 10 times a day, but on Election Day everyone gets just one vote."

Fay's firm has teamed with *National Journal* to evaluate conversations offline as well as online by conducting weekly surveys of people who match the demographics of the total U.S. adult population. They are asked the topics of conversations they had face-to-face, over the phone and online and whether the tone was positive or negative.

Stanford University about 360 miles up the California coast.[23] The UCLA computer was logging into the Stanford computer on Oct. 29, 1969, to create the first link in a network that now serves about 2 billion users.[24]

The $19,800 contract that funded the first Internet research was paid for by the federal government's Defense Advanced Research Projects Agency (ARPA) to facilitate information exchange among military research facilities.

As more computers joined the network, it became known as ARPANET.

To facilitate civilian research, the federal government's National Science Foundation (NSF) created the Computer Science Network (CSNET) in 1981. Five years later, the foundation established the faster NSFNET. As these early networks began to link to each other, they created a network of networks that became known as the Internet.

An interesting finding of "Conversation Nation," as the project is called: Political polling results tend to be stable while "we find the conversation changes quite a bit," Fay says.[8]

The project does not pretend to be predictive, Fay says. But when Keller Fay did the same surveying as an R&D project four years ago, Obama "was running away with the conversation, both in the amount of conversation and the positive nature of the conversation. It was very clear in that data who was leading on Election Day."

For the week ending Sept. 30, Fay's survey found 52 percent of conversations about Romney were mostly negative, 23 percent mostly positive and the rest neutral or mixed. It was the Republican's most negative score since the surveying began in late May. Obama recorded his highest positive score, 47 percent, to 30 percent negative.[9]

The Twitter index showed tweets about the candidates were much more negative than all tweets on Sept. 30. Obama scored higher than Romney, 20-19, and led for most of the entire preceding week.

Others attempting to measure online sentiment include CNN, in a collaboration with Facebook, and NBC News.

CNN's "Election Insights" simply reports the number of Facebook posts about the presidential and vice presidential candidates, broken down by state and various demographics.[10] Obama and Romney ran close together through most of the week ending Sept. 30, with each spiking occasionally. GOP vice presidential nominee Paul Ryan inspired many more posts than Vice President Joe Biden.

NBC analyzes social media posts using a tool developed by Crimson Hexagon, a Boston firm that monitors and analyzes social media activity. The analysis appears on the network's "Politics" page.[11] On Sept. 29, Romney received more expressions of support than Obama in all tweets and a sample of Facebook posts.

— *Tom Price*

Mitt Romney's Twitter site registers more than 1.3 million followers. The new Twitter Political Index attempts to measure Twitter users' opinions about the presidential candidates by evaluating their tweets.

[1] "The Twitter Political Index," https://election.twitter.com.

[2] "Topsy Analytics for Twitter Political Index," Topsy, http://about.topsy.com/election.

[3] Adam Sharp, "A new barometer for the election," Twitter Blog, Aug. 1, 2012, http://blog.twitter.com/2012/08/a-new-barometer-for-election.html.

[4] Ariel Edwards-Levy and Mark Blumenthal, "Twindex, New Twitter Polling System, Tracks Opinions On Presidential Candidates," *The Huffington Post*, Aug. 1, 2012, www.huffingtonpost.com/2012/08/01/twindex-twitter-polling-candidates_n_1730488.html.

[6] *Ibid.*

[5] *Ibid.*

[7] Sharp, *op. cit.*

[8] "Conversation Nation," http://nationaljournal.com/conversation-nation.

[9] "Conversation Nation," *National Journal*, Oct. 3, 2012, http://nationaljournal.com/conversation-nation.

[10] www.cnn.com/election/2012/facebook-insights.

[11] "NBC Politics," www.msnbc.msn.com/id/3032553/#.UGoWZVGruSq.

The general public didn't acquire Internet access until the late 1980s, when MCI Mail and CompuServe began selling email services. Earlier in the '80s, companies offered slow phone-line connections to private networks. In 1989, a service called "The World" offered the public its first full-service access to the Internet.

Hints at the Internet's eventual wide popularity appeared in the early '90s, when companies were allowed to conduct commercial operations online and scientists invented the point-and-click navigation system and the graphical browser — a web browser that allows interaction with both graphics and text.

The Internet found an early congressional advocate in Tennessee Sen. Al Gore, who helped turn the Web into a campaign tool when he joined presidential nominee Bill Clinton on the Democratic ticket in 1992.

Shortly after they took office in 1993, Clinton and Gore launched the first White House website. Two years later, the Library of Congress created an online legislative information system named "Thomas," after President Thomas Jefferson, who sold his personal book collection to the library after British troops burned it during the War of 1812. Following the White House lead, members of Congress began to create websites and use email.

Political use of the Web was spreading by the time Clinton and Gore ran for re-election in 1996. Candidates' websites now contained graphic elements, links to other sites and capabilities for exchanging email with voters. The Republican presidential nominee, Sen. Bob Dole of Kansas, became the first candidate to promote a website on television, doing so during a debate with Clinton.

Two years later, professional wrestler Jesse Ventura demonstrated the Internet's political value when he used it in running a successful upstart campaign for Minnesota governor. To help overcome doubts about his qualifications, he posted detailed position papers online. He raised $50,000 in cyberspace — nearly 10 percent of his treasury — and used email to help manage far-flung volunteers.

"We didn't win the election because of the Internet," Phil Madsen, Ventura's webmaster, said. But Ventura "could not have won the election without the Internet."[25]

The Federal Election Commission (FEC) greatly boosted the Internet's political value in 1999 when it ruled that campaign contributions charged to credit cards online would be eligible for matching federal funds. Sen. Bill Bradley of New Jersey raised more than $600,000 online that year as he prepared to challenge Gore in the 2000 Democratic presidential primaries, and Arizona Sen. John McCain raised $260,000 in the runup to the GOP contest. McCain then raised $2.7 million online in three days following his upset win over George W. Bush in the Feb. 2 New Hampshire primary.

Gore and Bush won the nomination, but the losers demonstrated the Web's political potential, which Howard Dean exploited dramatically in 2004.

Dean made the Internet central to his campaign, using its ever-strengthening capabilities to organize, motivate and manage his paid and volunteer workers. His supporters organized meetings at Meetup.com. He used the Internet to become the most prolific Democratic fundraiser in history up to that point.

Massachusetts Sen. John Kerry won the nomination but learned from Dean's Internet prowess. He and Bush both developed sophisticated websites with video and audio files, search capabilities and interactive features. In addition to raising funds online, they recruited volunteers, encouraged supporters to bring their friends and neighbors into the campaign, distributed good news about themselves and attacked their opponent.

Kerry and Bush also:

- Used their Senate and White House websites to supplement their campaigns' online activities;
- Placed targeted advertising on others' websites;
- Used email to deploy workers shortly before and on Election Day; and
- Guided their canvassers with information about individual voters that was gleaned from analyzing huge computer databases.

By voting day, they — along with nearly every other serious effort to influence the election — campaigned online.

Empowering the People

Steve Murphy — managing partner at Murphy Vogel Askew Reilly, the Democratic campaign consulting firm — described online campaigning as a new, more effective way to conduct old-style grassroots campaigning.

"You can't call them on the phone any more because nobody wants to talk on the phone because they've been inundated by telemarketers," he said. "You can't knock on the door anymore because nobody's ever home. But everybody's always home on the Internet."[26]

Bush press secretary Scott Stanzel agreed. "Our Internet effort empowers people to go to their neighbors and distribute information on their email lists," he said. "So we are bringing the campaign back to a very grassroots, neighbor-to-neighbor effort."[27]

Four years later, then-Sen. Barack Obama of Illinois took Internet campaigning to heights not dreamed of by the 2004 activists. McKinnon, the Bush media adviser, called Obama's 2008 campaign a "seminal, transformative race" and "the year campaigns leveraged the Internet in ways never imagined."[28]

Obama turned down public financing, which, according to FEC rules, would have limited his spending to $126 million in the primary and general elections, and raised $745 million, including $500 million online — unheard-of figures.[29]

Obama collected more than 13 million email addresses and compiled a million-member audience for text messages. He hired 90 people to run his online operations — Web developers, bloggers, videographers and others — and put them to work on communication, fundraising, grassroots organizing and other tasks. (GOP nominee John McCain hired four.)[30] Obama spent tens of millions of dollars on Internet ads. He campaigned on Facebook, Twitter and YouTube, as well as on lesser-known sites such as AsianAvenue and BlackPlanet. He even bought ads in video games, such as billboards along the highways of the Xbox racing game "Need for Speed: Carbon."[31] He also "killed public financing for all time," in the words of Steve Schmidt, McCain's chief campaign strategist.[32]

Although social media had far less reach in 2008 than 2012, they offered hints of their potential. Black Eyed Peas singer will.i.am's "Yes We Can" video and "I've Got a Crush on Obama" composed and sung by Leah Kauffman and lip-synched by actress Amber Lee Ettinger (better known as "Obama Girl") went spectacularly viral. On a more serious note, Hollywood film producer Robert Greenwald created several videos showing McCain contradicting himself. Dean's online manager Trippi says the songs showed, importantly, that social media enable private citizens to become a notable part of the campaign discussion with no assist from the candidates.

Conservative Victories

In the 2010 elections, social media contributed to many conservative victories at all levels of government. ComScore said Twitter "played a key role, providing a broadcast channel for candidates to voice their thoughts, ideas and opinions directly to their constituents and public at large."[33]

According to Facebook's Harbath, social media helped unhappy, unorganized conservatives locate each other and make the Tea Party a political force. "There wasn't a single group that said: 'Let's create the Tea Party,'" she said. "It was a lot of people finding themselves through social media."[34]

YouTube and Facebook had cosponsored debates with CNN and ABC during the 2008 presidential campaign, and the YouTube sessions included viewer questions submitted through the platform. They cosponsored debates again during the 2012 GOP presidential campaign, with Facebook also enabling viewer-submitted questions. In addition, an entire GOP debate took place on Twitter. The candidates made two or three 140-character Twitter posts in response to the questions.[35]

The GOP candidates made extensive use of social media, and some political analysts say that probably helped keep this year's Republican primary contest going for an unusually long time.

"Chunks of the Republican base, including Tea Partiers, anti-abortion activists and evangelicals, are using social media to form self-reinforcing factions within the larger party that are less and less susceptible to what nominal party leaders may want them to do," according to Micah Sifry, a networking consultant who studies how the Internet and other technologies are changing politics.[36] As a result, the various conservative factions were less likely to heed pleas to unite around frontrunner Romney, Sifry said.

That's not the sole reason the primary race lasted so long, Harbath says, but "it allowed [less-established] candidates like Herman Cain a lot of momentum because of something they said that was spread on social media."

According to Deutsch of Jones Public Affairs, social media enabled underdogs to continue raising money, finding supporters and engaging with them.

Rep. Michele Bachmann, R-Minn., for instance, credited Facebook with playing an important role in her surprise victory in the Iowa straw poll. Former Republican Pennsylvania Sen. Rick Santorum created a Facebook page for every state and used the pages to organize supporters. He also used Fundly, a social media fundraising site, to collect more than $230,000 through nearly 3,000 supporters who created Fundly pages of their own to seek contributions from friends.[37] And Gingrich created the #250 Twitter category to promote his promise to lower gasoline prices to $2.50 a gallon.

But candidates don't get to campaign by themselves in social media. Obama bought advertising that sent an Obama tweet on energy policy to everyone who searched for #250 gas.[38] Similarly, Romney bought Google

Social Media Give a Dark Horse the Edge

"The Internet allowed him to compete with someone with deep pockets."

Lt. Gov. David Dewhurst was supposed to be the next U.S. senator from Texas, succeeding the retiring Kay Bailey Hutchison. He had money. He had experience. He had name recognition and the support of Gov. Rick Perry and the rest of the state's Republican establishment.

Paul Burka, longtime columnist for *Texas Monthly* magazine, questioned if the race would be worth covering.

"Dewhurst has the money and the name I.D. Dewhurst has already driven most of the hopefuls out of the race," Burka wrote in mid-2011 as candidates jockeyed for positions in the 2012 campaign. "He will win in November. . . . The only way Dewhurst loses is if someone with more money and better conservative credentials than he has gets into the race. And that would be . . . who?"[1]

It turns out that would be Ted Cruz, a 40-year-old lawyer who had never held elected office, was not well known to the public, who might have had better conservative credentials but who certainly didn't have more money. Cruz won the GOP nomination for many reasons, one of the most important being his mastery of social media.

"For Ted Cruz to be outspent in the huge state of Texas, people thought he could never win," says Vincent Harris, digital consultant to Cruz's campaign. "But the Internet allowed him to raise money in small-dollar donations and to compete with someone with deep pockets."

Katie Harbath, an associate manager for policy in Facebook's Washington office, says Cruz's GOP primary victory demonstrates that "just having a ton of money doesn't matter. He used Facebook and other social media to help build up his ID and to talk to voters, and he ended up winning."

Cruz understood the power of social media from the beginning and integrated them throughout his campaign, says Harris, a Texas-based consultant who ran online operations for Perry and then Newt Gingrich in this year's Republican presidential primaries. Eventually the campaign dedicated three staff members to digital operations and received frequent help from Harris' consulting firm.

The campaign tapped social media and other online resources to raise money, recruit and engage supporters, organize campaign activities, distribute Cruz's messages and respond to opponents' attacks, Harris says. Cruz was especially effective in connecting with Tea Party members, who tend to be quite active online, Harris says.

Cruz announced his candidacy during a conference call with conservative Texas bloggers at the beginning of 2011, then tweeted the announcement.[2] He maintained an active relationship with the bloggers throughout the campaign, meeting with them individually and encouraging them to keep in touch with his staff.[3]

---

advertising that displayed criticism of Gingrich to anyone who searched for information on the former House speaker.[39]

CURRENT SITUATION

Courting 'Likes'

As the Nov. 6 election draws near, Obama and Romney are locked in battle to rack up as many YouTube subscribers, Facebook "likes" and Twitter retweets as possible. But political analysts view the importance of such metrics in different ways, and some say the data can be unreliable or even bogus.

Trying to enhance his social media presence, Romney sent a plea to his Facebook friends on Aug. 21: "We're

almost to 5 million likes — help us get there! 'Like' and share this with your friends and family to show you stand with Mitt!"[40]

That same day, Obama's Facebook page boasted more than 27 million likes — more than five times Romney's and just one piece of evidence that the president is running far ahead of his Republican challenger in online popularity.[41]

By the second week of October, Obama had 29.4 million Facebook "likes" to Romney's 8.6 million, 20.7 million Twitter followers to Romney's 1.3 million and 237,000 YouTube subscribers to Romney's 23,000.[42]

Moffatt, the digital director of Romney's campaign, dismisses those statistics as "vanity metrics" that don't tell how much effect the candidate's online efforts are having. "List size has no bearing," he said during the GOP

To engage supporters from the beginning, Cruz conducted an online poll to choose the campaign bumper sticker. As Cruz began to collect endorsements from prominent conservatives and conservative organizations — such as former vice presidential candidate Sarah Palin, U.S. Sen. Jim DeMint of South Carolina, the Club for Growth and FreedomWorks — the campaign would place search engine ads around their names and Facebook ads directed at users who liked them. The ads promoted Cruz's candidacy and solicited donations.

The campaign used advertising on search engines to respond to attacks. The ads — containing Cruz's answer to an attack — appeared with results that would likely be found by someone searching for information about the attack.

In addition, Cruz's supporters used social media on their own to respond to attacks.

Online advertising tends to raise more money than it costs — a key advantage, Harris says. "When was the last time a television advertisement raised money back?" he asks.

On election days — the initial primary and a two-candidate runoff — the campaign used social media posts and ads to encourage supporters to vote. Supporters were invited to virtually join Cruz's victory celebration when he wrapped up the nomination by watching live streaming of his election-night party on his Facebook page.[4]

Cruz had to use social media effectively, Harris says, because he didn't have the money to compete with Dewhurst in television advertising early in the race. Eventually Cruz "caught fire" and raised enough funds to compete on TV as well, Harris says. Substantial contributions from conservative organizations added to the small donations the campaign received online.

Cruz finished second in the May primary with 34 percent of the vote to Dewhurst's 45 percent in a field of nine.[5] Cruz won the runoff with 57 percent.[6] He's favored in the general election against Democrat Paul Sadler, a former state legislator.

"Ted Cruz is the Barack Obama of 2012," University of Texas political scientist Sean Theriault said, referring to Obama's groundbreaking use of the Internet in 2008. "It is a great case study of using these tools in politics."[7]

— *Tom Price*

[1] Paul Burka, "The Senate race," *Texas Monthly*, July 5, 2011, www.texasmonthly.com/blogs/burkablog/?p=10803.

[2] Steve Friess, "Ted Cruz's secret: Mastering social media," *Politico*, July 31, 2012, http://dyn.politico.com/printstory.cfm?uuid=0BC9A312-8A76-4517-B003-7BBF5AA4613D.

[3] Rick Dunham, "Q&A with Vincent Harris, the mastermind behind Ted Cruz's social media success," *The Houston Chronicle*, Aug. 6, 2012, http://blog.chron.com/txpotomac/2012/08/qa-with-vincent-harris-the-mastermind-behind-ted-cruzs-social-media-success.

[4] Alicia M. Cohn, "Ted Cruz wins social media victory," *The Hill*, Aug. 1, 2012, http://thehill.com/blogs/twitter-room/other-news/241643-ted-cruz-wins-social-media-victory.

[5] Friess, *op. cit.*

[6] Anna M. Tinsley, "A Texas stunner: Cruz beats Dewhurst in Senate runoff," *Fort Worth Star-Telegram*, Aug. 1, 2012, www.star-telegram.com/2012/08/01/4145441/a-texas-stunner-cruz-beats-dewhurst.html.

[7] Friess, *op. cit.*

convention. "It really doesn't matter how many people you have following you if you don't have people really engaged with your campaign."

Moffatt prefers measures such as Facebook's "talking about" metric, which is the weekly total of the number of unique visitors who interact with a Facebook page by taking such actions as "liking," commenting or sharing, plus the viral effect of their friends doing such things as resharing.[43] At the beginning of October, Romney's "talking about" number was 1.7 million, Obama's 1.4 million. But on Oct. 8 Obama had pulled ahead, 3.2 million to 2.9 million.

Moffatt also likes to compare those kinds of statistics with the candidate's fan base. Those 2.9 million interacting with Romney's site represented 34 percent of his likes, compared with Obama's 11 percent.[44]

Complicating assessments of the campaigns' relative standing in social media are companies that will create fake Twitter followers for as little as a penny apiece.[45] Two companies say they have developed methods for detecting fake followers.

Barracuda Labs, a threat-assessment firm, said most of a 117,000 jump in Romney followers in one day in July were fake.[46] StatusPeople, which develops tools for managing use of social networks, alleged that 30 percent of Obama's followers are fake and 40 percent are inactive. For Romney it's 15 percent fake and 31 percent inactive, StatusPeople said.[47]

Both campaigns deny buying followers, and others have questioned the accuracy of the analysis. Barracuda research scientist Jason Ding said it is impossible to determine who is responsible for buying the fake

President Obama's Facebook page has more than 29 million "likes." Candidates this year are using social media sites such as Facebook, Twitter and YouTube to identify and organize supporters and raise funds. Using such platforms also allows them to bypass traditional news media and send their messages unfiltered to the public.

followers — the campaigns, campaign supporters or opponents trying to embarrass the campaigns.[48]

As hazy as social media metrics may sometimes seem, both Obama and Romney have made huge strides in building online support, though Obama is widely perceived as still having the edge.

It appears Republicans have made "a great amount of progress in closing the technology gap," says Hendricks of Stephen F. Austin State University. "But I do not believe Romney and the Republicans have quite caught up with the Obama campaign."

Costas Panagopoulos, an assistant professor of political science at Fordham University and editor of the book *Politicking Online*, says counting Obama's social media contacts may overstate the president's current Internet strength. "Much of Obama's online following is a result of the 2008 election cycle," and some may no longer be in his camp, Panagopoulos notes.

But having the older operation can give Obama a head start on activities that matter now, Hendricks points out, saying that Obama released a smart-phone app to promote his campaign in 2010, something Romney's organization didn't do until 2012. This year, Obama distributed an app that gives door-to-door canvassers access to voter registration lists, neighborhood maps, talking points and the ability to process contributions.[49]

Incumbency Edge

And Obama benefits from incumbency online as well as off. His weekly radio addresses also appear as videos on YouTube, where they can be viewed at any time. Press briefings and other White House events also are posted to YouTube. Videos are made available at the White House Facebook site as well.

Obama also leads in other recent statistical measures.

His convention acceptance speech generated 52,756 tweets in the minute following its conclusion, the highest per-minute rate ever recorded for a political event, while Romney's acceptance speech generated 14,289. The figures were 28,003 when the president joined Michelle Obama on stage in the first minute following her speech, 6,195 when Romney joined his wife Ann.[50]

As of Sept. 24, Obama's acceptance speech had been viewed 4.9 million times on YouTube, compared with Romney's 1.1 million. Michelle Obama's convention speech had outdrawn Ann Romney's YouTube audience, 3.2 million to 560,000. Perhaps even more troubling for Romney: Clint Eastwood's lecture to an empty chair drew three times the YouTube viewers as Romney's speech, as did the surreptitiously recorded video that shows Romney saying 47 percent of Americans don't "take personal responsibility" for their own lives.[51]

One of the most interesting developments in this election, according to George Washington University's Cornfield, is the campaigns' ability to use social media and powerful computers to conduct on-the-fly experiments that can lead to rapid changes in campaign tactics.

Likening it to medical research, Cornfield describes a campaign delivering a message to a "treatment group" while a "control group" doesn't get the message. The campaign then measures how well the message worked. Or the campaign tries variations on a message with more than one group and determines which works better. "It's hard to know, when a campaign switches from message to message, whether they're undisciplined or experimenting," Cornfield says.

Moffatt, Romney's digital director, termed Facebook "a way for us to test messages for online advertising and other platforms, because it's instant feedback."[52] Twitter, also, "helps us keep our finger on the pulse of the fast-moving pace of new media," Romney spokesman Ryan Williams said.[53]

Should government restrict online data collection to protect voters' privacy?

YES
Jeffrey Chester
Executive Director, Center for Digital Democracy

Written for *CQ Researcher*, October 2012

A political campaign sends a striking digital ad personalized to your age, gender, race, spending habits, location and favorite musician or TV show. That interactive ad later appears on your mobile device, gaming platform and computer screen as you surf the Web. Its message and visual content keep changing, as if it learned about you — including what you had most recently done online. Your best friend gets an ad from the same candidate, but with a different message. It seems you care about the economy, your friend about the Middle East.

Such scenarios are no longer fantasy. Campaigns, candidates and special-interest groups, tapping into the personalized data-mining capabilities of digital marketing, now can "shadow" or track voters wherever they go or whatever they do online — including using their mobile phones. Political groups can buy individual profiles that contain information culled from both online and offline data brokers, producing a "road map" to the specific issues likely to sway a particular voter.

Our digital dossier can include our race and ethnicity, gender, relationships, events that have affected us (a loan application or a medical treatment, for example), favorite websites and even our past actions (products purchased or videos viewed). It can access the torrent of social media information that tells not only about us but also about our relations with friends. New, interactive multimedia tools perfected for selling cars, computers and entertainment on websites and mobile phones make data-enabled voter ads even more effective.

We shouldn't allow voter decisions to be influenced by digital micro-targeting tactics that invade our privacy and set the stage for potential manipulation. As campaigns increasingly have the ability to tell each of us what they think we want to hear, the truth can easily become a victim. As tens of millions of finely tuned, personalized interactive ads are delivered to mobile phone screens, how will news organizations and other watchdogs effectively monitor the information to say what's right or misleading?

We are allowing powerful special interests — campaigns, candidates, super Pacs and the like — to build a vast data mining and targeting apparatus that is transforming our political process without public debate. Congress must step in to both protect the rights of voters and enact fair ground rules for digital political campaigns. Voters — not the K Street complex — should have the power to decide what online information can be collected and used.

NO
Jim Harper
Director, Information Policy Studies, Cato Institute

Written for *CQ Researcher*, October 2012

Just like marketers do year in and year out, political campaigns are doing everything they can at election time to learn the interests of voters and how to reach them. Is democracy better served by campaigns that know less about voters or by campaigns that know more?

Nobody loves the tawdry tone of electoral politics, and some of the obscure techniques campaigns use to gather voter information leave us squirming. But this is hardly a justification for laws that could blinder our political system.

Political privacy is an interesting beast. Some people are reticent to speak even with family members about their politics and their votes. Others put on garish costumes and post signs on their lawns and cars to advertise what they think. No law regulating how campaigns can collect and use information would hit the right notes for communities this diverse.

Instead of taking privacy off the table as a campaign issue, why not push it forward? This problem should be put to the politicians vying for votes. Their tact and skill in handling voter information is a signal of how they might handle things they oversee, such as government agencies' collection and use of citizen data.

It's not likely to be a top issue, but the use of data in campaigns might sway privacy-sensitive voters. A campaign data law would prevent this competition. Voters couldn't learn which candidates demonstrate sensitivity toward personal information. These are skills elected officials should have.

The best way to learn voters' preferences, just like consumers' preferences, is to hash things out through real-world experience. Rather than having lawmakers decide for all of us how data can be used in society, let voters and consumers render their judgments, casting their ballots and dollars with the candidate or marketer who satisfies them the most.

Privacy regulation is impossible to write well, easy to sidestep and, in the campaign area, contrary to free-speech principles, if not the actual First Amendment. The long-term solution for privacy problems has always been consumer empowerment and awareness, so that sensitive voters can hide their politics online as well as off.

Over time, people will learn how their electronic devices work to protect or expose them. Social practices will catch up with the rapid advance of personal information technology. And people will have political privacy to the extent they want it.

The campaigns use the experiments' findings to guide advertising in all media. Both have sophisticated strategies for advertising beside the results of online searches.[54] Keeping an ear to what people were talking about earlier this year, for instance, Obama bought advertising beside Google results for "Warren Buffett," "Obama singing," "Obama birthday" and "Obama [NCAA basketball tournament] bracket."[55]

That strategy isn't restricted to presidential campaigns, notes Deutsch of Jones Public Affairs. After Rep. Todd Akin, R-Mo., sparked a nationwide furor by saying victims of "legitimate rape" don't get pregnant, Sen. Claire McCaskill, his Democratic opponent in the Missouri U.S. Senate race, put fundraising solicitations next to searches on Akins' name, Deutsch says.

Obama even repeated his 2008 tactic of advertising on video games — this year in the "Madden NFL 13" football game, the free online game site Pogo.com and mobile phone games such as "Tetris."[56]

Close and Personal

Candidates are tapping new social media to connect with voters on a personal level.

At Pinterest — which resembles a scrapbook or a refrigerator door and appeals primarily to women — Ann Romney and Michelle Obama emphasize their roles as wife and mother. Romney identifies herself as "Mom of five boys, Grandmother of 18." Among her posts are recipes, crafts and family photographs.[57] Michelle Obama also posts recipes and family photos as well as pictures of "people who inspire me."[58]

The candidates also created Pinterest pages. Romney's includes lists of his favorite movies, television shows and books — including the science fiction novel *Battlefield Earth* by Scientology founder L. Ron Hubbard. Obama's includes family photos but focuses primarily on the campaign.

Gingrich online director Harris called Pinterest "a great way to humanize a candidate. The Romney campaign has done a very good job of using Pinterest to showcase that Ann Romney's interests are very similar to the interests of average female voters in this country."

Both candidates also post favorite songs on the music site Spotify and participate on other social media, Hendricks of Stephen F. Austin State University says. "Both the Democrats and the Republicans realize that

they need to adopt those platforms and reach the demographic groups who are using them," he says.

During the presidential campaign's last big events — the October debates — social media provided platforms for users to watch, evaluate and discuss the clashes while they were in progress. The first debate, on Oct. 3, for instance, generated more than 10 million tweets during its 90-minute run, making it the most-tweeted-about event in U.S. politics.[59]

The debates illustrate one challenge to traditional news media that Twitter's Adam Sharp noticed during the conventions. Tweets would spike at points during a speech, peak in the first minute after the speech ended, then decline rapidly over 10 or 15 minutes, he said in a panel discussion during the Democratic convention.

During the first debate, tweeting peaked when Obama and Romney clashed with moderator Jim Lehrer over control of the proceedings and when they discussed Medicare.[60]

"By the time the pundits have actually gotten on the air and are sitting around the round table talking about it, the audience's conversation has already moved on," Sharp said. "Viewers are no longer waiting for that post-game analysis. They are participating in it in real time."

OUTLOOK
Creative Approaches

Candidates are poised to end this election year with a big bang as they deploy social media to get voters to the polls.

"I expect we're going to see a social-media-based campaign geared toward turnout that is like something we've never seen before," says Pinkham of the Public Affairs Council. "There probably will be a lot of creative approaches to how social media can be used to get people to show up to vote. They'll be saving some of their best ideas for last."

"It's not just connecting people online," says Trippi, the architect of Democrat Howard Dean's 2004 presidential campaign. "It's connecting the online army to do the hard work of getting out in the community, knocking on doors and making phone calls."

The effort will be especially important for Democrats, Trippi says, because of recently enacted voter-ID laws and cutbacks in early voting that are expected to make voting more difficult for Democrat-leaning young people, minorities and the elderly.[61]

"I suspect this is going to be a very close election," Trippi says, "and the ability of Obama to activate his network could very well be the difference in Ohio or Florida," which are viewed as key swing states. "If Romney's beating Obama by 10 points" — which polls indicate is unlikely — "no social network makes that up."

Experts say it's difficult to foresee what's likely to occur in future elections.

"One thing we know for sure is that the social media landscape is continually changing and evolving," Panagopoulos of Fordham University points out, "and campaigns and political parties will have to adapt to the changing circumstances."

Trippi envisions "a lot of kids in their garages who are working on really compelling technology. We're going to wake up in two months and there will be something that will totally change and empower people in a completely different way from what Twitter has. These networks, as big as they are, are going to be dwarfed four years from now."

Because of the technology they've developed, Obama, Romney and their social media experts will remain influential by helping candidates in future campaigns, Hendricks of Stephen F. Austin State University says.

"The Obama camp has been constantly building on and improving their platform," he notes. "They'll continue to do that beyond the 2012 campaign, and the Republicans will continue to build on what they started this year. This does not end after 2012."

Trippi also sees a "lasting impact" from this year's campaigns. "The Dean campaign had a lasting impact, and I think it laid the foundation for Obama," he says. "They took that and went far higher in orbit than we ever did. We were like the Wright brothers, and they landed a guy on the moon."

Technological developments will continue to make nuts-and-bolts campaigning more effective and efficient, says Harris, the Gingrich campaign's online director. For example, he says, "Campaign advertising is going to get to a degree of accuracy that was almost unimaginable when direct mail was started in the '80s."

"Big Data" will grow even bigger, Trippi says. Panagopoulos sees online fundraising becoming more

dominant. Rapid improvement in mobile devices will continue, and their popularity will continue to grow, Pew's Smith says. As a result, campaigns will acquire continually improving capabilities for "getting out political messages and encouraging people to take action where they are."

At some point, Trippi says, "an independent candidacy or a new party is going to happen, [because] there are only two reasons left to be in a party from a tactical point of view: money and organization." Both increasingly can be addressed outside the old institutions, he notes.

Television's influence will diminish gradually, and the Internet's importance will increase, Harris says. But Smith warns against predicting television's demise any time soon.

"People layer the new things on top of their existing communication," Smith says. "Just because we have text messaging doesn't mean people don't talk on the phone anymore. All of these things fit into the same big basket, and people pick the tool that's right for them based on their needs of the moment."

Hendricks says that won't happen until social media "are perceived by the citizens as being a reliable source of information," which they aren't now.

All of this will make old-fashioned campaigning more important, Pinkham says. "More and more money is going to be allocated toward the ground game to encourage turnout and to get volunteers who will try to help persuade undecided voters." But much of that will occur through social media.

"Personal contact still matters," Pinkham adds. "There's still no substitute for the candidate making personal appearances. What Obama did on reddit was the social media equivalent of making a personal appearance."

NOTES

1. "President Obama," reddit, undated, www.reddit.com/user/PresidentObama.
2. "POTUS IAMA Stats," reddit, Aug. 31, 2012, http://blog.reddit.com/2012/08/potus-iama-stats.html; www.reddit.com/user/PresidentObama.
3. See Tom Price, "Cyberpolitics," *CQ Researcher*, Sept. 17, 2004, pp. 757-780.
4. Jake Tapper, Richard Coolidge and Sherisse Pham, "#Campaign: How Twitter is Playing Politics

in 2012," *Yahoo News*, May 7, 2012, http://news.yahoo .com/blogs/power-players-abc-news/campaign-twitter-playing-politics-2012-101813518.html;_ ylt=A0LkuK2N6adPPD0AyACs0NUE;_ylu= X3oDMTNtdDY0NGs2BG1pdANKdW1ib3Ryb2 4gRlAEcGtnA2Q3YzBkNDE1LTU0YzUtM2Jh Ni1hNGU5LWU1MzFiZWJlNWM4NgRwb 3MDMQRzZWMDanVtYm90cm9uBHZlcgNm NTQ2OTc2MC05ODJkLTExZTEtOWU3Zi00 YmJiODJmODVmZjA-;_ylg=X3oDMTFlam ZvM2ZlBGludGwDdXMEbGFuZwNlbi11cw Rwc3RhaWQDBHBzdGNhdAMEcHQDc2Vjd GlvbnM-;_ylv=3.

5. Ronald Brownstein, "Communications is changing the relationship between business, government, and individuals," *National Journal*, June 7, 2012, http:// nationaljournal.com/magazine/how-the-internet-is-reshaping-us-and-our-government-20120607? page=1. Jenna Wortham, "Winning Social Media Votes," *The New York Times*, Oct. 8, 2012, p. B1, www.nytimes.com/2012/10/08/technology/ campaigns-use-social-media-to-lure-younger-voters .html?_r=1.

6. Pew Research Center Internet & American Life surveys, www.pewinternet.org/~/media/Files/Reports/ 2011/PIP-SNS-Update-2011.pdf and www.pewinter net.org/~/media/Files/Reports/2012/PIP_Older_ adults_and_internet_use.pdf.

7. Allstate/*National Journal* Heartland Monitor Poll XIII, Conducted May 19-23, 2012, www.allstate .com/Allstate/content/refresh-attachments/Heartland_ XIII_data.pdf.

8. T. W. Farnam, "Obama has aggressive Internet strategy to woo supporters," *The Washington Post*, April 6, 2012, www.washingtonpost.com/politics/obama-has-aggressive-internet-strategy-to-woo-supporters/ 2012/04/06/gIQAavB2zS_story.html.

9. Adam Mazmanian, "The Underdogs? Inside the Romney Campaign's Digital Efforts," *The Atlantic*, Aug. 22, 2012, www.theatlantic.com/politics/archive/ 2012/08/the-underdogs-inside-the-romney-campaigns-digital-efforts/261435.

10. For background, see Marcia Clemmitt, "Assessing the New Health Care Law," *CQ Researcher*, Sept. 21, 2012, pp. 789-812.

11. Patrick Gaspard, https://twitter.com/patrickgas-pard, and David Nakamura, "In a vicious campaign year, apologies are in the air," *The Washington Post*, Aug. 3, 2012, www.washingtonpost.com/politics/in-a-vicious-campaign-year-apologies-are-in-the-air/2012/08/03/cfe47e14-dd70-11e1-8e43-4a3c 4375504a_story.html.

12. Alyson Ward, "The politics of friendship: Have you unfriended someone over their views?," *The Houston Chronicle*, Sept. 24, 2012, p. 1, www.chron.com/ life/article/The-politics-of-friendship-Have-you-unfriended-3881766.php.

13. "Politics on Social Networking Sites," Pew Research Center, Sept. 4, 2012, p.19, http://pewinternet .org/~/media//Files/Reports/2012/PIP_PoliticalLifeon SocialNetworkingSites.pdf.

14. Tom Price, "Beyond Control: How Social Media and Mobile Communication Are Changing Public Affairs," Foundation for Public Affairs, 2011, http:// pac.org/system/files/FINAL%20Beyond%20 Control%20Report_0.pdf.

15. "The Digital Politico," ComScore Inc., April 2012, www.comscore.com/Press_Events/Press_Releases/ 2012/4/comScore_Releases_The_Digital_Politico_ Report.

16. "Social networking sites and politics," Pew Research Center, March 12, 2012, p. 8, http://pewinternet .org/~/media//Files/Reports/2012/PIP_SNS_and_ politics.pdf.

17. Allstate/*National Journal* Heartland Monitor Poll, *op. cit.*

18. Mark McKinnon, "How a Tweet Can Beat a PAC," *The Daily Beast*, April 1, 2012, www.thedailybeast .com/articles/2012/04/01/how-a-tweet-can-beat-a-pac-social-media-gives-voters-muscle-in-politics.html.

19. For background, see Kenneth Jost, "Campaign Finance Debates," *CQ Researcher*, May 28, 2010, pp. 457-480.

20. Brownstein, *op. cit.*

21. "2011 Public Affairs Pulse Survey," Public Affairs Council, http://pac.org/pulse/report.pdf.

22. James Rainey, "Voters still tuned in to traditional news media, poll finds," *Los Angeles Times*, Aug. 24, 2012, latimes.com/news/nationworld/nation/la-na-media-poll-20120824,0,3396454.story.

23. Except where noted, information in this historical section was drawn from the following: Price, "Cyberpolitics," *op. cit.* Marcia Clemmitt, "Social Networking," *CQ Researcher*, Sept. 17, 2010, pp. 749-772; and John Allen Hendricks and Robert E. Denton Jr., *Communicator-in-Chief: How Barack Obama Used New Media Technology to Win the White House* (2010).

24. Josh Catone, "The Staggering Size of the Internet," *Mashable*, Jan. 25, 2011, http://mashable.com/2011/01/25/internet-size-infographic.

25. Price, "Cyberpolitics," *op. cit.*

26. *Ibid.*

27. *Ibid.*

28. Adam Nagourney, "The '08 Campaign: Sea Change for Politics as We Know It," *The New York Times*, Nov. 4, 2008, p. 1, www.nytimes.com/2008/11/04/us/politics/04memo.html.

29. "2008 Election: Presidential Candidate Barack Obama," Center for Responsive Politics, www.opensecrets.org/pres08/summary.php?cycle=2008&cid=N00009638. Chris Cillizza, "Is Obama overrated as a candidate?" *The Washington Post*, Oct. 7, 2013, www.washingtonpost.com/politics/decision2012/is-obama-overrated-as-a-candidate/2012/10/07/316c40f6-1087-11e2-ba83-a7a396e6b2a7_story.htm.

30. Philip Rucker, "Romney advisers, aiming to pop Obama's digital balloon, pump up online campaign," *The Washington Post*, July 13, 2012, www.washingtonpost.com/politics/romney-advisers-aiming-to-pop-obamas-digital-balloon-pump-up-online-campaign/2012/07/13/gJQAsbc4hW_story.html.

31. Sami Yenigun, "Presidential Campaigns Rock The Gamer Vote," "All Things Considered," NPR, Oct. 1, 2012, www.npr.org/2012/10/01/162103528/presidential-campaigns-rock-the-gamer-vote.

32. Nagourney, *op. cit.*

33. "The Digital Politico," ComScore Inc., April 30, 2012, www.comscore.com/DigitalPolitico.

34. Price, "Beyond Control," *op. cit.*

35. Jason Donner, "GOP Presidential Candidates to Debate in the 'Twitter-Sphere,'" foxnews.com, July 15, 2011, http://politics.blogs.foxnews.com/2011/07/15/gop-presidential-candidates-debate-twitter-sphere.

36. Micah Sifry, "How grass-roots social media are extending the GOP race," CNN, March 1, 2012, http://articles.cnn.com/2012-03-01/tech/tech_social-media-gop-sifry_1_social-media-conservative-voters-and-activists-social-networking?_s=PM:TECH.

37. *Ibid.*

38. Daniel Malloy, "Gingrich engages his 'tweeples' on social media," *The Atlanta Journal-Constitution*, March 10, 2012, www.ajc.com/news/news/local-govt-politics/gingrich-engages-his-tweeples-on-social-media/nQR5x.

39. Mazmanian, *op. cit.*

40. Romney-Ryan campaign, www.mittromney.com/we039re-almost-5-million-likes-x2013-help-us-get-there-quotlikequot-and-share.

41. Mazmanian, *op. cit.*

42. Data taken from the following sources: www.facebook.com/barackobama?ref=ts&fref=ts; www.facebook.com/mittromney; https://twitter.com/BarackObama; https://twitter.com/MittRomney; www.youtube.com/user/BarackObamadotcom?feature=g-all-a; and www.youtube.com/user/mittromney?feature=results_main.

43. Brittany Darwell, " 'People Talking About This' defined," *Inside Facebook*, Jan. 10, 2012, www.insidefacebook.com/2012/01/10/people-talking-about-this-defined.

44. "Inside Network," *PageData*, Sept. 30, 2012, http://pagedata.appdata.com/pages/leaderboard/fc/fan_count/type/78.

45. Alex Fitzpatrick, "Obama Has Millions of Fake Twitter Followers," *Mashable*, Aug. 24, 2012, http://mashable.com/2012/08/24/obama-has-13-million-fake-twitter-followers-report.

46. Dara Kerr, "Mitt Romney suspiciously gets 116K Twitter followers in one day," CNET, Aug. 6, 2012, http://news.cnet.com/8301-1023_3-57487861-93/mitt-romney-suspiciously-gets-116k-twitter-followers-in-one-day.

47. Fitzpatrick, *op. cit.*

48. Kerr, *op. cit.*

49. Mazmanian, *op. cit.*

50. Simon Owens, "No Strong Evidence Romney Is Beating Obama in Digital Media," *U.S. News & World Report*, Sept. 7, 2012, www.usnews.com/opinion/articles/2012/09/07/no-strong-evidence-romney-is-beating-obama-in-digital-media; Leigh Ann Caldwell, "Ann Romney created buzz on Twitter," CBS News, Aug. 29, 2012, www.cbsnews.com/8301-503544_162-57502597-503544/ann-romney-created-buzz-on-twitter.

51. Henry Blodget, "Romney's 47% Video Has Been Viewed 3 Times As Often As His Convention Speech," *Business Insider*, Sept. 28, 2012, www.businessinsider.com/romneys-47-viewed-more-than-convention-speech-2012-9; Brad Plumer, "Romney versus the 47 percent," *The Washington Post*, Sept. 17, 2012, www.washingtonpost.com/blogs/ezra-klein/wp/2012/09/17/romney-my-job-is-not-to-worry-about-those-people.

52. Jennifer Moire, "How Mitt Romney Upgraded to Facebook Timeline," *AllFacebook*, March 15, 2012, www.allfacebook.com/facebook-timeline-romney-2012-03.

53. Beth Fouhy, "Twitter plays outsize role in 2012 campaign," The Associated Press, May 7, 2012, http://news.yahoo.com/twitter-plays-outsize-role-2012-campaign-073847636.html;_ylt=Am7NGDL.3RobLkBs3JIjnwqs0NUE;_ylu=X3oDMTNhMXFvNXZqBG1pdAMEcGtnAzRmN2M3Nz VlLWU0MWItMzA3Yy1hODBiLTI4NzQxMDAyN2M3NQRwb3MDNgRzZWMDbG5fQVBfZ2FsBHZlcgMwNzMyMyNGZlOS05ODU3LTExZTEtYmZiZi02NTMzZWYxYTZlZGQ-;_ylv=3.

54. Rucker, *op. cit.*

55. Farnam, *op. cit.*

56. Yenigun, *op. cit.*

57. Ann Romney, http://pinterest.com/annromney.

58. Michelle Obama, http://pinterest.com/michelleobama.

59. Adam Sharp, "Dispatch from the Denver debate," Twitter Blog, Oct. 4, 2012, http://blog.twitter.com/2012/10/dispatch-from-denver-debate.html.

60. *Ibid.*

61. For background see Peter Katel, "Voter Rights," *CQ Researcher*, May 18, 2012, pp. 449-476.

BIBLIOGRAPHY
Selected Sources
Books

Hendricks, John Allen, and Robert E. Denton Jr., eds., *Communicator in Chief: How Barack Obama Used New Media Technology to Win the White House*, Lexington Books, 2010.
This collection of scholarly essays looks at specific aspects of President Obama's 2008 campaign online, from email and YouTube to Twitter and video games.

Issenberg, Sasha, *The Victory Lab: The Secret Science of Winning Campaigns*, Crown Publishers, 2012.
A Washington journalist reveals the practical side of winning elections in the age of the Internet and powerful computers. One fascinating vignette: how, in the age of electronic communication, the Obama campaign decided to buy cardboard ads on buses on certain routes in 10 cities.

Panagopoulos, Costas, ed., *Politicking Online: The Transformation of Election Campaign Communications*, Rutgers University Press, 2009.
This collection of scholarly essays about politics and the Internet addresses campaigns in 2008 and earlier and elections in Europe as well as in the United States.

Trent, Judith S., Robert V. Friedenberg and Robert E. Denton Jr., *Political Campaign Communication: Principles and Practices*, Rowman & Littlefield Publishers, 2011.
Three communications scholars explore the full range of political communication, including various kinds of speeches, fundraising appeals, debates, advertising, communication among voters and use of the Internet.

Articles

Darwell, Brittany, "Does Romney have a better Facebook strategy than Obama?" *Inside Facebook*, Aug. 28, 2012, www.insidefacebook.com/2012/08/28/does-romney-have-a-better-facebook-strategy-than-obama.
Darwell, lead writer for an online magazine that covers all things Facebook, looks at Mitt Romney's and President Obama's Facebook operations and concludes that Romney is ahead.

McKinnon, Mark, "How a Tweet Can Beat a PAC," *The Daily Beast*, www.thedailybeast.com/articles/2012/04/01/how-a-tweet-can-beat-a-pac-social-media-gives-voters-muscle-in-politics.html.

A campaign communication adviser to both Democrats and Republicans argues that social media have the potential to "return power to all of the people."

Nagourney, Adam, "The '08 Campaign: Sea Change for Politics as We Know It," *The New York Times*, Nov. 4, 2008, p. 1, www.nytimes.com/2008/11/04/us/politics/04memo.html.

Writing on the eve of the 2008 general election, a veteran reporter reflects on how much the 2008 race changed campaigning.

Sifry, Micah, "How grass-roots social media are extending the GOP race," *CNN*, March 1, 2012, http://articles.cnn.com/2012-03-01/tech/tech_social-media-gop-sifry_1_social-media-conservative-voters-and-activists-social-networking?_s=PM:TECH.

An expert on politics and the Internet argues that social media played a key role in lengthening the race for the 2012 Republican presidential nomination.

Owens, Simon, "No Strong Evidence Romney Is Beating Obama in Digital Media," *U.S. News & World Report*, Sept. 7, 2012, www.usnews.com/opinion/articles/2012/09/07/no-strong-evidence-romney-is-beating-obama-in-digital-media.

The magazine's assistant managing editor examines the major presidential candidates' digital campaigns and concludes that despite Romney's best efforts, Obama has the edge.

Ward, Alyson, "The politics of friendship: Have you unfriended someone over their views?" *The Houston Chronicle*, Sept. 24, 2012, p. 1, www.chron.com/life/article/The-politics-of-friendship-Have-you-unfriended-3881766.php.

Texans describe how they're coping with the sometimes not-so-friendly political conversations encountered on Facebook and other social media.

Reports and Studies

"The Digital Politico: 5 Ways Digital Media is Shaping the 2012 Presidential Election," ComScore Inc., April 2012, www.comscore.com/Press_Events/Press_Releases/2012/4/comScore_Releases_The_Digital_Politico_Report.

ComScore, a firm that measures online activity, analyzes the impact of social media, digital advertising, Internet fundraising and actions online that earn coverage from traditional news organizations.

Price, Tom, "Beyond Control: How Social Media and Mobile Communication Are Changing Public Affairs," Foundation for Public Affairs, 2011, http://pac.org/system/files/FINAL%20Beyond%20Control%20Report_0.pdf.

The research and educational foundation examines how social media and mobile communications are causing businesses and activist groups to accept a more freewheeling world of public affairs. The author also is the author of this *CQ Researcher*.

Rainie, Lee, and Aaron Smith, "Social networking sites and politics," Pew Research Center, March 12, 2012, http://pewinternet.org/Reports/2012/Social-networking-and-politics.aspx; and "Politics on Social Networking Sites," Pew Research Center, Sept. 4, 2012, http://pewinternet.org/~/media//Files/Reports/2012/PIP_PoliticalLifeonSocialNetworkingSites.pdf.

Companion reports, based on a public opinion survey conducted early this year, explore how Americans use social media for political purposes.

For More Information

Association of Internet Researchers, 910 W. Van Buren St., #142, Chicago, IL 60607; www.aoir.org. Cross-disciplinary international academic association of scholars who study the Internet; conducts conferences and makes some research papers available for free on its website.

Berkman Center for Internet and Society at Harvard University, 23 Everett St., 2nd Floor, Cambridge, MA 02138; 617-495-7547; www.cyber.law.harvard.edu. Research center for studying the Internet and its impact on society; associates include faculty, students, fellows, entrepreneurs, lawyers and Internet practitioners.

Center for Democracy and Technology, 1634 I St., N.W., #1100, Washington, DC 20006; 202-637-9800; www.cdt.org. Advocacy group that promotes Internet freedom and individual privacy.

Center for Digital Democracy, 1621 Connecticut Ave., N.W., Suite 550, Washington, DC 20009; 202-986-2220; www.democraticmedia.org. Research, education and advocacy organization that promotes consumer protection and privacy.

Congressional Management Foundation, 513 Capitol Court, N.E., Suite 300, Washington, DC 20002; 202-546-0100; www.congressfoundation.org. Nonprofit organization that provides advice aimed at improving the way Congress works; publications include periodic reports on how Congress is — and should be — using the Internet.

Interactive Advertising Bureau, 116 East 27th St., 7th Floor, New York, NY 10016; 212-380-4700; www.iab.net. Trade association for companies that sell online advertising; website contains information about industry codes, public policy positions and research.

Personal Democracy Media, www.personaldemocracy.com. Promotes discussion about technology's impact on government, politics and society; publishes news and information on its website.

9

Internet Regulation

Marcia Clemmitt

Protesters in New York City demonstrate on Jan. 18, 2012, against the proposed Protect Intellectual Property Act (PIPA) and the Stop Online Piracy Act (SOPA), which would block the unauthorized use of movies, TV shows, recorded music and other copyrighted material. The bills' opponents — including Wikipedia co-founder Jimmy Wales — argue they are too draconian and will lead to censorship.

From *CQ Researcher*,
April 13, 2012

Wikipedia, the online encyclopedia written by its users, has become a dependable web presence — always there to answer questions on just about every conceivable subject, from aardvarks to Zoroaster. But on Jan. 18 Wikipedia disappeared, abruptly shutting down its U.S. site in a self-proclaimed "day of darkness."

The blackout came in protest of two Hollywood-backed proposals in Congress — the Stop Online Piracy Act (SOPA) and the Protect Intellectual Property Act (PIPA) — aimed at combating the unauthorized use or reproduction of movies, TV shows, recorded music and other copyrighted material.

Such pirating, which typically occurs on foreign-based rogue websites, has mushroomed into a global enterprise costing the entertainment industry and others billions of dollars a year in lost revenues and royalties.

But opponents of the proposed bills — including Wikipedia co-founder Jimmy Wales — argued they were so vague and draconian that they would force any website carrying user-generated content perceived to violate copyright laws to shut down at nearly a moment's notice.

What's more, opponents said, the bills would effectively block search engines from connecting to those sites and allow copyright owners to stop advertisers from doing business with them.

"I hope we send a broad global message that the Internet as a whole will not tolerate censorship in response to mere allegations of copyright infringement," said Wales.[1] Thousands of other websites also shut down in protest, while Google and Facebook, among

Top-Speed Internet Options Limited

Only about 15 percent of Americans will have a choice among top-speed broadband Internet service providers (ISPs) in 2012. Advocates of net neutrality, which would prevent ISPs from slowing delivery of some websites' content, say consumers won't be able to pressure ISPs to treat all content equally if they can't threaten to switch their business to other providers.

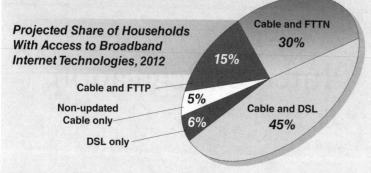

Projected Share of Households With Access to Broadband Internet Technologies, 2012

* Some telephone companies offer very high-speed broadband, but most service is slower. Fiber-to-the-premises (FTTP) is fastest — roughly as fast as current, upgraded cable. Fiber-to-the-node (FTTN) is somewhat slower, and digital subscriber line (DSL) is about a third as fast as top-speed cable and FTTP.

** Figures do not total 100 because of rounding.

Source: "Broadband Competition and Innovation Policy," Federal Communications Commission, 2010, www.broadband.gov/plan/4-broadband-competition-and-innovation-policy/

others, remained in operation but expressed support for Wikipedia's stand.

Debates on Internet regulation are heating up as cyber companies gain clout in Washington and the Internet penetrates every area of life. Besides the fight over copyright enforcement, a battle is raging over government attempts to bar Internet-service providers (ISPs) from delivering some websites' content to customers more slowly than others.

Government advocates argue that such "net neutrality" rules are needed to keep broadband ISPs — mostly cable TV and phone companies that provide high-speed Internet services but also are interested in supplying content to customers — from hurting small or upstart competitors in the content business. But the ISPs argue that such legislation impinges on their free-speech rights: After all, they argue, they own the transmission lines that carry the data. And besides, they say, slowing the flow of online traffic wouldn't be in their financial interest because it might make customers go elsewhere.

While the net neutrality debate can descend into the technical and arcane, Internet piracy is a subject that anyone who has knowingly watched a bootleg movie or illegally downloaded a Top 10 hit song can understand. Two days after Wikipedia's online protest, on Jan. 20, Congress postponed long-expected floor votes on House and Senate bills requiring online-payment companies, search engines and ISPs to cut their ties with websites alleged to be posting copyrighted material.

"The growing number of foreign websites that offer counterfeit or stolen goods continues to threaten American technology, products and jobs," said Rep. Lamar Smith, R-Texas, chief sponsor of the House bill. "Congress cannot stand by and do nothing while some of America's most profitable and productive industries are under attack."[2]

The 1998 Digital Millennium Copyright Act (DMCA) currently governs copyright infringement. Advocates of new legislation say it is outmoded because it doesn't cover the full range of Internet-piracy issues that have emerged over the past decade.

But others say the new bills go too far. "I'm not exactly a fan" of the DMCA, but it "has a process that at least gives people a hearing," says Jon Ippolito, an associate professor of new media at the University of Maine, in Orono. In contrast, proposed legislation risks "poisoning the very nature of the Internet" as a participatory medium by authorizing near-immediate shutdowns of websites with user-generated content, he says.

Meanwhile, after years of wrangling, the Federal Communications Commission (FCC), the federal agency that writes and enforces rules for telecommunications, last November required ISPs that deliver high-speed Internet service to observe "net neutrality" in managing their networks. While it's understood that ISPs may sometimes need to slow some data to avoid network congestion, they must publicly disclose the methods they use to manage traffic and may not block lawful websites or "unreasonably" discriminate among sites.

A congressional resolution to stop the regulation passed the House last year, but not the Senate, and lawmakers continue to fight over the issue.

The net neutrality rules are an unwarranted intrusion into an Internet market that functions well, wrote Gerald R. Faulhaber, professor emeritus of business and public policy at the University of Pennsylvania's Wharton School, and David J. Farber, professor of computer science and public policy at Carnegie Mellon University in Pittsburgh. The FCC's "successful policy of no regulation" for the past two decades has led to "the wildly successful Internet we have today" and should not be abandoned, they said.[3]

But net-neutrality advocates argue that broadband ISPs might have significant business motives for slowing some websites' traffic. The ISPs, too, would like to get into the Internet content game, which has brought big financial rewards to companies such as Facebook and Amazon. But the online services they could offer — video and phone service — also have competitors, such as the video company Netflix and the Internet phone company Skype.

Therefore, regulation advocates say, ISPs might consider it in their financial interest to slow content traffic to those competitors to gain an edge over them. For example, a phone company that offers broadband might be motivated to slow delivery of Internet-telephone services such as VoIP, and, in fact, several ISPs have been accused of such blocking in the past.[4]

"I don't pay Comcast for making Netflix inferior to [Comcast's] pay-per-view," says Robert Frieden, a professor of telecommunications and law at Pennsylvania State University, in University Park. "I don't want the intermediaries tilting things to favor their own content."

Edward W. Felten, a professor of computer science and public affairs at Princeton University and chief

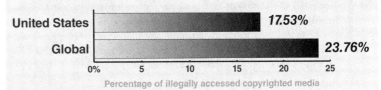

One-Fourth of Downloads Are Illegal

Roughly one-fourth of global Internet traffic, and about 18 percent of U.S. traffic, illegally accesses copyrighted media through downloading methods that include file-sharing, video streaming and use of torrents, which are files that reveal the online location of copyrighted items.

Internet Traffic Illegally Accessing Copyrighted Media

United States **17.53%**

Global **23.76%**

Percentage of illegally accessed copyrighted media

* Percentages do not include pornography because its status can be difficult to assess.

Source: "Technical Report: An Estimate of Infringing Use of the Internet," Envisional, January 2011, pp. 2-3, documents.envisional.com/docs/Envisional-Internet_Usage-Jan2011.pdf

technologist at the Federal Trade Commission, says it remains an "open question whether government can police favoritism by Internet network operators." Nevertheless, he says that keeping the Internet neutral by some means would help small Internet providers get off the ground or thrive against their bigger rivals.

"The next generation of innovators, who need neutrality the most, are not at the bargaining table. They're hard at work in their labs or classrooms, dreaming of the next big thing, and hoping that the Internet is as open to them as it was to the founders of Google."[5]

As lawmakers, entrepreneurs and policy analysts consider the future of Internet regulation, here are some of the questions being debated:

Is Internet piracy harming the economy?

For advocates of tougher copyright regulation, the domino effect may be the most compelling argument for toughening anti-piracy laws: Piracy of copyrighted material not only robs creative artists of due compensation but harms the whole economy as lost revenues in one industry decrease sales in others, they argue.

However, many analysts argue that economic- and job-loss estimates cited by copyright-owners' groups such as the Recording Industry Association of America

New Technology Spurs Innovation — and Resistance

Critics say "dinosaurs" seek veto power over the future.

Jesse Jordan, a freshman at Rensselaer Polytechnic Institute in Troy, N.Y., got the idea for his new search engine in 2003. It would be a useful and harmless way for his fellow students to search each others' files in the "public file" section of the school's internal computer system.

But after some searches turned up copyrighted music files that students had stowed on the system, the Recording Industry Association of America (RIAA) — the music-industry trade group — sued Jordan for music piracy, demanding millions of dollars in damages. Ultimately, Jordan — who said his program wasn't intended for sharing music — paid $12,000 to settle the suit, without admitting wrongdoing.[1]

Jordan wasn't alone. In the early 2000s, RIAA filed or threatened dozens of lawsuits against college students around the country. The campaign was needed, said RIAA General Counsel Steven Marks, because "the enormous damage compounded with every illegal download is alarming — thousands of regular, working class musicians . . . out of work, stores shuttered, new bands never signed."[2]

But there was more to the lawsuit blitz than simply an effort to scare pirating students straight, says Kevin J. Greene, a professor at Thomas Jefferson School of Law,

in San Diego. Among the schools where lawsuits were threatened were many that produce highly skilled technology majors, including Rensselaer, the Massachusetts Institute of Technology (MIT) and Carnegie Mellon University, in Pittsburgh. "That was not by chance," says Greene. RIAA officials "were trying to send a message to these high-tech kids" to back off from inventing new technology that would make it easier to copy and share music.

Attempts to slow the commercial impact of new communications technology have a long history.

In the 1930s, AT&T banned one of its engineers, Clarence Hickman of the telephone giant's famous research facility, Bell Labs, from continuing to work on an answering machine he'd invented that used magnetic tape to record messages. Worried that having conversations recorded would "lead the public to abandon the telephone," AT&T shut down Bell research on magnetic tape — the eventual source of audiocassettes, videocassettes and the first computer-storage systems. Eventually, "magnetic tape would come to America via imports of foreign technology, mainly German," wrote Tim Wu, a professor at Columbia Law School who specializes in technology issues.[3]

(RIAA) and the Motion Picture Association of America (MPAA) are inflated and based on minimal data.

"The accumulative impact of millions of songs downloaded illegally . . . is devastating" to a whole group of workers, including "songwriters, recording artists, audio engineers, computer technicians, talent scouts and marketing specialists, producers, publishers and countless others," said the RIAA.[6]

"More than 2.2 million hard-working, middle-class people in all 50 states depend on the entertainment industry for their jobs, and many millions more work in other industries that rely on intellectual property," Michael O'Leary, MPAA senior executive vice president,

said in lauding the House Judiciary Committee's strong bipartisan support for SOPA.[7]

"Rogue websites that steal America's innovative and creative products . . . threaten more than 19 million American jobs," wrote Mark Elliot, executive vice president of the U.S. Chamber of Commerce.[8]

"The independent music community is impacted by . . . illegal downloading, even more so in many cases than major music labels or movie studios because [profit] margins are so thin for independent labels," according to the American Association for Independent Music (A2IM), a trade group that represents smaller, independent record labels. "Because we are not part of larger

Also in the 1930s, the young broadcast industry — at the time limited to AM radio — stymied the emergence of FM radio. David Sarnoff, president of RCA, a radio manufacturer and broadcast company, assigned noted inventor Edwin Armstrong of Columbia University to devise a way to eliminate the static that plagued AM broadcasts. Armstrong went one better, inventing an entirely new form of transmission that reduced broadcast noise and made high-fidelity music broadcasts possible. It did so by modulating radio waves' frequency, rather than their amplitude. It was called FM (frequency modulation) radio.

Because FM radio also operates at a much lower power, Armstrong's invention opened the way for more small broadcasters to get into the game. "You might think that the possibility of more radio stations with less interference would be generally recognized as an unalloyed good," wrote Wu. But, he added, "by this point the radio industry . . . had invested heavily in the status quo of fewer stations," which pleased advertisers by reaching many listeners with one ad buy.

To preserve their business model, industry leaders convinced federal regulators that FM transmission was not ready for prime time, and for six years the government banned its commercial use and limited its experimental use to one narrow band of frequencies. "There was no way for an FM station even to get started without breaking the law," Wu wrote.

In the 21st century, the RIAA successfully fought for new music-licensing rules to hamper expansion of so-called "Internet radio," wrote Harvard Law School Professor Lawrence Lessig. Internet technology allows a virtually unlimited number of "Internet radio stations" to "broadcast,"

potentially allowing a much wider range of musicians to find a worldwide audience.

But what technology does not limit, laws can, according to Lessig. The RIAA fought to expand copyright law to require Internet stations to pay licensing fees to both composers and the recording artists who perform their songs. Ordinary broadcast-radio stations pay composers only. (In an earlier amendment to the law, Congress had reasoned that radio play acts as advertising for singers and bands, so payment isn't needed.) [4]

The financial burden Internet stations face from the rule "is not slight," Lessig wrote. By one estimate, an Internet station delivering "ad-free popular music to ten thousand listeners, twenty-four hours a day," would owe $1 million a year in recording-artists' fees, while a traditional station doing the same thing would not, he argued.

It's not surprising that existing businesses fight technological change, Lessig wrote. But, he added, the resistance comes with a cost: "It gives dinosaurs a veto over the future."

— *Marcia Clemmitt*

[1] For background, see "Music Settlement," transcript, "American Morning," CNN.com, May 6, 2003, http://transcripts.cnn.com/TRANSCRIPTS/0305/06/ltm.03.html.

[2] "RIAA Sends More Law Pre-Lawsuit Letters to Colleges With New School Year," press release, RIAA, www.riaa.com/newsitem.php?id=36CA9067-8061-3114-41BB-491B8B32A357.

[3] Tim Wu, *Master Switch: The Rise and Fall of Information Empires* (2010), p. 106.

[4] Lawrence Lessig, *Free Culture: The Nature and Future of Creativity* (2005), p. 197.

corporations which might be able to offset losses during leaner years, making a living becomes that much more difficult."[9]

Recorded-music sales have declined significantly in most years since the advent of Internet downloading. In 2010, for example, worldwide music sales dropped by 8.4 percent — $1.45 billion. The decrease comes "as the industry continues to struggle with piracy and winning consumers over to legal download models," observes *The Guardian* newspaper in Britain.[10]

"The demand for new music seems as insatiable and diverse as ever, and record companies continue to meet it. But they are operating at only a fraction of their

potential because of a difficult environment dominated by piracy," said Frances Moore, chief executive of the music-industry trade group International Federation of the Phonographic Industry (IFPI).[11]

"Piracy remains an enormous barrier to sustainable growth in digital music," according to IFPI. "Globally, one in four internet users (28%) regularly access unlicensed services," said the group.[12]

"I made a film called 'Naked Ambition: An R-rated Look at an X-rated Industry' " that Apple, Netflix and Warner Brothers distributed but that was widely pirated anyway, wrote photographer and independent filmmaker Michael Grecco. He received 107 Google alerts about online references to his movie that each named multiple websites where his film was available for free. The sites, which Grecco had not authorized to host his film, "made all the money; I have never seen a dime," he wrote.[13]

Piracy-related monetary and job losses are difficult to estimate, but the conservative, Lewisville, Texas-based think tank, Institute for Policy Innovation (IPI), founded by former House Majority Leader Dick Armey, R-Texas, has published perhaps the most oft-cited statistics. In 2005, industries that sell material whose copyrights they own, such as the film, TV and recording industries, lost at least $23.5 billion to piracy of music, video games and software, and retailers lost another $2.5 billion, the IPI calculated. The group also estimated that lost sales from pirating cost the United States the chance to add 373,375 jobs to the economy, about 120,000 in media- and software-creating industries and the rest in jobs that would have been supported by the 120,000 new media-industry workers.[14]

Skepticism about those estimates abounds, however. The Government Accountability Office (GAO), Congress' nonpartisan auditing arm, concluded in 2010 that while economic losses likely are "sizable," no existing estimates can be trusted. No public agencies collect their own data on piracy, industry groups often don't disclose the methods behind their estimates and numerous uncertainties cloud such questions as how much pirated material actually translates into lost sales, the GAO said. For example, a consumer who pays a low price for a counterfeit DVD wouldn't necessarily have paid the price of a non-counterfeit copy, it noted.[15]

Essentially, IPI argued that when a movie studio makes $10 selling a DVD, then passes on $7 to the company that manufactured it and $2 to the trucker who shipped it, the total value of the DVD is $10 plus $7 plus $2, or $19, wrote Timothy B. Lee, an adjunct scholar at the Cato Institute, a libertarian think tank in Washington. "Yet some simple math shows that this is nonsense," he wrote. After paying its subcontractors, "the studio is $1 richer, the trucker . . . $2, and the manufacturer . . . $7. . . . That adds up to $10."[16]

Sales of music CDs dropped steadily in the 2000s, but while the RIAA pins the blame on Internet piracy, the conclusion doesn't hold up because too many other factors likely play into the decrease, argued Lawrence Lessig, a Harvard Law School professor. For example, in the early 2000s, when RIAA reported a substantial drop in the number of CDs sold, fewer CDs than previously were being released and the per-CD price was rising, both solid reasons to expect fewer sales, Lessig wrote.[17]

Free downloading does sometimes replace a music sale, but it's misleading to count every free Internet download as an act of piracy that deprives a copyright owner of dollars, Lessig argued. For example, a large number of "pirated" downloads are of older music that has been taken off the market and is impossible to obtain legally, he wrote.

"This is still technically a violation of copyright, though because the copyright owner is not selling the content anymore, the economic harm is zero — the same harm that occurs when I sell my collection of 1960s 45-rpm records to a local collector."[18]

Figures about lost jobs from piracy don't add up, wrote Cato Institute Research Fellow Julian Sanchez. Research suggests that, for as many as 80 percent of free music downloads, the consumer would not actually have bought the music, even if a pirated copy had been unobtainable, he wrote. Those acts of piracy, then, cost the industry nothing, since they didn't replace potential sales, he said.

Meanwhile, in the 20 percent of cases in which piracy does replace a sale, the result is a loss to the music industry, "but not a [net] loss to the economy, since the money just ends up being spent elsewhere," Sanchez argued. That being the case, "there is no good reason to think eliminating piracy by U.S. users would yield any jobs on net."[19]

Should Congress crack down harder on digital piracy?

The entertainment industry argued forcefully over the past year that a much tougher system of copyright enforcement is imperative. However, critics of the stalled SOPA and PIPA bills contend that the legislation gives a few large businesses unwarranted power to shut down websites without due process.

SOPA and PIPA "would provide needed tools to combat foreign rogue websites," said MPAA's CEO, former Sen. Christopher Dodd, D-Conn.[20]

PIPA puts "muscle behind closing down foreign sites whose main purpose is to steal" and that cost "working professionals (not just corporations) hundreds of millions of dollars every year," wrote Grecco, the photographer and independent filmmaker.[21]

"Let's all agree that doing nothing is not an option any intellectual property creators can live with," said the independent-label group A2IM.[22]

Even some SOPA/PIPA critics want Congress to quickly craft tougher laws to combat piracy.

"While I'm relieved that the flawed SOPA and PIPA bills seem unlikely to pass in their current forms . . . rogue websites dedicated to the infringement of U.S. copyrights pose a public policy problem that merits . . . prompt (albeit prudent) legislative action," said Ryan Radia, associate director of policy studies at the Competitive Enterprise Institute, a free-market-oriented think tank.[23]

Others argue for more caution, however.

Trying to simply shut down sources of content is "bound to fail in today's increasingly interactive world," where new technologies and channels that facilitate information sharing come along continually, said Cato's Sanchez. "As the success of services like [the ad-supported video-streaming site] Hulu and [movie and TV-program distributor] Netflix suggests, consumers are only too happy to pay for content that's made available in a convenient form, and at a reasonable price," he said. "If the content industries want a genuinely effective way to reduce global piracy, they should spend less time and money lobbying for new regulations and focus on providing innovative services that make piracy unattractive."[24]

Many SOPA/PIPA critics view the bills as part of a long-running power grab by big media companies.

"I have first-hand knowledge of what the large media companies think of the Internet. They will never like it until they can control it 100 percent; of course ruining it in the process," wrote Joe Escalante, an entertainment lawyer and bassist for the punk band The Vandals. Escalante's band is being sued by the entertainment newspaper *Daily Variety* because websites unconnected to the band have posted images of album-cover art that the band withdrew from the market and scrubbed from

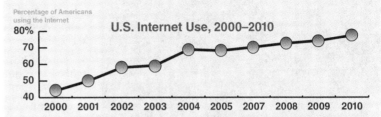

U.S. Internet Use Soars

More than three-fourths of Americans use the Internet, compared with fewer than half in 2000. About 240 million people are online, up from 124 million at the turn of the century.

Percentage of Americans using the Internet

U.S. Internet Use, 2000–2010

Source: "United States of America: Internet Usage and Broadband Usage Report," Internet World Stats, February 2011, www.internetworldstats.com/am/us.htm

their own website after *Variety* complained that it constituted trademark infringement.[25]

"The *Daily Variety* will claim in front of a jury, presumably with a straight face, that mere 'links' to a site that posted artwork from a discontinued CD displaying an 'infringing parody' should result in the four members of the Vandals paying . . . upwards of a million dollars" in damages, Escalante said. "If the fear is that under SOPA, the media companies will take advantage of a legal anomaly that will permit them to shut down entire websites, with the burden of proving innocence placed on the defendant, based on trumped up claims and theories, I can tell you, it's not paranoia. It is a real-world certainty."[26]

Historically, media and entertainment companies have sought legal protection against every technology that has given the public freer access to copyrighted content, wrote Clay Shirky, a professor at New York University's interactive-telecommunications program, in New York City. "This is an industry that tried to kill Tivo [a device for recording TV shows]. . . . They tried to kill player pianos. They do this whenever a technology increases user freedom over media. Every time. Every single time."[27]

Should the government require Internet-service providers (ISPs) to treat all websites the same?

The FCC and some technology analysts want the government to enforce rules preventing ISPs, mainly phone and cable companies, from treating different

www.newline.com

The 2005 horror movie "Snakes on a Plane," starring Samuel L. Jackson, received a major marketing boost from bloggers and Internet movie-fan communities. After advance word of the movie leaked out, online fans distributed parodies, doctored photographs and mock videos, which the producers used to market the film and shape its plot.

websites differently by slowing data from some websites. The aim of the enforcement, they say, would be to prevent ISPs from slowing the flow of content from companies such as video distributors or Internet phone companies that compete with an ISPs' other lines of business or with its business partners. But others argue that such "net neutrality" rules would violate ISPs' rights to conduct business as they see fit over wires and cables they own.

Advocates of net-neutrality regulation have turned traditional arguments for free-speech protections on their head, said Adam Thierer, a senior research fellow in technology policy at George Mason University's Mercatus Center, which researches free markets. They argue that barring ISPs from treating different websites differently would guarantee free speech to website owners that supply content to users. But this is a "twisted theory" of the Constitution's free-speech guarantee, said Thierer. The Constitution is written to stop government from becoming the enemy of free speech and doesn't envision "private platforms" such as ISPs taking that role, he wrote.[28]

In fact, new rules would abridge ISPs' freedom of speech, Thierer said. ISPs are in the business of delivering content to consumers, and "the First Amendment . . . was not intended as a tool for government to control the editorial discretion of private . . . institutions."[29]

"Disappointing one's paying end-user customers is unlikely to be a great business model over time," so "it seems unlikely that broadband ISPs are going to intentionally make a practice of slowing or blocking access to select websites," wrote technology analyst Barbara Esbin, a former special counsel at the Federal Communications Commission. Thus net-neutrality rules are unnecessary, she said.[30]

The so-called "takings clause" in the Fifth Amendment to the Constitution bars the government from taking private property "for public use, without just compensation" to the owner, says Daniel Lyons, an assistant professor at Boston College Law School. Cable- and phone-company ISPs own the wires and cables that bring Internet data into individual homes and businesses — the so-called "last mile" of Internet-content delivery — and because of that, the takings clause may apply to Internet regulations, Lyons says. "Since the 1920s there's been a branch of law that says regulations that go too far are like a taking," and net-neutrality rules may fall into that category, meaning that the government would have to pay ISPs to abide by them, he argues.

(In 1982, the Supreme Court ruled that the public interest required a New York landlord to give a cable-TV company access to his roof to install a cable box, as state law required, but that he was entitled to "just compensation" for doing so. The court deemed "just compensation" in the case to be just one dollar; nevertheless, the court established the principle that regulatory requirements are similar to an actual taking, says Lyons.[31])

Many net-neutrality advocates argue that ISPs have solid business reasons for slowing some data relative to others, but that rules to control the behavior are necessary.

A cable-TV company that offers broadband might be strongly motivated to slow the online delivery of movies from a competing video vendor such as Netflix, for example, says Frieden, of Pennsylvania State.

Furthermore, it's already been done, Frieden says. ISPs have said, "We'll never do this. We have no incentive to throttle" traffic. But in 2007, when Comcast was accused of deliberately slowing data transmitted with peer-to-peer file-sharing technology — computer programs that allow individuals to send and receive digital-media files, including music and games — first the company "said it didn't do it, then it said it did. Players do have incentives to distort the market," says Frieden.

(Comcast has argued that many users of file-sharing technology were transferring very large files and that slowing them was necessary in order to keep Internet traffic overall flowing. Subsequently, the company has worked to develop methods of traffic management that would not depend on blocking content from specific websites.[32])

Furthermore, such distortion can be consequence-free for an ISP, Frieden says. "All the consumer knows is that Netflix isn't working well, and they'll blame Netflix," even if the real culprit were an ISP slowing traffic, he says.

ISPs enter contracts with consumers to deliver certain amounts of Internet content at certain rates of speed, and the government could establish some kind of consumer-protection system for those contracts, says Frieden. For example, Congress could explicitly give the FCC authority to do "light-handed" conflict resolution of specific consumer complaints about ISPs hindering traffic, he says.

Opponents of net-neutrality regulation argue that the consumer marketplace is the proper place to handle such problems, but that may not be feasible, says Jonathan Zittrain, a Harvard Law School professor of Internet law.

"If access to Facebook is important to you, and an ISP provides poor (or no) connectivity to Facebook, you can fire your ISP. That is how markets work." But there's a catch, he continues. "There have to be meaningful alternatives" to your nonperforming ISP, and "you have to *know* that you are getting less than you want so you are motivated to switch. Both assumptions may turn out to be wrong." There is less ISP competition than many had hoped for, and rather than blaming one's ISP for slow connections, "you might just think the site itself doesn't have its act together."[33]

BACKGROUND

Communications Wars

Struggles over control of communications and media businesses have been among the most intense in economic history. Owners of older, dominant technologies have repeatedly fought innovations that threatened their businesses.[34]

In the mid-19th century, for example, Americans communicated long distances using a single technology — the telegraph — controlled by a single company, Western Union. When, around 1880, the fledgling telephone caused telegraphy to lose its role as virtually the only swift, viable distance-communications technology, Western Union faced potential collapse. Thus, "no sooner had the firm realized the potential of the Bell company's technology to overthrow the telegraph monopoly" than it made an all-out attempt "to kill or devour Bell," wrote Tim Wu, a professor of Internet, media and communications law at Columbia Law School in New York.[35]

Western Union's effort failed, but the pattern would repeat itself many times, frequently slowing development of innovations, sometimes for decades.[36]

At times, the government has stepped in to keep communications companies from snuffing out new competitors.

Beginning in the 1890s, some entrepreneurs strung their own wires through communities — attaching them to supports such as farms' barbed-wire fences — to provide local phone service. The companies prospered, especially in rural areas and small remote towns not served by the Bell system, and in the early 1900s began banding together into larger systems.

AT&T President Theodore Vail feared for his business and believed the small companies would provide inferior service. He began offering independent companies membership in the Bell system, on the condition that they adopt its technical standards and pay to use its long-distance lines. Many companies, which knew they were hamstrung without long-distance service, took the deal, even though AT&T did not promise to connect any calls to non-Bell customers.

The federal government, however, viewed the deals as antitrust violations, intended to snuff out AT&T's competition. To avoid sanctions, Vail agreed to allow independents access to AT&T's lines without joining the company and, more important, to operate AT&T henceforth as a "common carrier" — a company deemed so important to the public good that it must be required to do business in a nondiscriminatory way.[37]

Copyright Disputes

Over the years, numerous legal fights have arisen over protecting the rights of copyright owners, such as composers and filmmakers, when emerging technology has provided new ways for others to copy, alter or publish their intellectual property.

In 1909, Congress amended copyright law for music to ensure that composers were paid for "mechanical reproductions" of their works, such as phonograph records and player-piano rolls. Previous law had granted composers the exclusive right to control whether, when and how their music was performed in public. Under the new law, however, once a composer authorized any recording of a composition, subsequent musicians had the right — the "license" — to record and distribute new recordings of the piece, as long as they paid the composer a fee set by law.

Such licensing arrangements still prevail, and over time lawmakers have expanded their use in an attempt to balance the interests of original intellectual-property owners and those of others who want to use the works. Without such balance, "the monopoly power of rights holders . . . would stifle follow-on creativity," such as the creativity of musicians arranging old music into a new style, wrote Harvard's Lessig.[38]

In recent years, intellectual-property owners have argued for controlling or even banning the use of some technology.

Soon after VCRs — machines that could record TV shows and play tapes of movies for home viewing — hit the market in the 1970s, for example, the movie and television industries sought a ban. "The VCR is to the American film producer and the America public as the Boston strangler is to the woman home alone," Motion Picture Association of America (MPAA) President Jack Valenti told Congress in 1982.[39]

Movie studios sued VCR inventor Sony Corp., alleging that the machines were made for the sole purpose of copyright infringement. In 1984, the Supreme Court narrowly decided the case in Sony's favor, ruling that the recorders were most likely to be used to record TV programs to watch when convenient, a benign purpose that wouldn't harm original creators.[40]

Media Converging

The birth of digital media intensified past struggles.

When the digital revolution began, communications and media executives, like most people, viewed computers as calculating tools and scientific instruments. They missed the fact that, as computers gained more memory, everyday users not only would be able to access all kinds of media — including sound, graphics and video — through a single computer but also could manipulate those media as they wished.

The secret is "digitization" — the fact that a photograph, audio recording or any other piece of information can be converted into a two-digit "binary code" that computers can store, process and manipulate.

Coded digital information, no matter how complex, is expressed as a sequence containing only zeroes and ones. Digital technology means that "I don't use . . . different kinds of digits for representing music than I use for representing video or . . . documents," said Princeton's Felten. So "where I previously had . . . separate sets of technology" for producing and viewing video and audio, for example, a home computer now becomes "a universal machine" that can access any media and "cause a great earthquake in the media business."[41]

Peer-to-peer file-sharing (P2P) was one of the quake's first tremors.

Via cassette tapes and photocopiers, people have long shared their favorite copyrighted media with friends, but in 1999, the first P2P website for music sharing, Napster, came on the scene. Within months millions were using the site. Some downloaded others' copies of hard-to-obtain music, such as older songs that record companies had taken off the market, and amateur recordings, such as bootleg concert recordings.

But many also downloaded new music without paying for it. Heavy-metal band Metallica sued Napster after leaked copies of their unreleased music appeared on the site. The trade association Recording Industry Association of America (RIAA) also sued Napster for copyright infringement, and in 2000 a federal court ordered the website to close.[42]

The universal power of digital computing has led to a boom in the so-called "remix" culture — the creation of new art by copying and manipulating the old. Amateur and professional artists can manipulate photographs and paintings to create their own collages and animated videos, and young movie buffs intercut scenes from digitized commercial films with their own video to create unauthorized sequels to classic movies such as "Star Wars."

To blunt computers' power to share and remix media, one bill introduced in Congress — but not enacted — would have required that computers come with software that can determine whether online content is copyrighted and keep copyrighted material from being shared.[43]

CHRONOLOGY

1990s *Introduced in 1969 as a network linking a few research centers, the Internet attracts millions of users.*

1996 Phone companies unsuccessfully seek congressional ban on Internet telephone service. . . . Congress passes the Telecommunications Act, classifying cable-TV broadband Internet providers as lightly regulated "information services" but saying little else about the Internet.

1998 Congress passes Digital Millennium Copyright Act, toughening penalties for online piracy.

1999 Millions of users begin sharing music, much of it copyrighted, on Napster, first peer-to-peer file-sharing website.

2000s *Copyright owners worry as online file-sharing booms. Advocates push for requiring broadband Internet service providers (ISPs) to practice "net neutrality" by not blocking lawful content.*

2000 Judge orders Napster to shut down in wake of lawsuits by musicians and the Recording Industry Association of America (RIAA).

2003 RIAA sues or threatens lawsuits against thousands of students for alleged music piracy; Rensselaer Polytechnic Institute freshman Jesse Jordan is among those sued.

2005 Supreme Court rules that cable broadband providers don't have to open their lines to competitors. . . . FCC announces that phone companies providing broadband Internet service can operate under the same rules as cable broadband ISPs. . . . FCC will monitor all broadband ISPs to ensure that consumers can access the websites and applications they choose.

2006 Congress considers net-neutrality legislation.

2008 FCC orders cable broadband provider Comcast to stop blocking peer-to-peer file-sharing programs; Comcast complies but sues, arguing the FCC had no authority to issue the order. . . . RIAA announces it will end mass lawsuits against college students.

2009 Congress is split on net neutrality. Sen. John McCain, R-Ariz., introduces legislation to prohibit the FCC from regulating the Internet; Rep. Edward Markey, D-Mass., introduces a bill to make net neutrality national policy.

2010s *As Internet speeds rise and video streaming increases, movie and TV studios worry about illegal downloads.*

2010 Federal appeals court overturns FCC ruling in 2008 Comcast case. . . . FCC announces an "Open Internet Order," requiring ISPs to disclose their methods for managing Internet traffic and to not discriminate among websites; because of their capacity limitations, wireless broadband providers get more leeway to slow traffic.

2011 FCC Open Internet Order takes effect. . . . House passes resolution calling for the order to be rescinded; a similar measure fails in the Senate. . . . Phone company ISP Verizon sues the FCC over the order, arguing that the agency has no authority to issue it. . . . Countries including the United States, Australia, Canada, Japan and South Korea sign the Anti-Counterfeiting Trade Agreement (ACTA), requiring stronger cross-border antipiracy enforcement.

2012 Motion Picture Association of America urges Congress to toughen anti-piracy legislation. . . . Congress puts two anti-piracy bills, the Stop Online Piracy Act (SOPA) and the Protect Intellectual Property Act (PIPA), on a fast track, but House and Senate leaders pull the measures from consideration two days after Wikipedia and other websites close for a day to protest them. . . . After protests, several European countries delay signing the Anti-Counterfeiting Trade Agreement (ACTA). . . . Department of Justice shuts down Hong Kong-based Megaupload file-sharing site for violating the Digital Millennium Copyright Act. . . . Comcast announces that traffic from its Xbox streaming video service won't count against users' monthly data caps, but other video-streaming will; net-neutrality advocates say Comcast's policy endangers the Internet's standing as a neutral medium fostering economic competition.

'Remix' Culture Worries Copyright Owners

Software allows anyone to manipulate works of art.

After young fans of British author J. K. Rowling began posting renditions of her wildly popular *Harry Potter* story on their own Potter-related websites, Warner Brothers — producer of the book's film version — fought back.

Even though Rowling and her publisher, Scholastic, said they supported the young fans' creative impulses, Warner Brothers tried to block some of the websites, many of them run by children or teenagers, arguing that it wanted to prevent audience confusion about which sites were official.[1]

Heather Lawver, a young American fan, circulated a petition to stop Warner's crackdown and debated a company executive on television. "There are dark forces afoot, darker even than [Potter's evil nemesis] He-Who-Must-Not-Be-Named, . . . daring to take away something so basic, so human, that it's close to murder," she wrote. "They are taking away our freedom of speech."[2]

Warner Brothers backed off.

The episode underscored the increasingly uneasy relationship between copyright owners and others with a financial stake in creative works and a so-called "remix" culture that creates new art by copying, building upon and altering older art.

"Remix culture is in fact not an invention of the digital age," noted Edward W. Felten, a professor of computer science and public affairs at Princeton University.[3] Shakespeare, after all, famously borrowed virtually every plot twist of his play "Julius Caesar" from the Roman historian Plutarch.

New, however, is the breadth of older works that artists can incorporate, now that all art can be digitized and software allows virtually anyone to access, remix and manipulate it, altering visual art pixel by pixel, for example.

Furthermore, while the ability to publish was once the province of professionals, today everyone can publish their creations online.

As a result, traditional distinctions between artist and audience are breaking down.

"Once upon a time . . . the edge of the stage was there. The performers are on one side. The audience is on the other side, and never the twain shall meet," said Eric Kleptone, a Brighton, England-based producer of mashups — recordings that blend tracks from other songs into new music. As media-manipulating software such as Pro Tools, for music, and Photoshop, for graphics, allows people to put their own stamp on art they love, the creator-audience dichotomy is changing, he said. Increasingly, the media-buying public expect "that they should be able to personalize [purchased media] or manipulate it in some way. Or at least have the freedom to do so."[4]

By allowing amateurs to share their creations and get feedback, the Internet spurs more amateur remixes — and makes it easier for copyright owners to find — and object to — such uses of their creative output, according to Henry Jenkins, a professor of communications at the University of Southern California. In the past, "nobody minded, really, if you copied a few songs and shared the dub tape with a friend," he wrote. "But, as those transactions came out from behind closed doors, they represented a visible, public threat to the absolute control the culture industries asserted over their intellectual property."[5]

For the most part, copyright owners' response has been to ask Congress to "massively" increase "regulation

Such attempts are doomed, however, according to Lessig. Any technological fix "will likely be eclipsed" in short order by new technologies that make it even easier for consumers to access and adapt media, he wrote.[44]

Net Neutrality

The Internet was born in the 1960s when engineers at the Rand Corp., a think tank that focused on military issues, sought to devise a communications network that could survive a nuclear war.

Traditional networks — like the phone system and U.S. Postal Service — route messages through central switching points and can break down completely if vital nodes are knocked out. Rand's Paul Baran proposed a network with no central switch points but merely many smaller, widely dispersed nodes, each of which could route of creativity in America," wrote Lawrence Lessig, a professor at Harvard Law School. As a result, "To build upon or critique the culture around us one must ask . . . for permission first. Permission is, of course, often granted — but it is not often granted to the critical or the independent."[6]

Crackdowns on amateur expression risk snuffing out a vital source of cultural progress, argued Lessig. In the past, "The ordinary ways in which ordinary individuals shared and transformed their culture — telling stories, reenacting scenes from plays or TV, participating in fan clubs, sharing music, making tapes — were left alone by the law." It was "a tradition that, for at least the first 180 years of our Republic, guaranteed creators the right to build freely upon their past."[7]

As the realization dawns that the Internet is nearly impossible to control, some copyright holders may be casting a friendlier eye on remixers, some analysts say.

Warner Brothers' subsidiary New Line Cinema, for example, actually collaborated with bloggers and Internet movie-fan communities in the making and marketing of the 2005 horror movie "Snakes on a Plane," wrote Aram Sinnreich, an assistant professor at Rutgers University's School of Communication and Information.

"After advance word of the film was leaked . . . the one-two punch of its absurd title and a star turn by Samuel L. Jackson (perhaps the most remixed and mashed-up actor in cyberspace) attracted legions" of fans to share online "video mash-ups and remixes, doctored photographs," parodies and more, which the studio used to shape both its marketing campaign and the plot of the film itself, Sinnreich said.[8]

— *Marcia Clemmitt*

Getty Images/Jeff J. Mitchell

Young fans of *Harry Potter* author J. K. Rowling posted their own *Harry Potter* spin-offs, raising copyright concerns.

[3] Edward Felten, quoted in Carlos Ovalle, transcript, "Rip, Mix, Burn, Sue: Technology, Politics and the Fight to Control Digital Media," a lecture, Oct. 12, 2004, (transcript by Carlos Ovalle), www.cs.princeton.edu/~felten/rip.

[4] Quoted in Aram Sinnreich, *Mashed Up: Music, Technology, and the Rise of Configurable Culture* (2010), p. 109.

[5] Jenkins, *op. cit.*, p. 137.

[6] Lawrence Lessig, *Free Culture: The Nature and Future of Creativity* (2005), p. 71.

[7] *Ibid.*, p. 8.

[8] Sinnreich, *op. cit.*, p. 79.

---

[1] Henry Jenkins, *Convergence Culture: Where Old and New Media Collide* (2006), p. 137.

[2] Quoted in *ibid.*, p. 87.

---

data to another node until a message finally reached its destination. Each message would be chopped into tiny "packets" of digital code, and each separately addressed packet would travel on its own to the destination, where a computer would reassemble all the packets into a coherent message.

Each digital packet "would be tossed like a hot potato from node to node to node, more or less in the direction of its destination, until it ended up in the proper place," explained technology and science fiction writer Bruce Sterling. "If big pieces of the network had been blown away, that simply wouldn't matter; the packets would still stay airborne, lateralled wildly across the field by whatever nodes happened to survive."[45]

Soon the fledgling network was up and running, with packets traveling over telephone wires. The seven

Entertainment Industry Seeks New Business Plan

"There is a slow and grudging march toward progress."

You might say the pirate hunters engaged in a little piracy of their own. At the Sundance Film Festival, in Park City, Utah, this past January, VEVO — a video website owned by music-industry giants Sony Music Entertainment and Universal Music Group — streamed a pirated ESPN football game for guests, according to technology writer Jason Kincaid. Like many who pirate, VEVO likely streamed the game illegally because doing so was convenient and because a legal stream at a reasonable price wasn't available, Kincaid said.[1]

Sony and Universal have been at the forefront of protecting profits and fighting music and movie piracy, but as VEVO's display of the game underscores, they could be fighting a losing battle. Eventually, the Internet could make a wide variety of media — movies, TV programs, music CDs and other offerings — more easily and cheaply accessible to everyone, on demand, even if it means streaming content illegally.

Yet, while conventional wisdom says that such a trend would be financially devastating for media companies, the sales effects of piracy — and of laws that crack down on it — aren't as clear-cut as they might seem, some experts argue.

For example, in one study, researchers found that while pirated movies released before a film's debut significantly reduce opening-weekend box-office revenues, the piracy had no impact on the box-office take after that. That might have been because only fervent fans who attend openings want to see movies pre-release.[2]

In France, where an ultra-tough three-strikes-and-you're-banned-from-the-Internet law was adopted in 2009, aimed at individual users, piracy rose after enactment, as illegal downloaders switched to websites not explicitly targeted by the law. Furthermore, some of the most active music pirates in the study were also among the most frequent music buyers, so banning them from the Internet could wind up depressing sales, the researchers said.[3]

Of course, big media companies that rely on above-the-board sales of movies and music would rather see piracy disappear. But Internet sales of creative works may not be as gloomy as some may think, thanks in large part to an expanding online marketplace.

"It's true that CD sales are down precipitously," but the size of the music sector overall "actually grew last year," says Aram Sinnreich, an assistant professor at Rutgers University's School of Communication and Information. While some

research-university computers that constituted the entire network in 1969 expanded to thousands by the early 1970s and millions by the early 1990s. Users paid to use phone lines to transmit their data, but, otherwise, phone companies showed no interest in the medium.

As a result, the Internet initially developed without the strife that attended the early spread of such technologies as the telephone.

"There were no . . . Internet service providers . . . no commercial anything. So nobody . . . saw the original Internet initiative as a threat to their business," said Robert Kahn, an early Internet developer.[46]

In 1972, AT&T actually turned down an offer from the federal government to run the Internet.[47]

As late as 1996, when Congress undertook its first major overhaul of telecommunications law since 1934, lawmakers, too, ignored the Internet, mentioning it only a handful of times. Instead, the Telecommunications Act of 1996 focused on provisions lawmakers hoped would create more competition within each of the different forms of data transport, such as cable-TV or local landline phone service. The law also set up different regulatory structures for the various modes of information transfer, with cable companies operating under a completely different set of rules than telephone companies.[48]

growth came from a rebounding economy, he said, the rest was likely due to the growing universe of online venues for accessing music conveniently and economically.

At Apple's iTunes site, listeners can buy the exact songs they like for a wallet-friendly $1.29 per tune. At the London-based ad- and subscription-supported website Spotify, users can stream and share songs the company has licensed from record labels, without buying, if they choose, says Sinnreich.

In addition, "music publishers are having a field day," as downloads provide an unprecedented opportunity to sell the reams of older music to which they own rights, Sinnreich says. "Back catalogs used to be a hassle. You wouldn't distribute [CDs by 1970s singer-songwriter] Dan Fogelberg to Walmart" because too few would buy them, he says. But the CDs can be sold as downloads because no manufacturer or store shelf space is needed. And with computer tools that break recorded music into individual tracks and put it back together in new ways, "you can have [digital music producer] Danger Mouse do a remix of Dan Fogelberg" that may sell to a new generation.

What's needed, say many Internet experts, are new business and copyright models that reasonably compensate artists while helping consumers take advantage of online streaming, sharing and buying.

Such models might involve "licensing" — with websites buying the right to distribute songs, films or TV shows by selling ads or subscriptions and forwarding payment to industry groups such as the Recording Industry Association of America (RIAA) to distribute among the artists in proportion to how much their creative works were used.

Historically, that's been the solution to disputes between copyright holders and new technology, says David Touve, an assistant professor of business administration at Washington and Lee University, in Lexington, Va. "Radio is a massive infringer of copyright — except that they have a license," he quips. The challenge is "figuring out at what license value both copyright owners and others will be willing to participate," then devising an appropriate licensing scheme, he says.

Online technologies could help more artists get paid for their work, says Sinnreich. According to the RIAA, under "today's copyright-intensive system, only one in 10 albums make back their money" and, "if they don't, artists don't get paid. Can we develop a model that compensates a greater number of musicians?"

Websites such as TuneCore, which helps musicians place music on retail download sites such as Amazon, and CD Baby — a sales site for independent artists — show that payment can be distributed more widely and fairly among individual copyright holders, Sinnreich says. "There is a slow and grudging march toward progress on the economic front."

— *Marcia Clemmitt*

[1] Jason Kincaid, "Music Labels' Joint Venture, VEVO, Shows Pirated NFL Game at Sundance," *TechCrunch*, Feb. 9, 2012, http://techcrunch.com/2012/02/09/music-labels-joint-venture-vevo-shows-pirated-espn-game-at-sundance.

[2] "Selected Research Findings," "Digital Media," Heinz College iLab website, www.heinz.cmu.edu/ilab/research/digital-media/index.aspx.

[3] For background, see David Murphy, "French Anti-Piracy Law Actually Increasing Piracy," *PC Magazine*, March 28, 2010, www.pcmag.com/article2/0,2817,2361925,00.asp.

Lawmakers failed to grapple with the rapidly materializing prospect that the Internet would soon become a competitor to cable-TV and phone companies, transmitting video and audio data. They also did not foresee that Internet data would soon be carried by numerous modes, including TV cables, phone wires, high-speed wires, fiber-optic cables and wireless transmitters, some of which their new law had put under separate, very different, systems of regulation.

The main Internet-related provision in the 1996 law, which continues to have significant consequences, stems from these different levels of regulation. Specifically, the law states that cable-TV companies' broadband — or "high-speed" — Internet service will operate as a loosely regulated "information service" rather than a tightly regulated "telecommunications carrier," such as a phone company.

"Telecommunications carriers" — like the "common carriers" of old — must offer access to their lines to anyone who seeks it, including competing businesses. For this reason, slow, dial-up Internet service — which travels over regular phone lines — has been offered by many independent ISPs to whom phone companies are required to open their lines.

By contrast, in dubbing cable broadband Internet an "information service," Congress lumped it with "luxuries, non-essentials that don't need the same level of protection," says Pennsylvania State's Frieden. That decision — plus

German Web entrepreneur Kim Dotcom, founder of Megaupload
.com, a file-sharing website, leaves an Auckland, New Zealand,
court on Feb. 22, 2012, after being released on bail. He was
arrested at the request of the U.S. Justice Department, which is
seeking to extradite him on online piracy charges.

fast-moving technological change — set up the so-called
"net neutrality" debate that has raged ever since.

For one thing, soon after passage of the 1996 law,
phone companies joined cable TV companies as providers
of high-speed Internet, laying down their own technologically advanced networks — DSL, or digital subscriber
lines, and, later, wireless networks and fiber-optic cable.

Furthermore, in the late 1990s and accelerating in the
2000s, the Internet's importance to public life and business soared as it became a one-stop shop for media and
communications, as well as business functions such as
shopping and banking. For many observers, this raised
the question of whether the public's growing political and
economic dependence on online access required all ISPs
to operate as a kind of common carrier.

Further complicating matters, so-called packet-sniffing
technology was developed that gave ISPs the ability to
find out what kind of data a website was transmitting
and, to some degree at least, slow or speed up that data.

In the early 2000s, calls began for the government to
require all ISPs — including the lightly regulated cable
companies — to abide by a principle of "net neutrality,"
treating data from all websites the same. In 2005, however,
the Supreme Court and the FCC moved the other way.
In a key ruling based on Congress' classification of cable
broadband as an "information service," the Supreme Court

ruled 6-3 that a cable company had no obligation to open
its lines to a competing, independent ISP.[49]

The ruling opened the door for telephone companies
to argue that if cable broadband was not obliged to follow
common-carrier-type rules, their broadband services
shouldn't be required to do so either.

In 2005, the FCC agreed. Beginning in August 2006,
phone companies would no longer be required to offer
competing ISPs, such as AOL, free access to their DSL
connections. Dial-up Internet would still travel free over
regular phone lines, however.[50]

The FCC was not entirely comfortable with leaving
ISPs with so much discretion to block competitors, however. It announced that it would monitor ISPs to protect
consumers' right to access and run any lawful websites,
applications or services and link to the Internet any devices
that would not harm the ISP network.

In 2008, the U.S. Court of Appeals for the District of
Columbia ruled that cable giant Comcast had violated those
policies when it selectively blocked some users' peer-to-peer
file-sharing, which Comcast said it did to prevent Internet
bottlenecks. In 2010, however, the same court decreed that,
under the 1966 law, the FCC had no authority to impose
common-carrier-type rules on cable broadband.[51]

Lawmakers are sharply divided. In 2009, Sen. John
McCain, R-Ariz., introduced a bill that, with a few exceptions, would have banned the FCC from issuing any rules
governing the Internet. That same year Rep. Edward
Markey, D-Mass., introduced legislation to establish net
neutrality as national policy.

Technical complexity hampers the progress, says
Princeton's Felten. "There's a general consensus" that
requiring ISPs to be evenhanded has value, "but how do
you draw the line between reasonable network management and discrimination? That's hard to talk about" in
legislative language, he says.

In December 2010, the FCC adopted an "Open
Internet Order," proposing to maintain net neutrality
through three rules. Network operators must:

- publicly disclose methods for managing network
traffic;
- not block legal applications or websites, except as
required for network management;
- not practice "unreasonable discrimination" among
websites.

Only the "no blocking" and public-disclosure rules will apply to wireless broadband. Unlike wired transmission, wireless leaks a large amount of its signal into the air, experiences significant signal interference and can't easily add more capacity, as wired networks can. Therefore, as Internet traffic increases, wireless networks might become hopelessly congested without aggressive traffic management, the agency noted.[52]

The order took effect on Nov. 20, 2011.

CURRENT SITUATION

Going Dark

After seeming to be on the fast track toward enacting strict new online copyright enforcement, Congress has backed away amid protests by individuals and some major Internet players, including Google and Wikipedia. Meanwhile, some lawmakers are vowing to stop the FCC's net-neutrality order.

In January, Congress postponed long-expected floor votes for SOPA (H.R. 3261), introduced last year in the House by Smith, the Texas Republican — and PIPA — the Protect Intellectual Property Act (S. 968), introduced last year by Sen. Patrick Leahy, D-Vt.[53]

The bills were intended to help copyright owners fight media piracy that websites such as the Swedish site The Pirate Bay facilitate. The Pirate Bay and other sites host so-called bit-torrent files and other software that allow users to share massive audio and video files, many of which are copyrighted. Entertainment industries want enhanced enforcement to stop it.

Posting copyrighted files online without paying is already illegal under the 1998 Digital Millennium Copyright Act (DMCA).[54] The entertainment industry argues, however, that, because the law is tougher on individual copyright infringers than on websites where the material is posted, it goes after small-time pirates while passing up the chance to shut off piracy at its source by forcing entire piracy-facilitating websites offline.

SOPA would give the government a quick path to order advertising networks and online-payment companies such as PayPal to cut off service to websites where copyright infringement is alleged to occur. It would bar search engines from linking to those sites and require ISPs to block access to them. Copyright owners themselves could order advertising and payment companies to stop doing business with websites that post copyrighted material and sue if companies don't comply.

PIPA takes a similar approach but differs in some particulars. For example, it would not require search engines to remove infringing sites from their indexes and would set up a different legal process for seeking court orders.

PIPA is "a strong and balanced approach to protecting intellectual property through a . . . system that leverages the most relevant players in the Internet ecosystem," Leahy said in early January.[55]

Only a few days later, though, thousands of website owners staged a dramatic protest against what many called copyright owners' overreach. On Jan. 18, sites including Wikipedia, the social-media site Reddit, and Boing Boing shut down for the day, redirecting visitors to explanations of their objections to the bills. Other sites, including Google, expressed support for the protests, and millions signed online petitions against the legislation.[56]

"It's not hard to imagine . . . that a service provider, acting with abundance of caution and out of its own self-interest, will simply cut off services to entire sites that have been accused of infringement, even if the court order only applies to a portion of the site," wrote Christine Montgomery, president of the Online News Association, a digital journalists' organization.[57]

The ferocity of the fight is driven by the movie industry, says Kevin J. Greene, a professor of intellectual-property and entertainment law at Thomas Jefferson School of Law, in San Diego. The MPAA spent around $1 million a month fighting for the legislation during the last four to six months before Congress dropped the bills, he says. "Their fears are legitimate," though, especially when it comes to how piracy affects global sales, he says. "In the online world, it's said that if you have a video game to sell in China, you'll sell one copy" because the rest will be pirated.

Nevertheless, the MPAA "said that the problem they were going after was foreign websites, but the language in the bill was so broad" that it casts doubt on that claim, says Greene. "It looks more like they just wanted more weapons in their arsenal" against copyright infringement in general, even though "that arsenal has been getting bigger and bigger for years." (The MPAA did not respond to *CQ Researcher*'s request for comment.)

On Jan. 20, congressional leaders withdrew the bills from consideration.[58]

Should lawmakers support the FCC's net-neutrality rules?

YES
Gigi B. Sohn
President, Public Knowledge

From testimony before the House Judiciary Subcommittee on Intellectual Property, Competition and the Internet, Feb. 15, 2011

An open Internet is vitally important to political discourse, societal interactions, commercial transactions, innovation, entrepreneurship and job creation in the United States. However, past actions by incumbent broadband Internet access providers have threatened the preservation of an open internet resulting in the need for clear, enforceable baseline network-neutrality rules.

Network-neutrality rules are necessary to protect consumers against the monopoly and duopoly behavior of broadband Internet access providers in our country. Contrary to assertions by industry incumbents that consumers enjoy competition when it comes to broadband access choice and can simply switch, the Federal Communications Commission's (FCC's) National Broadband Plan reported that 13 percent of Americans have only one broadband access provider, and 78 percent of Americans have only two broadband Internet access providers.

Cable and telephone incumbents have asserted that network-neutrality rules are unnecessary and that the market has never demonstrated the need for rules. However, there is a documented history of harmful actions taken by broadband Internet access providers. The commission observed that it had acted on two high-profile incidents of blocking but recounted evidence of numerous other incidents. . . .

AT&T blocked certain applications, such as SlingBox video streaming, Skype and Google voice, from its mobile network while permitting its own streaming and voice products to use the same network. Cox and RCN both admitted to slowing or degrading Internet traffic at times. Both providers deny wrongdoing and claim that these practices are designed to handle congestion, but in neither case did providers disclose their traffic-management practices to subscribers. It is ironic that providers which publicly proclaim they have no intention of ever actually blocking or degrading content routinely include statements in their terms of service that would allow them to engage in precisely these practices — and without prior notice to consumers.

I want to mention Public Knowledge's concern with recent discussions in Congress to invoke the Congressional Review Act (CRA) to repeal the FCC network-neutrality rules. Enactment of a CRA repeal of the FCC's network-neutrality rules would virtually eliminate the agency's authority to protect an open Internet.

I urge members of the committee to recognize that the economic benefits of the Internet are entirely based on ensuring that it remains an open and free marketplace and that the federal government has an integral role to play in that regard.

NO
Larry Downs
Senior Adjunct Fellow, TechFreedom

From testimony before the House Judiciary Subcommittee on Intellectual Property, Competition and the Internet, Feb. 15, 2011

Proponents of net-neutrality regulation argue that the Internet's defining feature — and the key to its unarguable success — is the content-neutral routing and transport of individual packets throughout the network by Internet service providers, Internet backbones and other individual networks that make up the Internet.

As evidenced in all of my writings on the digital revolution, I share the enthusiasm for the open internet. I just don't believe there is any evidence of a need for regulatory intervention to "save" this robust ecosystem, or that the Federal Communications Commission (FCC) had the authority to do so.

As with any lawmaking involving disruptive technologies, moreover, the risk of unintended consequences is high.

There was no need for new regulation. Despite thousands of pages of comments from parties on all sides of the issue, in the end the [FCC] majority could only identify four incidents in the last 10 years of what it believed to be non-neutral behavior. All four were quickly resolved outside the agency's adjudication processes. Yet these four incidents provide the sole evidence of a need to regulate. With no hint of market failure, the majority instead has issued what it calls a "prophylactic rule" it hopes will deter any actual problems in the future.

But maybe these four incidents are not what's really driving the push for FCC regulation of Internet access. Maybe the real problem is, as many regulatory advocates argue vaguely, the lack of "competition" for broadband. According to the National Broadband Plan, 5 percent of the U.S. population still doesn't have access to any wireless broadband provider. In many parts of the country only two providers are available, and in others the offered speeds of alternatives vary greatly, leaving users without high-speed alternatives.

If lack of competition is the problem, though, why not solve the problem? Multiple technologies have been used to deliver broadband access to consumers, including DSL, coaxial cable, cellular, wireless and broadband over power lines (BPL). But rather than promote multiple technologies, the FCC has done just the opposite. For example, the agency has sided with some state governments who argued successfully that they can prevent municipalities from offering telecommunications service. And the commission has dragged its feet on approving trials for BPL.

Why does anyone believe the FCC can "prophylactically" solve a problem dealing with an emerging, rapidly evolving new technology that has thrived in the last decade in part because it was unregulated?

The protests themselves were a kind of watershed in Internet history — "the first time the Internet rose to defend itself," says Ippolito, of the University of Maine.

Others doubt that grassroots activism played much of a role, however. In the end, the dispute was "monopoly against monopoly, a clash of very big players," with Google and Facebook pitted openly against entertainment-industry giants such as Sony for the first time, says Robert W. Gehl, an assistant professor of communication at the University of Utah, in Salt Lake.

Progress toward an anti-piracy treaty once thought to be on the fast track to adoption also slowed this year.

In October 2011, countries including Australia, Canada, Japan, Morocco, New Zealand, Singapore, South Korea and the United States signed the Anti-Counterfeiting Trade Agreement (ACTA), which would set tough international standards for pursuing copyright enforcement and other anticounterfeiting actions.[59] This year, however, protests in countries such as the U.K., Germany, Poland and the Netherlands have led several European countries to postpone signing the measure.[60]

The White House Office of the U.S. Trade Representative promises that the compact will "support American jobs in innovative and creative industries."[61]

But opponents argue that while the treaty targets "commercial-scale piracy," its language is so vague that it might criminalize small-scale noncommercial file-sharing that involves no financial gain and is handled in civil courts today.[62]

Net Neutrality in Court

The FCC's plan to monitor ISPs for possible discrimination against particular websites remains under fire. In 2011, a joint congressional resolution disapproving the rule — and ordering the agency to refrain from regulating the Internet altogether until Congress issues directions for how to do so — passed the House but failed in the Senate.[63]

Lawsuits questioning the order are proceeding.

On Sept. 30, 2011, New York City-based Verizon Communications filed suit, arguing that the order is unnecessary and that the FCC had no legal authority to promulgate it. "We are deeply concerned by the FCC's assertion of broad authority to impose potentially sweeping and unneeded regulations on broadband networks and services and on the Internet itself," said Senior Vice President Michael E. Glover.[64]

Boing Boing and thousands of other websites, including Wikipedia and Reddit, shut down on Jan. 18, 2012, to protest proposed legislation to block pirating of online copyrighted material. The sites oppose the Stop Online Piracy Act and the Protect Intellectual Property Act, which they claim would amount to censorship. Posting copyrighted files online without paying is already illegal, but supporters of the legislation, principally the entertainment industry, argue tougher laws are needed to stop piracy at its source.

Yet, the Massachusetts-based media-reform advocacy group Free Press also has filed suit, arguing that the rule doesn't go far enough. "The final rules . . . fail to protect wireless users from discrimination," an "arbitrary distinction" between regulations for wireless and wired Internet that is "unjustified," said Policy Director Matt Wood.[65]

Some analysts say Congress must act to clarify the situation for consumers, the FCC and the courts.

ISP subscribers "don't expect anybody to mess with" their data delivery, says Frieden, of Pennsylvania State. For that reason, "Congress needs to clarify the law," stipulating exactly what power the FCC has to settle disputes between consumers and ISPs, he says. "You can revile government and hate the courts but you need some kind of referee here."

OUTLOOK
Continuing Battles

It's anybody's guess how the ongoing battles over control of digital intellectual property and management of the Internet's traffic flows will turn out.

This year's heated debate over SOPA and PIPA, however, did reveal something new, says Greene, of Thomas

Jefferson Law School. For the first time in a fight over copyrights, "the motion picture industry was up against somebody as well financed as they are" — Internet giants such as Google and Facebook — and that fact is what slowed the bills down, he says.

If SOPA or PIPA were enacted, it would break a "deal cut in 1998" when Congress, the entertainment industry and Internet businesses negotiated the Digital Millennium Copyright Act, Greene says. At that time, everyone agreed that "there's a lot of piracy online but also that we don't want ISPs to actually have to police it," he says.

Recently, however, MPAA came back with new proposals, asking Congress to require ISPs to do just that. In the past, they've gotten what they wanted through backroom channels, Greene says. This time, though, the Internet industry "has more power and money than the entertainment industry."

Many analysts worry that the concerns of the public and of small business won't be heard in the debates.

"Nobody, except for some poorly funded organizations" such as the San Francisco-based Electronic Frontier Foundation — which advocates on civil-liberties issues related to computers —"are standing up for the consumer and citizen," says Aram Sinnreich, an assistant professor at Rutgers University's School of Communication and Information. And those groups have trouble enlisting support "since it's difficult to make these arguments in terms that make sense to non-policy wonks," he says.

Ironically, while the goal of net-neutrality advocates is ensuring that new, small organizations with good ideas get a chance to grow online, such organizations are left out of legislative discussions, says Felten, of Princeton. "When it comes to small companies in the startup culture, and small business as an engine of growth, there's less understanding than there could be" of what's needed. "People in government look to large, established companies" for guidance on shaping the laws, he says.

Most alarming to some is the likelihood that powerful industries' desire to control online behavior — such as by detecting downloads of copyrighted media — "will overlap with a political interest in overseeing citizens' online behavior," says Sinnreich.

"As committed as we are to freedom, our government and every other government in the world has a prevailing interest in surveillance and control, which is truly scary if it aligns with corporate interest in the same thing."

NOTES

1. Quoted in Emma Barnett, "Wikipedia Founder Jimmy Wales Defends SOPA Protest Blackout," *The Telegraph* [UK], Jan. 17, 2012, www.telegraph.co.uk/technology/wikipedia/9020053/Wikipedia-founder-Jimmy-Wales-defends-SOPA-protest-blackout.html.

2. Lamar Smith, "Why We Need a Law Against Online Piracy," CNN.com, Jan. 20, 2012, www.cnn.com/2012/01/20/opinion/smith-sopa-support/index.html.

3. Gerald R. Faulhaber and David J. Farber, "The Open Internet: A Customer-Centric Framework," *International Journal of Communication*, 2010, pp. 302-342, http://ijoc.org/ojs/index.php/ijoc/article/view/670/388.

4. For background, see "10 ISPs and Countries Known to Have Blocked VoIP," *VoIP Providers List*, Feb. 2, 2009, www.voipproviderslist.com/articles/others/10-isps-and-countries-known-to-have-blocked-voip.html.

5. Edward Felten, "'Neutrality' Is Hard to Define," Room for Debate blog, *The New York Times*, Aug. 10, 2010, www.nytimes.com/roomfordebate/2010/8/9/who-gets-priority-on-the-web/net-neutrality-is-hard-to-define.

6. "Who Music Theft Hurts," Recording Industry Association of America, www.riaa.com/physicalpiracy.php?content_selector=piracy_details_online.

7. "MPAA Statement on Strong Showing of Support for Stop Online Privacy Act," Motion Picture Association of American, Inc., press release, Dec. 16, 2011, www.mpaa.org/resources/5a0a212e-c86b-4e9a-abf1-2734a15862cd.pdf. See also, "Intellectual Property and the U.S. Economy: Industries in Focus," U.S. Commerce Department, March 2012, www.esa.doc.gov/sites/default/files/reports/documents/ipandtheuseconomyindustriesinfocus.pdf.

8. Mark Elliot, letter to the editor, *The New York Times*, Nov. 18, 2011, www.nytimes.com/2011/11/19/opinion/rogue-web-sites.html.

9. "Protect IP and SOPA Legislation — Obama Administration Announcement," A2IM website, Jan. 16, 2012, http://a2im.org/tag/sopa.

10. Mark Sweney, "Global Recorded Music Sales Fall Almost $1.5 bn Amid Increased Piracy," *The Guardian* [UK], March 28, 2011, www.guardian.co.uk/business/2011/mar/28/global-recorded-music-sales-fall.

11. Quoted in *ibid.*

12. "IFPI Publishes Digital Music Report 2012," press release, International Federation of the Phonographic Industry, Jan. 23, 2012, www.ifpi.org/content/section_resources/dmr2012.html.

13. Michael Grecco, "Michael Grecco Is Pro Protect IP and SOPA," MichaelGrecco.com, Jan. 20, 2012, http://michaelgrecco.com/michael-grecco-blog/michael-grecco-is-pro-protect-ip-and-sopa.

14. Stephen E. Siwek, "The True Cost of Copyright Industry Piracy to the U.S. Economy," Institute for Policy Innovation, October 2007, www.ipi.org/IPI%5CIPIPublications.nsf/PublicationLookupFullTextPDF/02DA0B4B44F2AE9286257369005ACB57/$File/CopyrightPiracy.pdf?OpenElement.

15. "Observations on Efforts to Quantify the Economic Effects of Counterfeit and Pirated Goods," Government Accountability Office, April 2010, www.gao.gov/new.items/d10423.pdf.

16. Tim Lee, "Texas-sized Sophistry," The Technology Liberation Front website, Oct. 1, 2006, http://techliberation.com/2006/10/01/texas-size-sophistry.

17. Lawrence Lessig, *Free Culture: The Nature and Future of Creativity* (2005), p. 71.

18. *Ibid.*, p. 67.

19. Julian Sanchez, "How Copyright Industries Con Congress," Cato at Liberty blog, Jan. 3, 2012, www.cato-at-liberty.org/how-copyright-industries-con-congress.

20. Christopher Dodd, "These Two Bills Are the Best Approach," Room for Debate blog, *The New York Times*, Jan. 18, 2012, www.nytimes.com/roomfordebate/2012/01/18/whats-the-best-way-to-protect-against-online-piracy/these-two-bills-are-the-best-approach.

21. Grecco, *op. cit.*

22. "Protect IP and SOPA Legislation — Obama Administration Announcement," *op. cit.*

23. Ryan Radia, "Are Rogue Websites Really So Bad After All?" The Technology Liberation Front, Jan. 23, 2012, http://techliberation.com/2012/01/23/are-rogue-websites-really-so-bad-after-all.

24. Julian Sanchez, "Focus on Innovation Instead," Room for Debate blog, *The New York Times*, Jan. 18, 2012, www.nytimes.com/roomfordebate/2012/01/18/whats-the-best-way-to-protect-against-online-piracy/the-content-industry-should-focus-on-innovation-instead.

25. For background, see Vickie Chang, "Painful Parody," *OC Weekly*, Sept. 9, 2010, www.ocweekly.com/2010-09-09/music/vandals-vs-daily-variety/.

26. Joe Escalante, "Does Daily Variety Validate SOPA Fears?" *Huffington Post*, Jan. 23, 2012, www.huffingtonpost.com/joe-escalante/sopa-copyright_b_1222058.html.

27. Clay Shirky, "Pick up the Pitchforks: David Pogue Underestimates Hollywood," Shirky.com, Jan. 20, 2012, www.shirky.com/weblog/2012/01/pick-up-the-pitchforks-david-pogue-underestimates-hollywood.

28. Adam Thierer, "Net Neutrality Regulation & the First Amendment," The Technology Liberation Front, Dec. 9, 2009, http://techliberation.com/2009/12/09/net-neutrality-regulation-the-first-amendment.

29. *Ibid.*

30. Barbara Esbin, "Net Neutrality: A Further Take on the Debate," The Progress & Freedom Foundation, December 2009, http://papers.ssrn.com/sol3/papers.cfm?abstract_id=1529090.

31. For background, see *Loretto v. Teleprompter Manhattan CATV Corp.*, 458 U.S. 419, 434-35 (1982), http://caselaw.lp.findlaw.com/cgi-bin/getcase.pl?navby=case&court=US&vol=458&invol=419&pageno=436.

32. For background, see K. C. Jones, "Comcast Removes Blocks on File Sharing," *Information Week*, Jan. 7, 2009, www.informationweek.com/news/internet/policy/212701122; Ryan Paul, "FCC to Investigate Comcast BitTorrent Blocking," *Ars Technica*, http://arstechnica.com/tech-policy/news/2008/01/fcc-to-investigate-comcast-bittorrent-blocking.ars.

33. Jonathan Zittrain, "Net Neutrality as Diplomacy," Jan. 23, 2011, http://papers.ssrn.com/sol3/papers.cfm?abstract_id=1729424.

34. For background, see Tim Wu, *Master Switch: The Rise and Fall of Information Empires* (2010); Marcia

Clemmitt, "Controlling the Internet," *CQ Researcher*, May 12, 2006, pp. 409-432; Kenneth Jost, "Copyright and the Internet," *CQ Researcher*, Sept. 29, 2000, pp. 769-792.

35. Wu, *op. cit.*, p. 27.

36. *Ibid.*, p. 10.

37. *Ibid.*, p. 58.

38. Lawrence Lessig, *Free Culture: How Big Media Uses Technology and the Law to Lock Down Culture and Control Creativity* (2004), p. 57.

39. Quoted in Carlos Ovalle, transcript, "Rip, Mix, Burn, Sue: Technology, Politics and the Fight to Control Digital Media," a lecture by Edward Felten, Oct. 12, 2004, www.cs.princeton.edu/~felten/rip.

40. *Sony Corp. v. Universal City Studios*, 464 U.S. 417 (1984), http://supreme.justia.com/cases/federal/us/464/417.

41. Ovalle, *op. cit.*

42. For background, see Steve Knopper, "Napster Wounds the Giant," *Rocky Mountain News*, Jan. 2, 2009, www.rockymountainnews.com/news/2009/jan/02/napster-wounds-the-giant.

43. Lessig, *Free Culture: How Big Media Uses Technology*, *op. cit.*, kindle location 5476, Chap. 12, footnote 11.

44. *Ibid.*, p. 193.

45. Bruce Sterling, "Internet," *The Magazine of Fantasy and Science Fiction*, February 1993, archived at Electronic Frontier Foundation website, w2.eff.org/Net_culture/internet_sterling.history.txt.

46. Quoted in "Putting It All Together With Robert Kahn," Computer and Computer History website, http://66.14.166.45/history/network/Robert%20Kahn%20Interview%20-%20Putting%20it%20all%20Together%20with%20Robert%20Kahn.pdf.

47. For background, see Scott Bradner, "Blocking the Power of the Internet," *Network World*, Jan. 16, 2006, www.networkworld.com/columnists/2006/011606bradner.html.

48. For background, see Charles B. Goldfarb, "Telecommunications Act: Competition, Innovation, Reform," Congressional Research Service, Aug. 12, 2005, http://digital.library.unt.edu/ark:/67531/metacrs7798/m1/1/high_res_d/RL33034_2005Aug12.pdf.

49. For background, see *National Cable & Telecommunications Assn. v. Brand X Internet Services*, 545 U.S. 967 (2005), www.law.cornell.edu/supct/html/04-277.ZS.html.

50. For background, see Angele A. Gilroy, "Access to Broadband Networks: The Net Neutrality Debate," Congressional Research Service, Oct. 25, 2011, www.fas.org/sgp/crs/misc/R40616.pdf.

51. For background, see *Comcast Corp. v. FCC*, 600 F.3d 642, www.cadc.uscourts.gov/internet/opinions.nsf/EA10373FA9C20DEA85257807005BD63F/$file/08-1291-1238302.pdf.

52. For background, see Matthew Lasar, "It's Here: FCC Adopts Net Neutrality (Lite)," *Ars Technica*, 2011, http://arstechnica.com/tech-policy/news/2010/12/its-here-fcc-adopts-net-neutrality-lite.ars, and Elliott Drucker, "Tech Insights — Sizing Up Wireline Vs. Wireless Performance," *Wireless Week*, Jan. 16, 2011, www.wirelessweek.com/Articles/2011/02/Drucker-Sizing-Up-Wireline-Vs-Wireless-Performance.aspx.

53. For background, see bill text, H.R. 3261, Thomas, Library of Congress, http://thomas.loc.gov/cgi-bin/query/z?c112:H.R.3261:, and bill text versions, S. 968, Thomas, Library of Congress, http://thomas.loc.gov/cgi-bin/query/z?c112:S.968.

54. For background, see "The Digital Millennium Copyright Act of 1998," U.S. Copyright Office, December 1998, www.copyright.gov/legislation/dmca.pdf.

55. Quoted in Mike Masnick, "Senator Leahy Hopes to Rush Through PIPA By Promising to Study DNS Blocking . . . Later?" *TechDirt*, Jan. 12, 2012, www.techdirt.com/articles/20120112/14322317392/senator-leahy-hopes-to-rush-through-pipa-promising-to-study-dns-blocking-later.shtml.

56. For background, see Sean Poulter and Rob Waugh, "Wikipedia Protest Hits Home: U.S. Senators Withdraw Support for Anti-piracy Bills as 4.5 Million Sign Petition," *Daily Mail Online* [UK], Jan. 19, 2012, www.dailymail.co.uk/news/article-2087673/Wikipedia-blackout-SOPA-protest-US-senators-withdraw-support-anti-piracy-bills.html.

57. Christine Montgomery, "Letter from the President: Why ONA Opposes Sopa," Online News Association

website, Jan. 5, 2012, http://journalists.org/2012/01/05/ona-on-sopa.

58. For background, see SOPA/PIPA Timeline, *Pro Publica*, http://projects.propublica.org/sopa/timeline.

59. For background, see "Anti-Counterfeiting Trade Agreement," www.mofa.go.jp/policy/economy/i_property/pdfs/acta1105_en.pdf.

60. For background, see "Timeout for Finland in Ratifying ACTA," *Valtioneuvosto*, Finnish Government, March 9, 2012, http://valtioneuvosto.fi/ajankohtaista/tiedotteet/tiedote/fi.jsp?oid=352766&c=0&toid=1802&moid=1803; Dave Lee, "ACTA Protests: Thousands Take to Streets Across Europe," BBC News, Feb. 11, 2012, www.bbc.co.uk/news/technology-16999497; Raphael Satter and Venssa Gera, "Anonymous Protests ACTA, Attacks FTC and Other U.S. Agencies' Sites," Associated Press/*Huffington Post*, Feb. 17, 2012, www.huffingtonpost.com/2012/02/17/anonymous-acta-ftc_n_1285668.html; Anti-Counterfeiting Trade Agreement, Foreign Affairs and International Trade Canada, www.international.gc.ca/trade-agreements-accords-commerciaux/fo/intellect_property.aspx?view=d; Glyn Moody, "Brazil Drafts and 'Anti-ACTA': A Civil-Rights-Based Framework for the Internet," *Tech Dirt*, www.techdirt.com/articles/20111004/04402516196/brazil-drafts-anti-acta-civil-rights-based-framework-internet.shtml.

61. "Anti-Counterfeiting Trade Agreement," Office of the U.S. Trade Representative, www.ustr.gov/acta.

62. Dan Mitchell, "Meet SOPA's Evil Twin, ACTA," CNN Money, Jan. 26, 2012, http://tech.fortune.cnn.com/2012/01/26/meet-sopas-evil-twin-acta.

63. For background, see S.J.Res. 6, Open Congress, www.opencongress.org/bill/112-sj6/show.

64. Quoted in Marguerite Reardon, "Verizon Sues Again to Block Net Neutrality Rules," CNET, Sept. 30, 2011, http://news.cnet.com/8301-30686_3-20114142-266/verizon-sues-again-to-block-net-neutrality-rules.

65. Quoted in Grant Gross, "Free Press Files Lawsuit on FCC's Net Neutrality Rules," *Computer World*, Sept. 28, 2011, www.computerworld.com/s/article/9220367/Free_Press_files_lawsuit_on_FCC_s_net_neutrality_rules.

BIBLIOGRAPHY

Selected Sources
Books

Downes, Larry, *The Laws of Disruption: Harnessing the New Forces that Govern Life and Business in the Digital Age*, Basic Books, 2009.
A business and legal consultant describes how digitization and the Internet are disrupting the traditional economy. He argues against hasty government regulation of new technologies and for allowing a new legal system suitable to the digital era to emerge on its own.

Lessig, Lawrence, *Free Culture: The Nature and Future of Creativity*, Penguin, 2004.
A Harvard University law professor argues that copyright law favors copyright owners, empowering media companies to strangle creative digital opportunities.

Wu, Tim, *The Master Switch: The Rise and Fall of Information Empires*, Vintage, 2011.
A Columbia University law professor describes the history of American communications industries as one in which inventors create powerful industries that then fight to suppress competing innovations.

Articles

Ferreira, Heather, "What Do Directors Think When People Make a Torrent for Their Movie?" *Huffington Post*, Feb. 22, 2012, www.huffingtonpost.com/quora/what-do-directors-think-w_b_1292760.html.
An independent filmmaker argues that anti-piracy legislation serves the interests of big film studios and the highest-paid tier of Hollywood talent but not those of independent creators.

Hachman, Mark, "Comcast's Xfinity-on-Xbox Plans Draw Net Neutrality Fire," *PCMag.com*, March 26, 2012, www.pcmag.com/article2/0,2817,2402149,00.asp.
Net-neutrality advocates say Comcast's policy of not counting video streaming from its Xbox subsidiary toward customers' monthly data-usage caps violates the principle of an open Internet.

Jardine, Nick, "Meet the Man Who Founded the Pirate Party That Is Spreading Through European Parliaments,"

Business Insider, Dec. 5, 2011, http://articles.business insider.com/2011-12-05/europe/30477454_1_new-movement-young-voters-protest.
A Swedish-based political movement that aims to legalize online file-sharing is gaining support, especially among young people.

Wortham, Jenna, and Amy Chozick, "The Piracy Problem: How Broad?" *The New York Times*, Feb. 8, 2012, www.nytimes.com/2012/02/09/technology/in-piracy-debate-deciding-if-the-sky-is-falling.html?pagewanted=all.
Copyright-owning industries such as the movie and music businesses cite huge financial losses from piracy, but many consumers say they resort to pirating only when they can't conveniently access what they want at a reasonable price.

Reports and Studies

Benkler, Yochai, "Seven Lessons from SOPA/PIPA/Megaupload and Four Proposals on Where We Go From Here," techpresident, Jan. 25, 2012, http://techpresident.com/news/21680/seven-lessons-sopapipamegauplaod-and-four-proposals-where-we-go-here.
A Harvard law professor argues that anti-piracy bills in Congress this year were an over-reach by copyright-owning industries and that protests that slowed the bills' progress show how consumers are learning to use the Internet to accomplish political goals.

Esbin, Barbara S., "Net Neutrality: A Further Take on the Debate," Progress on Point, The Progress and Freedom Foundation, December 2009, http://papers.ssrn.com/sol3/papers.cfm?abstract_id=1529090.

A media lawyer and former Federal Communications Communication official argues that the fast-evolving nature of the Internet and its openness to new businesses and new ideas would be hampered if the government chose to regulate it.

Felten, Edward W., "Rip, Mix, Burn, Sue: Technology, Politics, and the Fight to Control Digital Media," video lecture, Princeton University, Oct. 12, 2004, www.cs.princeton.edu/~felten/rip; transcript, www.ischool.utexas.edu/~i312co/copyright/felten.html.
A Princeton University professor of computer science and public affairs discusses how digitization changes the game for media and communications businesses.

Gilroy, Angele A., "Access to Broadband Networks: The Net Neutrality Debate," *Congressional Research Service*, April 15, 2011, http://opencrs.com/document/R40616.
An analyst for Congress' nonpartisan research office describes the history and legislative, regulatory, judicial and commercial issues involved in the debate over net neutrality.

Thierer, Adam, "Net Neutrality Regulation & the First Amendment," The Technology Liberation Front, Dec. 9, 2009, http://techliberation.com/2009/12/09/net-neutrality-regulation-the-first-amendment.
A libertarian telecommunications analyst argues that net-neutrality advocates turn the Constitution's First Amendment on its head when they argue that in order to preserve freedom of speech Internet service providers (ISPs) must treat all content the same. In fact, he writes, net-neutrality rules would assault ISPs' free-speech rights by substituting government rules for ISPs' own editorial judgment.

For More Information

Chilling Effects Clearinghouse, www.chillingeffects.org. University-supported website that provides information on and analysis of digital-media issues.

Electronic Frontier Foundation, 454 Shotwell St., San Francisco, CA 94110-1914; 415-436-9333; www.eff.org. Advocates for media-related civil liberties, such as open access to the Internet.

Federal Communications Commission, 445 12th St., S.W., Washington, DC 20554; 888-225-5322; www.fcc.gov. Federal agency that sets rules for communications industries.

Motion Picture Association of America, 1600 Eye St., N.W., Washington, DC, 20006; 202-293-1966; www.mpaa .org. Trade association that represents the major American motion-picture and television studios.

Progress and Freedom Foundation, www.pff.org. Archives of a free-market-oriented think tank that analyzed digital media policy until October 2010.

Public Knowledge, 1818 N St., N.W., Suite 410, Washington, DC 20036; 202-861-0020; www.publicknowledge.org. Advocates for net neutrality and copyright policies that balance the interests of intellectual-property owners and media consumers.

Recording Industry Association of America, 1025 F St., N.W., 10th Floor, Washington, DC 20004; 202-775-0101; www.riaa.com. Trade association that represents major music-recording companies.

Technology Information Front, techliberation.com. Website of commentary by libertarian analysts that opposes government regulation of the Internet.

10

Internet and Media

Carol Kaufmann

Protestors outside of the Federal Communications Commission headquarters in May 2014 call for the commission to maintain "net neutrality," the policy that gives all websites equal access to the Internet.

Getty Images/Bloomberg

The most pressing issue confronting Internet service providers, content providers and end users revolves around the concept of net neutrality — the idea that all data on the Internet should be treated equally and that service providers can't favor, or provide faster service, to certain websites. The Federal Communications Commission (FCC), the courts and Congress have waded into this complicated regulatory terrain and — not surprisingly — created a firestorm of controversy.

It began in January, when a federal appeals court ruled that content providers, such as Amazon and Netflix, could pay service providers such as Verizon or Comcast for faster Internet access to their websites.[1] The decision invalidated most of the "open Internet order" adopted by the FCC in 2010.[2]

That order was the FCC's first attempt to maintain net neutrality by forbidding big cable and DSL providers from blocking or slowing Internet traffic. The court ruled the FCC didn't have that authority, but did give the regulatory body a general power to regulate the Internet. This opened the door to the possibility of a two-tiered system: a fast lane for big companies that can afford to pay for faster speeds, and a slower lane for all others. Since then, the FCC has scrambled to create a new regulatory role for itself that will stand up in court.[3]

This spring, FCC Chairman Tom Wheeler proposed new regulations that critics say would maintain the practice of allowing large content providers to pay for faster Internet speeds.[4] When

Getty Images/Bloomberg/Andrew Harrer

David Frederick, a lawyer for Aereo Inc., speaks to reporters outside the Supreme Court, with Chet Kanojia, chief executive officer of Aereo, left, and Brenda Cotter, Aereo's general counsel, right. The court ruled in June 2014 that the company's technology violated copyright laws.

these proposed rules were released for comment in May, critics pounced. Groups such as the American Civil Liberties Union (ACLU) argue that giving large companies access to faster speeds would doom small websites and allow large, well-funded corporate ones to monopolize the Web.[5]

Members of Congress have joined the debate. This summer, Democrats introduced the Online Competition and Consumer Choice Act, which would force the FCC to ban fast lanes for large content providers. Although it would not give the FCC new powers, the measure's passage would show strong support for a "neutral Internet" that favors no one.[6]

Patrick Leahy, D-Vt., held a field hearing on the act in July.[7] The controversy will come to a head this winter after the FCC's public comment period ends and the new regulations come up for more discussion and a final FCC vote.

TV Industry

The stakes are just as high for television's future. The industry is struggling to adapt as many viewers move away from watching live content on cable and broadcast channels and watch more programs on the Internet.

But the broadcast networks scored a big victory when the Supreme Court on June 25 ruled in their favor in one of the first challenges to their control of the airwaves. The company Aereo had been recording broadcast content by using a tiny antenna that works like TV rabbit ears did decades ago. Aereo's antenna receives shows and stores them in the cloud. Paying subscribers could log in, choose to watch live TV or stream saved content.[8]

Aereo was available in a number of large U.S. cities and, not surprisingly, the broadcast networks didn't like it, so they sued Aereo, claiming it was violating copyright protection on their program content. In *American Broadcasting Cos., Inc. et. al. v. Aereo, Inc.,* the Supreme Court justices found that there was little difference between Aereo and the cable companies that pay more than $3 billion annually for the right to rebroadcast network content.

Aereo had argued that it used the Internet in the same way consumers do: by storing programs and documents in the cloud to watch or read them when they want. The court disagreed, which leaves the future of Aereo very much in doubt. After the ruling, the company announced it was pausing operations, but in a July letter to a lower court judge, Aereo argued that it could resume business if it is legally treated as a cable company.[9]

Despite the Aereo ruling, broadcast networks and content providers of all kinds are fighting for eyeballs (and thus, advertising dollars) as viewers abandon appointment viewing — sitting down in front of the television to watch a program live at its designated broadcast time — in favor of watching content on their own schedules, via their video recorders or by downloading the programs from the Internet onto their computers or mobile devices. This trend has been a big boost for streaming services such as Hulu, Netflix and Amazon Prime. A study released in April by the marketing firm Millward Brown, an international company based in New York, is the first quantitative evidence that Americans are spending more screen time on their phones than in front of the television.[10]

Advertising Innovations

Advertisers are also working to adapt to the digital world, trying innovative ways to get their products in front of consumers in the online marketplace. Google AdWords — a

CHRONOLOGY

2010

December Federal Communications Commission (FCC) adopts the Open Internet Order, attempting to keep large Internet and DSL providers from blocking or slowing internet traffic.

2012

February Aereo Inc. launches a service that allows subscribers to watch live and delayed broadcast content on devices with an Internet connection.

March 1 U.S. broadcasters, including Fox, Univision and PBS, sue Aereo in federal court, claiming copyright infringement.

2013

January California and Illinois join four other states banning employers from demanding employees' social media passwords. . . . U.S. Federal Trade Commission closes antitrust investigation of Google, finding no violation of U.S. laws, but European antitrust inquiry continues. . . . Facebook begins rolling out tool that searches for people by such criteria as hometown, hobbies and "likes."

February FTC asks mobile industry to build better privacy safeguards into software and smartphone apps.

March U.S. copyright chief asks Congress to enact comprehensive copyright reform for the digital era.

April *Cleveland Plain Dealer* newspaper announces plans to cut home delivery to three days a week, expand Internet presence. . . . Fox CBS and Univision threaten to

become cable channels if they can't stop free transmission of their programming over the Internet. Electronic Frontier Foundation asks Washington state Supreme Court to give text messages the same privacy protections as phone calls.

2014

January U.S. Court of Appeals for the D.C. Circuit strikes down FCC's Open Internet Order in *Verizon v. FCC*.

February Comcast and Time Warner Cable announce proposed $45.2 billion merger.

March Millward Brown, an international brand management firm, releases study showing that Americans are spending more screen time on their smartphones than in front of the television.

April Supreme Court hears arguments in *American Broadcasting Cos. v. Aereo*. . . . Netflix CEO Reed Hastings announces his opposition to proposed Comcast-Time Warner merger.

May FCC Chairman Tom Wheeler proposes new net neutrality regulations for the Internet in an attempt to create a regulatory role for the FCC that will stand up in court.

June Supreme Court rules against Aereo; company pauses operations.

July Sen. Patrick Leahy, D-Vt., holds field hearing on the Online Competition and Consumer Choice Act, which would force the FCC to ban a two-tiered Internet system.

Late 2014 Comment period ends on new FCC rules proposed in May; the regulations come up for a vote in the FCC.

service through which companies pay for their advertising to pop up alongside general Google searches — is the primary source of Google's revenue.[11] In April Google announced new changes to AdWords that tighten its restrictions on advertising alcohol, tobacco, firearms and adult content.[12]

Another way for advertisers to reach consumers is through native advertising — ads that mimic the content on certain websites. Native ads are usually seen as sponsored content on popular social media websites such as Facebook, BuzzFeed and Twitter, where they appear alongside the postings of users and friends.[13] While budgets for native ads have seen double-digit growth in the past few years, this year marked the first time native ads appeared on *The New York Times'* website, which until January had refused to post advertising in its editorial space.[14] The decision to host native ads created some ethical questions about how readers can tell the difference between journalism and ads. *The Times'* solution was to send viewers who clicked on an ad for Dell Computers, for instance, to a separate section of *The Times'* website that is clearly labeled as an advertisement. Nonetheless, journalists continue to express concern about this type of advertising, fearing the ads allow companies to purchase access to readers in ways they couldn't before.[15]

Cable Merger

The proposed merger of two of the largest cable TV corporations could also affect how consumers watch television and interact online. In February, Comcast offered $45 billion for Time Warner Cable. If approved, the merger would result in a company that controls about 30 percent of paid TV subscribers, a huge market share.[16] That translates to more than 30 million cable subscribers, and as many broadband consumers.[17] But critics and some analysts worry about the influence such a mega-corporation would have. Critics say the resulting company could corner the cable and broadband market and have too much influence on the future of content delivery by controlling the viewing options for a significant number of consumers. The other concern is that the merger could set cable market rates simply because no other companies would be big enough to compete.[18]

The deal is subject to approval by the FCC and either the Federal Trade Commission (FTC) or Department of Justice.[19]

Netflix CEO Reed Hastings took an aggressive stance against the merger in his April letter to shareholders, saying it would give the new company access to "over 60 percent of U.S. broadband households, . . . with most of those homes having Comcast as the only option for truly high-speed broadband."[20] Comcast responded that Netflix's opposition is "about improving Netflix's business model by shifting costs that it has always borne to all users of the Internet and not just to Netflix customers."[21] Congress has held hearings on the matter, and the agencies involved are still investigating the proposed merger.

— Carol Kaufmann is a freelance writer living in the Washington, D.C., area.

NOTES

1. Edward Wyatt, "Rebuffing F.C.C. in 'Net Neutrality' Case, Court Allows Streaming Deals," *The New York Times*, Jan. 14, 2014, http://tinyurl.com/on355l3.

2. "D.C. Circuit Strikes Down Net Neutrality Rules, Affirms FCC Has Limited Authority to Regulate Broadband," Edwards Wildman Client Advisory, January 2014, http://tinyurl.com/qbaldej.

3. Tom Wheeler, "Finding the Best Path Forward to Protect the Open Internet," Official FCC Blog, April 29, 2014, http://tinyurl.com/o4jp52j.

4. "Tell the FCC: Preserve Net Neutrality!," ACLU Action, April 25, 2014, http://tinyurl.com/mljcaew.

5. *Ibid.*

6. "Senator Leahy and Congresswoman Matsui Introduce Landmark Net Neutrality Legislation," Sen. Patrick Leahy press release, June 17, 2014, http://tinyurl.com/jvmbnbt.

7. "Vermonters Urge Washington To Support An Open Internet," Sen. Patrick Leahy press release, July 1, 2014, http://tinyurl.com/pxpsxem.

8. Kyle Chayka, "What the Aereo Decision Means for You," *The Daily Beast*, June 25, 2014, http://tinyurl.com/mqsa8c8.

9. "American Broadcasting Companies, Inc. v. Aereo, Inc.," *SCOTUSblog*, June 25, 2014, http://tinyurl.com/l2bumby; Chet Kanojia, "A letter to our consumers," Aereo Inc., undated, http://tinyurl.com/826sxyd; and Eriq Gardner, "Aereo Lays Out New Survival Strategy in Letter to Judge," *The Hollywood Reporter*, July 9, 2014, http://tinyurl.com/mdouvec.

10. Greg Sterling, "Study Confirms Smartphones Now #1 Screen, Beating TV," *MarketingLand*, March 20, 2014, http://tinyurl.com/nyh3avd.

11. "2014 Financial Tables," Google Inc., undated, http://tinyurl.com/2wbmxne.

12. Larry Kim, "4 Things You Need to Know About Google's New AdWords Policies," *The Wordstream Blog*, June 17, 2014, http://tinyurl.com/q7nudye; and "AdWords policies," Google, undated, http://tinyurl.com/lx4wvga.

13. "Native Advertising," Sharethrough Inc., 2014, http://tinyurl.com/ldhmfee.

14. Aaron Taube, "Here's The New York Times' First Ever Native Ad," *Business Insider*, Jan. 8, 2014, http://tinyurl.com/knm72se.

15. Brian Braiker, "Andrew Sullivan on native ads: Journalism has surrendered," *Digiday*, May 7, 2014, http://tinyurl.com/qzjp5ot.

16. Liana B. Baker, "Comcast takeover of Time Warner Cable to reshape U.S. pay TV," Reuters, Feb. 13, 2014, http://tinyurl.com/oyth94o.

17. Cecilia Kang, "Comcast, Time Warner agree to merge in $45 billion deal," *The Washington Post*, Feb. 13, 2014, http://tinyurl.com/k5qakj8.

18. *Ibid*.

19. David Goldman, "Comcast deal to face antitrust hurdles," CNN Money, Feb. 13, 2014, http://tinyurl.com/nekggvq.

20. Brian Solomon, "Why Netflix Stands Alone Against The Comcast-Time Warner Merger," *Forbes*, April 22, 2014, http://tinyurl.com/lf6loz9.

21. Todd Spangler, "Comcast: Netflix's Opposition to Time Warner Cable Deal Is About Shifting Costs To All Broadband Users," *Variety*, April 21, 2014, http://tinyurl.com/luznvkj.

11

Big Data and Privacy

Tom Price

Actor Kunal Nayyar wears Google glasses to the 65th Annual Primetime Emmy Awards in Los Angeles on Sept. 22, 2013. Part of the big data revolution, the glasses contain a computer that can take pictures, respond to voice commands, search the Internet and perform other functions. Along with the nonstop collection of data come concerns about loss of privacy.

From *CQ Researcher*,
October 25, 2013

When Peter Higgs and François Englert won the Nobel Prize for physics this month, they were honored for a theory they published nearly a half-century ago but was not confirmed until March.

Higgs, of Scotland's University of Edinburgh, and Englert, of Belgium's Université Libre de Bruxelles (Free University of Brussels), had independently theorized that matter obtains mass from an unknown energy field that permeates the universe. Higgs suggested it is composed of an undiscovered subatomic particle, which became known as the Higgs boson. To confirm the theory, scientists needed to find that particle.

They finally succeeded largely with the help of so-called big data — the collection and analysis of enormous amounts of information by supercomputers, often in real time. Physicists analyzed trillions of subatomic explosions produced at the European Organization for Nuclear Research's Large Hadron Collider, a 17-mile circular underground tunnel that crosses the border between Switzerland and France. There, protons are fired at each other at nearly the speed of light, shattering them into other subatomic particles, including the Higgs.[1]

To analyze the results of those collisions, scientists needed computing capability that was "of larger scale and faster than ever before," says Joe Incandela, a University of California, Santa Barbara, physics professor who led one of the two collider teams searching for the Higgs. The collider can generate up to 600 million

Big Data Reveals Sources of Racist Tweets

Geographers at Humboldt State University in Arcata, Calif., used big data to create an interactive "Geography of Hate" map revealing where racist Twitter traffic originated. Hot spots predominated in the Midwest, South and Northeast, often in rural areas.

Where Most Racist Tweets Originated, June 2012–April 2013

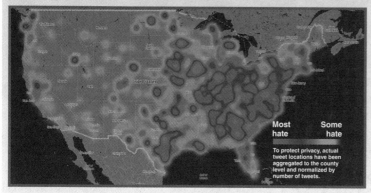

Source: Monica Stephens, "Geography of Hate," Humboldt State University, http://users.humboldt.edu/mstephens/hate/hate_map.html#

medical conditions; correlations among illnesses, their causes and potential cures; and the mapping of the human genome.

Big data also is a boon to businesses, which use it to conduct consumer marketing, figure out when machines will break down and reduce energy consumption, among other purposes. Governments mine big data to improve public services, fight crime and track down terrorists. And pollsters and political scientists use it to analyze billions of social media posts for insights into public opinion.

Even humanities scholars are embracing big data. Historians tap big data to gain new perspectives on historical figures. Other scholars use it to study literature. In the past, researchers investigating literary trends might read 10 books and conclude that "these books from this era show us how literature is different" from another era, says Brett Bobley, director of the National Endowment for the Humanities Office of Digital Humanities. "Today, a researcher could study thousands of books and look at how language changes over time, how the use of gender changes, how spelling changes."

Uses of big data involve businesses, governments, political organizations and other groups vacuuming up massive amounts of personal information from cell phones, GPS devices, bank accounts, credit-card transactions, retail purchases and other digital activities. The data often are gleaned from search engines, social networks, email services and other online sources. The mountains of information compiled in this manner — and the way they are analyzed and put to use — generate much of the criticism of big data, particularly after former NSA computer specialist Edward Snowden revealed in June that the agency has been collecting Americans' telephone and email records, and *The New York Times* revealed that the Drug Enforcement Administration had ordered AT&T to hand over vast amounts of records about its customers' telephone and computer usage.[3]

collisions per second, and the teams' servers can handle 10 gigabytes* of data a second.[2]

The search for the Higgs boson is just one of a vast array of discoveries, innovations and uses made possible by the compilation and manipulation of big data. The explosively emerging field could radically advance science, medicine, social science, crime-fighting and corporate business practices. But big data is controversial because of its potential to erode individual privacy, especially in the wake of recent revelations that the National Security Agency (NSA) is collecting massive amounts of personal information about Americans and others around the world. Critics want privacy controls on big data's use, while proponents say its benefits outweigh its risks.

Big data has led to cutting-edge medical discoveries and scientific breakthroughs that would have been impossible in the past: links between genetic traits and

*A gigabyte is 1 billion bytes. A byte is eight bits. A bit is one action of a computer switch. A byte commonly is equivalent to a single alphanumeric character.

Most Americans View Data Collection Negatively

More than half of Americans polled in May and June said the massive collection and use of personal information by government and business have a "mostly negative" impact on privacy, liberty and personal and financial security.* The polling was done just before former National Security Agency computer specialist Edward Snowden in June revealed widespread NSA domestic spying. Fewer than 40 percent of the respondents see the use of big data as "mostly positive." Fewer than half trust how the government uses their personal data, and nearly 90 percent support the so-called "right to be forgotten."

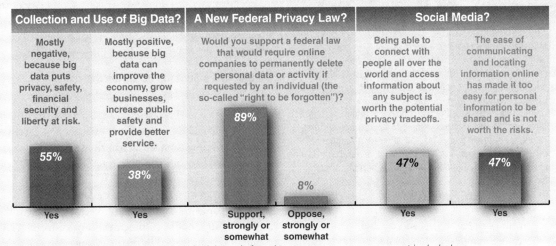

What is your viewpoint on . . .

Collection and Use of Big Data?		A New Federal Privacy Law?		Social Media?	
Mostly negative, because big data puts privacy, safety, financial security and liberty at risk.	Mostly positive, because big data can improve the economy, grow businesses, increase public safety and provide better service.	Would you support a federal law that would require online companies to permanently delete personal data or activity if requested by an individual (the so-called "right to be forgotten")?		Being able to connect with people all over the world and access information about any subject is worth the potential privacy tradeoffs.	The ease of communicating and locating information online has made it too easy for personal information to be shared and is not worth the risks.
55%	**38%**	**89%**	**8%**	**47%**	**47%**
Yes	Yes	Support, strongly or somewhat	Oppose, strongly or somewhat	Yes	Yes

Note: Totals do not add to 100 because don't know/refused to answer responses are not included.

* *Pollsters contacted 1,000 people by telephone between May 29–June 2, 2013.*

Source: *"Allstate/National Journal/Heartland Monitor* Poll XVII," June 2013, www.theheartlandvoice.com/wp-content/uploads/2013/06/HeartlandTopline-Results.pdf

"I don't really want to live in a total surveillance state where big brother knows everything I do and has all that information at its fingertips," says John Simpson, privacy project director for Consumer Watchdog, a consumer advocacy organization in Santa Monica, Calif. Sen. Jay Rockefeller, D-W.Va., has introduced a measure to allow Internet users to prohibit websites from collecting any of their personal information except when needed to provide a requested service to that person. Even then, the identity of the user would have to be kept secret or the information would have to be deleted after the service was performed. The bill awaits action in the Senate Committee on Commerce, Science and Transportation.[4]

Big data differs from old-fashioned data partly in the massive volume of the information being collected. But other distinctions exist as well. Big data computers often crunch vast amounts of information in real time. And they can reach beyond structured databases — such as a company's customer list — to make sense of unstructured data, including Twitter feeds, Facebook posts, Google searches, surveillance-camera images and customer browsing sessions on Amazon.com.

As a result, Internet platforms, such as Facebook or Google, act as big data "sensors," gathering information about people just as a thermometer gathers temperature information. In addition, Internet-connected optical,

Getty Images/John Moore

Police at New York City's counterterrorism center monitor more than 4,000 security cameras and license plate readers in the Financial District and surrounding parts of Lower Manhattan. Vast amounts of data are collected and stored by police departments and other government agencies. For example, law enforcement agencies store photos taken by cameras mounted on patrol cars and on stationary objects. Governments store photos made for driver's licenses and other identification documents. Many images are stored indefinitely and can now be searched with facial-recognition technology across multiple databases.

electronic and mechanical sensors are being installed in ever-increasing numbers and locations.

Viktor Mayer-Schonberger and Kenneth Cukier offer striking illustrations of the size of the data being collected — and the speed with which the volume of that information is growing — in their 2013 book *Big Data: A Revolution that Will Transform How We Live, Work, and Think.* If all the world's data were distributed among everyone on Earth, they write, each person would have 320 times more information than existed in third-century Egypt's Alexandria Library. If today's information were stored on stacks of compact disks, the stacks would stretch from Earth to the moon five times.

In 2000, only one-fourth of the world's information was stored digitally. Today 98 percent is, and the amount of digital data is doubling every two to three years, according to Mayer-Schonberger, a professor at Oxford University's Internet Institute, and Cukier, data editor of *The Economist.*[5] According to IBM, 90 percent of the world's data has been created in the last two years, and that information is growing by 2.5 quintillion bytes each day.[6] (A quintillion is 1 followed by 18 zeroes.)

For example, rapidly improving telescopes linked to powerful computers and the Internet are doubling the world's compilation of astronomical data each year and making it available to astronomers around the globe. Until it suffered a major malfunction in May, the Kepler Space Telescope, for instance, measured the light of 170,000 stars every 30 minutes in search of changes indicating the presence of planets, according to Alberto Conti, a scientist for the Space Telescope Science Institute at Johns Hopkins University.[7]

As advances in technology relentlessly expand big data's capabilities, here are some questions that scientists, business executives, privacy advocates and government officials are debating:

Do big data's benefits outweigh the risks?

Mario Costeja was shocked when a Google search on his name returned an 11-year-old Spanish newspaper notice about a financial transgression. Costeja, a Spaniard, had become delinquent on social security contributions, creating a debt that landed him in legal trouble in 1998 but that he had long since paid.

In a case still pending, Costeja asked a court to order the newspaper to remove the notice from its online archives and Google to block the notice from search results. The court ruled in the newspaper's favor, but the Google ruling remains undecided.[8]

Costeja's plight reveals a key drawback to big data: Once something enters an online database, it can be impossible to erase. Before digital databases and powerful search engines, the newspaper notice that Costeja encountered in 2009 would have existed only as a yellowed clipping in the newspaper's "morgue," or perhaps been buried in microfilm or old newspapers stored in a few libraries.

But with today's search engines capable of instantly exploring every database connected to the Internet, old transgressions can be found by anyone with a computer connection. And polls indicate that people are concerned about losing control of information once it gets collected and stored.

Of 1,000 Americans surveyed this year, 55 percent perceive a "mostly negative" impact from the collection and use of personal information. Two-thirds complain they have little or no control over information collected about them. Three-fifths believe they can't correct erroneous data. Conducted for the Allstate insurance company and *National Journal*, and just before the NSA domestic spying became public, the poll found that only 48 percent of Americans trust how governments, cell-phone companies and Internet providers use that information.[9]

Simpson of Consumer Watchdog says big data can harm individuals, especially if the information is erroneous or used to draw incorrect conclusions. Organizations can collect information from a variety of sources, then use it to "put together a profile about you that potentially could be used against you," he says. Analysis might conclude, for example, that "you're probably a health risk because you go to all these sites about losing weight, and we can see you're buying too much booze.

"Similarly, you can slice and dice the data you get from the Web and other sources and produce something that might be used to determine whether you should get a job, whether you should get a loan, or what rate you have to pay if you get the loan."

With sophisticated enough analysis, organizations might "red-line people," just as neighborhoods, suggests Jules Polonetsky, executive director and co-chair of the Future of Privacy Forum, a Washington-based think tank. Such "Web-lining," as some are calling it, can cause people to pay more for health insurance if they have traits associated with certain illnesses, he explains, or a person's credit rating could be affected by his Facebook friends' financial histories.

Those are "probabilistic predictions that punish us not for what we have done, but what we are predicted to do," said Mayer-Schonberger, the Oxford professor.[10]

But Jeff Jarvis, a City University of New York journalism professor who writes frequently about big data, says critics focus too much on the negatives while ignoring the positives. For example, while many deplore facial recognition technology as an invasion of privacy that can empower stalkers and other predators, Jarvis explains, "facial recognition technology also can be used to find lost children or people on Alzheimer's alert or criminals or terrorists."

And despite the negative attitudes toward big data uncovered by the Allstate/*National Journal* survey, some poll respondents saw value in the technology. Nearly half said the privacy tradeoffs are a fair price for being able to connect with people around the world and access information about almost any subject within seconds. More than two-thirds said the collection and analysis of information about them would likely lead them to receive more information about interesting products and services and better warnings about health risks. Nearly two in five said big data could enable government and business officials to make better decisions about expanding businesses, improving the economy, providing better services and increasing public safety.[11]

Scientists in Boston, for example, are using probabilistic predictions to try to prevent suicide. Funded by the federal government's Defense Advanced Research Projects Agency, the scientists are monitoring social media and text postings by volunteers who are active-duty military personnel or veterans. The scientists' computers watch for keywords associated with suicide in an effort to create an automated system that will alert caregivers, relatives or friends when suicide-linked expressions are observed.[12]

The Financial Industry Regulatory Authority — a self-regulating body for the securities industry — has turned to big data to catch up with the rapid technological changes occurring in financial markets. In August 2012, the agency employed software that scans trading activity for patterns that indicate suspicious practices. Results led the agency to launch 280 investigations by July 2013.[13]

Is big data speeding the erosion of privacy?

Security technologist Bruce Schneier, who has declared that "the Internet is a surveillance state," is doubtful about protecting privacy in the era of big data.

"If the director of the CIA can't maintain his privacy on the Internet," Schneier said, "we've got no hope."[14]

Schneier, a fellow at Harvard Law School's Berkman Center for Internet and Society, was referring to David Petraeus, who stepped down as director of the spy agency last November as his extramarital affair with former military intelligence officer Paula Broadwell was becoming public. The couple — presumably experts in covert actions — had taken steps to conceal their relationship. To avoid blazing email trails, they left messages to each other in the draft folder of a shared Gmail account. And when Broadwell sent threatening emails to a woman she thought was a rival for Petraeus' attention, she used a fake identity and accessed the Internet from hotel networks rather than her home. But big data tripped them up.[15]

Analyzing email metadata — addresses and information about the computers and networks used by the senders (but not message content) — the FBI traced Broadwell's threatening messages to several hotels. From hotel records, they found one guest who had stayed at those hotels on the dates the emails were sent: Broadwell.[16]

Combining Internet data with offline data occurs constantly across the globe, as companies build dossiers on their customers to offer personalized products and services and to target advertising or sell the information to others.

"This is ubiquitous surveillance," Schneier said. "All of us [are] being watched, all the time, and that data [are] being stored forever. . . . It's efficient beyond the wildest dreams of George Orwell," whose novel *1984* introduced the world to the all-seeing "Big Brother."[17]

Internet users voluntarily post photos of themselves and their friends on social media. Surveillance cameras take photos and videos of people in public and private places. Police departments store photos taken by cameras mounted on patrol cars and on stationary objects. Governments store photos made for driver's licenses and other identification documents. Some police cruisers are equipped with devices that enable remote searches of photo databases. Many of those images are stored indefinitely and can now be searched with facial-recognition technology across multiple databases.

Phone companies store call records, and mobile phone companies store records of where phones were used. Analysis of those records can reveal where a phone was at any time, down to a specific floor in a specific building.[18]

Big-data companies say they protect the identities of individuals behind the data. But scientists say even "anonymized" phone records — those with users' names removed — can reveal identities.

Many phone numbers are listed in public directories. Researchers at the Massachusetts Institute of Technology (MIT) and Belgium's Université Catholique de Louvain discovered that they could identify anonymized cell phone users 95 percent of the time if they knew just four instances of when and where a phone was used.[19] Companies' privacy policies also can be meaningless if

they accidentally release information or if their business partners don't honor the policies.

For example, due to a computer bug, Facebook allowed unauthorized people to access the phone numbers and email addresses of 6 million users and nonusers between mid-2012 and mid-2013. The social network admitted that it had been secretly compiling data about users from sources beyond Facebook and had been gathering information about nonusers as well.[20]

In 2010, the network had admitted that many third-party applications available through Facebook were collecting data on users and that the apps' makers were passing the information on to advertisers and tracking companies, contrary to Facebook's stated policy. Some also were collecting and distributing information about the app-users' friends.[21]

Such revelations have left many Americans worried about their privacy. In the Allstate/*National Journal* poll, 90 percent of Americans said they have less privacy than previous generations, and 93 percent expect succeeding generations to have even less.[22] An 11-nation survey by Ovum, a London-based business and technology consulting firm, found that two-thirds of respondents would like to prevent others from tracking their online activities.[23]

"Everything we do now might be leaving a digital trail, so privacy is clearly on the way out," says David Pritchard, a physics professor at MIT who studies teaching effectiveness by mining data gathered during massive open online courses (MOOCs), which MIT and other universities offer for free over the Internet.[24]

By recording and analyzing students' keystrokes, Pritchard can see what page of an online textbook they viewed, for how long and what they did before and after that. He can also see who participated in the course's online forum. Comparing such study habits with performance on tests will enable him to "figure out what tools students use to get problems right or wrong," he says. But he is quick to note that he obtains students' permission to monitor their keystrokes for the study.

While many people value their personal privacy, he says, "We're going to have to work a lot harder to maintain some aspects of it."

Others say concerns about big data speeding the loss of privacy are overblown.

Patrick Hopkins, a philosopher who focuses on technology, advocates a pragmatic approach. "We need to get realistic about privacy in the information age. This notion of privacy being an inalienable right is recent," says Hopkins, who chairs the Millsaps College Philosophy Department in Jackson, Miss., and is an affiliate scholar with the Institute for Ethics and Emerging Technologies, an international organization based in Hartford, Conn., that studies technology's impact on society. "It's not in the Constitution. It's not in the French Declaration of Rights," he says, referring to the "Declaration of the Rights of Man and of the Citizen," adopted by the French National Assembly in 1789.[25] "I'm only worried about privacy if there's something that's going to harm me."

"These days, I know if I drive down a street I will be monitored," says Hopkins. "That does not bother me. There's no harm to me, and I might benefit" if surveillance catches a criminal.

Similarly, he's not bothered by the government mining big data in search of terrorists. "Asking if you're willing to give up your privacy for security is a false dilemma," Hopkins says. "It's not like you have 100 percent of one and zero percent of the other. I would be willing to give up a bit of privacy for security."

Citing surveys showing that young people are less worried about privacy than their elders, Mike Zaneis, senior vice president for public policy at the Interactive Advertising Bureau, a New York-based trade association for the online advertising industry, says, "It's not because they don't care about privacy. It's that they understand the value of the exchange, and they are willing to give up more information as long as they are receiving some benefit."

Andreas Weigend — former chief scientist at Amazon .com who now directs Stanford University's Social Data Lab — says many people's notion of privacy is "romantic" and "belongs in the Romantic Age. We need to understand a 21st-century notion of privacy, and it can't be what some people wish was the case."

Health Care Providers, Employers Most Trusted to Protect Data

Consumers said they trusted doctors, hospitals and employers the most to handle individuals' personal data responsibly, according to a poll taken in late May and early June. Political parties, the media and social media websites were trusted the least. The poll was conducted just before Edward Snowden's revelations that the National Security Agency has been spying on private citizens.

How much do you trust these groups or people to use information about you responsibly?

	A great deal/some	Not much/ not at all
Health care providers	80%	20%
Employers	79	19
Law enforcement	71	28
Insurance companies	63	35
Government	48	51
Cell phone/Internet providers	48	50
Political parties	37	61
Media	29	69
Social media sites	25	70

Note: Totals do not add to 100 because don't know/refused to answer responses are not included.

Source: "Allstate/*National Journal/Heartland Monitor* Poll XVII," June 2013, www.theheartlandvoice.com/wp-content/uploads/2013/06/Heartland Topline-Results.pdf

Should the federal government strengthen its regulation of big data?

Privacy advocates and big data businesses both view Europe as instructive in debates about government regulation — but in different ways. Many privacy advocates want the United States to adopt Europe's stronger regulatory approach, and business advocates want Europe to become more like the less-regulated U.S.

The United States has laws that protect certain kinds of data, such as financial and medical records, while all European countries have broad right-to-privacy laws. For example, many European countries require

Getty Images/Burda Media/Sean Gallup

Jeff Jarvis, a City University of New York journalism professor, says critics focus too much on the negatives of big data while ignoring the positives. While many deplore facial recognition as an invasion of privacy that can empower stalkers, the technology also can be used to find lost children, as well as criminals or terrorists, he says.

organizations to obtain permission before collecting information about an individual and allow those individuals to review and correct the data.[26] Last year, the United Kingdom forbade online organizations from tracking individuals' Web activities without consent. And the European Union (EU) is considering regulations that would apply to all 28 member states.[27]

Zaneis, of the Interactive Advertising Bureau, says U.S. residents' privacy is guarded adequately by the laws regulating data gathered for specific purposes, including protecting children's online privacy.

The Federal Trade Commission is charged with protecting Americans' privacy, Zaneis says, and the marketing industry has an effective self-regulatory regime. For instance, he says, more than 95 percent of online advertising companies participate in a program that enables consumers to prevent their information from being sent to third parties for marketing purposes.

That's not good enough for many privacy advocates, however. Individuals should not have to opt out of data-collection programs, they argue. Instead, they contend, companies should have to ask individuals to opt in. Critics also maintain that self-regulation is inadequate.

"This isn't something the free market can fix," argued Schneier, of Harvard's Berkman Center for Internet and Society. "There are simply too many ways to be tracked" by electronic devices and services. "And it's fanciful to

expect people to simply refuse to use [online services] just because they don't like the spying."[28]

Supporting Schneier's contention, Forrester Research reported that just 18 percent of Internet users set their browsers to ask organizations not to track their online activities — a request the organizations can, however, legally ignore.[29] Zaneis says most people don't change their default settings — whether to opt in or opt out.

Privacy advocates want to do much more than block information to third parties. In the United States, Consumer Watchdog supports Sen. Rockefeller's proposal to enable individuals to ban Internet sites from collecting information about them online except when the collection is necessary to provide a requested service to the individual.[30]

Americans "should be empowered to make their own decisions about whether their information can be tracked and used online," Rockefeller said when he introduced the legislation in March.[31] Consumer Watchdog's Simpson would extend that right to all data, not just online data. "You as a consumer should have the right to control what data companies collect from you and how to use it, and if you don't want them to collect it you ought to be able to say 'no,' " he argues. "Right now, we have this insidious ecosystem that's based on spying on people without them really knowing who's looking and what they're doing and that they're putting together giant dossiers on you."

Americans also want the right to remove online data that they don't like. Fully 89 percent of respondents in the Allstate/*National Journal* survey supported this so-called "right to be forgotten."[32]

Computer scientist Jaron Lanier — an early developer of virtual reality technology who currently works at Microsoft Research — suggests that people should be paid for their data. The value of that personal information probably runs to $1,000 or more a year, he estimates. Companies already compensate consumers for the information they give up when using club cards at grocery stores and other retailers, by giving them "member" discounts, he notes.

But it's not just the value of online advertising that counts, Lanier says. "What if someone's medical records are used to make medicine?"

Zaneis argues that Internet users already are compensated via the services they receive free on the Web.

"Ninety-nine percent of the content and services that we consume online are offered for free to the consumer," he says. "They're paid for by the consumer giving something. Sometimes it's data. Sometimes it's their eyeballs on advertising." If many people blocked access to their data, he says, it could kill the Internet as we know it.

Stanford's Weigend calls that "the underlying concept [of the Internet]: Give to get."

Jim Harper, director of information policy studies at the Cato Institute, a libertarian think tank in Washington, says government should stay out of the debate. "I put the burden on people to maintain their own privacy," he says. "It's the responsibility of Web users to refuse interaction with sites they don't want to share information with, to decline to share cookies," which are small files that a website places in a computer's browser to identify the browser on future visits. "Don't post online things you don't want posted online.

"When you walk outside your house, people can see you and gather what they learn and use it any way they want. I think the online world has to work the same."

Jarvis, the journalism professor, argues that Internet users have an obligation to share their information with the websites they use. "You have an impact on the sustainability of the properties whose content you're getting," he says. By blocking your information, "you are choosing to make yourself less valuable to that property. You've made this moral choice not to support these sites." News media, which are struggling to survive as it is, would be especially damaged if readers withheld information needed to make ads more valuable, he adds.

Jarvis does not argue against all privacy laws, such as those protecting medical records, for instance. And he favors extending first-class mail's privacy guarantee to all private communication. But "we should not be legislating according to technology, because [technology] can be used for good as well as bad," he continues. "We shouldn't regulate the gathering of information" online because that would be restricting what people can learn and know. "We should regulate behavior we find wrong."

Jarvis also calls for respecting "publicness" as well as privacy. "The right to be forgotten has clear implications for the right to speak," he says. "If I take a picture of us together in public, and you, say, force me to take that picture down [from the Internet], you're affecting my speech."

Deciding how to regulate big data is "quite complex," Hopkins, of Millsaps College, says. "We need to recognize what the costs would be."

BACKGROUND

Data Overload

In mid-1945, as World War II slogged toward its end, Vannevar Bush, director of the U.S. Office of Scientific Research and Development and later a key advocate for creation of the National Science Foundation, conjured up the future of big data and the so-called Information Age.

In a lengthy essay in *The Atlantic* entitled "As We May Think," Bush wrote:

"The summation of human experience is being expanded at a prodigious rate, and the means we use for threading through the consequent maze . . . is the same as was used in the days of square-rigged ships. . . . The investigator is staggered by the findings and conclusions of thousands of other workers — conclusions which he cannot find time to grasp, much less to remember."[33]

Technology probably will solve the problem, Bush suggested, hinting at future inventions such as desktop computers, search engines and even Google's new Glass headgear, eyeglasses that contain a computer that can take pictures, respond to voice commands, search the Internet and perform other functions as wearers move from place to place. Bush envisioned a miniature automatic camera that a researcher would wear on his forehead to make microfilm photographs as he worked. He also predicted that one day a microfilmed *Encyclopaedia Britannica* could be kept in a matchbox and a million books in part of a desk.

Perhaps most striking, he suggested the personal computer and the search engine in a desk-sized contraption he dubbed the "memex." "On the top are slanting translucent screens, on which material can be projected for convenient reading," he wrote. "There is a keyboard, and sets of buttons and levers." Inside are all those compressed documents, which the memex user will call to a screen the way the brain remembers — through "association of thoughts" rather than old-fashioned indexing, as search engines do today.

Bush knew a great deal about data, having invented the differential analyzer — a mechanical computer for working

CHRONOLOGY

1960s–1995 *Development of Internet opens new ways to create and gather data.*

1967 Defense Department's Advanced Research Projects Agency (ARPA) funds research that leads to creation of the Internet.

1969 UCLA and Stanford Research Institute establish the first ARPANET link.

1980 Computer scientist I. A. Tjomsland declares that data expand to fill the available storage space. . . . Phrase "big data" is first used in print.

1989 Internet opens to general public.

1991 Commercial activities are allowed on Internet for first time. . . . Point-and-click navigation invented. . . . World Wide Web name coined.

1992 Bill Clinton-Al Gore presidential/vice presidential campaign makes Internet an effective political tool.

1994 First White House website launched.

1995 Library of Congress puts legislative information online.

1997–Present *Big data becomes major force through use of search engines, social media and powerful computers.*

1998 Google search engine goes online. . . . American information scientist Michael Lesk predicts increase in storage capacity will mean no data will have to be discarded.

2000 A quarter of the world's stored data has been digitized.

2002 LinkedIn business-networking site launched.

2003 More data created this year than in all previous human history.

2004 "TheFacebook" is launched for Harvard undergraduates. . . . Flickr photo-sharing platform goes online. . . . Walmart is storing 460 terabytes (460 trillion bytes) of data about its customers. Other large retailers also are storing large amounts of data.

2005 YouTube video-sharing site created.

2006 Twitter goes online. . . . Facebook opens to anyone age 13 or over.

2007 AT&T begins giving police access to U.S. phone records dating back to 1987 for use in criminal investigations.

2008 Sen. Barack Obama uses big data to win presidential election.

2010 Super-secret National Security Agency (NSA) processes 1.7 billion intercepted communications daily. . . . Google discloses that cars taking street-level photos for Google maps also captured information from unprotected Wi-Fi networks. . . . Conservative activists turn Tea Party into political force using social media.

2012 Google fined $22.5 million for bypassing browser privacy controls. . . . U.S. government launches $200 million Big Data Research and Development Initiative to advance technologies needed to analyze and share huge quantities of data. . . . Financial Industry Regulatory Authority taps big data to uncover suspicious securities practices. . . . NSA begins building $2 billion facility for processing big data. . . . Federal Trade Commission (FTC) begins inquiry into data brokers' activities. . . . Social media activism helps prolong Republican presidential nominating process. . . . Obama intensifies use of big data to win re-election.

2013 After strong negative customer reaction, Facebook temporarily backs away from plan to utilize users' pictures and postings in ads. . . . Google fights lawsuit over reading Gmail content. . . . Survey reveals 55 percent of Americans see "mostly negative" impact from collection of big data about people. . . . FTC official says people should be able to restrict use of their data in commercial databases. . . . Acxiom data broker lets people correct and delete information in its database. . . . Tapping Medicare's big data, U.S. government reports what 3,000 U.S. hospitals charge for 100 different treatments. . . . Ninety percent of world's data have been created in the last two years, and data are growing by 2.5 quintillion bytes daily. . . . Ninety-eight percent of world's data are stored digitally.

complex equations — in 1931. But he was far from the first to bewail data overload and to seek ways of addressing it. The Old Testament book of Ecclesiastes laments: "Of making many books there is no end; and much study is a weariness of the flesh."[34] The first-century AD philosopher Lucius Annaeus Seneca grumbled that "the abundance of books is distraction."[35] By the 15th century, Europeans felt crushed under information overload after German printer Johannes Gutenberg invented mechanical printing with moveable type — the printing press.

"Suddenly, there were far more books than any single person could master, and no end in sight," Harvard University historian Ann Blair observed of Europe after Gutenberg's invention around 1453.

Printers "fill the world with pamphlets and books that are foolish, ignorant, malignant, libelous, mad, impious and subversive," the Renaissance humanist Erasmus wrote in the early 16th century, "and such is the flood that even things that might have done some good lose all their goodness. . . . Is there anywhere on earth exempt from these swarms of new books?"[36]

The products rolling off the presses did not overwhelm scholars for long, however. New technologies were developed to address the challenges the presses had created: public libraries, large bibliographies, bigger encyclopedias, compendiums of quotations, outlines, indexes — predecessors of *Reader's Digest*, *Bartlett's Familiar Quotations* and Internet aggregators, Blair noted.

That always happens, the late science historian Derek Price said, because of the "law of exponential increase," which he propounded while teaching at Yale University in 1961. Scientific knowledge grows exponentially because "each advance generates a new series of advances," he said.[37]

Before the Internet and powerful computers made today's big data possible, some scholars saw it coming. In 1980, computer scientist I. A. Tjomsland proclaimed a corollary to Parkinson's First Law. (Work expands so as to fill the time available for its completion.) "Data expands to fill the space available," he said, because "users have no way of identifying obsolete data," and "the penalties for storing obsolete data are less apparent than are the penalties for discarding potentially useful data."[38]

In 1997, while working on an electronic library project called CORE (Chemical Online Retrieval Experiment),

information scientist Michael Lesk predicted that advances in storage capacity would create unlimited space for data.

"In only a few years, we will be able [to] save everything — no information will have to be thrown out, and the typical piece of information will never be looked at by a human being," said Lesk, who now is a professor of library and information science at Rutgers University.[39]

Birth of Big Data

Technological advances often come about through government initiatives. For instance, the 1890 U.S. Census used machine-read punch cards for the first time to tabulate the results, enabling the complete census to be reported in one year instead of eight. That, according to *Big Data* co-authors Cukier and Mayer-Schonberger, was the beginning of automated data processing.[40]

In Vannevar Bush's time, government demand drove the development of computing machines in efforts to crack enemy codes during World War II. After the war, U.S. spy agencies sought ever-more-powerful technology to collect, store and process the fruits of their espionage.

By 2010, the NSA was processing 1.7 billion intercepted communications every day. In 2012, it began construction of a $2 billion facility in Utah designed to deal with the huge amounts of data it collects.[41]

U.S. national security concerns also drove the creation and initial development of the Internet. The Defense Advanced Research Projects Agency funded the efforts in order to facilitate information exchange among military research facilities. The first Internet link occurred when a University of California, Los Angeles, computer logged onto a Stanford Research Institute computer 360 miles away on Oct. 29, 1969.

Although the concept of an "information explosion" had been around since 1941, the phrase "big data" was used first by the late University of Michigan sociologist Charles Tilly in a 1980 paper for the university's Center for Research on Social Organization, according to the *Oxford English Dictionary.* "None of the big [social history] questions has actually yielded to the bludgeoning of the big-data people," Tilly wrote of historians using computers and statistics.[42]

The Internet didn't open to the general public until the late 1980s, when MCI Mail and CompuServe offered

Crunching Data Sheds New Light on History

"Big data allows us to ask questions that were not possible before."

Big data can be used for more than plumbing databases for consumer preferences about dish soap or spying on citizens' phone calls. Sometimes supported by grants from the National Endowment for the Humanities, scholars in history and literature, for example, are digging into new databases of old documents to reexamine common assumptions about authors and important historical figures.

Researchers at Stanford University, for instance, have discovered that England was much less important to French philosopher Voltaire and the French Enlightenment than was commonly thought.

Tapping into Oxford University's digitized collection of 64,000 letters written by 8,000 historical figures from the early 17th to mid-19th centuries, the Stanford team analyzed the letters' metadata — the names, addresses and dates, but not their content — and discovered little communication between Voltaire and the English.

Using big data "allows us to ask questions that were simply not possible to be asked in a systematic manner before, and to analyze our data in ways that would have been impossible or incredibly difficult to do," explains Dan Edelstein, a Stanford associate professor of French and history. The analysis of the Oxford papers "allowed me to see Voltaire's correspondence network in a new light and to formulate hypotheses that I probably would not have hit upon."

Similarly, Caroline Winterer, a Stanford history professor and director of the Stanford Humanities Center, and her colleagues probed the papers of Benjamin Franklin, collected by Yale University scholars beginning in 1954 and digitized with support from the Packard Humanities Institute, in Los Altos, Calif. Their findings challenged the perception of Franklin as a cosmopolitan figure, at least before 1763, when he returned to America after a six-year stay in England. Almost all of the letters Franklin received while in England were from England or America.[1]

Living in London made Franklin "a typical Anglo-Atlantic figure" rather than "an international man of mystery," Edelstein explains, because "the American colonies and England really had shared a culture at this time."

email services. The public's first full-service Internet access came through a provider called "The World" in 1989.

The early '90s saw the beginnings of commercial activity on the Internet and the coining of the term World Wide Web. The additions of point-and-click browsing and graphics increased the Internet's popularity.[43]

Data and Politics

During the 1992 presidential campaign, former Arkansas Gov. Bill Clinton and his running mate, Sen. Al Gore of Tennessee, turned the Web into a campaign tool, then launched the first White House website in 1994. In 1995, the Library of Congress started an online legislative information website — Thomas.gov — named after former President Thomas Jefferson, who sold his personal book collection to the library after the British burned Congress' original holdings during the War of 1812.

In 2003, Vermont Gov. Howard Dean scaled new heights in Internet campaigning by organizing supporters, publicizing campaign events and raising funds online. The efforts made him the most successful fundraiser in the history of the Democratic Party and enabled him to take an early lead in the campaign for the 2004 Democratic presidential nomination.

Dean's quest for the nomination failed. But four years later, Illinois Sen. Barack Obama took a quantum leap over Dean, winning the White House after raising a record $500 million online and making the Internet and big data an integral part of his campaign. Obama compiled more than 13 million email addresses, attracted a million-member audience for text messages, and created a 90-worker digital staff to contribute to communication, fundraising and grassroots organizing. He campaigned on Facebook, Twitter and YouTube, and even bought ads in video games.[44]

Mark McKinnon, an adviser to George W. Bush's 2000 and 2004 campaigns, described the Obama run as a "seminal, transformative race" that "leveraged the Internet in ways never imagined."[45]

Analyzing big data, however, does not replace traditional scholarship, Edelstein says. "To find out if you're on the right track, you need to contextualize your results and to interpret them, and that means being very familiar with your data and with the scholarship of your period. When you see England doesn't seem to be that important in Voltaire's map [of correspondence], that only means something if you already are familiar with certain scholarship about Voltaire that establishes England as an important place for him.

"What does it mean that you don't see a lot of letters there?" he asks. "It could mean he didn't care about England. It could mean he had other sources of information about England. Could it be we just lost the letters to England? You have to spend time in rare-books collections figuring out these questions." They concluded that "there's not really a good reason why more of the English letters would have been lost than his [other] letters."

Brett Bobley, who runs the national endowment's Office of Digital Humanities, says big data techniques greatly expand what humanities scholars can accomplish.

"Humanities scholars study books, music, art — and those very objects that they study are increasingly in digital format," he explains. "If you study the Civil War and you read old newspapers, now you can digitally access thousands and thousands of newspaper pages from the Civil

Computer analysis of letters received by Benjamin Franklin during a six-year stay in England challenged perceptions of the famed founding father as a cosmopolitan figure.

War era, and you can use digital tools to analyze the data in those newspapers far more than you could possibly read in your lifetime."

— *Tom Price*

[1]Claire Rydell and Caroline Winterer, "Benjamin Franklin's Correspondence Network, 1757-1763," Mapping the Republic of Letters Project, Stanford University, October 2012.

Two years later, conservative activists employed online social media to turn the Tea Party into a political force that helped Republicans take control of the U.S. House. In 2012, social media activism helped dark-horse candidates stay alive to prolong the 2012 Republican presidential nominating contest. But Obama — adding a robust social media presence to his big-data mix of information-collection, data-processing and Internet communication — won a second term.

Social media — now a major source of big data — emerged in the early 2000s, with the LinkedIn business networking site launching in 2003 and Facebook (first called TheFacebook) beginning to serve Harvard undergraduates in 2004. The Flickr photo-sharing platform went online in 2004 and the YouTube video-sharing site in 2005. Twitter launched in 2006, and Facebook opened to anyone 13 or older that same year.[46]

A decade earlier, Stanford University graduate students Larry Page and Sergey Brin began to build a search

engine. They went online in 1997 with the name Google, a play on the number googol, which is 1 followed by 100 zeroes. Page and Brin chose the brand to represent the massive challenge of trying to search the entire Internet.[47] Google became the most profitable Internet company on the *Fortune* 500 list by continually innovating and adding new products and services, such as the Google+ social media platform, Google Maps and the street-level and satellite photos that accompany the maps.[48]

It also stumbled into some significant controversies, such as when it was discovered that Google cars taking street-level photos in 2010 also were collecting information from unprotected Wi-Fi networks, including email addresses and passwords. The Federal Trade Commission (FTC) fined the company $7 million for improper data collection that Google said was unintentional.[49] Last year, the FTC fined Google another $22.5 million for bypassing privacy controls on Apple's Safari browser.[50]

In the days before electronic computers, keypunch operators entered data on machine-readable cards. The U.S. government used punch cards in 1890 to tabulate census results, enabling the complete results to be reported in one year instead of eight, which some scholars mark as the beginning of automated data processing.

While online businesses such as Google and Facebook are famous — or infamous — for their use of big data today, brick-and-mortar retailers have been mining customer data since before some online companies were born. By 2004, for example, Walmart had loaded 460 terabytes of customer data onto its computers — more than twice as much information as was then available on the Internet and enough to begin predicting consumer behavior "instead of waiting for it to happen," according to Linda Dillman, the company's chief information officer.[51]

Target, too, has collected vast amounts of information about its customers for years and uses it to focus its marketing. For example, having determined what products pregnant women frequently buy at which stage of pregnancy, the retailer can predict which of its customers are pregnant and send promotions to them precisely when they'd likely be interested in certain products.

The process can have unintended consequences, however, such as when an angry father demanded to know why Target was sending coupons for baby clothes to his teenage daughter, only to learn later that she was expecting.[52]

CURRENT SITUATION
Hunting Criminals

After a summer-long public focus on the National Security Agency's surveillance practices, September brought additional revelations about government spying — this time by domestic law enforcement agencies employing big data strategies, primarily to hunt for criminals.

The New York Times reported that since 2007 AT&T had given federal and local police access to U.S. phone records — including phone numbers, locations of callers and date, time and duration of the calls — dating back to 1987.[53] Under the federally funded program, called the Hemisphere Project, four AT&T employees are embedded in joint federal-local law enforcement offices in Atlanta, Houston and Los Angeles, the newspaper said. They tap into AT&T's database whenever they receive "administrative subpoenas" from the Drug Enforcement Administration. The data are used to investigate a variety of crimes, however, not just drug cases.

The AT&T database contains records of every call that passes through the company's switches, including those made by customers of other phone companies. The AT&T's database may be larger than the NSA's — which stores records of phone numbers, date, time and duration of almost all U.S. calls but deletes them after five years — and it grows by about 4 billion calls a day. Justice Department spokesman Brian Fallon said the project "simply streamlines the process of serving the subpoena to the phone company so law enforcement can quickly keep up with drug dealers when they switch phone numbers to try to avoid detection."

Officials said the phone records help them find suspects who use hard-to-trace throwaway cell phones. Daniel Richman, a former federal prosecutor who teaches law at

Columbia University, described the project as "a desperate effort by the government to catch up" with advancing cell-phone technology.

September also brought disclosures that the NSA surveillance looked at more Americans' records than had previously been reported. Documents released in a lawsuit revealed that, from May 2006 to January 2009, the NSA improperly revealed phone numbers, date, time and call duration information about Americans who were not under investigation. The NSA gave the results of database queries to more than 200 analysts from other federal agencies without adequately shielding the identities of the Americans whose records were revealed.

The agency also tracked phone numbers without establishing "reasonable and articulable suspicion" that the numbers were tied to terrorists, as was required by a federal court order that allowed the NSA data collection.[54]

'Reclaim Your Name'

Just as the Justice Department is trying to catch up with criminals using cell-phone technology, regulatory agencies are trying to keep up with the technology employed by industries they oversee. The Federal Trade Commission, for instance, is investigating how data brokers operate. Such companies collect information about people, then sell it to others.

The commission asked nine companies about the kind of information they gather, the sources of the information, what they do with it and whether they allow individuals to view and correct the information or to opt out of having their information collected and sold.[55]

In August, FTC Commissioner Julie Brill called on the data broker industry to adopt a "Reclaim Your Name" program, which would enable people to see their information stored in companies' databases, learn how the information is gathered and used, prevent companies from selling it for marketing purposes and correct errors.

The proposal would not allow individuals to demand that the companies erase the information. Nevertheless, Brill said, it would address "the fundamental challenge to consumer privacy in the online marketplace: our loss of control over our most private and sensitive information."[56]

One data broker is opening the curtain on some of its practices — perhaps to its detriment. Scott Howe, chief executive of Arkansas-based Acxiom Corp., announced in late August that people can visit a new website, aboutthedata.com, to see and even change some of the information Acxiom has collected about them. Site visitors can discover the sources of the data, correct errors, delete some information and even tell the company to stop collecting and storing data about them, though to do so they first must provide Acxiom with personal information, including their address, birth date and last four digits of their Social Security number.

Acxiom collects a wide range of information about some 700 million individuals worldwide, including contact and demographic information, types of products purchased, type and value of residence and motor vehicles and recreational interests.[57] It gathers the information from public records, directories, Internet activity, questionnaires and from other data-collection companies. Acxiom sells the information to companies, nonprofits and political organizations that use it in marketing, fundraising, customer service, constituent services and outreach efforts.

Howe acknowledged Acxiom is taking a risk by letting people review their information. They could falsify information about themselves, for instance. And, if a significant number asked to be deleted from the database, "it would be devastating for our business," he said. "But I feel it's the right thing to do."

Aboutthedata.com also could lead to new business opportunities, Howe added. In the future, the site might invite visitors to volunteer more information about themselves. And Acxiom could make its database more valuable by allowing visitors to specify what kinds of advertising they'd like to see.[58]

Others in the marketing industry disagree. Adopting Brill's proposals "would lead to more fraud and limit the efficacy of [marketing] companies," according to Linda Woolley, CEO and president of the Direct Marketing Association, a trade organization for the direct marketing industry.[59]

Big data companies also are clashing with Web browser producers who make it easier for Internet surfers to keep their information secret and prevent tracking of their online activities. Microsoft now ships Internet Explorer with its do-not-track feature turned on. Mozilla plans to ship new versions of its Firefox browser with a default setting to block third-party cookies, but it's still working out the details. Internet Explorer, Firefox and other browsers allow users to set other restrictions on cookies. Randall

From Yottabytes to Googolplexes: Big Data Explained

For some, it's "writing zeroes until you get tired."

The term big data showed up this year in an old-school database — the *Oxford English Dictionary*, which defined it as "data of a very large size, typically to the extent that its manipulation and management present significant logistical challenges; [also] the branch of computing involving such data."[1]

Big data's information databases are so massive they require powerful supercomputers to analyze them, which increasingly is occurring in real time. And big data is growing exponentially: The amount of all data worldwide is expanding by 2.5 quintillion bytes per day.

In addition to analyzing large, traditional databases, big-data practitioners collect, store and analyze data from unstructured databases that couldn't be used in the past — such as email messages, Internet searches, social media postings, photographs and videos. The process often produces insights that couldn't be acquired in any other way.

Analyses of big data can uncover correlations — relationships between things that may or may not establish cause and effect. Some analysts say the lack of clear cause and effect is a weakness, but others say mere correlations often are sufficient to inform decisions.

"Correlations are fine for many, many things," says Jeff Hawkins, cofounder of Grok, a company that makes software for real-time data analysis. "You don't really need to know the why . . . as long as you can act on it." For instance, he continues, "You don't really need to understand exactly why people consume more energy at 2 in the afternoon" in order to decide whether to buy or sell it at that time of the day. "If I'm just trying to make a better pricing strategy," the correlation is enough.

Databases are measured in "bytes," which describe the amount of computer action required to process them. A byte is eight bits. A bit is one action of a computer switch. A byte commonly is equivalent to a single alphanumeric character.

Discussing big data requires huge numbers with unfamiliar names, such as:

- **Quadrillion:** 1 followed by 15 zeroes.
- **Quintillion:** 1 followed by 18 zeroes.
- **Sextillion:** 1 followed by 21 zeroes.
- **Septillion:** 1 followed by 24 zeroes.
- **Terabyte:** 1 trillion bytes.
- **Yottabyte:** 1 septillion bytes.
- **Googol:** 1 followed by 100 zeroes (the inspiration for the Google search engine's name).

Rothenberg, president and CEO of the Interactive Advertising Bureau (IAB), called Microsoft's do-not-track decision "a step backwards in consumer choice." Because it is set by default, he said, it doesn't represent a consumer's decision.[60]

The digital advertising industry's code of conduct currently does not require companies to honor do-not-track signals, but the Digital Advertising Alliance established a committee in October to formulate a policy on do-not-track settings by early next year. The alliance is a consortium of six advertising industry trade groups.[61]

The IAB also charged that Mozilla's plan to block third-party cookies would disrupt targeted advertising.

"There are billions and billions of dollars and tens of thousands of jobs at stake in this supply chain," Rothenberg said.[62] Blocking the cookies would be especially damaging to small online publishers that depend on the cookies to sell ads to niche audiences, he added. "These small businesses can't afford to hire large advertising sales teams [and] can't afford the time to make individual buys across thousands of websites."[63]

Brendan Eich, Mozilla's chief technology officer, defended the planned cookie-blocking. "We believe in putting users in control of their online experience, and we want a healthy, thriving Web ecosystem, [and] we do not see a contradiction," he said.[64]

- **Googolplex:** 1 followed by a googol zeroes — that is, 1 followed by 100 zeroes 100 times.

Googol and googolplex exist primarily for mathematical amusement. The 9-year-old nephew of Columbia University mathematician Edward Kasner, Milton Sirotta, coined the terms. The boy defined googolplex as a 1 followed by "writing zeroes until you get tired," Kasner related in the 1940 book *Mathematics and the Imagination*, which he wrote with fellow mathematician James Newman.[2]

Other big data jargon includes:

- **Metadata:** Information about information. With email, for instance, metadata include the addresses, time sent, networks used and types of computers used, but not the message content.

Many who collect metadata — including companies and government investigative agencies — say they don't invade privacy because they don't collect the content or identify specific individuals. But critics say metadata can reveal a great deal about an individual. Analyzing records of phone calls between top business executives could suggest a pending merger, calls to medical offices could hint at a serious illness and records of reporters' communications might reveal the identity of confidential sources, according to mathematician Susan Landau, a former Sun Microsystems engineer and author of *Surveillance or Security? The Risks Posed by New Wiretapping Technologies.*[3]

- **Cookie:** A small file, inserted into a computer's browser by a website, which identifies the browser. Different kinds of cookies perform different functions. They can relieve users of the need to provide the same identification information each time they visit a website. Cookies also can track the browser's activities across the Internet. A visited website can allow another, unvisited website to place a cookie — which is called a third-party cookie — into a computer without the Web surfer's knowledge.

- **Do not track:** A request a browser can send to a visited website asking that the site not set a tracking cookie. The site can ignore the request.

- **The cloud:** Computing and computer storage capabilities that exist beyond the user's computer, often accessed through the Internet.

- **Opt in and opt out:** Telling a website that you do or don't want to do something. Online companies tend to prefer the opt-out system, because the Web surfer specifically has to request that a site not set a cookie or track a browser. Privacy advocates tend to prefer the opt-in system.

- **Analytics:** The process of finding insights in data.

— *Tom Price*

---

[1] *Oxford English Dictionary* (2013), www.oed.com/view/Entry/18833#e id301162177.

[2] Edward Kasner and James Newman, *Mathematics and the Imagination* (2001), p. 23; Eric Weisstein, "Edward Kasner (1878-1955)," *Eric Weisstein's World of Science*, Wolfram Research, http://scienceworld .wolfram.com/biography/Kasner.html.

[3] Jane Mayer, "What's the Matter with Metadata?" *The New Yorker*, June 6, 2013, www.newyorker.com/online/blogs/newsdesk/2013/06/ verizon-nsa-metadata-surveillance-problem.html.

Privacy advocates applauded. "This is a really good move for online consumers," said Jeff Chester, executive director of the Center for Digital Democracy, a consumer-privacy advocacy group in Washington.[65]

While spying and advertising by big data companies stir up controversies, many big-data accomplishments go unnoticed by the public. Because of super-speedy computers, enormous databases and powerful sensors, scientists, technicians, business managers and entrepreneurs daily push out the frontiers of science, business and daily life. Some are even pushing past databases — employing computers, sensors and software to collect and analyze data simultaneously.

Maximizing big data's benefits requires real-time analysis of information streamed from sensors, says Jeff Hawkins, cofounder of Grok, a company that has developed software to do just that. The data explosion is happening in part because of an increase in data sources, he says, noting that "pretty much everything in the world is becoming a sensor." Sensors are collecting data from buildings, motor vehicles, streets and all kinds of machinery, Hawkins says, and much of it needs to be analyzed immediately to be worthwhile.

"Data coming off a windmill might get (analyzed) every minute," Hawkins explains. "Server data might be every 10 seconds. Trying to predict pricing in some marketplace

Are new laws needed to prevent organizations from collecting online personal data?

YES
John M. Simpson
Director, Privacy Project,
Consumer Watchdog

Written for *CQ Researcher*, October 2013

Privacy laws simply have not kept pace with the digital age and must be updated to protect us as we surf the Web or use our mobile devices. People must be able to control what, or even whether, organizations collect data about them online.

Suppose you went to the library and someone followed you around, noting each book you browsed. When you went to a store, they recorded every item you examined and what you purchased. In the brick-and-mortar world, this would be stalking, and an obvious invasion of privacy.

On the Internet such snooping is business as usual, but that is no justification. Nearly everything we do online is tracked, often without our knowledge or consent, and by companies with whom we have no relationship. Digital dossiers may help target advertising, but they can also be used to make assumptions about people in connection with employment, housing, insurance and financial services — and for government surveillance.

Americans increasingly understand the problem. The Pew Research Center released a poll in September that found 86 percent of Internet users have taken steps online to remove or mask their digital footprints. Some 68 percent of respondents said current laws are not good enough to protect our online privacy.

So, what can be done? In February 2012 President Obama issued a report, *Consumer Privacy in a Networked World*, that called for a Consumer Privacy Bill of Rights that includes the right of consumers "to exercise control over what personal data companies collect from them and how they use it." He called for legislation to enact those rights. It is long past time to introduce and pass it.

All four major browsers can now send a "do not track" message to sites their users visit. However, companies are not required to comply, and most do not.

Sen. Jay Rockefeller, D-W.Va., has introduced a "do not track" bill that would require compliance. But with Congress mired in partisan gridlock, state-level "do not track" legislation — perhaps enacted through the ballot initiative process in a progressive state such as California — is another option.

Stopping Internet companies from tracking users online will not end online advertising or break the Internet, but it will force advertisers to honor our personal boundaries. A "do not track" mechanism would give consumers better control and help restore everyone's confidence in the Internet. That's a win-win for consumers and businesses alike.

NO
Jim Harper
Director, Information Policy Studies,
The Cato Institute

Written for *CQ Researcher*, October 2013

There is no question that Internet users should be able to stop organizations from collecting data about them. The question is how.

Most people think that new sets of legal rights or rules are the way to put Internet users in the driver's seat. Ideas range from mandatory privacy notices, to government regulation of data collection, to a radical new legal regime in which people own all data about them. But these ideas founder when it comes to administration, and their proponents misunderstand what privacy is and how people protect it.

We can learn about online privacy from offline privacy. In the real world, people protect privacy by controlling information about themselves. We have ornate customs and habits around how we dress; when and where we speak; what we say, write or type; the design of houses and public buildings; and much more. All of these things mesh our privacy desires with the availability of information about us. Laws, such as contract and property laws, back up the decisions we make to protect privacy.

Protecting privacy is harder in the online world. Many people do not understand how information moves online. And we don't know what consequences information sharing will have in the future. What's more, privacy interests are changing. (Make no mistake: People — even the young — still care about privacy.)

The way to protect privacy online is by using established legal principles. When Internet service providers, websites or email services promise privacy, the law should recognize that as a contract. The law should recognize that a person's data — contact information in a phone or driving data in a car — belong to that person.

Crucially, the government should respect the contracts and property concepts that are emerging in the online environment. This is not an entirely new idea. In a 1929 Fourth Amendment case, U.S. Supreme Court Justice Pierce Butler weighed in against wiretapping, saying, "The contracts between telephone companies and users contemplate the private use of the facilities employed in the service. The communications belong to the parties between whom they pass."

When Internet users learn what matters to them and how to protect it, the laws and the government should protect and respect their decisions. This is the best way to let Internet users stop organizations from collecting data about them.

Statement of Ownership
Management, Circulation

Act of Aug. 12, 1970: Section 3685,
Title 39, United States Code

Title of Publication: CQ Researcher. Date of filing: October 25, 2013. Frequency of issue: Weekly (Except for 3/29, 5/24, 7/5, 8/16, 8/23, 11/22, 12/20, 12/27/13). No. of issues published annually: 44. Annual subscription price for high schools: $977. Annual subscription price for college/university: $1,054. Location of known office of publication: SAGE Publications, Inc., 2455 Teller Road, Thousand Oaks, CA 91320. Names and addresses of publisher, editor and managing editor: Publisher, SAGE Publications, Inc., 2455 Teller Road, Thousand Oaks, CA 91320; Managing Editor, Thomas J. Billitteri, CQ Press, an imprint of SAGE Publications, Inc., 2300 N Street, N.W., Suite 800, Washington, D.C. 20037. Owner: SAGE Publications, Inc., McCune Inter-Vivos Trust, David F. McCune, 2455 Teller Road, Thousand Oaks, CA 91320. Known bondholders, mortgagees and other security holders owning or holding 1 percent or more of total amount of bonds, mortgages or other securities: None.

Extent and Nature of Circulation	Average Number of Copies of Each Issue During Preceding 12 months	Actual Number of Copies of Single Issue Published Nearest to Filing Date
A. Total number of copies printed (Net press run)	606	550
B. Paid and/or requested circulation		
(1) Paid/requested outside-county mail subscriptions stated on Form 3541	449	435
(2) Paid in-county subscriptions stated on Form 3541	0	0
(3) Sales through dealers and carriers, street vendors, counter sales, and other non-USPS paid distribution	0	0
(4) Other classes mailed through the UPPS	0	0
C. Total paid and/or requested circulation	449	435
D. Free distribution by mail (Samples, complimentary, and other free copies)		
(1) Outside-county as stated on Form 3541	0	0
(2) In-county as stated on Form 3541	0	0
(3) Other classes mailed through the USPS	0	0
E. Free distribution outside the mail (Carriers or other means)	0	0
F. Total free distribution	0	0
G. Total distribution	449	435
H. Copies not distributed	157	115
I. Total	606	550
J. Percent paid and/or requested circulation	100%	100%

or demand for energy use in a building might be hourly or every 12 to 16 minutes."

Grok never runs into privacy issues because "we don't save data," Hawkins says. "We look at data, we act upon it and we throw away the data."

OUTLOOK

'Internet of Things'

People familiar with big data agree that the amount of information processed and the speed and sophistication with which it can be analyzed will increase exponentially. Huge amounts of data will be generated by what many are calling the "Internet of Things" — the online linking of sensors installed on more and more inanimate objects.

"There are going to be billions of sensors," Grok's Hawkins says, "maybe hundreds of billions. We are going to see the world become more efficient, more reliable. In the future, your refrigerator should be able to say: I should precool myself by about 3 degrees so, when the price of electricity goes up in the afternoon, I don't have to run."

Google Chairman Eric Schmidt predicts that everyone on Earth will be online by the end of the decade, but he concedes that won't be all good. In a book written with Jared Cohen, director of Google Ideas, the company's think tank, Schmidt acknowledges that threats to privacy and reputation will become stronger.[66]

Noting the old advice to not write down anything you don't want to read on a newspaper's front page, Schmidt and Cohen broaden it to "the websites you visit, who you include in your online network, what you 'like,' and what others who are connected to you say and share." They foresee privacy classes joining sex-education classes in schools and parents sitting children down for "the privacy-and-security talk even before the sex talk."[67]

The Cato Institute's Harper expects the collection of personal data to increase indefinitely, but "there still remain huge amounts of information that people keep to themselves, and that's not going to change. From every thought that crossed your mind at breakfast to your reasons for watching the television programs you did tonight — all that personal information that's part of what gives your life meaning — nobody knows that unless you tell them."

Hopkins from Millsaps College says, "it will become easier and cheaper to find information out about people in ways that our laws and ancestors never conceived of," noting the threat to privacy that would occur if nefarious individuals [such as peeping Toms or thieves "casing a joint"] could own drones.[68]

"Courts and public policymakers are going to have to decide if we're going to try to limit technology to things you could have done in 1950 or 1750, or are we going to have to give up the notion that we could have the same kinds of privacy expectations that we had a century ago," Hopkins says. People probably will accept less privacy, he says, "because of the incredible ease of use and personal benefits" that come from sharing the data. "I suspect we'll just get used to it."

Zaneis, of the Interactive Advertising Bureau, also doesn't expect tighter data controls, because government can't keep up with the speed of technological advances. "There's going to be evolution and change at such a rapid pace that legislators and regulators can't keep pace," he says, contending that industry self-regulation will fill the gap.

Consumer Watchdog's Simpson concedes that privacy advocates won't get everything they want. "But I think we're going to see some serious protections put in place," he says, because the NSA revelations have generated "tremendous pushback" against privacy invasion.

But Polonetsky, of the Future of Privacy Forum, says, "Technology probably is going to solve this before policymakers do," citing how browser manufacturers are developing privacy protections for their users.

Similarly, Mark Little, the principal consumer analyst for the Ovum consulting firm, warns big data companies that they could run into "hurricane-force disruptions" of their data collection. "Marketers should not be surprised if more and more consumers look to alternative privacy ecosystems to control, secure and even benefit from their own data," he said.[69]

NOTES

1. For background, see Tom Price, "Globalizing Science," *CQ Global Researcher*, Feb. 1, 2011, pp. 53-78.

2. "Computing," European Organization for Nuclear Research, Http://home.web.cern.ch/about/computing.

3. For background, see Chuck McCutcheon, "Government Surveillance," *CQ Researcher*, Aug. 30, 2013, pp. 717-740.

4. "Bill Summary & Status, 113th Congress (2013-2014), S.418, All Congressional Actions," Library of Congress, http://thomas.loc.gov/cgi-bin/bdquery/D?d113:1:./temp/~bd9qWL:@@@X|/home/LegislativeData.php.

5. Viktor Mayer-Schonberger and Kenneth Cukier, *Big Data: A Revolution that Will Transform How We Live, Work, and Think* (2013); James Risen and Eric Lichtblau, "How the U.S. Uses Technology to Mine More Data More Quickly," *The New York Times*, June 9, 2013, p. 1, www.nytimes.com/2013/06/09/us/revelations-give-look-at-spy-agencys-wider-reach.html?_r=0.

6. Risen and Lichtblau, *ibid.*

7. Ross Andersen, "How Big Data Is Changing Astronomy (Again)," *The Atlantic*, April 19, 2012, www.theatlantic.com/technology/archive/2012/04/how-big-data-is-changing-astronomy-again/255917.

8. Juliette Garside, "Google does not have to delete sensitive information, says European court," *The Guardian*, June 25, 2013, www.guardian.co.uk/technology/2013/jun/25/google-not-delete-sensitive-information-court; Katherine Jacobsen, "Should Google be accountable for what its search engine unearths?" *The Christian Science Monitor*, June 25, 2013, www.csmonitor.com/Innovation/2013/0625/Should-Google-be-accountable-for-what-its-search-engine-unearths.

9. "New Poll Shows Americans Anxious About Privacy," Allstate/*National Journal/The Atlantic/Heartland Monitor* Poll, June 13, 2013, www.magnetmail.net/actions/email_web_version.cfm?recipient_id=615749555&message_id=2731423&user_id=NJG_NJMED&group_id=526964&jobid=14264751.

10. Farah Stockman, "Big Data's big deal," *The Boston Globe*, June 18, 2013, p.11, www.bostonglobe.com/opinion/2013/06/18/after-snowden-defense-big-data/7zH3HKrXm4o3L1HIM7cfSK/story.html.

11. "New Poll Shows Americans Anxious About Privacy," *op. cit.*

12. Vignesh Ramachandran, "Social Media Project Monitors Keywords to Prevent Suicide," *Mashable*, Aug. 20, 2013, http://mashable.com/2013/08/20/durkheim-project-social-media-suicide.

13. Dina ElBoghdady, "Wall Street regulators turn to better technology to monitor markets," *The Washington Post*, July 12, 2013, www.washingtonpost.com/business/economy/wall-street-regulators-turn-to-better-technology-to-monitor-markets/2013/07/12/ab188abc-eb25-11e2-aa9f-c03a72e2d342_story.html.

14. Bruce Schneier, "The Internet Is a Surveillance State," CNN, March 16, 2013, www.schneier.com/essay-418.html.

15. Max Fisher, "Here's the e-mail trick Petraeus and Broadwell used to communicate," *The Washington Post*, Nov. 12, 2012, www.washingtonpost.com/blogs/worldviews/wp/2012/11/12/heres-the-e-mail-trick-petraeus-and-broadwell-used-to-communicate.

16. Schneier, *op. cit.*

17. *Ibid.*

18. Risen and Lichtblau, *op. cit.*

19. Niraj Chokshi and Matt Berman, "The NSA Doesn't Need Much Phone Data to Know You're You," *National Journal*, June 6, 2013, www.nationaljournal.com/nationalsecurity/the-nsa-doesn-t-need-much-phone-data-to-know-you-re-you-20130605.

20. Gerry Shih, "Facebook admits year-long data breach exposed 6 million users," Reuters, June 21, 2013, www.reuters.com/article/2013/06/21/net-us-facebook-security-idUSBRE95K18Y20130621; Violet Blue, "Firm: Facebook's shadow profiles are 'frightening' dossiers on everyone," ZDNet, June 24, 2013, www.zdnet.com/firm-facebooks-shadow-Fprofiles-are-frightening-dossiers-on-everyone-7000017199.

21. Emily Steel and Geoffrey A. Fowler, "Facebook in Privacy Breach," *The Wall Street Journal*, Oct. 17, 2010, http://online.wsj.com/article/SB10001424052702304772804575558484075236968.html.

22. "New Poll Shows Americans Anxious About Privacy," *op. cit.*

23. Mark Little, " 'Little data': Big Data's new battle-ground," *Ovum*, Jan. 29, 2013, http://ovum.com/2013/01/29/little-data-big-datas-new-battleground.

24. For background, see Robert Kiener, "Future of the Public Universities," *CQ Researcher*, Jan. 18, 2013, pp. 53-80.

25. For background, see "Declaration of the Rights of Man and of the Citizens," "Lectures in Modern European Intellectual History," *The History Guide*, www.historyguide.org/intellect/declaration.html.

26. Bob Sullivan, " 'La difference' is stark in EU, U.S. privacy laws," MSNBC, Oct. 19, 2006, www.nbcnews.com/id/15221111/ns/technology_and_science-privacy_lost/t/la-difference-stark-eu-us-privacy-laws/#.UlxnkhDhDpc.

27. Thor Olavsrud, "EU data protection regulation and cookie law — Are you ready?" *ComputerworldUK*, May 24, 2012, www.computerworlduk.com/in-depth/security/3359574/eu-data-protection-regulation-and-cookie-law—are-you-ready.

28. Schneier, *op. cit.*

29. Natasha Singer, "A Data Broker Offers a Peek Behind the Curtain," *The New York Times*, Aug. 31, 2013, www.nytimes.com/2013/09/01/business/a-data-broker-offers-a-peek-behind-the-curtain.html?adxnnl=1&ref=natashasinger&adxnnlx=1378241984-ftuN93sEdSPgKXyXIEdZZw.

30. "Section-by-Section Summary of the Do-Not-Track Online Act of 2013," U.S. Senate Committee on Commerce, Science and Transportation, www.commerce.senate.gov/public/?a=Files.Serve&File_id=95e2bf27-aa9b-4023-a99c-766ad6e4cf12.

31. "Rockefeller Introduces Do-Not-Track Bill to Protect Consumers Online," Office of Sen. Jay Rockefeller, March 1, 2013, www.rockefeller.senate.gov/public/index.cfm/press-releases?ID=deb2f396-104e-46a0-b206-8c3d47e2eed3.

32. "New Poll Shows Americans Anxious About Privacy," *op. cit.*

33. Except when noted otherwise, information for this historical section was drawn from Uri Friedman, "Big Data: A Short History," *Foreign Policy*, November 2012, www.foreignpolicy.com/articles/2012/10/08/big_data; Gil Press, "A Very Short History of Big Data," *Forbes*, May 9, 2013, www.forbes.com/sites/gilpress/2013/05/09/a-very-short-history-of-big-data; Ann Blair, "Information overload, the early years," *The Boston Globe*, Nov. 28, 2010, www.boston.com/bostonglobe/ideas/articles/2010/11/28/information_overload_the_early_years/?page=1.

34. Ecclesiastes 12:12, Holy Bible: King James Version, University of Michigan Library Digital Collections, http://quod.lib.umich.edu/cgi/k/kjv/kjv-idx?type=DIV1&byte=2546945.

35. Blair, *op. cit.*

36. *Ibid.*

37. Press, *op. cit.*

38. *Ibid.*

39. Michael Lesk, "How Much Information Is There In the World?" 1997, www.lesk.com/mlesk/ksg97/ksg.html.

40. Mayer-Schonberger and Cukier, *op. cit.*, p. 22.

41. Jessica Van Sack, "Nothing to fear now, but soon . . ." *The Boston Herald*, June 11, 2013, p. 2.

42. *Oxford English Dictionary* (2013), www.oed.com/view/Entry/18833#eid301162177. Gil Press, "Big Data News: A Revolution Indeed," *Forbes*, June 18, 2013, www.forbes.com/sites/gilpress/2013/06/18/big-data-news-a-revolution-indeed.

43. For background, see Marcia Clemmitt, "Internet Regulation," *CQ Researcher*, April 13, 2012, pp. 325-348.

44. Tom Price, "Social Media and Politics," *CQ Researcher*, Oct. 12, 2012, p. 922.

45. For background, see Tom Price, "Social Media and Politics," *CQ Researcher*, Oct. 12, 2012, pp. 865-888.

46. For background, see Marcia Clemmitt, "Social Media Explosion," *CQ Researcher*, Jan. 25, 2013, pp. 81-104.

47. "Our history in depth," Google, www.google.com/about/company/history. For background, see David Hatch, "Google's Dominance," *CQ Researcher*, Nov. 11, 2011, pp. 953-976.

48. "Fortune 500, 2013," CNN Money, http://money.cnn.com/magazines/fortune/fortune500/2013/full_list/index.html?iid=F500_sp_full.

49. Brian Fung, "Google Street View's covert collection of consumers' Wi-Fi data in 2010," *National Journal*, June 21, 2013, www.nationaljournal.com/tech/

you-know-who-else-inadvertently-gathered-your-electronic-data-20130621.

50. Phil Rosenthal, "Deeper into data mine we go, privacy plundered," *Chicago Tribune*, Aug. 12, 2012, p. 1, http://articles.chicagotribune.com/2012-08-12/business/ct-biz-0812-phil-privacy—20120812_1_apple-s-safari-google-privacy.

51. Constance L. Hays, "What Wal-Mart Knows About Customers' Habits," *The New York Times*, Nov. 14, 2004, www.nytimes.com/2004/11/14/business/yourmoney/14wal.html?_r=1&pagewanted=all&position=.

52. Mayer-Schonberger and Cukier, *op. cit.*, p. 57.

53. Scott Shane and Colin Moynihan, "Drug Agents Use Vast Phone Trove, Eclipsing N.S.A.'s," *The New York Times*, Sept. 1, 2013, www.nytimes.com/2013/09/02/us/drug-agents-use-vast-phone-trove-eclipsing-nsas.html?_r=1&.

54. Ellen Nakashima, Julie Tate and Carol Leonnig, "NSA broke privacy rules for 3 years, documents say," *The Washington Post*, Sept. 11, 2013, p. 1.

55. "FTC to Study Data Broker Industry's Collection and Use of Consumer Data," Federal Trade Commission, Dec. 18, 2012, www.ftc.gov/opa/2012/12/databrokers.shtm.

56. Julie Brill, "Demanding transparency from data brokers," *The Washington Post*, Aug. 15, 2013, www.washingtonpost.com/opinions/demanding-transparency-from-data-brokers/2013/08/15/00609680-0382-11e3-9259-e2aafe5a5f84_print.html.

57. Adam Tanner, "Finally You'll Get To See The Secret Consumer Dossier They Have On You," *Forbes*, June 25, 2013, www.forbes.com/sites/adamtanner/2013/06/25/finally-youll-get-to-see-the-secret-consumer-dossier-they-have-on-you/.

58. Singer, *op. cit.*

59. Linda Woolley, letter to FTC Commissioner Julie Brill, Aug. 19, 2013, http://blog.thedma.org/2013/08/19/dma-responds-to-op-ed-attacking-commercial-data-use.

60. "'Do Not Track' Set to 'On' By Default in Internet Explorer 10 — IAB Response," Interactive Advertising Bureau, May 31, 2012, www.iab.net/InternetExplorer.

61. Al Urbanski, "New Do Not Track Group Makes Progress in San Francisco," *Direct Marketing News*, Oct. 11, 2013, www.dmnews.com/new-do-not-track-group-makes-progress-in-san-francisco/article/315995.

62. Craig Timberg, "Firefox moves forward with tracking blocker," *The Washington Post*, June 20, 2013, p. 14.

63. "IAB Accuses Mozilla of Undermining American Small Business & Consumers' Control of Their Privacy with Proposed Changes to Firefox," Interactive Advertising Bureau, March 12, 2013, www.iab.net/about_the_iab/recent_press_releases/press_release_archive/press_release/pr-031213?gko=2dce8.

64. Brendan Eich, "C is for Cookie," Mozilla, May 16, 2013, https://brendaneich.com/2013/05/c-is-for-cookie.

65. Timberg, *op. cit.*

66. Eric Schmidt and Jared Cohen, *The New Digital Age: Reshaping the Future of People, Nations and Business* (2013).

67. Doug Gross, "Google chairman: 6 predictions for our digital future," CNN, April 23, 2013, www.cnn.com/2013/04/23/tech/web/eric-schmidt-google-book.

68. For background, see Daniel McGlynn, "Domestic Drones," *CQ Researcher*, Oct. 18, 2013, pp. 885-908.

69. Little, *op. cit.*

BIBLIOGRAPHY

Selected Sources

Books

Jarvis, Jeff, *Public Parts*, Simon & Schuster, 2011.
A journalism professor who writes frequently about big data and the Internet makes the case for sharing, which he calls "publicness," and putting aside certain notions of privacy.

Lanier, Jaron, *Who Owns the Future?* Simon & Shuster, 2013.
A Microsoft Research computer scientist argues that people should be paid for the information they share online and off.

Mayer-Schonberger, Viktor, and Kenneth Cukier, *Big Data: A Revolution That Will Transform How We Live, Work, and Think,* **Houghton Mifflin Harcourt, 2013.**

An Oxford professor (Mayer-Schonberger) and *The Economist*'s data editor examine big data's impact on the world, highlighting both its opportunities and threats.

Morozov, Evgeny, *To Save Everything, Click Here: The Folly of Technological Solutionism,* **Public Affairs, 2013.**

A self-described "digital heretic" challenges the utopian visions of "digital evangelists" and warns that many fruits of cutting-edge technology come with high costs.

Smolan, Rick, and Jennifer Erwitt, eds., *The Human Face of Big Data,* **Against All Odds Productions, 2012.**

Combining photographs, illustrations and essays, this remarkable coffee-table book shows big data at work in the real world, from obtaining new insights into health care costs to compiling detailed statistics from every Major League Baseball pitch.

Articles

Blair, Ann, "Information overload, the early years," *The Boston Globe,* **Nov. 28, 2010, www.boston.com/ bostonglobe/ideas/articles/2010/11/28/information_ overload_the_early_years/?page=1.**

A Harvard historian explains how since biblical times humankind has felt oppressed by too much data, then learned to cope.

Egan, Erin, "Proposed Updates to our Governing Documents," Facebook, Aug. 29, 2013, www.face book.com/notes/facebook-site-governance/proposed- updates-to-our-governing-documents/101531 67395945301.

Facebook officials announce plans for a revised privacy policy that says users automatically permit their posts and photos to be used in ads. Thousands of users express outrage.

Scola, Nancy, "Obama, the 'big data' president," *The Washington Post,* **June 14, 2013, www.washing tonpost.com/opinions/obama-the-big-data-presi dent/2013/06/14/1d71fe2e-d391-11e2-b05f- 3ea3f0e7bb5a_story.html.**

A journalist who covers technology and politics documents President Barack Obama's embrace of big data in both his campaign and his administration.

Stahl, Lesley, "A Face in the Crowd: Say goodbye to anonymity," CBS News, May 19, 2013, www .cbsnews.com/2102-18560_162-57599773.html.

In a report on facial-recognition surveillance, the veteran CBS correspondent walks into a store, is recognized by a surveillance camera and, moments later, her cell phone receives a text with a special deal offered by the store, based on her shopping history and Facebook "likes."

Reports and Studies

"Big Data, Big Impact: New Possibilities for International Development," World Economic Forum, 2012, www3.weforum.org/docs/WEF_TC_ MFS_BigDataBigImpact_Briefing_2012.pdf.

An organization best known for annually convening international leaders in Davos, Switzerland, explores how analyzing big data could predict crises, identify needs and help devise ways to aid the poor.

"Kenneth Cukier and Michael Flowers on 'Big Data,'" Foreign Affairs Media Conference, Council on Foreign Relations, May 9, 2013, www.cfr.org/ health-science-and-technology/foreign-affairs-media- conference-call-kenneth-cukier-michael-flowers-big- data/p30695.

The Economist's data editor (Cukier) and New York City's chief analytics officer discuss how the city uses big data to improve services, as well as some downsides to the massive collection and analysis of information.

"Self-Regulatory Principles for Online Behavioral Advertising," American Association of Advertising Agencies, American Advertising Federation, Association of National Advertisers, Direct Marketing Association, Interactive Advertising Bureau, July 2009, www.aboutads.info/resource/download/seven- principles-07-01-09.pdf.

Five advertising industry trade associations join together to issue "consumer-friendly standards" for collecting information online and using it to target advertising to individuals. The organizations said they would report uncorrected violations to government agencies and the public.

Rainie, Lee, Sara Kiesler, Ruogu Kang and Mary Madden, "Anonymity, Privacy, and Security Online," Pew Research Center, Sept. 5, 2013, www.pewinternet.org/Reports/2013/Anonymity-online.aspx.

A survey by the nonpartisan think tank finds that most Americans want the ability to be anonymous online, but many don't think it's possible.

For More Information

Berkman Center for Internet and Society at Harvard University, 23 Everett St., 2nd Floor, Cambridge, MA 02138; 617-495-7547; www.cyber.law.harvard.edu. Research center that studies aspects of the Internet, including commerce, governance, education, law, privacy, intellectual property and antitrust issues.

Consumer Watchdog, 2701 Ocean Park Blvd., Suite 112, Santa Monica, CA 90405; 310-392-0522; www.consumerwatchdog.org. National consumer advocacy organization that promotes privacy of personal data.

Future of Privacy Forum, 919 18th St., N.W., Suite 901, Washington, DC 20006; 202-642-9142; www.futureofprivacy.org. Think tank that convenes discussions, publishes papers and advocates policies to protect privacy of data on and offline.

Institute for Ethics and Emerging Technologies, Williams 119, Trinity College, 300 Summit St., Hartford, CT 06106; 860-297-2376; 860-297-2376; www.ieet.org. Think tank that studies and debates ethical implications of new technologies.

Interactive Advertising Bureau, 116 East 27th St., 7th Floor, New York, NY 10016; 212-380-4700; www.iab.net. Trade association for companies that sell online advertising; promulgates an industry code of conduct.

Pew Internet & American Life Project, 1615 L St., N.W., Suite 700, Washington, DC 20036; 202-419-4500; www.PewInternet.org. Research center that conducts frequent public opinion surveys as it studies how the Internet affects Americans.

12

Media Violence

Christina L. Lyons

Nelba Márquez-Greene and Jimmy Greene embrace on the one-month anniversary of the death of their 6-year-old daughter, Ana Grace, who was among 20 children and six teachers killed by Adam Lanza at Sandy Hook Elementary School in Newtown, Conn., on Dec. 14, 2012. Because Lanza, 20, and other high-profile school shooters reportedly have been fans of violent video games, such incidents have reignited a perennial debate about whether violence in the media can cause aggressive behavior.

From *CQ Researcher*,
February 14, 2014

Teenage girls flooded movie theaters last fall to watch the PG-13-rated "Hunger Games: Catching Fire," the second in a series based on a tale of kids killing kids.

"It's a heady and disturbing concept," one reviewer said of the theme. "As executed here, it's often a bloody and gruesome one, as well."

But another movie critic wrote: "Keenly aware of his adolescent audience, the director always manages to look away before the violence becomes too icky." The critic commended screenwriters for toning down the graphic violence of Suzanne Collins' series, which two years before had appeared on the American Library Association's list of the 10 most "challenged" books — those that parents or others most frequently sought to have pulled from library shelves.[1]

A month earlier, Syracuse University administrators came under fire for inviting Florida rapper Ace Hood to perform during the school's annual Orange Madness event launching the basketball season. Local parents who typically take their children to the community celebration were hesitant because Hood's lyrics include such lines as, "Know I keep that .45, turn you into Cabbage Patch/Hit you right between the eyes and leave you like an alley rat."[2]

In November, gamers rushed to buy "Grand Theft Auto V," the latest edition of a popular video game about three violent criminals who commit burglaries and corporate crimes, gun down police officers and drive over civilians. Using their mobile devices, enthusiasts can play from anywhere —"at the bar, on the beach, on the toilet," one ad said. "This is the future, we're almost sure of it."[3]

TV Rating System Called Inconsistent

Television broadcast programs have long been considered less violent than cable shows. But a recent report found that some broadcast programs are more violent than cable shows and that the TV ratings system does not consistently warn of explicit adult content. For example, NBC's "Revolution," a post-apocalyptic drama rated as appropriate for viewers 14 and older, contained more violence than any of the cable shows studied that were aimed at mature audiences, defined as viewers over 17.

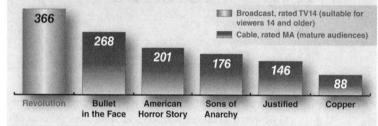

Total Acts of Violence on "Revolution" (TV-14) vs. Adult-Rated Cable Shows
(during four hours of programming, 2012–13 season)

Broadcast, rated TV14 (suitable for viewers 14 and older)
Cable, rated MA (mature audiences)

Revolution: 366
Bullet in the Face: 268
American Horror Story: 201
Sons of Anarchy: 176
Justified: 146
Copper: 88

Source: "An Examination of Violence, Graphic Violence and Gun Violence in the Media (2012-2013)," Parents Television Council, December 2013, http://w2.parents tv.org/main/Research/Studies/CableViolence/vstudy_dec2013.pdf

Rapid technological advances allow today's consumers, including children, to easily access — anywhere, anytime — media content that some critics say depicts unprecedented levels of blood and gore and moral depravity. Mass shootings such as the 2012 Sandy Hook Elementary School massacre in Newtown, Conn., repeatedly have prompted lawmakers, parents, researchers and educators to question whether such content contributes to aggressive behavior among youths and whether the entertainment industry's self-regulation is sufficient to protect young consumers from the effects of media violence. Moreover, as shown by reviews of "Hunger Games," many observers have differing opinions on the acceptable level of violence in young viewers' entertainment.

Researchers disagree on whether media violence can lead young people to mimic violent behavior, a lack of consensus that industry officials have cited in defending their entertainment products. "There's no medical or scientific research showing that video games cause people to be violent in real life — even our most ardent critics agree

with that," Dan Hewitt, vice president of media relations and event management for the Entertainment Software Association (ESA), which represents video game producers, said in an e-mail.

But some researchers contend that studies have long shown that exposure to media violence at least correlates with aggressive behavior. "Right now, the research is so overwhelmingly consistent that there are negative effects on the tendency to behave violently — [causing] desensitization and lowering of empathy — [that] it's a shame we are still fighting this battle," says Joanne Cantor, a professor emeritus of communications and outreach director for the Center for Communication Research at the University of Wisconsin–Madison.

Concerns about media violence are hardly new. In the 1930s children watched movies, listened to radio thrillers and read comic books — all of which sparked alarms among community leaders worried about rising juvenile crime rates. By the 1980s, studies increasingly examined television dramas and musical lyrics for violent content, while story creators and some psychologists defended such entertainment for helping children overcome fears.

Besides watching television, today's children use computers, tablets and smartphones to access movies, books, the Internet, video games and music — at any time. Children ages 8 to 18 consume, on average, 10 hours and 45 minutes per day when the simultaneous use of multiple devices is taken into account. By contrast, in the 1930s, children were exposed to 10 hours of media per week.[4]

The Parents Television Council (PTC), which monitors prime-time television shows and PG- and G-rated movies for violent content, said that because of the ubiquity of portable media devices a great deal of children's television consumption today occurs "outside the watchful eye of a parent." In a special report released in December, the organization complained that the increasingly graphic nature of today's TV violence is "as alarming as the volume of violence." The report cited examples such as child molestation, rape, mutilation, disfigurement, dismemberment, graphic killings or injuries by gunfire and stabbings, cannibalism and burning flesh. And the most graphic violence airs when children were more likely to be watching, said the report.[5]

Moreover, the report said, parents can no longer assume that broadcast shows are less violent than cable shows or rely on TV ratings to warn of explicit adult content. For example, the study found that NBC's broadcast show "Revolution," which is rated TV-14 (appropriate for viewers 14 and older) contained more violence than all of the cable shows studied that were rated for "mature adults."

"Cable is probably pushing the envelope . . . and [violence is] moving into the regular broadcast," says Dan Romer, director of the Adolescent Communication Institute at the University of Pennsylvania's Annenberg Public Policy Center. "I think there is more violence on broadcast TV as a result of cable."

Studies do not indicate how much of children's overall media consumption entails violent content, although some researchers say the number of violent actions in modern bestselling adolescent novels has risen significantly since the advent of the "young adult novel" in the 1960s. Others say violence has been a central component of children's books since the first fairy tales were published.[6]

A study in November showed that violent content in PG-13 movies more than doubled between 1950 and 2010, and the level of gun violence exceeds that in

Youths' Weekly Media Use Soars

In the 1930s children and teens spent about 10 hours per week using popular media, such as radio, movies, magazines and records. Today, children ages 8 to 18 spend about 75 hours weekly using media devices, including television, computers, tablets, game consoles, MP3 players and smart phones.

Weekly Media Exposure of Youths Ages 8 to 18

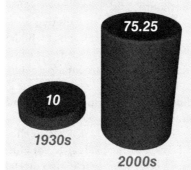

Source: Aviva Lucas Gutnick, et al., "Always connected: the new digital media habits of young children," The Joan Ganz Cooney Center at Sesame Workshop, 2010, www.joanganz cooneycenter.org/wp-content/uploads/2011/03/jgcc_alwaysconnected.pdf

R-rated films (as determined by "coders" who counted violent sequences in 945 top-grossing films). But Joan Graves, senior vice president and chairman of the Classification and Rating Administration at the Motion Picture Association of America (MPAA), questions what actions the coders are identifying as violent. The unrealistic "superhero" actions depicted in most of the PG-13 movies studied are not the same as the graphic violence depicted in R-rated movies, she says. "We're not comparing apples to apples here," she says.[7]

Many parents, lawmakers and experts worry that violent video games, such as "Call of Duty," "Killzone 3" and "Battlefield 3," may be more dangerous because of their interactive nature and because they reward players for shooting people onscreen or they depict sexual violence. "The thing I find incredibly personally upsetting is the amount of violence against women in these games . . . and a lot of the roles are prostitutes and rape victims. It's staggering," says April McClain-Delaney, Washington director of Common Sense Media, a nonprofit that provides information for educators and parents about media content.

"Research on the background of our juvenile mass murderers [shows] they have one thing in common: They all dropped out of life and filled their lives with nothing but violent movies and violent video games," said Lt. Col. Dave Grossman, author of *On Killing: The Psychological Cost of Learning to Kill in War and Society.* "The sickest video games and the sickest movies are very, very sick indeed. And the sick, sick kids who immerse themselves in this 'entertainment' are very sick indeed." The Sandy Hook massacre, in which 20-year-old Adam Lanza shot and killed 20 elementary school students and six adults, had been "building for years," he added, "and there is much, much worse yet to come."[8]

Lanza reportedly had an appetite for violent video games, as did the two Columbine High School seniors who massacred 13 classmates and teachers in 1999, and Anders Breivik, who killed 77 people in Norway in 2011.[9]

When the National Rifle Association found itself a target of legislators after the Sandy Hook shootings, it too blamed the producers of violent video games and music videos. "There exists in this country, sadly, a callous, corrupt and corrupting shadow industry that sells . . . violence against its own people," NRA CEO and Executive Vice President Wayne LaPierre said. Several members of Congress also wanted to take a closer look at the media — among them, West Virginia Democratic Sens. John "Jay" Rockefeller and Joe Manchin and Republicans Sen. Tom Coburn of Oklahoma, Tennessee Rep. Marsha Blackburn, and others.[10]

The investigation of the shootings revealed that Lanza had played violent video and online games such as "Combat Arms" and "World of Warcraft." He also incessantly played the nonviolent game "Dance Dance Revolution," had a history of mental illness, access to firearms and a fascination with mass murder. A federal investigation of a series of school shootings that occurred between 1974 and 2000 found that 87 percent of the shooters were interested in violent movies, 12 percent in violent video games and 24 percent in violent books, but there was no common type of interest in media violence.[11]

President Obama and several states have called for further study into the risk factors of readily available firearms, violent video games and media images and lack of mental health care. But when addressing media laws, the courts routinely reject regulations that infringe on free speech rights, so lawmakers and parent advocacy groups see limited options beyond calling for more research, encouraging more parental oversight of children's media consumption and considering new labeling or ratings systems.[12]

The Supreme Court in 2011 struck down a 2005 California law that would have barred minors from buying or renting violent video games that give the player options for "killing, maiming, dismembering, or sexually assaulting an image of a human being," if those actions

are created to appeal to "a deviant or morbid interest." The court said the law violated the First Amendment's protection of free speech and that studies had not proved that exposure to violent video games causes children to act aggressively.

"Video games qualify for First Amendment protection," Justice Antonin Scalia wrote in the court's decision. "This country has no tradition of specially restricting children's access to depictions of violence."[13]

As researchers, advocacy groups, lawmakers, industry leaders and parents continue to debate the issue, here are key questions being debated:

Does media violence cause aggressive behavior?

"I think media violence is part of the mix that's producing a mean world," says John Murray, a research fellow in psychology at Washington College in Chestertown, Md., and visiting scientist at the Center on Media and Child Health at Children's Hospital in Boston.

Murray, who also is emeritus professor of developmental psychology at Kansas State University, helped coordinate research for a 1972 surgeon general's report that he says concluded children who regularly viewed violence on television demonstrated aggressive behavior. He also cites a 1982 National Institute of Mental Health conclusion that "television violence is as strongly correlated with aggressive behavior as any other behavioral variable that has been measured. That should have ended this constant bickering" on this question, he says.[14]

In a more recent study, Murray and colleagues used magnetic resonance imaging (MRIs) to determine that the brain-activation patterns of children who viewed boxing scenes from "Rocky IV" suggested they were storing the images in a part of the brain that could potentially allow them to instantly recall the images when deciding how to respond to threatening situations.[15]

In a study published in 2012 in the *British Journal of Social Psychology*, people who read stories about "physical aggression," for example, were then more physically aggressive.[16] And various studies on the impact of violent and misogynistic lyrics in rap music found that they could desensitize listeners to sexual harassment and domestic violence and lead to aggressive responses to certain scenarios.[17]

Researchers increasingly are focusing on interactive video games. "We know that video game violence is correlated with violence — just like smoking is correlated with lung cancer," Brad J. Bushmann, co-chair of a National Science Foundation committee studying media violence research, told a House panel in March 2013.[18]

Bushman, an Ohio State University communication and psychology professor, helped lead a 2012 study that found that participants who played a violent video game 20 minutes per day for three days displayed increased aggressive behavior. That matched his analysis of hundreds of earlier studies concluding such games increased aggressive thoughts and behavior while decreasing empathy among males and females of all ages. The International Society for Research on Aggression also concluded that exposure to all types of media violence has negative effects, regardless of "age, gender, or where the person lives in the world."[19]

"The link with aggression has been proven," says Victor Strasburger, a professor of pediatrics and family and community medicine at the University of New Mexico School of Medicine. The correlation between aggression and video games is as conclusive as it is for violent TV programming, he says, and some studies suggest interactive games are more influential.[20]

Bushman is a bit more circumspect. "We haven't 'proven' that violent video games directly cause violence because it can't be proven," he says. "There is no way to ethically run experiments that see if playing a violent game . . . can push a person into violence. But that doesn't mean we are left without evidence."

At the other end of the spectrum, Jonathan Freedman, emeritus psychology professor at the University of Toronto, says, "Those who believe in the harmful effects of media violence . . . have enormously overstated their findings, ignored negative findings that don't agree with them, and to some extent . . . they pick and choose what they report." Freedman argues in a 2002 book that fewer than half of existing studies at the time showed a causal connection between media violence and actual crime. The MPAA helped finance the book, he says, but had no say in its conclusions.[21]

"What we're doing isn't really science anymore," says Stetson University psychology professor Christopher Ferguson. "It may be well-intentioned advocacy, but it's

no longer science. The core of science is skepticism." Ferguson helped coordinate a study in which pairs of college students (most of them Hispanic) played an Xbox 360 game for 45 minutes — either the shooter game "Borderlands," "Lego Star Wars III," which is a cartoon but involves shooting, or the nonviolent "Portal II." Results showed video games did not influence aggressive behavior or perceptions of empathy, but cooperative play correlated with less aggressive behavior.[22]

Ferguson also "didn't find much," he says, when he studied teenagers who read books banned for "edgy" violent, sexual or occult content. "There was no correlation with aggression," although some correlation with mental health problems was reported primarily within a small group of girls. Reading for pleasure was associated with civic engagement and higher grades, he says.[23]

Free-speech advocates say the Supreme Court closed the debate in 2011 when it overturned California's video game sales law and said research had not proved a causal link between violent video games and violent behavior. The advocates also point out that even though violent video games are played globally, few other countries match the United States in the rate of homicides.[24]

"Our position is supported by common sense," the Entertainment Software Association's Hewitt wrote in an e-mail. "The video games played in this country are played worldwide, and ours is the only country that sees our society's level of violence."

Are there benefits from media violence?

Cantor, of the University of Wisconsin–Madison, says, "There is an innate sense that violence is important in any organism." In nature, she says, if organisms don't "pay attention to violence, they would be dead pretty soon."

Some researchers suggest that males' innate attraction to violent scenes represents a desire to learn about war, to see justice done or for social entertainment. Moreover, some experts say such exposure can prepare children for real-world events and help them address their fears.

Cartoon creator Gerard Jones said all forms of media provide a safe fantasy world where children can deal with their emotions and understand violence and sexuality.[25]

Violence has been a central theme of children's books from *Grimm's Fairy Tales* (1812) to today's

Violent Video Games Are Among Top Sellers

Half of the 10 top-selling video games of 2012 were rated M for Mature, meaning they were deemed suitable only for those ages 17 and older because they contained intense violence, blood and gore, sexual content or strong language. The rest were rated E, or suitable for Everyone.

Top 10 Video Games and Their Ratings, 2012

1. **Call of Duty: Black Ops II (M)**
2. **Madden NFL 13 (E)**
3. **Halo 4 (M)**
4. **Assassin's Creed III (M)**
5. **Just Dance 4 (E)**
6. **NBA 2K13 (E)**
7. **Call of Duty: Modern Warfare 3 (M)**
8. **Borderlands 2 (M)**
9. **Lego Batman 2: DC Super Heroes (E)**
10. **FIFA Soccer 13 (E)**

Source: "Essential Facts About the Computer and Video Game Industry," Entertainment Software Association, 2013, www.theesa.com/facts/pdfs/esa_ef_2013.pdf

young-adult fiction, literature experts say. Lauren Myracle, author of several young adult novels on the American Library Association's list of widely challenged books, defends her books, which content critics say contain too much sex or violence. She said she addresses a range of topics teens are grappling with, including "bullying, suicide, homophobia and social injustice," among other things.[26] And racial violence has long been a theme of rap music, which some researchers say fosters solidarity among black youths and serves as an artistic outlet.

Other researchers theorize that violent video games challenge the brain, allow participants to face their fears, act out aggression in a fantasy world and — in the case of multiplayer games — encourage social behavior. However, few studies have proved such theories.

Lawrence Kutner and Cheryl K. Olson, cofounders of the Harvard Medical School Center for Mental Health and Media, said in their 2008 book *Grand Theft Childhood* that most young players understand that games like "Grand Theft Auto" are fantasy. And, unlike a movie, players can change the story — turning a "scary story into something where someone is saved," Olson says. "You always know it's a fantasy; if you want to stop

doing it, you can stop." Video games also offer children a chance for social interaction and an ego boost when they beat adults — benefits that have not been thoroughly studied, Olson says. And children they surveyed said playing the game reduced their stress.[27]

But Cantor is skeptical. She says Kutner and Olson discounted their own study results indicating increased aggressive behavior among teenagers who played M (Mature) rated video games. The authors, she says, instead emphasized the kids' own opinions about why they play games and their own statements that they felt less aggressive afterwards. "[I]t doesn't take a research expert to have doubts about a child's willingness to admit that something he or she loves to do is harmful," she wrote in a review.[28]

Steven J. Kirsh, a psychology professor at The State University of New York at Geneseo, said research shows players can gain a sense of independence and accomplishment when they rack up points and are cheered by their peers.[29] And Stetson's Ferguson says some studies have indicated that violent games may improve hand-eye coordination, increase social involvement and be educational, but he says more research is needed in that area.[30]

James Paul Gee, an Arizona State University professor of literacy studies who has analyzed the educational value of video games, said many games portray warfare as heroic and a confirmation of various cultural models, which provides pleasure and allows players to experience the world from different perspectives.[31]

In *Everything Bad Is Good For You*, journalist Steven Johnson described an underlying "sleeper curve" effect of new technology. "The most debased forms of mass diversion — video games and violent television dramas and juvenile sitcoms — turn out to be nutritional after all" by increasing cognitive abilities, he wrote.[32]

But Murray says he hasn't seen evidence that violent video games are psychologically beneficial and says there must be other ways to improve focus, reaction time and eye-hand coordination without violence.

Some critics say only depictions of violence in which good reigns over evil can provide positive lessons for consumers. Others disagree. "Unfortunately, the entertainment industry seems to confuse the fact that people like *action*, not violence," the University of New Mexico's Strasburger said. "Action doesn't have to involve shooting, blood spurting or bones breaking."[33]

Common Sense Media's McClain-Delaney decries some video games' "almost pornographic" depictions of violence against women, including raping and maiming, such as in the M-rated game "Manhunt 2."

The effects of such media are not yet thoroughly understood, she says. "This is the No. 1 important messenger to our kids . . . so I find it interesting that we are doing a big experiment on our kids, in a way."

Should the government regulate violence in media?

The Supreme Court has said over the years — beginning in 1968 in *Ginsberg v. New York* — that the government can regulate sexual content in media, but the court has never permitted restrictions on media violence. And while some media industries voluntarily provide ratings to help parents monitor their children's entertainment, critics increasingly suggest they need to do more to better inform parents and limit children's access to the most violent media content.[34]

The University of Pennsylvania's Romer says network programs and movies "should have more warnings, just as they do with drugs. Watch a drug ad on TV, and half the ad is about the side effects." Viewing violence likely has a different effect on different people, but so do drugs, he says. "Even tobacco doesn't kill everybody, but we have a lot of regulation on that."

Romer advocates "giving people full disclosure" about the level of violence in PG-13 movies. "What we have now is just false advertising," he says of the current movie rating systems. "It's true for video games, too."

Bushman agrees the current rating system is "confusing to parents," and Rockefeller, the West Virginia Democrat, said, "Overworked and stressed parents cannot be expected to always prevent their kids from viewing inappropriate content across a variety of devices."[35]

Strasburger, at the University of New Mexico, says "the onus should be on the makers of violent video games. It should be a product-liability issue." Video game producers "should have to show it is safe for a 13-year-old."

The University of Wisconsin's Cantor has several recommendations, including:

• Having the government fund or require media producers to finance public education programs;
• Requiring creation of a new uniform ratings system for all media formats;
• Allowing local communities to restrict sales of highly violent video games to young children; and
• Requiring the television industry to build a user-friendly v-chip — technology that allows individuals to block certain content on their channels — which would accommodate an improved rating system.

The media industries say their current ratings systems are adequate. A 2013 survey by the Entertainment Software Ratings Board (ESRB), a self-regulatory body which establishes ratings on video games, found that 85 percent of parents are aware of the ratings system for games.

"The extensive tools and programs that ESRB provides to help parents are one reason that government efforts to regulate computer and video games are unlawful," the Entertainment Software Association says on its website. "The First Amendment protects interactive entertainment software, and the government generally cannot restrict their sale, any more than it can ban books or movies."[36]

The MPAA's Graves defends the film ratings system, which is run by a panel of parents with children ages 5 to 15 who, she says, are attuned to the views of their communities. The members view up to three films a week, she says. The reviewers judge the levels of violence by what looks realistic. Typically brutal, graphic or persistent violence that is deemed "realistic" is rated R, and more "action-oriented" movies are PG-13.

"It's all subjective, obviously, to some degree . . . because all are parents, and they are reacting, hopefully, as parents would," she says.

Modern computer graphic imaging effects produce a new kind of onscreen violence, permitting depictions of flying robots and superheroes, Graves says. "So we have more frenetic type action violence [that] just didn't exist in that form a couple decades ago," she says. But that violence typically is rated PG-13 because "there's not a lot of brutality in it. I think there's an unreality to it that both parents and kids . . . don't see as threatening."

In MPAA surveys and focus groups, Graves says, "We hear we're getting the right information about the level of [violence] so [parents] can make the best choices." She has seen society's tolerance for certain material change over the past 20 years, she says, but if parents complain, it's typically about sexual material, not violence.

Graves acknowledges that it's easy for children to access movies online but says parents can limit access to computers and the Internet. "They can regulate what their children see," she says. "I don't think [the ratings] are outmoded."

McClain-Delaney suggests that rather than require the industry to create new ratings systems, for example, evaluating media content should remain the role of a nonprofit such as Common Sense Media, which provides its own detailed media ratings systems.

Gabe Rottman, legislative counsel for the American Civil Liberties Union, which defends free-speech rights, also doesn't want the government involved. "The government shouldn't be in the business of policing access, be it by children or adults."[37]

BACKGROUND

Early Media

Parents, educators, community and political leaders have raised concerns about violent imagery in entertainment for centuries, particularly in response to waves of social disorder. In ancient Greece, Plato and his mentor Socrates warned about the impact on young minds of repeated images and lines in poetry and plays. In the 18th and 19th centuries the novels of many writers, including Edgar Allan Poe and Nathaniel Hawthorne, sparked cries for censorship.[38]

In the early 20th century, broadsheet and tabloid newspapers offered sensationalized crime stories and comic strips some regarded as tools for teaching youth lawlessness. On Christmas Eve 1908, New York Mayor George B. McClellan Jr. closed the nickelodeons (small indoor movie exhibition spaces that cost 5 cents to enter) and called for an investigation of whether they were showing films on the Sabbath, in violation of city law. Several states created censorship laws, which the Supreme Court upheld in 1915 when it ruled that free speech protections in Ohio's constitution did not extend to motion pictures.[39]

By the late 1930s, kids could buy 10-cent comic books such as *Superman Quarterly Magazine*, gather around the radio to hear crime-packed thriller stories such as "Dig My Grave" and "Crimson Corpse" and watch films such as "The Great Train Robbery" that contained themes clergy feared glorified criminal behavior.[40] As radio, movies and comic books increasingly pervaded everyday life and crime rates increased, more communities questioned whether there was a link between violent content and aggressive behavior. The entertainment industries promised self-regulation, and Congress failed to advance legislation similar to what the states had done.[41]

To avoid censorship, the movie industry created the National Board of Censorship of Motion Pictures, but it was perceived as ineffective. In response it created the Motion Picture Production Code, known as the Hays Code, in 1930, requiring that "the sympathy of the audience should never be thrown to the side of crime, wrongdoing, evil or sin" in movies shown in American theaters.[42]

By the 1940s, lawmakers in nearly 50 cities were trying to ban the sale of crime comics, so in 1948 the comic-book industry formed the Association of Comics Magazine Publishers with a code of editorial practices.

In 1952 the Supreme Court overturned its 1915 decision upholding movie censorship, stating: "If there be capacity for evil, . . . it does not authorize substantially unbridled censorship such as we have here."[43]

Yet, with juvenile crime rising sharply in the postwar years, complaints continued with each new movie with a violent theme, such as the 1955 film "Rebel Without a Cause." Congress by that time had decided to thoroughly review the potential causes of juvenile crime — including media violence — under the guidance of a new Senate panel chaired by Tennessee Democrat Estes Kefauver.

"The volume of delinquency among our young has been quite correctly called the shame of America," Kefauver said in opening the hearings in 1954. "If the rising tide of juvenile delinquency continues, by 1960 more than one-and-a-half million American youngsters from 10 through 17 years of age will be in trouble with the law each year." The panel was not solely looking at media as the cause of the problem, Kefauver said, and it was "not a subcommittee of blue-nosed censors. We want to find out what damage, if any, is being done to our children's minds by certain types of publications which contain a substantial degree of sadism, crime and horror."[44]

Some of the hearings focused on the potential influence of violence in comic books. Fredric Wertham, a psychiatrist and author of *Seduction of the Innocent*, pointed at comic books as a major cause of juvenile crime. Holding up a comic book during a hearing, he said, "This is a baseball game where they play baseball with a man's head; where the man's intestines are the baselines."[45]

The committee found the link between comic books and juvenile crime unclear, but laid responsibility for oversight on parents and encouraged the industry to self regulate. The industry then agreed to beef up its earlier standards, creating the Comics Code Authority in 1954 that said "scenes of brutal torture, excessive and unnecessary knife and gun play, physical agony, gory and gruesome crime shall be eliminated."[46]

The panel also scrutinized the motion picture and television industries. William Mooring, media editor for *Catholic Tidings* in Los Angeles, complained that "criminal violence, human brutality, sadism and other psychopathic disorders" were increasingly portrayed in such films as "Blackboard Jungle" and "Black Tuesday." But actor Ronald Reagan, the future U.S. president, testified that films "are theatrical entertainment. . . . you cannot have successful theater unless your audience has an emotional experience of some kind. If it is comedy, they must laugh. If it is tragedy, they must cry."[47]

NBC Vice President Joseph V. Heffernan told the panel, "We are an organization of human beings. We make no claim to perfection in every program we broadcast." But he urged that television be allowed to remain a "free-enterprise competitive business."[48]

In the 1960s and '70s, several studies and government inquiries analyzed the effects of television and film violence on children and adolescents, as leaders worried about civil rights demonstrations, war protests and the assassinations of President John F. Kennedy, Robert Kennedy and civil rights leader the Rev. Martin Luther King Jr. President Lyndon B. Johnson created the National Commission on the Causes and Prevention of Violence, and Newton Minow, chairman of the Federal Communications Commission (FCC), famously called commercial television a "vast wasteland" of crime, violence and advertising directed at children.[49]

In 1968 the Supreme Court upheld a New York law barring the sale of "obscene" materials to minors. That same year, Massachusetts parent Peggy Charren created the grassroots organization Action for Children's Television (ACT), to lobby the FCC and Congress for better children's programming.[50]

The momentum led to creation of the Public Broadcasting System (PBS) in 1970 to offer educational programming. Jack Valenti, former special assistant to President Johnson who was named head of the MPAA, pushed for revisions in the movie industry's code to include new movie ratings to better inform parents of movie content.[51]

Media Debate Expands

In 1969, a report by President Johnson's violence commission portrayed exposure to media violence as a cause of aggression and urged networks to reduce time given to violent programming. Congress resumed its hearings, but again was unable to come to a clear conclusion and asked the surgeon general to study the issue. The series of reports that followed in 1972 did not provide further clarity on whether children's viewing of violence on television leads them to behave aggressively.[52]

Meanwhile, violence in cartoons such as "Road Runner," TV crime-fighting series such as "Starsky and Hutch" and "Hawaii Five-O" and made-for-TV movies such as "Born Innocent" brought more negative attention to the networks. The FCC received thousands of complaints from parents.[53]

In the 1980s President Reagan encouraged the industry to address the issue on its own. Under FCC pressure, the networks created a "family hour," during which only material deemed appropriate for children would be shown. The ACT pushed for more, resulting in the Children's Television Act of 1990, which called for all televisions to have v-chips. The broadcast industry followed in 1992 with its own guidelines on violent content. About that time, however, cable TV companies began to increase their offerings of violent-themed shows and movies, putting pressure on broadcast networks to boost their violent content to compete for viewers, according to some critics.[54]

Movies also remained under scrutiny. In 1984, the release of "Indiana Jones and the Temple of Doom" led to an outcry among parents for its PG rating. Director Steven Spielberg called on the MPAA to create a new tier, and a year later it created the PG-13 rating.

C H R O N O L O G Y

1900–1948 *Media industry begins to regulate itself.*

1915 Supreme Court allows states to restrict motion picture industry.

1930 Movie industry creates the Motion Picture Production Code.

1948 Supreme Court rules magazines depicting crime and bloodshed are "as much entitled to the protection of free speech as the best of literature."

1950s–1960s *Congress investigates link between media violence and juvenile crime.*

1952 Supreme Court overturns decision on state censorship.

1952–1955 House and Senate committees hold hearings on media violence.

1968 President Lyndon B. Johnson creates commission on violence following political assassinations. . . . Congress holds hearing on media violence.

1970s–1980s *Federal agencies seek to reduce TV violence.*

1972 Surgeon general's committee reports TV violence can encourage aggressive behavior among youth.

1975 Federal Communications Commission (FCC) mandates a family viewing hour on TV.

1982 National Institute of Mental Health concludes TV violence contributes to increased aggression in youth.

1985 Senate hearings result in music industry agreement to label albums containing explicit content.

1990s *Media violence concerns shift to video games.*

1990 Childrens' Television Act requires networks to provide educational programming.

1993 Lawmakers hold hearings on violent video games.

1996 Telecommunications Act requires content ratings and "v-chips."

1999 Mass shooting at Columbine High School in Colorado; the teenage shooters reportedly were influenced by violent movies and video games.

2000s *Media violence targeted following rampages.*

2000 Senate Commerce Committee investigates violent video games.

2001 Surgeon general says exposure to media violence can increase a child's aggressive behavior but that specific predictions are impossible.

2002 U.S. Secret Service finds no common link among mass shootings.

2005 Senators offer bills to require labeling of indecent and violent TV programming, evaluate the v-chip and to bar sales of graphically violent video games to minors. . . . American Psychological Association calls for reduction in violence in video and computer games.

2007 FCC seeks to regulate TV violence; 10 days later, Virginia Tech student kills 32 people on campus. . . . Senate holds hearing on media violence.

2009 Federal Trade Commission investigates marketing of violent entertainment to children.

2011 Supreme Court rejects California law barring sale of certain violent video games to minors.

2012 Mass shootings in Aurora, Colo., theater and at Sandy Hook Elementary School in Connecticut heighten focus on violent media.

2013 White House calls for study into causes of gun violence, including violent video games and media images. Flurry of federal and state bills address media violence but stall due to industry opposition.

2014 School and mall shootings further intensify debate about effects of media violence on youth.

Meanwhile, young-adult novels, which had emerged in the 1970s,were growing in popularity, even as they were criticized for focusing on teen issues such as drug use and the Vietnam War. The American Library Association inaugurated its annual "Banned Book Week" in 1982, a series of events held in September each year to raise national attention to the ALA's anticensorship efforts.

That same year, the Supreme Court ruled that students' First Amendment rights were violated when junior and senior high school libraries removed from their shelves Kurt Vonnegut's 1969 World War II novel *Slaughterhouse Five* and eight other titles for portrayals of violence and other reasons.[55]

Video games became popular in the 1970s, when children began frequenting video arcades offering coin-operated games. "Death Race," in which the player controlled a car to run down gremlins, led the National Safety Council in 1976 to state, "The person is no longer a spectator, but now an actor in the process of creating violence."[56]

Over the next 15 years, video games grew in popularity and attracted the attention of researchers and lawmakers. But courts again ruled that laws limiting violent content violated the First Amendment. In 1992, the Eighth U.S. Circuit Court of Appeals invalidated a statute restricting minors' access to violent video games, stating, "Unlike obscenity, violent expression is protected by the First Amendment."[57]

Sen. Joseph Lieberman, D-Conn., was undeterred and warned of the negative impact on youth of such games as "Mortal Kombat" and "Night Trap." Lieberman (who later became an independent) and Sen. Herb Kohl, D-Wis., held hearings in 1993 and called for industry regulations. The next year, game producers responded by creating the Entertainment Software Ratings Board and a voluntary standard for age ratings on video games.[58]

Meanwhile, clergy and parents voiced concerns about violence in music lyrics. Critics in the 1960s and '70s had protested violent imagery in lyrics by heavy metal groups such as Judas Priest and Motorhead. In 1979 rap music was introduced in America, and music videos began to be broadcast on television's MTV network, upsetting parents with their sometimes violent lyrics and imagery. In 1985, the new Parents Music Resource Center led by

Tipper Gore — wife of then-Sen. Al Gore, D-Tenn. — encouraged the Senate to consider legislation requiring record labeling. The Recording Industry Association of America (RIAA) responded by voluntarily labeling albums containing explicit content.

In 1996 the American Academy of Pediatrics issued guidelines for parents, warning particularly against heavy metal and "gangsta rap" — a type of hip-hop music with lyrics reflecting urban crime.[59] A Senate panel the following year looked into whether such music might be related to violent juvenile crime. Sen. Sam Brownback, R-Kan., said such crime had spiked more than 500 percent over 30 years. He raised concerns about contemporary music, citing such songs as "Don't Trust a Bitch" by the group Mo Thugs, "Slap a Ho" by Dove Shack and "Stripped, Raped and Strangled" by Cannibal Corpse.

One parent cried as he described how his 15-year-old son committed suicide while listening to his favorite Marilyn Manson song, "The Reflecting God." The song included the lyrics: "Each thing I show you is a piece of my death/One shot and the world gets smaller/Shoot here and the world gets smaller/Shoot shoot shoot."

"I would say the lyrics to this song contributed directly to my son's death," the father said.[60]

Concerns about Manson's music resurfaced after the 1999 Columbine High School massacre, in which students Eric Harris and Dylan Klebold shot and killed 12 other students and a teacher before committing suicide. Lieberman and conservative pundit William Bennett blamed Manson's violent lyrics, which the students reportedly had listened to. But the boys also allegedly had repeatedly watched the movie "Natural Born Killers" and played the violent video game "Doom." Parents of some of the victims unsuccessfully sued the video game manufacturers for contributing to their children's deaths.[61]

In a 2000 report requested by President Bill Clinton, the Federal Trade Commission (FTC) concluded that the music, film and video game industries marketed violent content directly to children and teenagers. It recommended they improve self-regulation, establish marketing guidelines and enforce retail restrictions, but few changes were made.[62]

Increasing Pressures

At that point, the research and medical community was strongly promoting studies showing a correlation between

Teaching Kids to Be Media Savvy

Special curricula teach how media influence attitudes and behaviors.

Eighth-graders in Brad Koepenick's class quietly watch a scene from the 1985 R-rated film "Witness." Actor Harrison Ford's character, John Book, a New York cop undercover as an Amish farmer, rides a wagon into a town where suddenly a group of local youths block the street to taunt an Amish family in another wagon.

An Amish elder accompanying Book warns, "It happens sometimes. Do nothing. It's not our way." Book responds, "But it's my way." He saunters up to one of the young men, who knocks Book's hat off his head and laughs. Book says, "You're making a mistake," then punches him to the ground.

The students cheer loudly until Koepenick asks them how someone else might respond to the scene. How would a 6-year-old boy view it? A New York cop? An Amish man? Quickly the students quiet down, and the lesson proceeds. Later students reconstruct the scene with different endings — negotiation, surrender, avoidance or a search for help.

"I believe one of the most engaging elements of this is teaching students about breaking the cycle of violence," says Koepenick. Now a communications teacher at Charter High School of the Arts, Multimedia and Performing, in the Los Angeles suburb of Van Nuys, Koepenick participated in a 2007-'08 study of middle school students to test the effectiveness of a curriculum titled "Beyond Blame," developed by the Center for Media Literacy, an educational organization based in Malibu, Calif.

The curriculum is intended to increase students' awareness of media violence, reduce associated aggressive behavior and encourage a change in media-consumption habits. Positive results from the initial study, though slightly more limited than researchers desired, nonetheless led them to conclude that the curriculum may "prompt youth to protect themselves by changing the types of media they use or by reducing total consumption."[1]

As courts repeatedly reject efforts to limit children's exposure to media violence, some researchers, lawmakers and medical associations advocate approaches that help educate students about media influences. And an increasing number of studies indicate such approaches can be effective.[2]

Koepenick this year is incorporating "Beyond Blame" into his ninth-grade communications class. He says the curriculum helps him teach filmmaking while turning many students into "media-literate foot soldiers" eager to teach others about the use and effects of media messages.

Koepenick's lessons entail viewing clips from movies and television shows such as "South Park" and video games like "Grand Theft Auto." Students analyze scenes of conflict or violence and discuss whether they are realistic, appropriate or excessive. They also tackle questions on producers' use of creative techniques, different interpretations of the same message and lifestyles shown or omitted. In addition, students discuss news articles about violence in American society and potential media influence.

media violence — in television, film, video games and music — and real-life aggression.[63]

Rap and punk rock music continued to worry parents and lawmakers, triggering more hearings on the effects of violent lyrics by performers such as Eminem and others.

"If you think that this type of graphic violence has no effect on our kids, well, think again," House Energy and Commerce Subcommittee Chairman Fred Upton, R-Mich., said in July 2001. "If you don't believe me, ask the parents at Columbine." He said while hundreds of

kids aren't shooting others, many are "pushing, shoving and assaulting each other with greater frequency and greater anger than ever before."[64]

In Colorado Springs in 2007, police publicly blamed gangsta rap for contributing to the city's growing murder rate. Meanwhile, Mexican and Mexican-American singers grew in popularity with songs glorifying drug war violence south of the U.S. border.[65]

A series of reports concluded that solutions such as the v-chip and self-regulation were not taming primetime television viewing among children. TVs in most households

The lesson is not that media violence is bad, Koepenick says. "My favorite movie is 'Godfather Part II.' I'm also a filmmaker, so I'm not going to tell you media violence is bad." Instead, the lesson is to critically analyze scenes and language. "We talk about the fact that nothing is random and everything is intentional."

After discussing media examples, the students use computers or other available technology to create their own videos, cartoons or other productions. In the final lesson, students divide into teams representing government, media producers, teachers, community leaders and parents to discuss next steps. Answers range from censoring one's own habits to teaching younger children about media violence.

Meanwhile, elementary schools in New Hampshire are seeking to use a similar curriculum devised and tested by Media Power Youth (MPY), a nonprofit organization in Manchester, N.H. In December, Democratic Gov. Maggie Hassan announced an initiative between the state Department of Education and MPY to help the nonprofit further develop its media-literacy curriculum for fifth-graders and train interested elementary faculty. A $100,000 state grant will cover expenses to train faculty and incorporate the curriculum into any elementary schools interested in the program.

By January, 75 New Hampshire communities had shown interest in the curriculum, which also includes instruction on bullying, alcohol and tobacco use and unhealthy foods. News of the announcement prompted phone calls from schools outside the state, although they would need to seek separate funding to pursue the coursework and training, according to MPY.

The curriculum uses clips of commercials, television shows, films and video games as well as paintings to prompt discussion about media messages and alternatives to conflict resolution. It was tested three times, according to MPY Executive Director Rona Zlokower, most recently during the 2009-'10 school year in fifth-grade health and art courses at two elementary schools in Manchester.

Some of the results were unexpected. One analysis showed a small increase in the reported likelihood to be verbally aggressive among students taking the curriculum. But researchers found that critical thinking among students in the program had improved, and they concluded prospects for the curriculum were promising.[3]

"It helps children understand how media influence their attitudes and behaviors," Zlokower says. "By doing so, it reduces their vulnerability to how media influence them. The reality is kids are surrounded by this all day, all night. We are not really showing them things they haven't seen before. We are slowing it down for them and making them think about it."

— Christina L. Lyons

[1] Kathryn R. Fingar and Tessa Jolls, "Evaluation of a school-based violence prevention media literacy curriculum," *Injury Prevention*, Aug. 16, 2013.

[2] See, for example Victor C. Strasburger, "Pediatricians, Schools, and Media," *Pediatrics*, 2012; Jeff Share, "The Earlier the Better; Expanding the Deepening Literacy with Young Children" in J. Share, *Media Literacy is Elementary; Teaching Youth to Critically Read and Create Media* (2009).

[3] David S. Bickham and Ronald G. Slaby, "Effects of a media literacy program in the U.S. on children's critical evaluation of unhealthy media messages about violence, smoking, and food," *Journal of Children and Media*, 2012.

---

were not equipped with v-chips, according to several reports, and increasing levels of violence appeared on broadcast television, according to the Parents Television Council, which suggested that Congress consider including violence in the category of "indecent" content to be regulated by the FCC.[66]

Access to violent cable television shows outside the traditional "family hour" slot, a growing number of youths watching late-night television and new recording technologies made the v-chip useless. In 2007, the FCC said it could further regulate TV if Congress passed legislation that essentially called for restrictions on "excessively violent programming that is harmful to children" and that also applied to cable and satellite. It also suggested that broadcasters pledge to air violence-free programming during prime time hours, and that cable and satellite operators offer customers "a la carte" menus of stations.[67]

Ten days after the FCC's statement, Virginia Tech University student Seung-Hui Cho shot and killed 32 people on campus. The massacre sparked new congressional hearings, in which Parents Television Council President Tim Winter advocated that Congress grant FCC

Entertainment Firms Spend Big on Lobbying

Legislation to curb media violence has stalled.

Video game manufacturers and other entertainment companies are spending millions of dollars a year on lobbying, in part to fend off new laws and regulations on violent content.

The Center for Responsive Politics, a nonprofit research group in Washington that tracks political spending, ranked the television, movie and music industries as ninth in lobbying expenditures for 1993-2013, with spending totaling nearly $1.2 billion. That was close to what the oil and gas industries spent, though less than half the pharmaceutical industry's lobbying expenditures.

The National Cable and Telecommunications Association, which has sought to monitor a range of issues affecting the cable industry, including potential legislation regarding programming, spent nearly $19.9 million on lobbying in 2013 alone, more than four times its 1998 level.[1] The Motion Picture Association of America (MPAA), a trade association representing the six major Hollywood studios, spent nearly $2.2 million. The Entertainment Software Association (ESA), which represents video game makers and other technology companies, spent more than twice that much — $5.21 million, not including money paid to outside lobbyists. The ESA's lobbying focused not only on issues related to video game violence but also on a range of other matters.[2]

Michael Gallagher, chief executive of ESA, acknowledged his organization's role last year in helping to block several proposed state laws designed to encourage further study into the effects on youth of violent video games — primarily because they singled out his industry, he said. He cited one such proposal in Maryland. "Why would the movie 'The Godfather' not be included?" he asked.[3]

Last July, the U.S. Senate Commerce Committee advanced a bill by Sen. John "Jay" Rockefeller, D-W.Va., calling for a study on whether violent video games and other programming have a negative effect on youths. The ESA, as well as the movie, cable and TV industries, issued statements saying they welcomed "further academic examination of the reasons behind societal violence." But the ESA has pushed for any study to take into account research that shows little or no link between video game violence and actual violence. The measure remained stalled early this year.[4]

Lawmakers hoping to protect children from violent entertainment appear frustrated at what they see as the entertainment industry's power to thwart new laws. Sen. Frank Wolf, a Virginia Republican, complained last year that the video game industry had "so many" lobbyists in Washington, he could become wealthy working for them.

Wolf and Rockefeller for several years have aimed to limit children's exposure to violent media content, particularly video games, only to see their measures stall. "Major corporations, including the video game industry, make billions on marketing and selling violent content to children,"

greater regulatory authority over TV content. But Harvard law professor Laurence Tribe warned the FCC's recommendations would violate the First Amendment.[68] Two years later, FCC Chairman Julius Genachowski told senators the commission would investigate the state of programming for kids.

Meanwhile, Sen. Rockefeller and others grew increasingly concerned about violent video games. In 2000, the Senate Commerce Committee held a hearing on the impact of such games, but legislative options remained limited because courts repeatedly ruled that violent video games were protected expression under the First Amendment and that research had not shown a causal link to actual violence.[69]

Brownback expressed frustration with industry expectations that the media could not be regulated. "The First Amendment guarantees the right to free speech," he said in March 2006. "What too many in the industry fail to realize is that this right is not without limits, particularly when it comes to minors." He referred to two Supreme Court cases, *Sable Communications v. FCC* and *Ginsburg v. New York*, which had permitted the government to intervene when concerned about the well-being of minors.[70]

Rockefeller said. "They have a responsibility to protect our children."[5]

Many critics of the entertainment media who want to see a reduction in children's exposure to media violence suggest the video game industry is battling laws calling for further studies because it is more interested in preserving profits. The adult-rated video game "Grand Theft Auto V" grossed $800 million in the first 24 hours of sales last fall and more than $1 billion in its first three days on the market.[6]

The ESA, MPAA and National Cable and Television Association launched public awareness campaigns about their ratings systems after the December 2012 shooting at Sandy Hook Elementary School in Newtown, Conn., in which 20-year-old Adam Lanza, reportedly a heavy consumer of violent video games, shot and killed 20 students and six adults.

The industry has found support among some members of Congress, who in 2011 formed the Caucus for Competitiveness in Entertainment Technology, in part to support the video game industry. Moreover, Constance Steinkuehler, a professor of digital media at the University of Wisconsin who served briefly as senior policy analyst for the White House Office of Science and Technology, told Vice President Joseph Biden after the Sandy Hook shootings that research findings on links between violence and video games were inconclusive.

Until recently, several video game producers had ties to wealthy gun manufacturers, promoting brand-name assault rifles and pistols in their games, such as those made by Colt, found in Electronic Arts' game "Battlefield 2." Electronic Arts parted ways with Colt after the National Rifle Association

(NRA) targeted the video game industry for blame following the Newtown shootings. However, Electronic Arts spokesman Jeff Brown denied the company's decision was in response to NRA comments.[7]

Such examples underscore the difficulty of passing strong regulations, suggests April McClain-Delaney, Washington director of Common Sense Media, a non-profit that provides information for educators and parents about media content. "It's hard," she says, "because there are so many competing interests lobbying on all these issues."

— Christina L. Lyons

[1] Center for Responsive Politics, www.opensecrets.org/lobby/.

[2] U.S. Senate Lobbying Disclosure Database, http://tinyurl.com/djbc2e.

[3] Jennifer Levitz, "Videogame Makers Fight Efforts to Study Link to Violence," *The Wall Street Journal*, Dec. 10, 2013, http://tinyurl.com/k2ap3wo.

[4] "Sen. Jay Rockefeller's Violent Content Research Act Gets Greenlight from Senate Committee, Includes Video Games," Game Politics.com, July 30, 2013, http://tinyurl.com/jwtncz7.

[5] "Rockefeller Introduces Bill to Study Violent Video Games Impact on Children," press release, http://tinyurl.com/cb5josw.

[6] Erik Kain, "'Grand Theft Auto V' Crosses $1 B in Sales; Biggest Entertainment Launch in History," *Forbes*, Sept. 20, 2013, http://tinyurl.com/kqfmloo.

[7] Malathi Nayak, "Electronic Arts severing ties with gun manufacturers, but not their guns," *Financial Post*, May 8, 2013, http://tinyurl.com/lleahn2; and Barry Meier and Andrew Martin, "Real and Virtual Firearms Nurture a Marketing Link," *The New York Times*, Dec. 24, 2012, http://tinyurl.com/c5j4wde.

More shootings further heightened the public debate. In July 2011, Norwegian mass murderer Breivik bombed government buildings in Oslo, killing eight, then opened fire on summer vacationers at a lakeside resort, killing 69, mostly teenagers. A year later, gunman James E. Holmes opened fire in a movie theater in Aurora, Colo., killing 12 people and wounding 70. That December, the mass shooting at Sandy Hook Elementary School again launched investigations into the cause of youth violence. Parent advocacy groups urged that media standards be strengthened, and federal lawmakers sought avenues for further regulation, such as requiring certain video games to carry health warnings.[71]

But in the wake of the Supreme Court's 2011 decision striking down the California law, regulatory solutions seemed elusive to many.

CURRENT SITUATION

Federal Efforts

Federal and state lawmakers seeking ways to limit children's and adolescents' exposure to media violence face continued divided opinion on whether their concerns are supported by the science. In addition, courts remain averse to infringing on free speech rights, even as public pressure intensifies for lawmakers to do something to prevent school shootings and other massacres.

The Centers for Disease Control and Prevention (CDC) is studying the causes and prevention of gun violence, including the impact of gun safety technology, mental health care and violent video games and media images. A report, ordered by President Obama after the Sandy Hook massacre, is expected within three to five years.[72]

Several lawmakers want the entertainment industry to shoulder more responsibility. "As a grandparent or parent, to pretend these violent video games don't make a difference — it's crazy," said Rep. Frank Wolf, R-Va., who favors action against the video game industry. "Ever seen 'Grand Theft Auto?' It is violent," he said. "Garbage in, garbage out."[73]

Wolf, who will retire from Congress in 2015, reportedly is considering legislation to require reduced-violence versions of video games with less realistic images. In a report requested by Wolf, the National Science Foundation recommended further study on the connection between youth violence and exposure to media violence, including how violent media affect certain vulnerable individuals and the potential benefit of a universal rating system for all media.[74]

Rockefeller, who is also retiring next year, has proposed a bill that would have the National Academy of Sciences examine the impact on children of violent video games and "violent video programming" and whether there is a causal connection to actual violence. He remains concerned about controlling youth's access to other violent content as well.

Rep. Jim Matheson, D-Utah, wants to ban sales and rentals of video games rated M (Mature) and AO (Adults Only) to anyone younger than 17 or 18, respectively.[75]

Rep. Kevin Brady, a Texas Republican, believes "the relentless, in-your-face glorification of violence promoted on our TV screens and in the movies" is of greater concern than video games in general, which he said are "a healthy form of education and entertainment for our family."

Meanwhile, the Parents Television Council supports legislation offered by Sen. John McCain, R-Ariz., that would force cable providers to offer channels "a la carte," permitting parents to choose Disney but not MTV, for instance.[76]

Federal officials indicate they are open to solutions. "Even without legislation, Congress can play an important oversight role that pushes the industry to do a better job of policing itself," Rockefeller said. White House Press Secretary Jay Carney said government didn't necessarily have to intervene, but could "elevate issues that are of concern."[77]

The Media Coalition, which represents a range of media industries, strongly opposes censorship, but said, "The good news is that the debate may be slightly more measured than in years past. This time around, most proposals tend more toward scholarship than censorship. Not all politicians are jumping on the media-causes-violence bandwagon."[78]

The MPAA, National Association of Broadcasters, National Cable and Telecommunications Association and Independent Film and Television Alliance have said they are willing to help address the issue. MPAA chairman and CEO Christopher Dodd, a former Democratic senator from Connecticut, said he had reached out to the administration after the Newtown shooting.

"Those of us in the motion picture and television industry want to do our part to help America heal," Dodd said. Meanwhile, both the MPAA and the ESA began campaigns in 2013 to better educate the public about their ratings systems while continuing to oppose federal or state regulation.[79]

State Efforts

Several states are seeking ways to address media violence in the wake of court rulings. Attorneys general from 11 states filed a brief supporting California's video game law when it was being considered by the Supreme Court.* They defended the law, written by Democratic California state senator and child psychologist Leland Yee, and said their own states "are vitally interested in protecting the welfare of children and in helping parents raise them."

States continue to pursue solutions. New Jersey Republican Gov. Chris Christie in 2013 signed into law a measure requiring the state Department of Education to provide information for parents on how to limit children's exposure to violent images or themes. Two other bills

---

* The states were Connecticut, Florida, Hawaii, Illinois, Louisiana, Maryland, Michigan, Minnesota, Mississippi, Texas and Virginia.

offered in 2013 but that did not reach the governor's desk would have required parental consent for minors to purchase games labeled Adult or Mature.

Several other states considered video game laws in 2013, but they were not enacted. Some were versions of earlier proposals, and some likely will be reintroduced this year. They included:

- A Massachusetts Senate measure to create a commission to study the social benefits of video games, their potential connections to violence and First Amendment issues related to the games.

- A Connecticut law to impose a 10 percent sales tax on video games rated M (Mature), with proceeds going to state mental health services and for training on the warning signs of video game addiction. The legislature also considered a bill to bar minors from playing violent video games at public arcades.

- An Oklahoma measure that would have imposed a 1 percent excise tax on violent video games.

- A Missouri proposal by a Republican lawmaker for a 1 percent sales tax on violent video games. The tax would have been used to help pay for mental health programs and law enforcement measures aimed at preventing mass shootings.

Latest Research

An American Psychological Association (APA) task force is analyzing peer-reviewed research on the impact of media violence and is reviewing its previous policy statements on the issue. Its work is expected to be complete in 2014.[80]

One group of scholars hopes the APA will revise its 2005 policy stating that research had shown clear negative effects from exposure to violence, including sexual violence, in interactive video games. In a written statement to the APA last September, the scholars (who include Ferguson, Freedman and others), said: "We are of the belief that the task force has a tremendous opportunity to change the culture of this research field to one which is less ideological and open to new theories, data and beliefs."[81]

Meanwhile, researchers continue to analyze the effects of media violence. Romer, Bushman and others are collaborating on a study analyzing whether gun violence in video games has a different effect on players than violence on television or in a movie has on viewers. They also are

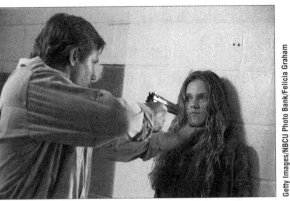

Canadian actress Tracy Spiridakos plays Charlotte "Charlie" Matheson in the post-apocalyptic science fiction series "Revolution." Although the NBC broadcast drama is rated as appropriate for viewers 14 and older, a recent study showed it contained more violence than any of the cable shows examined — including "Bullet in the Face" and "American Horror Story" — that were aimed at mature audiences, defined as viewers over 17.

comparing the effects of games with gun violence to other games, Romer says.

Researchers at Indiana University, the National Institutes of Health and other institutions are advancing studies using neuroimaging — contrast imaging that maps brain activity and the storage of images.

Meanwhile, some video game developers are testing new types of games. Video game director Navid Khonsari, who worked on "Grand Theft Auto III" and other games, has been leading a team in building a documentary game about the 1979 Iranian Revolution. Instead of just shooting back, players can help the wounded, sneak around to take photographs and smuggle evidence. "If I had conflict thrown at me in this particular situation, I'm not going to pick up a gun and charge soldiers, I'm going to try to get to safety, and I'm going to try to find the closest people to me and get them to safety," Khonsari said.[82]

Richard Davidson, a neuroscientist and founder of the Center for Investigating Healthy Minds at the University of Wisconsin–Madison, received a $1.39 million grant from the Bill and Melinda Gates Foundation to develop games that teach empathy and compassion rather than violence. Test results of the games, targeted at 8th-graders, are expected to be released this spring.

Should the entertainment industry be required to help reduce children's access to media violence?

YES
Sen. John "Jay" Rockefeller
Chairman,
Senate Commerce Committee

Written for *CQ Researcher*, February 2014

Protecting children from questionable video content, especially content filled with violence, has been a deeply personal and important issue to me during my time as a senator. For years I have questioned why the nation's media conglomerates continue to include so much violence in their video programming and have called on them to show restraint in how much violence they sell. Yet each year they seem to increase the violence to the point where such content is virtually unavoidable.

Today, children often consume hours of video content — both through television programming and video games. By the time they are 18, they have seen tens of thousands of violent images on television, the Internet and in video games. I strongly believe — as do many parents, researchers and doctors — that these images have a negative effect on our children's mental and emotional well-being, especially during their formative years.

Video content of all forms permeates our everyday life. It has the power to inform, educate, entertain and better our society. But it also can expose children to the coarser side of human nature and affect their development in ways we still do not fully understand.

And as television programming and video games increasingly migrate to mobile devices and new distribution platforms, parents have even less control over what their children see. These changes in technology could amplify the impact of violent content on our society's most vulnerable members — a very disturbing development.

Although many researchers and doctors express certainty that violent media can harm children, no consensus exists. More work must be done. So, I introduced a bill that directs the National Academy of Sciences to conduct a comprehensive study on the impact of violent video games and programming on children. This legislation was passed unanimously out of the Commerce Committee, and I am looking at every possible avenue to pass it in the full Senate.

I am calling for this study because we seek answers — not blame. We all share a collective goal of keeping our children healthy and safe. The more we know about how the minds of our young are shaped and formed, the more we can do to help them thrive. The more we know about whether and how violent content affects different children in different ways, the more we can do to protect them from its harms.

NO
Joan E. Bertin
Executive Director,
National Coalition Against Censorship

Written for *CQ Researcher*, February 2014

Violence has always been a fact of life and remains a reality for many people. It also has occupied a central place in art and literature, including children's stories ("Hansel and Gretel"), classic texts ("The Odyssey") and religious art (Gustave Doré's illustrations in Dante's "Inferno"). If violence is an accepted subject of timeless art and literature, why question it in contemporary modes of expression?

New forms of expression have always aroused anxiety and calls for restrictions, often accompanied by pseudo-scientific claims of harm. For example, in the 1950s psychiatrist Fredric Wertham's now-discredited claims of harm nearly wiped out comic books in America.

Recently, the Supreme Court considered similar claims about video games and found that studies on the effects of violent games "show at best some correlation between exposure to violent entertainment and minuscule real-world effects [which] are both small and indistinguishable from the effect [of watching] cartoons starring Bugs Bunny or the Road Runner." Official reports from Sweden, Norway, Australia and Great Britain have reached similar conclusions.

A federal appeals court rejected such arguments about media violence even more emphatically, holding that shielding children "from exposure to violent descriptions and images would not only be quixotic, but deforming," leaving them "unequipped to cope with the world as we know it."

That doesn't mean individuals have to like media violence or watch it or allow their children to do so. They're free to make their own choices. However, they're not entitled to impose their view on others, or to expect the government or anyone else to do it for them.

If the question is whether the *government* should require the media and communications industries to reduce children's exposure to media violence, the answer is clearly "no." As Supreme Court Justice Anthony Kennedy said in the 2000 majority opinion in *United States v. Playboy Entertainment Group*, the First Amendment "exists precisely so that opinions and judgments, including esthetic and moral judgments about art and literature, can be formed, tested and expressed. . . . [T]hese judgments are for the individual to make, not for the government to decree, even with the mandate or approval of a majority."

If not the government, who else? The idea of a private watchdog or industry group acting as culture czar to dictate taste is both implausible and chilling. There are all kinds of ratings and reviews for anyone who wants to use them. Isn't that good enough?

Other researchers are considering further studying the effects of interactive games as well as exposure to online hate groups, violent radical groups and sexual violence.

OUTLOOK

Debate Rages On

Court rulings have led to calls for more studies, and many researchers agree more could be done — including closer examinations of brain imaging techniques, more focus groups or refined studies on newer media. Murray of Washington College says he would like to see more detailed neuroimaging of where violent images are stored in the brain and how they are processed.

Ferguson of Stetson University hopes the Supreme Court's decision overturning California's video game sales law encourages scholars to be more cautious and conservative in their statements, which previously "expressed high certitude, made spurious comparisons with medical research . . . and increasingly spoke beyond what the data could support."[83]

But Strasburger from the University of New Mexico and McClain-Delaney of Common Sense Media say tight federal budgets mean little money is available for media research. "The only research being funded is by the industry," he says. "It's a pretty bleak picture."

Murray contends research already shows a link between entertainment violence and actual violence. "The future is really in education, media literacy and talking to parents," he says. Groups such as the Center for Media Literacy and Media Power Youth are seeking to promote media literacy in all schools across the country.

Regardless, Murray, Wisconsin's Cantor, Ferguson and others believe the public debate will continue, and a resolution will be difficult to reach.

"These things tend to run in obvious cycles," Ferguson says. "For a while it was television. Even back to the 1930s, a lot of people were panicking about movies. Then it was rock [music] in the 1980s, then pornography and now video games." Most adults fear video games because they are unfamiliar with them, he says.

McClain-Delaney believes legislative remedies will be slow but hopes some answer is found — particularly in light of children's growing access to online media. "We

don't allow kids to drive until they are 16, drink until 21. They can't be legally bound in a contract until they are 18," she says. "But at 13, they are totally an adult in a digital world? That makes no sense, and that's exactly the time the parent begins to retreat because they can't track them.

"What do we do? What does the FCC do? It's a hard one," she says. "I think the next step is to look at how we as a country want to balance our children's well-being. How do we want to help them navigate the very violent content?"

But the industries and free speech advocates will continue to oppose media restrictions.

"States can't target emerging media: As new technologies are invented, states cannot target them for restriction because of concern about the potential influence on children," said Ken Paulson, president of the First Amendment Center, a program associated with The Freedom Forum, a nonpartisan foundation in Washington, D.C.

The Supreme Court's 2011 ruling in the California case "is a vibrant application of 219-year-old principles to cutting-edge technology and asserts that any new forms of communication or media to come will be protected by the First Amendment," he says.[84]

NOTES

1. Christy Lemire, "Parental Guidance: The Hunger Games: Catching Fire and Delivery Man, Plus Planes and Paranoia," *Rotten Tomatoes*, Nov. 22, 2013, www .rottentomatoes.com/m/the_hunger_games_catch ing_fire/news/1929025; Ann Hornaday, "Jennifer Lawrence dominates 'The Hunger Games: Catching Fire' sequel," *The Washington Post*, Nov. 21, 2013, http://tinyurl.com/kptx5ot.

2. Chris Baker, "Rapper Ace Hood brings violent lyrics to the 'friendly' Orange Madness," *The Syracuse Post-Standard*, Oct. 11, 2013, http://tinyurl.com/lez43oo.

3. Ryan Leas, "Move over, Kerouac! 'Grand Theft Auto' is the American Dream narrative now," *Salon*, Jan. 5, 2014, http://tinyurl.com/pocn2p5.

4. Aviva Lucas Gutnick, *et al.*, "Always Connected: The new digital media habits of young children," The Joan Ganz Cooney Center at Sesame Workshop, 2011, http://tinyurl.com/br6an8q.

5. "An Examination of Violence, Graphic Violence and Gun Violence in the Media (2012-2013)," Parents Television Council, December 2013, http://tinyurl.com/mhfwwxm.

6. Sarah M. Coyne, *et al.*, "A Mean Read: Aggression in Adolescent English literature," *Journal of Children and Media*, 2011; Michelle Ann Abate, *Bloody Murder: The Homicide Tradition in Children's Literature* (2013).

7. Brad J. Bushman, *et al.*, "Gun Violence Trends in Movies," *Pediatrics*, Nov. 11, 2013.

8. Dave Grossman, "Videogames as 'murder simulators,' " *Variety Special Report: Violence and Entertainment*, 2013.

9. N. R. Kleinfeld, Ray Rivera and Serge F. Kovaleski, "Newtown Killer's Obsessions in Chilling Detail," *The New York Times*, March 28, 2013, http://tinyurl.com/d9v2uyy.

10. See "Remarks from the NRA press conference on Sandy Hook school shooting (Transcript)," *The Washington Post*, Dec. 21, 2012.

11. Stephen J. Sedensky III, "Report of the State's Attorney for the Judicial District of Danbury on the Shootings at Sandy Hook Elementary School and 36 Yogananda Street, Newtown, Connecticut on December 14, 2012," Office of the State's Attorney, Judicial District of Danbury, Nov. 25, 2013; "The Final Report and Findings of the Safe School Initiative: Implications for the Prevention of School Attacks in the United States," U.S. Secret Service and U.S. Department of Education, May 2002.

12. "Now is the Time: The President's Plan to Protect Our Children and Our Communities by Reducing Gun Violence," White House, http://tinyurl.com/ab3jauw.

13. *Brown vs. Entertainment Merchants Assn.* (formerly *Schwarzenegger v. EMA*), 131 S. Ct. 2729, June 27, 2011.

14. "Television and Growing Up: The Impact of Televised Violence," Office of the Surgeon General, 1972; "Television and Behavior: Ten Years of Scientific Progress and Implications for the Eighties," National Institute of Mental Health, 1982.

15. J. P. Murray, *et al.*, "Children's brain response to TV violence: Functional Magnetic Resonance Imaging (fMRI) of video viewing in 8-13 year-old boys and girls," *Media Psychology*, 2006, pp. 25-37.

16. S. M. Coyne, *et al.*, "Backbiting and bloodshed in books: Short-term effects of reading physical and relational aggression in literature," *British Journal of Social Psychology*, 2012, pp. 188-196. S. M. Coyne, *et al.*, "Two sides to the same coin: Relational and physical aggression in the media," *Journal of Aggression, Conflict and Peace Research*, 2012, pp. 186-201.

17. Gretchen Cundiff, "The Influence of Rap/Hip-Hop Music: A Mixed-Method Analysis on Audience Perceptions of Misogynistic Lyrics and the Issue of Domestic Violence," *The Elon Journal of Undergraduate Research in Communications*, Spring 2013, pp. 71-93.

18. Testimony of Brad J. Bushman before the House Subcommittee on Commerce, Justice, Science and Related Agencies, March 19, 2013.

19. Youssef Hasan, Laurent Begue, Michael Scharkow and Brad J. Bushman, "The more you play, the more aggressive you become: A long-term experimental study of cumulative violent video game effects on hostile expectations and aggressive behavior," *Journal of Experimental Social Psychology*, 2012, pp. 224-227; C. A. Anderson, *et al.*, "Violent video game effects on aggression, empathy, and prosocial behavior in Eastern and Western countries: A meta-analytic review," *Psychological Bulletin*, 2010; "Report of the Media Violence Commission," Media Violence Commission, International Society for Research on Aggression, 2012, pp. 335-341.

20. See Victor C. Strasburger, Barbara J. Wilson and Amy B. Jordan, *Children, Adolescents, and the Media* (3rd edition) (2014); Victor C. Strasburger, and Ed Donnerstein, "The New Media of Violent Video Games; Yet Same Old Media Problems?" *Clinical Pediatrics*, Aug. 22, 2013.

21. Jonathan L. Freedman, *Media Violence and its Effect on Aggression: Assessing the Scientific Evidence* (2002).

22. Jessica M. Jerabeck and Christopher J. Ferguson, "The influence of solitary and cooperative violent video game play on aggressive and prosocial behavior," *Computers in Human Behavior*, 2013.

23. Christopher J. Ferguson, "Is Reading 'Banned' Books Associated with Behavior Problems in Young Readers? The Influence of Controversial Young Adult Books on the Psychological Well-Being of Adolescents," *Psychology of Aesthetics, Creativity, and the Arts*, forthcoming, 2014.

24. "Gun Homicide Rate Down 49% Since 1993 Peak; Public Unaware," Pew Research Center, May 7, 2013, http://tinyurl.com/d9de4jn/. "Trends in Homicide Rates: United States, 1994-2010," Centers for Disease Control and Prevention, http://tinyurl.com/k7xv8qg; "Global Study on Homicide: 2011," United Nations Office on Drugs and Crime, 2011, http://tinyurl.com/72blpzw.

25. Gerard Jones, *Killing Monsters: Why Children Need Fantasy, Super Heroes, and Make-Believe Violence* (2003).

26. Lauren Myracle, "And the Banned Played On," *The Huffington Post*, April 16, 2012, http://tinyurl.com/le2rdvx.

27. Lawrence Kutner and Cheryl K. Olson, *Grand Theft Childhood: The Surprising Truth about Violent Video Games* (2008).

28. Joanne Cantor, "Review of Grand Theft Childhood: The Surprising Truth about Violent Video Games and What Parents Can Do," accessed at yourmindonmedia.com/wp-content/uploads/gtc_review.pdf.

29. Steven J. Kirsh, *Children, Adolescents, and Media Violence, A Critical Look at the Research* (2012), p. 97.

30. Christopher J. Ferguson, "Blazing Angels or Resident Evil? Can Violent Video Games Be a Force for Good?" *Review of General Psychology*, 2010, pp. 68-81.

31. James Paul Gee, *What Video Games Have to Teach Us About Learning and Literacy* (2003), pp. 199-200.

32. Steven Johnson, *Everything Bad Is Good For You* (2005), p. 9.

33. In "Sunday Dialogue: Violence in the Media," *The New York Times*, Sept. 28, 2013.

34. *Ginsberg v. New York*, 390 US 629, 1968.

35. "Rockefeller Works to Reduce Violence and Indecency on Television," U.S. Senate, March 14, 2005, http://tinyurl.com/k6aawq4.

36. Entertainment Software Association, "Computer and Video Game Ratings and the Law," www.theesa.com/policy/effective_ratings_system_argument.asp.

37. Gabe Rottman, "Worst Facts Make Worst Law With Violent Video Games," American Civil Liberties Union, http://tinyurl.com/nyhjy96.

38. H. B. Shaffer, "Violence in the Media," *Editorial Research Reports*, May 17, 1972, available at *CQ Researcher Plus Archive*, http://library.cqpress.com/.

39. *Mutual Film Corporation v. Industrial Commission of Ohio*, 236 US 230, 1915; Ford H. MacGregor, "Official Censorship Legislation," *Annals of the American Academy of Political and Social Science, The Motion Picture in Its Economic and Social Aspects*, November 1926, pp. 163-174.

40. "Interim Report of the Committee on the Judiciary Pursuant to S. Res. 89 and S. Res. 190, A Part of the Investigation of Juvenile Delinquency in the United States," Committee on the Judiciary, 1954.

41. MacGregor, *op. cit.*; Kirsch, *op. cit.*

42. Christopher J. Ferguson, *Adolescents, Crime, and the Media: A Critical Analysis* (2013).

43. *Joseph Burstyn Inc. v. Wilson, et al.*, 343 U.S. 495, May 26, 1952, www.law.cornell.edu/supremecourt/text/343/495.

44. "Hearings before the Subcommittee to Investigate Juvenile Delinquency of the Committee on the Judiciary," U.S. Senate, April 21, 22 and June 4, 1954.

45. "Comic Books and Juvenile Delinquency," Interim Report of the Committee on the Judiciary Pursuant to S. Res. 89 and S. Res. 190, A Part of the Investigation of Juvenile Delinquency in the United States, 1954." Also see "Hearing on comic books and children," Subcommittee on Juvenile delinquency, https://archive.org/details/juveniledelinque54unit.

46. "Interim Report of the Committee on the Judiciary," 1954.

47. "Juvenile Delinquency (Motion Pictures)," hearings before the Subcommittee to Investigate Juvenile Delinquency of the Committee on the Judiciary, U.S. Senate, June 15-18, 1955, http://tinyurl.com/kn8tm7v.

48. "Juvenile Delinquency (Television Programs)," hearings before the U.S. Senate Committee on the Judiciary, Subcommittee to Investigate Juvenile Delinquency in the U.S., 1955.

49. For background, see Charles S. Clarke, "TV Violence," *CQ Researcher*, March 26, 1993, pp. 265-288.

50. *Ginsburg v. New York* 390 US 629, April 22, 1968, http://tinyurl.com/mta8gym.

51. "History of Motion Picture Association of America," www.mpaa.org/about/history; surgeon general's report, 1972, *op. cit.*

52. R. K. Baker and S. J. Ball, "Mass Media and Violence: A staff report to the National Commission on the Causes and Prevention of Violence," 1969.

53. The show portrayed actress Linda Blair being sexually assaulted in prison with a mop handle.

54. In 1996, Congress amended Title III of Communications Act to require all television sets sold in the United States to incorporate v-chip technology to block violent, sexual or other programming. The act also provided cable subscribers with ways to block unwanted programming. See *Action for Children's Television v. FCC.*

55. Ashley Strickland, "A brief history of young adult literature," CNN.com, Oct. 17, 2013; *Board of Education, Island Trees Union Free School District v. Pico*, 457 U.S. 853, 1982.

56. Carly A. Kocurek, "The Agony and the Exidy: A History of Video Game Violence and the Legacy of Death Race," *The International Journal of Computer Games Research*, September 2012; "Death Race Video Game Outrages U.S. Safety Council," *Eugene Register-Guard*, Dec. 26, 1976.

57. *Video Software Dealers Assn. v. Webster*, 8th Circuit, 968 F.2d 684, July 1, 1992.

58. Chris Kohler, "This Day in Tech: July 29, 1994: Videogame Makers Propose Ratings Board to Congress," *Wired*, July 29, 2009.

59. For background, see Peter Katel, "Debating Hip-Hop," *CQ Researcher*, June 15, 2007, pp. 529-552.

60. "Music Violence: How Does it Affect Our Children," hearing before the Subcommittee on Oversight of Government Management, Restructuring and the District of Columbia of the Senate Committee on Governmental Affairs, Nov. 6, 1997, http://tinyurl.com/mnuw8m3.

61. Jerald Block, "Lessons From Columbine: Virtual and Real Rage," *American Journal of Forensic Psychiatry*, July 2007; Mark Ward, "Columbine Families sue computer game makers," BBC News, May 1, 2001; The Associated Press, "Columbine lawsuit over video games dismissed," Nov. 14, 2007.

62. "Marketing Violent Entertainment to Children: A Review of Self-Regulation and Industry Practices in the Motion Picture, Music Recording & Electronic Game Industries," U.S. Federal Trade Commission, Sept. 11, 2000.

63. "Joint Statement on the Impact of Entertainment Violence on Children," Congressional Public Health Summit, July 26, 2000, www2.aap.org/advocacy/releases/jstmtevc.htm.

64. "Hearing on Children and Media Violence, House Energy and Commerce Subcommittee on Telecommunication and Finance," July 2001.

65. Dan Frosch, "Colorado Police Link Rise in Violence to Music," *The New York Times*, Sept. 3, 2007, http://tinyurl.com/4jjsam6. Stephen Holden, "Singing of the Cartels, and Investigating Them," *The New York Times*, Nov. 21, 2013.

66. "Home Technology Monitor Survey," Knowledge Networks SRI, Spring 2004; "Dying to Entertain: Violence on Prime Time Broadcast Television 1998-2006," Parents Television Council, January 2007.

67. Federal Communications Commission, "In the Matter of Violent Television Programming and Its Impact on Children," April 6, 2007.

68. "The Impact of Media Violence on Children," hearing before the Committee on Commerce, Science and Transportation, U.S. Senate, June 26, 2007, http://tinyurl.com/lyhapv3.

69. "The Impact of Interactive Violence on Children," hearing before the Committee on Commerce, Science and Transportation, U.S. Senate, March 21, 2000, Washington, D.C., 2003. Also see *American Amusement Machine Association vs. Kendrick*, 7th Circuit, 2001; *Interactive Digital Software Assn. vs.*

St. Louis, 8th Circuit, 2003; *Video Software Deals Assn. v. Maleng*, 325 F. Supp. 2d 1180, 1188 (W.D. Wash., 2004); *Entertainment Software Assn. v. Blagojevich*, 404 F. Supp. 2d 1051, N.D. Ill. 2005; *Entertainment Software Assn. vs. Hatch*, 8th Circuit, 2008.

70. "What's In a Game? Regulation of Violent Video Games and the First Amendment," hearing before the Subcommittee on Civil Rights, Property Rights and Constitutional Rights, Committee on the Judiciary, U.S. Senate, March 26, 2006.

71. Joe Baca, D-Calif., The Video Game Health Labeling Act of 2011.

72. See "Priorities for Research to Reduce the Threat of Firearm-Related Violence," Institute of Medicine, June 2013.

73. Josh Gerstein, "Wolf lashes out at violent video games," *Politico*, March 14, 2013, http://tinyurl.com/lxconza.

74. "Youth Violence: What We Need to Know," Report of the Subcommittee on Youth Violence of the Advisory Committee to the Social, Behavioral and Economic Sciences Directorate, National Science Foundation, Feb. 1 and 2, 2013.

75. "Video Games Ratings Enforcement Act," H.R. 287, introduced by Jim Matheson, D-Utah, Jan. 15, 2013.

76. Eric Lichtblau, "Makers of Violent Video Games Marshall Support to Fend Off Regulation," *The New York Times*, Jan. 11, 2013.

77. "Biden seeks video game industry input on guns," The Associated Press, Jan. 11, 2013; Sen. Jay Rockefeller, "Does videogame violence have an impact on children?" *Variety Special Report: Violence and Entertainment*, 2013, http://variety.com/2013/voices/opinion/rockefeller-2476/.

78. "Only a Game: Why Censoring New Media Won't Stop Gun Violence," 2013, executive summary, Media Coalition.

79. Xan Brooks, "Gun Control: Hollywood ready to 'help America heal,' says MPAA head," *The Guardian*, Dec. 21, 2012, www.theguardian.com/film/2012/dec/21/gun-control-hollywood.

80. "Violence in the Media — Psychologists Study TV and Video Game Violence for Potential Harmful Effects," American Psychological Association, undated, http://tinyurl.com/cqzd8h8.

81. "Resolution on Violence in Video Games and Interactive Media," American Psychological Association, 2005, http://tinyurl.com/bpn3p5n; "Scholars' Open Statement to the APA Task Force on Violent Media," delivered to the APA Task Force 9/26/13, http://tinyurl.com/mvd2c5n.

82. Alan Yu, "Game Director Shifts From Grand Theft Auto To Iranian Revolution," NPR's All Tech Considered, Dec. 13, 2013, http://tinyurl.com/kdkz5dj.

83. Douglas A. Gentile and John P. Murray, "Media Violence and Public Policy: Where we have been and where we should go," in Douglas A. Gentile (ed.), *Media violence and children: A complete guide for parents and professionals* (2003); Christopher J. Ferguson, "Violent Video Games and Supreme Court: Lessons for the Scientific Community in the Wake of Brown v. Entertainment Merchants Association," *American Psychologist*, February-March 2013.

84. Ken Paulson, "Court's video-game ruling shields emerging media," First Amendment Center, June 27, 2011, http://tinyurl.com/3qmgk64.

BIBLIOGRAPHY

Selected Sources

Books

Abate, Michelle Ann, *Bloody Murder: The Homicide Tradition in Children's Literature*, Johns Hopkins University Press, 2013.
An Ohio State University professor of literature compiles a list of literary hits that entail violence, from *Grimm's Fairy Tales* to modern young-adult novels.

Ferguson, Christopher J., *Adolescents, Crime, and the Media: A Critical Analysis*, Spring Science+Business Media, 2013.
A Stetson University psychology professor examines the debate about whether media consumption is related to

youth crime and arguments over whether restrictions should be placed on media.

Gentile, D. A., ed., *Media violence and children: A complete guide for parents and professionals***, 2nd ed., Praeger Publishing, in press.**

The director of the Media Research Lab at Iowa State University presents a range of articles on recent research regarding the effects of television, film, video game, music and Internet violence.

Singer, Dorothy G., and Jerome L. Singer, Eds., *Handbook of Children and the Media***, 2nd ed., Sage Publications, 2012.**

The codirectors of the Yale University Family Television Research and Consultation Center affiliated with the Zigler Center for Child Development and Public Policy provide a collection of essays examining children's use of new media technology and summarizing research on children and the media.

Strasburger, Victor C., *et al.***,** *Children Adolescents and the Media***, 3rd ed., Sage Publications, 2014.**

A University of New Mexico School of Medicine pediatrics professor (Strasburger), with a University of Illinois communications professor and a University of Pennsylvania communications professor discuss research on how media impact the lives of children and adolescents.

Articles

"Special Report: Violence and Entertainment," *Variety***, 2013, http://variety.com/violence.**

This lengthy report includes a compilation of guest columns from media producers, writers, researchers, lawmakers and others addressing the issue of violence in entertainment media from various angles.

Pozios, Vasilis K., *et al.***, "Does Media Violence Lead to the Real Thing?"** *The New York Times***, Aug. 23, 2013, www.nytimes.com/2013/08/25/opinion/sunday/does-media-violence-lead-to-the-real-thing.html?_r=0.**

In an op-ed, three forensic psychiatrists who founded the consulting group Broadcast Thought say research shows that media exposure is a risk factor for violence that could be easily modified but should be further studied along with other risk factors.

Reports and Studies

"Media and Violence: An Analysis of Current Research," Common Sense Media, Winter 2013, www.commonsensemedia.org/research/media-and-violence-an-analysis-of-current-research.

A nonprofit organization that provides educational materials for teachers and parents regarding media content and ratings explores existing research on the effects of exposing youths to media violence and notes where research is lacking.

"Priorities for Research to Reduce the Threat of Firearm-Related Violence," Institute of Medicine, June 2013, www.iom.edu/Reports/2013/Priorities-for-Research-to-Reduce-the-Threat-of-Firearm-Related-Violence.aspx.

In response to an executive order by President Obama after the December 2012 Sandy Hook school shooting, the Centers for Disease Control and Prevention, the Institute of Medicine and the National Research Council assembled a committee of experts to develop a potential research agenda focused on firearm-related violence.

"Youth Violence: What We Need to Know," Report of the Subcommittee on Youth Violence of the Advisory Committee to the Social, Behavioral and Economic Sciences Directorate, National Science Foundation, Feb. 1-2, 2013. http://wolf.house.gov/sites/wolf.house.gov/files/documents/Violence_Report_Long_v4.pdf.

The National Science Foundation Subcommittee on Youth Violence reviews existing research on the potential causes of youth violence and where more research is needed.

Bushman, Brad J., *et al.***, "Gun Violence Trends in Movies,"** *Pediatrics***, Nov. 11, 2013.**

A study focusing on the top 30 films since 1950 concludes that violence in films has more than doubled and that gun violence in PG-13 rated films has more than tripled since the rating was introduced in 1985.

DeLisi, Matt, *et al.***, "Violent Video Games, Delinquency, and Youth Violence: New Evidence,"** *Youth Violence and Juvenile Justice***, April 2013.**

A study of institutionalized juvenile delinquents shows that playing violent video games is associated with some measures of delinquency and antisocial behavior.

For More Information

American Academy of Pediatrics, 141 Northwest Point Blvd., Elk Grove Village, IL 60007-1098; 847-434-4000 or 800-433-9016; www.aap.org. Provides background on media use and guidance for pediatricians, parents and educators.

American Psychological Association, 750 First St., NE, Washington, DC 20002-4242; 800-374-2721 or 202-336-5500; www.apa.org. Publishes research on the effects of violent media on children and adolescents.

Center for Media Literacy, 22837 Pacific Coast Highway, #472, Malibu, CA 90265; 310-804-3985; www.medialit .org. Provides research, professional development and educational resources to support media literacy education.

Center on Media and Child Health, Children's Hospital Boston, Harvard Medical School and Harvard School of Public Health, 300 Longwood Ave., Boston, MA 02115; 617-355-2000; www.cmch.tv. Researches the effects of media on the physical, mental and social health of children.

Common Sense Media, 650 Townsend, Suite 435, San Francisco, CA 94103; 415-863-0600; www.commonsense media.org. Provides educational materials about media for classrooms, ratings and reviews of books, movies, music, video and computer games, websites and apps.

Entertainment Software Ratings Board, 317 Madison Ave., 22nd Floor, New York, NY 10017; www.esrb.org. Self-regulatory body created by the Entertainment Software Association that assigns ratings for video games and apps and enforces industry-adopted advertising guidelines.

Media Coalition, 19 Fulton St., New York, NY 10038; 212-587-4025; mediacoalition.org. Defends the First Amendment rights of booksellers, publishers, librarians, video game manufacturers and retailers and the recording industry.

Media Power Youth, 1245 Elm St. Manchester, NH 03101; 603-222-1200; mediapoweryouth.org. Works with public-health programs, schools and communities to teach media literacy to young people.

Motion Picture Association of America, 15301 Ventura Blvd., Building E, Sherman Oaks, CA 91403; 818-995-6600; www.mpaa.org. Provides a guide to film ratings and list of ratings of specific films.

Parents Television Council, 707 Wilshire Blvd., No. 2075, Los Angeles, CA 90017; 213-403-1300 or 800-882-6868; w2.parentstv.org. Monitors prime time television shows and PG and G-rated movies; provides summaries for parents of certain films and shows, campaigns for TV ratings.

Recording Industry Association of America, 1025 F St., N.W., 10th Floor, Washington, DC 20004; 202-775-0101; www.riaa.com. Opposes efforts to censor music, including efforts to restrict sales to minors and to create a uniform labeling standard for the entertainment industry.

13

Digital Journalism

Kenneth Jost

Former *Washington Post* star reporter Ezra Klein is one of several top journalists who have jumped from traditional print publications to explore new frontiers in digital journalism. Klein, who launched the *Post*'s popular site *Wonkblog*, started *Vox* — "a general news site for the 21st century" — with the main goal of explaining the news.

From *CQ Researcher*,
May 30, 2014

M any news junkies who logged onto their computers Sunday night, April 6, went straight to a site with a full-screen image of the U.S. Capitol under ominously gray clouds. A headline superimposed over the scene declared: "How politics makes us stupid."

The foreboding tableau marked the eagerly awaited launch of the newest of a growing number of digital-only news sites: *Vox*, the brainchild of journalistic wunderkind Ezra Klein, who turned 30 on May 9. For the debut, Klein wrote a 4,000-word essay built around research suggesting that political partisanship makes people impervious to new information contradictory to their views.[1]

Klein had launched *Vox* after a storied, five-year run at *The Washington Post* as the founder and main writer for the newspaper's political site, *Wonkblog*. After *The Post* refused Klein's request for a multimillion-dollar expansion of the must-read site, he left in January to practice what he calls a new kind of journalism. Its mission would be "to explain the news" and to move readers "from curiosity to understanding."

In years past, would-be Clark Kents and Lois Lanes aspired to work at nationally recognized newspapers such as *The Washington Post* or *The New York Times*. Today, however, newspapers are often dismissed as "legacy media," and stars such as Klein are jumping ship to explore new frontiers in digital journalism. Their sites are drawing mixed reviews for design, even as they attract attention and traffic for their content and their role as experiments in how to present news and run a successful news business today. They join

Most Americans Get Their News Online

Percentage who say they get their news sometimes or often from a digital source.

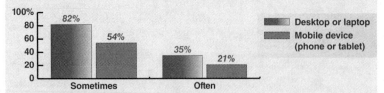

Source: Kenneth Olmstead, "5 key findings about digital news audiences," Pew Research Center, March 17, 2014, http://tinyurl.com/lr7tqb9.

other digital-only general news sites that over the past decade have been luring news consumers onto the Web.

"The vast majority of Americans now get news in some digital format," the Pew Research Center's Journalism Project notes in its most recent report "State of the News Media 2014."[2]

Others, who like Klein are making closely watched transitions, include Nate Silver, who built a name for himself as a data-crunching political handicapper at *The New York Times*' blog *FiveThirtyEight*, and veteran technology reporters Walt Mossberg and Kara Swisher, who founded the closely watched tech blog *AllThingsD* at Dow Jones, publisher of *The Wall Street Journal*. Silver left *The Times* last year and launched a data-journalism site, also called *FiveThirtyEight*, on March 17 under sponsorship of the sports network ESPN. Mossberg and Swisher launched their technology news site *Re/code* on Jan. 2 with financial backing from NBCUniversal and the investment operation of former Yahoo chief executive Terry Semel.

In another high-profile start-up, Glenn Greenwald is editor of *The Intercept*, launched on Feb. 2 and funded by Pierre Omidyar, the billionaire founder of eBay, the Internet auction site. Greenwald, who previously worked with the U.S. website of the British newspaper *The Guardian*, made international headlines over the past year with Pulitzer Prize-winning disclosures of U.S. and British global surveillance based on documents leaked by former National Security Agency (NSA) contractor Edward Snowden.

"It seems like not a week goes by without an announcement of a new project online headed by a prominent journalist," says Jim Romenesko, a veteran newspaperman who tracks media on the eponymous website *jimromenesko.com*. "A lot of legacy journalists want to try something new, something that's maybe a little bit edgy and experimental."

Among the best known of the older so-called digital natives, *The Huffington Post* mimics conventional newspapers in format and tone, while the virally popular *BuzzFeed* traffics in irreverent entertainment even while adding serious journalism. Other popular sites include what are known as news aggregators — sites that republish stories from other news media. Two of the most widely viewed are maintained by the established Internet search engine companies, *Google News* and *Yahoo News*. By contrast, two newer aggregators — *Mashable* and *Flipboard* — are the built-from-scratch creations of entrepreneurially minded techies, both tied to the explosion in social media. *Mashable* says it "covers top social media news," meaning both news about social media and news popular on social media; *Flipboard* self-identifies as "Your social magazine for iPad, iPhone and Android."[3]

Meanwhile, traditional print and broadcast media are putting more energy, effort and resources into their websites amid declining news readership and viewership.[4] "There's no stopping the migration from print to digital," says Tom Rosenstiel, executive director of the newspaper industry-affiliated American Press Institute and a former reporter with the *Los Angeles Times* and *Newsweek*.

These trends amount to "a virtual digital revolution," according to Tim McGuire, a longtime newspaperman and now a professor at Arizona State University's Walter Cronkite School of Journalism in Phoenix. "There is no choice," he explains. "It's the set of tools we have today. We didn't keep driving horses and buggies when cars came along."

The digital revolution has changed the economics of the newspaper, magazine and television industries. Classified advertising in print newspapers has shriveled, while retail and national advertising have shrunk as well, though less dramatically. Newspapers and other media have shed thousands of jobs, but the losses have not been offset by employment at digital publications.

The developments have prompted alarmed hand-wringing. The total number of newspaper reporters, editors and other journalists fell to 38,000 in 2012 — down nearly one-third from a peak of 56,400 in 2000, according to the American Society of News Editors' annual census.[5] Nearly 60 percent of journalists surveyed recently by Indiana University's School of Journalism say journalism is headed in the wrong direction. Slightly more than 60 percent say their newsrooms have shrunk in the past few years. Those interviewed worked for online media as well as traditional print, television, radio and news services.[6]

Digital Sites Debut to Mixed Reviews

New digital-only news sites include several launched by prominent journalists that debuted with great fanfare and high expectations for their content. But the sites drew mixed reviews from design experts surveyed by *Digiday,* a site for digital media, marketing and advertising professionals.

Name	Founder(s)	Review of Design
Vox	Ezra Klein	"Accessible"; "best job" of creating brand identity
FiveThirtyEight	Nate Silver	"Straightforward" look, but "a lot of scrolling" required
The Intercept	Glenn Greenwald	"Looks . . . like a bare-bones blog"
Re/code	Walt Mossberg, Kara Swisher	"Hard to read," but good information

Source: Lucia Moses, "Which new digital news publisher designed it best?" *Digiday,* April 9, 2014, http://tinyurl.com/om2r5ms.

Some journalism experts see a bright side even while acknowledging the wrenching changes. "News for the most part is in fine shape," writes Mitchell Stephens, a professor at New York University's Arthur L. Carter Journalism Institute, in his new book *Beyond News.*[7]

Technology has been "a boon for news," Stephens explains in his book. Despite the job losses, he writes, technology has allowed fewer hands to gather more information on "an extraordinarily wide variety of events" from "an extraordinarily wide variety of sources" and to disseminate the information "in a wide variety of formats fast and far."

Others agree. "Digital has made it possible for people to do different things that they were not able to do before," says Pablo Boczkowski, director of the Program in Media, Technology and Society at Northwestern University in Evanston, Ill. Among other changes, Boczkowski notes that people can now access news around the clock — at work, at home or on the go — and can comment on articles without being filtered by editors. Digital "has broadened the possibility of public engagement," he says.

At the same time, some experts and critics say the new digital-only news sites have some less attractive features — in particular, a higher degree of political partisanship. Mark Jurkowitz, associate director of the Pew Research Center's Journalism Project and a former ombudsman for *The Boston Globe,* complains of the "proliferation of argumentative ideological media" in the digital world.

For instance, *The Huffington Post* is widely seen as having a left-liberal tilt, although founder Arianna Huffington minimizes the importance of any political slant.[8] Other sites, however, are overtly partisan, such as the progressive *Think Progress Memo* or its conservative counterpart *Red State.*

McGuire agrees on the increase in partisanship, but sees market demand as driving the trend. "You've got people seeking affirmation, not information," he says.

As traditional news organizations still strive to find their place in the new digital world, some of the older digital-only publications have shown signs of health. *The Huffington Post* was acquired by the Internet service provider AOL in February 2011 in a $315 million deal. AOL chief executive Tim Armstrong has said the publication may be profitable in 2014, taking into account the conferences it organizes and other associated businesses.[9] *BuzzFeed* has expanded its editorial staff to 170 since hiring the rising journalistic star Ben Smith as editor late in 2011. Jurkowitz says he asked Smith in a telephone interview to explain the phenomenal growth. Smith's answer: "The business staff has overperformed."

Magazine Industry Tries to Adjust to Digital Age

Going all-digital is "like life support — before we pull the plug."

For millions of African-Americans, *Jet* has been essential reading for the past six decades — a weekly chronicle of events and issues that were barely covered, if at all, in the nation's predominantly white news media. Starting in July, however, *Jet* will no longer be delivered in the mail or available at newsstands and grocery store checkout lines.

Instead, *Jet* will switch from print to an all-digital format. In announcing the move on May 7, Johnson Publishing Co., which also publishes the black-oriented magazine *Ebony*, called the step a "proactive decision to adapt to the changing needs of its readers" as they increasingly want information quickly and easily.[1]

Jet, launched in 1951, was an invaluable source of information for black Americans during the most tumultuous decades of the civil rights revolution. The pocket-sized magazine was a weekly until it cut back to every three weeks last year.

Jet's move is evidence that the magazine industry, like the newspaper industry, is trying to adjust to the digital age.

The magazine industry's trade association changed its name in 2010 to recognize the change: the Magazine Publishers Association became instead MPA —the Association of Magazine Media.

"The industry can no longer by judged by print alone," says Meredith Wagner, the association's executive vice president for communications. "Magazine media is an evolving industry that is not tied to any one single format or medium."

Jet's move does not sit as well, however, with one expert on the industry. "It's very bad news," says Samir Husni, director of the Magazine Innovation Center at the University of Mississippi in Oxford and a consultant to magazine companies. "Instead of investing in the magazine, they say, 'We are going to be cutting the magazine.'"

For Husni, print remains an essential part of what he calls the "total experience" of subscribing to a magazine, even as readers also want immediate access to continually updated content online. The digital-only route, he says, "has been like life support — before we pull the plug."

The newer sites — *Vox*, *FiveThirtyEight* and others — are works in progress at this point. Experts differ on their financial prospects. "Some will win, and some will lose," Arizona State's McGuire says. In the meantime, however, news and information consumers are able to choose from among an ever-expanding number of news sources. "The more, the merrier," says media tracker Romenesko.

As the news industry continues to adapt to change, here are some of the questions being debated:

Do digital-only publications benefit readers?

The digital media site *Mashable* scored a coup of sorts last fall by hiring Jim Roberts, a longtime editor at *The New York Times*, as executive editor and chief content officer. Roberts announced his arrival in an open letter posted on *Mashable* on Oct. 30 that extolled the benefits

of digital technology in reporting news faster, combining text and video and allowing the site's users to help tell and spread stories via interactions with the site and social media.

"In other words," Roberts wrote, "as disruptive as certain technologies have been to the news business, they have created much greater benefits for those of us who make a living as communicators — and for our audience."[10]

Mashable's "community" — as Roberts termed the site's users — are greeted daily by a kaleidoscopic display of changing headlines and images on stories both weighty and light. The home page sorts stories under conventional headings such as U.S. & World, Tech, Business and Entertainment and newer usages such as Must Reads and Water Cooler.

The home pages of other digital sites offer users similarly wide arrays of options. *The Huffington Post* divides

Like newspapers, magazines have been in a challenging environment for decades. The weekly editions of such general-interest magazines as *Saturday Evening Post* and *Life* are distant memories from the 1960s and '70s. *Time* is a shrunken relic of its former self; *Newsweek*, which once had a circulation of 3.3 million, dropped its print edition at the end of 2012, only to return in March with a limited print run of only about 70,000 copies.[2] Monthly titles have also churned, with launches and closures as publishers feel out the changing environment.

Overall industry figures show that magazine circulation revenue peaked at $10.5 billion in 2005 and declined to $8.3 billion in 2011.[3] Total ad pages have fallen for the past two years, according to an MPA press release, but the decline slowed in 2013 to 4 percent from an 8 percent drop in 2012. Print ad revenue overall rose 1 percent, to $19.7 billion — presumably thanks to rate increases. But the trade association called 2013 a "growth year," primarily because of a 16 percent increase in tablet advertising revenue.[4]

Despite economic uncertainties, Husni says the magazine industry overall has a positive future, but only if it takes care of its print legacy. "The future of digital begins with print," he says. "The rumors of our demise," he adds, "have been greatly exaggerated."

— *Kenneth Jost*

Courtesy Johnson Publishing Co.

The pocket-size print version of *Jet* was once a staple for millions of African-American readers, but starting in July the magazine will switch from print to an all-digital format.

[1] "Johnson Publishing Company Announces Transition of JET Magazine to Digital Magazine," press release, Johnson Publishing, May 7, 2014, http://tinyurl.com/q2xtuwb; and Rem Reider, "'Jet' comes in for a digital landing," *USA Today*, May 8, 2014, p. 2B, http://tinyurl.com/nqgweh2.

[2] Leslie Kaufman, "Newsweek to Restart Printing Process," *The New York Times*, March 3, 2014, p. B1, http://tinyurl.com/k6y28up.

[3] "Top Statistics about Magazine Industry in the U.S. — Statista Dossier 2013," *Statista*, http://tinyurl.com/ms9f978.

[4] "2013 a Growth Year for Magazine Media Across Platforms," MPA — The Association of Magazine Media, Jan. 9, 2014, http://tinyurl.com/q737v3v.

topics into 44 general news and nine local categories, or "verticals" — to use the current news jargon. Users who click on "Sports," for example, find not just daily scores, standings and highlights, but also a wealth of features, commentaries and the like — many with reader comments numbering into the hundreds or beyond. In contrast to print newspapers or magazines, digital readers can never really "finish" exploring a site because there is always more to read, view, link to or share.

"There are obviously some real advantages to producing content in the digital space, which is infinite," says Pew's Jurkowitz. "It allows news consumers to do a much deeper dive into news content than they could in traditional platforms. You can click on links that can take you to original documents, links to everything that's been written about on that subject for the last three to four years, links to related issues or timelines."

Other veterans of print media also wax ecstatic. "Digital news is richer, more convenient," says Rosenstiel at the American Press Institute. "It's in my pocket when I want it. It's not confined to one medium."

At the same time, the wealth of news, information and commentary threatens overload, according to Jurkowitz. "It's obviously more difficult to be a news consumer in this digital age because there are so many choices," he explains.

"There are so many outlets now, so many information gatherers and distributors," says Jane McDonnell, executive director of the Online News Association, an organization for online journalists founded in 1999. "How do you know where your accurate journalism is coming from?"

The change reduces the agenda-setting and educational roles that news media have played for decades.

"People consume more of what they're interested in and less of what they're not interested in," says Northwestern professor Boczkowski. "That exacerbates the gap between what the public wants to know and what the media considers they should know about."

McGuire, the Arizona State professor, agrees. "You are no longer talking about the kind of mass publications that you and I are familiar with," he says. "The idea of mass has largely evaporated."

Social media tools contribute to the phenomenon. Computer-generated algorithms funnel stories on particular subjects or from particular viewpoints to users based on profiles developed from stories they followed in the past. Increasingly, people are referred to news via their friends on Facebook, Twitter, Instagram or other services rather than seeking out news sites on their own.[11] "Another question looming over developments in social media," the Pew report says, "is whether the self-selective process combined with algorithmic feeds are narrowing the kinds of information Americans are exposed to."[12]

Roberts voiced none of these concerns, however, as he assumed his new post at *Mashable*, where news is inextricably linked to social media. In his vision, the site's users are an essential part of newsgathering and reporting in the 21st century.

"[T]he *Mashable* community is not just a bunch of passive consumers, but are also active and thoughtful participants in the conversation, creators and contributors of unique content, and an essential part of the distribution chain," Roberts wrote. "The members of *Mashable*'s community are smart and voracious; they like to share, and it's *Mashable*'s mission to create smart material for them to do so."

Do digital-only publications have drawbacks for readers?

Visitors to *BuzzFeed* are greeted on the home page's left side by such conventional section headings as "News," "Entertainment" and "Life." On the right side, however, are headings such as "cute," "trashy" and "fail." Others are acronyms — "OMG" (for "Oh, my God"), "LOL" (for "laughing out loud") and "WTF," which uses a common obscenity to express surprise and disappointment.

The headings hark to *BuzzFeed*'s birth in 2006 as a social media site specializing in creating posts that would go viral and leave "buzz" in their wake. *BuzzFeed*'s most distinctive contribution to 21st-century journalism is the creation of the "listicle" — numbered combinations of images and text such as "43 Things That Will Make You Feel Old." But even as *BuzzFeed* has increased its editorial staff and moved into serious reporting and analysis, editor-in-chief Smith makes no apologies for relying on the whimsical to draw traffic.

"The fabric of politics has always been gossip and jokes and crazy personality stuff and memes," Smith, who came to *BuzzFeed* from the hyperpolitical website *Politico*, snapped at a *New York Times* interviewer in February 2013. "Political coverage that wants to be solely high-minded," he continued, "is missing huge chunks of the actual interplay of personality and power that is what actually drives things."[13]

The approach produces mixed reactions from media watchers. "Cat videos don't do anything for me," Pew's Jurkowitz remarks, referring to another common BuzzFeed feature. But he adds that traditional newspapers also offered less-than-serious fare, including comics, crossword puzzles and horoscopes. "There's always been part of American media that's been trivial and light," he says. "There's enough substantive content out there."

Arizona State's McGuire agrees. "*BuzzFeed* does some things that make journalistic traditionalists squint a lot, but they are talking about doing more serious journalism," he says. "Us [sic] grand pooh-bahs have worried about the trivialization of the news for the past 30 years," he adds. "With every tool you can do bad things."

Media watchers raise concerns about more serious downsides of digital journalism — most notably, inaccuracies and ideological biases. As Jurkowitz notes, digital journalism's emphasis on speed increases the possibility that some information will prove inaccurate.

"The newspaper newsroom, the television newsroom — editors had time to think about what they had, what they didn't have, what they needed to fill holes," Jurkowitz says. With digital publications, "there's a built-in error rate," he says.

McDonnell, with the Online News Association, acknowledges the increased risk of errors in digital journalism's emphasis on speed. But she notes that some of the mistakes are spread online by nonjournalists. "It's a journalist's job to figure out what's real and what's not," she says. Digital also has an offsetting advantage: the possibility of instantaneous corrections, unlike in print publications or scheduled radio or television newscasts.

Jurkowitz also complains about what he calls "the hybrid mix of fact and opinion" found in some digital sites. "You get a lot of ideology in digital news," he says. News sites on both sides of the ideological spectrum "play loose with the facts because they are in service to a particular idea."

Stephens, the NYU professor, also sees more ideology in digital journalism, but views the trend more favorably. "There's great opinionated analysis that appears all over in this news ecology," he says. In his book, Stephens argues that journalism in the 20th century became too wedded to "the religion of objectivity." He calls instead for "wisdom journalism" — journalism that "includes and even emphasizes informed, interpretive, explanatory, even opinionated takes on current events."[14]

Stephens is also untroubled by the cat videos and the like. "Newsstands were and are still filled with a lot of very dumb magazines which are mostly concerned with celebrities and other trivialities," he says. "Obviously, we're going to get a lot of that on line."

For his part, *BuzzFeed*'s Smith believes that humor, done well, is one of the keys to the success of digital journalism. To reach people these days, he wrote in an essay in *Playboy*, "you have to write an article so funny, so revelatory or so trenchant that they will actively share it with their friends. To go viral, you have to do something excellent."[15]

Will the new digital news sites succeed financially?

Swisher and Mossberg created a money-making business under Dow Jones's auspices with their "All Things Digital" technology conferences, which began in 2003 and gave birth to the *AllThingsD* blog four years later. Now that they have gone out on their own with a digital tech news site, *Re/code*, Swisher acknowledges that the financial prospects are uncertain.

In every year they were with Dow Jones, "*AllThingsD* was profitable," Swisher told an interviewer with *San*

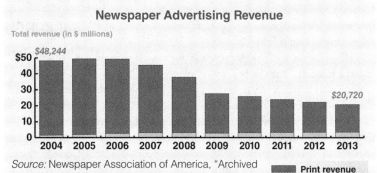

Newspaper Ad Revenue Plummeted

Revenue for newspaper print and online advertising fell 57 percent from 2004 to 2013.

Newspaper Advertising Revenue

Source: Newspaper Association of America, "Archived Advertising & Circulation Revenue Data," undated, http://tinyurl.com/d83po24; 2013 figures from "Business Model Evolving, Circulation Revenue Rising," Newspaper Association of America, April 18, 2014, http://tinyurl.com/kljkoj7.

Francisco magazine in April. "We'll probably lose money this year, and that will be upsetting. I'm focused on getting to a place where we can prove that journalism can make good money on the web. So we'll see about that."[16]

Klein was similarly reluctant to make financial predictions one week after the launch of his brainchild *Vox*. "You've gotta give this stuff some time to play out," he told an interviewer for *New York* magazine. "People are just constantly pronouncing on business strategies or content strategies. We're all going to be different organizations a year from now than we are today."[17]

The four most buzz-producing new sites — *Vox*, *FiveThirtyEight*, *Re/code* and the Intercept — all start with solid financial backing, but most media watchers are hesitating to make specific forecasts about their long-term viability. "Some will win, some will lose," says McGuire, the Arizona State professor. "You're at a high stage of experimentation."

Among those more skeptical is media watcher Michael Wolff, who writes for, among other publications, *GQ*. In a chat with Hearst Magazines president David Carey in early April just as *Vox* was being launched, Wolff was openly contemptuous of the likely fortunes of journalists-turned-entrepreneurs such as Klein and others.

"There is not a chance in the world," said Wolff, who wrote a 1998 book, *Burn Rate*, about the failure of his own Internet media company. "It's just preposterous. I don't know what they're thinking, what they're smoking. Nobody knows anything about selling an ad, nobody knows anything about aggregating an audience. So I think this is, to put it kindly, a bubble."[18]

Fellow media watcher Romenesko, for one, dismisses Wolff's forecast. "I think he's a kind of negative Nancy," Romenesko says. "They're smart people. I don't think they're going to throw buckets of money out the window."

The new sites follow in the steps of older publications that have made money with digital journalism. "*BuzzFeed* says they're profitable now," Romenesko notes. "The secret is to stay lean and be cautious."

Boczkowski, the Northwestern professor, also emphasizes the need to be cautious and keep expectations low. "Sure, there is a way to make money — the question is how much money," he says. "Making money involves having costs less than the income. The question is how to keep the costs low and how to get revenue."

Vox, *FiveThirtyEight*, *Re/code* and *The Intercept* are all starting out as free sites seeking revenue from advertising and other sources. An exception to that pattern is *The Information*, a tech industry news site launched in December by former *Wall Street Journal* reporter Jessica Lessin, with an annual subscription cost of $399. "Instead of chasing the highest number of eyeballs," Lessin explained in a blog post, "we will chase and deliver the most valuable news."[19]

Digital advertising revenue could prove disappointing for digital sites, as it has so far for legacy media. A recent survey notes that companies are spending a relatively small portion of their digital marketing budgets — only 12.5 percent — on digital advertising. A much bigger portion — around 40 percent — was spent on social networks, email marketing, mobile marketing and company websites and blogs.[20]

Romenesko notes, however, that digital sites do not need to rely solely on advertising. "The conference business is very lucrative for them, too," he notes, citing All Things Digital as an example. "They're finding ways to get revenue beyond advertising."

The new sites are not alone in trying to figure out the new economics of the journalism business, according to the experts. "All of these startups — have they figured out

some kind of business model?" Jurkowitz asks rhetorically. "Frankly, the consensus is no. They have not figured out what the legacy organizations haven't figured out either."

BACKGROUND
Changing Technologies

The technology now transforming journalism may seem revolutionary, but it is only the latest in a succession of innovations since the invention of the printing press that have helped disseminate news ever faster and ever wider. Newspapers became a daily, household commodity in the United States by the turn of the 20th century thanks to the steam-powered cylindrical press. Radio brought the sound of history into the living room by the 1920s and '30s; television added pictures in the 1940s and '50s. And with the launch of the World Wide Web in 1990, people around the world gained a tool for nearly instantaneous access to the events of the day.[21]

The German blacksmith Johannes Gutenberg made handwritten manuscripts and woodblock prints obsolete when, sometime around 1439, he combined the essential elements of what was once "modern" printing: movable type, oil-based inks and a screw-driven press. The printers of 18th-century colonial America, such as Benjamin Franklin and John Peter Zenger, used much the same technology to print the often highly partisan newspapers that played an important part in unifying colonists around the cause of independence.

The 19th-century invention of the steam-driven cylindrical press made newspapers widely accessible and the newspaper business reliably profitable, according to NYU professor Stephens. Printer Benjamin Day, in 1835, was first in the United States to use a steam-driven press to mass-produce his newspaper, the *New York Sun*, and sell copies for a penny each. The great turn-of-the-century publishers — William Randolph Hearst and Joseph Pulitzer, among others — showed that the so-called penny press could bring news to the masses at a healthy profit. Those newspapers depended on another 19th-century advance, the telegraph, for news accounts written by far-flung reporters and published not after months, weeks or even days, but the very next day.

In the 20th century, radio and then television erased even that delay. Americans listened in their living rooms to President Franklin D. Roosevelt's fireside chats delivered from the White House in the 1930s. Beginning with Harry S. Truman in 1949, Americans grew accustomed to watching their president take the oath of office via live television — first in black and white and then, in the 1960s, in "living color." In 1969, millions around the world viewed the first man to step onto the moon via televised images delayed only by the time required for radio waves to travel 240,000 miles across space.

Newspapers and the news divisions of what were then the three commercial TV networks built profitable businesses by selling news written and edited for mass audiences. Americans had more information about events of the day than ever before, but Stephens rues what was missing. "They're mostly recounting the facts," he says of mid- and late 20th-century U.S. journalists. "They didn't provide anywhere near the ability to understand the facts."

The World Wide Web, which allows users to link easily to information via the global network of computer systems, created new opportunities for journalists to disseminate news farther and faster. The transformation now so apparent materialized only slowly. Credit for inventing the Web goes to the British computer scientist Tim Berners-Lee, now Sir Timothy. Working as an independent contractor at the European Organization for Nuclear Research, known as CERN, Berners-Lee developed the now-familiar hypertext transfer protocol (HTTP), hypertext markup language (HTML) and Web browser to facilitate communication among the center's dispersed facilities. The first site outside CERN was brought online in January 1991.[22]

The "handful" of newspapers publishing on the Web before 1995 grew to 175 that year and more than quadrupled to 702 by mid-1997, according to Northwestern professor Boczkowski.[23] *USA Today* boasted 2.5 million Web visitors in December 1998 — pitifully small in comparison to the newspaper's current figure of 35 million unique visitors a month. And the "online newspapers" of the period differed little from the print editions.

"They had not really figured out what was native to the digital space," Pew's Jurkowitz recalls. "They weren't doing any special thinking about the digital world."

Exploiting the Web

Within a few years of its launch, the World Wide Web was drawing interest from a growing array of companies,

Kara Swisher is among the print journalists making closely watched transitions to digital news. Along with Walt Mossberg, also a veteran technology reporter at *The Wall Street Journal*, she founded the much-heralded tech blog *AllThingsD* at Dow Jones, publisher of *The Journal*. Swisher and Mossberg left Dow Jones to start tech news site *Re/code*.

organizations and computer-savvy individuals. Over time, the number of websites worldwide grew into the hundreds of millions and the number of users to more than 2 billion by 2010.[24] The growing popularity of the Web hurt other media, especially newspapers, by diverting both advertising revenue and readers' time and attention.

The economic impact of Web advertising on newspapers began to materialize early in the 21st century. Print retail advertising peaked at $22.2 billion in 2005 and fell by nearly half by 2011, according to the Newspaper Association of America, while print national advertising crested at $8.1 billion in 2004 and fell by more than half by 2011. Classified ad revenue was siphoned off by Web

Getty Images/Bloomberg/Matt Nager

Traditional newspapers, such as *The Dallas Morning News*, above, have seen their popularity dwindle as digital media have become increasingly popular. "There's no stopping the migration from print to digital," says Tom Rosenstiel, executive director of the American Press Institute. As a result, so-called "legacy media" are putting more effort and resources into developing their websites.

innovations such as Craigslist, a free online marketplace, and the Web auction site eBay. Print revenue from classifieds, which peaked at $19.6 billion in 2000, had plummeted by more than 70 percent by 2011. Online ad revenue gains offset less than 10 percent of the print revenue losses.[25] At the same time, to attract as many viewers as possible to those ads, almost all sites offered their news content for free.

The rapidly multiplying number of websites also contributed to the continuing decline in newspaper circulation and readership, which had begun in the 1970s. Free Web-based news aggregators — such as *Yahoo News*, launched in 2001, and *Google News*, launched in 2002 — gave audiences continually updated access to multiple news sources with no need for print copies. Government websites provided official information at the federal, state and local levels. Professional sports leagues created websites — such as *NFL.com* and *MLB.com* — as early as the mid-1990s for fans to follow games in real time and keep track of standings, scores, statistics and much more than any sports section could provide.

Special-interest blogs became essential reading for specific audiences. For example, two legal blogs launched in 2002 — *SCOTUSblog* on the Supreme Court and *How Appealing* on appellate litigation — provide news and analysis that judges, lawyers and legal affairs journalists

depend upon today. For health policy news, the Kaiser Family Foundation launched a free health-news site in 2009 that is similarly invaluable for people in and around the nation's largest industry sector.

Gawker was founded in 2003 as a Manhattan-oriented celebrity gossip site; Gawker Media developed seven other blogs, including the sports site *Deadspin*. Another popular sports site is *Grantland*, created by sports journalist Bill Simmons in 2011 and named in honor of one of the great sportswriters of the print era, Grantland Rice, whose daily column was syndicated across the country. For business audiences, the *Business Insider* is now a popular site with some original content after having been launched in 2009 as a blog and financial and tech news aggregator.

Newspapers were challenged more directly by new digital-only general news publications even as they tried to innovate online and simultaneously tend to the print editions that yielded roughly 80 percent of their revenue. In the clearest head-to-head matchup, the author and syndicated columnist Arianna Huffington launched *The Huffington Post* in May 2005 with financial backing from venture capitalist Kenneth Lehrer. The site's design mimicked to some extent the various sections of print newspapers. The site grew to become a 24/7 operation, with local and international editions, before the legacy Internet service provider AOL bought it in 2011 for $315 million.[26]

Within a year after *HuffPost*'s debut, two more of today's most popular sites were launched, both more as social media than the general news sites that they were to become. *Mashable* was the brainchild of Pete Cashmore, a college dropout in Aberdeen, Scotland. Three months shy of his 20th birthday, Cashmore launched *Mashable* in July 2005 as a tool for collecting news about social media and about what users were sharing. By 2009, *The Huffington Post* hailed Cashmore as one of the globe's "top game changers," crediting him with taking social media mainstream and "translating geek-speak for the curious and converted."[27]

BuzzFeed debuted in November 2006, created as "the Internet popularity contest" by Jonah Peretti, a graduate of the MIT Media Lab and co-founder of *The Huffington Post* along with Huffington and Lehrer. Peretti developed technologies for searching out items being posted and shared — creating "buzz," that is. He left *The Huffington Post* after the AOL purchase in 2011 to devote full time

CHRONOLOGY

Early 1990s *The World Wide Web is invented; online news publications are born.*

1990–1991 British computer scientist Tim Berners-Lee develops World Wide Web so his colleagues can collaborate; first site outside his institution comes online January 1991.

Mid-1990s Newspapers with online editions grow from 175 in 1995 to more than 700 by mid-1997. . . . Professional sports leagues establish websites for fans.

1999 Online News Association is founded.

2000s *More news goes online. . . . Classified ad revenue for print newspapers reaches peak and then declines by more than 70 percent over the decade.*

2001 Yahoo launches *Yahoo News* as news aggregator. . . . Annual classified ad revenue for print newspapers peaks at $19.6 billion and begins to decline; retail, national advertising begin less drastic declines in 2004, 2005.

2002 Google launches *Google News* as news aggregator. . . . *How Appealing* and *SCOTUSblog* launched as legal news websites.

2003 *Gawker.com* launches as Manhattan-based celebrity gossip site (January).

2005 *Huffington Post* launches as digital-only, national news source (May 9). . . . *Mashable* is founded as social media news aggregator (July).

2006 *BuzzFeed* launches as site to chronicle events, trends "on the rise and worth your time" (Nov. 17).

2007 Walt Mossberg and Kara Swisher launch *AllThingsD* blog at *The Wall Street Journal* (April 18).

2008 *The Wall Street Journal* adds reader comment section; *The New York Times* allows users to share stories from site (September).

2009 Ezra Klein hired as economics and domestic policy blogger at *The Washington Post* (June); develops *Wonkblog*. . . . Kaiser Family Foundation launches online health news website.

2010s *Star journalists launch online news sites.*

2010 Nate Silver moves political forecasting blog *FiveThirtyEight.com* to *The New York Times* under three-year licensing agreement (June 3). . . . *Flipboard* debuts as news aggregator app for iPad (July 21).

2011 AOL acquires *Huffington Post* for $315 million (Feb. 7). . . . Sportswriter Bill Simmons launches sports website *Grantland* (June 8). . . . *BuzzFeed* hires political reporter Ben Smith as editor; news staff begins expansion (Dec. 11).

2012 Upworthy launches as website for viral content (March). . . . *Huffington Post*'s military correspondent David Wood wins Pulitzer Prize for national reporting (April 16). . . . *Newsweek* announces plan to end print edition at end of year (Oct. 18).

2013 Gadfly journalist Glenn Greenwald breaks news of U.S., U.K. global surveillance with leaked documents from National Security Agency contractor Edward Snowden (June 5). . . . Silver's plan to leave *The New York Times* becomes public (July 19). . . . eBay founder Pierre Omidyar announces plans to bankroll Greenwald, others in new online publication, eventually named *The Intercept* (Oct. 17). . . . Veteran newspaperman Jim Roberts hired as *Mashable* executive editor (Oct. 31). . . . Mossberg, Swisher leave Dow Jones (Dec. 31).

2014 Mossberg and Swisher launch *Re/code* (Jan. 2). . . . Klein's departure from *The Washington Post* is announced (Jan. 21). . . . Greenwald's team launches *The Intercept* (Feb. 10). . . . *Newsweek* announces plan to resume print edition, with limited run (March 3). . . . Silver launches *FiveThirtyEight* (March 17). . . . Study finds vast majority of news consumers get news in digital format "sometimes," roughly one-third "often" (March 26). . . . Klein launches *Vox.com* (March 9). . . . Newspaper industry group releases figures showing revenue losses are slowing, digital-only subscription revenue is up (April 18). . . . Poll by Indiana University finds 60 percent of journalists say profession is headed "in wrong direction" (May 5). . . . *Jet* magazine announces it will end print edition (May 7).

Hyperlocal News Sites
Cover What Others Don't

"Mark every death. Remember every victim. Follow every case."

Laura Amico broke into journalism in her home state of California and put in two years on the crime beat at the Santa Rosa *Press Democrat*. But when she moved to Washington, D.C., in 2009 with her husband, Chris, for his new job at PBS's "NewsHour," she could not find a journalism position that she wanted.

Five years later, however, Amico is founder and publisher of an award-winning local digital news site that covers every homicide in the District of Columbia from the killing through the end of legal proceedings. *Homicide Watch D.C.* greets visitors with a promise of unremitting thoroughness: "Mark every death. Remember every victim. Follow every case."[1]

The combined effects of electronic commerce and online journalism have been hard on coverage of local news. Advertisers and readers alike have been drawn away from local newspapers that previously were the principal source for coverage of local news, whether it be crime and justice, business and real estate or local government.[2]

At the same time, however, technology reduces the barriers to entry for start-up local news operations, like the one Amico and her web-developer husband began in 2010 and relaunched in 2011. The site provides coverage and a searchable database of D.C. homicides based on original reporting, court documents and social media.

Start-up operations practicing what has come to be called "hyperlocal journalism" are an antidote to the long-term decline in local reporting that has concerned journalists, community activists and others who follow local government. "Many of them are covering statehouses, city halls or local neighborhoods at a very granular level, compensating for the decline in reporting from legacy media," says Mark Jurkowitz, associate director of the Pew Research Center's Journalism Project.

Columbia Journalism Review's Guide to Online News Startups lists around 60 "hyperlocal" sites from *ARLNow* .com (Arlington, Va.) to *West Seattle Blog*. That number does not count *Homicide Watch* and affiliated sites in Chicago and Trenton, N.J., which are listed in other categories, as are most of the numerous sites devoted to local high school sports.[3]

Two dozen of the hyperlocal listings are state entries for *Patch*, described in Feb. 24, 2012, postings as "AOL's fast-growing hyperlocal network." AOL sold the financially troubled operation in January to Hale Global, an investment firm that specializes in turning around ailing businesses. Hundreds of *Patch* employees were laid off, but those who remained were told that all 900 *Patch* sites would be continued.[4]

Community newspapers have long provided some of the hyperlocal coverage of neighborhoods, schools, zoning boards and the like that metropolitan dailies do not cover. But most of the community papers are weekly and have limited space, at least in their print editions. Digital sites offer the advantage of continual updating and unlimited space.

to *BuzzFeed*. His decision to hire political journalist Smith as editor in December 2011 marked the site's evolution into a serious news site with its buzz-creating features still intact.[28]

Flipboard came along in 2010, designed by creators Mike McCue and Evan Doll to bring magazine-like graphics to a social media aggregator, which pulls together feeds from a user's various social networks.[29] McCue had been head of a voice-recognition company, Tell Me, which was acquired by Microsoft in 2007; Doll was an Apple iPhone engineer McCue met after leaving Microsoft in 2009. Their app was released first for Apple's iPad in 2010 and then for iPhone late in 2011. *The New York Times* marked the iPhone debut of the app with a headline describing it as useful "for killing time standing in line."[30]

Yet another entrant in the attention-grabbing competition was born in 2012: *Upworthy*, launched by Eli Pariser, a liberal political activist, and Peter Koechley, former managing editor of the satirical newspaper *The Onion*. With financial backing from one of Facebook's founders,

The Amicos had been financing *Homicide Watch* themselves, but they raised $47,450 in 2012 through a Kickstarter online crowd-funding campaign, allowing the site to hire student interns to take over some of the reporting.[5] Amico prides herself on thoroughness. In a recent story on a mistrial in a homicide case, she noted that local news media had covered the killing but only *Homicide Watch* reported on the no-verdict trial.

The site's home page also makes an unmistakable allusion to the widespread feeling in Washington's African-American and Latino communities that the District's major news media devote more time, attention and space to homicides in predominantly white neighborhoods than in their communities. "If we are to understand violent crime in our community, the losses of every family, in every neighborhood must be recognized," the introductory statement reads.

Digital technology is what makes the operation work, as Laura and Chris Amico explained to an interviewer in 2013.[6] "Having the platform speeds up my workflow by creating a pattern out of my work," Laura Amico said. By checking the database regularly, she continued, she is able to fill in holes as new information becomes available.

"Some of what makes the site work is really fundamental to the web," Chris Amico added. The site allows links to profile pages, he explained, eliminating the need to include background in each story. He also built a database application that creates maps showing where each homicide occurred.

Laura Amico saw a concrete advantage to that database recently when the District recorded three homicides in one night. With a quick check, she determined that it had been the deadliest week of the year for Washington. "I haven't seen any other reporter with a database robust and agile enough to do that," she said.

— *Kenneth Jost*

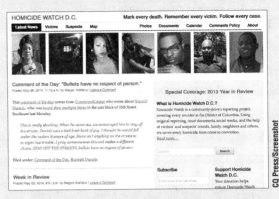

The hyperlocal news site *Homicide Watch D.C.* covers every homicide in the city from the killing through the end of legal proceedings.

[1] *Homicide Watch D.C.*, http://homicidewatch.org.

[2] Some background drawn from Paul Farhi, "Is local reporting in a death spiral?" *The Washington Post*, March 27, 2014, p. C1, http://tinyurl.com/mmx8zcg.

[3] "CJR's Guide to Online News Startups," accessed May 2014, http://tinyurl.com/7oebz3d.

[4] Leslie Kaufman, "New Owner of Patch Lays Off Hundreds," *The New York Times*, Jan. 30, 2014, p. B7, http://tinyurl.com/mqpywdb.

[5] "A One-Year Student Reporting Lab within Homicide Watch DC," Kickstarter, http://tinyurl.com/kg72l6q .

[6] Erin Kissane, "Homicide Watch: An Interview," *Contents*, Issue 4 (2013), http://tinyurl.com/kbpcqem.

Chris Hughes, the site announced its mission of becoming "the place to find awesome, meaningful, visual things to share." By deft use of virally appealing headlines, it grew with phenomenal speed.[31]

Gaining Respect

Digital publications such as *The Huffington Post* and *BuzzFeed* slowly gained respect and proved their worth, editorially and financially, as the 21st century moved into its second decade. Meanwhile, major newspapers discovered that they could increase their audience by expanding their digital products, including some digital-only content. Meanwhile, some journalists who had become stars on the newspapers' platforms outgrew their employers and decided to venture into the digital world on their own.

In their early years, *The Huffington Post* and *BuzzFeed* were held in low regard by some in the traditional media. In retrospective pieces, leading media writers have recalled *The Huffington Post* in its early days as "a viral aggregation

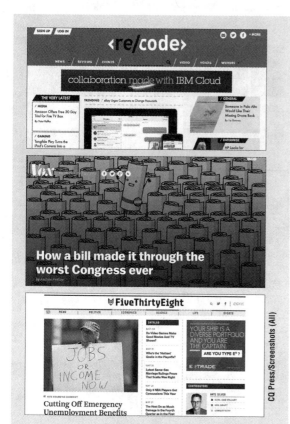

Digital Newcomers

New digital news sites such as *Re/code, Vox* and *FiveThirtyEight* were launched by high-profile print reporters with high expectations for their content, but they have drawn mixed reviews from design experts. *FiveThirtyEight* is the brainchild of Nate Silver, who built a name for himself as a data-crunching political handicapper at *The New York Times*. *The Washington Post*'s Ezra Klein started *Vox* when *The Post* refused his request to invest more in *Wonkblog*, his *Post* digital site. *Wall Street Journal* tech reporters Kara Swisher and Walt Mossberg started *Re/code* on Jan. 2 with backing from NBCUniversal and the investment operation of former Yahoo chief executive Terry Semel. How they will do financially remains to be seen.

scoop: Arizona Republican Sen. John McCain's endorsement of Mitt Romney for the GOP presidential nomination. A few months later, *The Huffington Post* gained new stature when its senior military correspondent David Wood won the Pulitzer Prize — the first ever for work by a for-profit, digital-only publication. The prize, for national reporting, was for a 10-part series on the plight of wounded veterans from the Afghanistan and Iraq wars.

In the meantime, major U.S. newspapers were expanding their digital presence, adding some features and content that appeared only online and not in their print editions. At Dow Jones, Mossberg and Swisher launched the *AllThingsD* blog on April 18, 2007, as an extension of the tech conferences that they had begun hosting in 2003.[33] Klein, who had blogged for the liberal magazine *The American Prospect*, came on board at *The Washington Post* in 2009. He was introduced to *The Post*'s readers in June as writing a blog about domestic and economic policy.[34] A year later, *The New York Times* announced plans to host the political blog that statistician Silver had created in 2008, *FiveThirtyEight.com. The Times* announcement on June 3, 2010, noted that under a three-year licensing agreement, Silver will retain all rights to the blog and will run it himself.[35]

Greenwald, a political gadfly blogger and columnist for the British-based newspaper *The Guardian*, made worldwide headlines beginning in June 2013 with sensational disclosures about U.S. and British global surveillance. Greenwald and his colleague documentary filmmaker Laura Poitras were recipients — along with *The Washington Post*'s Barton Gellman — of classified documents leaked by Snowden, the whistle-blowing onetime NSA contractor. Four months after the first of the stories was published, eBay founder Omidyar announced that he would bankroll Greenwald and others, to the tune of $250 million, in a new digital-only venture into serious journalism.[36]

Silver's plan to leave *The Times* leaked on July 19, 2013, in the form of a post by its then-media reporter Brian Stelter on another of the newspaper's branded blogs, *Media Decoder*.[37] Stelter, who later left the newspaper for CNN, noted that Silver's affiliation with ESPN would allow him to return to sports and statistics, the area where he had first gained prominence, and to cover politics in election years for ABC. ESPN and ABC are both owned by the Disney Company.

factory and unpaid-blogger's paradise" and *BuzzFeed* as "something like *The Huffington Post* without the pretension of producing news and commentary."[32]

Not long after *BuzzFeed* got a new editor and a $15.5 million infusion of new capital late in 2011, it turned heads in the world of political journalism with a good

Mossberg and Swisher left Dow Jones at the end of the year. In a final jointly bylined post on *AllThingsD* on Dec. 31, they took credit for writing more than 40,000 posts, testing "hundreds" of new products and services and drawing "millions" of readers. But they closed —"taking a page from the industry we cover" — by saying, "It's once again time to refresh, reimagine, remake and reinvent." They launched *Re/code* on Jan. 2, as principal owners of the newly formed company Revere Digital, and took all of the *AllThingsD* staff along with them.[38]

Klein's departure from *The Post* was confirmed on Jan. 21, 2014, in a memo distributed to the newspaper's staff and reported in *The New York Times* and elsewhere.[39] Klein was quoted as expressing gratitude to *The Post*, but it was later disclosed that he had unsuccessfully pitched to the newspaper's editors and its new owner, Amazon.com founder Jeffrey Bezos, a plan for an expanded *Wonkblog* that he would run as a stand-alone site still with *The Post*. Instead, Klein started his new policy-oriented site under the aegis of Vox Media, parent of digital-only sports site *SB Nation* and tech site *The Verge*.[40]

"We are just at the beginning of how journalism should be done on the web," Klein told *New York Times* media writer David Carr. "We really wanted to build something from the ground up that helps people understand the news better. We are not just trying to scale *Wonkblog*, we want to improve the technology of news, and *Vox* has a vision of how to solve some of that."[41]

CURRENT SITUATION

Starting Up

The new stars of digital news are filling their sites with lots of content, but keeping mum on how much traffic they are getting and generally steering clear of broad pronouncements about how they are doing.

Of the high-profile sites that launched this year — *Re/code*, *The Intercept*, *FiveThirtyEight* and *Vox.com* — none responded to requests for figures on visitors to the sites. Mossberg, co-founder of *Re/code*, was the only one of the principals to agree to an interview to discuss the post-launch output and impact. And media watchers appear to be slow so far in offering detailed reviews of the sites.

At *Vox.com*, the most recent of the four to launch, Klein oversees an editorial staff of roughly 20 reporters

Getty Images/Andrew Burton

One of the newest entrants into the digital news field is Glenn Greenwald, an investigative reporter for *The Guardian* who won a Pulitzer Prize for his disclosures of U.S. and British global surveillance, based on documents leaked by former National Security Agency consultant Edward Snowden. Greenwald, here with colleague Laura Poitras, a documentary filmmaker, launched *The Intercept* on Feb. 2. The national security publication was funded by the billionaire founder of eBay, Pierre Omidyar.

who write stories or conduct interviews that could just as easily appear in a conventional newspaper or news website.[42] But in the interest of what he calls "persistent explanatory journalism," Klein has created two distinctive features: numbered yellow "card stacks" that explain a subject step-by-step, in primer-like terms; and VoxExplains videos, such as a two-minute piece on income inequality narrated by Klein.

One week after launch, Klein told an interviewer he was "really, really happy with week one," but hoped that week two would be better and week three better still.[43] Most of the stories are on serious, policy-oriented subjects, but *Vox*'s readers are not necessarily wedded to the high-brow. One afternoon early in May, the top three "most read" stories dealt with sex, beer and the NFL draft.

At *FiveThirtyEight*, Silver used a launch-day "manifesto" to announce the hiring of more than 20 people described as skilled not only in "statistical analysis" but also in "data visualization, computer programming and data-literate reporting." Silver said the site would apply data-journalism

Getty Images/Bloomberg/David Paul Morris

Nate Silver, 36, who ran his political data blog *FiveThirtyEight* at *The New York Times*, left the paper to relaunch the site in March under the same name at the sports network ESPN.

techniques to five areas: politics, economics, science, life and sports.[44]

In the two months since, *FiveThirtyEight* has explored such issues as whether white Republicans are more racist than white Democrats (yes, but only a little); whether children born to older fathers are at greater risk of attention deficit disorder (unclear); and whether cheerleading is unsafe compared with other high school and college sports (in the middle).[45]

Mossberg says he and Swisher named their new product *Re/code* to combine an abstract word with tech connotations and the importance of "reinvention," which he says characterizes the tech and media industries the site covers. "We're off to an excellent start," Mossberg says four-and-a-half months after launch. Mossberg and Swisher have majority control of the new company, Revere Digital, but financing from NBC and Semel's company, Windsor Media, has allowed an expanded editorial staff. Reporters cover such beats as Washington tech policy and tech and society. The total staff count, including Web developers, is 30.

Along with *Re/code*, Revere will be sponsoring what Mossberg says will be "lucrative" conferences about tech issues. The first is being held at the end of May in Rancho Palos Verdes, Calif. "The conference sold out in hours," Mossberg says. Advertising, however, is slow so far. "We haven't built out the business staff," he explains.

At *The Intercept*, Greenwald and his co-founders — documentary filmmaker Poitras and investigative reporter

Jeremy Scahill — have assembled a team of 13 others to carry on what the trio described at launch as a "central mission . . . to hold the most powerful governmental and corporate factions accountable." Two months after the launch, however, the newly appointed editor-in-chief John Cook acknowledged the site had been slow to gear up and so far had published only more material from Snowden's leaked documents.[46]

Cook, former *Gawker* editor in chief, acknowledged organizational start-up problems in his message, published the same day the liberal blog *Daily Kos* suggested the site was "stalled."[47] The site had published three dozen stories as of mid-April and also cached a trove of national security-related documents. A month later, only three new stories had appeared.

Going Mobile

Major newspapers are redesigning their websites to tailor them for mobile devices, just as the industry is reporting an increase in digital revenue that is helping to slow the bottom-line slide of the past decade.

The *Los Angeles Times* is touting a website redesign announced on May 6 that promises to be user-friendly on all devices: desktop, tablet or smartphone. Meanwhile, top editors at *The New York Times* are studying a specially commissioned internal report that sets out a five-step plan to what the report's authors call a "digital-first transition" — a report that surfaced only days before the tumultuous firing of executive editor Jill Abramson and the appointment of her deputy, Dean Baquet, to succeed her.

The latest figures from the Newspaper Association of America show a 2.6 percent decrease in total revenue in 2013 — the smallest decrease since 2006. Even though advertising fell by 6.5 percent, the decrease was offset somewhat by a 3.7 percent increase in circulation revenue. That increase came mostly from digital-only subscriptions as more newspapers instituted so-called "paywall plans" that require users to pay for access to websites.[48]

Instead of bemoaning the demise of print, industry spokesman Jim Conaghan touts the revenue potential from digital and the benefits to newspapers' audiences. "We are really a multiplatform business," says Conaghan, the Newspaper Association of America's vice president for industry research and analysis. "The distribution system has gotten much wider for newspaper media companies, which certainly is an advantage to the public."

Are print publications adapting to online journalism?

YES — Caroline Little
President and CEO,
Newspaper Association of America

Written for *CQ Researcher*, May 2014

When I joined the Newspaper Association of America in 2011, I said that newspapers were going to transform. As we survey the industry in 2014, it is clear that this transformation has taken place, and the numbers bear this out.

According to comScore, a company that measures Internet use, digital newspaper content was accessed by 161 million Americans in March 2014. That is an increase of 19 percent from April 2013. It shows that print publications have put an emphasis on digital content, and that emphasis is being rewarded with growing audiences.

When you look at newspaper financials, you see that circulation revenue has increased the past two years and that this was driven largely by digital subscriptions. This is another example of print publications adapting to a changing landscape and how it is paying off.

Our members are no longer looking at their newspapers as "print publications," because that is now just one part of the larger business model. That is why I like to discuss "newspaper media" instead of simply "newspapers" because a successful newspaper media company will focus on both print and digital, which includes the website, social media channels and mobile capability.

The younger generation remains engaged with newspaper content; they are simply doing so in a different way. We see that a majority of young adults, ages 18 to 24, access newspaper content exclusively through mobile devices. This is obviously a drastic change from how content was accessed even five years ago, when it was all on the desktop.

There are now more than 450 newspapers that offer digital subscriptions, and that number is increasing every day. We are seeing that readers will pay for good, trusted content, which is exactly what newspapers deliver.

Additionally, digital platforms have provided newspapers a better way to tell stories. When I look at the future of journalism, I see journalists who have an eye for telling stories in the best possible manner. That can be a written article and a video. Or it can be in a long-form package with accompanying infographics. At the Newspaper Association of America, our members no longer focus solely on print. To continue our recent success, print publications must continue to balance between print, digital and mobile. So far, so good — and I expect even more good things in the future.

NO — Mitchell Stephens
Author, Beyond News: The Future of Journalism; *Journalism Professor at New York University*

Written for *CQ Researcher*, May 2014

Newspapers and magazines have two problems as they attempt to survive in a world where information can move fast and far digitally.

The first and least interesting is practical. These publications are going to have to complete their "migration," to use the jargon, to the new "platform." It is hard to imagine much justification for continuing to go to the expense and trouble of printing on and schlepping around paper, when it is possible to distribute equally attractive publications more or less for free, more or less instantly, online.

As the printing press was first being used in Europe, there were those who insisted that there would always be a place in libraries for handwritten books. They were wrong. Those who — succumbing to a similar nostalgia — think there will always be a place for journalism in print are similarly wrong.

The more interesting question is how journalism originally designed for print will change as it completes this inevitable journey into a new form. Here the issue is mindset, not technology. And mindsets usually change more slowly than technologies.

For a century after the arrival of the printing press in Europe, books were still being printed with typefaces that imitated the thick, black letters of handwritten manuscripts and with illuminations that were hand painted on each page. Online journalism sites are similarly stuck. Their "pages," story formats and "headlines" haven't changed much — even in magazines, where more creativity might be expected. They make little use of the fluidity of the Web. The content of their articles has stayed mostly true to the print model, too.

Newspapers today, even online, still announce the day's events as if there weren't numerous other places — Twitter, Facebook, blogs, dozens of other easily available websites — that are announcing those events at the same time. They persist in the assumption that they are selling news, although in a world where information is available fast and free that is about as good a business as selling encyclopedias. They are figuring out only slowly that they need to sell something else — interpretations of the news, what I call "wisdom journalism."

New forms — the novel, the newspaper — were eventually invented to take best advantage of the printing press, but it took a century and a half. New approaches to journalism will have to be invented to take best advantage of digital communication. That process is just getting started.

Former *New York Times* executive editor Jill Abramson makes the commencement address at Wake Forest University on May 19, 2014, in Winston-Salem, N.C. Days earlier, *Times* Publisher Arthur Sulzberger fired Abramson, the paper's first female executive editor, and replaced her with Dean Baquet, who became the first African-American to hold the post. Sulzberger attributed the firing to "newsroom management issues," but one source of friction between Abramson and Baquet was said to be Abramson's attempt to recruit a new managing editor for digital content who would have equal standing with Baquet.

Digital-only advertising for the industry — that is, ads that are not sold in combination with print advertising — now accounts for about one-fourth of digital advertising. Conaghan acknowledges that digital advertising growth has been "slower than we would like." A new challenge, he says, is "how to monetize the growing mobile audience." The statistics show a growing reliance on mobile devices to read newspaper content: Among online readers age 34 or younger, the number who rely exclusively on mobile devices more than doubled over the past year.[49]

The *Los Angeles Times*, the fourth-largest U.S. newspaper by circulation, had the mobile device readership in mind as it redesigned its website. Visitors touring the site are greeted by the slogan, "designed to fit your life > as it happens," and later are promised that the website is "smart enough for all your devices." A laptop, tablet and smart phone are used to illustrate. The site tour shows that users can "share effortlessly," "explore further," "join the conversation" and "find news near you." The result is described as "a completely reinvented latimes.com."

The redesign draws warm praise from Mario García, a renowned newspaper designer who is president of a Tampa-based media consulting company, as "clean"

and "easy to navigate." Newspapers need to "stop regretting print," he says, and instead "learn to cope with storytelling."[50]

Closer to home, however, a writer for *L.A. Weekly* was less impressed with the redesign. Denis Romero complained of what he called the residue of "print DNA," pointing to the list of newspaper-style sections on the left side of the desktop version of the home page. He called the redesign "formulaic."[51]

The Los Angeles newspaper's online redesign comes about 20 months after a similar revamping by *USA Today*, another of the nation's biggest newspapers. In announcing the change on Sept. 18, publisher Larry Kramer said the "bold redesign" amounted to "an evolution" of the newspaper's brand "in print and across all our digital platforms."[52] Today, the newspaper says it has reclaimed its status as the nation's largest-circulation newspaper, based on a new industry standard of including digital-only readers in subscription figures.[53]

The New York Times, third-largest in circulation after *USA Today* and *The Wall Street Journal*, needs to do more to transition to the digital world, according to the 11-page internal report submitted by a team of editors and reporters in early May. The task force was headed by Arthur Gregg Sulzberger, a metro reporter and son of publisher Arthur Sulzberger Jr.[54]

The report recalls that *The Times* print and digital news staffs were once housed in separate buildings but have since been partly consolidated. But it calls for a more complete transition and a determined focus on spreading its journalistic content through social media with the creation of, among others, a "newsroom audience development team."

In a jointly signed memo to the staff, executive editor Abramson and managing editor Baquet said the report represented "another milestone in our digital transformation." They indicated changes were likely, but set no timetable.

Only a few days later, however, publisher Sulzberger summarily fired Abramson, the newspaper's first female executive editor, and replaced her with Baquet, who became the first African-American to hold the post. Sulzberger attributed the dismissal to a "newsroom management issue," but news accounts said that one source of friction between Abramson and Baquet was the attempted recruitment of a new managing editor for digital content, who was to have equal standing with Baquet.[55]

OUTLOOK

"Golden Age"?

Many baby boomer journalists are known to recall their days as youngsters delivering newspapers by saying that they "started out in circulation." Today, millions of newspaper readers still pick up a print edition. But the vast majority also read the news sometimes on screens: laptop, tablet or smartphone. And a growing number of younger news readers are "mobile-exclusive" — weaned completely off print and accustomed to news and information in their pockets.

Print-era veterans acknowledge or even embrace the change. "I've pretty much abandoned print," says media watcher Romenesko. At NYU, Stephens says, "I teach journalism students. I've stopped asking them whether they read the print version of *The New York Times.*"

Stephens professes not to be discouraged. "There's tremendous hope for journalism," he says. Another print veteran agrees that news is faring well in the digital age. "People are consuming news differently," says the American Press Institute's Rosenstiel, "but consuming more."

For much of the second half of the 20th century, news audiences were in fact disadvantaged by consolidation in the newspaper industry — the fading away of the two-newspaper town — and by the limited number of radio and television outlets until the rise of cable in the 1980s and '90s.

In the digital age, however, the barriers to entry have come down. A digital news organization needs no printing press, warehouse or fleet of delivery trucks, only a computer infrastructure and a team of good Web developers to work with so-called content producers. "The news ecosystem has increased," says the Pew Center's Jurkowitz. "There are a lot of new players."

"The largest legacy media have the advantage of having a brand," says Boczkowski, the Northwestern professor. "They have the disadvantage of being associated with traditional ideas and the disadvantage of having very high fixed costs."

With lower fixed costs, *The Huffington Post* has eclipsed *The New York Times* in total readership "in just a few years,"

according to *The Times'* innovation study completed in April. The report warns that all of *The Times'* competitors — traditional newspaper rivals, social media such as Facebook and LinkedIn and start-ups such as *Vox* and *First Look Media* — are becoming more "digitally sophisticated."

The impact on legacy media of the newest digital-only news sites — *Vox, FiveThirtyEight, Re/code* and *The Intercept* — has yet to be seen. Nate Silver's prediction in March that Republicans were favorites to gain control of the Senate in the November elections — a reversal of his previous forecast — created instantaneous waves among politicians and political junkies.[56] Otherwise, however, none of the four new sites appears to have launched a story yet that went on to become a major item of watercooler conversations or public policy debate.

"All of these things are young and still in experimental form," says Stephens. "It's going to take a while."

With the digital age barely in its third decade, news organizations that invested time, energy and resources in websites are already being forced to adapt to the new formatting requirements of mobile devices. "Certainly mobile is going to present a whole new set of challenges," says McGuire, the Arizona State professor. "With that smaller screen, there is so much going on. We need to develop mobile-only designs that communicate with audiences more effectively." And Conaghan, of the newspaper industry association, acknowledges that advertisers are yet to be persuaded that mobile is such a great venue for their messages.

Of the new ventures, Boczkowski thinks most will fail — just as most business startups do. Jurkowitz, too, thinks the odds of survival for any particular one are not necessarily high. "There's going to be churn," he says. For his part, though, McGuire shies away from a bearish forecast. "People are trying new things," he says.

"It's a golden age of media experimentation," McGuire concludes. "I think that's cool."

NOTES

1. Ezra Klein, "How politics makes us stupid," *Vox,* April 6, 2014, http://tinyurl.com/ocdwzru.

2. Amy Mitchell, "State of the News Media 2014," Pew Research Center Journalism Project, March 28, 2014, http://tinyurl.com/kk2opwy.

3. For background, see Marcia Clemmitt, "Social Media Explosion," *CQ Researcher*, Jan. 25, 2013, pp. 81-104.

4. For background, see these *CQ Researcher* reports: Peter Katel, "Future of TV," April 18, 2014, pp. 313-336; Tom Price, "Future of Journalism," March 27, 2009, pp. 273-296; Kenneth Jost, "The Future of Newspapers," Jan. 20, 2006, pp. 49-72.

5. Rick Edmonds, "ASNE census finds 2,600 newsroom jobs were lost in 2012," Poynter.org, June 25, 2013, http://tinyurl.com/pymo9fx.

6. Lars Willnat and David H. Weaver, "The American Journalist in the Digital Age," Indiana University School of Journalism, May 5, 2014, http://tinyurl.com/q5fjk85.

7. Mitchell Stephens, *Beyond News: The Future of Journalism* (2014), p. xii.

8. Dana Milbank, "Arianna Huffington's ideological transformation," *The Washington Post*, Feb. 9, 2011, http://tinyurl.com/p2wjtg7.

9. See Joe Pompeo, "The Huffington Post, nine years on," *Capital*, May 8, 2014, http://tinyurl.com/n7spoh6.

10. "Jim Roberts Is Mashable's Executive Editor and Chief Content Officer," *Mashable*, Oct. 31, 2013, http://tinyurl.com/qxc63xl.

11. Derek Thompson, "The Facebook Effect on News," *The Atlantic*, Feb. 12, 2014, http://tinyurl.com/o7ev4jv.

12. "State of the News Media 2014," *op. cit.*

13. Douglas Quenqua, "The Boy Wonder of BuzzFeed," *The New York Times*, Feb. 17, 2013, p. ST1, http://tinyurl.com/bhprs3c.

14. Stephens, *op. cit.*, p. xxvi.

15. Ben Smith, "Tweet Victory: How Twitter and Facebook will save journalism (mostly)," *Playboy*, January 2014, http://tinyurl.com/oxmxpah.

16. Ellen Cushing, "I Think Google's Pretty Dangerous and Thuggish. I've Always Said That," *San Francisco* (magazine), April 29, 2014, http://tinyurl.com/kbua2g9.

17. Joe Coscarelli, "Ezra Klein on Vox's Launch, Media Condescension, and Competing With Wikipedia," *Daily Intelligencer*, *New York* magazine, April 11, 2014, http://tinyurl.com/onw8plt.

18. Lucia Moses, "Michael Wolff: 'Online journalism can't pay for itself,' " *Digiday*, April 7, 2014, http://tinyurl.com/nh2nfpp. Wolff's appearance with Carey was part of Hearst's Master Class series; others who have recently appeared include Arianna Huffington of *The Huffington Post* and Jonah Peretti of *BuzzFeed*.

19. Jessica Lessin, "Introducing The Information!" Dec. 4, 2013, http://tinyurl.com/qyluqxq; and Jenna Wortham, "A Missing Revenue Stream From Mobile Apps," *The New York Times*, Dec. 15, 2013, p. BU3, http://tinyurl.com/nn7ksm7.

20. "Key Findings From U.S. Digital Marketing Survey 2013," Gartner for Marketing Leaders, March 6, 2013, http://tinyurl.com/d4tqjfd.

21. Background drawn in part from Stephens, *A History of News* (3d. ed.), 2007; Pablo J. Boczkowski, *Digitizing the News: Innovation in Online Newspapers* (2004).

22. Tim Berners-Lee, "Frequently asked questions," undated, http://tinyurl.com/b4zy79 (accessed May 2014). See also Tim Berners-Lee, *Weaving the Web: The Original Design and Ultimate Destiny of the World Wide Web* (2000).

23. Boczkowski, *op. cit.*, p. 8.

24. Estimate by the International Telecommunications Union, a United Nations agency, quoted by Jonathan Lynn, "Internet users expected to exceed 2 billion this year," Reuters, Oct. 19, 2010, http://tinyurl.com/o37q7dz.

25. "State of the News Media 2012," Pew Research Center Project for Excellence in Journalism, http://tinyurl.com/6rjxylx.

26. David Carr and Jeremy W. Peters, "Big Personality and Behind-the-Scenes Executive Prove a Top Media Team," *The New York Times*, Feb. 8, 2011, p. B1, http://tinyurl.com/oxmq9rm.

27. Arianna Huffington, "HuffPost Game Changers: Your Picks for the Ultimate 10," *The Huffington Post*, Nov. 19, 2009, http://tinyurl.com/ndx6on9.

28. David Carr, "Significant and Silly at BuzzFeed," *The New York Times*, Feb. 6, 2012, p. B1, http://tinyurl.com/7utu8pb.

29. Michael Liedtke, "New iPad app mines Web links for 'social magazine,'" The Associated Press, July 21, 2010, http://tinyurl.com/nu922ma. See also Richard McManus, "How Flipboard Was Created and its Plans beyond iPad," *readwrite*, Oct. 6, 2010, http://tinyurl.com/nocht4l.

30. Claire Cain Miller, "Flipboard Introduces an iPhone App for Killing Time Standing in Line," Bits (*New York Times* blog), Dec. 7, 2011, http://tinyurl.com/ph8wgo8.

31. Ed Pilkington, "New media gurus launch Upworthy — their 'super basic' internet startup," *The Guardian*, March 26, 2012, http://tinyurl.com/o3pzylx.

32. Pompeo, *op. cit.*; Carr, "Significant and Silly at Buzzfeed," *op. cit.*

33. Walt Mossberg and Kara Swisher, "You Say Goodbye and We Say Hello," *AllThingsD.com*, Dec. 31, 2013, http://tinyurl.com/lxbpd4a.

34. "Economy Department with Ezra Klein," *The Washington Post*, June 11, 2009, http://tinyurl.com/medwqn.

35. Brian Stelter, "Times to Host Blog on Politics and Polls," *The New York Times*, June 4, 2010, p. B2, http://tinyurl.com/oqhcbjl.

36. Noam Cohen and Quentin Hardy, "Snowden Journalist's New Venture to Be Bankrolled by eBay Founder," *The New York Times*, Oct. 17, 2013, p. B1, http://tinyurl.com/q9etmuw.

37. Brian Stelter, "Blogger for Times Is to Join ESPN Staff," *The New York Times*, July 20, 2013, p. B6, http://tinyurl.com/nympltn.

38. Mossberg and Swisher, *op. cit.*; and Brian Stelter, "Re/code: new site launched by AllThingsD founders," CNNMoney, Jan. 2, 2014, http://tinyurl.com/lakbw9d.

39. Ravi Somaiya, "Top Wonkblog Columnist to Leave Washington Post," *The New York Times*, Jan. 22, 2014, p. B6, http://tinyurl.com/plhq4ar.

40. David Carr, "A Big Hire Signals Web News Is Thriving," *The New York Times*, Jan. 27, 2014, p. B1, http://tinyurl.com/k58kx3k.

41. *Ibid.*

42. Leslie Kaufman, "Vox Takes Melding of Journalism and Technology to New Level," *The New York Times*, April 7, 2014, p. B1, http://tinyurl.com/ms97rhe.

43. Joe Coscarelli, "Ezra Klein on Vox's Launch, Media Condescension, and Competing With Wikipedia," *New York Magazine*, http://tinyurl.com/onw8plt.

44. Nate Silver, "What the Fox Knows," *FiveThirtyEight.com*, March 17, 2014, http://tinyurl.com/q6cduqb.

45. Nate Silver, "Are White Republicans More Racist Than White Democrats?" *FiveThirtyEight.com*, April 24, 2014, http://tinyurl.com/k35qs6a; Emily Oster, "Are Older Men's Sperm Really Any Worse?" *FiveThirtyEight.com*, April 24, 2014, http://tinyurl.com/k9m8exp; and Walt Hickey, "Where Cheerleading Ranks in Safety Among High School Sports," *FiveThirtyEight.com*, May 11, 2014, http://tinyurl.com/kjg7bxp.

46. Glenn Greenwald, Laura Poitras and Jeremy Scahill, "Welcome to The Intercept," *The Intercept*, Feb. 10, 2014, http://tinyurl.com/m9bt2u5; and John Cook, "Passover Greetings from the Editor," *The Intercept*, April 14, 2014, http://tinyurl.com/puykfzf.

47. Richard Lyon, "First Look Media/The Intercept Appears to Be Stalled," *dailykos*, April 14, 2014, http://tinyurl.com/ntnehxo.

48. "Business Model Evolving, Circulation Revenue Rising," Newspaper Association of America, April 18, 2014, http://tinyurl.com/kljkoj7; and Rick Edmonds, "Newspaper industry narrowed revenue loss in 2013 as paywall plans increased," Poynter, April 18, 2014, http://tinyurl.com/mtj7vnv.

49. Jim Conaghan, "Mobile-Exclusive Surges Among Young Adults," Newspaper Association of America, April 28, 2014, http://tinyurl.com/o3t5w23.

50. Mario R. Garcìa, "New Los Angeles Times website: innovative, inspiring," Garcìa Media, May 7, 2014, http://tinyurl.com/qfjam6w.

51. Dennis Romero, "Los Angeles Times Website Redesign Is Meh," *L.A. Weekly*, May 6, 2014, http://tinyurl.com/qcvm7xx.

52. "Welcome to USA Today — again," *USA Today*, Sept. 14, 2012, p. 1A.

53. "USA Today regains national circulation lead," *USA Today*, Oct. 21, 2013, http://tinyurl.com/qzd5cj5.

54. Joe Pompeo, "New York Times Completes 'Innovation Report' by Sulzberger Scion," *Capital*, May 8, 2014, http://tinyurl.com/l2z5bds. Pompeo's story includes this link to the report itself: http://tinyurl.com/q39y9wz ("Innovation Study").

55. David Carr, "Abramson's Exit at The Times Puts Tensions on Display," *The New York Times*, May 18, 2014, http://tinyurl.com/odc557x.

56. Nate Silver, "FiveThirtyEight Senate Forecast: GOP Is Slight Favorite in Race for Senate Control," *FiveThirtyEight.com*, March 23, 2014, http://tinyurl.com/lskyb92; and Catalina Camia, "Senate Democrats Debunk Nate Silver's GOP-favored Forecast," *On Politics* (*USA Today*), March 24, 2014, http://tinyurl.com/ommef5s.

BIBLIOGRAPHY

Selected Sources

Books

Boczkowski, Pablo, *Digitizing the News: Innovation in Online Newspapers*, **MIT Press, 2004.**
A professor and director of the Program in Media, Technology and Society at Northwestern University examines the early days of electronic newspaper publishing. Includes detailed notes, bibliography.

Boler, Megan, ed., *Digital Media and Democracy: Tactics in Hard Times*, **MIT Press, 2008.**
A professor of the history and philosophy of education at the University of Toronto examines, via essays by scholars, journalists and activists, the role of digital media in creating new avenues for exploring truth and practicing media activism.

Palfrey, John, and Urs Gasser, *Born Digital: Understanding the First Generation of Digital Natives*, **Basic Books, 2008.**
The authors explore philosophical and practical issues about "digital natives," children born into and raised in a digital world. Palfrey, head of school at Phillips Academy in Andover, Mass., was formerly executive director of Harvard University's Beekman Center on Internet and Society; Gasser is a professor at Harvard Law School and current executive director of the Beekman Center.

Stephens, Mitchell, *Beyond News: The Future of Journalism*, **Columbia University Press, 2014.**
A professor at New York University's Arthur L. Carter Institute argues that in the digital age there is a need for what he calls "wisdom journalism" – providing analysis and opinion along with fact-based reporting. Stephens also wrote *A History of News* (3d. ed., Oxford University Press, 2007).

Usher, Nikki, *Making News at* **The New York Times, University of Michigan Press, 2014.**
An assistant professor at George Washington University's School of Media and Public Affairs examines the inner workings of *The New York Times*, including the tension between print and digital content, based on unique access to the *Times*' newsroom from January to June 2010.

Articles

Gapper, John, "Silicon Valley gets excited about a small story," *Financial Times*, **April 9, 2014, http://tinyurl.com/l9uval8.**
Columnist Gapper questions the potential profitability of digital start-ups *Vox.com* and *FiveThirtyEight.com*.

Grabowicz, Paul, "The Transition to Digital Journalism," Knight Digital Media Center, University of California-Berkeley Graduate School of Journalism, updated March 2014, http://tinyurl.com/kd5gnun.
This comprehensive tutorial on digital journalism covers major digital tools and trends; it includes embedded links to a vast number of resources from a variety of research organizations, news media and scholars and experts.

Packer, George, "Telling Stories About the Future of Journalism," *The New Yorker*, **Jan. 28, 2014, http://tinyurl.com/lqy682c.**
The article discusses Ezra Klein's plan to launch a new digital news site, *Vox.com*.

Scott, Ben, "A Contemporary History of Digital Journalism," *Television and New Media*, **February 2005, pp. 89-126.**
The article traces the history of online journalism from its birth in the mid-1990s to a period of relative stabilization early in the 21st century.

Reports and Studies

"State of the News Media 2014," Pew Research Journalism Project, March 26, 2014, http://tinyurl .com/kk2opwy.

The annual report by the Washington-based research center examines the growth and growing importance of digital news media.

Grueskin, Bill, Ava Seaves, and Lucas Graves, "The Story So Far: What We Know About the Business of Digital Journalism," Tow Center for Digital Journalism, Columbia University Graduate School of Journalism, May 2011, http://tinyurl.com/6aumlu3.

The 140-page comprehensive report examines the economics of digital journalism at for-profit news organizations.

Stencel, Mark, Bill Adair, and Prashanth Kamalakanthan, "The Goat Must Be Fed: Why digital tools are missing in most newsrooms: A report of the Duke Reporters' Lab," May 2014, http://tinyurl .com/o8qkwd7.

The 21-page report finds that newsrooms are slow in using digital tools to find and sift government information, analyze social media and crunch data.

On the Web

"CJR's Guide to Online News Startups," *Columbia Journalism Review*, http://tinyurl.com/l8b3xg7 (accessed May 2014).

The site features a continually updated database of digital news outlets across the country.

For More Information

American Press Institute, 4401 Wilson Blvd., Suite 900, Arlington, VA 22203; 571-366-1200; www.americanpressin stitute.org. Journalism research and training organization founded in 1946 and affiliated with Newspaper Association of America since 2012.

Arthur L. Carter Journalism Institute, New York University, 20 Cooper Square, 6th floor, New York, NY 10003; 212-998-7980; www.journalism.nyu.edu. Graduate program in journalism.

MPA — The Association of Magazine Media, 757 Third Ave., 11th Floor, New York, NY 10017; 212-872-3700; www.magazine.org. Trade association for the magazine industry, formerly known as Magazine Publishers Association.

Newspaper Association of America, 4401 Wilson Blvd., Suite 900, Arlington, VA 22203; 571-366-1000; www .newspapers.org. Trade association for the newspaper industry.

Online News Association; journalists.org. Membership organization for digital journalists.

Pew Research Center Journalism Project, 1615 L St., N.W., Suite 700, Washington, DC 20036; 202-419-4300; www .journalism.org. Publishes annual reports — "State of the News Media."

Tow Center for Digital Journalism, Columbia University Graduate School of Journalism, Pulitzer Hall, 6th floor, 116th St. and Broadway, New York, NY 10027; 212-854-1945; www.towcenter.org. Institute established in 2012 to foster development of digital journalism.

14

Media Bias

Robert Kiener

Conservative talk show hosts such as Sean Hannity have found huge audiences — mainly among Republicans — at Fox News. Some media critics trace the rise of partisan programming to the government's 1987 decision to abandon the Fairness Doctrine, which required broadcasters to devote airtime to policy debates and offer contrasting views on those issues. The government said the rapid growth of cable outlets made the rule unnecessary.

From *CQ Researcher*,
May 3, 2013

"A total embarrassment." "A fawning interview." "A targeted barrage of softballs."

A wide variety of journalists and media critics used those disparaging terms to attack CBS reporter Steve Kroft's Jan. 27 "60 Minutes" interview with President Obama and outgoing Secretary of State Hillary Rodham Clinton.[1]

The Atlantic compared it to Scott Pelley's earlier, much tougher "60 Minutes" interview with President George W. Bush and proclaimed "a glaring double standard" favoring Democrats.[2] *The Washington Post* called Kroft's sit-down with Obama and Clinton a "soft-as-premium-tissue" interview.[3]

Fox News claimed the interview "totally epitomizes liberal media bias in the modern era."[4] *The Wall Street Journal's* editorial page dubbed it "embarrassing" evidence of "the mainstream media fawn-a-thon toward the current president."[5]

The complaints are only the latest in a rising chorus of charges that the nation's mainstream media — major newspapers, news-weeklies and broadcasters — lean either to the left or to the right. And polls show that the perception of media bias is growing, and that it comes from both sides of the political spectrum.

For example, some mainstream media outlets were accused of slanting their coverage of the Senate's recent refusal to mandate background checks on gun purchases. "Television hosts, editorial boards and even some reporters have aggressively criticized and shamed the 46 Senators who opposed the plan, while some have even taken to actively soliciting the public to contact [the senators]

Coverage of Democrats Was More Negative

Republican-oriented sources accounted for about 60 percent of the partisan quotes during three months of media coverage of the 2012 presidential campaign, according to the 4thEstate Project, which conducts statistical analysis of the media. It also found that media coverage of health care, the economy and social issues was more negative for President Obama than for GOP challenger Mitt Romney. Thirty-seven percent of total election coverage during the period was negative for Obama, compared to 29 percent for Romney.

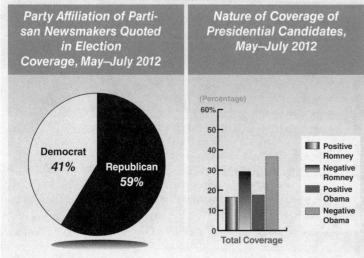

Party Affiliation of Partisan Newsmakers Quoted in Election Coverage, May–July 2012

Democrat 41%
Republican 59%

Nature of Coverage of Presidential Candidates, May–July 2012

(Percentage)

- Positive Romney
- Negative Romney
- Positive Obama
- Negative Obama

Total Coverage

Source: "Liberal Media Bias: Fact or Fiction," 4thEstate Project, July 2012, specialreports.4thestate.net/liberal-media-bias-fact-or-fiction/

Palin calls them, the "lamestream" media — lean to the left has been a favorite theme of the Republican Party for years. "As a conservative I've long believed that there is an inherent media bias, and I think that anyone with objectivity would believe that that's the case," vice presidential candidate Rep. Paul Ryan, R-Wis., said last September. "I think most people in the mainstream media are left of center."[8]

The media are "out of control with a deliberate and unmistakable leftist agenda," the Media Research Center, a conservative media watchdog group in Alexandria, Va., charged in an August 2012 "open letter" to the "biased" news media during last year's presidential race. "To put it bluntly: you are rigging this election and taking sides in order to pre-determine the outcome."

During the 2012 presidential election, however, Democrats received more negative coverage than Republicans, according to the 4thEstate Project, which examined three months' worth of 2012 election coverage. It found that 37 percent of Obama's coverage was negative, compared to 29 percent of Romney's. About 60 percent of the partisan quotes came from GOP-oriented sources.[9]

Others see a conservative, pro-GOP slant at some popular media outlets. Fox News is "vital" to the conservative movement, said Republican Jim Gilmore, former governor of Virginia.[10] And a 2009 Pew Research poll found that Fox News is considered the most ideological channel in America, with 47 percent of respondents saying Fox is "mostly conservative."[11]

Measuring media bias is an inexact science, and researchers who try to quantify it have found mixed results, with some studies showing a left-leaning bias and some a rightward tilt.

A Media Matters survey found that about 60 percent of the nation's newspapers publish more conservative syndicated columnists than liberal ones every week,

directly" to express their displeasure, reporter Dylan Byers wrote in *Politico*. "The decision by some members of the media to come down so firmly on one side of a policy debate has only served to reinforce conservatives' longstanding suspicions that the mainstream media has a deep-seated liberal bias."[6]

The Sunday talk shows also are criticized for hosting Republican and conservative guests more often than Democrats or liberals. Of 400 guests hosted by the major Sunday morning talk shows on ABC, CBS, NBC and Fox during the first three months of 2013, 40 percent were either Republicans or conservatives, and only 29 percent were Democrats or liberals, complained the left-leaning media watchdog group Media Matters. Centrist, nonpartisan and ideologically neutral guests made up 31 percent.[7]

The claim that the mainstream media — or as former vice presidential candidate and Alaska governor Sarah and among the country's top 10 columnists (as ranked by the number of papers that carry them), five are conservative, two centrist and three liberal.[12]

A classic study by the media watchdog group Fairness & Accuracy in Reporting (FAIR) found in 1998 that most journalists were relatively liberal on social policies but significantly more conservative than the general public on economic, labor, health care and foreign policy issues. Journalists "nearly always" turn to government officials and business representatives — rather than labor representatives or consumer advocates — when covering economic policy, a practice that critics say led to the nation's business reporters being blindsided by the 2007-09 recession.[13]

Tim Groseclose, a political science professor at the University of California, Los Angeles (UCLA), has developed a statistical model for measuring the "slant quotient" of news stories. In his 2012 book *Left Turn: How Liberal Bias Distorts the American Mind*, he concludes that "every mainstream national news outlet in the United States has a liberal bias." Of the 20 news sources he studied, 18 were left of center, he said.[14]

But David D'Alessio, an assistant professor of communications sciences at the University of Connecticut, Stamford, says his research shows that "while some individuals may produce biased reporting, over time both sides tend to balance one another. There is no clear bias for one side or the other."

Most Americans See Media as Politically Biased

More than three-fourths of Republicans consider the media politically biased, a perception shared by 54 percent of Democrats and 63 percent of Independents. Sixty percent of Americans say they have little or no confidence in the media to report news fully, accurately and fairly.

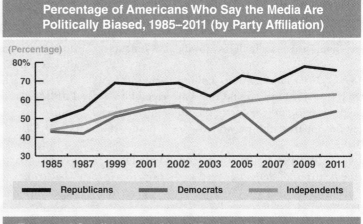

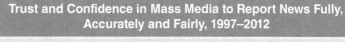

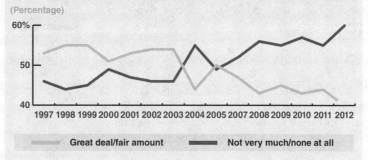

Sources: Lymari Morales, "U.S. Distrust in Media Hits New High," Gallup, September 2012, www.gallup.com/poll/157589/distrust-media-hits-new-high.aspx; "Views of the News Media: 1985-2011," Pew Research Center, September 2011, p. 11, www.people-press.org/files/legacy-pdf/9-22-2011%20Media%20Attitudes%20Release.pdf

Many observers agree that distrust of the media often depends on one's political leanings. "Democrats trust everything except Fox, and Republicans don't trust anything other than Fox," said a Public Policy Polling press release announcing its latest survey of media credibility.[15]

"If Fox tilts right, that doesn't bother conservatives; they don't necessarily see it as bias," said Bernard Goldberg, a Fox contributor and author of *Bias* and other books on media partiality. "And when MSNBC goes left, liberals . . . see it as 'truth.'"[16]

"Fox is perfectly entitled to be a conservative news organization" said former *New York Times* executive editor Bill Keller. "I will always defend their right to be that. My criticism of Fox is that a lot of the time they pretend that they're not. And I think that just tends to contribute to cynicism about the media. All news organizations, including the ones that try very hard to play fair and to be even-handed in their reporting and writing, get tarred by the Fox brush."[17]

Despite the inconclusiveness of the studies, skepticism about media credibility is growing. For instance:

• A 2013 Public Policy Polling survey of news media trustworthiness found that Fox's credibility had dropped significantly: 46 percent of those surveyed said they do not trust the network — up 9 points since 2010.[18]

• A 2011 Pew Research Center poll found that 77 percent of respondents believed news organizations "tend to favor one side" — up from 53 percent in 1985.[19]

• A September 2012 Gallup survey found that 60 percent of respondents said they had "not very much" or no trust or confidence that the mass media report the news fully, accurately and fairly — up from 46 percent in 1998.[20]

"These are big increases," says Mark Jurkowitz, a former *Boston Globe* journalist and media reporter and now the associate director of the Pew Research Project for Excellence in Journalism. "For the last three decades there has been a seriously embedded, growing thought among the public that the media, especially the liberal media, are biased."

Larry Light, editor-in-chief of the financial website AdviceIQ.com, contended that public antipathy toward the news media is the result of what he called the right-wing's ongoing "war against journalists," which he maintained has stepped up its tempo recently. The perception of bias "has nothing to do with people's individual observations" but everything to do with "a juggernaut of conservative, anti-media propaganda that has grown more and more powerful," he wrote. "The propagandists repeat the phrase 'biased liberal media' a zillion-fold everywhere. That it is a crock of baloney is beside the point."[21]

Some observers blame the changing perceptions on the rise of cable television, radio talk shows and Internet sites and blogs, which have enabled thousands of new players to spread their often partisan messages. Commentators such as conservatives Sean Hannity of Fox News and radio personality Rush Limbaugh, and liberals such as Rachel Maddow of MSNBC, along with news sites such as the right-leaning Drudge Report and left-leaning *Huffington Post*, have helped blur the line between straight news and opinion. "The public does not always differentiate between these partisan outlets and the more objective mainstream media," says S. Robert Lichter, director of the Center for Media and Public Affairs at George Mason University in Annandale, Va., and co-author of the 1986 book *The Media Elite*.

Indeed, 63 percent of respondents cited cable news — particularly CNN and Fox — when asked what comes to mind when they hear the term "news organizations," according to Pew.[22] Pew also found that opinion and commentary, as opposed to news reporting, fill 85 percent of MSNBC's airtime, 55 percent of Fox's and 46 percent of CNN's.[23]

Some say the public's perceptions about media bias may also have been influenced by the growth of media watchdog groups, such as Media Matters and the Media Research Center, which track inaccurate reporting, media bias and political gaffes. Often financed by wealthy partisans, the groups comb the media searching for examples of perceived right- or left-wing bias.

"Part of their message is, 'The other guy is lying to you,'" says Jurkowitz. That helps to convince the public that "the media are biased," he says.

Others say fact-checking groups such as PolitiFact and FactCheck.org may also have increased the perception that the media are biased.

Surveys repeatedly have shown that most mainstream journalists in New York City and Washington, D.C., have liberal leanings, but most reporters say they separate their personal views from their reporting.[24] "An opinion is not a bias," said Michael Kinsley, former editor of the online publication *Slate*.[25] Longtime *Washington Post* political reporter David Broder once famously declared that "the charge of ideological bias in the newsroom [is] laughable. There just isn't enough ideology in the average reporter to fill a thimble."[26]

As scholars, journalists and news consumers explore bias in the quickly changing media world, here are some questions they are asking:

Should journalists try to be objective?

As the media landscape grows more varied — with cable broadcasters, bloggers, Twitterers and others adding their often-partisan views to those of the established media — many media analysts are asking if journalistic objectivity is becoming passé.

But for many mainstream media organizations, objectivity is a core part of their brand and very much worth preserving. "Objectivity is like virtue; it's . . . the thing that you always strive toward" in search of the truth, said *New York Times* conservative columnist David Brooks.[27]

He and other journalists say being objective means not playing favorites, regardless of one's personal views. "It means doing stories that will make your friends mad when appropriate and not doing stories that are actually hit jobs or propaganda masquerading as journalism," said Alex S. Jones, director of Harvard University's Joan Shorenstein Center on the Press, Politics and Public Policy and a Pulitzer Prize-winning journalist. "It is essential that genuine objectivity should remain the American journalistic standard."[28]

In its *Handbook of Journalism*, the Reuters news service warns journalists: "As Reuters journalists, we never identify with any side in an issue, a conflict or a dispute."[29]

But many media specialists today question whether journalists can ever be truly objective or neutral. "No journalist is completely objective," says Pew's Jurkowitz. "There are subjective judgments made in every story: what quote a reporter uses in his lead, the prominence he gives to certain facts, who gets one or two quotes, the language used, etc."

"Objectivity is in the eye of the beholder," says Barrie Dunsmore, a former ABC News foreign correspondent. "It's not just reporting both sides, which often aren't equivalent in terms of moral, legal or sociological balance. It has to be coupled with knowledge of a subject. It's easy to be objective if you don't know anything."

"The big problem with objectivity is that it has no bias toward truth," says Eric Alterman, a journalism history professor at the City University of New York (CUNY) Graduate School of Journalism and a liberal

journalist. "You can quote both sides of an issue, and they can both be false. This doesn't bring readers any closer to the truth."

"Good journalism, like good science, starts out with a hunch, not with an observation, and then builds its case from there" says Reuters media critic Jack Shafer. "It's the method the journalist uses to arrive at his conclusion that has to be objective."

Some journalists have held that being objective means producing "balanced" stories — stories that give various sides of an issue. But many now see that approach as misleading and often producing weak reporting.

"There is no such thing as objectivity, and the truth . . . seldom nestles neatly halfway between any two opposing points of view," the late Texas columnist Molly Ivins declared. "The smug complacency of much of the press . . . stems from the curious notion that if you get a quote from both sides . . . you've done the job. In the first place, most stories aren't two-sided, they're 17-sided at least. In the second place, it's of no help to either the readers or the truth to quote one side saying, 'cat,' and the other side saying 'dog,' while the truth is there's an elephant crashing around out there in the bushes."[30]

After seeing his reporting reduced to a formulaic, he-said-she-said news story, former *Los Angeles Times* reporter Ken Silverstein complained to his editors that "balanced" reporting can be "totally misleading and leads to utterly spineless reporting." In the end, he continued, "It's just an easy way of avoiding real reporting and shirking our responsibility to inform readers."[31]

Constantly demanding balance can lead to a false equivalence, critics argue. "Al Gore says about 97 percent of climate scientists agree that global warming is real and manmade, but only about 50 percent of news reporting will say that, because they . . . want to give equal weight to both sides," says Alterman.

"The term 'balance' implies equal time, and that's not sufficient for accurate and fair reporting," says Dunsmore. "It is more important to be accurate and fair than merely showing both sides of an issue in order to be balanced."

Longtime Washington observers Norman Ornstein, a resident scholar at the conservative American Enterprise Institute, and Thomas Mann, a senior fellow at the centrist Brookings Institution, recently excoriated the mainstream press for insisting on writing balanced news stories that gave equal weight to often-outlandish political views, such as the comment by former Rep. Allen West, R-Fla., that "78 to 81" members of Congress are communists.

"Our advice to the press: Don't seek professional safety through the even-handed, unfiltered presentation of opposing views," they said. Instead, reporters should ask: "Which politician is telling the truth? Who is taking hostages, at what risks and to what ends?"[32] Choosing balance over common sense does the public a disservice, they said. Taking a "balanced treatment of an unbalanced phenomenon distorts reality."[33]

Others, such as George Mason's Lichter, differentiate between objectivity and balance. Objectivity is "such a valuable gift from America to the world of journalism that I'd hate to lose it," he says. "We owe a debt of gratitude to the wire services and papers such as *The New York Times* for making objectivity their goal."

But some journalists today argue that reporters should not be afraid to declare their biases. With many new-media platforms producing journalism that is increasingly laced with opinion, it's more important than ever to know a reporter's agenda, says Jurkowitz. "Organizations have to be clear about their motives and agendas. Transparency is the new objectivity," he says.

Has the proliferation of media watchdog groups fostered perceptions of media bias?

Much of the criticism of the "biased right-wing press" and the "lamestream media" has originated with self-styled media watchdog groups that exist mainly to monitor the media in hopes of discovering bias, inaccuracies or inconsistencies. Often funded by politically inspired financial backers such as conservative billionaire brothers Charles and David Koch or liberal financier George Soros, these groups comb the media searching for examples of bias.

"An entire cottage industry exists to highlight the media's alleged failings," wrote Paul Farhi, a reporter at *The Washington Post*.[34]

By publicizing failings, groups such as the Media Research Center (MRC), Media Matters for America, Fairness & Accuracy in Reporting and others also have ratcheted up the volume in the national conversation about media bias. "Their message that the media are biased has certainly seeped into the public consciousness," says Pew's Jurkowitz.

For example:

- L. Brent Bozell, founder and president of the conservative MRC, said the mainstream media are "the 'shock troops' of the Obama administration because they are the ones doing all the dirty work for him so that he doesn't have to do it."[35]
- Left-leaning Media Matters said Fox News often uses "offensive words" to refer to undocumented immigrants. The group claimed that between Nov. 7, 2012, and Feb. 15, 2013, Fox's prime-time hosts and their guests used what Media Matters called anti-immigrant language — such as "illegals," "illegal aliens" and "anchor babies" — 99 times.[36] (Recently The Associated Press dropped the term "illegal immigrant" from its *AP Stylebook*.)[37]
- Fairness & Accuracy in Reporting complained that the mainstream media "failed" to properly question the Bush administration's justification for the Iraq War by neglecting to sufficiently question the existence of weapons of mass destruction and other assertions.[38]

These groups have "created the perception that the media is more biased than it really is," says Si Sheppard, an assistant professor of political science at Long Island University and author of *The Partisan Press: A History of Media Bias in the United States*. "That's their objective. They like to say that the media play favorites, but studies have shown that there has not been consistent favoritism in reporting over the last few decades."

Others say that because these groups are open about their own biases, their findings do not unfairly taint the press. "Everyone has to parse everyone's arguments for themselves," says Reuters media critic Shafer. "I find these groups valuable."

But others say the groups have crossed the line from unbiased critics to political partisans. "When watchdog groups push their political agenda to the detriment of facts, they are becoming biased political operators," says Andrew R. Cline, associate professor of journalism at Missouri State University, in Springfield. "They stop doing a good service."

"Media criticism has become political criticism by another name," says George Mason's Lichter.

But the MRC's Bozell disagrees. "Data is data, numbers are numbers. While our interpretation of those facts may be subjective, we aren't forcing the public to see bias everywhere. We are showing them what different news organizations are reporting and the way they are reporting and let them decide."

"By awakening the public to bias, these watchdogs are doing a favor," says UCLA's Groseclose. "They are moving people's perceptions closer to the truth that the media is biased."

However, some media observers say the groups make the media look more biased than they really are. "These groups' criticisms are certainly reinforcing that opinion," says Lichter. "Instead of just beating up the other side, there is more beating up on the media for being biased."

This is more than politically oriented criticism. "The new part of some of these groups' message is, 'the media are lying to you,'" says Jurkowitz. "That has become a significant element of the message that goes out on both sides of the spectrum."

Lichter and others blame the public's declining trust in media in part on the watchdog groups' repeated allegations of bias.

Media Matters executive vice-president Bradley Beychok disagrees. "The fact that public trust in the media continues to fall says more about the media than it does about media watchdogs. The media landscape is expanding beyond television and newspapers. As it does, there is more of a need to combat misinformation from new sources."

Are the media biased in favor of President Obama?

During the Sept. 16, 2012, presidential debate, Republican candidate Mitt Romney implied that Obama's personal funds likely included investments in China, a charge that had been leveled at Romney.

"Mr. President, have you looked at your pension?" asked Romney.

Negative Views of Press Growing

The public's assessment of the press has become increasingly negative since the mid-1980s. Two-thirds of Americans say reports often are inaccurate, compared to about one-third in 1985. Seventy-seven percent say the press shows bias on political and social issues, while 80 percent say the media often are influenced by powerful people and organizations. Experts say the rise of cable television and the Internet has led more media outlets to engage in partisanship, with less regard for accuracy.

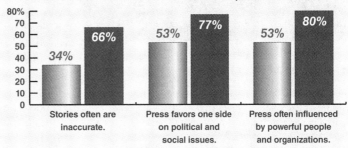

Public Views on Press Performance, 1985 and 2011

Source: "Views of the News Media: 1985-2011," Pew Research Center, September 2011, p. 1, www.people-press.org/files/legacy-pdf/9-22-2011%20Media%20Attitudes%20Release.pdf

■ 1985
■ 2011

Obama shot back, "You know, I don't look at my pension. It's not as big as yours, so it, it doesn't take as long."

In a nearby room where reporters were watching the debate, a round of applause broke out.[39]

While conservative commentators used this outburst as proof of their oft-repeated claim that much of the media favored Obama, others said all it showed was that reporters, like anyone else, enjoy a good debate comeback.

Many conservatives, such as the Media Research Center's Bozell, say the media are pro-Obama and his administration. "Saying the media aren't Obama-biased is like saying ducks don't waddle," says Bozell.

David Freddoso, editorial page editor of the conservative *Washington Examiner* and author of *Spin Masters: How the Media Ignored the Real News and Helped Reelect Barack Obama*, echoes the bias claims but believes that much of it is unintentional. "A lot of the mainstream media's pro-Obama bias is a product of the 'liberal bubble world' most journalists live in," he says. "When you and most of your colleagues are liberal, that can easily skew your perceptions."

AFP/Getty Images/Saul Loeb

Conservatives claimed moderator Candy Crowley (center) of CNN favored President Obama when she intervened on his behalf during the Oct. 16, 2012, presidential debate. GOP candidate Mitt Romney repeatedly asserted that Obama took "days" to call the Sept. 11, 2012, attack on the Benghazi consulate in Libya an "act of terror," while Obama insisted he did so the day after the incident. When Romney refused to accept Obama's answer, Crowley said the president "did in fact" call the incident an act of terror on Sept. 12. Crowley later said she was only trying to move the debate along to other topics.

Freddoso believes the mainstream media have "misrepresented Obama's so-called economic recovery" in Obama's favor and "emphasized Romney's gaffes during the campaign instead of attacking Obama's handling of the Benghazi attack," in which the American diplomatic mission in Benghazi, Libya, was attacked by insurgents in September, 2012.

Some conservative journalists claim there has been a double standard in coverage of the Obama and George W. Bush administrations. "There was no fear of affronting Bush," said Fred Barnes, executive editor of the conservative *Weekly Standard*. "He faced relentless scrutiny . . . . The media raised questions about his motives, the constitutionality of his policies, his brainpower . . . . Obama's adoption of these same policies has drawn minimal attention."[40]

Lichter disagrees. "While Obama did get extremely positive coverage during his extended honeymoon period in 2009, the press since then has been fairly balanced in its coverage of him and his administration."

Other media critics claim journalists are so swayed by Obama's personal story that it is hard to "resist" him.

"He is liberal, Ivy League and a person of color. That is simply too powerful a combination for the media to resist," wrote Peter Wehner, a senior fellow at the conservative Ethics and Public Policy Center. "One gets [the] sense that journalists not only like Mr. Obama; they are in awe of him."[41]

But NBC chief White House correspondent Chuck Todd called such charges "mythology." He said conservatives increasingly believe, without cause, that the "big, bad non-conservative media is out to get conservatives."

However, Light, the editor of AdviceIQ.com, wrote, "anti-media critiques are often absurdly one-sided. Their anti-media world is one where you whine about perceived slights to your side and conveniently ignore bad press that Democrats get. Anything that doesn't embrace the right-wing line is, by definition, biased."[42]

Likewise, Romney strategist Stuart Stevens said after Romney's loss in the election that the media were not "in the tank" for Obama nor were they too sympathetic to him.[43]

The public as a whole believes the press was fair in its coverage of the candidates. During the 2012 election, 46 percent of those polled by Pew said the coverage of Obama was fair, and an equal percentage said Romney's coverage was fair. However, when only Republicans were polled, 60 percent said the press coverage of Obama was "too easy," compared to just 4 percent of Democrats.[44]

While critics point to negative coverage of Romney as an example of media bias, others say it reflected the nature of political reporting: Journalists tend to cover politics as a horse race, and gaffes make for entertaining copy. A lot of Romney's negative coverage, they say, was due to his numerous gaffes, such as his critical comments about how London was handling security for the Olympics or his blaming Palestine's lack of economic success on cultural differences with Israel.

The 4thEstate study found no pro-Obama bias during the election period it examined. From May 1 to July 15, 2012, Republicans were quoted in news reports 44 percent more often than Democrats, and negative coverage of Obama was 17 percent higher than such coverage of Romney, the group said. "Our data does not support the thesis of a liberal media bias as it relates to Election 2012 coverage," 4thEstate said. "If anything, our analysis suggests a media bias towards both Mr. Romney and Republicans."[45] The organization also found that the media discussed Romney more than Obama: 41.8 percent of the time versus 36.8 percent.[46]

However, a Pew Research poll found that Obama enjoyed a surge in positive coverage during the last week of the campaign.[47]

"But on the whole, both candidates got equally negative coverage," says George Mason's Lichter.

BACKGROUND

Journalism's 'Dark Ages'

Historians are quick to point out that the roots of American journalism were deeply embedded in partisan soil. Bias was the norm during journalism's formative years in this country. Indeed, the very idea of an unbiased press was anathema to the nation's early citizens.

Newspapers reflected the opinions of their owners and publishers. "For most of American history . . . there was only opinion, and highly partisan opinion at that," said Sheppard of Long Island University.[48] In *The Partisan Press*, Sheppard cites several early newspaper owners and publishers who attacked the ideas of balance and objectivity:

• On Sept. 4, 1798, the *Newark Gazette* described giving equal time to both sides of the political divide a "'folly that should not be tolerated.'"[49]

• On July 17, 1799, *The Washington Mirror* said treating parties equally was impossible, and that "printers who 'pretended' neutrality succeeded only in willfully misleading the people."[50]

• On March 10, 1800, the *New York American Citizen* called impartiality "'injurious to the best interests of mankind.'"[51]

Newspapers and their political pamphlet cousins were "mouthpieces" for the political parties of the era.[52]

Many newspapers were even supported directly by politicians. For example, Thomas Jefferson helped pay for the startup and running of the *National Gazette*, and Alexander Hamilton supported the *Gazette of the United States.*

"This gave an acrimonious tone to public discourse, since newspapers had no incentive to temper the language they used to criticize opponents," wrote George Mason

Antiwar demonstrators protest the mainstream media's Iraq War coverage outside NBC headquarters in New York City on March 15, 2006. Critics said the press was too willing to accept the Bush administration's assertions that Iraq had weapons of mass destruction before the U.S.-led invasion of the country in 2003. No such weapons were ever found.

University's Lichter.[53] In addition, newspapers often had lucrative government printing contracts, which also promoted biased reporting.

To temper the political bias of the press, the government — led by President John Adams' Federalist Party — passed the Sedition Act of 1798, which made it a crime to publish "false, scandalous and malicious writing" about the president or Congress. It enabled the government to close down many opposition Republican newspapers but caused such a voter backlash that Adams was not re-elected. The act expired in 1801.[54]

The partisan press also placed party above accuracy. Some editors and reporters even worked part-time for politicians.[55] Others were key party leaders.[56] Some have called the first quarter of the 19th century the "Dark Ages of American journalism."[57]

"Even Jefferson, who famously preferred newspapers without government to government without newspapers, later complained that newspapers made their readers less well informed because 'he who knows nothing is nearer to truth than he whose mind is filled with falsehood and errors,'" wrote Lichter.[58]

'Penny Papers'

The rise of the "penny papers" in the 1830s transformed journalism's partisan character. Edited for the middle and working classes rather than for the elites, cheap,

CHRONOLOGY

1690–1798 *Newspapers move from partisan approach to more independence.*

1690 *Publick Occurrences* becomes first newspaper published in America.

1702 *Daily Courant* becomes first English-language daily newspaper.

1791 First Amendment is added to U.S. Constitution, guaranteeing the right to publish news, information and opinions without government interference.

1798 The Alien and Sedition Acts prohibit publishing anything "false, scandalous and malicious" about the president or Congress. More than 20 editors are arrested; some are imprisoned. The laws later expired or were repealed.

1800s–1900 *Newspapers flourish as the "penny press" gains in popularity; journalism becomes a profession.*

1830 United States has 715 newspapers.

1833 *New York Sun* is launched, marking beginning of "penny press."

1846 Newspapers with varied political views create the nonpartisan Associated Press wire service.

1850 Only 5 percent of U.S. newspapers are "neutral and independent."

1851 Believing that a free, independent press is important to an educated populace, the Post Office offers a cheap mailing rate for newspapers.

1870 Nearly 5,100 newspapers are published in the United States.

1878 University of Missouri begins offering nation's first journalism courses.

1896 Adolph Ochs buys *The New York Times* "to give the news impartially, without fear or favor, regardless of any party, sect or interest."

1900–2000 *Government regulates, then deregulates, the broadcast media. Radio, television and then the Internet change the face of media.*

1934 Communications Act creates Federal Communications Commission (FCC) to regulate radio.

1940 American Institute of Public Opinion says 52 percent of Americans rely on radio for political information; 38 percent rely on newspapers.

1949 FCC's "Fairness Doctrine" requires broadcasters to devote airtime to controversial issues and to offer contrasting views.

1963 TV surpasses newspapers as the leading source of daily news.

1981 Survey by George Mason University journalism professor S. Robert Lichter shows that 81 percent of mainstream journalists voted for Democrats for president between 1964 and 1976.

1985–1986 Non-journalistic corporations buy all three major television networks, sparking cost cutting and staff reductions in the news departments.

1987 FCC drops Fairness Doctrine, saying the growth of cable and broadcast outlets make it unnecessary.

2000–2013 *Newspaper circulation drops; many papers cease publication. Cable broadcasting surges; social media play an increasing role in opinion journalism.*

2001 Fox becomes most-watched cable-news network.

2007 Nearly 1,500 newspapers sell 55 million copies daily.

2012 Gallup survey finds 60 percent of Americans have no or not very much trust that the mass media report the news accurately and fairly, up from 46 percent in 1998. Pew Research Center finds that 36 percent of Twitter users follow the news, compared with 19 percent of social media users.

2013 Pew Research Center finds that opinion and commentary fill 85 percent of MSNBC's airtime, 55 percent of Fox's and 46 percent of CNN's.

tabloid-style papers such as the *New York Sun* were able to prosper by offering an entertaining, informative product less dependent on partisan politics — for a penny apiece.

This was largely an economic decision. A partisan approach would inevitably alienate a large sector of a paper's potential readership, while a less political approach was more inclusive and could, in turn, attract more advertising. By mid-19th century the penny press' less partisan approach dominated journalism.

"Henceforth the reader would typically be viewed as a consumer rather than a partisan, and the nostrums of private enterprise would replace those of political ideology in paying the bills," wrote Lichter.[59]

But the penny papers were not apolitical. They often endorsed candidates, sometimes from more than one party. With "a business model incorporating the independence of action afforded by financial self-reliance, the critical first steps towards objectivity had been established," explained Sheppard.[60]

Toward the end of the 19th century, rapid industrialization and urban growth increased the audience for newspapers. Entrepreneurial publishers such as Joseph Pulitzer and William Randolph Hearst helped develop a profitable formula that relied heavily on a sensationalist mix of sex, crime and gossip that came to be known as "yellow journalism."

A combination of factors soon pushed newspapers to become less sensational. Their increased reliance on advertising made them reluctant to offend readers and led papers to improve their product and expand circulation. The expansion of the railroad and telegraph created new demand for instantaneous news from isolated communities where political sentiments might differ from the paper's hometown. Wire services, such as The Associated Press, formed in 1846, prospered by supplying subscribing newspapers with concise, accurate and objective copy.

When Adolph Ochs purchased *The New York Times* in 1896, he announced his intention, "to give the news impartially, without fear or favor, regardless of any party, sect, or interest involved."[61] As journalism history professor Alterman says, "We can date the beginning of serious, objective reporting in America with Ochs' purchase of *The New York Times*."

In part because of Ochs' paper, objectivity began to play a more important role in journalism. Journalism schools proliferated after the turn of the 20th century and taught the importance of objectivity along with accuracy and ethical reporting. According to a study cited by Lichter, the proportion of objective stories in newspapers and on wire services doubled from 1897 to 1914. "Having previously served the common good by standing aside from the world of politics, the press would now do so by standing above it," noted Lichter.[62]

Electronic Media

Radio, which burst onto the scene in the 1920s, soon transformed the media landscape. Between 1927 and 1934 the number of homes with radios jumped from 25 percent to 65 percent. Politicians, some angered by what they perceived as a biased press, saw radio as a medium to get their unfiltered message directly to the public. President Franklin D. Roosevelt famously used his iconic "fireside chats" to circumvent what he considered to be a hostile Republican press and speak directly to the people.

Because the airwaves were considered a public resource, radio was regulated. Under the Communications Act of 1934, created by the Federal Communications Commission (FCC), stations could lose their licenses if their broadcasts were considered too controversial, and stations had to offer equal time for political candidates.

By the 1940s radio was the main source of political information for 52 percent of the public, compared to 38 percent who relied on newspapers, according to a 1940 American Institute of Public Opinion poll.[63]

Meanwhile newspapers continued to become more objective. As publishers realized readers were attracted by objective, authoritative reporting, a church-state-style wall separated the advertising and news sides of the business. Robert McCormick, publisher of the *Chicago Tribune*, took this separation so seriously that he had two sets of elevators installed in his headquarters building in the early 20th century; one was for reporters and editors, the other for the business side.[64]

After World War II, television emerged as the dominant news medium. Nearly half the nation's households had a television as early as 1953, and by 1963 television was America's leading source of daily news.[65]

To guarantee that the public airwaves exposed audiences to a variety of viewpoints, the FCC's 1949 Fairness Doctrine required broadcasters to devote airtime

Media Bias Seen as Threat to Democracy

"I don't know if democracy can survive without an actively free press."

How important is a free and vibrant press to a healthy democracy? The nation's founders, even though they were not always pleased with the partisan newspapers that proliferated at the time, thought it was vital.

"No government ought to be without censors, and where the press is free, no one ever will," Thomas Jefferson told George Washington in 1792.[1] The First Amendment to the Constitution offered special protection to the press by barring Congress from abridging its freedom.

Throughout American history, the press has been viewed as such an important source of checks and balances on the government that it became known as the "Fourth Estate" — as important to democracy as the legislative, executive and judicial branches of government. However, while the founders stressed the need for a free press, they never claimed, for example, that the press should be nonpartisan.

As Americans increasingly complain that the media are becoming more biased, some media critics are asking if such a trend is healthy for democracy.

"We designed a constitutional system with many checks and balances," said Democratic pollster Patrick Caddell. "The one that had no checks and balances was the press, and that was done under an implicit understanding that, somehow, the press would protect the people from the government and the power by telling — somehow allowing — people to have the truth. That is being abrogated as we speak, and has been for some time."[2]

Caddell and others argue that an increasingly partisan press not only is slanting the news but choosing not to cover news that could cast an ideology or party in a bad light. Such bias by omission, said Caddell, has led the media to make "themselves a fundamental threat to the democracy, and, in my opinion, made themselves the enemy of the American people."[3]

At the 2013 Conservative Political Action Conference (CPAC), an annual political conference attended by conservative activists and elected officials, Rep. Lamar Smith, R-Texas, said, "When the media don't report the facts, Americans can't make good decisions. And if Americans can't make good decisions, our democracy is at risk. So media bias, to me, is a major threat to our democracy."[4]

"If society doesn't have knowledge of the workings of government, how can it pass judgment on government?" asks L. Brent Bozell, president of the Media Research Center, a conservative media watchdog group "I don't know if democracy can survive without an actively free press."

Not everyone agrees that today's media threaten democracy. "When anyone tells me that the media is so biased that democracy is at risk, I remind them that even at the beginnings of our democracy the media was much, much more partisan," says S. Robert Lichter, director of the Center for Media and Public Affairs at George Mason University and

to controversial matters of public interest and to offer contrasting views on those issues. The act also forbade stations from censoring campaign or political ads. Another FCC rule, calling for "equal time" for political candidates, did not apply to newscasts, documentaries, entertainment programs or political advertising.

Television's popularity was a factor in the closure of the nation's afternoon newspapers, which could not compete with the immediacy of the evening news broadcasts. However, many papers responded to the new journalistic competitor by "expanding their interpretative coverage and news analyses, where print held a competitive advantage," wrote Lichter. "Mainstream journalism began to take on a sharper point of view, often including opinion and advocacy in its reporting.... For the next decade, reporters were thrown onto the front lines of political battlegrounds that ranged from the civil rights movement to campus protests, the Vietnam War and the Watergate scandal."[66]

New Media

The 1980s were marked by major changes in American media. In 1985 and '86, non-journalistic corporations bought all three major television networks, leading to sweeping cost-cutting and staff reductions in the news departments.

co-author of *The Media Elite*. "There were no boundaries then, and people were accused of all sorts of heinous, outlandish things. We survived then, and we will now."

A continuing decline in the number of journalists and the closure of print and broadcast outlets in recent years could be more of a threat to democracy than partisan media, say other observers. "There is no end in sight to job losses in journalism," says Eric Alterman, a journalism history professor at CUNY Graduate School of Journalism. "Losing journalists means people will be far less informed as citizens, and that's bad for democracy. Also, the bad guys will be able to get away with a lot more because there won't be as many people watching them."

Others are concerned about the growing concentration of media ownership, which could result in corporate influence on what is covered and how it is covered. Six corporations (Disney, News Corp, Viacom, Time-Warner, Comcast and CBS) control 90 percent of the nation's news and entertainment media, up from 50 percent in 1983.[5] "Rupert Murdoch owns *The Wall Street Journal* and *The New York Post*, and he and the Koch brothers are reportedly trying to buy the Los Angeles Times," says Alterman, referring to wealthy, conservative billionaire brothers who have donated millions of dollars to libertarian, free-market advocacy groups and conservative politicians. "That would result in much less of a national conversation."

Former "CBS Evening News" anchor Dan Rather, who recently described a free and independent press as "the red, beating heart of democracy and freedom," warned of the dangers of such concentrated ownership.

"These big corporations, for whom news is only a small part of their business — they manufacture defense products and weapons, they run theme parks, they have all kinds of interests — this makes them dependent in large measure on whoever is in power in Washington," said Rather, who now anchors the news on the cable channel AXS TV. "I think we can all agree that we don't want to have a few very large corporations, working in concert with a powerful political apparatus in Washington, deciding what we see, read and hear — and they do, to a very large degree."[6]

— *Robert Kiener*

[1] *The Jeffersonian Cyclopedia* (1900), p. 130, http://books.google.com/books?id=ZTIoAAAAYAAJ&pg=PA130&lpg=PA130&dq=%E2%80%9CNo+government+ought+to+be+without+censors,+and+where+the+press+is+free,+no+one+ever+will,%E2%80%9D+Thomas+Jefferson+told&source=bl&ots=vamgnUacT4&sig=gHinV3U0Chb16W3EjRdujaEhRo4&hl=en&sa=X&ei=X7x2UZu6IcXy0QGL9oD4Ag&ved=0CEMQ6AEwAzgK#v=onepage&q=%E2%80%9CNo%20government%20ought%20to%20be%20without%20censors%2C%20and%20where%20the%20press%20is%20free%2C%20no%20one%20ever%20will%2C%E2%80%9D%20Thomas%20Jefferson%20told&f=false.

[2] Patrick Caddell, "Mainstream media is threatening our country's future," Fox News, Sept. 29, 2012, www.foxnews.com/opinion/2012/09/29/mainstream-media-threatening-our-country-future/.

[3] *Ibid.*

[4] "Congressman Smith speaks at CPAC 2013 Re: media bias," press release, March 14, 2013, http://lamarsmith.house.gov/news/documentsingle.aspx?DocumentID=324058.

[5] Ashley Lutz, "These 6 companies control 90% of the media in America," *Business Insider*, June 14, 2012, www.businessinsider.com/these-6-corporations-control-90-of-the-media-in-america-2012-6.

[6] Brad Martin, "Dan Rather warns of media control," *American Libraries*, June 24, 2012, http://americanlibrariesmagazine.org/annual-conference/dan-rather-warns-media-control.

Meanwhile, public perceptions that the media were fair were plummeting. By 1984, 38 percent of those surveyed said newspapers were "usually fair," down from two-thirds who felt the press was "fair" in 1937.

The FCC dropped the Fairness Doctrine in 1987, arguing that the growth of cable and broadcast outlets made it unnecessary. The decision, favored by Republicans, is seen as one of the main causes of the rise of conservative talk radio in the 1980s and '90s.[67] Legislation that liberalized media-ownership restrictions, such as the 1996 Telecommunications Act, led to widespread broadcast media consolidation via mergers and buyouts.

Meanwhile, competitive constraints and government regulation of cable channels were relaxed by the Cable Communications Policy Act of 1984. The industry boomed, with hundreds of stations reaching households across the country. Soon, thanks to advances in cable and satellite technology, all-news "24/7" cable channels such as CNN and later Fox News and MSNBC would change the face of television journalism. Outspoken conservative hosts such as Sean Hannity and Bill O'Reilly would find a lucrative audience, mainly among Republicans, on Fox News. And equally sharp-tongued hosts on talk radio, no longer hampered by the need to present both sides of an issue, filled the airwaves and prospered.

Fact Checkers Proliferate — and So Do Their Critics

Media services expose deception, but partisans often ignore them.

"Here's the truth the president won't tell you," said Rep. Michele Bachmann, R-Minn., at this year's Conservative Political Action Conference (CPAC), an annual political conference attended by conservative activists and elected officials. "Of every dollar that you hold in your hands, 70 cents of that dollar that's supposed to go to the poor doesn't. It actually goes to benefit the bureaucrats in Washington, D.C. — 70 cents on the dollar."[1]

True? Not exactly.

The Washington Post's "Fact Checker" column found that Bachmann was off by at least a factor of 10 — or even a factor of 200 — depending on what was included in her figures. It awarded her four "Pinocchios" — its worst rating —"for such misleading use of statistics in a major speech."[2]

Written by veteran reporter Glenn Kessler, "Fact Checker" is just one of many fact-checking operations that have sprung up over the last decade or so — including those at CNN, The Associated Press, Fox and ABC — to examine the accuracy of statements made by politicians and public officials. Such operations also fact-check major speeches, most notably after presidential debates, major addresses such as the State of the Union and claims made in campaign ads.

Groups such as PolitiFact, the Pulitzer Prize-winning site started in 2007 and a project of the *Tampa Bay Times* (formerly *St. Petersburg Times*), and FactCheck.org, a project of the Annenberg Public Policy Center of the University of Pennsylvania, describe themselves as nonpartisan. FactCheck.org, for example, says it is a "nonpartisan, nonprofit 'consumer advocate' for voters that aims to reduce the level of deception and confusion in U.S. politics."[3]

But as fact-checking programs have proliferated, so have their critics. Not surprisingly, many of these criticisms fall along ideological lines. On its conservative-leaning editorial page, *The Wall Street Journal* argued that fact checking is "overwhelmingly biased toward the left," while liberals, such as City University of New York journalism professor Eric Alterman, often claim there is a growing conservative bias among the fact checkers.[4]

Likewise, candidates have been accusing the fact checkers of bias. During the 2012 presidential election, fact checkers labeled as deceptive a Mitt Romney campaign advertisement depicting President Obama as saying, "If we keep talking about the economy we're going to lose." Although the fact checkers explained that Obama was merely quoting Republican Sen. John McCain, Romney's strategists quickly went on the offensive. "We're not going to let our campaign be dictated by fact-checkers," said Romney campaign pollster Neil Newhouse.[5] After Romney lost the election, Media Research Center's research director, Rich Noyes, said his defeat was due partly to opponents "pounding Romney with partisan fact checking."[6]

In fact, both parties often attacked or simply ignored fact checkers' claims of inaccuracy or deceit. "Both candidates' campaigns laid out a number of whoppers, got clobbered for

Many journalists were shocked "that they were widely perceived as just another cog in a distant establishment, an elite group of wealthy and influential snobs who had forgotten their roots," said Lichter.[68] Surveys repeatedly confirmed that the mainstream media were generally to the left of the American public on such hot-button issues as gun control and abortion.[69]

Many GOP politicians agreed with the perception that the media were left-leaning and fanned the flames. For example, during the 1996 presidential election, Republican candidate Bob Dole exhorted, "We've got to stop the liberal bias in this country . . . . Don't read that stuff! Don't watch television! Don't let them make up your mind for you!"[70]

Also in 1996, Fox News was launched by Australian-born news magnate Rupert Murdoch, who appointed former GOP media consultant Roger Ailes as CEO.

doing so, and then kept right on saying them," said *New York Times* media critic David Carr.[7]

Bill Adair, the departing editor of PolitiFact, agrees. "I think there has always been a calculation by political campaigns to forge ahead with a falsehood if they think it will score the points they want to score."[8]

A recent rise in partisan fact-checking organizations, such as Conservative Fact Check and the Media Matters-sponsored Political Correction, has led to even more charges of bias.

"The term 'fact check' can easily be devalued, as people throw it onto any sort of an opinion that they have," said Brendan Nyhan, an assistant professor of government at Dartmouth College. "The partisans who pay attention to politics are being conditioned to disregard the fact checkers when their own side gets criticized."[9]

Fact checking has proved to be a valuable resource, but media experts warn that it is no substitute for sampling a diverse range of news and views. As Northeastern University journalism professor Dan Kennedy noted, "Perhaps the biggest lie of all is that fact-checking can act as some sort of short-cut to the truth. For news consumers, there's really no getting around the time-intensive work of paying attention to multiple sources of information and making their own judgments."[10]

— *Robert Kiener*

The online fact-checking organization PolitiFact — a Pulitzer Prize–winning site started in 2007 by the *St. Petersburg Times* (now the *Tampa Bay Times*) — uses a "pants on fire truth-o-meter" to show when a politician is not telling the truth.

[1] Glenn Kessler, "Bachmann's claim that 70 percent of food stamps go to 'bureaucrats,' " *The Washington Post*, March 19, 2013, www.washingtonpost.com/blogs/fact-checker/post/bachmanns-claim-that-70-percent-of-food-stamps-go-to-bureaucrats/2013/03/18/3f85d042-8ff5-11e2-bdea-e32ad90da239_blog.html.

[2] *Ibid.*

[3] "About Us," Factcheck.org, www.factcheck.org/about.

[4] James Taranto, "The Pinocchio press," *The Wall Street Journal*, Sept. 4, 2012, http://online.wsj.com/article/SB10000872396390444301704577631470493495792.html.

[5] As *The New York Times* pointed out, "The truncated clip came from a speech Mr. Obama gave in 2008 talking about his opponent, Senator John McCain of Arizona." The full Obama quote was: "Senator McCain's campaign actually said, and I quote, 'If we keep talking about the economy, we're going to lose.' " See Michael Cooper, "Campaigns play loose with truth in a fact-check age," *The New York Times*, Sept. 1, 2012, www.nytimes.com/2012/09/01/us/politics/fact-checkers-howl-but-both-sides-cling-to-false-ads.html.

[6] Mike Burns, "Fox blames Romney loss on the 'biased' fact-checkers," Media Matters, Nov. 7, 2012.

[7] David Carr, "A last fact check: It didn't work," *The New York Times*, Nov. 6, 2012, http://mediadecoder.blogs.nytimes.com/2012/11/06/a-last-fact-check-it-didnt-work.

[8] Cooper, *op. cit.*

[9] *Ibid.*

[10] Dan Kennedy, "PolitiFact and the limits of fact checking," *The Huffington Post*, Dec. 13, 2011, www.huffingtonpost.com/dan-kennedy/politifact-and-the-limits_b_1144876.html.

Says Lichter, "The idea that journalists were presenting news from their own point of view was growing among the public."

Blurring the Lines

The growing belief that the media were biased, coupled with liberalizing legislative changes and technological developments, opened a new chapter in the history of the American media. Television and radio airwaves were soon populated with a growing band of commentators and pundits who helped blur the line between journalism and opinion for many media consumers.

The media landscape changed dramatically. Talk radio, cable news networks, Internet-based websites and blogs fragmented the media but also have made them more populist. The new partisan media, much like their historic predecessors, the *National Gazette* and other 18th century publications, have offered a wide variety of ideological slants on the news.

As former-University of Wisconsin–Madison journalism school director James Baughman wrote, "In contrast to the fractious newspaper culture of the mid-19th century, today's media culture is in fact divided between the new partisan media of the radio, Internet and cable, and those news outlets that still endeavor to report the news seriously. Serious news services won't, for example, provide platforms for those who insist the president was born in Kenya, or that the Bush administration was behind the destruction of the World Trade Center."[71]

While new media outlets sometimes offer biased slants on the news, the mainstream — or what some term the "elite" — media that still strive to be nonpartisan attract the larger audiences. But, some media experts say, as the media landscape becomes more partisan, that grip may become more and more tenuous.

CURRENT SITUATION

Agenda-Driven News

Each day in more than 20 states across the country, some 35 reporters are investigating topics such as government waste, corruption and fraud. But they are not employed by traditional newspapers or television stations.

Rather, they are part of a nonprofit media program that has quietly been hiring and training reporters in state capitals. The Franklin Center for Government and Public Integrity is an investigative nonprofit based in Alexandria, Va., that is funded by the State Policy Network — a group of conservative think tanks — and other conservative organizations such as the Richmond, Va.-based Sam Adams Alliance and by the Koch brothers.

The center, which the *Columbia Journalism Review* (*CJR*) called "the most ambitious conservative news organization you've never heard of," hires journalists to report on government waste and public unions, usually from a pro-free-market, anti-labor viewpoint. Its news stories are published on its website, Watchdog.org, and elsewhere.[72] Often, the stories are picked up by blogs and by often-understaffed regional newspapers, but only some of the papers tell readers the stories originated with the center.

Although the center describes itself as nonpartisan, the liberal *Washington Monthly* called it "more like a political attack machine than a traditional news machine."[73] A Pew

Research study of Franklin Center-sponsored stories found that 41 percent were pro-conservative versus 11 percent that favored the left.[74]

Some media observers also accuse the center of not being transparent. *CJR* said "a reader of one of the local and regional newspapers that run Franklin Center statehouse reporting might not even be aware of the Franklin Center and its agenda or 'point of view.'"[75]

Says Steven Greenhut, Franklin's vice president of journalism, "I reject the description of us as partisan. We have a free-market philosophy and have done plenty of stories that have offended both conservatives and liberals, Republicans and Democrats."

This sort of nonprofit, sometimes agenda-driven, news organization is a relatively new phenomenon. Since 2000, cash-strapped newspapers have lost 30 percent of their news personnel, according to Pew, and few can afford the personnel for complex or investigative stories. Nonprofit organizations have moved in to fill some of that void.

Think tanks and partisan organizations, such as the conservative Heritage Foundation, also have begun hiring "news reporters" to help spread their messages to a wider audience. "This is the wave of the future," says George Mason's Lichter. "Heritage Foundation and others have realized they don't need to depend on a few gatekeepers at major media outlets to run their material. They merely have to put it on the Web themselves."

Nonprofit organizations such as ProPublica produce nonpartisan, non-ideological investigative journalism, often in partnership with other major media outlets. The Kaiser Health Foundation produces objective health-related news stories under the brand *Kaiser Health News*. The stories are regularly published by newspapers such as *The Washington Post*, but the stories are clearly identified as coming from those sources.

For-profit ideologically driven journalistic operations also are proliferating. In 2010 the conservative online news site *Daily Caller* was launched with 21 reporters and editors. Other sites such as Breitbart.com report news with a conservative agenda. Liberal, for-profit news sites include *The Huffington Post* and the *Talking Points Memo* political blog.

"Efforts by political and corporate entities to get their messages into news coverage are nothing new," according to Pew. "What is different now . . . is that news organizations are less equipped to question what is coming to

AT ISSUE

Do mainstream outlets have a political bias?

YES Tim Graham
Director of media analysis, Media Research Center, Alexandria, Va.

NO S. Robert Lichter
Director, Center for Media and Public Affairs, George Mason University; co-author, The Media Elite

Written for *CQ Researcher*, May 2013

Written for *CQ Researcher*, May 2013

One can tell the tilt of the "mainstream" media merely by listening to conservatives and liberals complain about the tone of the news. Conservatives demand that the media cover both sides of public policies and controversies. Liberals such as President Obama lament that the media too often present a "false balance" — that conservatives get any air time to be blatantly incorrect. This suggests the media's default is to favor liberal views and downplay or ignore conservative ones.

In 2011, former *New York Times* executive editor Bill Keller wrote, "If the 2012 election were held in the newsrooms of America and pitted Sarah Palin against Barack Obama, I doubt Palin would get 10 percent of the vote. However tempting the newsworthy havoc of a Palin presidency, I'm pretty sure most journalists would recoil in horror from the idea."

In 2008, the Pew Research Center surveyed 222 journalists and news executives at national outlets. Only 6 percent said they considered themselves conservatives, compared to 36 percent of the overall population that describes itself as conservative. Most journalists — 53 percent — claimed they are moderate; 24 percent said they were liberal and 8 percent very liberal.

Only 19 percent of the public consider themselves liberal. And it's not much of a leap to presume many of the 53 percent who describe themselves as "moderate" are really quite liberal, since Keller thinks most are horrified by a President Palin.

Our studies of TV news repeatedly show a liberal tilt. Media Research Center news analysts reviewed all 216 gun-policy stories on the morning and evening shows of ABC, CBS and NBC in the month after the Newtown, Conn., school shooting. The results showed staggering imbalance: Stories advocating more gun control outnumbered stories opposing gun control by 99 to 12, or a ratio of 8 to 1. Anti-gun sound bites were aired almost twice as frequently as pro-gun ones (228 to 134). Gun-control advocates appeared as guests on 26 occasions, compared to seven for gun-rights advocates.

But the most insidious bias is what the national media choose *not* to cover. For example, in 2012 there was only one network mention (on ABC) that Obama promised to cut the deficit "by half by the end of my first term in office."

Inconvenient clips of tape go missing, while network anchors can find the time to ask the president about Dr. Seuss books and which superhero's power he would like to possess.

Liberal media bias is an article of faith to conservatives, who see the news as a reflection of journalists' well-documented liberal perspectives and Democratic voting preferences. However, the truth is more complicated.

First, the media aren't the closed shop they used to be. The Internet hosts a thriving competition between left-wing and right-wing websites and blogs, and any reasonable definition of the "mainstream media" would have to include Fox News and conservative-dominated talk radio.

Second, both conservative and liberal media watchdog groups have long lists of complaints about biased stories. What's missing is evidence of a broad pattern of coverage that consistently favors one side. For example, a meta-analysis of every scholarly study of election news found no systematic bias in the amounts of good and bad press given to Republican and Democratic presidential candidates. Another study compared news coverage of measurable conditions, such as unemployment and murder rates, under Democratic and Republican administrations at every level of government. It too found no consistent evidence of partisan favoritism.

Journalists do suffer bouts of "irrational exuberance," when they wear their feelings on their sleeves. Yet, even Barack Obama's well-documented media honeymoon in 2008 and 2009 soon gave way to the highly critical coverage that every recent president has suffered. By 2012 Obama's campaign coverage was as negative as Mitt Romney's.

So why do conservatives see liberal bias at every turn? One answer is what's called the "hostile media effect." Partisans treat criticisms of their own side as bias, while assuming criticisms of the other side are well-founded.

But some aspects of political journalism don't affect both sides equally. In their role as a watchdog over the rich and powerful, journalists see the world in terms of competing economic and political interests, with the media standing above the battle and serving the public interest. They are sympathetic toward those who define themselves the same way, such as "public interest" groups or social movements demanding equality for excluded groups.

Thus, what conservatives see as liberal bias is often the byproduct of a professional norm that runs parallel to liberal values. And journalists can filter their personal political views out of their stories more easily than their professional identities. So the problem for conservatives is not *just* that journalists are liberals, it's that they're journalists.

Getty Images/Bill Pugliano

Former Republican vice presidential candidate and Alaska governor Sarah Palin has been highly critical of the nation's major newspapers and other mainstream media, calling them the "lamestream media" and alleging they are biased against conservatives. Studies on media bias have produced mixed results.

them or to uncover the stories themselves, and interest groups are better equipped and have more technological tools than ever."[76]

More is not necessarily better. "I have warned conservatives to be careful what they wish for," explains the Media Research Center's Bozell. "With the old media, at least there were rules, such as the two-source rule. In the new media there's the no-source rule. Stories can be written by innuendo. The public is finding it harder to differentiate between news and conjecture."

Tweeting and More

About 35 percent of Americans turn to online sources for news, and as more and more do so, journalists have responded by using blogs, social media sites like Facebook and, more recently, Twitter to reach their audience.

"Tweet your beat" is a common refrain among online journalists. According to recent surveys, only 3 to 4 percent of the public gets its news either regularly or sometimes via Twitter, but that number is reportedly growing.[77]

Twitter's immediate and direct (and usually unedited) nature creates a more intimate relationship between journalist and reader than existed in the past. As a Pew

Research Center report noted, "Twitter users appear to be more closely connected to professional journalists and news organizations than their social-networking counterparts when it comes to relying on them for online news."[78]

"Twitter is a venue for news but also opinion," says Pews' Jurkowitz. "It's tempting to say something memorable and pithy in 140 characters or less." As some journalist have found, however, tweeting and blogging opinion can prove disastrous:

• CNN's senior editor for Middle Eastern Affairs, Octavia Nasr, was fired after posting this comment on Twitter: "Sad to hear of the passing of Sayyed Mohammad Hussein Fadallah. One of Hezbollah's giants I respect a lot." CNN called her tweet "an error of judgment," and said, "It did not meet CNN's editorial standards."[79]

• *The Washington Post* rebuked managing editor Raju Narisetti for tweeting, "Sen. Byrd (91) in hospital after he falls from 'standing up too quickly.' How about term limits. Or retirement age. Or common sense to prevail."[80]

Narisetti — who has since moved to Rupert Murdoch's News Corp as a senior vice president and deputy head of strategy — subsequently closed his Twitter feed. *The Post* promptly drew up new guidelines, saying its journalists "must refrain from writing, tweeting or posting anything — including photographs or video — that could be perceived as reflecting political, racial, sexist, religious or other bias or favoritism that could be used to tarnish our journalistic credibility."[81]

Other papers have drawn up similar conduct codes. "I think that the same guidelines for reporters would hold true in social networking or any other ways they conduct themselves in their life outside of work," said Martin Kaiser, editor of the *Milwaukee Journal Sentinel*. "It's the same way [that] we don't want reporters putting bumper stickers on their cars for candidates."[82]

Those who get their news from social networks prefer unbiased reports, according to a recent Pew poll. More than half of the respondents preferred nonpartisan news: 52 percent of those who get their news on Twitter and 56 percent of those who get news on social networks prefer news sources without a particular point of view.[83]

Not all journalists agree that opinion should be banned from reporters' social media outlets. "It's time to get rid of the hoax that all reporters are objective," says journalism professor Alterman. "I am all for journalists exposing their personal biases on Twitter, their blogs or wherever."

Reuters takes a more balanced approach in its social media policy. Acknowledging that posting on Twitter and blogging can be like "flying without a net," it reminds its reporters that "social networks encourage fast, constant, brief communications; journalism calls for communication preceded by fact-finding and thoughtful consideration. Journalism has many 'unsend' buttons, including editors. Social networks have none."[84]

Whatever side a journalist takes on the social media debate, there's no denying the power of the new technology. This February, moments after NBC's Todd claimed that charges of a liberal media bias were "a mythology," his Twitter feed and others were filled with tweets, pro and con. After watching the messages pour in, he tweeted, "when you want to spark a conversation on Twitter, simply talk about media bias."[85]

OUTLOOK

Dizzying Changes

The numbers are grim. Nearly every week brings news of another newspaper or magazine cutting staff, shrinking the publication, reducing frequency or even closing. Television stations, especially local operations, are trimming staff, and national networks are downsizing and closing bureaus.

The Internet has essentially "blown up" the old media world and transformed the way news is delivered and consumed. Given the dizzying changes in the media world and the speed with which they have altered the landscape, many experts say it's impossible to know the future of bias.

"Remember, it wasn't until the 1990s that we even had Web browsers," says George Mason University's Lichter. "Since then, YouTube, Twitter and Facebook have completely changed the way people interact with media. One thing is sure: We will see a lot more innovations that change the way people think about the media and its biases. It is difficult to see what's ahead, but if current trends continue it looks like the media will be becoming increasingly partisan."

Some even see an end of traditional "hard news" coverage. Bozell believes "journalism is losing its seriousness. The line between news and infotainment is being blurred." Others worry that as newspapers continue cutting back and producing less hard and investigative

news, readers will continue to desert them, as the Pew surveys and others suggest.

"Infotainment is luring more and more people away from solid journalism, so I think the news will be playing a lesser role in people's lives than it does today," says Sheppard, the Long Island University journalism professor. "Kim Kardashian has over 17 million Twitter followers, and many of those people are probably following her instead of reading the news. There's a worry for the future of the republic!"

Many media experts claim the media will grow increasingly partisan, resembling the early days of journalism. "I see the wheel turning, not full circle, but toward more partisan narrow-casting," says Sheppard. "We will see the media creating more partisan information, which will then be seized upon by ideological audiences."

According to Sheppard and others, the financial success of Fox News and talk radio will likely spawn even more imitators, each hoping to serve a niche, partisan market. However, if the ideological middle disappears in the media, some worry that new media will merely be "preaching to the choir."

A more fragmented media will offer more choice but would also further change the public's perceptions of the press. "The decay of the traditional agenda-setting function of the press will continue, and with it the idea of 'the public' as a large, interconnected mass of news-consuming citizens," said a recent Columbia School of Journalism study. "Choice in available media outlets will continue to expand, leading not so much to echo chambers as to a world of many overlapping publics of varying sizes."

"Seen in this light, the long-term collapse of trust in the press is less a function of changing attitudes toward mainstream media outlets than a side effect of the continuing fragmentation of the American media landscape."[86]

Will there be an increase in transparency? "The media will be more open about their views because they realize people want a point of view in their news," says CUNY journalism professor Alterman. "There will always be an audience for trustworthy news organizations such as *The New York Times*, but media with strong points of view will increase. Fewer people will complain about media bias."

As long-established and valued newspapers face closure or purchase by partisan owners, many journalists believe the nation will be worse off. Many question how democracy can continue to function if voters become so inundated by "advocacy journalism" that they give up trying to even make an objective, informed decision or simply disengage from the democratic process altogether.

"The world will not be a better place when these fact-based news organizations die," said former *New York Times* correspondent Chris Hedges. "We will be propelled into a culture where facts and opinions will be interchangeable, where lies will become true and where fantasy will be peddled as news. I will lament the loss of traditional news. It will unmoor us from reality."[87]

NOTES

1. "Obama and Clinton: The 60 Minutes interview," "60 Minutes," CBS News, Jan. 27, 2013, www.cbsnews.com/8301-18560_162-57565734/obama-and-clinton-the-60-minutes-interview/.

2. Conor Friedersdorf, "Steve Kroft's Softball Obama Interviews Diminish '60 minutes,'" *The Atlantic*, Jan. 29, 2013, www.theatlantic.com/politics/archive/2013/01/steve-krofts-softball-obama-interviews-diminish-60-minutes/272611/.

3. Erik Wemple, "Kroft on Obama-Clinton interview: 30 minutes not enough!" *The Washington Post*, Jan. 28, 2013, www.washingtonpost.com/blogs/erik-wemple/wp/2013/01/28/kroft-on-obama-clinton-interview-30-minutes-not-enough/.

4. Noel Sheppard, "The transformation of '60 Minutes' — now the place for swooning, softball interviews," Fox News, Jan. 30, 2013, www.foxnews.com/opinion/2013/01/30/transformation-60-minutes-now-place-for-swooning-softball-interviews/.

5. Peggy Noonan, "So God Made a Fawner," *The Wall Street Journal*, Feb. 7, 2013, http://online.wsj.com/article/SB10001424127887323452204578290363744516632.html.

6. Dylan Byers, "Gun vote triggers media outcry," *Politico*, April 18, 2013, www.politico.com/story/2013/04/gun-debate-triggered-media-bias-90306.html#ixzz2Rsfg1FgP.

7. "REPORT: Partisanship And Diversity On The Sunday Shows In 9 Charts," Media Matters, April 5, 2013, http://mediamatters.org/research/2013/04/05/report-partisanship-and-diversity-on-the-sunday/193482.

8. "Ryan: As a Conservative I've long believed there's inherent media bias," *Real Clear Politics*, Sept. 30, 2012, www.realclearpolitics.com/video/2012/09/30/ryan_as_a_conservative_ive_long_believed_theres_inherent_media_bias.html.

9. "Liberal Media Bias: Fact or Fiction," 4thEstate Project, July 2012, specialreports.4thestate.net/liberal-media-bias-fact-or-fiction/.

10. Quoted in Reed Richardson, "GOP-Fox Circus Act," *The Nation*, April 29, 2013, pp. 11-15.

11. "Fox News Viewed as Most Ideological Network," Pew Research Center for People & the Press, Oct. 29, 2009, www.people-press.org/2009/10/29/fox-news-viewed-as-most-ideological-network/.

12. "Black and White and Re(a)d All Over: the Conservative Advantage in Syndicated Op-Ed Columns," Media Matters, 2007, http://mediamatters.org/research/oped/.

13. "Examining the 'Liberal Media' Claim," Fairness & Accuracy in Reporting, June 1, 1998, http://fair.org/press-release/examining-the-quotliberal-mediaquot-claim/.

14. David Freddoso, "Press pass: In a new book a journalist explains how the media tilts the scales for Obama," *New York Post*, Jan. 7, 2013, www.nypost.com/p/news/opinion/books/press_pass_CAbPXffNvA4ntrqbMNIkOI.

15. "4th Annual TV News Trust Poll," Public Policy Polling, Feb. 6, 2013, www.publicpolicypolling.com/main/2013/02/4th-annual-tv-news-trust-poll.html.

16. Joseph Cotto, "Bernie Goldberg on media bias in the 'Unites States of Entertainment,'" *The Washington Times*, Oct. 25, 2012, http://mobile.washingtontimes.com/neighborhood/conscience-realist/2012/oct/25/bernie-goldberg-media-bias-united-states-entertain/.

17. Joe Strupp, "Bill Keller Speaks Out On Judy Miller, Iraq War Coverage, And Fox News," Media Matters, June 3, 2011, http://mediamatters.org/blog/2011/06/03/bill-keller-speaks-out-on-judy-miller-iraq-war/180289.

18. "4th Annual TV News Trust Poll," *op. cit.*

19. "Pluralities Say Press is Fair to Romney, Obama," Pew Research Center for the People & The Press,

Sept. 22, 1012, www.people-press.org/files/legacy-pdf/9-22-2011%20Media%20Attitudes%20Release.pdf.

20. Lymari Morales, "U.S. distrust in media hits new high," Gallup Politics, Sept. 21, 2012, www.gallup.com/poll/157589/distrust-media-hits-new-high.aspx.

21. Larry Light, "The right's propaganda victory over the 'liberal' media," *The Huffington Post*, Dec. 11, 2012, www.huffingtonpost.com/larry-light/the-rights-propaganda-vic_b_2279625.html.

22. "The State of the News Media 2013," The Pew Research Center's Project for Excellence in Journalism, 2013, Key Findings, http://stateofthemedia.org/2013/overview-5/key-findings/.

23. *Ibid.*

24. Tim Groseclose, *Left Turn* (2011), pp. 99-110.

25. Michael Kinsley, "Gore Carries Slate," Nov. 7, 2000, *Slate*, www.slate.com/articles/news_and_politics/readme/2000/11/gore_carries_slate.html.

26. David Broder, *Behind the Front Page* (2000), p. 332.

27. David Brooks, "Objectivity in Journalism," Catholic Education Resource Center, www.catholiceducation.org/articles/media/me0054.html.

28. Alex S. Jones, "An Argument Why Journalists Should Not Abandon Objectivity," Nieman Reports, Fall 2009, www.nieman.harvard.edu/reports/article/101911/An-Argument-Why-Journalists-Should-Not-Abandon-Objectivity.aspx.

29. "Freedom from Bias, Reuters Handbook of Journalism," Reuters, http://handbook.reuters.com/index.php?title=Freedom_from_bias.

30. Chris Hedges, "The Creed of Objectivity Killed the News," TruthDig, Feb. 1, 2010, www.truthdig.com/report/item/the_creed_of_objectivity_killed_the_news_business_20100131.

31. Ken Silverstein, "The Question of Balance: Revisiting the Missouri Election Scandal of 2004," *Harpers*, May 8, 2007, http://harpers.org/blog/2007/05/the-question-of-balance-revisiting-the-missouri-election-scandal-of-2004/.

32. Thomas E. Mann and Norman J. Ornstein, "Let's just say it: The Republicans are the problem," *The Washington Post*, April 27, 2012, http://articles.washingtonpost.com/2012-04-27/opinions/35453898_1_republican-party-party-moves-democratic-party/3.

33. *Ibid.*

34. Paul Farhi, "How biased are the media, really?" *The Washington Post*, April 27, 2012, http://articles.washingtonpost.com/2012-04-27/lifestyle/35451368_1_media-bias-bias-studies-media-organizations.

35. "MRC launches $2.1 million campaign demanding liberal media 'tell the truth!'" Newsbusters, Oct. 5, 2010, http://newsbusters.org/blogs/nb-staff/2010/10/05/new-2-1-million-campaign-demands-liberal-media-t0ell-truth.

36. Salvatore Colleluori, "Roger Ailes' Latino outreach at odds with Fox News' anti-immigrant rhetoric," Media Matters, Feb. 19, 2013, http://mediamatters.org/research/2013/02/19/roger-ailes-latino-outreach-at-odds-with-fox-ne/192714.

37. Paul Colford, "'Illegal immigrant' no more," *The Definitive Source*, April 2, 2013, http://blog.ap.org/2013/04/02/illegal-immigrant-no-more/.

38. Jim Naureckas, "The media didn't fail on Iraq; Iraq just showed we have a failed media," Fairness & Accuracy in Reporting, March 25, 2013, www.fair.org/blog/2013/03/25/the-media-didnt-fail-on-iraq-iraq-just-showed-we-have-a-failed-media/.

39. Stephen Dinan, "Reporters applaud Obama's slam on Romney's wealth," *The Washington Times*, Oct. 17, 2012, www.washingtontimes.com/blog/inside-politics/2012/oct/17/reporters-applaud-obamas-slam-romneys-wealth/.

40. Fred Barnes, "The four-year honeymoon," *The Weekly Standard*, Jan. 14, 2013, www.weeklystandard.com/articles/four-year-honeymoon_693769.html.

41. Peter Wehner, "Media bias in the age of Obama," *Commentary*, Jan. 30, 2013, www.commentarymagazine.com/2013/01/30/media-bias-in-the-age-of-obama/.

42. Light, *op. cit.*

43. Jon Nicosia, "Top Romney strategist Stuart Stevens says media not 'in the tank' for President Obama," Mediate, Feb. 24, 2012, www.mediaite.com/tv/

top-romney-strategist-stuart-stevens-says-media-not-in-the-tank-for-president-obama/.

44. "Pluralities say press is fair to Romney, Obama," Pew Research Center for the People & the Press, Sept. 25, 2012, www.people-press.org/2012/09/25/pluralities-say-press-is-fair-to-romney-obama/.

45. "Liberal media bias: fact or fiction?" *op. cit.*

46. "Romney discussed more than Obama in election coverage," 4thEstate, Aug. 1, 2012, http://election2012.4thestate.net/romney-discussed-more-than-obama-in-election-coverage/.

47. "Low marks for the 2012 election," Pew Research Center for the People & the Press, Nov. 15, 2012, www.people-press.org/2012/11/15/section-4-news-sources-election-night-and-views-of-press-coverage/press.

48. Si Sheppard, *The Partisan Press* (2008), p. 19.

49. *Ibid.*, pp. 18-19.

50. *Ibid.*

51. *Ibid.*

52. Quoted in *ibid.*, pp. 22-23.

53. S. Robert Lichter, "The Media," in Peter H. Schuck, *Understanding America: The Anatomy of an Exceptional Nation* (2009), p. 187.

54. Geoffrey R. Stone, *Perilous Times* (2004), p. 73.

55. James L. Baughman, "The Fall and Rise of Partisan Journalism," Center for Journalism Ethics, University of Wisconsin-Madison, April 20, 2011.

56. Paul Starr, "Governing in the age of Fox News," *The Atlantic*, Jan. 1, 2010, www.theatlantic.com/magazine/archive/2010/01/governing-in-the-age-of-fox-news/307845/.

57. Sheppard, *op. cit.*, p. 22.

58. Lichter, p. 187.

59. *Ibid.*, p. 188.

60. Sheppard, *op. cit.*, p. 76.

61. William Safire, "On language; default, Dear Brutus," *The New York Times*, Dec. 10, 1995, www.nytimes.com/1995/12/10/magazine/on-language-default-dear-brutus.html.

62. Lichter, *op. cit.*, p. 190.

63. *Ibid.*, p. 32.

64. Bill Kovach and Tom Rosenstiel, *The Elements of Journalism* (2001), p. 62.

65. Alan Greenblatt, "Media Bias," *CQ Researcher*, Oct. 15, 2004, p. 866.

66. Lichter, *op. cit.*, p. 194.

67. Peter J. Boyer, "Under Fowler, FCC treated TV as commerce," *The New York Times*, Jan. 19, 1987, www.nytimes.com/1987/01/19/arts/under-fowler-fcc-treated-tv-as-commerce.html.

68. Lichter, *op. cit.*, p. 205.

69. For survey results, see Sheppard, *op. cit.*, p. 284.

70. Quoted in *ibid.*, p. 280.

71. Baughman, *op. cit.*

72. Justin Peters, "Serious, point of view journalism?" *Columbia Journalism Review*, Sept. 13, 2012, www.cjr.org/united_states_project/serious_point-of-view_journalism.php?page=all.

73. Laura McGann, "Partisan Hacks," *The Washington Monthly*, May/June 2012, www.washingtonmonthly.com/features/2010/1005.mcgann.html.

74. "Non-profit News: Assessing a New Landscape in Journalism," Pew Research Center, July 18, 2011, p. 11, www.journalism.org/sites/journalism.org/files/Non-profit%20news%20study%20FINAL.pdf.

75. Peters, *op. cit.*

76. "The State of the News Media 2013," *op. cit.*

77. "In Changing News Landscape, Even Television Is Vulnerable," Pew Research Center for the People & The Press, Sept, 27, 2012, www.people-press.org/2012/09/27/section-2-online-and-digital-news-2/.

78. *Ibid.*

79. James Poniewozik, "CNN, Twitter and Why Hiding Journalists' Opinions Is (Still) a Bad Idea," *Time*, July 8, 2010, http://entertainment.time.com/2010/07/08/cnn-twitter-and-why-hiding-journalists-opinions-is-still-a-bad-idea/.

80. John Morton, "Staying Neutral," *American Journalism Review*, Dec./Jan. 2010, www.ajr.org/article.asp?id=4837.

81. Stephanie Gleason, "Going Public," *American Journalism Review*, December/January 2010, www.ajr.org/article.asp?id=4846.

82. *Ibid.*

83. "In Changing News Landscape, Even Television is Vulnerable," *op. cit.*

84. *Handbook of Journalism*, Reuters, http://handbook .reuters.com/index.php?title=Reporting_From_the_ Internet_And_Using_Social_Media.

85. "Chuck Todd discusses the 'mythology' of media bias against conservatives," *Twitchy*, Feb. 19, 2013, http://twitchy.com/2013/02/19/chuck-todd-dis cusses-the-mythology-of-media-bias-against-con servatives/.

86. C. W. Anderson, Emily Bell and Clay Shirky, "Post-Industrial Journalism," Columbia Journalism School, 2013, p. 108, http://journalistsresource.org/ wp-content/uploads/2013/01/TOWCenter-Post_ Industrial_Journalism.pdf.

87. Hedges, *op. cit.*

BIBLIOGRAPHY

Selected Sources

Books

Alterman, Eric, *What Liberal Media? The Truth About Bias and the News*, **Basic Books, 2004.**
A City University of New York journalism professor and liberal journalist says the news media are far more slanted toward conservative than liberal thought, contrary to the claims of many conservative media critics.

Freddoso, David, *Spin Masters: How the Media Ignored the Real News and Helped Reelect Barack Obama*, **Regnery Publishing, 2013.**
The editorial page editor of the conservative *Washington Examiner* contends the mainstream media manipulated coverage of the 2012 presidential candidates, were obsessed with Mitt Romney's gaffes and refused to cover stories that could have portrayed President Obama in a negative light.

Groseclose, Tim, *Left Turn: How Liberal Media Bias Distorts the American Mind*, **St. Martin's Press, 2011.**
A UCLA political science and economics professor concludes that nearly all mainstream media have a liberal bias, based on a formula he uses to analyze political content in news stories.

Hunnicut, Susan (ed.), *At Issue: Media Bias*, **Greenhaven Press, 2011.**
Media experts explore the history of bias, the meaning of objectivity, whether the mainstream media are biased toward Democrats or Republicans, whether bias in financial reporting contributed to the nation's financial crisis and more.

Sheppard, Si, *The Partisan Press: A History of Media Bias in the United States*, **McFarland & Co., 2008.**
An assistant political science professor at Long Island University places the debate about media bias in historical context. He tracks media bias from the early days of the nation's partisan press to the rise of objectivity in the 20th century to today's technology-driven media alternatives.

Stroud, Natalie Jomini, *Niche News: The Politics of New Choice*, **Oxford University Press, 2011.**
A journalism professor at the University of Texas-Austin explores how consumers navigate the increasingly crowded and diverse new-media market and investigates the political implications of those choices.

Articles

Alterman, Eric, "Think Again: Why Didn't the Iraq War Kill the 'Liberal Media'?" American Progress, April 4, 2013, www.americanprogress.org/issues/ media/news/2013/04/04/59288/why-didnt-the-iraq-war-kill-the-liberal-media.
In reporting on the Iraq War, reporters ignored traditional journalistic practices in order to dismiss counter-evidence provided by numerous experts, says the author. Because of these lapses, the author claims, the bulk of the mainstream media and much of the blogosphere showed bias in favor of the war.

Carr, David, "Tired Cries of Bias Don't Help Romney," *The New York Times*, **Sept. 30, 2012, www.nytimes .com/2012/10/01/business/media/challenging-the-claims-of-media-bias-the-media-equation.html?_r=0.**
Although the press is frequently accused of exhibiting a liberal bias when conservative candidates drop in the polls, the media increasingly are made up of right-leaning outlets, says the *Times* media critic.

Chozik, Amy, "Conservative Koch brothers turning focus to newspapers," *The New York Times*, April 21, 2013, www.nytimes.com/2013/04/21/business/media/koch-brothers-making-play-for-tribunes-newspapers.html?pagewanted=all.

Charles and David Koch, the billionaire supporters of libertarian causes, reportedly are considering trying to buy the Tribune Co.'s eight regional newspapers, including the *Los Angeles Times* and *Chicago Tribune*. Some in the media industry are asking whether they would use the papers to further a conservative agenda.

Friedersdorf, Conor, "Steve Kroft's Softball Obama Interviews Diminish '60 Minutes,'" *The Atlantic*, Jan. 29, 2013, www.theatlantic.com/politics/archive/2013/01/steve-krofts-softball-obama-interviews-diminish-60-minutes/272611.

An *Atlantic* staff writer argues that "60 Minutes," which prides itself on tough investigations and probing interviews, limited its interview with President Obama and Secretary of State Hillary Rodham Clinton to "softball" questions.

Stray, Jonathan, "How do you tell when the news is biased? It depends on how you see yourself," *Nieman Journalism Lab*, June 27, 2012, www.niemanlab.org/2012/06/how-do-you-tell-when-the-news-is-biased.

Recent research shows that people detect and judge bias in news reporting based on such factors as how they see themselves, not on what journalists write.

Reports and Studies

"The State of the News Media 2013: An Annual Report on American Journalism," The Pew Research Center's Project for Excellence in Journalism, March 18, 2013, http://stateofthemedia.org.

The nonpartisan research group's annual study includes reports on how news consumers view the media's financial struggles, how the news landscape has changed in recent years, an analysis of the main media sectors and an essay on digital journalism.

For More Information

Accuracy in Media, 4350 East West Highway, Suite 555, Bethesda, MD 20814; 202-364-4401; www.aim.org. Conservative media watchdog organization that searches for potential liberal bias.

American Society of News Editors, 209 Reynolds Journalism Institute, Missouri School of Journalism, Columbia, MO 65211; 573-884-2405; www.asne.org. Promotes ethical journalism, supports First Amendment rights, defends freedom of information and open government.

Center for Media and Public Affairs, 933 N. Kenmore St., Suite 405, Arlington, VA 22201; 571-319-0029; www.cmpa.com. Nonpartisan research and educational organization that studies the news and entertainment media.

Fairness & Accuracy in Reporting, 104 W. 27th St., Suite 10B, New York, NY 10001; 212-633-6700; www.fair.org. Liberal media watchdog organization that monitors bias and censorship.

Media Matters, P.O. Box 52155, Washington, DC 20091; 202-756-4100; www.mediamatters.org. Liberal media watchdog group that looks for potential conservative bias.

Media Research Center, 325 S. Patrick St., Alexandria, VA 22314; 703-683-9733; www.mrc.org. Conservative media watchdog group that searches for potential liberal bias.

Pew Research Center for the People & the Press, 1615 L St., N.W., Suite 700, Washington, DC 20036; 202-419-4300; www.people-press.org. Nonpartisan media research organization funded by the Pew Charitable Trusts.

Poynter Institute for Media Studies, 801 Third St. South, St. Petersburg, FL 33701; 727-821-9494; www.poynter.org. Journalism education and research organization; ethics section of its website (www.poynter.org) includes articles, discussions, tips and case studies.

Society of Professional Journalists Ethics Committee, 3909 N. Meridian St., Indianapolis, IN 46208; 317-927-8000; www.spj.org/ethics.asp. Advises journalists on ethical matters; website contains ethics resources and a blog.

15

Free Speech at Risk

Alan Greenblatt

Egyptian political satirist Bassem Youssef arrives at the public prosecutor's office in Cairo on March 31. Police questioned Youssef for allegedly insulting President Mohammed Morsi and Islam. The government filed charges against hundreds of Egyptian journalists but dropped them earlier this month. Free-speech advocates worry that journalists, bloggers and democracy supporters worldwide are being intimidated into silence.

From *CQ Researcher*,
April 26, 2013

It wasn't an April Fool's joke. On April 1, "Daily Show" host Jon Stewart defended Egyptian political satirist Bassem Youssef, who had undergone police questioning for allegedly insulting President Mohammed Morsi and Islam.

"That's illegal? Seriously? That's illegal in Egypt?" Stewart said on his Comedy Central show. "Because if insulting the president and Islam were a jailable offense here, Fox News go bye-bye."

Stewart was kidding, but Youssef's case has drawn attention from free-speech advocates who worry Egypt's nascent democracy is according no more respect toward freedom of expression than the regime it replaced.

The U.S. Embassy in Cairo, which had linked to Stewart's broadcast on its Twitter feed, temporarily shut down the feed after Egyptian authorities objected to it. Egypt's nascent government also has filed charges against hundreds of journalists, although Morsi asked that they all be dropped earlier this month.

Concerns are widespread that commentators, journalists, bloggers — and, yes, even comedians — are being intimidated into silence. And not just in Egypt.

Free speech, once seen as close to an absolute right in some countries, is beginning to conflict with other values, such as security, the protection of children and the desire not to offend religious sensibilities, not just in the Middle East but in much of the world, including Western Europe.

In many cases, freedom of speech is losing. "Free speech is dying in the Western world," asserts Jonathan Turley, a George Washington University law professor. "The decline of free speech has come not

Democracies Enjoy the Most Press Freedom

Democracies such as Finland, Norway and the Netherlands have the most press freedom, while authoritarian regimes such as Turkmenistan, North Korea and Eritrea have the least, according to Reporters Without Borders' 2012 index of global press freedom. European and Islamic governments have enacted or considered new press restrictions after a recent phone-hacking scandal in Britain and Western media outlets' irreverent images of the Prophet Muhammad triggered deadly protests by Muslims. Myanmar (formerly Burma), which recently enacted democratic reforms, has reached its greatest level of press freedom ever, the report said.

Press Freedom Worldwide, 2013

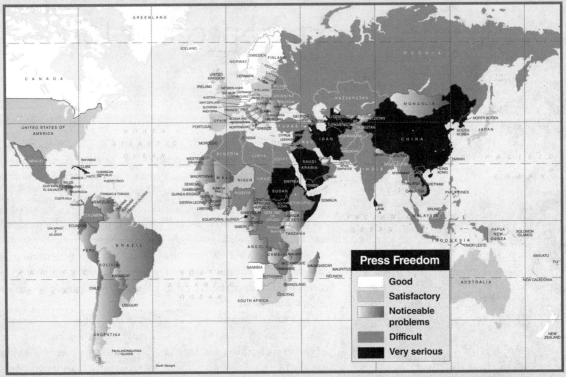

Source: "Freedom of the Press Worldwide in 2013," Reporters Without Borders, http://fr.rsf.org/IMG/jpg/2013-carte-liberte-presse_1900.jpg

from any single blow but rather from thousands of paper cuts of well-intentioned exceptions designed to maintain social harmony."[1]

In an era when words and images can be transmitted around the world instantaneously by anyone with a cell phone, even some American academics argue that an absolutist view of First Amendment protections couldn't be expected to prevail. Several made that case after protests broke out in several Muslim countries last September over an American-made video uploaded to YouTube defamed the Prophet Muhammad.

Even the administration of President Obama, who defended the nation's free-speech traditions at the United Nations in the wake of video backlash, supports a proposed U.N. resolution to create an international standard to restrict some anti-religious speech. And, under Obama, the Justice Department has prosecuted a record number of government employees who have leaked sensitive documents, discouraging potential whistleblowers from exposing government waste, fraud or abuse.[2]

"Wherever you look, you see legislation or other measures seeking to reassert state control over speech and the means of speech," says John Kampfner, author of the 2010 book *Freedom for Sale.*

In the United Kingdom and Australia, government ministers last month proposed that media outlets be governed by new regulatory bodies with statutory authority, although they ran into opposition. Two years ago, a new media law in Hungary created a regulatory council with wide-ranging powers to grant licenses to media outlets and assess content in a way that Human Rights Watch says compromises press freedom.[3]

"Not only is legislation such as this bad in and of itself, but it is crucial in sending a green light to authoritarians who use these kind of measures by Western states to say, whenever they are criticized by the West, 'Hey, you guys do the same,'" says Kampfner, former CEO of Index on Censorship, a London-based nonprofit group that fights censorship.

Some observers have hoped the growth of social media and other technologies that spread information faster and more widely than previously thought possible could act as an automatic bulwark protecting freedom of expression. "The best example of the impact of technology on free speech is to look at the Arab Spring," says Dan Wallach, a computer scientist at Rice University, referring to the series of upheavals starting in 2011 that led to the fall of autocratic leaders in Tunisia, Egypt, Yemen and Libya.[4]

But as studies by Wallach and many others show, countries such as China and Iran are building new firewalls to block sensitive information and track dissidents. "The pattern seems to be that governments that fear mass movements on the street have realized that they

Number of Journalists Killed on the Rise

Seventy journalists were killed in 2012, nearly half of them murdered, a 43 percent increase from 2011. A total of 232 journalists were imprisoned in 2012, the highest number since the Committee to Protect Journalists began keeping track in 1990. Experts say a select group of countries has fueled the increase by cracking down on criticism of government policies.

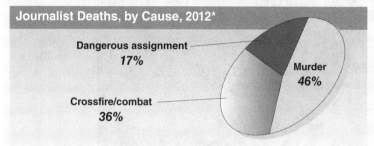

Journalist Deaths, by Cause, 2012*

Dangerous assignment 17%

Murder 46%

Crossfire/combat 36%

* Figures do not total 100 because of rounding.

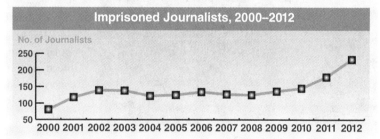

Imprisoned Journalists, 2000–2012

No. of Journalists

250
200
150
100
50

2000 2001 2002 2003 2004 2005 2006 2007 2008 2009 2010 2011 2012

Source: "Attacks on the Press," Committee to Protect Journalists, 2013, www.cpj.org/attacks/

might want to be able to shut off all Internet communications in the country and have started building the infrastructure that enables them to do that," said Andrew McLaughlin, a former White House adviser on technology.[5]

In January, a French court ordered Twitter to help identify people who had tweeted racist or anti-Semitic remarks, or face fines of 1,000 euros (about $1,300) per day. The San Francisco-based company refused to comply, citing First Amendment protections for free speech.[6]

But even as Twitter appeals the French court order, the microblogging site in October blocked the account of a neo-Nazi group called Besseres Hannover, or Better Hanover, which had been charged with inciting racial hatred. Twitter said it was the first time it had used

AFP/Getty Images/Attila Kisbenedek

A free-speech activist in Budapest, Hungary, protests against a new media law on March 15, 2011. The law set up a regulatory council with wide control over media outlets and content, a power that Human Rights Watch says compromises press freedom. Pictured on the poster is the revered poet of Hungary's 1848-1849 revolution, Sandor Petofi.

technology to monitor and withhold content based on a given country's concerns and laws.

Meanwhile, government arrests of journalists and mob attacks against them are on the rise. Journalists are being arrested more often than in previous years in countries such as Russia and Turkey, and in 2012, mobs attacked journalists in Mali and Canada — among other countries — for what the protesters perceived as their blasphemous coverage of Islam. Blasphemy prosecutions have become more common, especially in predominantly Islamic countries such as Pakistan, where blasphemy laws apply only to comments about Islam or Muhammad, not to derogatory comments about Christianity, Judaism or other world religions.[7]

"There have been attempts to pass so-called religious-sensibility laws, which are, in fact, a way of curbing press freedom and expression," says Robert Mahoney, director of the Committee to Protect Journalists, a New York–based nonprofit group that promotes press freedom.

In one widely covered case, three members of the Russian punk rock band Pussy Riot were found guilty of hooliganism motivated by religious hatred last year. They had been arrested in March after a performance in Moscow's main cathedral, in which they profanely called for the Virgin Mary to protect Russia against Vladimir Putin, who was returned to the presidency soon after the performance. The three were sentenced to two years in a prison colony, but one member was released on probation before being sent to prison.[8] In more open societies, laws meant to protect against hate speech, Holocaust denial and offenses against religious sensibilities also can end up limiting what people can talk and write about.

Free-speech laws traditionally have been about the protection of unpopular and provocative expression. Popular and uncontroversial opinions usually need no protection. But in recent years, free-speech protections have been fading away.

"The new restrictions are forcing people to meet the demands of the lowest common denominator of accepted speech," Turley contends.

As people monitor the health of free expression around the globe, here are some of the questions they're debating:

Has technology made speech freer?

As Arab protesters took to the streets — and the Internet — in 2011 in countries such as Tunisia and Egypt, everyone from commentators for serious foreign-policy journals to "The Daily Show" asked whether the world was witnessing a "Twitter revolution."

Social-media sites such as Twitter and Facebook were used by activists both as organizing tools and as a means of communication with the outside world.

"Tunisians got an alternative picture from Facebook, which remained uncensored through the protests, and they communicated events to the rest of the world by posting videos to YouTube and Dailymotion," Ethan Zuckerman, a researcher at Harvard University's Berkman Center for Internet and Society, wrote in 2011. "It's likely that news of demonstrations in other parts of the country disseminated online helped others conclude that it was time to take to the streets."[9]

Unquestionably, new-media tools make it easier for activists to spread their messages farther and faster than was conceivable during the days of the mimeograph machine, or even the fax. "What's happening with new technology is that it's making publication of these stories easier, and they're reaching a bigger audience," says Mahoney, the Committee to Protect Journalists deputy director.

"Twenty years ago, you'd struggle to get published in a local newspaper," Mahoney says. "Now, as a journalist, you've got far more platforms open to you, and you can get it out."

And not just journalists. From Libya and Iran to Syria and Myanmar, activists and average citizens are able to disseminate text, images and video all over the world, ensuring that their voices can be heard even at moments when regimes are violently cracking down on them.

Social media and other technological tools have become so omnipresent that former Rep. Tom Perriello, D-Va., worries that people become addicted to the online dialogue rather than reaching out to broader populations. "My pet peeve is that people think that social media can replace traditional organizing," says Perriello, President of the Center for American Progress Action Fund, part of a liberal think tank in Washington.

And even free-speech advocates readily admit that, in a broader sense, technology can be a two-edged sword. "Suddenly, you have the ability to reach people all over the world and communicate in ways that you never could before, and that's wonderful," says Eva Galperin, global policy analyst with the Electronic Frontier Foundation (EFF), a San Francisco-based group that promotes an unrestricted Internet. "But it also allows government surveillance on a scale that was never before possible."

Journalists find that their e-mail accounts have been hacked by "state-sponsored attackers" in countries such as China and Myanmar.[10] Mobile phones become surveillance devices.

"Modern information technologies such as the Internet and mobile phones . . . magnify the uniqueness of individuals, further enhancing the traditional challenges to privacy," according to a recent study by researchers from MIT and other universities that exposed the ease of tracking individual cellphone users. "Mobility

data contains the approximate whereabouts of individuals and can be used to reconstruct individuals' movements across space and time."[11]

Authoritarian regimes also use technology to access dissidents' computers, installing malware that tracks their movements online, according to Galperin. "It records all of their keystrokes and can use the microphones and cameras on the computers, circumventing all attempts to use encryption," she says.

It's not just dictatorships. Galperin notes that EFF's longstanding lawsuit against the National Security Agency for using warrantless wiretaps in the United States is "now old enough to go to school." And many of the surveillance tools used by authoritarian regimes are made by U.S. companies, she points out.

In the United Kingdom, in response to a phone-hacking scandal that has led to government investigations and a national debate about press abuses, a communications data bill has been proposed by Home Secretary Theresa May to require Internet service providers and mobile phone services to collect and retain data on user activity. The measure is "designed to give the state blanket rights to look at e-mails and IMs [instant messages] and requires all companies to retain the data for a year and hand it over [to the government]," says Kampfner, the former editor of *New Statesman* magazine. "It was halted a few months ago, but will be reintroduced this year."

Iran, which saw its own "Twitter revolution" during a spasm of post-election protests in 2009, has attempted to keep a "Halal Internet," free of unclean influences and information from the outside world.

In March, Iran's Ministry of Information and Communications Technology blocked software used by millions of Iranians to bypass the state's elaborate Internet filtering system. "A collection of illegal virtual private networks, or VPNs, was successfully closed off by the ministry, making visits to websites deemed immoral or politically dangerous — like Facebook and Whitehouse.gov — nearly impossible," *The New York Times* reported.[12]

Governments and Internet users are engaged in an unending game of cat and mouse, Kampfner says, with each trying to advance technology in ways that gives its side the upper hand.

"There's something called Tor, an open-source project that aims to break through all those barriers, whether in

Blasphemy Laws Proliferate

Videos and cartoons mocking the Muslim Prophet Muhammad have prompted many countries to enact strict anti-blasphemy laws. Christians and Muslims have used the laws to prosecute people seen as insulting religion. Blasphemy laws in Muslim countries usually refer only to defaming Islam, and punishments can include the death penalty. Many cases involve comments or videos posted on social media such as Twitter and YouTube.

Examples of Recent Blasphemy Cases

Country	Law
Austria	Prohibits disparaging a religious object, society or doctrine.
On Dec. 11, 2010, Helmut Griese, 63, was convicted for offending his Muslim neighbor by yodeling while mowing his lawn; the neighbor claimed Griese was imitating the Muslim call to prayer. On Jan. 22, 2009, politician Susanne Winter was fined $24,000 for saying Muhammad was a pedophile because he had a 9-year-old wife.	
India	Allows up to three years in prison for insulting religion or religious beliefs.
On April 21, 2012, the Catholic Church filed a complaint against Sanal Edamaruku, the founder of the reason-based organization Rationalist International, after he exposed a "miracle" by showing water from a statue of Jesus was coming from a leaky drain. On Nov. 19, 2012, college student Shaheen Dhada and a friend were arrested for complaining on Facebook that Mumbai had been shut down for the funeral of the leader of the Hindu nationalist party.	
Iran	Bars criticism of Islam or deviation from the ruling Islamic standards.
Web designer Saeed Malekpour, 35, a Canadian, served four years on death row in Iran for "insulting Islam." He was arrested while visiting his dying father in Iran in 2008 because a photo-sharing program he created while in Canada was used by others to download pornography. The death sentence was suspended in 2012 after Malekpour "repented."	
Netherlands	Penalizes "scornful blasphemy" that insults religious feelings.
On March 19, 2008, Dutch cartoonist Gregorius Nekschot was arrested for insulting Muslims in his drawings. On Jan. 21, 2009, politician Geert Wilders was put on trial because his film "Fitna" compared Islam and Nazism. He was acquitted.	
Pakistan	Bans blasphemy, including defiling the Quran and making remarks against the Prophet Muhammad.
In 2011 the governor of Punjab and the minister for minority affairs were assassinated because they opposed the country's blasphemy laws. On June 22, 2011, 29-year-old Larkana resident Abdul Sattar was sentenced to death and fined $1,000 for sending text messages and blaspheming the Quran, Muhammad and other Islamic figures during a phone conversation.	
United Kingdom	Prohibits "hate speech" against religious groups.
On March 4, 2010, philosophy tutor Harry Taylor was sentenced to six months in prison, 100 hours of community service and fined €250 ($337 at the time) for leaving anti-Christian and anti-Islam cartoons in an airport prayer room.	

Source: International Humanist and Ethical Union, December 2012

China or Iran or anywhere else," says Wallach, the computer scientist at Rice University. "Tor keeps getting more and more clever about hiding what they're doing, and regimes like Iran get more and more clever about blocking them regardless."

But as many commentators have noted, free speech online depends not only on government policies and court rulings, but on private companies such as Twitter, Facebook and Google. Increasingly, these companies are being called on to block posts by terrorists and unpopular or banned political parties.

"At the end of the day, the private networks are not in any way accountable if they choose to censor or prevent individuals from accessing services," says Katherine Maher, director of strategy and communications for Access, a New York-based digital-rights group.

"The Internet is not something different," Maher says. "It is just an extension of the area in which we live."

Should religious sensibilities be allowed to limit free expression?

When an assassin's bullet narrowly missed the head of Lars Hedegaard, suspicion immediately fell on Muslims, since Hedegaard, a former newspaper editor in Denmark, has been an anti-Islam polemicist.

But a number of Danish Muslims condemned the February attack and rose to defend Hedegaard. "We Muslims have to find a new way of reacting," said Qaiser Najeeb, a Dane whose father had emigrated from Afghanistan. "We don't defend Hedegaard's views but do defend his right to speak. He can say what he wants."[13]

For free-speech advocates, it was a refreshing reaction — particularly in a country where Muslim sensitivities have run high since the 2006 publication of cartoons caricaturing the Prophet Muhammad in a Danish newspaper.

"For those, like me, who look upon free speech as a fundamental good, no degree of cultural or religious discomfort can be reason for censorship," writes British journalist and author Kenan Malik. "There is no free speech without the ability to offend religious and cultural sensibilities."[14]

In recent years, a growing number of people around the globe have been prosecuted on charges of blasphemy or offending cultural sensibilities through hate speech. According to the International Humanist and Ethical Union (IHEU), only three people were arrested for committing blasphemy via social media between 2007 and 2011, but more than a dozen such arrests occurred in 10 countries last year.[15]

Turkish pianist Fazil Say, for instance, was given a suspended sentence of 10 months in jail on April 15 for posting tweets considered blasphemous, while Gamal Abdou Massoud, a 17-year-old Egyptian, was sentenced to three years for posting blasphemous cartoons on Facebook.

"When 21st-century technology collides with medieval blasphemy laws, it seems to be atheists who are getting hurt, as more of them go to prison for sharing their personal beliefs via social media," says Matt Cherry, editor of the IHEU report.

In Pakistan, those accused of blasphemy often fall victim to violence — before they even get their day in court. Dozens have been killed after being charged with blasphemy over the past 20 years. Last November, a mob burned Farooqi Girls' High School in Lahore after a teacher assigned homework that supposedly contained derogatory references to Muhammad.

"Repeating the blasphemy under Pakistan law is seen as blasphemy in itself," says Padraig Reidy, news editor for the Index on Censorship. "You have these bizarre cases where evidence is barely given but people are sentenced to death."

Even criticizing Pakistan's blasphemy law can be dangerous. Sherry Rehman, the Pakistani ambassador to the United States, has received death threats since calling for changes in the law, while two like-minded politicians have been assassinated.[16]

In Pakistan, free speech is pretty much limited to those hanging around cafes and literary festivals, says Huma Yusuf, a columnist for the Pakistani newspaper *Dawn.* "The threat of blasphemy — a crime that carries the death penalty — has stifled public discourse," she writes.[17]

Indians protest against the American-made anti-Muslim video "Innocence of Muslims" in Kolkata on Oct. 5, 2012. The film incited a wave of anti-U.S. violence in Libya, Egypt and other countries across the Muslim world. Speaking at the United Nations after the protests, President Obama explained that such films could not be banned in the United States because of the U.S. Constitution's free-speech rights.

YouTube has been blocked throughout Pakistan since September, when an anti-Muslim video was uploaded to the site. Thousands of other websites also have been blocked, allegedly for containing pornographic or blasphemous content. "In truth, most had published material criticizing the state," according to Yusuf.

In counties such as Pakistan and Egypt, the line between blasphemy laws designed to protect against religious offense and those meant to punish minorities and stifle dissent is highly porous. "There have been attempts to protect religious sensibility which are in fact a way of curbing press freedom and expression," says Mahoney, of the Committee to Protect Journalists.

In the West, worries about offending religious and cultural sensibilities have sometimes trumped free-speech concerns. "Denigration of religious beliefs is never acceptable," Australian Prime Minister Julia Gillard stated before the United Nations in September. "Our tolerance must never extend to tolerating religious hatred."[18]

Gillard emphasized her disdain for speech that incites hatred and violence, which has become a common concern among Western politicians. "Western governments seem to be sending the message that free-speech rights will not protect you" when it comes to hate speech, writes Turley, the George Washington University law professor.[19]

Hate speech is intended to incite discrimination or violence against members of a particular national, racial or ethnic group, writes Aryeh Neier, a former top official with the American Civil Liberties Union, Human Rights Watch and the Open Society Institute.

But, Neier notes, "It is important to differentiate blasphemy from hate speech. The proclivity of some elsewhere to react violently to what they consider blasphemous cannot be the criterion for imposing limits on free expression in the U.S., the United Kingdom, Denmark or the Netherlands (or anywhere else)."[20]

In recent months, the human rights group American Freedom Defense Initiative (AFDI) has been running anti-Muslim ads on public transportation systems around the United States. Posters that appeared on San Francisco buses last month, for example, included a picture of Osama bin Laden and a made-up quote from "Hamas MTV" that said, "Killing Jews is worship that brings us closer to Allah."

After New York's Metropolitan Transit Authority tried to block the ads last summer, Federal District Judge Paul A. Engelmayer ruled that the agency had violated AFDI's First Amendment rights.

"Not only did [he] rule that the ads should be 'afforded the highest level of protection under the First Amendment,' he went on to offer some eye-opening examples," writes *San Francisco Chronicle* columnist C. W. Nevius. "Engelmayer said an ad could accuse a private citizen of being a child abuser. Or, he suggested, it could say, 'Fat people are slobs' or 'Blondes are bimbos' and still be protected."[21]

Rather than put up a legal fight, San Francisco's Municipal Railway decided to put up peace posters of its own and donate the AFDI's advertising fee to the city's Human Rights Commission.

Should the United States promote free speech abroad?

Because of the First Amendment and the history of its interpretation, the United States has what comes closest to absolute protection of free speech of any country on Earth. And many believe free expression is not only essential to democracy but a value Americans should help export to other countries.

At a 2011 Internet freedom conference in The Hague, then-Secretary of State Hillary Rodham Clinton said,

"The United States will be making the case for an open Internet in our work worldwide.

"The right to express one's views, practice one's faith, peacefully assemble with others to pursue political or social change — these are all rights to which all human beings are entitled, whether they choose to exercise them in a city square or an Internet chat room," Clinton said. "And just as we have worked together since the last century to secure these rights in the material world, we must work together in this century to secure them in cyberspace."[22]

But the right to free expression that is taken for granted in the United States is not shared around the world. Some people — including some Americans — worry that the United States risks offending governments and citizens in other nations by preserving free-speech rights — including the right to racist and blasphemous speech — above nearly every other consideration.

Such voices have been prominent when Americans have exercised their free-speech rights in ways that offend others. Threats to burn the Quran — as well as actual Quran burnings — by Florida pastor Terry Jones led to deadly riots in the Muslim world in 2010 and 2011. Last fall, video portions from an anti-Muslim film called "Innocence of Muslims" triggered riots in several predominantly Muslim nations.

Speaking to the United Nations two weeks later, President Obama explained that the U.S. government could not ban such a video because of free-speech rights enshrined in the U.S. Constitution.

"Americans have fought and died around the globe to protect the right of all people to express their views, even views that we profoundly disagree with," Obama said. "We do not do so because we support hateful speech, but because our founders understood that without such protections, the capacity of each individual to express their own views and practice their own faith may be threatened."[23]

But Obama noted that modern technology means "anyone with a cellphone can spread offensive views around the world with the click of a button."

While reality, some commentators said it was foolish to expect other nations to understand the American right to unbridled speech. "While the First Amendment right to free expression is important, it is also important to remember that other countries and cultures do not have to understand or respect our right," Anthea Butler, a University of Pennsylvania religious studies professor, wrote in *USA Today*.[24]

Americans must remember that "our First Amendment values are not universal," cautioned Eric Posner, a University of Chicago law professor.

"Americans need to learn that the rest of the world — and not just Muslims — see no sense in the First Amendment," Posner wrote in *Slate*. "Even other Western nations take a more circumspect position on freedom of expression than we do, realizing that often free speech must yield to other values and the need for order. Our own history suggests that they might have a point."[25]

Access' Maher, who has consulted on technology issues with the World Bank and UNICEF, notes that even other Western nations tend to hold free-speech rights less dear, viewing them within a context not of personal liberty but a framework where they risk infringing on the rights of others. "This often leads to robust debates about incitement, hate speech, blasphemy and their role in the political discourse, often in a manner more open to possible circumscription than would be acceptable in the United States," she says.

Even some who promote free expression worry about the United States taking a leading role in its promotion, because of the risk of it being seen elsewhere as an American value being imposed from without.

"The problem is freedom of expression has come to be seen as either an American or Anglo-Saxon construct, whereas we would all like to see it as a universal principle," says Kampfner, the British journalist. "There is a danger that if this value is seen as proselytized primarily by the United States, it will reinforce those who are suspicious of it."

But it may be that America's staunch adherence to free speech makes the United States uniquely well-suited to promote and defend the idea.

"The United States values a free press and should promote those values abroad," says Robert Mahoney, deputy director of the Committee to Protect Journalists.

"No Western country wants to appear to be lecturing other countries to uphold its values, but it's not an American construct," he says. "We have a duty to remind them of that, and we expect international bodies like the U.N. and countries like the United Kingdom and the European Union to do the same thing."

During his first trip abroad as secretary of State, John Kerry in February defended free speech — including the "right to be stupid" — as a virtue "worth fighting for."[26]

It's important that individuals and groups in foreign countries take the lead in explaining free-speech rights, "so it's not seen as a Western concept," says Reidy, the Index on Censorship editor.

"Certain human rights are not Western," he says, "they're universal. That's the whole point of human rights."

BACKGROUND

Refusal to "Revoco"

The struggle for free speech has been a long story about testing limits. Many of the most famous moments in the development of free speech in the Western world involved notable figures such as the French philosopher Voltaire, the Biblical translator William Tyndale and the Italian astronomer Galileo, who were variously exiled, executed or forced to recant things they had said or written.

"Governments in all places in all times have succumbed to the impulse to exert control over speech and conscience," writes Rodney A. Smolla, president of Furman University.[27]

The first great flowering of democracy and free speech occurred 500 years before the birth of Christ in the Greek city-state of Athens. The city pioneered the idea of government by consent, allowing the people the freedom to choose their own rules.

"Free speech was an inseparable part of the new Athenian order," Robert Hargreaves, who was a British broadcaster, writes in his 2002 book *The First Freedom*. "Never before had ordinary citizens been given the right to debate such vital matters as war and peace, public finance or crime and punishment."[28]

But although Athens embraced, off and on, the concept of government by consent, it did not yet accept the idea of individual free speech that might upset the prevailing order. Athens now may be remembered less for pioneering free speech than for trying and executing the great philosopher Socrates in 399 B.C., after he refused to recant his teachings.

Demanding that critics and heretics recant has been a persistent theme throughout history. After Martin Luther printed his *Ninety-Five Theses* in 1517, which criticized

CHRONOLOGY

1940s–1980s *New laws, international entities and court decisions expand free-speech rights.*

1946 French constitution upholds principle that "free communication of thought and of opinion is one of the most precious rights of man."

1948 United Nations adopts Universal Declaration of Human Rights, declaring "the right to freedom of opinion and expression" for all.

1952 U.S. Supreme Court extends First Amendment protections to movies.

1954 Congress effectively criminalizes the Communist Party.

1961 British jury allows Penguin to publish the novel *Lady Chatterly's Lover*, which had been on a list of obscene material.

1964 In landmark *New York Times v. Sullivan* decision, U.S. Supreme Court rules that public officials must prove "actual malice" on the part of journalists in order to sue for libel. . . . Free Speech Movement at University of California, Berkeley, insists that administrators allow campus protests.

1968 U.K. abolishes 400-year-old laws allowing for government censorship of theater performances.

1971 In the first instance of prior restraint on the press in U.S. history, a court blocks *The New York Times* from publishing the Pentagon Papers, but the Supreme Court OKs publication of the classified Vietnam War history.

1989 Iran's Islamic government issues a fatwa, or kill order, against *Satanic Verses* author Salman Rushdie forcing him into hiding for years. . . . Supreme Court upholds the right to burn the U.S. flag in protest.

2000s *In response to terrorist attacks, many Western countries limit civil liberties.*

2000 At the first meeting of the post-Cold War Community of Democracies, 106 countries pledge to uphold democratic principles, including freedom of expression.

2005 George W. Bush administration ultimately fails in its year-long campaign to pressure *New York Times* not to publish a story about warrantless wiretaps.

2006 More than 200 people die in violent protests across the Muslim world after the Danish newspaper *Jyllands-Posten* publishes cartoons satirizing the Prophet Muhammad. . . . United Kingdom bans language intended "to stir up religious hatred." . . . In response to July 2005 terrorist bombings of bus and subway system that killed more than 50 people, U.K. enacts Prevention of Terrorism Act, which curtails speech in the name of security. . . . Crusading Russian journalist Anna Politkovskaya, known for her coverage of the Chechen conflict, is assassinated.

2010s *In an age of new media, both rich and developing countries restrict speech that may offend.*

2010 WikiLeaks publishes thousands of sensitive documents related to U.S. diplomatic efforts in Iraq, Afghanistan and elsewhere. . . . Google announces it is pulling out of China due to government censorship of its service.

2012 U.S. Supreme Court finds the Stolen Valor Act unconstitutional; the 2006 law made it a crime to falsely claim to have won military decorations. . . . Members of the Russian punk band Pussy Riot are convicted of hooliganism for protesting President Vladimir Putin's policies in a Moscow church. . . . "Innocence of Muslims," an anti-Muslim video posted on YouTube, triggers riots in several Middle Eastern and North African countries. . . . Twitter blocks German access to posts by a banned neo-Nazi party, its first bow to "country-withheld content" regulations. . . . Inquiry on press abuses in Britain spurred by telephone-hacking scandal by media outlets calls for greater regulation. . . . Egyptian court sentences to death in absentia Florida pastor Terry Jones, who had offended Muslims through Quran burnings and promotion of an anti-Muslim film.

2013 Pfc. Bradley Manning pleads guilty to 10 charges of giving government secrets to WikiLeaks (Feb. 28). . . . Due to lack of support, Australia's ruling party withdraws a proposal to regulate the press (March 21). . . . Privately owned newspapers are distributed in Myanmar for the first time in 50 years (April 1). . . . Egyptian court drops charges against popular comedian Bassem Youssef, who had been accused of insulting the president (April 6).

clerical abuses, Cardinal Thomas Cajetan, the papal legate in Rome, asked him to say *revoco*, or "I recant," and all would be well. Luther refused.

Cajetan wanted to turn Luther over to Rome on charges of heresy, but Frederick III, the elector of Saxony, allowed him to stay. Luther's works became bestsellers. Not only was he a celebrity, but his writings helped spark the Protestant Reformation.

Eventually, Pope Leo X and the Holy Roman Emperor Charles V also asked Luther to recant his writings. He argued that he was defending works about the teachings of Christ and therefore was not free to retract them. He offered this famous defense: "Here I stand; God help me; I can do no other."[29] As a result, the pope excommunicated him, and the emperor condemned him as an outlaw.

Controlling the Press

Luther's writings were spread thanks to the advent of the printing press, a new technology that governments sought to control. The Star Chamber of the British Parliament in 1586 strictly limited the number of master printers, apprentices and printing presses that could operate in London. All books were required to be licensed by the archbishop of Canterbury or the bishop of London.

A few decades later, members of Parliament won the ability to speak and vote without royal restraint. This led to a freer press, as London printers began publishing journals that were largely accounts of Parliament but also contained news. By 1645, the printers were putting out an average of 14 separate weekly titles.[30]

A year earlier, the English poet John Milton had published his *Aereopagitica*, remembered as one of the most eloquent pleas for a free press ever penned. "Truth is strong next to the Almighty, she needs no policies, no stratagems nor licensing to make her victorious," Milton wrote in the treatise. "Give her but room, and do not bind her."

Although it grew out of ongoing debates about press licensing and limiting free speech, the *Aereopagitica* had little influence in its day. The press remained heavily regulated both in the United Kingdom and in its American colonies.

In 1734, a German-born printer in New York named John Peter Zenger published criticism of royalist Gov. William Cosby, calling him "a governor turned rogue" who was undermining the colony's laws. At Zenger's trial

the following year, attorney Andrew Hamilton argued that the judge and jury should not separately consider the questions of whether he had published the material and whether it was libelous, as was the practice at the time, but rather simply determine whether it could not be libel because it was true.

The jury's verdict of not guilty was considered an important precedent, but it would be 70 years before New York changed its libels laws so the question of truth could be entered into evidence.

William Blackstone, in his *Commentaries on the Laws of England* of 1769, laid the groundwork for the idea that there should be no licensing or prior restraint of the press, but that publishers could still face punishment after publication. This formed the basis for the thinking of the American Founders, who remained skeptical about a completely free press.

"License of the press is no proof of liberty," John Adams wrote in his *Novanglus Letters* of 1774. "When a people are corrupted, the press may be made an engine to complete their ruin . . . and the freedom of the press, instead of promoting the cause of liberty, will but hasten its destruction."

As U.S. president, Adams signed the Alien and Sedition Acts, which led to multiple arrests and convictions of printers and publicists (all Republicans, or political opponents of Adams). The law was overturned under Thomas Jefferson, who had been skeptical about the need for unbridled press but embraced it in his second inaugural, stating that the press needed no other legal restraint than the truth.

The principle that there was a right to disseminate facts in a democracy was crystallized in British philosopher John Stuart Mill's *On Liberty* of 1859. "News, independently gathered and impartially conveyed, was seen to be an indispensable commodity in a society where the people ruled themselves," Mill wrote.

Expanding Rights

The U.S. Supreme Court seldom examined the question of free speech during the 19th century, but justices began to expand its sense in the 20th century.

During World War I, more than 1,900 Americans were prosecuted under the Espionage Act of 1917 and the Sedition Act of 1918, which banned printing, writing and uttering of statements deemed disloyal or abusive of the U.S. government.

Free Speech Can Be Deadly in Russia

"Many journalists end up dead, assaulted or threatened."

Aleksei A. Navalny expects to go to jail. Last month, a Russian court announced it would schedule a trial against Navalny, who is accused of embezzling from a timber company, even though the case was dismissed last year for lack of evidence. Still, Navalny said, "Honestly, I am almost certain I am going to prison."[1]

Many of Navalny's supporters believe his real crimes were organizing protests in Moscow in 2011 and 2012, blogging and running a nonprofit group that operates websites that allow citizens to report incidents of government corruption.

Navalny, who announced on April 4 that he will run for president, is not the only activist to come under pressure from Russia's government. Since Vladimir Putin returned to the presidency last May, new restrictions have been imposed on Internet content, and fines of up to $32,000 have been imposed for participating in protests deemed illegal.

International nonprofit groups such as Amnesty International, Human Rights Watch and Transparency International have been ordered to register as foreign agents. All have refused, and their offices recently have been raided by government investigators.

Last month, Dmitry Gudkov, an opposition politician and one of only two members of the Russian parliament to support public protests such as those organized by Navalny, was accused of treason by some of his colleagues after he visited the United States in March. Gudkov's father was stripped of his seat in parliament last fall.

While cracking down on opposition voices, Putin's government has been able to rely on friendly state-run media

coverage, including from Channel One, the nation's most widely watched television station. During his U.S. visit, Gudkov noted that Russian state-controlled media had accused him of treason and selling secrets.

While some countries try to crack down on independent media outlets through intimidation, Russia for the most part controls communications directly, with the state or its friends owning most of the major newspapers and broadcasters.

Arch Puddington, vice president for research at Freedom House, a Washington-based watchdog group, says what he calls the "Putin model" is widely practiced. "They buy television stations and turn them into mouthpieces of the government," he says.

It's a case of, "If you can't beat them, buy them," says Anthony Mills, deputy director of the International Press Institute in Austria.

Russia is not alone. In some Central Asian and Latin American countries, government-owned media are commonly used for propaganda and to negate foreign criticism.

In Turkey, most of the media are controlled by a few private companies, which leads more to collusion than intimidation, says former Rep. Tom Perriello, D-Va. "In Turkey, you have less of the situation of people being shaken down [or threatened] if they print this story," he says. "Instead, many of the TV companies are doing contracts with the government, so there's a financial interest in not wanting to irritate people in the . . . government."

In other countries, antagonism is the norm. According to Freedom House, Ecuadoran President Rafael Correa has

---

One case led to the famous formulation of Justice Oliver Wendell Holmes. "The most stringent protection of free speech would not protect a man in falsely shouting 'fire' in a crowded theater and creating a panic," Holmes wrote in his dissent in *Schenck v. U.S.* in 1919. "The question in every case is whether the words used are used in such circumstances and are of such a nature to create a clear and present danger that they will bring about the substantive evils that Congress has a right to prevent."

Although fewer dissenters were prosecuted during World War II there were still dozens. "The Roosevelt administration investigated suspects for their 'un-American' associations and employed a variety of legal devices to harass the dissenters and suppress the dissent," writes historian Richard W. Steele.[31]

During the 1940s and '50s, Congress did what it could to ban Communist Party activities in the United States, but after World War II, the sense that free speech was an inalienable right took deep hold in the called the press his "greatest political enemy," which he says is "ignorant," "mediocre," "primitive," "bloodthirsty" and "deceitful."[2]

"Ecuador under its president of the last five years, Rafael Correa, has become one of the world's leading oppressors of free speech," Peter Hartcher, international editor for *The Sydney Morning Herald*, wrote last summer. "Correa has appropriated, closed and intimidated many media outlets critical of his government. He has sued journalists for crippling damages."[3]

Analysts say the Venezuelan government tries to own or control nearly all media, while vilifying and jailing independent journalists.

And in Russia, government harassment of independent voices is common. Only a few independent outlets operate, such as *Novaya Gazeta*, a newspaper co-owned by former Soviet President Mikhail Gorbachev, but they aren't widely read or heard except by law enforcement agencies that often arrest, beat and — according to watchdog groups — even kill journalists.[4]

The 2006 killing of Anna Politkovskaya, a *Novaya Gazeta* reporter noted for her coverage of the Chechen conflict, drew international attention, although no one has been convicted of her murder. "Russia is among the most dangerous countries in which to be a journalist," says Rajan Menon, a political scientist at City College of New York. "Many journalists end up dead, assaulted or threatened for looking into hot-button issues, especially corruption."

Russian activist Aleksei Navalny, a leading critic of President Vladimir Putin, addresses an anti-Putin rally in St. Petersburg on Feb. 12, 2012.

In some countries, state-owned media criticize their own governments, says Robert Mahoney, deputy director of the Committee to Protect Journalists, citing the example of the BBC. But when nearly all media are owned by a few individuals or companies, it's not "good in the long term for a diverse and vibrant free press," he says.

Nor is it good when journalists fear they might be killed for digging into stories. In Russia, for instance, journalists are routinely killed with impunity. "There are 17 cases where journalists were killed in the last dozen years or so," Mahoney says, "and there have been no prosecutions."

— *Alan Greenblatt*

[1] Andrew E. Kramer, "With Trial Suddenly Looming, Russian Activist Expects the Worst," *The New York Times*, March 28, 2013, p. A4, www.nytimes.com/2013/03/28/world/europe/with-case-reopened-the-russian-activist-aleksei-navalny-expects-the-worst.html.

[2] "Freedom of the Press 2011: Ecuador," Freedom House, Sept. 1, 2011, www.freedomhouse.org/report/freedom-press/2011/ecuador.

[3] Peter Hartcher, "Hypocrisy Ends Hero's Freedom to Preach," *The Sydney Morning Herald*, Aug. 21, 2012, www.smh.com.au/opinion/politics/hypocrisy-ends-heros-freedom-to-preach-20120820-24ijx.html.

[4] Peter Preston, "Putin's win is a hollow victory for a Russian free press," *The Guardian*, March 10, 2012, www.guardian.co.uk/media/2012/mar/11/putin-win-russian-free-press.

country and the courts. It was even included in Article 19 of the Universal Declaration of Human Rights, adopted by the United Nations in 1948, which says: "Everyone has the right to freedom of opinion and expression; this right includes freedom to hold opinions without interference and to seek, receive and impart information and ideas through any media and regardless of frontiers."[32]

A series of lectures by American free-speech advocate Alexander Meiklejohn published in 1948 was hugely

influential as a defense of the notion that free speech and democracy are intertwined. "The phrase 'Congress shall make no law . . . abridging the freedom of speech,' is unqualified," Meiklejohn wrote. "It admits of no exceptions. . . . That prohibition holds good in war and peace, in danger as in security."[33]

In the 1960s, the U.S. Supreme Court protected racist speech, as well as speech by advocates of integration. "A decision protecting speech by a Ku Klux Klan member cited a decision that protected an African-American

China Opens Up — But Just a Crack

Journalists' and dissenters' activities are still monitored.

It's been decades now since China opened up to the West. But it's still not completely open, especially with regard to freedom of speech and the press.

In recent months, angered by coverage it viewed as hostile, such as reports that the families of top government officials have enriched themselves while the officials have been in power, China has denied entry visas to reporters from media organizations such as *The New York Times*, Al-Jazeera English and Reuters.

Since October, it has blocked access within China to *The Times*' website, while Chinese hackers have broken into email accounts belonging to reporters from *The Times* and *The Wall Street Journal*, possibly to determine the sources of stories critical of government officials.

China has long maintained a "Great Firewall," blocking its citizens from accessing critical content from foreign sources. But the Chinese government is also at pains to block internal criticism from its own citizens and media, as well.

In any given year, China typically ranks in the world's top two or three countries in terms of how many journalists it imprisons.[1] "There's a certain level of very localized dissent allowed, but it can never be expressed directly at the regime," says Padraig Reidy, news editor for Index on Censorship, a free-speech advocacy group.

"You can say a local official is corrupt — maybe," Reidy says. "But you can't say the party is corrupt. That's the end of you."

Besides tracking journalists' activities, China's government also monitors activists' online postings. A recent study by computer scientist Dan Wallach of Rice University and several colleagues found that China could be employing more than 4,000 censors to monitor the 70,000 posts per minute uploaded to Weibo, the Chinese version of Twitter.[2]

The censors tend to track known activists and use automated programs to hunt for forbidden phrases. "Certain words you know are never going to get out of the gate," Wallach says. "Falun Gong" — a spiritual practice China has sought to ban — "those three characters you can't utter on any Chinese website anywhere in the country."

Weibo users are "incredibly clever" at coming up with misspellings and neologisms to sneak past the censors, Wallach says. For instance, a colloquial phrase for China, the Celestial Temple, is sometimes rewritten as "celestial bastard," using similar-looking characters.

But once such usage becomes widespread, the censors are quick to catch on and such terms also are quickly eradicated from websites. "China is definitely the market leader in technical tools for clamping down on free expression," says British journalist John Kampfner.

Aside from imprisonment and hacking attacks, China uses self-censorship to suppress criticism of the state, says Robert Mahoney, deputy director of the New York-based Committee to Protect Journalists. Reporters and others constantly worry about what sort of statements could trigger a crackdown.

"With self-censoring, journalists tend to be more conservative," Mahoney says. Such sensitivity to what censors will think extends even to Hollywood movies. Given the

antiwar state legislator, and the case of the klansman was, in turn, cited [in 1989] to protect a radical who burned the American flag as a political protest," writes Wake Forest law professor Michael Kent Curtis.[34]

In 1964, the Supreme Court limited libel suits brought by public officials, finding that the First Amendment required "actual malice" — that is, knowledge that information published was false.[35] Seven years later, a lower court blocked *The New York Times* from publish further portions of the Pentagon Papers, a government history of

the Vietnam War — the first example in U.S. history of prior restraint.

The Supreme Court lifted the injunction. Justice Hugo Black wrote, "In revealing the workings of government that led to the Vietnam War, the newspapers nobly did precisely that which the Founders hoped and trusted they would do."[36]

After a long period of expansion, press freedoms and other civil liberties were challenged following the terrorist attacks of Sept. 11, 2001. Once again, free speech was growing importance of the Chinese film market, the country's censors now review scripts and inspect sets of movies filmed in China to make sure that nothing offends their sensibilities.

"There were points where we were shooting with a crew of 500 people," said Rob Cohen, director of "The Mummy: Tomb of the Dragon Emperor," which kicked off a recent wave of co-productions between Chinese companies and American studios. "I'm not sure who was who or what, but knowing the way the system works, it's completely clear that had we deviated from the script, it would not have gone unnoticed."[3] The Academy Award-winning "Django Unchained" was initially cut to delete scenes of extreme violence, but censors blocked its scheduled April 12 release due to shots of full-frontal nudity.

In addition to carefully inspecting Western content coming into the country, China is seeking to export its model for rigid media control to other countries. "It's fascinating to look at Chinese investment in Africa," says Anthony Mills, deputy director of the Austria-based International Press Institute. "They've bought into a variety of media outlets in Africa."

While China can't impose censorship in Africa, its control of media outlets there helps ensure favorable coverage. Beijing is actively promoting its image abroad through news-content deals with state-owned media in countries including Zimbabwe, Nigeria, Cuba, Malaysia and Turkey, according to the South African Institute of International Affairs. "Countries that need Chinese trade, aid and recognition, and those with tense relations with the U.S., are more likely to be influenced by China's soft power," the institute concluded in a report last year.[4]

"China has this model in which the economic welfare and the perceived welfare of the state as a whole trump individual freedoms," Mills says.

Some Western observers, such as Reidy, believe China will eventually have to become more open, because capitalist investment demands a free flow of information.

But others wonder whether China's more authoritarian approach represents a challenge to the transatlantic model that has been fairly dominant around the globe since World War II, with freedom of expression seen as essential to democracy and economic growth.

Already, says former Rep. Tom Perriello, D-Va., residents of countries such as Turkey complain less about individual freedoms while the economy is growing.

"If you actually get to a point where China is associated with economic prosperity more than Western countries are, then people look differently at democracy and human rights," he says. "I wish they didn't, but that's part of the fear, that we can't assume there's this natural march toward more liberalism."

— *Alan Greenblatt*

---

[1] Madeline Earp, "Disdain for Foreign Press Undercuts China's Global Ambition," Committee to Protect Journalists, March 11, 2013, www.cpj.org/2013/02/attacks-on-the-press-china-tightens-control.php.

[2] "Computer Scientists Measure the Speed of Censorship on China's Twitter," *The Physics arXiv Blog*, March 6, 2013, www.technologyreview.com/view/512231/computer-scientists-measure-the-speed-of-censorship-on-chinas-twitter.

[3] Michael Cieply and Brooks Barnes, "To Get Movies Into China, Hollywood Gives Censors a Preview," *The New York Times*, Jan. 15, 2013, p. A1, www.nytimes.com/2013/01/15/business/media/in-hollywood-movies-for-china-bureaucrats-want-a-say.html.

[4] Yu-Shan Wu, "The Rise of China's State-Led Media Dynasty in Africa," South African Institute of International Affairs, June 2012, p. 11, www.saiia.org.za/images/stories/pubs/occasional_papers_above_100/saia_sop_%20117_wu_20120618.pdf.

---

seen as possibly undermining the government at a time when security concerns had become paramount. "Press freedoms are positively correlated with greater transnational terrorism," write University of Chicago law professor Posner and Harvard University law professor Adrian Vermeule. "Nations with a free press are more likely to be targets of such terrorism."[37]

For example, they cited a 2005 *New York Times* story on the so-called warrantless wiretapping program at the National Security Agency, which they argue alerted

terrorists that the United States was monitoring communications the terrorists believed were secure.[38] The Bush administration made similar arguments to The *Times*, which held the story until after the 2004 presidential election.

Worried that the administration would seek a federal court injunction to block publication, *The Times* first published the story on its website. "In the new digital world of publishing, there were no printing presses to stop," notes Samuel Walker, a University of Nebraska law professor.[39]

Ku Klux Klan members in Pulaski, Tenn., participate in a march honoring Nathan Bedford Forrest, a Confederate general who helped found the Klan, on July 11, 2009. The U.S. Supreme Court has ruled that even hate groups like the Klan have a constitutional right to express their racist views publicly.

CURRENT SITUATION

Government Secrets

With so much speech, commerce — and terrorist activity — taking place online, Congress is struggling to find an appropriate balance between security on the one hand and privacy and free-speech concerns on the other.

On April 18, the House passed the Cyber Intelligence Sharing and Protection Act, known by the acronym CISPA. The bill would give military and security agencies greater access to Americans' online activity by making it easier for private companies to share cyberthreat information with the government, allowing government and businesses to help each other out when they get hacked.

The nation's networks are already under attack from countries such as Iran and Russia, Texas GOP Rep. Michael McCaul, chair of the House Homeland Security Committee, told his colleagues during floor debate.[40]

"I think if anything, the recent events in Boston demonstrate that we have to come together to get this done," McCaul said, referring to the bombs that exploded near the finish line of the Boston Marathon three days earlier. "In the case of Boston, they were real bombs. In this case, they're digital bombs."[41]

But the bill's opponents said it represented a violation of privacy and free-speech rights, giving government agencies such as the FBI and CIA easy access to online accounts without warrants, chilling free expression. On April 16, the Obama administration threatened to veto the bill, if it were to reach the president's desk.[42]

The bill would allow Internet companies "to ship the whole kit and caboodle" of personal information to the government, including that which does not pertain directly to cyberthreats and "is none of the government's business," said California Rep. Nancy Pelosi, Democratic leader of the House.[43]

"I am disappointed. . . we did not address the concerns of the White House about personal information," Pelosi said. "It offers no policies and did not allow any amendments and no real solutions to uphold Americans' right to privacy."

The measure now goes to the U.S. Senate. A similar bill was unable to muster enough Senate votes last year to overcome a filibuster, and this year's outcome is uncertain.

Information Explosion

The explosion of information on the Internet and in online databases has made legal concerns about free speech more complicated, says Randall Bezanson, a law professor at the University of Iowa. For most of U.S. history, such concerns turned largely on the question of whether the government had the power to censor speech. Now, he says, regulating speech involves the government not just quashing the speech of individuals but in protecting documents and databases — its own, and others — from disclosure.

The Obama administration has learned that lesson well, he says, and is doing its best to keep state secrets secret. "Eric Holder, attorney general under President Barack Obama, has prosecuted more government officials for alleged leaks under the World War I–era Espionage Act than all his predecessors combined," Bloomberg News reported last fall.[44]

The administration was disturbed by the leak of thousands of diplomatic cables, which were published in 2010 by the whistleblower website Wiki-Leaks, founded by former Australian computer hacker Julian Assange.[45]

"The Julian Assange episode and those disclosures of pretty well unfiltered information, I think, scared people in government and raised a whole different specter of

Should journalists be regulated?

YES — Steven Barnett
Professor of Communications, University of Westminster, London, England

Written for *CQ Researcher*, April 2013

In an ideal world, a free press should not be constrained any more than free speech. Unfortunately, this is not an ideal world. Would-be terrorists seek to recruit supporters, grossly offensive material can reap huge financial rewards and some publications try to boost circulation and scoop competitors using immoral and even downright malicious methods.

Some methods, such as hacking into voicemails, are illegal in Britain. Others are not. Public outrage was sparked by atrocious behaviour that some British newspapers have sanctioned in the name of "journalism," such as splashing on the front page the private and intimate diaries of Kate McCann after the disappearance of her daughter Madeleine. Although Mrs. McCann begged the *News of the World* not to publish the diaries, the newspaper ignored her pleas. Such callous indifference to people's feelings had become institutionalized in some of Britain's best-selling newspapers.

What is required is not state control or statutory regulation. But the press must be held accountable for egregious abuses of its own privileged position within a democracy.

In the United Kingdom, Sir Brian Leveson, who chaired a judicial inquiry into press practices and ethics as a result of the phone-hacking scandal, recommended the moderate solution of voluntary self-regulation overseen by an autonomous body that would assess whether self-regulation was effective and independent. If so, news organizations choosing to belong would be entitled to financial incentives such as lower court costs and exemption from exemplary damages if sued. It is, I repeat, a voluntary incentive-based system, which is needed to protect ordinary people from amoral and sometimes vindictive practices that have no place in journalism.

Such proposals might feel uncomfortable in the land of the First Amendment, but it is exceptionally mild by European standards. In Finland, a Freedom of Expression Act mandates, among other things, that aggrieved parties have a right of reply or correction without undue delay. In Germany, newspapers are required to print corrections with the same prominence as the original report. Scandinavian countries have passed legislation on press ethics.

These countries are not rampant dictatorships. But they all, as will Britain, find a proper balance between unconstrained journalism and the rights of ordinary people not to have their misery peddled for corporate profit.

NO — Anthony Mills
Deputy Director, International Press Institute, Vienna, Austria

Written for *CQ Researcher*, April 2013

In any healthy democracy, the media play a watchdog role, holding elected officials accountable and serving the public interest by satisfying citizens' right to know what is being done in their name in the often not-so-transparent corridors of power. In the United States, for instance, the Watergate scandal was unearthed and covered, at not inconsiderable risk, by two young *Washington Post* reporters.

Not surprisingly, there are those in office for whom such media scrutiny is, to put it mildly, unwelcome. And, lo and behold, they become advocates for state regulation of the media. They may very well point to one or more examples of egregious, even criminal, journalist behavior as evidence of the need to exert greater control.

No one suggests that journalists are above the law. But when they engage in criminal behavior, they should be held accountable in criminal courts. The profession must not be overseen by the very elected officials whom it is supposed to hold to account. Surely, from the perspective of the politicians, that would be a conflict of interest.

The answer is self-regulation. That could be accomplished through independent regulatory bodies with the teeth to hold journalists ethically accountable or through ethical standards rigorously and systematically imposed by media outlets themselves as is the case in the United States, where the First Amendment right to freedom of the press is fiercely guarded. Professional peers must lead by example.

In the absence of self-regulation, or where it is not effectively implemented, the path is easily paved for statutory regulation, whether direct, or roundabout, in form. The aftermath of the *News of the World* phone-hacking scandal in the U.K., and the ensuing inquiry by Lord Justice Leveson, have amply demonstrated this. The U.K. press is set to be bound by statutory legislation for the first time in hundreds of years. That cannot be healthy for democracy, and other countries tend to follow the lead of their democratic "peers."

So it is incumbent upon everyone in the profession to resist any efforts to impose statutory regulation of the press by those upon whom the press is supposed to be keeping its watchful eye. But it falls upon the press to ensure that the standards it embraces are of the highest order of professionalism and integrity. Anything less offers cannon fodder for those targeting a free media.

what could be done and what the consequences are, and that has probably triggered a more aggressive approach in the Justice Department," Bezanson says.

On Feb. 28, Army Pfc. Bradley Manning, who leaked thousands of diplomatic, military and intelligence cables to WikiLeaks, pleaded guilty to 10 charges of illegally acquiring and transferring government secrets, agreeing to spend 20 years in prison. Manning pleaded not guilty, however, to 12 additional counts — including espionage — and faces a general court-martial in June.

Manning's case has made him a cause célèbre among some on the left who see him as being unduly persecuted. A similar dynamic is playing out in memory of American online activist and pioneer Aaron Swartz, who committed suicide in January while facing charges that could carry a 35-year prison sentence in a case involving his downloading of copyrighted academic journals.

In March, the entire editorial board of the *Journal of Library Administration* resigned over what one member described as "a crisis of conscience" over the 26-year-old Swartz's death.[46] The librarians were concerned not only about the Swartz case but the larger issue of access to journal articles, feeling that publishers were becoming entirely too restrictive in their terms of use.

In general, Bezanson says, courts are becoming less accepting of the idea that "information wants to be free," as the Internet-era slogan has it. The courts are not only more supportive of copyright holders but seemingly more skeptical about free speech in general, with the Supreme Court in recent cases having curbed some of the free-speech rights it had afforded to students and hate groups in previous decisions.

"The doctrine of the First Amendment is going to be more forgiving of regulated speech," Bezanson says.

Regulating the Press?

In other countries, concern is growing that freedom of speech and of the press have been badly abused in recent years. A phone-hacking scandal involving the *News of the World*, a British tabloid, shocked the United Kingdom in 2011 and has led to more than 30 arrests, as well as a high-profile inquiry chaired by Sir Brian Leveson, then Britain's senior appeals judge. Leveson's report, released in November, called for a new, independent body to replace the Press Complaints Commission, the news industry's self-regulating agency. The recommendations

triggered difficult negotiations among leaders of the United Kingdom's coalition government, which announced a compromise deal in March.

"While Lord Leveson was quite correct to call for a regulator with more muscle that can impose substantial fines for future misconduct, [Prime Minister] David Cameron pledged that he would resist the clamor for such measures to be backed by law," the *Yorkshire Post* editorialized. "Given that to do so would be to take the first step on the slippery slope toward censorship of the press, a weapon that has been employed by many a corrupt dictatorship around the globe, he was right to do so."[47]

The U.K. is not the only country considering new media regulations. In March, Australia's government proposed tighter regulation of media ownership and a new media overseer with statutory authority. "Australians want the press to be as accountable as they want politicians, sports people and business people," said Stephen Conroy, Australia's communications minister.[48]

Media executives argued that the proposals were draconian and amounted to the government's revenge for hostile coverage. "For the first time in Australian history outside wartime, there will be political oversight over the conduct of journalism in this country," said Greg Hywood, the CEO of Fairfax Media.[49]

In response to such criticisms, Australia's government quickly withdrew the proposals.

Reporters Under Attack

If journalists, commentators, artists and writers are feeling embattled in the English-speaking world, they face worse fates elsewhere. According to the Committee to Protect Journalists, 232 journalists around the world were imprisoned as of Dec. 1 — the highest total since the group began its survey work in 1990. And 70 journalists were killed while doing their jobs in 2012 — a 43 percent increase from the year before.[50]

According to the group, 49 journalists were imprisoned in Turkey alone in 2012, a record high, and more than were in jail in either Iran or China. Francis J. Ricciardone, the U.S. ambassador to Turkey, has been openly critical about the country's approach to free speech. "The responsibility of Turkey's friends and allies is to . . . to point out, with due respect, the importance of progress in the protection of freedom of expression for journalists and blog writers," State Department spokeswoman Victoria Nuland said at a news conference in February.[51]

In India freedom of expression is enshrined in the constitution, but with many provisos. And lately, India's judiciary has appeared to show little concern when the government has arrested people over their Facebook posts and remarks made at literary festivals. "Writers and artists of all kinds are being harassed, sued and arrested for what they say or write or create," writes Suketu Mehta, a journalism professor at New York University. "The government either stands by and does nothing to protect freedom of speech, or it actively abets its suppression."[52]

India — the world's most populous democracy — has slipped below Qatar and Afghanistan in Reporters Without Borders' press freedom index.[53]

In emerging economic powerhouses such as Turkey and India, along with Brazil, Mexico, South Africa and Indonesia, governments are "kind of floating" between two different models, says Kampfner, the *Freedom for Sale* author: the open-society approach favored by transatlantic democracies and a more authoritarian approach.

"I slightly fear it's going in the wrong direction in all of them," Kampfner says.

But there also have been signs recently that things may be improving in places for free-speech advocates. On April 1, for the first time in half a century, privately owned daily newspapers hit newsstands in Myanmar.[54]

In Syria, new newspapers have emerged to cover the civil war, countering bias from both government-controlled media and opposition-friendly satellite channels based in Qatar and Saudi Arabia.

"We need to get out of this Facebook phase, where all we do is whine and complain about the regime," said Absi Smesem, editor-in-chief of *Sham*, a new weekly newspaper.[55]

OUTLOOK

Shame, Not Laws?

It's always impossible to predict the future, but it's especially difficult when discussing free speech, which is now inextricably bound up with constantly changing technologies.

"I don't know what's next," says Reidy, the Index on Censorship news editor. "None of us five years ago thought we would be spending our lives on Twitter." Still, Reidy says, the fact that so many people are conversing online makes them likely to equate blocking the Internet with more venerable forms of censorship, such as book burning.

"Within the next five years, you will have a lot of adults in the Western world who literally don't know what life is like without the Internet," he says. "That is bound to change attitudes and cultures."

Information technology is penetrating deeper into the developing world, says Kampfner, the British journalist and author. For instance, thanks to mobile technology African farmers can access more information they need about crop yields and prices. And with cell phones, everyone has better access to information on disasters.

However, "In terms of changing the political discourse, the jury is out," Kampfner says. "Every new technology, by its nature, is open to both use and abuse."

Activists wanting to use technology to spread information and governments trying to stop them play an ongoing "cat and mouse game," says Galperin, of the Electronic Frontier Foundation.

Given how easily commercial applications can track individuals' specific interests and movements online, it's not difficult to imagine that political speech will be tracked as well, Belarus-born writer and researcher Evgeny Morozov, a contributing editor at *The New Republic* and a columnist for *Slate*, contends in his 2011 book *The Net Delusion*. It's not the case, as some have argued, he says, that the need to keep the Internet open for commercial purposes will prevent regimes from stamping out other forms of online discourse.

"In the not so distant future, a banker perusing nothing but Reuters and *Financial Times,* and with other bankers as her online friends, would be left alone to do anything she wants, even browse Wikipedia pages about human-rights violations," he writes. "In contrast, a person of unknown occupation, who is occasionally reading *Financial Times* but is also connected to five well-known political activists through Facebook and who has written blog comments that included words like 'democracy' and 'freedom,' would only be allowed to visit government-run websites, or . . . to surf but be carefully monitored."[56]

In democratic nations, concerns about security and offending religious believers could lead to more restrictions — although not necessarily in terms of new laws, says Arch Puddington, vice president for research at Freedom House, but through shaming and "other informal methods" of disciplining unpopular ways of speaking.

"What you could have over the next 10 years in the U.S. and abroad is a distinction between rights and norms," says former Rep. Perriello, at the Center for American Progress Action Fund. "Having a legal right to say certain things does not actually mean one should say certain things."

Anthony Mills, the deputy director of the International Press Institute in Austria, suggests that the more things change, the more they will stay recognizably the same. "Unfortunately, in 10 years we'll still be having similar conversations about efforts by everyone from criminals to militants and government operatives to target the media and silence them," Mills says.

"But at the same time, . . . a variety of media platforms — of journalists and of media practitioners — will continue to defy that trend," he says. "I have no doubt that in the grand scheme of things, the truth will always come out. The dynamic of the flow of information is unstoppable."

Wallach, the Rice University computer scientist, is equally certain that despite all legal, political and technological ferment, the basic underlying tension between free expression and repressive tendencies will remain firmly in place.

"There will always be people with something to say and ways for them to say it," Wallach says. Likewise, "There will also always be people who want to stop them."

NOTES

1. Jonathan Turley, "Shut Up and Play Nice," *The Washington Post*, Oct. 14, 2012, p. B1, http://articles.washingtonpost.com/2012-10-12/opinions/35499274_1_free-speech-defeat-jihad-muslim-man.

2. For background, see Peter Katel, "Protecting Whistleblowers," *CQ Researcher*, March 31, 2006, pp. 265-288.

3. "Memorandum to the European Union on Media Freedom in Hungary," Human Rights Watch, Feb. 16, 2012, www.hrw.org/node/105200.

4. For background, see Kenneth Jost, "Unrest in the Arab World," *CQ Researcher*, Feb. 1, 2013, pp. 105-132; and Roland Flamini, "Turmoil in the Arab World," *CQ Global Researcher*, May 3, 2011, pp. 209-236.

5. Tom Gjelten, "Shutdowns Counter the Idea of a World-Wide Web," NPR, Dec. 1, 2012, www.npr.org/2012/12/01/166286596/shutdowns-raise-issue-of-who-controls-the-internet.

6. Jessica Chasmar, "French Jewish Group Sues Twitter Over Racist, Anti-Semitic Tweets," *The Washington Times*, March 24, 2013, www.washingtontimes.com/news/2013/mar/24/french-jewish-group-sues-twitter-over-racist-anti-.

7. Jean-Paul Marthoz, "Extremists Are Censoring the Story of Religion," Committee to Protect Journalists, Feb. 14, 2013, www.cpj.org/2013/02/attacks-on-the-press-journalism-and-religion.php. See also, Frank Greve, "Combat Journalism," *CQ Researcher*, April 12, 2013, pp. 329-352.

8. Chris York, "Pussy Riot Member Yekaterina Samutsevich Freed on Probation by Moscow Court," *The Huffington Post UK*, Oct. 10, 2012, www.huffingtonpost.co.uk/2012/10/10/pussy-riot-member-yekaterina-samutsevich-frees-probation-moscow-court_n_1953725.html.

9. Ethan Zuckerman, "The First Twitter Revolution?" *Foreign Policy*, Jan. 14, 2011, www.foreignpolicy.com/articles/2011/01/14/the_first_twitter_revolution.

10. Thomas Fuller, "E-mails of Reporters in Myanmar Are Hacked," *The New York Times*, Feb. 10, 2013, www.nytimes.com/2013/02/11/world/asia/journalists-e-mail-accounts-targeted-in-myanmar.html.

11. Yves Alexandre de Mountjoye, *et al.*, "Unique in the Crowd: The Privacy Bounds of Human Mobility," *Nature*, March 25, 2013, www.nature.com/srep/2013/130325/srep01376/full/srep01376.html.

12. Thomas Erdbrink, "Iran Blocks Way to Bypass Internet Filtering System," *The New York Times*, March 11, 2013, www.nytimes.com/2013/03/12/world/middleeast/iran-blocks-software-used-to-bypass-internet-filtering-system.html.

13. Andrew Higgins, "Danish Opponent of Islam Is Attacked, and Muslims Defend His Right to Speak," *The New York Times*, Feb. 28, 2013, p. A8, www .nytimes.com/2013/02/28/world/europe/lars-hede gaard-anti-islamic-provocateur-receives-support-from-danish-muslims.html.

14. Kenan Malik and Nada Shabout, "Should Religious or Cultural Sensibilities Ever Limit Free Expression?" Index on Censorship, March 25, 2013, www.index oncensorship.org/2013/03/should-religious-or-cul tural-sensibilities-ever-limit-free-expression/.

15. "Freedom of Thought 2012: A Global Report on Discrimination Against Humanists, Atheists and the Nonreligious," International Humanist and Ethical Union, Dec. 10, 2012, p. 11, http://iheu.org/files/ IHEU%20Freedom%20of%20Thought%202012 .pdf.

16. Asim Tanveer, "Pakistani Man Accuses Ambassador to U.S. of Blasphemy," Reuters, Feb. 21, 2013, http://news.yahoo.com/pakistan-accuses-ambassa dor-u-blasphemy-124213305.html.

17. Huma Yusuf, "The Censors' Salon," *Latitude*, March 14, 2013, http://latitude.blogs.nytimes .com/2013/03/14/in-lahore-pakistan-the-censors-salon/.

18. See "Speech to the United Nations General Assembly — Practical progress towards realising those ideals in the world," Sept. 26, 2012, www .pm.gov.au/press-office/speech-united-nations-gen eral-assembly-%E2%80%9Cpractical-progress-towards-realising-those-idea.

19. Turley, *op. cit.*

20. Aryeh Neier, "Freedom, Blasphemy and Violence," Project Syndicate, Sept. 16, 2012, www.project-syndicate.org/commentary/freedom--blasphemy--and-violence-by-aryeh-neier.

21. C. W. Nevius, "Free Speech Protects Offensive Ads on Muni," *The San Francisco Chronicle*, March 14, 2013, p. D1, www.sfgate.com/bayarea/nevius/article/ Offensive-ads-on-Muni-protected-speech-4352829 .php.

22. Clinton's remarks are available at www.state.gov/sec retary/rm/2011/12/178511.htm.

23. Obama's remarks are available at www.whitehouse .gov/the-press-office/2012/09/25/remarks-presi dent-un-general-assembly.

24. Anthea Butler, "Opposing View: Why 'Sam Bacile' Deserves Arrest," *USA Today*, Sept. 13, 2012, http:// usatoday30.usatoday.com/news/opinion/story/2012- 09-12/Sam-Bacile-Anthea-Butler/57769732/1.

25. Eric Posner, "The World Doesn't Love the First Amendment," *Slate*, Sept. 25, 2012, www.slate.com/ articles/news_and_politics/jurisprudence/2012/09/ the_vile_anti_muslim_video_and_the_first_amend ment_does_the_u_s_overvalue_free_speech_.single .html.

26. Eyder Peralta, "John Kerry to German Students: Americans Have 'Right to Be Stupid,'" NPR, Feb. 26, 2013, www.npr.org/blogs/thetwo-way/ 2013/02/26/172980860/john-kerry-to-german-stu dents-americans-have-right-to-be-stupid.

27. Rodney A. Smolla, *Free Speech in an Open Society* (1992), p. 4.

28. Robert Hargreaves, *The First Freedom* (2002), p. 5.

29. *Ibid.*, p. 51.

30. *Ibid.*, p. 95.

31. Richard W. Steele, *Free Speech in the Good War* (1999), p. 1.

32. See "The Universal Declaration of Human Rights," United Nations, www.un.org/en/documents/udhr/ index.shtml#a19.

33. Alexander Meiklejohn, *Free Speech and Its Relation to Self-Government* (1948), p. 17.

34. Michael Kent Curtis, *Free Speech, 'The People's Darling Privilege': Struggles for Freedom of Expression in American History* (2000), p. 406.

35. David W. Rabban, *Free Speech in Its Forgotten Years* (1997), p. 372.

36. "Supreme Court, 6-3, Upholds Newspapers on Publication of Pentagon Report," *The New York Times*, July 1, 1971, www.nytimes.com/books/ 97/04/13/reviews/papers-final.html.

37. Eric A. Posner and Adrian Vermeule, *Terror in the Balance: Security, Liberty and the Courts* (2007), p. 26.

38. James Risen and Eric Lichtblau, "Bush Lets U.S. Spy on Callers Without Courts," *The New York Times*, Dec. 16, 2005, www.nytimes.com/2005/12/16/politics/16program.html.

39. Samuel Walker, *Presidents and Civil Liberties From Wilson to Obama: A Story of Poor Custodians* (2012), p. 468.

40. For background, see Roland Flamini, "Improving Cybersecurity," *CQ Researcher*, Feb. 15, 2013, pp. 157-180.

41. Karen McVeigh and Dominic Rushe, "House Passes CISPA Cybersecurity Bill Despite Warnings From White House," *The Guardian*, April 18, 2013, www.guardian.co.uk/technology/2013/apr/18/house-representatives-cispa-cybersecurity-white-house-warning.

42. See the "Statement of Administration Policy" at www.whitehouse.gov/sites/default/files/omb/legislative/sap/113/saphr624r_20130416.pdf.

43. McVeigh and Rushe, *op. cit.*

44. Phil Mattingly and Hans Nichols, "Obama Pursuing Leakers Sends Warning to Whistle-Blowers," Bloomberg News, Oct. 17, 2012, www.bloomberg.com/news/2012-10-18/obama-pursuing-leakers-sends-warning-to-whistle-blowers.html.

45. For background, see Alex Kingsbury, "Government Secrecy," *CQ Researcher*, Feb. 11, 2011, pp. 121-144.

46. Russell Brandom, "Entire Library Journal Editorial Board Resigns," *The Verge*, March 26, 2013, www.theverge.com/2013/3/26/4149752/library-journal-resigns-for-open-access-citing-aaron-swartz.

47. "A Vital Test for Democracy," *Yorkshire Press*, March 19, 2013, www.yorkshirepost.co.uk/news/debate/yp-comment/a-vital-test-for-our-democracy-1-5505331.

48. Sabra Lane, "Stephen Conroy Defends Media Change Package," Australian Broadcasting Company, March 13, 2013, www.abc.net.au/am/content/2013/s3714163.htm.

49. Nick Bryant, "Storm Over Australia's Press Reform Proposals," BBC, March 19, 2013, www.bbc.co.uk/news/world-asia-21840076.

50. Rick Gladstone, "Report Sees Journalists Increasingly Under Attack," *The New York Times*, Feb. 15, 2013, p. A10, www.nytimes.com/2013/02/15/world/attacks-on-journalists-rose-in-2012-group-finds.html.

51. "U.S.: American Ambassador to Turkey Reiterating What Clinton Previously Said," *Today's Zaman*, Feb. 7, 2013, www.todayszaman.com/news-306435-us-american-ambassador-to-turkey-reiterating-what-clinton-previously-said.html.

52. Suketu Mehta, "India's Speech Impediments," *The New York Times*, Feb. 6, 2013, www.nytimes.com/2013/02/06/opinion/indias-limited-freedom-of-speech.html.

53. "Press Freedom Index 2013," Reporters Without Borders, fr.rsf.org/IMG/pdf/classement_2013_gb-bd.pdf.

54. Aye Aye Win, "Privately Owned Daily Newspapers Return to Myanmar," The Associated Press, April 1, 2013, www.huffingtonpost.com/huff-wires/20130401/as-myanmar-new-newspapers/.

55. Neil MacFarquhar, "Syrian Newspapers Emerge to Fill Out War Reporting," *The New York Times*, April 2, 2013, p. A4, www.nytimes.com/2013/04/02/world/middleeast/syrian-newspapers-emerge-to-fill-out-war-reporting.html.

56. Eugeny Morozov, *The Net Delusion* (2011), p. 97.

BIBLIOGRAPHY

Selected Sources

Books

Ghonim, Wael, *Revolution 2.0: The Power of the People Is Greater Than the People in Power*, Houghton Mifflin Harcourt, 2012.

A Google employee who became a leader in using social media to organize protests against the government in Egypt during the so-called Arab Spring of 2011 writes a memoir about those tumultuous times.

Hargreaves, Robert, *The First Freedom: A History of Free Speech*, Sutton Publishing, 2002.

The late British broadcaster surveys the long history of speech, from Socrates to modern times, highlighting the personalities and legal cases that eventually led to greater liberties.

Kampfner, John, *Freedom for Sale: Why the World Is Trading Democracy for Security*, Basic Books, 2010.
Visiting countries such as Russia, China, Italy and the United States, a British journalist examines how citizens in recent years have been willing to sacrifice personal freedoms in exchange for promises of prosperity and security.

Articles

Erdbrink, Thomas, "Iran Blocks Way to Bypass Internet Filtering System," *The New York Times*, March 11, 2013, www.nytimes.com/2013/03/12/world/middleeast/iran-blocks-software-used-to-bypass-internet-filtering-system.html.
Iran's Ministry of Information and Communications Technology has begun blocking the most popular software used by millions of Iranians to bypass the official Internet censoring system.

Malik, Kenan, and Nada Shabout, "Should Religious or Cultural Sensibilities Ever Limit Free Expression?" *Index on Censorship*, March 25, 2013, www.indexoncensorship.org/2013/03/should-religious-or-cultural-sensibilities-ever-limit-free-expression/.
An Indian-born British broadcaster (Malik) and an Iraqi art historian debate whether even the most offensive and blasphemous speech should be protected.

Mattingly, Phil, and Hans Nichols, "Obama Pursuing Leakers Sends Warning to Whistle-Blowers," Bloomberg News, Oct. 17, 2012, www.bloomberg.com/news/2012-10-18/obama-pursuing-leakers-sends-warning-to-whistle-blowers.html.
Attorney General Eric Holder has prosecuted more government officials for leaking documents than all his predecessors combined.

Posner, Eric, "The World Doesn't Love the First Amendment," *Slate*, Sept. 25, 2012, www.slate.com/articles/news_and_politics/jurisprudence/2012/09/the_vile_anti_muslim_video_and_the_first_amendment_does_the_u_s_overvalue_free_speech_.single.html.
In the wake of violent protests across the globe triggered by an anti-Muslim video that was produced in the United States, a University of Chicago law professor argues that freedom of expression must give way at times to other values.

Turley, Jonathan, "Shut Up and Play Nice," *The Washington Post*, Oct. 14, 2012, http://articles.washingtonpost.com/2012-10-12/opinions/35499274_1_free-speech-defeat-jihad-muslim-man.
A George Washington University law professor argues that freedom of speech is being eroded around the world as efforts to protect various groups against being offended become enshrined in law.

Reports and Studies

"Attacks on the Press: Journalism on the Front Lines in 2012," Committee to Protect Journalists, February 2013, www.cpj.org/2013/02/attacks-on-the-press-in-2012.php.
The latest edition of this annual report documents how more journalists are disappearing or being imprisoned in countries ranging from Mexico to Russia.

"Freedom of Thought 2012: A Global Report on Discrimination Against Humanists, Atheists and the Nonreligious," International Humanist and Ethical Union, Dec. 10, 2012, http://iheu.org/files/IHEU%20Freedom%20of%20Thought%202012.pdf.
The number of prosecutions for blasphemy is sharply on the rise, according to a global survey of laws regulating religious beliefs and expression.

Leveson, Lord Justice Brian, "An Inquiry Into the Culture, Practices and Ethics of the Press," The Stationary Office, Nov. 29, 2012, www.official-documents.gov.uk/document/hc1213/hc07/0780/0780.asp.
A judge appointed by the British prime minister to examine press abuses calls for greater regulation. "There is no organized profession, trade or industry in which the serious failings of the few are overlooked because of the good done by the many," Leveson writes.

Zhu, Tao, *et al.*, "The Velocity of Censorship: High-Fidelity Detection of Microblog Post Deletions," March 4, 2013, http://arxiv.org/abs/1303.0597.
A team of computer scientists examined the accounts of 3,500 users of Weibo, China's microblogging site, to see if it was being censored. The scientists found that thousands of Weibo employees were deleting forbidden phrases and characters.

For More Information

Access, P.O. Box 115, New York, NY 10113; 888-414-0100; www.accessnow.org. A digital-rights group, founded after protests against Iran's disputed 2009 presidential election, that fosters open communications.

Article 19, Free Word Centre, 60 Farringdon Road, London, United Kingdom, EC1R 3GA; +44 20 7324 2500; www .article19.org. A group named for a section of the Universal Declaration of Human Rights that designs laws and policies promoting freedom of expression.

Committee to Protect Journalists, 330 7th Ave., 11th Floor, New York, NY 10001; 212-465-1004; www.cpj.org. Documents attacks on journalists; publishes its findings and works to promote press freedom.

Freedom House, 1301 Connecticut Ave., N.W., 6th Floor, Washington, DC 20036; 202-296-5101; www.freedomhouse .org. An independent watchdog group founded in 1941 that advocates greater political and civil liberties.

Index on Censorship, Free Word Centre, 60 Farringdon Rd., London, United Kingdom, EC1R 3GA; +44 20 7324 2522; www.indexoncensorship.org. Founded in 1972 to publish stories of communist dissidents in Eastern Europe; promotes global free speech through journalistic reports and advocacy.

International Press Institute, Spielgasse 2, A-1010, Vienna, Austria; +43 1 412 90 11; www.freemedia.at. A global network of media executives and journalists founded in 1950, dedicated to promoting and safeguarding press freedoms.

Reporters Committee for Freedom of the Press, 1101 Wilson Blvd., Suite 1100, Arlington, VA 22209; 703-807-2100; www.rcfp.org. Provides free legal advice and other resources to journalists on First Amendment issues.